Introduction to Computers and Information Systems

Henry C. Lucas, Jr.

Schools of Business
New York University

INTRODUCTION TO
COMPUTERS AND
INFORMATION SYSTEMS

MACMILLAN PUBLISHING COMPANY
New York

Macmillan Publishing Company
866 Third Avenue, New York, New York 10022

Collier Macmillan Canada, Inc.

Library of Congress Cataloging in Publication Data

Lucas, Henry C.
    Introduction to computers and information systems.

    Includes index.
    1. Electronic digital computers.   2. Electronic data processing.   I. Title.
QA76.5.L76   1985   001.64   85-10536
ISBN 0-02-372210-X

Printing: 3 4 5 6 7 8   Year: 6 7 8 9 0 1 2 3 4 5

To Ellen

Preface

This text is intended for the introductory course on computers and information systems. Information processing is an integral part of our business and personal lives—today's student needs to be able to understand and apply this technology. This text is addressed to students who are entering their first course on computers, and its goal is to orient the reader to the uses of information systems in the business world.

Key Features

The book has several key features which distinguish it from other books in the field. The first is **integrated coverage of microcomputers** throughout the text. One reason for this enhanced coverage is that students are most likely to have encountered microcomputers in grade or high school, or at home. Also, micros are the easiest kind of computer to use and are less intimidating than minis or mainframes for a beginning student. Finally, and most importantly, many college graduates will face microcomputers when they enter the workforce, and they will be expected to know something about their use. While microcomputers are integrated throughout

the text, there remains thorough coverage of all types of computers and systems.

Most students taking a course in which this text is used will *not* become computer professionals. Therefore, the book has a strong **end-user flavor.** An end user is someone who works in an area of business, such as accounting, finance, marketing and the like, and needs to use a computer to solve problems. This person is not interested in computers per se, but instead wants to understand how to get computers and information processing systems to work for him or her. While the text does present an introduction to working as a computer professional, the majority of material is designed for the end user.

To further this goal of preparing the end user, the book has an extensive section on **systems analysis and design.** Chapter 14 is an in-depth example of the design of a microcomputer system for a small business. The chapter on alternatives to traditional design approaches introduces modern and timely material on Fourth Generation Languages, end-user programming and prototyping. It should be stressed that each of the Systems Analysis and Design chapters is self-contained, allowing instructors to choose the depth of coverage that most suits their course.

Besides being involved in Systems Analysis and Design, the other way in which an end user works with a computer is to actually sit behind one and work on problems. Section IV of the text introduces students to **"hands-on" uses of computers.** The discussion is very concrete and oriented toward microcomputers. Included are detailed key-stroke by key-stroke examples of the uses of Lotus 1-2-3 and a word processing system. This section also contains a chapter on BASIC; the reader will find a detailed appendix on this higher level language at the end of the text.

The end-user orientation of the text is balanced with a **clear explanation of the technology** and a **focus on business applications** and **management issues.** Some knowledge of computer *technology,* even for noncomputer professionals, is essential in order to understand the nature of business information processing as it occurs today and as it will occur tomorrow. Specifically, a solid grounding in the technology is required to adequately understand the computer *applications* (such as spreadsheets analysis) that have so influenced the business world in recent years. Within the technology section of the text, there is a chapter on file design followed by a discussion of data base management systems. The reader will also find a chapter on communications, one of the most important topics in the field now and in coming years.

On the management side, the book discusses both the positive and negative impact of computers on organizations. Of particular interest will be the ways in which companies have used information processing technology as a part of their competitive strategies. One of the themes of the management section is that the environment within an organization is one of the keys to successfully tapping the potential of modern information systems. Throughout the text this focus on management is supported by a wealth of examples and applications drawn from real companies. My goal here has been to select applications that both clarify and enliven the material in the book.

Few arenas are as dynamic and fast changing as that of computers and information systems. A final key feature of this text is that it is thoroughly **modern** and **up to date.** We have presented state of the art technology throughout the text. Even more importantly, we have focused on the most recent trends in information processing, and whenever possible, introduced students to anticipated future trends. Some of the more significant new developments covered in this text include the following:

- The uses of microcomputers
- End-user programming (Spreadsheets, Word Processing, Database Management Systems, Fourth Generation Language)
- Alternatives to traditional systems development techniques
- The uses of information technology as a part of corporate strategy (MIS, DSS)
- The proliferation of computers OF ALL TYPES in the firm
- Greater management attention to controlling information processing

The book describes these new trends and others and introduces them where appropriate throughout the text.

Contents and Organization

While writing the text, I kept reminding myself of the many ways an instructor can approach this course. Therefore, though there is an internal logic to the organization of the text, an effort was made to make each Part, and each chapter within each Part, independent and self-contained. An instructor can assign the chapters in any order and feel confident that continuity will be maintained.

The first chapter of the text is an introduction to computing; it shows the reader, among other things, some of the tasks that can be accomplished with an electronic spreadsheet package on a microcomputer. Chapter 2 is a survey of computer applications; it is intended to motivate the student to learn more about information processing. Chapter 3 presents the history of computing, emphasizing the reasons for, and the impact of, each new development.

Part II of the text deals with how computers function. In Chapter 4, we examine the rudiments of how a computer works, while in Chapter 5 the student reads about the arithmetic basis of a modern computer. Chapter 6 classifies the many different types of computers found today, from microcomputers to supercomputers.

In Chapter 7 we see some of the many peripheral devices one can use for input and output with computer systems. Chapter 8 is extremely important; it discusses software, the instructions that tell a computer what to do. Chapter 9 introduces files and the logic of secondary storage, while Chapter 10 shows how Data Base Management Systems have contributed markedly to productivity in developing applications. Chapter 11 is a primer on computer communications.

Part III contains three chapters. The first is a discussion of systems analysis and design, presented through the systems life cycle model. Chapter 13 describes alternatives to tradition, like the use of package programs, end-user programming and prototypes. These alternative techniques are significant because their objective is to reduce the amount of time required to develop a computer application, which can often be considerable when using the life-cycle approach. Chapter 14 is a comprehensive example of the design of a system for a small retail store.

Chapter 15 begins Part IV of the text with a hands-on demonstration of a spreadsheet package. It is followed in Chapter 16 by a similar treatment for word processing. Chapter 17 is a portfolio of photo essays on information systems technology and its application. The chapter begins by showing how a microchip is manufactured and then presents a number of examples of computer applications, such as computer aided manufacturing at an automated dishwasher factory. The chapter also illustrates the use of a popular Fourth Generation Language, Computer Aided Design, and the Uses of Business Graphics. Chapter 18, and the lengthy appendix at the end of the text, provide a solid introduction to programming in BASIC.

Part V explores the results; what has been the impact of the computer revolution? In Chapter 19 we look at the positive and negative impact of computers. Chapter 20 focuses on the effect of computers on the organization and especially on how to manage information processing. Chapter 21 raises a number of concerns about how computers interact with people. Chapter 22 deals with what the future holds in store. Finally, in Chapter 23 the student is introduced to the functions of an information services department and the career paths for computer professionals.

Teaching and Learning Aids

There are a number of aids to teaching and learning in the text. Some of these are the following:

- Concepts throughout the text are illustrated with numerous applications of the technology to actual business situations.
- A single, hypothetical company, Multicorp, is used as a vehicle to introduce new ideas throughout the text.
- Each important term is introduced in boldface.
- There is a list of keywords at the end of each chapter.
- Key words and terms are defined in a comprehensive glossary at the end of the book.
- There are both review and thought questions at the end of each chapter (except the introductory and photo essay chapters).
- Each chapter contains two business problems which give the students a chance to apply chapter material to a problem situation.
- Annotated, recommended readings at the end of the chapters tell the reader where to go for more information.
- Full color photographs are used to illustrate and fully depict the uses of computers today.
- Extensive line drawings and flow diagrams are an integral part of the book and are there to help students grasp the sometimes abstract nature of information systems.

The Package

Introduction to Computers and Information Systems is complemented by an extensive supplemental package:

For the Instructor:

Instructor's Manual—includes extensive **lecture outlines** for each chapter, and answers to all of the end-of-chapter question and problems in the text. Also, included are approximately 50 **transparency masters** based on figures found in the text.

Test Bank—includes approximately 1,400 objective test items to assist in the preparation of examinations. Some essay-type questions are also included. The test bank is available in two ways: in the form of a book, and on **microcomputer disks** for the IBM-PC, APPLE IIe, and TRS-80.

Transparency Acetates—consists of approximately 50 color acetates that represent original figures (they are not found in the text). These acetates have been designed to help show the relationship between the various components that make up information systems.

Update—the text will be supported by an annual Update that will provide coverage of current trends in Information Processing that have emerged since publication of the text. The first update will appear in the Spring of 1986.

For the Student:

Study Guide—for student review purposes, the Guide is designed to augment and help clarify each chapter in the text. Besides containing numerous objective and short answer study questions, the Guide also contains an extensive annotated glossary for each chapter. The Study Guide was prepared by Eli B. Cohen of California State University, Sacramento.

PC-Series Software and Student Manual For PC-Series Software

(1) PC-Series Software—Jim Button's user-friendly software, PC-Calc, PC-Type, and PC-File, is available along with a specially designed Student Manual (the software is IBM-PC/MS-DOS compatible). The software is commercial grade and is not modified. Thus, students can take away from this course a package, containing a working spreadsheet, word processor, and data base management system, that will be of use for many years to come. The software is being distributed in two ways: schools can opt for a site license which will allow for unlimited free copies to be made for student use; or, alternatively, Macmillan is making the multi disk package available to students at a low price. If the second option is chosen, students should feel free to get together in teams of 3 or 4 to make copies among themselves, thus keeping student costs down.

(2) The *Student Manual for PC-Series Software* provides complete directions on how to use the software, along with several worked-out exercises that serve as tutorials. Moreover, a number of supplementary assignment exercises are also included.

(3) The *Instructor's Manual* to the Student Manual for PC-Series Software contains answers to the exercises that appear in the Student Manual.

All in all, the supplements to the main text serve three purposes: to help students master the material in the texts, to allow instructors to use their preparation time efficiently, and, perhaps most importantly to provide students with a chance to apply and use their newly gained knowledge.

Acknowledgements

A number of fellow instructors have helped me immensely in the development of this text. Their comments have helped to shape the final product more than they probably realize. My thanks to

- Jack Baroudi, New York University
- Jack Becker, University of Missouri, St. Louis
- Frank Cable, Penn State University
- Donald Chand, Georgia State University
- Eli Cohen, California State University, Sacramento
- Karen Gardner, Golden Gate University
- Lou Goodman, University of Wisconsin, Madison
- Alka Harringer, Purdue University
- Jack Hogue, University of North Carolina, Charlotte

- Brian Honess, University of South Carolina
- Peter Irwin, Richland College
- Bob Keim, Arizona State University
- Paul Mulcahy, Morehead State University
- Bill Pracht, Texas Tech University
- Richard Redmond, Virginia Commonwealth University
- Bob Saldarini, Bergen Community College
- J. C. Shepard, Indiana University of Pennsylvania
- Ray Stone, James Madison University
- Tony Verstraete, Penn State University

Special thanks to Eli Cohen (who wrote the Study Guide for the text), Bob Saldarini (who prepared the BASIC appendix, Bob Keim, and Jack Baroudi, who read each successive draft of the manuscript—they provided some much needed continuity.

I would also like to thank those individuals who were thoughtful enough to respond to a questionnaire that was sent out early in the text's development:

Donald Chand, Georgia State University; Kim Troboy, Arkansas Tech University; D. F. Costello, University of Nebraska–Lincoln; R. J. Daigle, University of South Alabama; Patricia Boggs, Wright State University; Frank W. Connolly, The American University; Virginia Alvis, Virginia Highlands Community College; Donald D. Scriuen, Northern Illinois University; George Ledin, Jr., University of San Francisco; B. C. Day, University of Tennessee–Chatanooga; Thomas I. M. Ho, Purdue University; Andrew Suhy, Ferris State College; Peter L. Irwin, Richland College; Charles W. Drocea, Jersey City State College; Eugene F. Stafford, Iona College; William E. Grimsley, Jr., University of Charleston; Christopher Heil, Columbia Union College; Chuck Iliff, Anchorage Community College; David Russell, Western New England College; Carey Cooper, University of Alabama–Huntsville; Bob Broschat, South Dakota State University; Tom Kleen, Briar Cliff College; Murrell Gillan, Florida Southern College; Carl J. Clavadetscher, California State College–Stanislaus, Diana M. Michalke, Wright State University; James F. Dowis, Des Moines Area Community College; E. M. Teagarden, Dakota State College; Frank A. Chimenti, Southwestern Oklahoma State University; Clifford Pope, Atlantic Union College; Darrel R. Thoman, William Jewell College; L. A. Nicholas, Weber State College; Russell Anderson, Weber State College; Richard H. Lavoie, Providence College; Kenneth A. Smitz, Southwest Missouri State University; Priscilla K. McGill, Dickinson State College; Howard F. Aucoin, Suffolk University; Steven Thoede, Southwest Texas State University; Ellen Johnson, Delta State University; James W. Bannerman, Southern Technical Institute; Edward L. McClusky, University of Arkansas–Pine Bluff; Frank C. Grella, University of Hartford; Alan R. Hevner, University of Maryland; Robert L. Wrisley, Fayetteville State University; Howard Boyd, Shenandoah College and Conservatory of Music; Engming Lin, Eastern Kentucky University; J. F. Schleich, Northern Missouri State University; David J. Lewis, Ithaca College; Andrew Markoe, Rider College; A. R. Sorkowitz, University of the District of Columbia; Robert C. Aden, Middle Tennessee State University; Michael Koplitz, York College of Pennsylvania; Susan Traynor, Clarion University of Pennsylvania; Patricia H. Roth, Southern Tech Institute; O. J. Prather, Arkansas College; Milan Kaldenberg, Northwest Nazarene College; Joe Otterson, Missouri Valley College; Dave Rosenlof, Sacramento City College; Joseph Ofili, University of Arkansas–Pine Bluff; G. P. Novotny, Ferris State College; Harry Nagel, St. John's University; Jerold Isenberg, Hebrew Theological College; Robert Clark, University of the District of Columbia; J. H. Ruder, East Central University, Charles C. Clever, South Dakota State University; Robert D. Smith, Missouri Western State College; Fred Longren, Ferris State College; John Stock, Lawrence Institute of Technology; Herbert J. Mattord, Southwest Texas State University; George V. Poynor, Dallas Baptist College; Richard N. Bialac, Xavier University; Joseph J. Cebula, Community College of Philadelphia; Jerome W. Blaylock, East Texas State University; Allana R. Adams, University of New Haven; Richard M. Scroggin, Purdue University–North Central; Anthony Jack Carlisle, Huntingdon College; Mira Carlson, Northwestern Illinois University; Norman Jacobson, University of California; Mike McClurkin, University of Nebraska—Lincoln; Paul

A. McGloin, Rensselaer Polytechnic Institute; Alka Rani Harriger, Purdue University; David R. Lee, Golden Gate University; John A. Willhardt, Alabama State University; David Bernstein, University of Maryland–Baltimore County; Robert Saldarini, Bergen Community College; Royann S. Blodgett, SUNY–Albany; Irvin Lichtenstein, Drexel University; Brad Wilson, Western Kentucky University; Satya P. Saraswat, San Diego State University; Robert R. Nash, Central Wesleyan College; C. L. Callis, Troy State University; Tala R. Chlach, The American University; David B. Brown, Auburn University; J. McLellaio, Marymount Manhattan College; Robert Gordon, University of Hartford; Craig Van Lengen, Northern Arizona University; Carl C. Hommer, Jr., Purdue University–North Central; Paul J. Mulcahy, Morehead State University; Elias R. Callahan, Jr., Mississippi State University; Elizabeth H. Sparrow, East Carolina University.

I would especially like to thank Jack Repcheck of Macmillan for his boundless enthusiasm and excellent suggestions for this project. Thanks to Chip Price, Executive Editor of Macmillan, for helping to guide the project from its inception. Also, thanks are due to Ed Neve (production supervisor), Joan Greenfield (text designer), John Schultz (photo researcher), and Natasha Sylvester (manufacturing manager); not only were they professional and extremely flexible during the production of the text, they were also highly committed to producing the best book possible. Ms. Wanda Orlikowski of New York University was of invaluable assistance in preparing illustrations and critiquing drafts of the manuscript. I also would like to thank my wife Ellen and our sons, Scott and Jonathon, for their support and encouragement in writing the text. They provided both the peace and understanding needed to make the book possible.

Contents

PART I: INTRODUCTION *2*

Chapter 1. Introduction *4*

A First Job   The Computer Profession   Recommended Readings

Chapter 2. Current Uses of Computers *14*

The Role of the Citizen   Components of Information Systems   Multicorp
Manufacturing at Autosport   Survey of Applications   Observations
Summary
Review   Key Words   Business Problems   Review Questions
Thought Questions   Recommended Readings

Chapter 3. A Short History of Computing *44*

Introduction   Ancient History   The First Computers   The First
Generation   The Second Generation   The Third Generation   The Fourth
Generation   The Fifth Generation   Summary   History at Safehaven
Review   Key Words   Business Problems   Review Questions
Thought Questions   Recommended Readings

PART II: HOW COMPUTERS WORK *72*

Chapter 4. Hardware Concepts: A Journey into a Computer *76*

Introduction   The Nature of Design   Components of a Microcomputer
Other Computers   Summary   Applications

Review   Key Words   Business Problems   Review Questions
Thought Questions   Recommended Readings

Chapter 5. How a Computer Computes *96*

Introduction   The Number System   Binary Numbers   Coding   Moving on
to Software   Application
Review   Key Words   Business Problems   Review Questions
Thought Questions   Recommended Readings

Chapter 6. So Many Computers: Mainframes, Minis, and Micros *112*

Introduction   Types of Processing   How We Arrived   Original Equipment
Manufacturers   Micros   Minicomputers   Mainframes   Supercomputers
Implications   Application
Review   Key Words   Business Problems   Review Questions
Thought Questions   Recommended Readings

Chapter 7. Peripherals *134*

Introduction   Input   Storage   Output   Summary   Application
Review   Key Words   Business Problems   Review Questions
Thought Questions   Recommended Readings

Chapter 8. Software: The Key to Processing *164*

Introduction   Machine Language   Assembly Language   Higher Levels
Packages   Operating Systems   Strategy   Software for New Products
Review   Key Words   Business Problems   Review Questions
Thought Questions   Recommended Readings

Chapter 9. Data Storage and Retrieval *190*

Introduction   Operations   Records   Update   Data Structures   Chained
or Linked List   Changes   Applications
Review   Key Words   Business Problems   Review Questions
Thought Questions   Recommended Readings

Chapter 10. Database Management *214*

Introduction   More Data Structures   Database Management Systems
Application   Summary   Two Examples
Review   Key Words   Business Problems   Review Questions
Thought Questions   Recommended Readings

Chapter 11. Computer Communications *232*

Introduction   Data Communications   Fundamentals   Protocol
Networks   Sources of Service   Software   Some Examples
Review   Key Words   Business Problems   Review Questions
Thought Questions   Recommended Readings

**PART III:
SYSTEMS
ANALYSIS AND
DESIGN** *256*

Chapter 12. Building a System *258*

Introduction   Components of a System   Systems Life Cycle   Trade-offs
Hardware and Software Considerations   Providing Alternatives   A New
Venture   A Real Experience
Review   Key Words   Business Problems   Review Questions
Thought Questions   Recommended Readings

Chapter 13. Alternatives to Traditional Design *286*

Introduction   Packages   Generators and Nonprocedural Languages
Prototyping   Summary
Review   Key Words   Business Problems   Review Questions
Thought Questions   Recommended Readings

Chapter 14. An Example of an Application *306*

Introduction   The Environment   The Beginning and the End   The
Inventory Control System   Reporting   Database Contents   Summary
Review   Key Words   Business Problems   Review Questions
Thought Questions   Recommended Readings

**PART IV:
HANDS-ON
COMPUTING** *342*

Chapter 15. Electronic Spreadsheets *344*

Generic Features   An Example   Making Life Easier   Other Features
Summary
Review   Key Words   Business Problems   Review Questions
Thought Questions   Recommended Readings

Chapter 16. Word Processing *366*

Introduction   An Example   More Features   Other Commands
Summary   Some Applications   A Workstation
Review   Key Words   Business Problems   Review Questions
Thought Questions   Recommended Readings

Chapter 17. A Portfolio of Technology and Applications *384*

The Making of a Chip   The Manufacturing Process   End-User Computing in a Fourth Generation Language   Some Further Examples   Business Graphics   Computer-Aided Design   Application   Summary   Computers in Manufacturing   Summary

Chapter 18. BASIC: A High-Level Language *420*

Introduction   Overview   A Growing Program   Other Features   Review   Key Words   Business Problems   Review Questions   Thought Questions   Recommended Readings

PART V: COMPUTER BUSINESS AND SOCIETY *450*

Chapter 19. The Impact of Computers on Organizations *452*

Introduction   The Organization   Summary   Organizational Structure   Individuals
Review   Key Words   Business Problems   Review Questions   Thought Questions   Recommended Readings

Chapter 20. The Management Issue: Dealing with Computers in the Organization *478*

Introduction   The End-User   Management of Information Processing   Summary
Review   Key Words   Business Problems   Review Questions   Thought Questions   Recommended Readings

Chapter 21. The Computer, the Citizen, and Society *498*

Introduction   Some Useful Applications   Issues for Concern   Application   Summary
Review   Key Words   Business Problems   Review Questions   Thought Questions   Recommended Readings

Chapter 22. What's Coming *518*

Introduction   Hardware   Software   The Fifth Generation   Applications   Summary
Review   Key Words   Business Problems   Review Questions   Thought Questions   Recommended Readings

Chapter 23. The Computer Profession *550*

Preview   Introduction   The Computer Industry   A Typical Organization
Users   Career Paths
Review   Key Words   Business Problems   Review Questions
Thought Questions   Recommended Readings

APPENDIX: Programming in BASIC *566*

Glossary *619*

Index *625*

Introduction to Computers and Information Systems

Part I

Computers are bringing about a revolution in information processing. Historians in a hundred years will look back on the last half of the twentieth century as the "information revolution," a period that will be as important as was the Industrial Revolution of the last century. Computers are the engines of the information revolution.

The importance of these devices and their application to information processing in business and government is enough to warrant their study. For the student contemplating a career in any area of business, computers will be an integral part of the work environment.

The computer is the major capital investment for those of us who work in offices. What does this mean? The machines of the factory multiplied the output of the laborer. An individual worker could produce far more because the machine provided the factory worker with leverage. In the same way, computers and information systems provide leverage for the manager and other business professionals.

In this first part of the text, we describe some of the ways in which computers have been applied to solving problems in business. Chapter 1 is a brief introduction to the book. Chapter 2 presents several examples of different kinds of computer systems and is intended to demonstrate the diversity of computer uses; we are limited only by our creativity and imagination in using this technology.

Chapter 3 is a short history of computers. We want not to dwell on the past but to explore how dramatically conditions have changed from the time computers were first invented. These changes mean that today's decisions about how to use computers are quite different from decisions made only five years ago. Unfortunately, some individuals in the computer field have not adapted to this rapid progress. It may help the frustrated user to recognize why some computer professionals are not as modern in philosophy as the user.

INTRODUCTION

Chapter 1

We are living in a computer age, in the period of a revolution that historians will look back on as being as significant as the Industrial Revolution of the nineteenth century. Computers and information systems are an integral part of business and society today. Educated individuals must understand computers and information processing in order to function in their professional and private lives.

INTRODUCTION

Figure 1-1. Blank Lotus Screen Showing Rows and Columns. This is the screen a user sees after starting the Lotus program.

A FIRST JOB

Assume for a few minutes that you have just accepted a position with Multicorp and are in an employee orientation class when suddenly a worried employee rushes up to the instructor.

After a moment of whispered conversation the employee addresses the class: "My name is Ann Mason and I'm secretary to the controller of Multicorp. The president of the firm just called with some data he needs processed; the company is making a decision on whether to enter a new line of business."

She continues, "We have two people out sick, the controller is in London, and I've been here only two weeks. Does anyone here know how to use a *personal computer* with an *electronic spreadsheet package*?"

Naturally eager to make a good impression, you volunteer.

Ann Mason leads you to an office with a personal computer and says, "I've been trying to figure out how to use the computer with no luck. I have the program—or whatever it is that the controller did before leaving—right here, but it just won't work."

Spreadsheet Programs

The *program* Ann Mason wants to use is a type of spreadsheet application. A spreadsheet is a table of rows and columns and is used often in business for different kinds of analyses. For example, forming the first row of the spreadsheet might be a column for each of five years in the future with estimated sales for a new product. The second row would contain costs, and the third the profit. An electronic spreadsheet puts this form on a computer so that the calculations can be done automatically. We shall now see how this program actually works.

"It's easy," you reply. "First, we need a *diskette* with the spreadsheet program itself. Now we load the diskette drive and turn on the computer."

"What's this?" asks Ann.

"This looks like the controller's analysis program.

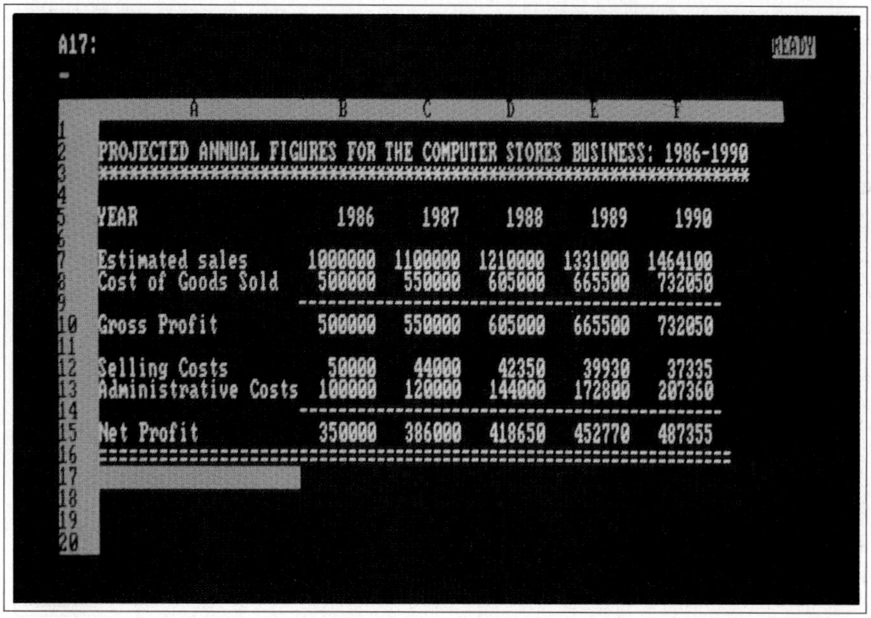

Figure 1-2. The microcomputer screen after loading the program STORE.

See the adhesive label on the outside of this little diskette?" you reply. "We'll put this in the second diskette drive to bring up his calculations."

The computer makes a few noises, and a display appears. After pressing the return key on the keyboard, we see Figure 1-1.

You explain to Ann, "This is like a grid. We can refer to the various cells where the columns and rows intersect, like A-1. Each of these cells can hold a number and each number can be tied to another with a formula."

"I don't think I understand," she replies.

"Do you have notes on the problem? Here they are. Now let's see . . . here the controller called his program STORE. Let's load STORE. By hitting the slash key, the one with the question mark, we get a list of commands on the screen called a **menu.** The commands tell the program what we want to do."

"OK. Hey, this is fun."

"Here we want to load a **file.**" You press a few keys and the display of Figure 1-2 appears. (We shall see how to build this model later.)

Ann says, "This looks good. Here are the num-

bers the president gave me. He thinks we have to be conservative with this new line of computer stores we are thinking of opening; we should start with $750,000 in annual sales for the first year and then go up by $200,000 per year."

You enter a few numbers, noticing that many of the other figures on the display change each time you enter a single number (see Figure 1-3 for two examples of how changes can be made very easily to the display).

"Wow!" exclaims Ann. "That's fantastic. You just put in a number and the whole rest of the screen changes."

You reply, "That's the power of this kind of program. Now let's run a few examples with different numbers, and you can phone the president with the results."

Computer programs like the one described offer tremendous power for many people in the world's economy: the **knowledge workers** who process information as a part of their jobs. *Knowledge workers* is a term applied to the many individuals in the work force who essentially process information.

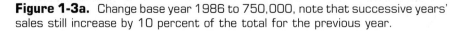

```
A17:                                                              READY
-
              A           B        C        D        E        F
1
2   PROJECTED ANNUAL FIGURES FOR THE COMPUTER STORES BUSINESS: 1986-1990
3   ****************************************************************
4
5   YEAR                 1986     1987     1988     1989     1990
6
7   Estimated sales     750000   825000   907500   998250  1098075
8   Cost of Goods Sold  375000   412500   453750   499125   549038
9                      ------------------------------------------
10  Gross Profit        375000   412500   453750   499125   549038
11
12  Selling Costs        37500    28875    27225    24956    24707
13  Administrative Costs 100000   120000   144000   172800   207360
14                      ------------------------------------------
15  Net Profit          237500   263625   282525   301369   316971
16                      ==========================================
17
18
19
20
```

Figure 1-3a. Change base year 1986 to 750,000, note that successive years' sales still increase by 10 percent of the total for the previous year.

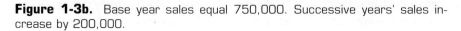

```
A17:                                                              READY
-
              A           B        C        D        E        F
1
2   PROJECTED ANNUAL FIGURES FOR THE COMPUTER STORES BUSINESS: 1986-1990
3   ****************************************************************
4
5   YEAR                 1986     1987     1988     1989     1990
6
7   Estimated sales     750000   950000  1045000  1149500  1264450
8   Cost of Goods Sold  375000   475000   522500   574750   632225
9                      ------------------------------------------
10  Gross Profit        375000   475000   522500   574750   632225
11
12  Selling Costs        37500    33250    31350    28738    28450
13  Administrative Costs 100000   120000   144000   172800   207360
14                      ------------------------------------------
15  Net Profit          237500   321750   347150   373213   396415
16                      ==========================================
17
18
19
20
```

Figure 1-3b. Base year sales equal 750,000. Successive years' sales increase by 200,000.

Figure 1-4. (a) Computer terminals have replaced typewriters at many newspapers. The example above is from the editorial offices of the *Toronto Star-Ledger* newspaper, Toronto, Canada. (b) A reporter is writing an eyewitness report of a plane crash on a computer at the *New York Post*. The editorial system at the *Post* allows the reporter to write stories about late-breaking news events and place them in any of the daily paper's eight editions.

These individuals do not supervise factories or make a product; they process information that enables others to make products. Computer devices are also being used to support workers in other sectors of the economy, like manufacturing. Computer-controlled tools and *robots* can improve product quality and reduce costs. There are very few areas of modern life that have not been touched in some way by computers.

This is a book about computers and information systems. We shall explore how computers work and the many different types of computers available. The techniques used to build computers are incredible, but we must remember that these devices are of most interest in business when they are applied to solve a problem. Therefore, we spend time on programs that make computers work and on systems that use computers to do some task in an organization. The text also contains a section on how to use two types of applications programs and how to program in BASIC. Finally, we look at the results of applying this technology. How have computers influenced the economy and corporations? What should

the citizen know and be concerned about in applying the technology? What does the future hold?

THE COMPUTER PROFESSION

Who uses computers? Almost every business professional uses computers now or soon will. IBM plans to have more than one computer-input device (either a terminal or a small computer) for each of its professional employees. Figures 1-4 to 1-7 are examples of computer applications in a number of settings. Other firms are following suit, so that any student in school today who chooses a business career can expect to use a computer. Much of this text is designed to prepare the reader to work with computers, to understand how to apply this technology to the solution of business problems.

The example we have given describes how a small computer can be used to support a decision in business. The people involved in this example would not be consider computer professionals; instead, they are employees of the firm who work in different

Figure 1-5. Livestock are valuable commodities whose sales are heavily influenced by their pedigrees. In this photo, a Missouri farmer tags a prize animal while the farmer's Apple II microcomputer in the foreground displays the animal's breeding record.

Figure 1-6. (a) This worker in the publishing industry uses a computer to manipulate photographic images to produce the exact image required by his client. The machinery automatically produces the film needed by the printer to print the final color image in a book or magazine (b) Bernhard Hurwood, in his study, is the author of *The Whole Earth Catalog*. He is learning to use the popular Wordstar word processing program on a Tandy microcomputer.

Figure 1-7. This photo shows the famous jazz musician Herbie Hancock in his studio working on the keyboard of an electronic piano while studying the display of the music on a computer screen.

areas, like accounting and finance.

We will see many examples in the text of how employees in various areas of a company use computers and information systems. Many readers will work with computers in a similar manner. Other students will decide to become members of the computer profession; they will work heavily with computers and will contribute to information processing in the firm in a number of different ways. In this chapter, we shall introduce some of the different careers for these computer professionals; Chapter 23 will describe the profession in more detail, after the reader has been exposed to the concepts in the rest of the text.

Most organizations have some type of information services department; in fact, some firms have several of these departments in different locations (see Figure 1-8). Typically, a manager directs the activities of the department and is responsible for seeing that two major activities in the department are completed: the design of computer applications and the operation of existing computer systems. A computer application is the use of a computer to help solve some business problem, for instance, processing a firm's payroll. A computer system to solve this problem has to be designed, a process known as *systems analysis and design.* Once the design is completed, the firm wants to use the computer and its programs (the commands that tell the computer what to do) on a regular basis to process the payroll. The regular run of the system falls under operations. The manager of the computer department is responsible for seeing that systems are both designed and operated satisfactorily.

This manager also has to work with managers and system users in other departments, like marketing, accounting, and manufacturing. The manager of the computer department has a very demanding job because he or she must interact with and try to satisfy users while managing two different types of employees. Typically, individuals who analyze systems and who program computers are quite different from operations personnel.

The systems analyst works with users to define the requirements for a new computer application. This work, as we shall see in Chapters 12 through 14, is conceptual in nature and requires creativity. Programming—that is, taking the requirements for

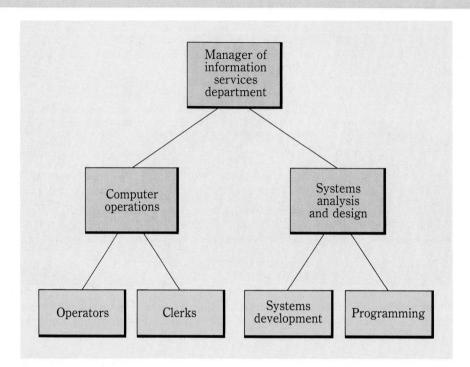

Figure 1-8. The structure of a typical information services department in a company.

a new application and writing a program to fit them— is a difficult task. The manager of the computer department must manage all of these systems analysts and programmers. Frequently, middle managers report to the department manager and are in charge of systems development, particularly in a large computer department.

The systems analysts and programmers often work in teams, and their work environment resembles that of an engineering department, whereas the operations area of the computer department is more like a production line.

In operations, the specifications are very clear: there are so many jobs to be done, and operations is responsible to see that existing computer applications are run as scheduled.

The head of the computer department manages a group of conceptual designers and a group of action-oriented operations personnel. Of course, he or she also has to keep the users and the management of

the firm happy at the same time.

Because it is often very difficult for a central computer department to provide all of the computer support that members of the firm desire, there has been a trend toward giving users in departments like finance, accounting, marketing, sales, and production more opportunities to use computers themselves. This trend is sometimes called **end user computing** and is intended to let users solve their own problems with minimal help from computer staff members. However, end users do need some help; they must be taught how to use the tools available to them for computing and how to locate the data that they want to access on the computer. There are new careers now in consulting with end users and in managing end user computing.

The positions described are typical of the computer department in a firm—any firm, like a manufacturing company, a bank, an insurance company, or a services firm such as a consulting company. A

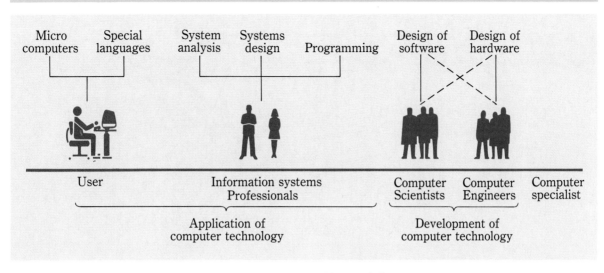

Figure 1-9. The drawing above shows the activities undertaken by some of the many individuals who work in the information processing industry.

number of people are also employed by companies that are in the computer industry; these firms make computers and their associated equipment or they write programs and sell them to others. These firms offer jobs to engineers, to computer scientists, and to some business-school graduates, who work in the development of programs to be sold to firms or individual computer users.

Where are the opportunities? For the business student, there are many ways to participate in the information systems profession (see Figure 1-9). First, we expect most business students to be users, even if they are not professionals. The material in this text will help you in this role. For the student who wants to become a professional, almost any of the careers described is open. It is unlikely that with only some computer courses a business student would actually design computer devices. However, a business student could easily work on the development of computer programs to be sold to businesses. A business student who concentrates on the study of computers could also work in a computer department in a company. Any of the jobs described above would be possible for the computer major, ranging from systems analyst through pro-

grammer to a manager in information processing. One of the greatest opportunities for the business student comes in helping end users. Business school provides the graduate with a variety of courses from different areas of business, so that she or he could help users with problems in marketing, finance, production, sales, and so on.

Whether you use computers casually in your work or whether they become the focus of your career, the opportunities are unlimited. In going through the text, the reader should gain an appreciation of the rapid progress in building and applying computers. We are, indeed, living in a remarkable technological age.

RECOMMENDED READINGS

Daily newspapers for articles on computing.

The Wall Street Journal for announcements of products and stories on the application of the technology.

Popular magazines, like *Business Week* and *Time*, for their articles on computers and information processing.

Chapter 2

This is a book about computers and information systems, two of the most exciting inventions of modern society. In three decades, this technology has created a revolution in how information is managed in homes, businesses, and government. We shall learn about how the computer, the engine that processes information, works, so as to gain an understanding of what can be accomplished with the technology. We also examine a number of different applications of computers to solving real problems. The common thread of the systems described in this chapter is their creativity, the fact that users and designers have been able to apply information technology to doing important and useful work.

After reading the chapter, you should be able to:

- Define a system.
- Describe at least one computer application.
- Discuss some of the problems in computer systems.
- Define each of the components of a computer system.
- Compare and contrast several different applications.
- Explain why it is important to understand computers and information systems.

CURRENT USES OF COMPUTERS

THE ROLE OF THE CITIZEN

Although much of our emphasis is on business problems, there are very serious computer-related issues for the concerned citizen. To motivate our analysis of computer-based information systems, we shall first describe several problem systems. If you understand how computers work and how they are applied to solving problems, you will be in a much better position to deal with the issues raised by the examples that follow.

For example, on several occasions, the U.S. defense command has experienced false alerts. On one of these occasions, it appeared on military command consoles that enemy missiles were approaching the United States. Senior military officers reviewing the situation did not obtain confirmation of an attack from a variety of different sensors and grew suspicious that the alert might be false.

It turned out that a technician had mounted a simulated test tape on a standby computer. This tape indicated on one of the U.S. sensor systems that land and sea missiles had been launched toward the United States. For some reason, the test computer was connected to the on-line defense computer, and the simulated data turned up as real. Because the simulation did not include all U.S. sensors, the military officers in charge of defense determined that the alert was false.

The frightening question is: What if the simulation had been better, if all sensors had been included in the simulation tape? Would the president have been notified? Would the United States have launched a retaliatory strike based on a false computer warning?

One of the largest frauds in the United States—the Equity Funding debacle—was carried out with the assistance of a computer. Although there were many parts to this fraud, one of the key aspects involved the creation of phony insurance policies. Equity Funding sold insurance on policyholders' lives. An individual buys insurance as a form of savings, if the insured lives, and as protection for his or her dependents. A few hundred dollars a year in premiums paid to the insurance company might provide a payment, if the insured dies, of thousands of dollars.

Equity Funding sold many of its insurance policies to reinsurance companies. It is customary in the insurance business to reinsure; that is, one company reduces its risk by selling some of its policies to another firm. The reinsurance company might have paid Equity Funding 190 percent of the first year's premium on the policy as the price for the business. However, in succeeding years, Equity Funding should have provided the reinsurance firm with the premiums on these policies, less a small administration fee.

The false policies, then, generated a great deal of cash in the beginning but required Equity Funding to come up with even more money in the future to avoid arousing suspicion. Evidently, the actuarial department created a simulation program to generate real-looking policy numbers for the fake policies. It is estimated that over sixty thousand false policies were created (see Figure 2-1).

Because the firm's auditors were not knowledgeable about computers, they were easily fooled during their audit. The accountants believed the computer staff when they said that a computer error prevented them from printing the full policy number for the policies being audited. If the program had printed the full number, there would have been duplicates because many of the false policies had the same numbers as existing policies, and the fraud would have been evident. The computer department also provided the addresses of company employees when the accountants sent letters to false policyholders to confirm the existence of their policies. The people in the company receiving the letters were part of the conspiracy, so they sent them back indicating that they owned the policies.

When the whole house of cards tumbled down, experts estimated that the cost of the fraud exceeded $100 million. Worse yet, thousands of shareholders were left with virtually worthless stock. The computer was not responsible for the fraud, but dishonest individuals used a computer to help them perpetrate one of the largest conspiracies in American business history.

How computers are used must concern citizens for a number of reasons. We have seen the possible dangers in defense systems and conspiracy. How-

Figure 2-1. One of the many newspaper stories about the huge computer-assisted fraud at Equity Funding Corporation of America. This story is from the front page of the *New York Times*, April 5, 1973.

Equity Funding to Petition Under the Bankruptcy Law

Concern to File Action Today—Banks Find Loans in Default

S.E.C. Plans Intensive Inquiry Into Methods Used by Company

By ROBERT J. COLE

The Equity Funding Corporation of America, caught up in a multimillion dollar scandal over bogus insurance policies and besieged by bankers for the immediate repayment of $50-million in loans, disclosed last night that it would petition the court today to file for reorganization under Chapter X of the Federal bankruptcy law.

Lawyers for the financial services conglomerate told Judge Harry Pregerson in United States District Court in Los Angeles that the step had been approved by the company's board of directors.

Judge Pregerson ordered the company to file after hearing from representatives of the California Insurance Department, the California Attorney General, the Securities and Exchange Commission, a lawyer for the Wells Fargo Bank and Lewis B. Merrifield, a Los Angeles lawyer named by the court as special investigator.

Equity Funding reported earlier that it had been notified officially by the bankers that the loans were in default and that the bankers planned to

By FELIX BELAIR Jr.
Special to The New York Times

WASHINGTON, April 4—The Securities and Exchange Commission's investigation of fraud charges it has brought against the Equity Funding Corporation of America promises to be the most intensive undertaken by the agency since its creation in 1933, officials reported today.

In addition to inquiring into the company's complex system of creating alleged spurious insurance business and fictitious assets, the commission's inquiry will extend to "inside information" that may have induced institutional investors and large brokerage firms to unload their Equity Funding shares on the market before trading was suspended last week.

Obviously disturbed by the magnitude of the alleged fraudulent practices of Equity Funding, the commission's enforcement staff plans to delve deeply in its interrogation of parent and subsidiary company personnel.

"Usually, our fraud investigations penetrate three layers of company executives,' a high official of the agency said. "But

Continued on Page 73, Column 3 | Continued on Page 73, Column 1

ever, there are also isolated instances where individuals have tried to abuse systems for their personal gain alone. In a recent case, an ex-employee of a Federal Reserve bank tried to extract important data from its files after leaving the bank. (The Federal Reserve system is the central U.S. banking system, and you will study its operations in courses on economics, finance, and/or banking.) The employee took a position with one of the Wall Street brokerage houses. These firms buy and sell stocks for their customers for a commission; they also perform a number of services for individuals and corporations.

In order to attract clients, they often conduct extensive research and make it available to the people who use their services. If clients and potential clients find the research useful, the firm hopes that they will do business with it.

Brokerage firms will also manage funds for an individual or a company. There are usually management fees involved, and the broker also earns commissions when stocks are bought and sold for the managed portfolio.

What did the ex-employee of the Federal Reserve stand to gain? The Federal Reserve publishes key monetary statistics, and these numbers often influence the stock market. For example, if traders are very optimistic based on these statistics, they might buy a lot of stock, causing the market price of stocks (measured by the market average) to rise. The opposite might occur as well. If we knew the Federal Reserve numbers in advance, we could buy or sell a lot of stock short, without actually owning it. (It is possible to sell stock at today's price without owning it. Then we must buy stock to deliver at a later date. If the price of the stock falls, then we make a profit. This practice is called *selling short* because we are short of the stock we are selling.) After the price change, we could cover our short position for a nice gain, assuming that the market reacted as expected once the Federal Reserve statistics were released.

How was the ex-employee caught? An alert supervisor at the Federal Reserve noticed that an account on the computer was active for an employee who she knew was absent that day. The supervisor notified other officials, and a separate data file was set up for just this account. The ex-employee then accessed incorrect data and was traced and apprehended.

The problems described are very serious. Computers have a tremendous potential to help improve the way organizations function and to enhance the quality of work life. The point of the examples given is that, as is true of any powerful tool, a computer can be misused. There is no magic to developing a computer system that is successful. Like any other human endeavor, designing and running computer systems requires sound thinking and great diligence. Whether we encounter them in business or at leisure, a good knowledge of how computers and information systems work is important for all of us. It is hard to imagine coping with the complexities of modern life without this kind of understanding.

COMPONENTS OF INFORMATION SYSTEMS

Before we look at some examples of information systems in detail, it is important to have a model of the various components of a system. Unfortunately,

the word *system* is used in a number of different ways. One definition is that a system is a set of interrelated parts that work together for some purpose. In common usage, you will find something like transportation described as a system. Yet within the transportation system we find many subsystems, like air, rail, and road. Someone focusing on one of these may call it a system as well. In the computer field, we have the same problems. One individual might call the organization a system, whereas another looks at some part—say, manufacturing—as a system. Computers and all of their parts are also sometimes called a *computer system*. Even more confusing, the application of a computer to solve a problem is also frequently called a *computer system*. Because this ambiguous use of the word *system* is so common, we shall also use it in several ways in the text. Hopefully, the context of the discussion will make clear which kind of system is being referenced.

Figure 2-2 presents four major aspects of a system. At the highest level, we find the organization itself. It is important to stress the role of the organization; except for the computer used at home, systems generally exist in the context of some organization. The goals of that organization and the individuals who work in it influence the type of systems developed and do a great deal to determine the success of each computer application.

Next, we see the user, who interacts with a system. For computer systems that process data and provide information, the user is crucial. Users provide many of the data processed; they also look at the output from a computer system and interpret it as information. Users also have to follow the manual procedures that are associated with a system. For example, the sales staff must fill out an order form and send it in for computer entry or there will be no record of their sales. The user and the procedures that he or she follows are vital components of the system.

The user interacts with something called the *application*, which is the task undertaken by a computer system. Examples of computer applications include a system in the university that keeps track of the courses taken by students, a system that pre-

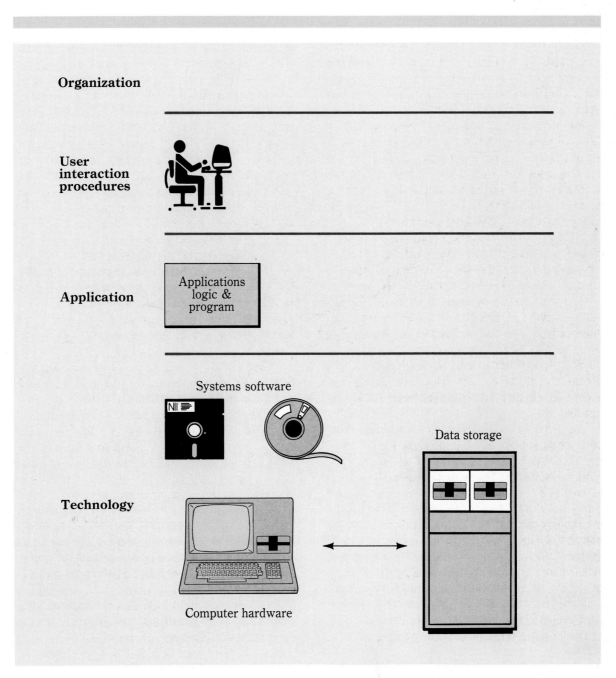

Organization

User interaction procedures

Application

Applications logic & program

Systems software

Data storage

Technology

Computer hardware

Figure 2-2. Components of a Computer-Based System. The organization provides the environment for a user who follows procedures while interacting with an application of a computer. The application draws on the technology including hardware and software.

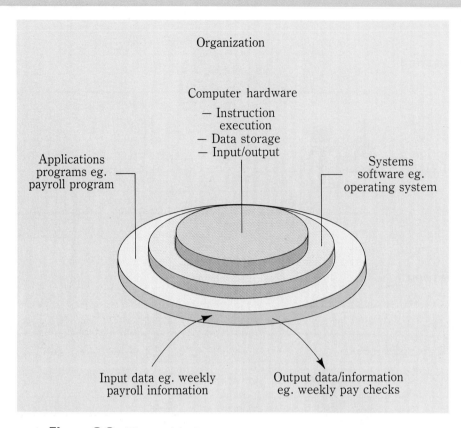

Figure 2-3. The model of a system applied to payroll processing.

pares payroll checks for the faculty and staff, and a system that pays the bills for the goods and services that the university buys. The application has logic; that is, the procedures and programs express how a task is done. The logic of the payroll application tells how a payroll is computed: the hours worked are multiplied by the wage rate, and then various deductions are subtracted from each person's pay.

The last layer in our model of a system consists of technology. Here we find the actual computer hardware, the parts of a computer that you can see. There is a computer that executes **instructions** and some kind of data **storage;** there may also be **communications** among computer devices. Succeeding chapters explore this technology in much greater detail. The computer must have a program or **software** to do anything useful. An **applica-**

tions program expresses the logic of a system; there are also programs known as **systems software.** These programs manage the resources of the computer. We shall discuss the most important of these, the **operating system,** in a subsequent chapter.

As you see different examples of computer applications and when you design an application, keep in mind these four levels:

- The organization
- The user
- Applications
- Technology

Figure 2-3 shows how a simple payroll application fits into our framework above.

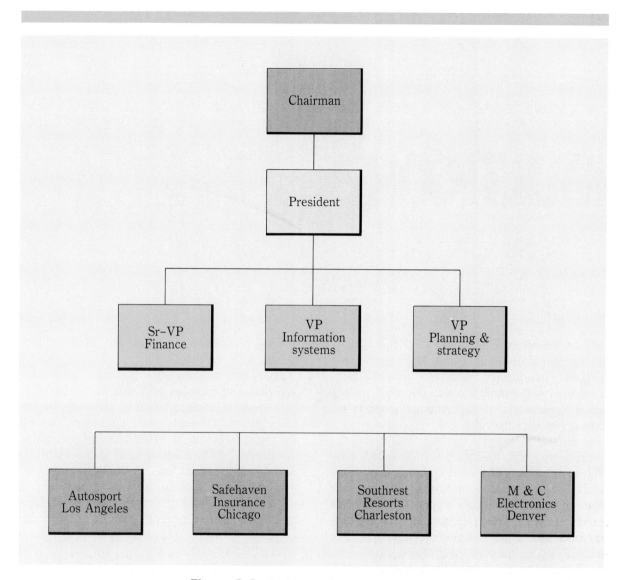

Figure 2-4. Multicorp Organization Chart.

The organization furnishes the environment for the design and operation of the system. The user is key in whether and how the system is used. Later, we shall explore the user's all-important role in design, as well. The application refers to the task that the system is to perform; it contains the logic of the system. Finally, we depend on the technology to operate the system; it is the engine that powers the application.

MULTICORP

Multicorp is a hypothetical company that we will use throughout the text to illustrate many of the points raised herein. Multicorp is a large conglomerate, a company that has many divisions that produce different products or services. An organization chart for the company may be found in Figure 2-4.

The firm has grown by purchasing companies in

different industries. Why is this a good idea? By having different kinds of businesses, Multicorp reduces its risks. For example, one type of business that it owns might suffer through a recession while another would be unaffected. Being in different products and markets spreads the risks. Also, the firm can shift resources to subsidiaries that are doing well.

Multicorp has its headquarters in New York City. The headquarters is relatively small because management believes in decentralization. The managers of the local subsidiaries have a great deal of freedom to run their businesses. Headquarters allocates capital funds among the various subsidiaries and, of course, decides on purchasing new firms (acquisitions) or selling off parts of the firm (divestiture).

There is a computer at headquarters for corporate applications. The various divisions also have computers for applications that are mostly local in nature. There are computer-department staff members working for the headquarters managers, and there are computer departments at each division that has a computer.

Currently, Multicorp has four major business lines. The first of these is Autosport, an automotive parts manufacturer and distributor based in Los Angeles. Autosport manufactures some products and buys others; it operates a line of retail stores that sell replacement parts and accessories to motorists.

Safehaven is Multicorp's insurance subsidiary. The president has high ambitions for this division: "The world is turning to financial services—we are no longer just someone selling insurance. Now we are trying to provide a whole family of services to our clients." With a strong base in the Midwest, Safehaven is headquartered in Chicago.

Five years ago, Multicorp bought Southrest, a major resort operator on the North and South Carolina coasts. With a central office in Charleston, South Carolina, the company has been growing at about 8 percent a year.

M&C Electronics Stores is the fourth Multicorp venture. This string of retail stores with headquarters in Denver sells electronic parts to consumers. The firm features items like stereo sets, games, television, and small appliances. Currently, the only computer equipment it sells is a small home computer, primarily for game playing.

MANUFACTURING AT AUTOSPORT

To illustrate how pervasive computers and information systems are at Multicorp, we shall look at the major systems in use at Autosport's largest manufacturing plant. We have two objectives in this review of Autosport. The first is to gain an understanding of how a business operates in general: What is a business? How does it make money? What services does it provide? Second, we want to see how a computer can contribute to the efficiency and effectiveness of a firm. Computers are used extensively throughout business and government; we want to understand their contribution to the user and to his or her organization.

A System

What is a system? We have used the term above assuming an intuitive knowledge on the part of the reader. A more formal definition is that a system is a set of interrelated parts that are organized to achieve some objective. A system is complex; it may have many parts that are related in different ways. However, a system, by definition, is not chaotic; its parts are organized to achieve some goal. There are many different types of systems; computer systems represent one type and they are the topic of this text.

Why is it hard to understand information systems?

1. You can see only part of an information system; most of what is important is invisible, for example, the data storage component.
2. Many people who work with computer-based systems (called *users*) deal with only a small part of the system; for example, a clerk at Autosport may only enter orders for parts.
3. Information systems are abstract.
4. Information systems have many components.
5. Information systems tend to be very complex; it is hard to understand all of their intricacies.
6. When information systems are computer-based, the computer processes data in millionths of a second so that a vast amount of information is operated on in a short period of time.

We shall look at an information system from the following perspective:
1. *The environment.* What is the nature of the business?
2. *The application area. Computer systems* are developed in some area of the firm such as marketing, accounting, and sales.
3. *The purpose.* What is the computer system supposed to do?
4. *The functions.* What functions does the computer system perform? For example, it may accept time cards and produce a payroll check to give to workers.

Logic

Logic is the step-by-step procedure followed by the system to transform input into output reports or answers to queries.

Input. What data are supplied by whom?

Update. Information systems have records like those kept in a file cabinet. How are they changed over time? As an example, the year-to-date wages are updated each time the payroll is computed.

Reporting. What formal reports are produced regularly? For the payroll, we have a register of payments, W-2 forms, tax reports, social security payments, and the check for the employee.

Query Capability. What questions will the system answer? We might allow payroll and personnel department employees to ask questions about the data stored for the payroll application.

Transactions

Many information systems process transactions; that is, the computer and its programs help with the basic data flow for the firm, such as entering orders and preparing reports. A transactions-processing system should be contrasted with other types of systems. For example, an inquiry system provides answers to users' questions, and a decision support system (DSS) helps a user with a decision problem like the spreadsheet program described in the first chapter.

Figure 2-5. These few symbols can be used to diagram procedures and information flows.

Figure 2-6 (opposite). Autosport Systems Overview. The major computer applications at Autosport, a manufacturing and distribution company.

Flow of information or documents

Figure 2-5 shows the symbols that we shall use to describe an information system. A rectangle represents the processing of some kind of information. The rectangle with rounded ends is an input. The third component, represented by a modified rectangle, is a file, a place where data are stored. The fourth item in the figure is a report, some type of output from a system. Finally, flow lines with arrows show the direction in which information moves.

Figure 2-6 shows the information systems at one of Autosport's manufacturing plants. We can actually see that many individual systems might be called subsystems of an entire manufacturing information-processing system.

The environment for all of the information systems we shall discuss here is an auto manufacturing firm. Our first application is production scheduling (see Figure 2-7). A production schedule shows what items are planned for production for each planning period; in the case of Autosport, the period is one week. The purpose of the production scheduling system is to take production forecasts and match them with the capacity of the factory to determine a feasible plan for manufacturing. The functions supported by the system include the input of forecast data, the matching of forecasts with production capacity, and the production of a planning report.

Let's look at the logic of the application. The marketing department supplies the forecast. The system processes the forecast data and any input adjustments made by the planners. It also updates the records of past plans based on what has actually

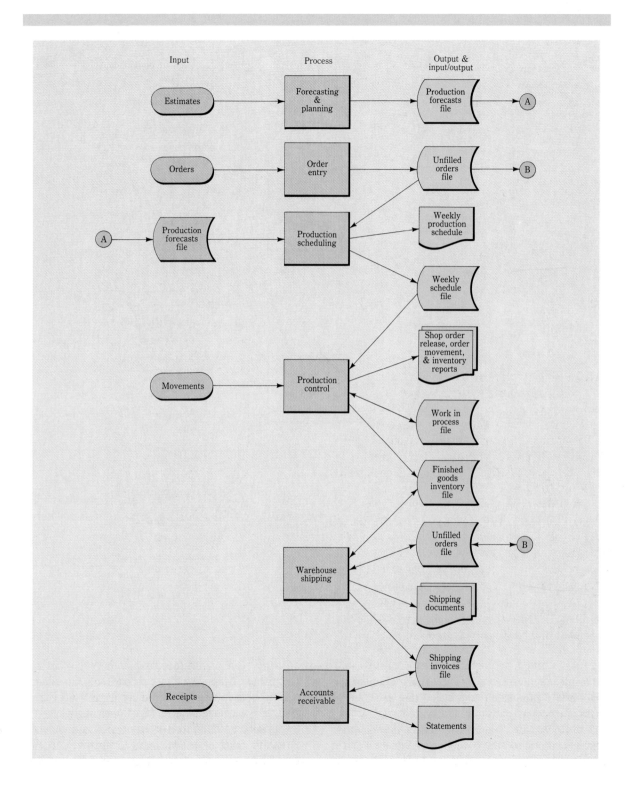

Input	Process	Output & input/output
Estimates	Forecasting & planning	Production forecasts file → A
Orders	Order entry	Unfilled orders file → B
A → Production forecasts file	Production scheduling	Weekly production schedule
		Weekly schedule file
Movements	Production control	Shop order release, order movement, & inventory reports
		Work in process file
		Finished goods inventory file
	Warehouse shipping	Unfilled orders file ← B
		Shipping documents
Receipts	Accounts receivable	Shipping invoices file
		Statements

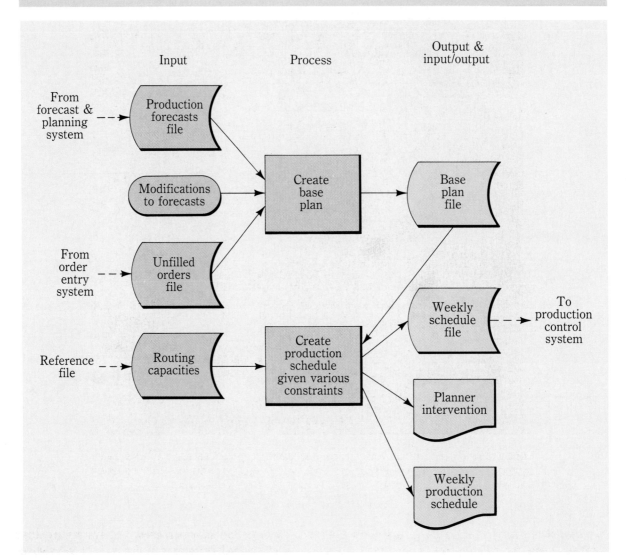

Figure 2-7. Autosport Production Scheduling. Production scheduling must balance planned production with orders from customers to tell the factory what and how much to produce.

been manufactured so far. The major output of the system is a production plan called the weekly production schedule; each time the system runs, it produces a new plan. Figure 2-8 shows how another firm has automated the collection of data or work in process.

Our next Autosport system is order processing, a system that is common in many firms (see Figure 2-9). The purpose of an order-processing system is to accept customer orders promptly and to place them in a machine-readable file for further processing. The functions of this system include entering

Figure 2-8. This employee of Omark Industries, a manufacturer of chain saw cutting bars, uses an Intermec bar code data collection system. The production control worker above uses a wand to input data on production.

orders and creating a record of what is ordered so that the items can be shipped from inventory. Also, the file of all orders is used by production control to release actual manufacturing instructions to the plant. Production control looks at the weekly production schedule and at the orders for particular products already received from customers and decides on what specific items to produce on each given day (see Figure 2-10).

The logic of the Autosport order-entry system begins with the input of the actual orders from customers. The system accepts data about the customer and each product ordered. It looks up the prices of the items and computes the total value of

the order for billing purposes. The system updates a file of all orders entered so far and not yet shipped (we usually leave completed orders in this file for a while, too, for inquiry purposes). Updates of the file also include changes in existing orders that customers phone in. The system generates a number of reports; two important ones are a listing of sales for the day, the week, and the month and a report of what items have been ordered to be shipped on a given date. The first report is used by sales and general management to compare actual orders to forecast; the second is used by production control to help decide what to produce. Finally, the logic of the system allows for inquiries about individual orders

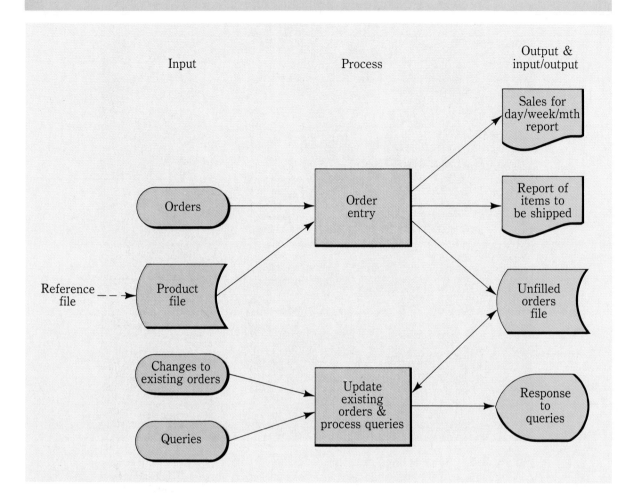

Input	Process	Output & input/output

Figure 2-9. Autosport Order Processing. Order entry involves keying orders from customers in to a computer. Orders represent the sales "booked" (put in the order book) while net sales represents goods shipped less returns.

Figure 2-10 (opposite). Autosport Production Control. Production control is responsible for implementing the production plan. This function releases work orders for manufacturing to begin and monitors work in the process of manufacture.

from a terminal; this feature is used extensively in customer services to answer customer questions that come by telephone.

Production control is an application that depends on the two systems that we have just discussed: production scheduling and order entry (see Figure 2-11). The purpose of this system is to assist the production control staff in releasing factory orders and monitoring the progress of orders. As discussed

under order processing, the production control staff starts jobs through the factory. It then watches progress; that is, the staff controls the work in process. The second part of the production control system moves the records of work in process into finished-goods inventory when the factory has completed a product. The functions of the system are to provide information about production scheduling on orders and on in-process inventory. A second

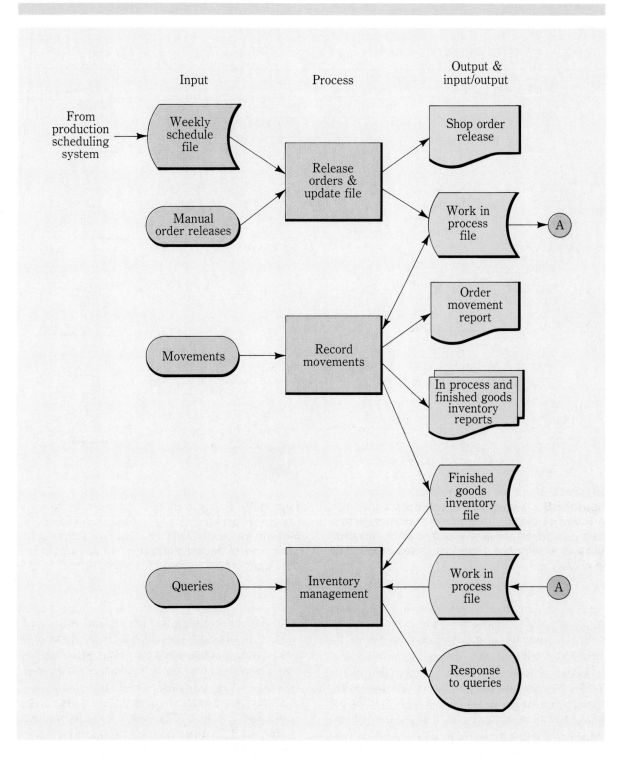

AUTOSPORT WORK CENTER WORK-IN-PROGRESS REPORT AS AT 7/25/86

Work Center: 1

ORDER NUMBER	PART NUMBER	HOURS COMPLETED	EST. HOURS REMAINING	CUSTOMER NAME	SHIP DATE
1006	TDF891	26	134	Metalico	8-30-86
1024	ABC111	218	62	Jacobsen Co.	7-31-86
1024	TDG675	90	5	Jacobsen Co.	7-31-86
1040	KJH004	133	26	Hunt & Cowe	7-31-86
1134	PLL220	290	288	Continental	8-30-86
1134	PLL221	2	198	Continental	8-30-86

Work Center: 2

ORDER NUMBER	PART NUMBER	HOURS COMPLETED	EST. HOURS REMAINING	CUSTOMER NAME	SHIP DATE
1002	DSE900	45	35	Premium Mfg.	8-30-86
1005	DSG808	30	10	Premium Mfg.	8-30-86
1232	SAF454	21	21	Continental	8-30-86
1056	GHF434	90	10	Roberts & Son	7-31-86
1565	GHL434	20	60	Yaydon Corp.	7-31-86
1565	GHS454	84	31	Yaydon Corp.	8-30-86
1602	ABC111	10	15	Pacific Inc.	8-30-86
1611	SAK900	45	15	Universal	7-31-86

Figure 2-11. Example of Autosport Order Movement Report. This report shows the orders in the process of manufacture at Autosport work centers. A work center is an organizational unit where some manufacturing process takes place.

function is to maintain an in-process inventory and a finished-goods inventory accurately.

The logic of the system includes input from the production schedule and the production scheduler. This staff member inputs new orders to be released to the factory and any changes in past orders. The factory also supplies data in the form of movement reports. The work in process actually consists of a number of different steps in the factory; at each major transfer, workers in the factory enter into a computer terminal the fact that the order has moved from one point to another. All of the information entered is used to update the order file and the in-process and finished-goods inventories. For example, the release of an order is of interest to customer services in case someone calls to find out when certain products will be available if none are in inventory. As the factory order moves through manufacturing, the in-process stages are updated as already described.

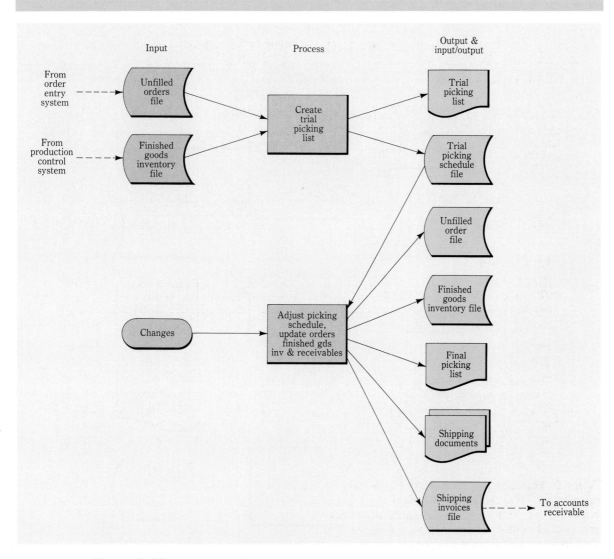

Figure 2-12. Autosport Warehouse Shipping. The final stage in processing a customer order is shipping. The goods are sent to the customer, which creates an entry in accounts receivable for Autosport. The receivable eventually produces a statement of what the customer owes Autosport.

Reporting from this production control system consists of movement reports that show where factory orders are located in the plant. There are also various reports of in-process and finished-goods inventory to be used by production control. The system features an inquiry function as well, so that various individuals at Autosport can check in-process and finished-goods balances for different products.

The purpose of the shipping system is to assist in filling orders and preparing them for shipment (see Figure 2-12). Its functions include the production of a trial picking list for the warehouse (a list of goods

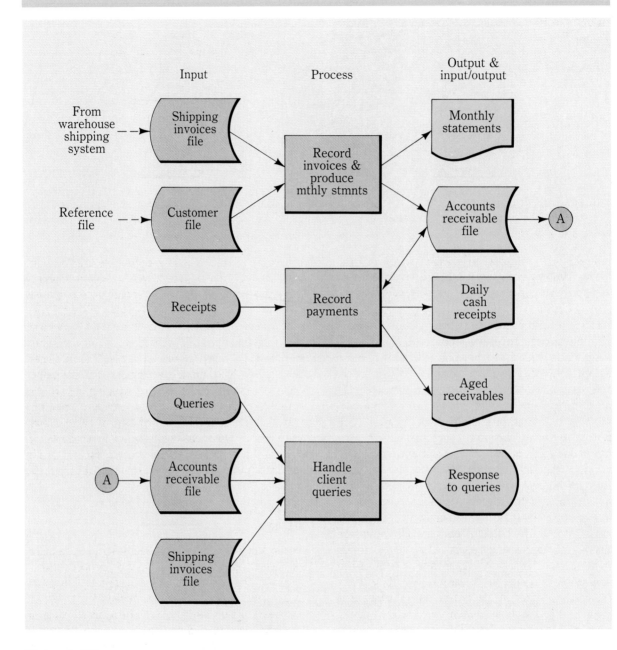

Figure 2-13. Autosport Accounts Receivable. On a monthly basis, Autosport sends statements to customers. When customers pay, the accounts receivable department has to record payment.

Figure 2-14. Autosport Accounts Receivable Display Screen.

AUTOSPORT ACCOUNTS
RECEIVABLE SYSTEM

Do you wish to:

1. Create a Receivable
2. Prepare Monthly Statements
3. Record a Payment
4. Make an Enquiry

Make your selection by typing the corresponding digit: ___ or press the ESCAPE key to return to the Main Menu.

to be shipped), the creation of a final picking list, and the preparation of shipping labels and invoices. The warehouse manager uses the system extensively in filling orders and shipping them.

The logic of the shipping system is based on input from the order processing and production control systems, at least in the beginning. The warehouse manager asks the system to compare unfilled orders with the finished-goods inventory to determine what can be picked and shipped and also to take into account the date that the customer asked for the shipment to be made. This processing produces the recommended picking list. The warehouse manager examines this list and then puts into the computer any changes that she or he wishes to make. Then the system updates its records of what is in inventory and updates the orders to show that they have been shipped. The output from the shipping system consists of the picking reports already described, plus labels for the cartons and an invoice to be placed in an envelope glued to the carton. A carbon of the invoice is enclosed in the carton, as a shipping list.

The last transactions system that we shall examine is accounts receivable. The purpose of this system is to keep track of the money that customers owe Autosport, a very critical function in any firm. The functions included in the system are the creation of a receivable, the preparation of statements, and the input of payments by customers (see Figures 2-13 and 2-14).

The input for the system comes from the shipping program and the accounts receivable clerks. The shipping program creates a receivable when goods are sent; the receivable corresponds to the invoice and shows each item and its cost plus the total cost of the shipment. Each month, the accounts receivable department runs a report consisting of statements which are mailed to customers. The customer is supposed to return the statement with payment; then the clerks retrieve the computer's record of the statement and mark it paid. The receipt of money, then, results in the major updating of the system. The clients' invoices and statements are available for inquiry, an especially useful feature for customer services, which must respond to questions from clients.

Design

The systems that have just been described are quite extensive, but they are still basically process transactions in the organization. One system at Autosport makes heavy use of computer technology to assist engineers and drafting people. The applications area is product design, and one function of the system is to provide a repository of engineering drawings. The system is a design aid for the engineer; a terminal that can display line drawings is the major part of the engineer's **workstation** (see Figure 2-15). (A workstation is a collection of computer-based tools to support the engineer's work.)

Suppose that the engineer is assigned a new part

Figure 2-15. A computer-aided design system at Autosport is used by an engineer during the early stages of product development. The operator is making changes on the computer to a design held in her hand that she developed earlier using the system.

to produce. First, the engineer might see if it is similar to an existing part; if so, he or she retrieves the part and displays it on the terminal. Then, using powerful commands, the engineer makes changes in the drawing; these changes update a copy of the part's drawing in computer memory. When done, the new drawing is stored in the computer under a new part number; the designer creates a picture of the part using a plotting device attached to the computer. The computer has saved many hours of drawing and drudgery associated with the creation and or modification of a part.

Decision Support

Not shown at Autosport are all of the ways in which computers and information systems can be used to help managers and professionals make specific decisions. The forecast, for example, helps management construct a budget that is used to determine what expenditures and new products to authorize.

The production control manager looks at various order summaries and reallocates factory capacity to different products. At headquarters, managers use spreadsheet programs to help evaluate new plans.

In this lengthy discussion of Autosport's computer systems, even though we have only touched the surface of Autosport's applications, it should be apparent that computers and information systems play a major role at Multicorp. In the rest of this text, we shall try to learn more about not just the role of systems, but how to design, use, and manage them. The firms that prosper in the coming years will be those that are able to control and take advantage of the powerful technology available today.

SURVEY OF APPLICATIONS

Multicorp is a hypothetical firm; the applications we have described are typical of those such a company would use. In this section, we briefly sketch some

Figure 2-16. A server at the Encroe Restaurant, Toronto, Canada, uses a Remanco system to enter her customer's order.

unusual and interesting uses of computers. In initiating computer applications and designing them, creativity is encouraged.

A Computer for Dinner

A number of fine food restaurants are using computers. The purpose of the system is to aid in accounting and to provide management with a way to keep track of the details that determine whether the restaurant will be profitable or not.

Input into the computer, shown in Figure 2-16, describes each meal; the program then deducts the items consumed from inventory. One report from the computer system compares the price of each dish with the cost of the raw materials used as ingredients. Another report from the system compares the prices from different vendors and allows the manager to choose the lowest-priced supplies consistent with quality standards. Although some restaurants use the computer to improve service to customers, most of the systems are intended to save on operating cost.

In the Pits

The technology of the automobile has been improved through competition. However, until recently, most of the technology has been automotive; now the computer is playing an increasingly important role. A relatively new entrant in auto racing, Shierson Racing, is using computers to catch up with more experienced racing teams.

The problem is to identify the forces that act on a race car so that the team can set the car up for each new race track. A "magic box" sits on the floor in front of the driver in the forwardmost part of the car. The box has a processor and a memory, which is used to store the data collected during a drive. The data are downloaded onto a digital tape when the car enters the pits, and then the tape is processed on an old Apple computer (see Figure 2-17).

At the Indianapolis 500, cars were having trouble with exploding gearboxes. Conventional wisdom was that, in the turns, the oil was being forced out of the gears by the g forces of cornering. The data collected on the computer indicated that the problem

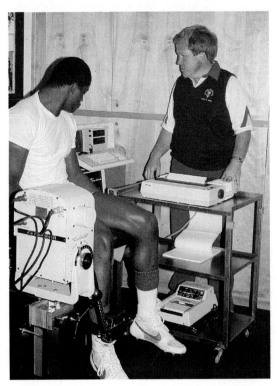

Figure 2-17. A Shierson racing car during a speed test in Florida.

Figure 2-18. San Diego Chargers trainer Ric Mc-Donald assesses the strength in the legs of Fred Robinson. The data from the test are analyzed using a computer system designed for training members of the Chargers football team.

was the opposite: in the long straightaway, the oil sump was being pumped dry. A minor change in the pickup for oil cured the problem. In another race, the driver complained of understeer at a top speed of 188 miles per hour. The data analysis showed that the front of the car was too high and the rear too low. A quarter of an inch solved the problem and produced a top speed of 198 miles per hour.

The racers say that the computer helps them arrive at a solution; the final answer is usually a compromise. The computer solution may result in a car that is too difficult to drive, so the needs of the human behind the wheel are also factored into the car's setup.

On the Gridiron

In a recent season, the San Diego Chargers, a professional football team, scored three touchdowns and had one long gain using one play: 372 F Shoot Pump. In this play, the tight end heads downfield eight yards and cuts to the outside while the fullback shoots to the same area to draw the strong safety. With the safety cleared out, the quarterback fakes a pass to freeze the linebacker covering the end. Then he throws to the tight end, who has darted upfield into the area left open by the departing safety. When the play works, the end usually scores a touchdown. This is certainly a tough play to draw on the blackboard! This play was designed with the help of a computer from Quantel Business Computers.

A number of professional sports teams use computers for accounting tasks and for keeping track of potential college-draft picks. Coaches are most excited today about computerized game analysis, which lets them identify formations, define pass patterns, examine player performance, and so on. The coaches also study the printouts to find holes in an opponent's defense. Figure 2-18 shows another application of computers in professional sports.

A Computer for Travel

Two major airlines, American and United, have placed terminals connected to their reservations computers in thousands of travel agencies around the country. The airlines have each invested an estimated $200 million to $250 million in these systems. An estimated sixty-five thousand terminals are connected to the American Sabre system, a system that has processed a peak load of 950 messages per second. The computers list flights and fares and make reservations, not just for the airlines' own flights, but for all major national and international carriers (see Figure 2-19). It has been estimated that $20 billion in travel is booked through computerized reservations systems each year.

Why is the travel agent interested? Access to these systems through a terminal at the travel agency means that the agent can make reservations directly without calling an airline. The systems also feature printers that produce the tickets, a tremendous savings compared with the cost of writing tickets by hand. One travel agent reported a 50 percent improvement in productivity for agents and has found that he was able to sell 41 percent more tickets per year after computerization.

The systems have been so successful for the airlines that the government is investigating whether they should be regulated! The airlines charge the travel agents for the terminals and the computer service. However, one of the biggest advantages for the airline is that its own flights show up first on the display when an inquiry is made.

Thus, the airline is more likely to get the business than a competitor. The government is concerned that the airlines have been too competitive with their systems; for example, if a system lists an airline last, its flights may seldom be chosen. Even worse, if an airline is omitted from the system, a large number of travel agents may not know that it exists.

Other computer systems aid the airlines in different ways. At American, a computer figures the most efficient flight plan and sets crew schedules. It computes overtime and pay for thirty-four thousand employees. Another American system keeps track of the entire history of every plane in the fleet, the flight numbers and destinations, and every maintenance action performed. Every two weeks, the computer adjusts American's flight schedules and

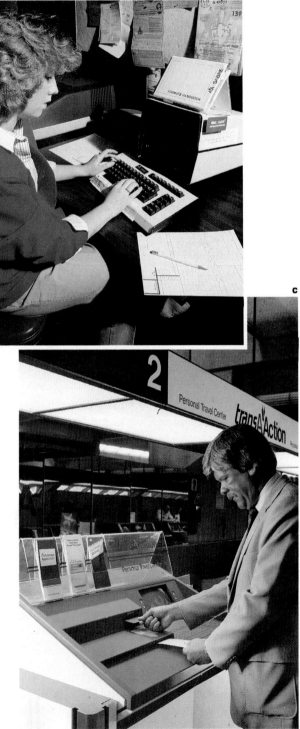

Figure 2-19. (a) A reservations agent at American Airlines examines data on reservations and flight availability. (b) A travel agent in Portland, Maine accesses the same Sabre system to display airline schedules and book convenient flights for her clients. (c) American has convenient "Personal Travel Centers." The traveler above orders a ticket and makes payment with a credit card using a center.

Figure 2-20. A behaviorist uses a hand-held computer to count repetitions of movements by monkeys at the San Diego Zoo.

matches the available planes to the most useful routes.

A computer keeps track of fuel prices at various locations and figures the cost of taking on fuel where prices are cheaper to avoid a fill-up at a fuel-expensive airport; computers also keep track of the amount of fuel used by each of American's four thousand pilots. A computer on board each of American's planes sends a message to the reservations computer in Tulsa as soon as the plane is airborne. The computer consults the plane's flight plan and weather and flashes an estimated time of arrival on the airport monitors at each of the flight's destinations.

Computers have been used by these airlines to obtain a competitive edge. More applications of this sort can be expected as firms learn how to manage technology and harness it as a part of their overall corporate strategy.

A Computer in the Zoo

Believe it or not, there is a system known as the International Species Inventory System. The system contains information on fifty-seven thousand captive birds and mammals in 175 locations around the world. The records include the animal's age, sex, and parentage; where it was caught or born; its current location; and any planned moves.

Why are we interested in this information? We go to the zoo to look at the animals, not a computer. The system is actually quite important for breeding. If there is too much inbreeding, the offspring are likely to die. One zoo's penguins were all dying. The zoo had been using its original penguins for breeding and selling off the offspring; no one had noticed until the original penguins started dying of old age.

Input for the system has to come from forms filled out by zoo directors. Now the system is limited by funds, but the sponsor's hope to expand it so that input will be easier and the information more readily accessible. Another use of computers at the zoo is shown in Figure 2-20.

OBSERVATIONS

We have reviewed a number of computer applications. Note that they all occur in some organizational context, from a firm to a racing team to a football squad. There are one or more users of the system and there are one or more applications with logic and programs. The applications rely on underlying technology that consists of systems software and hardware and data storage devices.

Beyond the components of the systems, the common aspects of these applications are the diversity and creativity they display. The computer has been used for thousands of different applications. Surely, there are common ones like payroll processing, but there are also unique systems like those found in the zoo and on the auto racetrack. The reader is encouraged to use his or her imagination, to be creative, and to learn enough about computer technology to use it to gain a competitive advantage.

SUMMARY

At this point, the reader should have a good idea of the many ways in which computers and information systems can be applied in a variety of situations. Computer-based systems are all around us, though they are often well concealed behind the scenes. Consider what the world would be like without them. How could banks process checks and provide services? How could any large corporation keep track of orders, budgets, bills, and other documents? How would a modern airline operate without a computerized reservations system? Because these systems are so pervasive, we must know enough about them to function in our business and private lives. This book is designed to help the reader gain a basic understanding of computers and information systems.

Review of Chapter 2

REVIEW

In this chapter we have covered a lot of material. Our objective has been to motivate you to learn more about the phenomenal power and potential of computers and information systems. At this point, you are not expected to understand the details in each component of our model of the organization, the user, the application, and the underlying technology. The rest of the book will fill in these details.

It is hoped, however, that at this point you have an appreciation of the variety of ways in which computers and information systems can make a contribution to individuals, organizations, and society. We are limited by our understanding of the components of a system and by our imagination. The text can help provide understanding, but only the reader can furnish creativity!

KEYWORDS

Accounts receivable	Computer
Application	Conglomerate

Decision support
Electronic
  spreadsheet
Environment
Finished goods
Forecast
Information system
Inventory
Logic

Order entry
Personal computer
Planning
Query
Report
Shipping
Transactions
Update

BUSINESS PROBLEM

2-1. This chapter has provided some examples of computer systems with control problems, for example, the missile warning system and the Equity Funding case. The control of computer systems is a major problem for the government and for business and other organizations. The incidents discussed in this chapter are only a few; there have been many more situations in which control failures have jeopardized a computer system and the organization running it.

What are some of the ways of preventing these problems? There are two specific examples that can focus your discussion. First, consider the missile warning system. What strategy should be take to be sure that there are no future false alarms? What is the likely cost of your suggested solution?

Next, consider the penetration of computer systems using telephone networks. How can the user of a time-sharing computer who wants to have widespread access prevent unauthorized entry into the system? What demands does your solution place on the telephone network?

2-2. A frequent question is: Do I need a computer to solve a particular problem, like managing inventory or forecasting sales for next year? In this chapter, we have seen a variety of computer applications, from large systems affecting many users to personal computers used by a single individual. How would you help someone who had asked the question above?

First, consider the information processing problem or problems that the potential computer user wants to address. What is the nature of the information? What is its source? How much is there? What processing does the user perform?

Next, think about how a computer would be employed to help this person in his or her tasks. What kind of computer seems appropriate? How would you decide between a small single-user computer and a large computer supporting a large number of users?

Write down a procedure or a checklist for tackling this problem. What are the key questions to ask, and what decisions will you make based on the answers?

REVIEW QUESTIONS

1. Define a *system*.
2. What is a subsystem of a computer system?
3. What are the advantages of an electronic spreadsheet program?
4. Why does Multicorp have so many different kinds of businesses?
5. Why did the president of Multicorp want to try different sales projections in the spreadsheet example in the text?
6. How was the computer used in the fraud at Equity Funding?
7. Describe the duties of the production control department.
8. What is the major purpose of an accounts re-

ceivable system? What are its functions at Autosport?
9. What advantages does a computer-aided design system like the one at Autosport provide for the engineer?
10. What is the difference between transactions processing and decision support?
11. Describe three reasons why it is hard to understand the concept of a computer system.
12. How are airlines using their reservations systems competitively? What kinds of unfair competition are made possible by these systems?
13. How does the zoo system described help in breeding?

THOUGHT QUESTIONS

14. Think of a computer application that you have seen. Describe its major components: its environment, purpose, function, and logic, including input, updating, output, and query capabilities.
15. Consider a system that is not based on a computer, for example, the transportation system. What is one of its subsystems?
16. How could the defense command prevent the

accident described in the text from happening again? (Hint: think about human checks for the two computers involved.)

17. Do you think the ex-employee of the Federal Reserve would have been caught if it had not been for an alert supervisor? How could the Federal Reserve prevent this from happening again?

18. Why would we want to have quick access to customer orders on a terminal?

19. Describe the process of developing a production plan for a factory. Does the process sound simple or difficult?

20. What would happen at Multicorp headquarters if the personal computer for spreadsheet work was broken?

21. What do you conclude from questions 19 and 20 about the importance of computer systems?

22. Why is it important for a firm to have good records of finished-goods inventory?

23. How do you think customers in a fine food restaurant would react to the use of computer terminals in the dining room to enter orders?

24. Describe the importance of computers and information systems to a typical firm.

25. Describe the importance of computers and in-

formation systems to the economy.

26. Explain why computer-based systems should be an integral part of a person's education.

RECOMMENDED READINGS

Business Week. This journal contains a section on information systems that often features interesting and unusual applications.

Computer World. This weekly newspaper presents a great deal of news about the computer industry. Each week, one or two computer applications are usually described. The paper is also a good general source of information about the industry.

PC World. This magazine is devoted to the IBM personal computer, a machine that has captured a significant share of the microcomputer market, especially in business. It contains occasional applications for small computers as well as articles about programs for personal computers.

Time. This general-interest publication now has a section on computers. The articles tend to be of more interest to individuals than to business; for example, one recent article talked about how computers are used to aid the handicapped.

Chapter 3

The electronic computer is a device invented during this century. Probably no other invention has had such a dramatic impact on organizations and the individuals who work in them. Inventors and mathematicians laid the groundwork for electronic computers prior to the breakthroughs that created the first such machine during World War II. We review history in order to learn about the significant trends that have influenced and that continue to influence the application of computers.

After reading the chapter, you should be able to:

- Describe the reasons for each step in the development of computers.
- Describe the motivation for each advance in computing.
- Identify the major trends in computing over the last three decades.
- Explain how the costs of various parts of computing have changed.
- Explain why computers are moving closer and closer to the end user.

A SHORT HISTORY OF COMPUTING

Figure 3-1. A picture of Charles Babbage at age 56 painted by Samuel Lawrence in 1845.

INTRODUCTION

Computers are relatively new devices, yet humans have long been interested in computation. Early mathematicians and inventors came up with some of the ideas that form the basis for modern computers; they just lacked the electronics to go further. In this chapter, we briefly review the history of computers to help place in perspective the tremendous power that modern computers possess today.

Some fields study history in order to avoid making the same mistakes again. In the history in this chapter, at least, we are not worried about mistakes. Certainly, there have been some, but the impressive progress in the computing field overshadows any mistakes that may have been made along the way. The pattern is one of steady cost reductions for computer hardware and increased performance at the same time.

We are interested in history because it is a part of our cultural heritage. However, besides satisfying our intellectual curiosity, the history of computing is important because it helps us understand the significant trends in the field. By examining the motivation for each advance in computing, we begin to develop an understanding of where we are today and why

there may be controversy in the field. Why do we advocate that users do more of their own computing? Why might a long-time computer-staff member resist the proliferation of personal computers?

ANCIENT HISTORY

Charles Babbage

One of the first people to envision a mechanical computation device was Charles Babbage, an Englishman who was born in 1792. Babbage, shown in Figure 3-1, was very curious about how various mechanical devices worked. Fortunately, he had inherited a substantial amount of money from his father, a successful banker. Babbage and a friend were checking calculations for the Royal Astronomical Society. Babbage, frustrated by the tedious work, exclaimed that he wished it were possible to perform the calculations by steam, as steam engines were the dominant form of power in the early 1800s.

From this experience, Babbage came up with some of the ideas for a computer over one hundred years before the first computer was constructed. In 1823, the British government provided a grant, and Babbage developed the design for a "difference en-

Figure 3-2. Pictured left is a portion of the mill or central processor of Babbage's analytical engine. In the late 1860s Babbage began building a scaled-down version of the engine, which was envisioned to be the size of a small locomotive, 15 feet tall and 20 feet long, consisting of hundreds of vertical axles and thousands of wheels or gears.

Figure 3-3. A painting of Ada Augusta, Countess of Lovelace, by Margaret Carpenter around 1835. Lady Lovelace, the daughter of Lord Byron, was a talented mathematician who met Babbage in 1833. She published a translation of an Italian scientific paper on the analytical engine to which she added many pages of notes.

gine," a machine that would calculate equations in the form of $y = a + ax + ax^2 + \ldots ax^6$. After ten years of work, the device was not completed. However, his experiences had led Babbage to propose an analytical engine that could compute any function, not just the formula he had begun with.

For eight frustrating years, Babbage corresponded with the government, trying to get them interested in dropping the difference engine first proposed and sponsoring the analytical engine. The analytical engine had a main memory, called the *store,* and could hold 1,000 numbers of 50 digits each. An arithmetic and logic unit was called the *mill,* and programs for it were to be written on punched cards. The machine was designed to drive a typesetter. The device was able to ring a bell and take action if a variable became less than zero or expanded beyond the maximum capacity of the machine. Babbage's machine, however, was all mechanical; there were no electronic components (see Figure 3-2).

One of Babbage's associates was Ada Augusta, the Countess of Lovelace, who also happened to be the only legitimate daughter of Lord Byron (see Figure 3-3). Lady Lovelace is sometimes credited with being the world's first systems engineer. As a competent mathematician in her own right, she worked with Babbage on his analytical engine, devising ways to program the machine. It has been said that at the time, because she was a woman, Lady Lovelace could claim only to have translated work, not to have originated it herself. However, the project was not able to get enough financial support, and the machine never reached a working stage. Unfortunately, Lady Lovelace died of cancer at thirty-six, but a recently developed programming language has been named Ada in her honor.

Babbage's plans were sweeping, and he suffered because there was no electronics industry to provide the mechanisms he needed for computations; his design presented requirements beyond the capabilities of mechanical fabricators of the time.

Motivation. Aside from his intellectual interest, the primary motivation for Babbage was to solve a computation problem. Business systems were not a major thought; he was interested in scientific computing. The analytical engine was intended to reduce the drudgery of computation, which is a major use of computers today.

Hollerith

Every ten years, the United States undertakes a new census, a count of the number of individuals living in the United States that includes various statistics on each of us. In 1888, the census of 1880 was completed; the tabulation of the results took seven and a half years. Census officials were worried that the next census in 1890 might take over ten years to tabulate and thus run into the 1900 census. As a result, the Census Bureau announced a competition for the design of devices to aid in enumerating the U.S. population.

A man named Herman Hollerith responded to the contest with a design for electromechanical machines that used punched holes in cards to represent data. Hollerith proposed machines that could punch holes in cards, read cards with holes already punched in them, sort the cards, and tabulate the number of cards that had a certain pattern of punches in a column. His reader featured a series of pins, one for each possible hole in a card. Where the card being read had a hole, a pin went through the card and contacted a bed of mercury under the card. The mercury and the pin then formed a closed electrical circuit indicating the presence of a hole (see Figure 3-4). The sorter was connected to the tabulator. The sorter advanced a counter and opened the lid of a box where the operator was to put the card.

Hollerith's design won the competition because his equipment required a tenth of the time for processing needed by the nearest competitor. The system was used with great success to count the population in the 1890 census. In fact, the first count of the census supposedly took only six weeks. However, New York State lost two representatives, and the newspapers bitterly criticized the Census Bureau. Hollerith's devices were described in *Scientific American* and were featured on its cover.

Hollerith built a business that sold his equipment to companies having a need for computation. He eventually sold the business to a firm that became International Business Machines, Inc. (IBM). Although the use of punched cards is slowly dying out, for almost one hundred years the familiar card has been a mainstay in data processing. The eighty-column punched card is called the ***Hollerith card*** after the man who developed electronic accounting equipment (EAM), Herman Hollerith.

It should be emphasized that this punched-card equipment was electromechanical; that is, many mechanical functions were involved. The equipment did not have sophisticated logic capabilities; it had to be rewired to perform different operations. One could say that the wiring was a form of programming, but certainly it was nothing close to what is done to direct a modern digital computer.

Motivation. Hollerith was motivated by an overwhelming amount of data that had to be processed and an estimate that the work could not be done within the given time frame. New ways of handling the data were required, and Hollerith came up with one approach. His cards and processing scheme were used until well after the first computers were installed, and they are still in use in some places today.

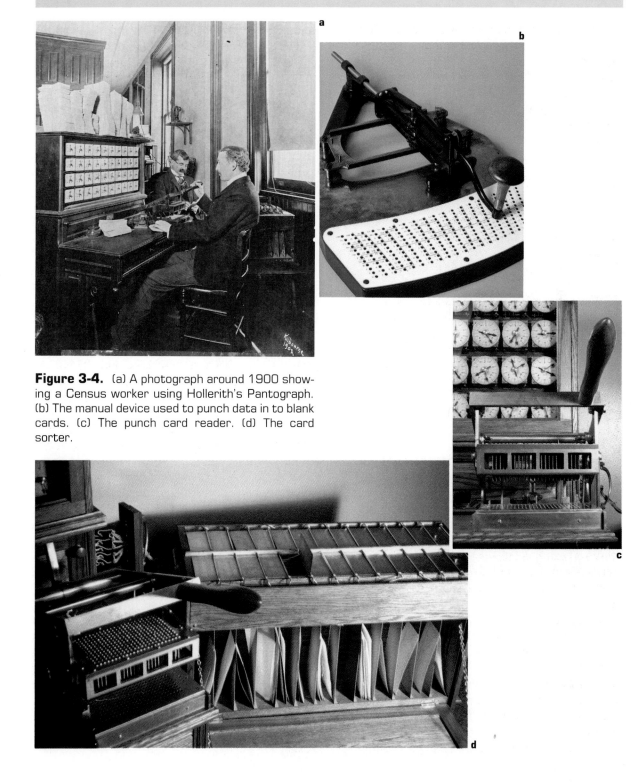

Figure 3-4. (a) A photograph around 1900 showing a Census worker using Hollerith's Pantograph. (b) The manual device used to punch data in to blank cards. (c) The punch card reader. (d) The card sorter.

Figure 3-5. (a) The Mark I computer at Harvard. The machine was built at an IBM plant in New York and assembled at Harvard. A long metal shaft turned 3000 number wheels to calculate based on input from a punched paper tape. (b) Howard Aiken, right, and one of his engineering colleagues from IBM examine a prototype of the number wheels for the Mark I.

Figure 3-6. (a) A top view of Atanasoff's computing machine showing the memory drum (center rear), the card readers (metal trays at left) and the control console (upper right). (b) A 1981 photo of John V. Atanasoff.

Figure 3-7. A rear view of two ENIACs' 36 panels. The machine had 19,000 vacuum tubes in all.

THE FIRST COMPUTERS

In 1937, a graduate student at Harvard, Howard Aiken, proposed an electromechanical device for calculations. IBM supported him with a grant, and in 1944, he completed the Mark 1 electronic-sequence calculator. This device used mechanical counters and was advanced over the tabulating equipment that preceded it (see Figure 3-5).

John Atanasoff, a professor at Iowa State University, developed many ideas for an all-electronic computer in 1939. In 1942, he and a graduate student built a device that could solve linear equations (equations with variables raised only to the first power). However, Atanasoff could not secure support from the university administration to continue his work. J. Presper Eckert and W. Mauchly, who are discussed later, are usually given the credit for building the first all-electronic computer. However, there is a great deal of dispute, and many historians now recognize that the significant credit should go to Professor Atanasoff (see Figure 3-6).

The government also had a contract with the University of Pennsylvania to develop a calculator for computing ballistics trajectories for artillery. The result of this project was the electronic numerical integrator and calculator (ENIAC), which was completed in 1942 (see Figure 3-7). This computer was the first device in which all the components were electronic; no mechanical components at all were involved in the computations. This computer, developed by W. Mauchly and J. Presper Eckert, used electronic circuits to turn vacuum tubes on and off. The ENIAC has 19,000 vacuum tubes, 70,000 resistors, and 500,000 solder connections. It could perform 5,000 additions a second and was programmed by changes in various wires, a time-consuming task. Supposedly, a graduate student with a shopping cart full of vacuum tubes attended the machine when it was running in order to replace any of the tubes that failed. Rumor has it that the lights in the university's area in Philadelphia dimmed when the machine was turned on because of its high power consumption.

In 1945, John von Neumann, a Princeton mathematician, proposed a theory that has formed the

THE INSTITUTE FOR ADVANCED STUDY
SCHOOL OF MATHEMATICS
PRINCETON, NEW JERSEY

March 29, 1944

Dear Professor Chaffee:

Last week I discussed with Dr. Warren Weaver, Chief of the Applied Mathematics Panel, N.D.R.C., the possibility of carrying out some gas dynamical calculations in which various branches of the N.D.R.C. and the Services are interested. We felt that the possibility of making these calculations on your new device was an exceedingly tempting one, and Dr. Weaver promised to get in touch with you on this matter. I have now learned from him that you have obligingly taken his proposal into consideration and suggested that I get in touch with you.

I appreciate this opportunity exceedingly, and would like to discuss the matter in detail with you at your convenience. I regret that I shall not be able to come to Cambridge this week or next; but may I ask you which days in the week after next (April 10-15) would suit you?

I am

Sincerely yours,

John von Neumann

Professor E. L. Chaffee
Electrical Engineering Department
Harvard University
Cambridge, Massachusetts
JvN:GR

a

b

Figure 3-8. (a) A copy of a letter from Von Neumann to a colleague at Harvard; the men corresponded about new electrical devices for computer storage. (b) A photo of John von Neumann in 1955 testifying before Congress on his appointment to the Atomic Energy Commission.

Figure 3-9. The components of a Von Neumann computer as they might be used to process a payroll.

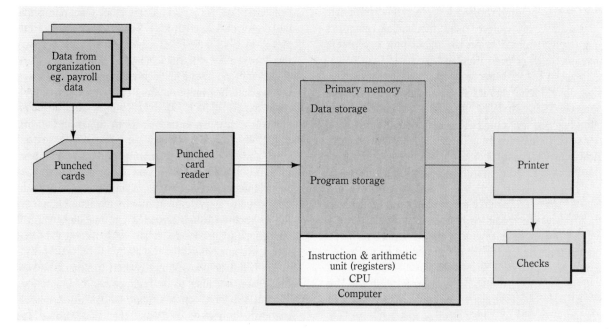

Figure 3-10. A 1953 Photo of the IBM 650 computer. The card reader is at right while the punch is to the left.

basis for modern computers (see Figure 3-8). Von Neumann suggested that a computer store programs in memory along with data. Until this time, clumsy panels with plugged wires had been used to program computers.

Another characteristic of von Neumann's design was a single instruction and arithmetic unit (see Figure 3-9). This control unit brought instructions and data to its registers and performed operations on them. (Registers are special locations in the computer that are able to perform logical operations on data.) The first computer based on this concept of a stored program was built in 1949–1950.

As is true of many new inventions, the world's reaction to computers was less than overwhelming. The faculty at the University of Pennsylvania who developed the ENIAC were not promoted, and as already stated, Atanasoff could not get support from his administration to pursue work on computing.

Motivation. The impetus for electronic computing came from the need to perform many computations in a short period of time. During World War II, the military needed to compute trajectories for artillery; a high-speed calculating device was very appealing. Now, unlike in Babbage's day, there was an electronics industry and components were available to build an analytical engine.

THE FIRST GENERATION

In 1946, Eckert and Mauchly formed a company that was eventually purchased by Sperry Rand. The company produced the Univac I, which was purchased by the Census Bureau. This computer was used from 1951 to 1963 and now resides at the Smithsonian Institution in Washington, D.C. Computers during this time could execute 10,000 instructions per second and had memories of about two thousand characters.

Other firms began to sense a market for computers, and IBM continued the development of the Mark 1. IBM emphasized business problems and developed a vacuum tube computer called the *650*. The company estimated that twenty of these computers would satisfy the world's demand for computation; eventually it sold two thousand of them (see Figure 3-10).

Computers of this generation were programmed in a language close to the electronics of the computer, called **machine language.** At this time, we began to see the use of **assembly language,** a language that was easier for humans to use than the cryptic numbers of machine language. (We shall discuss languages in more detail in Chapter 8.) In the first generation a team working with Jay Forrester at the Massachusetts Institute of Technology (MIT)

a   b

Figure 3-11. (a) Jay W. Forrester holding a magnetic-core memory plane. (b) The Whirlwind computer at MIT in 1951 with Forrester and an engineer, Norman Taylor at left examining plug in modules.

Figure 3-12. An IBM 1401 computer with tapes (far right) and a high speed printer (near man standing in the background). The card reader is at the far left.

developed *magnetic core storage,* an inexpensive way of storing large amounts of information. This breakthrough, shown in Figure 3-11, contributed greatly to the advancement of computer hardware.

Motivation. The computer industry was formed during this period, and we see considerations of the market entering into the decisions made by vendors. The first computers were scientific curiosities; soon companies became interested in offering them as products and in creating a market. Note the trend to severely underestimate the demand for computing. This tendency is still with us today: no one accurately predicted the explosive demand for microcomputers either.

THE SECOND GENERATION

The second generation of computers ran from about 1957 to 1963 and was characterized by the use of transistors rather than vacuum tubes for the logic circuits of the computer. Machines during this period could execute 200,000 instructions per second and might have 32,000 characters of memory. The second generation represented a major advance in speed over the first, and because the cost of transistors is lower than that of vacuum tubes, there was a cost–performance improvement as well. Figure 3-12 shows an IBM 1401 computer, one of the most popular business computers during the second generation.

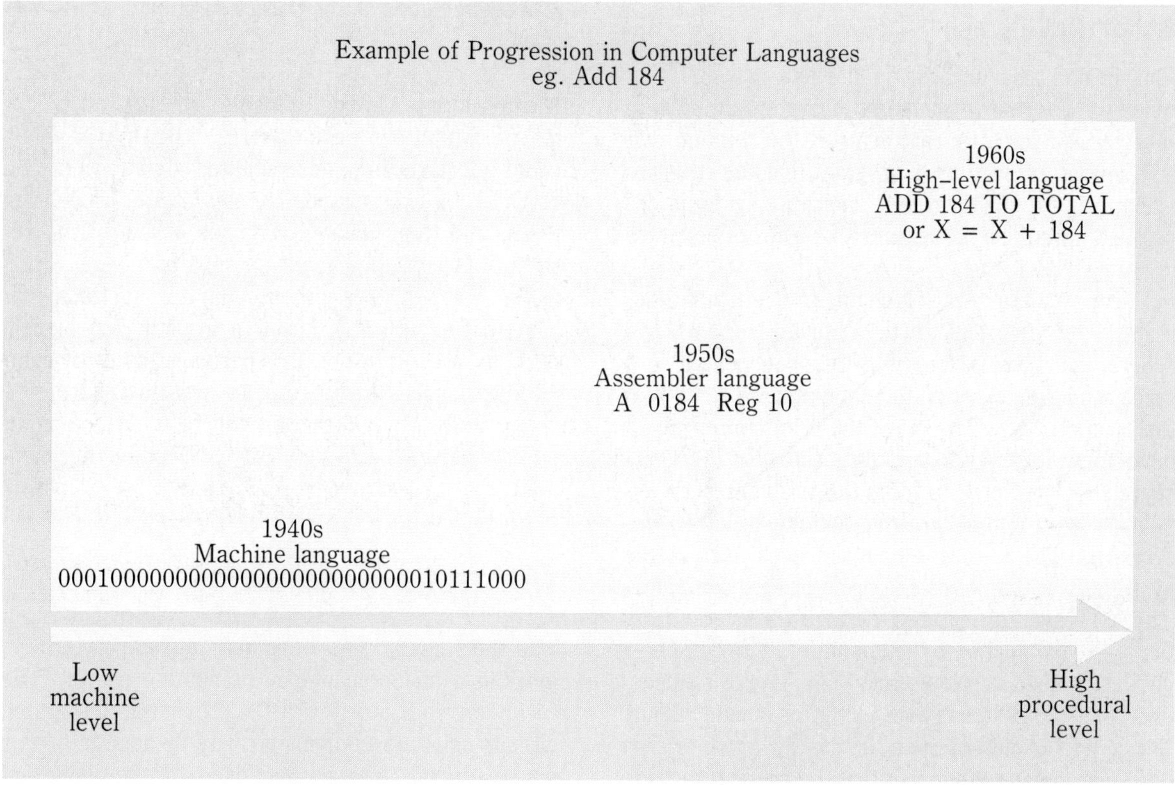

Example of Progression in Computer Languages
eg. Add 184

1960s
High–level language
ADD 184 TO TOTAL
or X = X + 184

1950s
Assembler language
A 0184 Reg 10

1940s
Machine language
0001000000000000000000000000010111000

Low
machine
level

High
procedural
level

Figure 3-13 Computer languages have progressed from machine language to assembler language to the higher-level languages of today.

Motivation. Marketing was again a consideration here: computer vendors were trying to reduce costs and to increase performance in order to expand the market for their products. As the price of computers dropped, more customers were encouraged to acquire them, and existing customers did more computing. In addition, the vendors faced competition that forced product improvements.

During this period, assembly language usage fell as **higher-level languages** were developed. A higher-level language is one in which each statement generates three or four assembly- or machine-language instructions. This higher level of language makes it easier for the programmer to concentrate on the solution to the problem rather than on how the computer works. The chief higher-level lan-

guage in use in business was (and is) COBOL for *COmmon Business-Oriented Language*. Engineers and scientists also began to make heavy use of a language developed in the first generation called FORTRAN for FORmula TRANslation. Figure 3-13 shows how computer languages have developed.

Motivation Here we see the first concerns with productivity for the individuals who worked with computers. The solution was higher-level languages to facilitate programming. It was also clear that to extend computers to end users like scientists and engineers, a language was needed that was at a higher level than assembly language. Professional programmers could be expected to use assembler, but not the casual end user.

Other Advances

This period also ushered in the use of something called an *operating system.* An operating system is a piece of software that controls the computer; it is in charge of each user program that the machine executes. We shall see that operating systems developed into much more complex pieces of software in later generations.

Because computers solved one problem at a time, it could be very difficult to write a program. The programmer wrote the program, punched it onto cards, and then ran it on the computer for testing. If the computer was very busy, the programmer might have to wait several days for each test. MIT researchers attempted to solve this problem by developing a new approach to computing called *time-sharing.* The idea was to make each user of the system think that he or she had a private computer. The MIT system featured *terminals,* typewriters that were connected to the computer. The computer gave each user a slice of time—say, one or two seconds—and then moved on to the next user. Many times, a user did not even use his or her time slice before stopping to think, so that the *response time* was quite good (the time between asking for service from the computer and receiving it).

Motivation. Programmer productivity was the key here. The developers of time-sharing were frustrated by the program development process; there had to be a better way. It took a good twenty years to move almost all program development on-line, and it all started with Project MAC at MIT.

IBM working with the U.S. Government developed the first command and control system featuring *on-line* computers for air defense. In this system the user also had a terminal of some kind. However, unlike time-sharing, the user of the system could only perform certain actions set up in the system's programs. Time-sharing was primarily designed for program development so that the user could write and test programs. In an on-line application, the user wants immediate response, but we certainly do not want the user writing programs. The task of the user is to work with the system to accomplish some

processing, such as the detection of unidentified aircraft.

Motivation. On-line systems are our first example of computers performing a task that probably could not have been done without a computer. The demands for accepting data in *real time,* processing them, and then making decisions based on the results of processing cannot be done by human action alone. We shall see other computer systems that have made a new approach to a problem possible and feasible. We often find this particular facet of computing associated with on-line systems; here, the speed and communications capability of the computer make possible new ways of conducting business.

THE THIRD GENERATION

The third generation, beginning in the early 1960s, marked a major change in computing power. The technology advanced with the creation of integrated circuits, circuits containing many components on a single *chip.* (The production of silicon chips that contain many electronic components will be discussed in Chapter 17.) No longer did one see the discrete components of the second generation: many transistors and other devices were now integrated into a single unit.

The result was computers that could execute (at the high end of the model line) some 5 million instructions per second and store up to 8 million characters of data (see Figure 3-14).

Motivation We are back to the market and competitive forces with the third generation. There was more power, and the growth pattern of customers' moving from one computer to a more powerful one was a little easier. Basically, the computer companies were betting that, with a major improvement in price and performance plus some new approaches to compatibility among computers, the market would expand again. Some of the business press has described IBM's decision to bring out its 360 line as a "you-bet-your-company" move. The new line was

Figure 3-14. The IBM 360 computer system using integrated-circuit technology.

Other Advances

Conversion to the third generation from the second provided a major challenge. The transition from the first generation to the second was really not very traumatic; there were few programs, and it was fairly easy to convert them to the new computers. Conversion was a requirement because the computers of the second generation were sufficiently different from those of the first so that they were unable to execute the programs of the first. Because programming was basically in machine language and one machine could not understand the language of another, organizations rewrote many programs.

By the end of the second generation, firms had developed a large number of programs for their computers. They were not eager to forfeit all of this

so important and costly to develop that its failure could have set the firm back many years. Instead, it was an outstanding success and helped make IBM the industry leader.

investment, so the manufacturers needed to find some way to ease the transition. IBM also wanted to develop a family of computers that all had roughly the same *instruction set* (the instruction set is the repertoire of instructions included in the computer at the machine language level). Until now, there had been different lines of computers with different machine languages. Scientific computers had a different architecture from that of business computers. Now, it appeared that all types of individuals were using computers and that it would be difficult to maintain such distinctions. When a customer needed a more powerful computer, it should not be necessary to move to an entirely new line; a family of computers would make it possible to grow without having to go through major conversions.

To create an entire family of computers that could run the same programs required that the instructions on each computer be essentially identical. However, in the past, a more expensive, faster machine had had more instructions than the least expensive computer in the line. How could one have the same instructions across all computers and offer a range of price and performance?

The answer to this question also helped to solve the conversion problem. Engineers figured out how to break the individual instructions in the computer into smaller pieces, pieces that could be put together again to make an instruction. The concept is like taking a series of different-shaped building blocks and cutting them into smaller pieces. The smaller pieces can be arranged in a number of different ways to form larger blocks. In the case of the computer, the smaller pieces are called *microinstructions,* and the process of putting microinstructions together is known as *microprogramming.*

By using these microprograms to form the instructions in the smaller versions of the line, IBM was able to offer essentially the same set of instructions for the top of the line as for the least expensive models. What does one give up with microprogramming? As you might guess, executing this sequence of microinstructions to produce one larger instruction takes more time than wiring the larger instruction directly into the computer. Therefore, we gain flexibility at the cost of speed; the higher end of the line features less microprogramming and more direct wiring of instructions (see Figure 3-15).

Now we can see how microprogramming helped develop a line of computers, but how did it ease conversion? The microinstructions could be put together (i.e., microprogrammed) to represent instructions from second-generation computers. With some of the instructions simulated in software and the rest microprogrammed, we had a third-generation computer that pretended it was a second-generation machine. The customer could run old software on the new computer without changing it right away, a process known as *emulation.*

Why dwell on microprogramming? Now we have a way of instructing a machine that is between building something in hardware and writing a program. In terms of speed, the fastest approach is still to wire the instruction into the hardware, the next fastest is microprogramming, and the slowest is a software program; that is, software is the most flexible and the easiest to change, and hardware is the least. Microprogramming falls between and thus gives the

manufacturer another tool to use in designing computers.

On the software front, the third generation required that one operate a computer with an operating system. What had begun as a simple program to help the operator had turned into a major piece of software to manage a computer complex. These new operating systems also featured something called *multiprogramming:* more than one program was in a semiactive state in memory at one time. The purpose of this technique was to get more use out of the central processing unit. When one program was, say, writing a tape, the operating system turned its attention to another program and worked on it. As a result, we obtained more *throughput;* that is, the computer processed more jobs per unit of time than before.

Because users were interested in more on-line systems, systems in which the user is connected to the computer directly and receives a rapid response to an inquiry, manufacturers began to build features into their hardware and software to facilitate the development of on-line applications. These on-line systems needed access to large databases, and vendors developed software programs to aid in the management of data called *database management systems (DBMS).*

The third generation also exhibited economies of scale; that is, as one acquired larger models of computers, the cost per computation dropped. A larger computer might have four times the power of a smaller one but cost only twice as much. As a result, companies replaced several second-generation computers with one of the third generation. Local computers were replaced with regional computer centers; the trend was toward the centralization of computer hardware.

In 1964, Professors John Kemeny and Thomas Kurtz at Dartmouth University developed a programming language called *BASIC* for time-sharing use. This language grew to become one of the most prevalent of the languages used by nonprofessional programmers.

Motivation. Although the MIT time-sharing system was a great success, it appealed primarily to

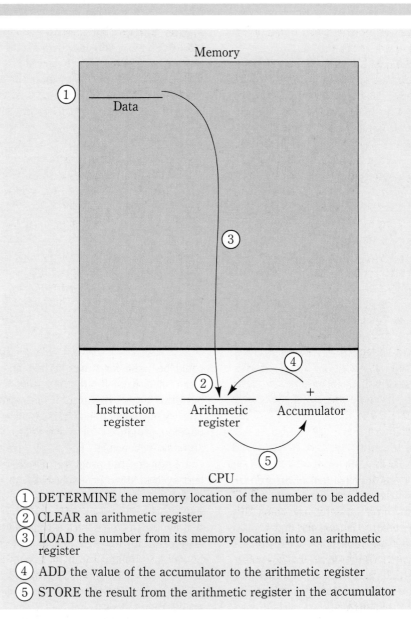

Memory

① Data

③

② Instruction register   Arithmetic register   + Accumulator

④

⑤

CPU

① DETERMINE the memory location of the number to be added

② CLEAR an arithmetic register

③ LOAD the number from its memory location into an arithmetic register

④ ADD the value of the accumulator to the arithmetic register

⑤ STORE the result from the arithmetic register in the accumulator

Figure 3-15. Example of Microinstructions to Implement the Operation to Add a Number to the Value in an Accumulator. The five steps listed above are required to execute the ADD instructions through a microprogram.

individuals with more than a casual interest in computing. The Dartmouth time-sharing language was developed to extend the power of the computer to the nonprofessional. BASIC was intended to become for businesspeople and other casual users what FORTRAN was for the scientist and engineer. Did it succeed? Today, BASIC is the most heavily used language on microcomputers and in time-sharing.

Minicomputers

This period also saw the development of ***minicomputers,*** computers that cost significantly less than the large mainframe computers that had been the sole choice available before. During the mid-1960s, scientists and engineers developed a process for fabricating circuits known as ***large-scale integration (LSI).*** Essentially, LSI is an extension of integrated circuits (many circuit elements fabricated together) in which thousands of components are placed on a silicon chip. Being able to place, say, 100,000 transistors on a chip suddenly made the central processing unit of the computer relatively inexpensive, whereas historically it had been the most valuable component of the computer (see Figure 3-16).

Minicomputer manufacturers like Digital Equipment Corporation (DEC) created a new market with relatively low-priced, powerful computers with flexible operating systems. Most of these computers could be used for time-sharing, and because they were specialized for this purpose, they might outperform larger mainframe time-sharing systems. Small firms began to buy these minicomputers and to develop programs for a particular application like accounts receivable. The small firm would sell the computer and the program to a customer as an on-line system devoted exclusively to processing accounts receivable. (Remember that an on-line system provides the user with a terminal or an interactive device to communicate with the computer. The user does not have the ability to write a program, however. The small firm then uses time-sharing to create an on-line system by programming a business application and denying users the ability to write programs themselves.)

Figure 3-17 shows the rapid advances that have been made in the development of electronics used in fabricating computers. From the first transistor to a computer on a chip, the power of computers has multiplied many times.

Motivation. Entrepreneurs saw a new market, one that was not being addressed by the mainframe manufacturers. They took advantage of advances in

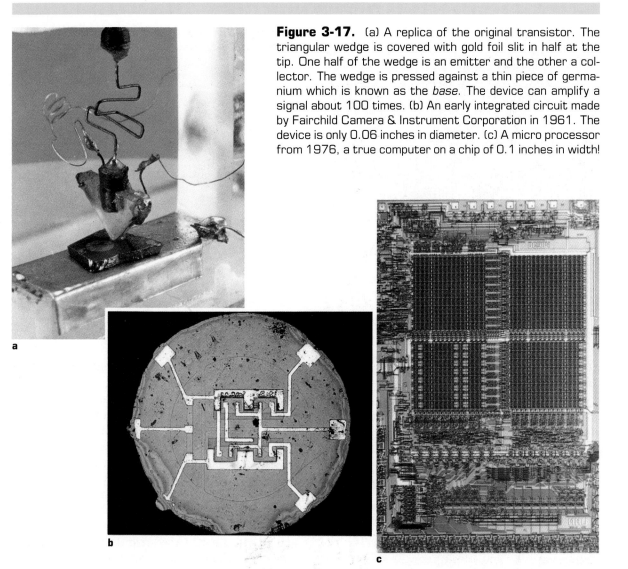

Figure 3-17. (a) A replica of the original transistor. The triangular wedge is covered with gold foil slit in half at the tip. One half of the wedge is an emitter and the other a collector. The wedge is pressed against a thin piece of germanium which is known as the *base*. The device can amplify a signal about 100 times. (b) An early integrated circuit made by Fairchild Camera & Instrument Corporation in 1961. The device is only 0.06 inches in diameter. (c) A micro processor from 1976, a true computer on a chip of 0.1 inches in width!

a

b

c

fabrication techniques for building computer components and came out with a new type of computer. Their actions extended computing again by creating a new market, and the computer became even more pervasive and more affordable than before.

Microcomputers

In 1977, Apple Computer marketed the Apple II, a personal computer (see Figure 3-18). (Other microcomputers existed, but Apple succeeded in selling its computer to a variety of customers and popularized the idea of a home computer that could do far more than play games.) The technology of LSI allowed a computer to be made from a few small silicon chips, and a vendor could manufacture a relatively inexpensive computer for use by only one person at a time. Soon entrepreneurs and small companies flooded the market with special-purpose programs to run on the Apple II. In the early 1980s, the personal computer market exploded as many companies built personal computers, vastly increas-

Figure 3-18. The Apple II Computer in use in an elementary school classroom.

ing the number of computers installed in a short period of time.

Motivation. As with the mini, we see here the desire to create a new market and to service it with a product. The low price and high power of the microcomputer made it very interesting to potential customers. However, it was the development of very powerful and easy-to-use programs that really helped the microcomputer create a market. There are thousands of programs for Apple's II series; the home user can probably buy a program to do almost anything needed. The computer has now been extended even farther: the nonprofessional can operate a computer using purchased software, and the user may never need to write a program.

THE FOURTH GENERATION

Large-scale integration gave way to **very-large-scale integration (VLSI).** By the end of the third generation, computers no longer had core memory but instead used all-semiconductor memory. The fourth generation is expected to extend from 1982 to about 1989 and will have machines at the high end of the performance spectrum capable of executing 40 million instructions per second. Primary memories will probably exceed 100 million characters (see Figure 3-19).

Software is becoming more oriented to the nonprofessional programmer. There will be less need to learn a procedural language like BASIC or COBOL to use a computer; software will be more like natural language (a restricted form of English) than a computer language. Organizations are keeping billions of characters of data on-line for inquiry; flexible software will be used to keep track of the data and make them available to users.

Motivation. The fourth generation is an incremental improvement on the third; the vendors are responding to competition and a desire to expand the market. Demands from customers for on-line systems and large databases also encourage the continued evolution of computers.

THE FIFTH GENERATION

There has been much recent publicity about the fifth generation of computers; Japan has set up a well-funded research group to develop the fifth generation. The fifth-generation computer will be a member of a large network of computers, each with differing capabilities. The user of the personal computer will also be connected to a network having large processors and access to huge databases.

The most dramatic change will be in the user interface with the system. A goal of the fifth generation is to have the computer understand natural language and to recognize voices; one will be able to talk to the machine instead of typing on a terminal. Such capabilities will require the use of techniques

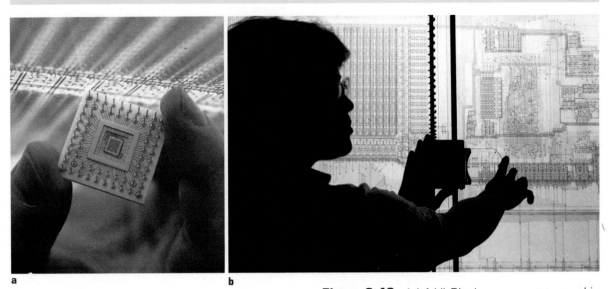

a   b

Figure 3-19. (a) A VLSI microprocessor on a chip from Sperry Corporation. (b) A designer working on a circuit plan for a custom VLSI chip at Sperry.

from **Artificial Intelligence (AI),** a field that stresses computation using symbols rather than numbers. AI is an approach to problem solving that tries to produce computer programs that exhibit what humans would call intelligence. Much AI programming involves finding rules used by humans to make decisions and then programming these rules into the computer to create an *"expert system."* Fifth-generation researchers talk not about instructions executed per second, but about rules interpreted per second.

Right now, the fifth generation is a design on paper. New hardware breakthroughs will be required to furnish the computer power for the interfaces envisioned for the system. We may have trouble delineating what finally is the fifth generation because many of its features are likely to appear gradually, by evolution (see Figure 3-20).

SUMMARY

In a relatively short time, we have seen tremendous advances in hardware and software. In the early days of computers, we were very concerned about expensive hardware and not very worried about software. Now, the balance has shifted completely: software is a huge bottleneck, and we care far less about how efficiently we use hardware. It takes too long to develop programs, so that now we use hardware inefficiently if such use contributes to greater productivity in developing software (see Figure 3-21).

Advances in technology, inventions, and production processes have contributed to the development of extremely powerful hardware. Unfortunately, it is unlikely that we shall see such dramatic breakthroughs in software. Programming is a human intellectual task that is not subject to the same kinds of inventiveness that produced transistors and integrated circuits. Instead, we shall expect more end users to access the computer themselves. These individuals will not use languages like COBOL for the most part but will communicate with the computer in something approaching English, having a few more rules and more structure than completely natural language. We simply cannot afford the time and the resources required to have a programmer

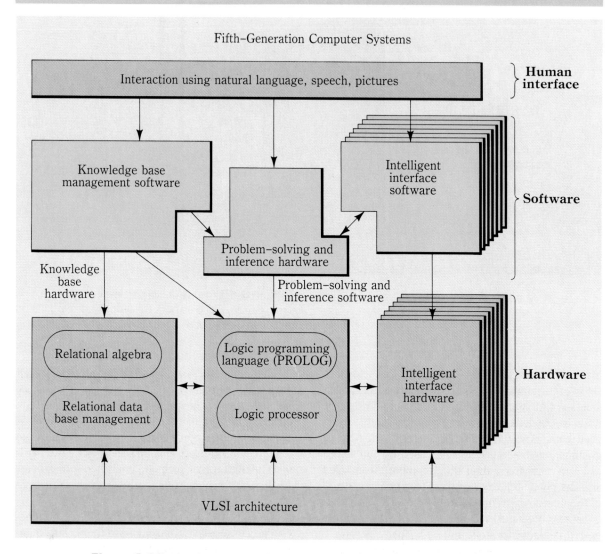

Fifth–Generation Computer Systems

Interaction using natural language, speech, pictures — Human interface

Knowledge base management software

Intelligent interface software — Software

Problem–solving and inference hardware

Knowledge base hardware

Problem–solving and inference software

Relational algebra

Relational data base management

Logic programming language (PROLOG)

Logic processor

Intelligent interface hardware — Hardware

VLSI architecture

Figure 3-20. The Fifth Generation as proposed by the Japanese will provide a more human-like interface to the computer. The machine will use Artificial Intelligence or more symbolic than numerical processing techniques.

write a program for every information request. If we are to obtain data, we shall have to get it ourselves.

HISTORY AT SAFEHAVEN

Safehaven, as you may remember, is the insurance subsidiary of Multicorp. This company took an early

interest in computing, along with other insurance companies and banks. Why? Think of the primary product of this industry: it is information. Insurance companies receive information from customers applying for insurance policies. They evaluate the applications and decide whether to issue the policies. Then the firm must service the policies: customers must be billed and the firm has to process informa-

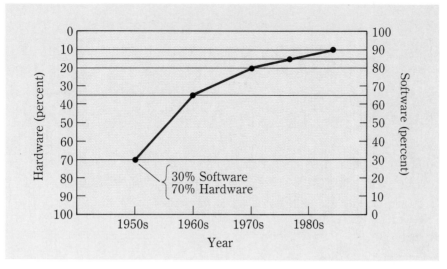

Figure 3-21. Relative Hardware and Software Costs. In the first generation of computers, the largest cost of computers was for hardware. Today, the cost picture has changed and software is the biggest expense.

tion on claims made for losses.

Large insurers look like factories, but the product is paper, not a consumer durable. At first, computers seemed like the answer to help automate this paperwork factory. Accordingly, Safehaven bought its first computer in 1955, an IBM 650. The first application on this computer was policy renewals. Because policies have different billing dates, bills are always being sent out and cash is always coming in. A computer seemed like an excellent way to keep track of renewals, so they were a high-priority application. Note that the firm was first interested in a high payoff, in processing transactions more efficiently.

In 1958, the computer was heavily loaded, so Safehaven bought an IBM 709; it added accounting applications to the billing application already running. In order to minimize conversion, and because Safehaven had purchased the machine, the 650 continued to execute its applications. In 1960, the second generation looked very appealing to Safehaven, and the firm ordered two 1401s to replace both the 650 and the 709.

The new computers did require conversion, so it took about a year to move all of the applications over to the 1401s. With that task completed, Safehaven set out to develop new systems on the new computers. The first was to implement sales reporting for the insurance agents. Now, the agents received a monthly report showing all of their activity. Once the historical data had been accumulated, the sales reports also showed the year-to-date compared with last year, so that the agent knew how well he or she was doing. The second application of the 1401s was the general ledger, which summarized all of the individual accounts or "books" of the firm.

By 1963, the two 1401s had grown to be two 1410s. New applications were being suggested, and there began to be a bit of a wait to get a new program. The third generation seemed to be an answer; Safehaven rented an IBM 360 Model 50 in 1966. In order to ease the transition, the firm also ordered a Model 40, which was devoted to emulating the programs that had run on the 1401s. The firm expected to convert within a year but found that a total of four years passed before the last 1401 assembly-language program was moved to COBOL on the 360s.

One of the reasons for renting the 360/50 was to

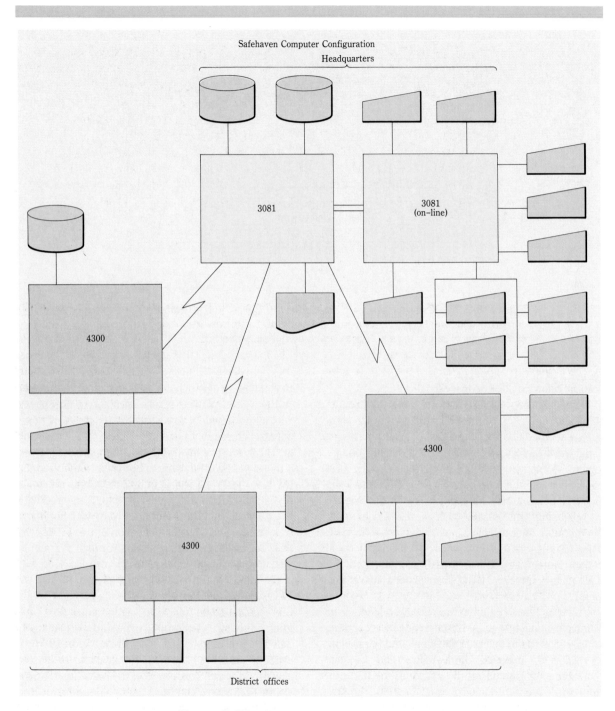

Figure 3-22. Computing today at Safehaven.

Year	Computer (IBM)	Primary New Applications
1955	650	Policy renewal notices
1958	709, IBM650	Accounting
1960	1401 (2)	Sales reporting, general ledger
1963	1410 (2)	Various applications
1966	360/40 and 50	Loss inquiries on-line
1970	370/168	Claims history on-line
1975	370/168 & 4300's in district office	Local access to customers data on-line
Present	3081 headquarters 4300's at districts (networked)	Local and central data access, PC applications underway

Figure 3-23. Safehaven's Computer History.

try to develop an on-line application. The particular need was to be able to make inquiries on policy numbers and record a loss. When a claim arrived at the office, the loss section needed to access a record of the customer's policy to determine what kind of coverage the customer had and how to process the claim. It took a two-and-a-half-year effort, but this system was finally developed on-line at Safehaven.

In 1970, a 370/168, the top of the line at that time, replaced the 360s. Now Safehaven was well into on-line processing. The claims inquiry system had grown to record a history of the year's claims against a policy. Marketing was using the computer to offer new products. For example, the company developed a new type of policy to insure firms against losses from employee accidents. The computer kept a record of all claims, and then a program analyzed the claims by customer. Company representatives met with customers to show them places where they had had claims and to point out safety hazards.

In 1975, IBM 4300s were placed in district offices with information on the policies and customers served in each district. The loss files were still maintained at headquarters, but the agents could access them with a phone call to an operator there. Within a year, the 370 at headquarters downloaded revised data to the district computers every night (downloading is putting data in the files of the local computer), and a study was under way to see if all new

customer applications for insurance policies could be entered by use of the 4300s.

Today, Safehaven is a major computer user. An IBM 3081 at headquarters continues to process huge amounts of data. Because there are so many on-line applications, there is a second 3081 dedicated to on-line work. The 4300s in the district offices have been upgraded several times and are now networked to the 3081 at headquarters. The firm is developing personal computer applications to be run on computers available to the sales agents. A research-and-development project is under way to see if enough functions can be included in a portable computer so that each agent should have one to use in making calls on potential customers (see Figures 3-22 and 23).

Safehaven mirrors the path taken by many firms that began using computers when they first became available. Computing has become a major part of the business. However, the technical staff has had a formidable task in providing service; much time has been required just to determine what computer to acquire next and to use a new machine when it arrives. Users continue to want more and more applications, and company management is always trying to determine how much money it wants to invest in computing. The computer has done a great deal for Safehaven, but managing information processing is a formidable challenge.

Review of Chapter 3

REVIEW

As we looked at the history of computing, we saw a number of trends. First, mathematicians were looking for a way to do computations quickly and accurately; early computers addressed this problem. Computers are also helpful when we have a great amount of data to analyze. The computer has helped do jobs that would not be possible manually, like centralizing airline reservations systems. Much of the industry has been driven by the marketplace. Vendors have responded to competition with new computer designs that have reduced costs dramatically; as a result, the market has expanded and created a seemingly insatiable demand for computing.

One important trend has been to extend the computer to the end user. We saw it first with FORTRAN for engineers and scientists; then BASIC entered the scene for casual time-sharing users. We shall see new languages and microcomputers in subsequent chapters that are also aimed at end users. As costs decline, the amount of computing one buys per dollar increases. The balance is shifting toward software; the cost of programs exceeds the cost of the hardware to run them. This change in cost struc-

ture is dramatic, as the early computers were characterized by expensive hardware and cheap software. The opposite is true today.

Who is the end user? What do the trends discussed in this chapter mean for him or her? *You* are the end user, and these trends mean that a computer is likely to be a major part of your future career. As hardware and software continue to become easier to use and the end user becomes the focus of design, working with a computer will become a natural part of your activities. There is no need to become a professional programmer. However, it is helpful to become computer-literate, to understand the essentials of how computers work and how they are applied in the organization.

KEY WORDS

Ada	COBOL
Aiken	Communications
Analytical engine	Core
Artificial intelligence	Database
Assembly language	ENIAC
Babbage	**Fifth generation**

FORTRAN	Operating system
IBM	Semiconductor
Integrated circuits	Software
LSI	Time-sharing
Mark 1	Transistors
Microcomputer	Univac 1
Microprogramming	VLSI
Multiprogramming	von Neumann
On-line	

BUSINESS PROBLEM

3-1. We have witnessed dramatic progress in computing power over the last three or four decades. Machines that could execute only thousands of instructions per second have given way to computers that execute millions of instructions per second. The cost per computation has dropped dramatically during this time.

Just the same, many corporate managers complain that they are spending more and more on computing. Costs seem to rise despite all of the gains in the productivity of the equipment itself. How do you reconcile these two seemingly contradictory positions? It is clear that computers are more powerful and cost less today.

As you organize a discussion, think about what companies are doing with computers and also about the components of the cost of a modern computer installation. How are systems designed? What is required to take the desires of a user and develop a system that runs on a computer?

3.2. In the early days of computing, everyone was very concerned about the speed of a computer. Elaborate techniques were devised to measure performance. In benchmarking, an evaluator would take a series of representative programs and run them on several computers that were under consideration for acquisition. The evaluator would then compare the performance of the computers so as to decide which one to order.

If hardware is becoming so inexpensive and so powerful at the same time, is there a need to be concerned about performance? We now talk about giving many users local personal computers of their own. Why? and where might performance be an issue? If we want users to program their own computers, should we aim for very efficient programs?

Remember that there are many different types of computer applications and programs, and there is still a place for performance considerations. Where do you think it is?

REVIEW QUESTIONS

1. Why did Babbage not succeed in developing an analytical engine?
2. Who was Ada Augusta, and what was her contribution to computing?
3. What prompted the Census Bureau to ask for help for the 1890 census?
4. What was Hollerith's response? What equipment did he propose?
5. How did the first card reader work?
6. What was the first electronic computer?
7. Who was Howard Aiken, and what computer did he construct?
8. What was the difference between the Mark 1 and the ENIAC?
9. Why was the government interested in computers in the 1940s?
10. What company came out of the work of Mauchly and Eckert?
11. What was important about von Neumann's suggestion for a stored program?
12. What was the Univac I used for originally?
13. What hardware breakthrough brought the second generation?
14. What is a high-level language? Give at least two examples.
15. What is an operating system?
16. Define *multiprogramming*.
17. How does time-sharing differ from on-line computing?

THOUGHT QUESTIONS

18. Why do you suppose early computer pioneers received so little support from their schools?
19. Why did IBM so underestimate the market for the 650? Have we learned anything from this mistake?
20. What is machine language? How does it differ from assembly language?

21. What was the major conversion problem when the third generation of computers was being planned?
22. Why would a company want a family of compatible computers?
23. What is a database?
24. Explain the concept of time-sharing.
25. What is the significance of the language BASIC?
26. What are LSI and VLSI? What do they mean for the computer industry?
27. What is end user computing? Why is it expected to increase?
28. What is the appeal of the personal computer?
29. What is so different about the fifth generation computer effort?
30. Define *artificial intelligence*. How does it improve the user interface with a computer?
31. Explain how hardware and software costs have changed since the first generation of computers.
32. What options are available for obtaining more software productivity?
33. What do you think will ultimately limit the speed of computers?
34. Explain the concept of microprogramming. Why is it important?
35. Why is the fifth-generation computer effort interested in the number of rules a computer can execute in a second?
36. Where do you think the computer industry is headed?

RECOMMENDED READINGS

"As Time Goes By," *Datamation*. (September 1983), pp. 65–122. A history of the computer industry.

"The Chip," *National Geographic*, Vol. 162, No. 4 (October 1982), pp. 421-456. An excellent article on how chips are made and used; requires no technical background to appreciate.

IBM Journal of Research and Development (Anniversary issue), Vol. 25, No. 5 (September 1981). A series of technical papers from the first several decades of computer science.

Kronke, D. *Business Computer Systems*. Santa Cruz, CA: Mitchell Publishing, 1981. Contains a readable chapter on the history of computers.

Part II

This part of the text will build your understanding of the technology. But why, if computers are as easy to use as advertised, do you need to understand technology? I can drive a car without understanding mechanics or thermodynamics. Why is it not as easy to use a computer?

In the early days of the automobile, the driver had to understand a lot more about how a car works than is necessary today. The early auto owner had to be a bit of a mechanic and a gas station attendant rolled into one. If there was a blowout, the driver pulled over to the side and fixed the tire with a patch and then inflated it with a pump. Have you ever advanced the spark for your engine? In the old days, that was a driver's job; today, it is done automatically. How about a manual choke? There are some around today, but very few. Most engines feature fully automatic chokes.

Computers have not evolved to the point where they are fully automatic; hopefully, in the future, they will continue to become easier to use. Today, we are at the beginning of the computer age; it is still helpful to know something about the technology in order to understand how to apply it. (If an automobile were an important part of how we earned a living, say, as to a racing driver, we would be very sure that we knew how it worked.)

This part of the text is intended to provide an understanding of computers. It is unlikely that every point will be clear on first reading. We recommend that you read a chapter and then put the book aside for a while. After thinking about the points made, reread the chapter.

There are a number of reasons to learn about technology:

- To select and buy computer hardware.
- To understand what a program is.
- To understand how programs direct the computer.
- To ask the appropriate questions of computer professionals.
- To make intelligent decisions about technological matters, such as where to install computers for what particular jobs.

HOW COMPUTERS WORK

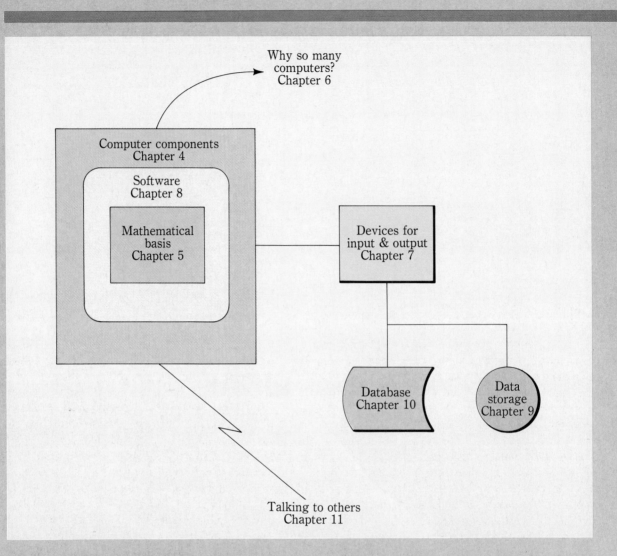

Part II, Figure 1. The organization of this part of the text: first we discuss computers themselves, then peripherals and finally data storage.

- To make design decisions when building new systems.
- To manage information processing in the firm.

Figure 1 shows how the chapters in this part of the text are organized. We begin with a description of the components of a computer in Chapter 4. This chapter is heavily concerned with the technology, that is, the realm of the physicist and the engineer responsible for building computer devices.

Chapter 5 presents the mathematical basis for computing. How do the engineers build circuits that actually perform arithmetic? How does one instruct the computer to do work?

Chapter 6 builds on what you have just learned about hardware to ask why there are so many different kinds of computers. It seems very confusing to have super-computers, mainframes, superminis, mini-computers, and microcomputers. How did the world get into this predicament? What are the uses for these computers, and how do you tell what kind of computer someone is trying to sell?

One of the real bottlenecks in computing is getting information into the machine and getting it back out again. Computers are extraordinarily fast; they do millions of operations in a second. Humans are terribly slow by comparison; human input is time-consuming. Even the use of high-speed scanning devices is not particularly fast compared to the internal speed of the computer. Chapter 7 explains some of the options for input and output. At the end of the chapter, we will all be wishing for good-quality voice recognition as one way to expedite communicating with computers.

At this point, we have explored computer hardware and how it functions in depth. Now for what makes it all work: software. Software encompasses the instructions that make the computer do useful tasks. Chapter 8 is devoted to an explanation of software.

We shall see how elaborate programming systems and languages have been constructed from quite rudimentary building blocks.

One facet of computers that makes them so valuable for business applications is their ability to store large amounts of data and to make them readily available, billions of characters, in fact. Chapter 9 talks about the major kinds of data storage. You will see that the idea of secondary storage is quite easy, but keeping track of the data and resolving the different views of data held by different users is another story. We shall see how simple file systems have expanded to something called *database management systems* in Chapter 10.

Finally, in Chapter 11, we discuss communications among computers and computer devices. Many experts in the field predict that networks of computers linked by communications will continue to grow in the future.

At the completion of this part of the text, the reader will have a strong foundation for using computers to solve problems, and we shall be ready to discuss the development of computer applications in the organization.

Chapter 4

This chapter begins our study of how a computer works. We shall start with a microcomputer, the kind of computer you might find at home or in a computing laboratory at a school. Microcomputers or personal computers are one of the most successful products ever developed in the computer industry. No one foresaw how great the demand would be for these powerful, easy-to-use machines. An understanding of how a computer works can help in using them and in making decisions about computers. Trying to buy your own computer can be a very frustrating task; a little knowledge can help a great deal in choosing equipment.

After reading the chapter, you should be able to:

- Describe the components of a microcomputer.
- Distinguish between hardware and software.
- Describe an instruction and a program.
- Explain the purpose of each component of a computer.
- Discuss the difference between a microcomputer and other kinds of computers.

HARDWARE CONCEPTS:
A JOURNEY INTO A COMPUTER

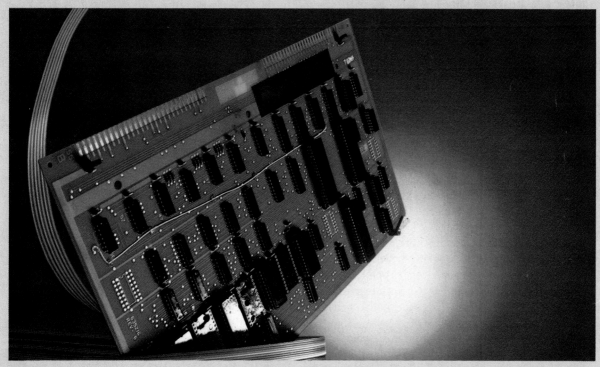

INTRODUCTION

In the last chapter, we saw how computers have developed in a constant quest for more computational power and speed. Now we explore the major components of hardware and how a computer actually works. Although few of us will ever build computers, a basic understanding of their components increases our ability to work with these machines. What are the pros and cons of different options in buying a computer? What are the key questions in looking at different kinds of programs (software)?

Beyond the casual home use of a computer, we expect that many, if not most, white-collar workers in the future will have their own *workstations.* A workstation is a computer-based device that supports the user's work. As an example, the workstation for a manager might provide the following capabilities:

1. A spreadsheet program of the type we saw in the first chapter for various kinds of financial analyses.
2. A *word-processing* program that helps the user to write documents. The user enters text in the word processor, which helps in editing, making changes, and printing out a final copy.
3. Presentation graphics. Many managers have to make presentations of their work to others; the term *presentation graphics* refers to programs that to help prepare overhead transparencies, graphs, and similar displays that help us to communicate with others.
4. Routines that download data from a mainframe computer. Many corporate data are on large computers; users want to access those data, move them to their workstations, and perform different analyses on them.
5. A communications terminal. When a *network* is used to connect local computers, or when the mainframe is used as a central switch, documents and messages can be sent to and received from other workstations. (A network is a series of computers connected over some path, such as phone lines.)
6. A file system. There are programs, which we shall study later, that help the user to set up files

like the ones in a filing cabinet, except that the computer version can be examined much more easily and different information can be retrieved based on user-defined indexes. For example, an index used to access transcripts of student grades might be based on the students' social security numbers.

These are just some of the uses of the workstation that incorporates a microcomputer. For the users of this technology, it helps to have an understanding of how it functions.

THE NATURE OF DESIGN

Why does a car have its transmission lever on the right of the steering wheel in most instances? Is there a theory or principle that explains this location? Originally, the transmission lever was located right on the transmission in the center of the floor. Why? Because the lever went directly to the gearbox. Later, designers thought that it would save space to move the lever from the floor to the steering-wheel post. Why put it on the right side? Because it was probably cheaper to do so; the right side is closest to the transmission.

This discussion shows an example of a trade-off. In this case, we would guess that the trade-off was between convenience and cost. From a human engineering standpoint, we would probably be better off with the shift lever on the left of the wheel because most of the population is right-handed. Now we use the right hand for shifting gears rather than for controlling the steering wheel, which is far more important than shifting gears.

Similarly, there are *trade-offs* in the design of computers, usually involving convenience, speed, and storage capacity versus cost. There is no rule of design as in the sciences; rather, the development of a computer is an engineering feat. Computers are created by humans, not by laws or rules. Of course, the designers do follow certain principles and practices that have been shown to work. However, they are always searching for innovations to improve the performance of the hardware and the software.

```
; KERMIT — KL10 Error-free Reciprocal
;          Micro Interconnect Program
;
;        Kermit Protocol Version 2
;
;        Based on the KERMIT Protocol.
; This program implements the Kermit
; Protocol developed at Columbia University.
; This version is being written specifically for
the DEC Rainbow 100.

             TITLE  'Kermit'

Memory
Address         ; Definitions:

0001       soh       EQU       010
0007       bell      EQU       070
0009       tab       EQU       110
000A       lf        EQU       120
000C       ff        EQU       140
000D       cr        EQU       150
0011       xon       EQU       210
0013       xoff      EQU       230
001B       esc       EQU       330
007F       del       EQU       1770

0000       parevn    EQU       00H
0001       parmrk    EQU       01H
0002       parnon    EQU       02H
0003       parodd    EQU       03H
0004       parspc    EQU       04H
0002       defpar    EQU       parnon
0001       ibmpar    EQU       parmrk

0018       defesc    EQU       'X'-1000

0000       diasw     EQU       00H
```

```
                        ; The actual program:
                                    CSEG

               Hexadecimal       Assembly
Memory         Memory            Language
Address        Contents          Instruction

0000    9C                       pushf
0001    58                       pop ax
0002    8CDB                     mov bx, ds
0004    8ED3                     mov ss, bx
0006    8D26A001                 lea sp, stack
000A    50                       push ax
000B    9D                       popf

000C    8D162909                 lea dx, versio
0010    E82C09       093F        call tcmsgc

                        ; This is the main
                             KERMIT loop.

0013    8D16C402     kermit: lea dx, kerm
0017    E8CA09       09E4        call prompt
001A    8D16A801                 lea dx, comtab
001E    8D1EB105                 lea bx, tophlp
0022    B402                     mov ah, cmkey
0024    E8360A       0A5D        call comnd
0027    E91000       003A        jmp kermt2
002A    FFD3                     call bx
002C    E91500       0044        jmp kermt3
002F    803EA40100               cmp extflg, 0
0034    74DD         0013        je kermit
0036    E84909       0982        call haltf
0039    C3                       ret

003A    8D168503     kermt2: lea dx,
                                     ermes1
```

```
003E    E8F508       0936        call tcrmsg
0041    E9CFFF       0013        jmp kermit

0044    8D16AD03     kermt3: lea dx,
                                     ermes3
0048    E8EB08       0936        call tcrmsg
004B    E9C5FF       0013        jmp kermit

                        ; This is the EXIT
                             command.

004E    B401         exit:       mov ah, cmcfm
0050    E80A0A       0A5D        call comnd
0053    E98D09       09E3        jmp r
0056    C606A40101               mov extflg, 1
005B    E97F09       09DD        jmp rskp

                        ; This is the HELP
                             command.

005E    B401         help:       mov ah, cmcfm
0060    E8FA09       0A5D        call comnd
0063    E97D09       09E3        jmp r
0066    8D16B105                 lea dx, tophlp
006A    E8E608       0953        call tmsg
006D    E96D09       09DD        jmp rskp

                        ; FINISH - tell remote
                             KERSRV to exit.

0070    B401         finish:     mov ah, cmcfm
0072    E8E809       0A5D        call comnd
0075    E96B09       09E3        jmp r
0078    B446                     mov ah, 'F'
007A    E8AA0F       1027        call gensen
007D    E95D09       09DD        jmp rskp
```

Figure 4-1. This figure contains an edited listing of a program in assembly language which we shall discuss in Chapter 8. The important part of the program for this Chapter is in the second column labeled "Hexadecimal Memory Contents." If we were to look inside the computer when this program is running, it would appear as a long string of digits beginning with 9C588CDB. . . . The circuits of the computer are able to interpret what these digits mean and to run the program. This particular program runs on the popular Intel 8086/8088 processor chip and is used for transmitting files between a microcomputer and a larger mini or main frame computer. The next several chapters of the text will describe these different types of computers and how programs are written and executed by computers.

Hardware Versus Software

By this time, you should have a general feeling for the difference between hardware and software. The *hardware* is what we can actually see when we look at the computer; we can walk up and touch the hardware. *Software* constitutes the instructions that tell the computer what to do. An instruction is an order; for example, there is usually an instruction in a computer to add two numbers together. This instruction commands the computer to add the numbers. The computer is built to add the numbers whenever it encounters the "add" instruction.

We can actually see one manifestation of software, a listing of the program steps on a screen or on paper. However, we cannot open up the computer's cabinet when a program is being executed and see it at work. Inside the computer, the program creates various electrical impulses that we have no way of detecting with the human eye (see Figure 4-1).

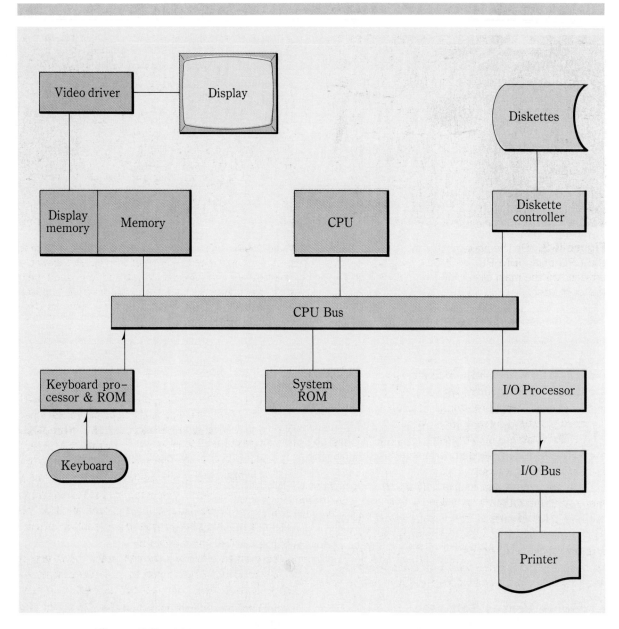

Figure 4-2. A Microcomputer. The microcomputer is usually built around a bus or data highway. Various units connect in a modular fashion to the bus.

There are trade-offs involving software as well as hardware. As we saw in the last chapter, we have three ways of accomplishing a task: the first is to wire it into the hardware, the second is to use micro-programming (called *firmware*), and the last is to use software. Do you remember the advantages and disadvantages of each approach? The fastest execution comes from direct wiring, the slowest from soft-

Figure 4-3. On the photograph above one can see the CPU of an IBM PC, an INTEL 8088 chip as it appears on the main circuit board (motherboard) of the computer.

Figure 4-4. Microcomputers are designed so that their functions can easily be expanded. For example one can add the card above with various electronic logic components to make an Apple IIe computer display 80 characters of text on a line on its CRT instead of 40.

ware. Microprogramming is in the middle in terms of speed, and in terms of flexibility as well. It is easiest to change a software program and hardest to change something that has been directly wired into the computer. The designer has to decide what is the best alternative given the design objectives and the cost constraints of the project.

Please remember as we proceed that the reasons for designing a computer in a particular way may not seem obvious. However, there were good engineering reasons for these design decisions despite how arbitrary they might appear. There is also much research today concerned with improving on present design practice with innovative computer *architecture.*

COMPONENTS OF A MICROCOMPUTER

We shall first look at the structure of a *microcomputer.* Because these devices are intended to be relatively inexpensive, their design is usually simpler than the design of a large mainframe computer (see Figure 4-2).

CPU

The *central processing unit (CPU)* is the heart of the computer; it contains the logic of the machine. The computer has a series of instructions wired into it; the CPU is the part of the computer that interprets the instructions and executes them (see Figures 4-3 and 4-4). *Logic* refers to the ability of a computer to follow instructions; the instructions usually reflect the logic of some procedure, like the logic of computing the payroll. An instruction is simply an order to the computer.

An example of how a human might represent a logical process will help you to understand instructions. Suppose that you want to tell a fellow student how to add two numbers. You might go through the following steps:

1. I will tell you the first number.
2. You write the number on the top of a paper.
3. I tell you the second number.
4. You write it down beneath the first number.
5. You add the two numbers together.
6. You write the result below the two numbers.
7. Tell me the answer.

This is a simple program, a list of instructions that, if

followed, will result in two numbers' being added together. The definition of a **program,** then, is a series of instructions to do some processing task. Programs are called *software* because the instructions are easily changed, particularly compared to hardware instructions, which are wired into the computer. Software has become the most expensive part of computer systems.

Your friend interprets the instructions and executes them: He or she reads Line 1 and thinks (interprets), "I will wait for a number." Next you say the number *12* and your colleague looks at Line 2 and reads it. He or she says, "Now I must write down *12*," thus interpreting your instruction. In writing down the *12*, he or she has actually executed the instruction.

Because the steps are numbered, your friend takes each one in order. At Line 5, you are assuming that your friend knows how to add two numbers together, that the procedure is well understood and "wired into" your friend's thought processes. Similarly, your friend is "wired" to do steps 6 and 7; he or she knows how to write down the answer and tell it to you.

How is all of this related to the CPU of a computer? First, your friend acted like a CPU; he or she read the instructions in your list, interpreted them, and executed them. The CPU does the same thing, except that we have to be a lot more precise and detailed in our instructions.

The instructions or programs are kept in **primary memory.** The memory of the computer is capable of holding data and programs; we shall discuss how shortly. The CPU takes each instruction in sequence from memory and tells memory to move the instruction to a **register** in the CPU. The instruction register is the part of the CPU that holds an instruction; it has electrical circuits that are able to examine the instruction and interpret its meaning. Then the CPU executes the instruction, doing whatever it says (*execution* means doing what the instruction says). Then the CPU requests the next instruction, and the whole process begins again.

The CPU has a series of registers that do various tasks. In general, a register is a storage location for data or instructions. The register has some kind of

logical capabilities, whereas primary memory simply stores information and has no logical capabilities. A register, on the other hand, often does some processing on the data.

Some registers can perform calculations. For example, there are registers that are capable of doing arithmetic. In a microcomputer, the typical kind of arithmetic is fixed-point arithmetic; that is, we assume that the decimal point is to the right of the last digit of the number (and there is no fraction). The number 127 means the same as 127.0. Fixed-point arithmetic is the simplest because we never have to worry about aligning the decimal points; they are always to the right of the last digit on the right. Generally, the CPU has registers that add, subtract, multiply and divide these fixed-point numbers. In the next chapter, we shall see how these arithmetic calculations are accomplished.

The CPU is the heart of a modern computer. The power of the computer is partially described by how much the CPU processes at one time and how fast it does the processing. For example, how many digits can the CPU fetch from memory at one time? The typical measure of this capacity is something called bits (binary digits, or a 0 or a 1), and today's computers process four, eight, sixteen, or thirty-two bits (bits are further explained in the next section and in Chapter 5). Very large computers may actually fetch more data than this at one time in order to speed up computations.

Memory

Memory is the second major element of the computer. Memory is passive; that is, all it does is store data and programs. But how do transistors store data? The key is our ability to record information in a series of bits (binary digits) that consist of 0's and 1's. If we use a 0 and a 1 to represent numbers, then the presence of a voltage on the transistor can be interpreted as a 1 and the absence of a voltage as a 0. No matter what is stored, this level of a 0 or a 1 is called a *bit.* The next chapter explains the mathematical basis for the **binary** number system. For now, assume that we can do computations if only we can store 1's and 0's and the CPU can process them.

Figure 4-5. The top cover of a TRS-80 Color Computer 2 from Radio Shack is removed in the photograph above. Which part do you think contains the CPU chip? Which components are the memory chips?

The advantage of using a 1 and a 0 is that we can easily represent these two symbols physically; for example, we can signal with a light. If the light is on, it represents a 1, and off means a 0. Naturally, we are rather limited in what can be represented with just a 0 or a 1. However, how about grouping several bits together to form a larger unit? If we put four bits together, what would that accomplish? We could have the following arrangement of patterns:

Bits	Code
00	N
01	S
10	E
11	W

If we assign a code to the bits, we see that four letters can be represented with two bits. The formula for the number of unique letters or symbols that can be represented by bits is 2 raised to the power of the number of bits. With 2 bits we have 2 squared or 4 symbols; with 5 bits it is 2 to the fifth, or 32, and so on.

Many computers today group 8 bits together and call it a **byte,** and this is the unit of storage that we will generally discuss. How many characters can we represent with a byte? The answer is 2 to the eighth power, or 256.

Now we see how symbols are stored in memory. The symbols can be data like "378 of Part Number AC112X are in inventory," or they can be instruc-

tions that form part of a program. It may seem confusing, but one can have instructions or data in memory. The program must, of course, be written to differentiate instructions from data, and we shall see how this is done in the next chapter.

As a review, think about the CPU. It brings one or more bytes of data at a time to its registers for processing. One indicator of speed and power is the number of bytes fetched at one time by the CPU. Why? The more bytes taken at a time, the fewer "trips" to memory and the faster computation proceeds.

Figure 4-2 shows a **bus** connecting various components of the computer. A bus is simply a communications path. The data and the instructions travel back and forth between the CPU and the memory on this bus.

The discussion so far has presented the concept of storage, but you will also hear several terms that describe particular kinds of semiconductor (transistor) storage. The first of these is *RAM,* which stands for *random access memory*. A RAM is the most versatile kind of memory and is used in the computer to store and retrieve data and programs. The CPU can write data into this memory and read from it (see Figure 4-5). Random access memory is used dynamically during computations; it will hold different data and instructions all day long as different programs are executed on the computer.

A **ROM** is a **read-only memory**; its contents are fixed by a computer vendor and the computer can

Figure 4-6. The main circuits of an Apple IIe showing RAM (bottom right edge) and ROM (center, right). Note that the packages for the various components tend to make them all look alike!

Figure 4-7 (opposite). Instruction Summary for the Intel 808 Processor Chips.

read only these contents. What good is such a memory? In the last chapter, we discussed microprogramming; a ROM is used to hold the various microinstructions (see Figure 4-6). The user of the computer does not want to change these instructions; rather, the CPU reads and executes them under microprogram control.

Figure 4-7 is the instruction set of one of the popular CPUs used in personal computers, the Intel 8088.

Addresses

How does the CPU know where to find data? By an *address.* In our computer, each byte has an address. The concept of an address should be very familiar; we all have one. My address tells the street where our house is located, and the number positions our house among all of the houses on the street. Knowing my address, you can find where I live, but not whether anyone is home. The address points to a house; to find out whether someone is in the house requires us to look inside.

The computer operates in the same way. A storage location has an address that refers to its position in memory. However, we must actually read the contents of that memory cell to find out what is there. A program must keep track of memory, of where data are stored, so that they can be processed.

Data in the 8080A is stored in the form of 8-bit binary integers. All data transfers to the system data bus will be in the same format.

$$D_7\ D_6\ D_5\ D_4\ D_3\ D_2\ D_1\ D_0$$
DATA WORD

The program instructions may be one, two, or three bytes in length. Multiple byte instructions must be stored in successive words in program memory. The instruction formats then depend on the particular operation executed.

One Byte Instructions

| $D_7\ D_6\ D_5\ D_4\ D_3\ D_2\ D_1\ D_0$ | OP CODE |

Two Byte Instructions

| $D_7\ D_6\ D_5\ D_4\ D_3\ D_2\ D_1\ D_0$ | OP CODE |
| $D_7\ D_6\ D_5\ D_4\ D_3\ D_2\ D_1\ D_0$ | OPERAND |

Three Byte Instructions

$D_7\ D_6\ D_5\ D_4\ D_3\ D_2\ D_1\ D_0$	OP CODE
$D_7\ D_6\ D_5\ D_4\ D_3\ D_2\ D_1\ D_0$	LOW ADDRESS OR OPERAND 1
$D_7\ D_6\ D_5\ D_4\ D_3\ D_2\ D_1\ D_0$	HIGH ADDRESS OR OPERAND 2

A logic "1" is defined as a high level and a logic "0" is defined as a low level.

TYPICAL INSTRUCTIONS

Register to register, memory reference, arithmetic or logical, rotate, return, push, pop, enable or disable Interrupt instructions

Immediate mode or I/O instructions

Jump, call or direct load and store instructions

Instruction Set Summary

Mnemonic	D_7	D_6	D_5	D_4	D_3	D_2	D_1	D_0	Operations Description
MOVE, LOAD, AND STORE									
MOV r1,r2	0	1	D	D	D	S	S	S	Move register to register
MOV M,r	0	1	1	1	0	S	S	S	Move register to memory
MOV r,M	0	1	D	D	D	1	1	0	Move memory to register
MVI r	0	0	D	D	D	1	1	0	Move immediate register
MVI M	0	0	1	1	0	1	1	0	Move immediate memory
LXI B	0	0	0	0	0	0	0	1	Load immediate register Pair B & C
LXI D	0	0	0	1	0	0	0	1	Load immediate register Pair D & E
LXI H	0	0	1	0	0	0	0	1	Load immediate register Pair H & L
STAX B	0	0	0	0	0	0	1	0	Store A indirect
STAX D	0	0	0	1	0	0	1	0	Store A indirect
LDAX B	0	0	0	0	1	0	1	0	Load A indirect
LDAX D	0	0	0	1	1	0	1	0	Load A indirect
STA	0	0	1	1	0	0	1	0	Store A direct
LDA	0	0	1	1	1	0	1	0	Load A direct
SHLD	0	0	1	0	0	0	1	0	Store H & L direct
LHLD	0	0	1	0	1	0	1	0	Load H & L direct
XCHG	1	1	1	0	1	0	1	1	Exchange D & E, H & L Registers
STACK OPS									
PUSH B	1	1	0	0	0	1	0	1	Push register Pair B & C on stack
PUSH D	1	1	0	1	0	1	0	1	Push register Pair D & E on stack
PUSH H	1	1	1	0	0	1	0	1	Push register Pair H & L on stack
PUSH PSW	1	1	1	1	0	1	0	1	Push A and Flags on stack
POP B	1	1	0	0	0	0	0	1	Pop register Pair B & C off stack
POP D	1	1	0	1	0	0	0	1	Pop register Pair D & E off stack
POP H	1	1	1	0	0	0	0	1	Pop register Pair H & L off stack
POP PSW	1	1	1	1	0	0	0	1	Pop A and Flags off stack
XTHL	1	1	1	0	0	0	1	1	Exchange top of stack, H & L
SPHL	1	1	1	1	1	0	0	1	H & L to stack pointer
LXI SP	0	0	1	1	0	0	0	1	Load immediate stack pointer
INX SP	0	0	1	1	0	0	1	1	Increment stack pointer
DCX SP	0	0	1	1	1	0	1	1	Decrement stack pointer
JUMP									
JMP	1	1	0	0	0	0	1	1	Jump unconditional
JC	1	1	0	1	1	0	1	0	Jump on carry
JNC	1	1	0	1	0	0	1	0	Jump on no carry
JZ	1	1	0	0	1	0	1	0	Jump on zero
JNZ	1	1	0	0	0	0	1	0	Jump on no zero
JP	1	1	1	1	0	0	1	0	Jump on positive
JM	1	1	1	1	1	0	1	0	Jump on minus
JPE	1	1	1	0	1	0	1	0	Jump on parity even
JPO	1	1	1	0	0	0	1	0	Jump on parity odd
PCHL	1	1	1	0	1	0	0	1	H & L to program counter
CALL									
CALL	1	1	0	0	1	1	0	1	Call unconditional
CC	1	1	0	1	1	1	0	0	Call on carry
CNC	1	1	0	1	0	1	0	0	Call on no carry
CZ	1	1	0	0	1	1	0	0	Call on zero
CNZ	1	1	0	0	0	1	0	0	Call on no zero
CP	1	1	1	1	0	1	0	0	Call on positive
CM	1	1	1	1	1	1	0	0	Call on minus
CPE	1	1	1	0	1	1	0	0	Call on parity even
CPO	1	1	1	0	0	1	0	0	Call on parity odd
RETURN									
RET	1	1	0	0	1	0	0	1	Return
RC	1	1	0	1	1	0	0	0	Return on carry
RNC	1	1	0	1	0	0	0	0	Return on no carry
RZ	1	1	0	0	1	0	0	0	Return on zero
RNZ	1	1	0	0	0	0	0	0	Return on no zero
RP	1	1	1	1	0	0	0	0	Return on positive
RM	1	1	1	1	1	0	0	0	Return on minus
RPE	1	1	1	0	1	0	0	0	Return on parity even

Instruction Set Summary

Mnemonic	D_7	D_6	D_5	D_4	D_3	D_2	D_1	D_0	Operations Description
RPO	1	1	1	0	0	0	0	0	Return on parity odd
RESTART									
RST	1	1	A	A	A	1	1	1	Restart
INCREMENT AND DECREMENT									
INR r	0	0	D	D	D	1	0	0	Increment register
DCR r	0	0	D	D	D	1	0	1	Decrement register
INR M	0	0	1	1	0	1	0	0	Increment memory
DCR M	0	0	1	1	0	1	0	1	Decrement memory
INX B	0	0	0	0	0	0	1	1	Increment B & C registers
INX D	0	0	0	1	0	0	1	1	Increment D & E registers
INX H	0	0	1	0	0	0	1	1	Increment H & L registers
DCX B	0	0	0	0	1	0	1	1	Decrement B & C
DCX D	0	0	0	1	1	0	1	1	Decrement D & E
DCX H	0	0	1	0	1	0	1	1	Decrement H & L
ADD									
ADD r	1	0	0	0	0	S	S	S	Add register to A
ADC r	1	0	0	0	1	S	S	S	Add register to A with carry
ADD M	1	0	0	0	0	1	1	0	Add memory to A
ADC M	1	0	0	0	1	1	1	0	Add memory to A with carry
ADI	1	1	0	0	0	1	1	0	Add immediate to A
ACI	1	1	0	0	1	1	1	0	Add immediate to A with carry
DAD B	0	0	0	0	1	0	0	1	Add B & C to H & L
DAD D	0	0	0	1	1	0	0	1	Add D & E to H & L
DAD H	0	0	1	0	1	0	0	1	Add H & L to H & L
DAD SP	0	0	1	1	1	0	0	1	Add stack pointer to H & L
SUBTRACT									
SUB r	1	0	0	1	0	S	S	S	Subtract register from A
SBB r	1	0	0	1	1	S	S	S	Subtract register from A with borrow
SUB M	1	0	0	1	0	1	1	0	Subtract memory from A
SBB M	1	0	0	1	1	1	1	0	Subtract memory from A with borrow
SUI	1	1	0	1	0	1	1	0	Subtract immediate from A
SBI	1	1	0	1	1	1	1	0	Subtract immediate from A with borrow
LOGICAL									
ANA r	1	0	1	0	0	S	S	S	And register with A
XRA r	1	0	1	0	1	S	S	S	Exclusive Or register with A
ORA r	1	0	1	1	0	S	S	S	Or register with A
CMP r	1	0	1	1	1	S	S	S	Compare register with A
ANA M	1	0	1	0	0	1	1	0	And memory with A
XRA M	1	0	1	0	1	1	1	0	Exclusive Or memory with A
ORA M	1	0	1	1	0	1	1	0	Or memory with A
CMP M	1	0	1	1	1	1	1	0	Compare memory with A
ANI	1	1	1	0	0	1	1	0	And immediate with A
XRI	1	1	1	0	1	1	1	0	Exclusive Or immediate with A
ORI	1	1	1	1	0	1	1	0	Or immediate with A
CPI	1	1	1	1	1	1	1	0	Compare immediate with A
ROTATE									
RLC	0	0	0	0	0	1	1	1	Rotate A left
RRC	0	0	0	0	1	1	1	1	Rotate A right
RAL	0	0	0	1	0	1	1	1	Rotate A left through carry
RAR	0	0	0	1	1	1	1	1	Rotate A right through carry
SPECIALS									
CMA	0	0	1	0	1	1	1	1	Complement A
STC	0	0	1	1	0	1	1	1	Set carry
CMC	0	0	1	1	1	1	1	1	Complement carry
DAA	0	0	1	0	0	1	1	1	Decimal adjust A
INPUT/OUTPUT									
IN	1	1	0	1	1	0	1	1	Input
OUT	1	1	0	1	0	0	1	1	Output
CONTROL									
DI	1	1	1	1	1	0	1	1	Enable Interrupts
DI	1	1	1	1	0	0	1	1	Disable Interrupt
NOP	0	0	0	0	0	0	0	0	No-operation
HLT	0	1	1	1	0	1	1	0	Halt

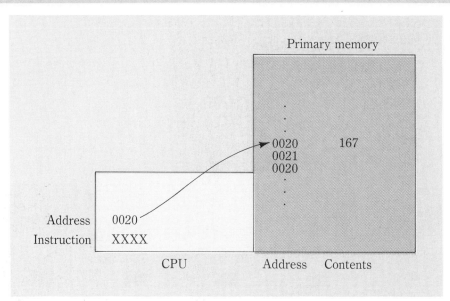

Figure 4-8. Addressing. The address in an instruction points to a location in memory, in this case location 20. Here, location 20 contains the number 167.

The CPU refers to data by its address. Consider the example in Figure 4-8: the number 20 is not the number to be added but is the address of the number in memory that we want to add (in this case 167). The address of 20 points to the location, just as your address points to where you live. Some computers group four bytes together and call them a **word;** usually, they can access either a whole word at a time or individual bytes in the word as long as each byte has an address.

Secondary Storage

Primary memory is directly addressed by the CPU; that is, an instruction like the one in Figure 4-8 refers to the location (address 20) in primary memory. Circuits in the computer instruct the memory to deliver the contents of location 20 to the CPU.

Primary memory is fast because of this direct routing capability. However, we also use something called **secondary storage** because we do not want to have all of our data in primary memory at once. First, primary memory would quickly become full,

given all of the billions of characters of data in a typical organization. Second, we want to be able to store data off-line, that is, not on the computer all the time. Sometimes we do not need data available all the time and sometimes we want to store sensitive data off the computer. This book was composed on a microcomputer; it is convenient to store different chapters on a medium away from the computer, such as on the **diskette** shown in Figure 4-9.

The computer cannot give one piece of data directly from a diskette; this device is read on a diskette drive, which spins the diskette just as a record player spins a record. Unlike a record, the diskette records the information magnetically, somewhat as a cassette tape does. The diskette rotates under **read** and **write heads** that, like a magnetic tape player, are capable of reading magnetically encoded data, and a block of data is transferred by the hardware to primary memory. Once the information is in primary memory, the CPU accesses it just as in Figure 4-8.

Using the diskette is many times slower than having data in primary memory. For example, on the average, it may take 100 to 300 milliseconds to

Figure 4-9. (a) A 3¼ inch floppy disk, with protective covering removed revealing the magnetic disk; (b) Inserting a floppy disk into a Sperry Corporation computer (5¼ inch disk); (c) A 5¼ inch floppy disk drive, with cover removed to reveal electronics.

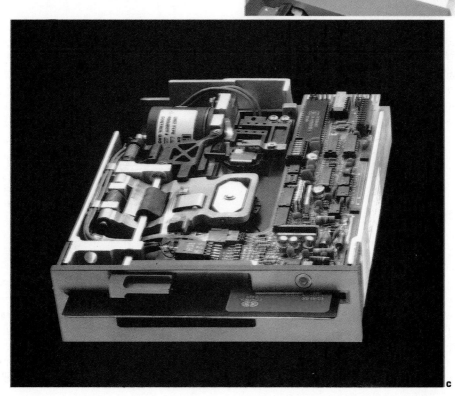

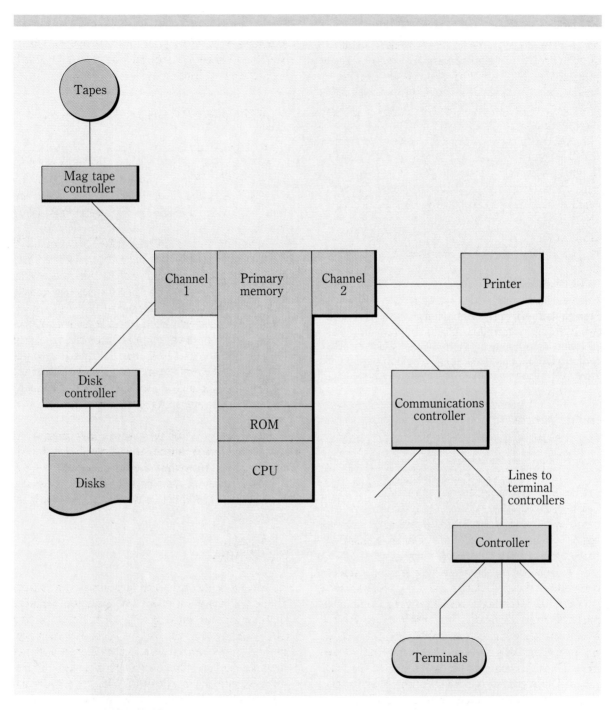

Figure 4-10. A Mainframe. A mainframe computer is often built with data channels, small processors themselves. Historically, the use of these channels and a direct memory connection instead of a bus architecture has produced the fastest computers.

move data from the diskette to primary memory, and then the CPU has to access primary memory to process the data. This two-step process is required because of the physical medium; a diskette drive is not capable of selecting a specific byte for transfer directly to the CPU.

A personal computer might have 256,000 to 512,000 bytes of primary memory and 720,000 bytes of diskette memory if there is a diskette on each of two drives. However, the diskettes can be removed and stored, so that the off-line capacity of the computer is very large. A box of ten diskettes could contain nearly 7 million characters of data, more than enough to hold all of the chapters in this text.

We shall discuss secondary storage more fully in Chapter 9; the important point is the concept of being able to *directly access* data in primary memory. Secondary storage requires an extra operation: first, the data must be located, and then they are brought into memory for further processing by the CPU.

Input/Output

The computer needs a way to communicate with the outside world, that is, people like us. *Input/output,* or I/O, refers to this communications process.

Microcomputers usually have a keyboard, which is like that of a typewriter, for entering data and some type of a printer to print output. For displaying results, we also have a display, or CRT (cathode ray tube), which is like a television set.

I/O is one of the biggest bottlenecks in modern computing. Why? Because I/O is very slow compared to the internal processing speeds of the computer. For many systems, humans have to type the input, and they must read and study the output. Even printing a report on a fast printer is many times slower than processing the information in the computer. There are many devices for input and output, and we shall discuss them in more detail in Chapter 7.

A communications capability is also found in many microcomputers; it allows the computer to send signals to and receive them from other computers. This exchange often takes place over regular telephone lines, and **communications,** too, is the topic of a later chapter (Chapter 11).

OTHER COMPUTERS

How do other computers differ from a microcomputer? We shall go into some of the differences later, but a glance at Figure 4-10 will show some of the major differences between a typical large (more expensive) *mainframe* computer and a microcomputer.

First, note the direct connection between CPU and memory in the mainframe; there is no bus. Then there are boxes called *channels,* which are very important for the I/O process; the channel actually has some logic capability and is usually a small computer in its own right. The CPU delegates input/output operations to the channel and goes on processing other data. The channel speeds up input and output and makes the entire computer faster. However, channel architecture is more complex and more costly than is warranted on most personal computers.

Finally, larger computers usually have an array of secondary storage devices with capacities in the billions of bytes. However, the principles of the CPU and its interaction with primary memory are the same for a micro or a mainframe machine, at least conceptually.

SUMMARY

We have seen the major components of a computer. There are many variations on this basic scheme. However, if one understands the basic parts (the CPU, the primary memory, the secondary memory, and the input/output devices), the different kinds of computer architecture should be easy to comprehend. Remember that design is a human activity and humans are very creative. A lot of innovative ideas have influenced computer design, so we will find numerous differences and additional features on different types of computers. The fundamentals, fortunately, remain the same.

Applications

A Casino System

We have been through some difficult material in this chapter, and it is important not to lose sight of why this information should be understood. We want to learn about computers in order to use them in solving a problem. One interesting application uses computers to control slot machines.

Resorts International is one of the most successful casino operators in Atlantic City, New Jersey. There is a microcomputer installed on each of the casino's slot machines. It sends information on the number of coins dropped into the slot, the number of times the handle is pulled and how much is paid out of the jackpot, the number of hits and the amount of time in which all this happens. Resorts uses two Digital Equipment Corporation (DEC) PDP 11/70 minicomputers in its New Jersey casino. Why? The system helps to pick up people called *stringers* and *yo-yos*, who are slot-machine con artists.

These entrepreneurs solder a wire onto a quarter and slip it into the machine. The operator dips the wire four times to make the machine think she or he is betting a dollar. If the quarter spends too much time on the trigger in the machine, the DEC computer is notified, and it, in turn, signals security that someone may be tampering with the machine.

In addition to the slot machine monitor, there is an IBM personal computer (PC) in each pit (each gaming area) on the casino floor; this system helps employees to control the complimentary meals or show tickets that casinos distribute to good customers. The PC system helps to keep track of comps; it shows who is a good customer and when the last comp was awarded.

Why computers? A casino is big business; the Resorts casino has 60,000 square feet of games, more than 1,700 slot machines, and 120 gaming tables. The cash flow hits $1 million a day on good days.

The 60 PCs connected to the DEC minis also help in checking credit status; pit bosses (game supervisors) or other floor employees can get all of the information they need about a client very quickly.

Resorts International has developed a complete system that they call the Casino Management System. In addition to the functions already described, it provides automatic accounting controls over chips and signature verification for credit requests and checks.

Why did someone at Resorts International need to know about computers? The interface between slot machines and a microcomputer is unique. Some individual had to work with the technical staff to design the application and to learn what technology was available to make it work. A superficial knowledge of the technology might have been satisfactory for a high-level manager approving the plan. However, the users and the computer professionals actually designing the system had to know some of the details about the technology.

The users and the managers were probably involved in defining what the application was to accomplish. Then it was necessary to conduct research to find out what computer devices were available. Custom programs and hardware modifications were required to make the system work. One expects the computer professional to understand this technology, but the user must be knowledgeable enough to make decisions like what microcomputer to use and what tasks to have done on the micro versus the DEC computer.

The computer system at Resorts International is not a typical application; it demonstrates the creativity of an organization with a problem. The computers offered a way to help improve the operations of the casino and have proved their worth. There are many applications, like accounting and inventory control, that look alike. However, we should not forget that clever computer applications are limited only by our imaginations. ∎

Multicorp

This example, as well as the Resorts International example, addresses the use of microcomputers linked to a larger computer to solve a business problem. Remember from Chapter 2 that Multicorp has a small mainframe computer at headquarters. This computer is used for processing financial information. At the end of each month, the subsidiaries send data on their monthly performance and the status of various balance sheet entries in a typed report to headquarters. Headquarters personnel key these data into the mainframe computer program, which produces a consolidated financial statement of sales and a balance sheet for Multicorp as a whole for that month.

The subsidiaries cannot send their data until they have processed it. Then the subsidiaries type the

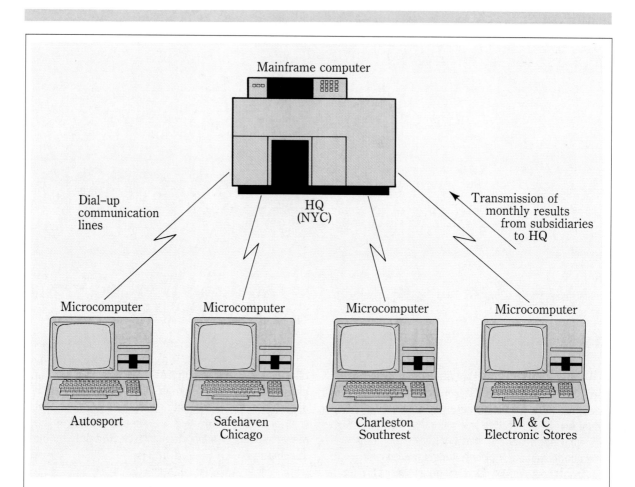

Mainframe computer

HQ
(NYC)

Dial–up
communication
lines

Transmission of
monthly results
from subsidiaries
to HQ

Microcomputer   Microcomputer   Microcomputer   Microcomputer

Autosport   Safehaven   Charleston   M & C
                     Chicago   Southrest   Electronic Stores

Figure 4-11. A possible solution to producing consolidated financial statements at Multicorp using a mainframe at headquarters and microcomputers at the subsidiaries.

reports and mail them to headquarters. At headquarters, the staff opens the reports and types the data into the computer. There is a lot of duplication of effort here.

The controller at headquarters has formed a design team to look at the possibility of automating this process. He envisions a series of programs running on microcomputers in each of the subsidiaries. These programs would help the local subsidiary to enter its figures for the month. For example, the local program would keep a record of last month's entries so that only an update would be necessary. (see Figure 4-11).

The local computer staff would then connect the micro over telephone lines to the headquarters computer and transmit the results. The controller estimates that this system would reduce the time needed to get the consolidated statements to headquarters management from three weeks to five working days. What do you think of the proposal? ∎

Review of Chapter 4

REVIEW

The basic purpose of this chapter has been to introduce computer hardware. We have seen the major components of the computer, and we have seen that these machines are dependent on the binary number system. The central processing unit (CPU) has the logic, the ability to follow instructions and process data. The primary memory of the computer is a passive store for data and instructions.

It is important to remember that hardware is what you can see and that software is the instructions inside the computer. Instructions are developed to solve some problem; such a group of instructions is known as a *program*. Computer memory contains the program and the data. The CPU retrieves instructions and executes them, accessing the data in memory.

Secondary storage is used to store large amounts of data; it is less expensive than primary memory, but more time is needed to read or write information on secondary storage.

Finally, one of the biggest bottlenecks in computing is input and output. We must have a way to input data, and this process often takes place at human typing speeds. Output is also important; output on a printer is faster than a human can type or read, but it is considerably slower than the computer's internal processing. Output on a CRT is limited only by human reading and comprehension speeds.

KEY WORDS

Address	Input/output
Architecture	Memory
Binary	Microcomputer
Bus	Primary memory
Byte	Program
Channel	RAM
CPU	Register
Communications	ROM
CRT	Secondary storage
Direct access	Software
Diskette	Trade-off
Hardware	Word

BUSINESS PROBLEMS

4-1. Computers are devices that have been designed by people. There are few laws or theorems that dictate this design, though designers do use rules and procedures developed over the years.

One area on which much attention is focused is the design of the user interface, that is, what the user of a computer sees. The term most popular today is *user friendly,* meaning that the system is very easy to use.

Consider a software program like the one for spreadsheet analysis described in the first chapter. What do you think allows a program to be user friendly? What are the desirable characteristics of a computer system's interface with a user? Can you think of any general design principles that should be applied? Make a list of the major points that a designer should consider when developing the user interface with a computer application.

4-2. In Chapter 11, we shall read about computer networks, computers that are connected to one another by some kind of communications link. A popular type of connection used today is a local area network, or LAN. The LAN connects various devices that are physically near each other.

In one environment, we might have a group of personal computers that share a single large storage device. The computers could communicate with each other and with the computer controlling the storage device.

At first, it may seem a little strange to connect microcomputers. After all, are they not intended for use by individuals? What reasons can you think of for use by individuals? What reasons can you think of for making this type of connection, for investing in a local area network? As a hint, think about how one uses a microcomputer. What are the most popular applications? What advantages would there be in having access to a single large storage device?

REVIEW QUESTIONS

1. Describe the functions of the CPU.
2. What is a register? What does it do?
3. What are instructions?
4. What is the purpose of a bus in a microcomputer?
5. What is an address?
6. Explain how the CPU retrieves and stores data in primary memory.
7. What does it mean to interpret an instruction?
8. What is a fixed-point number? Why is it relatively easy to do arithmetic using fixed-point numbers?
9. Why do we say that memory is passive?
10. What two entities are stored in memory?
11. What is the difference between primary and secondary storage?
12. Why do computers use 0's and 1's?
13. How many characters can a code represent

using six bits?

14. What is a byte?
15. What is RAM? What is ROM?
16. Why is secondary storage not directly addressable by the CPU?
17. Why do we want off-line storage capabilities?
18. What is a CRT?
19. What is a data channel?
20. Why do microcomputers usually not have a data channel?

THOUGHT QUESTIONS

21. Write a program in English to multiply two numbers together.
22. Assume that your friend in the example in the chapter did not know how to add numbers beyond two digits. Write a procedure for adding numbers of arbitrary size.
23. Why is design an arbitrary activity?
24. What is a trade-off? What are the major trade-offs in designing a computer system?
25. Consider a time-sharing system versus a personal computer. What are the trade-offs for a user deciding which kind of system to use?
26. Why is the CPU the heart of a computer?

27. Why might a microinstruction set be placed in a ROM rather than in a RAM?
28. Explain the difference between an address and the contents of the location addressed.
29. Why might a personal computer user want to communicate with other computers?
30. How might you increase the speed of a computer through changes in its architecture?

RECOMMENDED READINGS

Byte, published by McGraw-Hill, is a leading periodical on microcomputers with reviews of hardware and software products.

High Technology is an excellent popular journal on various forms of technology written for the layperson; it includes many articles on computer-related topics.

Lucas, Henry C., Jr. *Information Systems Concepts for Management,* 3rd ed. (New York: McGraw-Hill, 1986.) See the chapters on technology for more details on how computers work.

Toong, H., and A. Gupta. "Personal Computers," *Scientific American,* Vol. 247, No. 6 (December 1982), pp. 86–107. A good, but somewhat technical, article on the IBM personal computer.

Chapter 5

This chapter is designed for the reader who wants to understand how a computer works when it is doing calculations. The idea that a series of electrical signals performs arithmetic is a difficult one to contemplate. In this chapter, we shall try to explain the basis of computer arithmetic.

Our objective is to fill the gap between electrical signals, computer hardware, and the way computations take place. The goal of the chapter is not to make you an expert in binary arithmetic; instead, we want you to gain an understanding of how arithmetic can be done on a computer.

After reading this chapter, you should be able to;

- Discuss number systems like base 10 and base 2.
- Convert a number from decimal to binary and vice versa.
- Add two numbers in binary.
- Subtract two numbers in binary.
- Explain how a computer can do arithmetic.
- Describe a computer code and the reasons for it.

HOW A COMPUTER COMPUTES

INTRODUCTION

This chapter moves from the realm of the engineer and the hardware designer to the concerns of the mathematician. How can a computer perform arithmetic when all it has to work with is a series of electrical signals? We shall seek to answer this question by showing a relationship between electrical signals like "on" and "off" and one type of arithmetic.

The trick is to use a number **base** different from the one to which we are all accustomed, base 10. Base 10 happens to be very convenient for humans and will continue to be our favorite. In base 10, we can multiply by 10 simply by adding a 0 to the right of the number; division by a power of 10 is equally simple.

However, other number bases are possible, and one of these has only two digits, a 0 and a 1, and is called the **binary number system.** It is fairly easy to represent a 0 and a 1 physically. For example, we could decide that having the light on in the room is a 1, and that having it off is a 0. Something this simple has often been employed in computers; for example, the presence of a voltage on a transistor might be a 1, and no voltage a 0. An iron oxide magnetized in one direction might be a 1 and in the other a 0.

Given the ability to represent 0's and 1's, the next task is to perform arithmetic in binary. In this chapter, we shall see how mathematics is done in this base; it will turn out to be very similar to base 10 arithmetic, with which we are all familiar. The chapter addresses these topics:

- The number system: How are numbers represented?

- Base 2, or binary arithmetic: An easy system for computers.
  Arithmetic.
  Types of numbers: Where is the decimal point?
  Other bases besides binary: base 16 or hexadecimal.
  Rounding off.

- Coding: How do we represent symbols using binary digits?
  Error checking

THE NUMBER SYSTEM

You probably write a number like 6728 without thinking about what it means. Our number system uses positional notation; that is, the **position** of the digit tells us something. The 8 is in the units position, and it indicates that we have eight 1's. The 6 is in the thousands position, meaning that the number has six 1000's. The number 6728 is interpreted as follows:

6×1000	The thousands place
7×100	The hundreds place
2×10	The tens place
8×1	The units place

The first position is the units, the second the tens, the third the hundreds, and the fourth the thousands. Let us indicate the various positions by starting at 0 and counting by 1's. Thus, the 8 in the number 6728 is in the 0 position, the 2 in the first position, the 7 in the second, and the 6 in the third.

Look again at 6728; note that the position is the power to which the base is raised to determine the place. That is, 10 is raised to the first power at the tens place, 10 is raised to the second power in the hundreds place, and so on. For the number 6728:

Digit	Position	10 raised to position
6	3	1,000
7	2	100
2	1	10
8	0	1 (anything to the 0 power = 1)

Obviously, one can extend this analysis to larger and larger numbers. We could also define other bases, though most of us are used to working with base 10.

It is interesting to note that a single digit never represents the base. In base 10, the 10 is represented by two digits, not one. It takes two digits (i.e. another position) to represent the base, 10. (Ten is 0×10 to the $0 + 1 \times 10$ to the first.) It is a characteristic of all number bases that the base is not represented by a single digit.

BINARY NUMBERS

The example given features base 10; now we shall do the same with base 2, or the binary system. Note that there is no single digit for a 2, the base. Instead, 2 in binary is the number 10. Remember that our objective is to do arithmetic in binary because it is relatively easy to represent the two digits, 1 and 0, electrically in a computer.

If we are successful in building a number system using binary, think of what that means with respect to computers. Computers are very adept at representing "on" and "off"; we can assign 1 to on and a 0 to off. Remember, the presence of a small voltage across a semiconductor could represent a 1, whereas no voltage is a 0.

Let us try to see how the binary system relates to the more familiar base 10. Take the following binary number: 1001101. What is the decimal or base 10 equivalent? Remember the positional notation. Beginning at the right, the position indicates the exponent to which the base is raised. Thus, the rightmost position is a 0, or the units position, because any number raised to the 0 power is 1. What is the second position in base 2? That should be easy; it is numbered position 1, so it is 2 raised to the first power, which is 2. The next position is number 2, so we take the base 2 and raise it to the second power, which gives an answer of 4. To convert to base 10, then, begin at the rightmost digit of the binary number and work left.

	Digit	Position	2 raised to power	Decimal result
Rightmost	1	0	1×1	1
	0	1	0×2	0
	1	2	1×4	4
	1	3	1×8	8
	0	4	0×16	0
	0	5	0×32	0
Leftmost	1	6	1×64	64
Sum				77

Converting binary to decimal should be pretty easy;

just expand the number by the powers of 2 as in the table.

Conversion from decimal (base 10) to binary (base 2) can be accomplished by division (if there are no fractions). Divide the decimal number repeatedly by the base, in this case 2. If 2 goes evenly into the number, write a 0 on the next line in the remainder column. If 2 does not go evenly, so that 2 is left over, write the 1 on the next line in the remainder column. Keep going until the quotient is 0. The remainders in the opposite order in which they are found are the converted number. For an example, convert 75 base 10 to its binary equivalent.

Step	Division	Remainder
1	2⟌75	
2	2⟌37	1
3	2⟌18	1
4	2⟌9	0
5	2⟌4	1
6	2⟌2	0
7	2⟌1	0
8	0	1

Taking the remainders in reverse order gives 1001011. To check, convert the binary number back to decimal:

$$1 \times 2^0 + 1 \times 2^1 + 1 \times 2^3 + 1 \times 2^6 =$$
$$1 + 2 + 8 + 64 = 75$$

Will you ever have to do this kind of conversion except as an exercise? Probably not, but it is important to understand the analogy between base 10, which we use every day, and base 2, which is used by the computer. We can move easily and quickly from one number base to another. Thus, it is simple for the computer to perform all of its calculations using base 2, or binary, and then to convert the results for display purposes (i.e., for us to read) to base 10.

Arithmetic

One can do addition in binary the same way as in base 10, only there are fewer choices because there are only two digits. An addition table would look like this:

	0	1
0	0	1
1	1	0*

*carry of 1.

We shall try to add two numbers together in binary. Take the two numbers 1011 and 1001 as follows:

```
  1011
  1001
 ─────
 10100
```

To add, begin on the right-hand side and work left, just as in base 10. At the 0 position there are two 1's. Checking the addition table, we see that $1 + 1$ is a 0 with a carry of 1. Write down the 0 and carry the 1 to the first position. Here we find $1 + 0$, but we have the carry, which gives us $1 + 1$, so write down 0 and carry the 1. In the second position, we have two 0's and our carry, so we write the carry. In the third position, the last on the left, we find two 1's. Their sum is 0 with a carry, and as there is no fourth position, we can write the carry down directly. Our answer then is 10100.

To check in decimal, we must convert the two addends: 1011 is $1 + 2 + 8$, or 11, and 1001 is $1 + 8$, or 9. Adding together:

```
 11
  9
 ──
 20
```

The answer in binary 10100 is $4 + 16$, or 20, and the results check.

Now how about subtraction? Computers usually subtract differently from humans. Instead of subtracting directly, computers take the complement of the number being subtracted and add it to the minuend. This sounds confusing, but if we take one step at a time, it should be a little easier.

The **complement** of a number is the result of subtracting each digit from the base. For example, the base 10 complement of 6 is 4 because 4 must be added to 6 to get 10, the base.

10 base

  6 number to be complemented

  4 number added to 6 to get the base

To subtract using complements, it is first necessary to find the complement of the number to be subtracted. To subtract $8 - 6$, take the 10's complement of 6, which is 4, just as we did above. Add 4 to 8, giving 12:

```
   8
 + 4
 ───
  12
```

The answer is certainly not correct, $8 - 6$ is not 12. We must drop the carry (1) to give 2, the desired result.

Let us try another example; what is $6 - 3$ using 10's complement subtraction? The 10's complement of 3 is 7. Add 6 to 7, giving 13. Drop the carry to give an answer of 3.

What about the case where the result is negative? To compute $4 - 7$, take the 10's complement of 7, which is 3:

10 base

  7 number to be complemented

  3 number added to 7 to get the base

Add $3 + 4$, giving 7:

```
   4
 + 3
 ───
   7
```

There is no carry, so take the 10's complement of the answer and add a minus sign, giving -3.

10 base

  7 number to be complemented

  3 number added to 7 to get the base

Another example would be $3 - 9$. We take the complement of 9, which is 1. Add $3 + 1$, giving 4. We find no carry, so take the 10's complement of the answer and add a minus sign. The 10's complement of 4 is 6, so the answer is -6.

Why go to all of this trouble? Because it is very easy for a computer to add two numbers directly. We shall see that taking the complement of a binary number is very fast, and that instead of needing a special circuit to subtract, we simply complement the number and use the existing computer adder to get the answer.

In binary, we take the 2's complement by changing every 1 to a 0 and vice versa, and by finally adding 1 at the end. To subtract the following numbers in binary:

```
10010
01101
```

Take the 2's complement of 01101, which is 10010. (It turns out that we must make the subtrahend the same size as the minuend.) We formed the complement by changing each 1 to a 0 and each 0 to a 1. Starting on the right and working left, we change the first 1 to a 0, the first 0 to a 1, and then the two 1's to 0's. Finally, the leftmost 0 becomes a 1. Now add 1, giving 10011. The problem becomes one of adding:

```
 10010
 10011
100101
```

Now drop the carry of 1, giving 00101. The leading 0's are not needed, and removing them gives the final answer of 101.

To check: 10010 in decimal is 18, and 1101 is 13. The number 101 is their difference, or 5 in base 10. From this example, it is hopefully clear why computers often subtract by adding! Taking the complement of a binary number is very fast: Just reverse the digits and add 1. Then use the existing adder of the computer to add the numbers and drop the final carry. What could be easier?

Types of Numbers

In the previous discussion, we have been concerned with how arithmetic is done in binary, the actual ap-

proach taken by the computer. Most jobs on which humans work with computers are not done in binary. Instead, we work with base 10 numbers. We studied binary only so that you would understand what the term means and so that you would realize that at the lowest level in the computer, calculations occur in binary.

Now we can go beyond the internal operations of the hardware and look at what we will generally see at the level called **machine language,** the instructions that are built into the computer by its designers. Now we shall deal with decimal numbers in order to make things easier.

Two different types of numbers are necessary for computation. We have been using **fixed-point** numbers in our examples without considering any alternatives. In a fixed-point number, the decimal point is assumed to be to the right of the units or rightmost digit. A number of the form 3.4×10^1 is different and is called a **floating-point** number. The decimal point is free to float; its position is determined by the power to which the base is raised. In this example, the base is 10, which is raised to the first power and then multiplied by 3.4, giving 34. Computers usually represent floating-point numbers as the mantissa, the letter E and the exponent. For example .24E2 would be 24, and in computer memory the decimal point itself would not appear.

How does a computer add and subtract floating-point numbers? It must first align the decimal points to do addition or subtraction. For multiplication and division, the computer has to compute the proper location of the decimal point. For example $(2.4 \times 10^2)(4.3 \times 10^1) = 10.32 \times 10^3$, or 1.032×10^4, or in fixed-point, 10320. Do you see why there is a problem with addition? It would not be correct in this example to add 2.4 and 4.3 because those are a shorthand representation of the numbers 240 and 43. The computer must figure out where to align these numbers if they are to be added correctly. In this case, the right answer would be 283. Performing floating-point arithmetic is more complex than performing fixed-point arithmetic because we have to worry about locating the decimal points and managing the exponents.

Engineers can build hardware to do fixed- or floating-point arithmetic. Because floating-point is more complex, many small computers come with only fixed-point arithmetic. How do they perform floating-point computations? The answer is through software. Remember, we mentioned that a fundamental trade-off is whether or not to perform an operation using hardware or software. In this instance, the software solution to floating-point arithmetic is cheaper, but it is also slower.

The popular IBM personal computer comes without a floating-point-arithmetic hardware unit; the software simulates floating-point operations. However, for someone who does a lot of floating-point computations, another processor chip with floating-point hardware is available as an extra cost option. This chip is called a *coprocessor* because it works with the main **CPU** chip supplied with the computer.

Other Bases

Base 2 is a bit difficult to understand; it is hard to interpret long strings of 0's and 1's. By grouping various binary digits, we can form other number systems that are a little easier to process. We can view this process as one of combining chunks of details into a higher level. In this case, the chunks are binary digits that are grouped together to form a digit of a higher-level base. One second-generation computer grouped three binary digits to form base 8, or *octal.* The engineers who designed the computer agreed that its machine language would be base 8 and built the proper circuits for base 8 arithmetic out of binary components.

Binary	Octal
001	1
010	2
011	3
.	.
.	.
111	7

(As an exercise, complete the missing parts of the table.)

Remember that in octal there is no digit for the base and no digit greater than a 7. Therefore, when you add 7 + 1 in octal, the answer is 10. (If you have doubts, 10 in octal can be converted to base 10 as $0 \times 8^0 + 1 \times 8^1 = 8$ base 10.) A popular second-generation scientific computer was designed to use octal as its machine language.

Today, many computers, especially the large mainframes from IBM, use base 16, or ***hexadecimal*** (hex). Hexadecimal digits are created by grouping four binary digits together. (See Figure 5-1, which shows the binary, hexadecimal, and decimal equivalent of numbers. Note that because we need more than 9 single digits for base 16, hexadecimal numbers feature letters A through F standing for single digits 10 through 15.)

It is easy to convert from binary to hex:

Position	8	4	2	1	8	4	2	1	
Bits	0	1	0	1	0	1	1	0	Binary
Digit		5				6			Hex

In this example, the binary bits correspond to the numbers shown on the line above them. The hexadecimal 5 has a 1 in the ones position and a 1 in the fours position, giving 5. The hexadecimal 6 has a 1 in the twos position and in the fours position, giving 6. Hexadecimal is a lot easier to read than binary.

Why discuss hexadecimal? Now we are beginning to get to the numbers that a programmer might see. If one is writing a program and has a problem, the programmer frequently asks the computer to print the contents of memory in order to help find the error. The printout for a computer with a hexadecimal machine language will be in hexadecimal, which is the case in Figure 5-1.

Rounding Off

We are used to dealing with dollar amounts and calculating fractions in measurements. What are you supposed to do when you and a friend plan to split the dinner bill at a restaurant and the total is odd, say, $10.51? We do not have halfpennies, so you must round one half up and the other half down. One of you pays $5.25, and the other pays $5.26. One

Figure 5-1. Binary, Hexadecimal, and Decimal Equivalents.

Binary	Hexadecimal	Decimal
0000	0	0
0001	1	1
0010	2	2
0011	3	3
0100	4	4
0101	5	5
0110	6	6
0111	7	7
1000	8	8
1001	9	9
1010	A	10
1011	B	11
1100	C	12
1101	D	13
1110	E	14
1111	F	15

penny is not usually a problem, but what happens if this situation arises for thousands of people? Thousands of pennies do begin to add up after a while. Computers have this problem all of the time because they are calculating payments or bills owed to a company by thousands or hundreds of thousands of individuals.

One easy way to represent a fraction in a computer is as a floating-point number. We can also use fixed-point binary; that is, there is a definite position assumed for a decimal point on all of the numbers in the calculations.

Unfortunately, some numbers that can be expressed easily in one base cannot be represented exactly in another. It is difficult to represent the decimal 0.1 in binary. Thus $100.10 does not have an exact representation. If a computer adds $0.10 a thousand times, you may not get $100. Instead, the answer might come out $99.99.

There is an old story of a computer programmer working on a binary computer who supposedly used the round-off error to accumulate funds for an extra employee on the payroll run. At the end of the payroll, the program sent the leftover round-off amounts to the programmer's home in the form of an extra paycheck.

Many commercial computers and some languages allow the programmer to do computations in decimal arithmetic so that she or he does not need to worry about round-off errors.

CODING

In the previous sections, we have covered how computers do arithmetic. But computers do far more than just calculations; they also process a variety of symbols, like the letters in the alphabet. Certainly, we need to perform calculations to process the payroll. The computer must take the employee's wage rate times the hours worked and then subtract various deductions, like taxes, insurance, and pension contributions.

However, this arithmetic is not enough; the computer must also print out a check with the employee's name on it and must report taxes to the government, identified by employee. Arithmetic is important, but so is the ability to represent symbols.

EBCDIC CODE[a]

Bit Position	4	0	0	0	0	0	0	0	0	1	1	1	1	1	1	1	1
	3	0	0	0	0	1	1	1	1	0	0	0	0	1	1	1	1
	2	0	0	1	1	0	0	1	1	0	0	1	1	0	0	1	1
8 7 6 5	1	0	1	0	1	0	1	0	1	0	1	0	1	0	1	0	1
0 0 0 0		NUL	SOH	STX	ETX	PF	HT	LC	DEL			SMM	VT	FF	CR	SO	SI
0 0 0 1		DLE	DC1	DC2	DC3	RES	NL	BS	IL	CAN	EM	CC		IFS	IGS	IRS	IUS
0 0 1 0		DS	SOS	FS		BYP	LF	EOB	PRE			SM			ENQ	ACK	BEL
0 0 1 1				SYN		PN	RS	UC	EOT					DC4	NAK		SUB
0 1 0 0		SP								¢	.	<	(	+	|
0 1 0 1		&								!	δ	*	)	:	¬
0 1 1 0			/							.	%	-	>		?
0 1 1 1										:	#	@	.	=	..
1 0 0 0			a	b	c	d	e	f	g	h	i						
1 0 0 1			j	k	l	m	n	o	p	q	r						
1 0 1 0				s	t	u	v	w	x	y	z						
1 0 1 1																	
1 1 0 0			A	B	C	D	E	F	G	H	I						
1 1 0 1			J	K	L	M	N	O	P	Q	R						
1 1 1 0				S	T	U	V	W	X	Y	Z						
1 1 1 1		0	1	2	3	4	5	6	7	8	9						□

[a]ACK	Acknowledge	IGS	Interchange group separator
BEL	Bell, or alarm	IL	Idle
BS	Backspace	IRS	Interchange record separator
BYP	Bypass	IUS	Interchange unit separator
CAN	Cancel	LC	Lowercase
CC	Unit backspace (word processing)	LF	Line feed (printer to next line)
CR	Carriage return	NAK	Negative acknowledge
DC1	Device control 1	NL	New line (LF plus CR)
DC2	Device control 2	NUL	Null, or all zeros
DC3	Device control 3	PF	Punch off
DC4	Device control 4	PN	Punch on
DEL	Delete	PRE	Prefix
DLE	Data link escape	RES	Restore
DS	Digit select	RS	Record separator (or reader stop)
EM	End of medium	SI	Shift in
ENQ	Enquiry	SM	Start message
EOB	End of block	SMM	Repeat
EOT	End of transmission	SO	Shift out
ETX	End of text	SOH	Start of heading
FF	Form feed	SOS	Start of significance
FS	File Separator	SP	Space
HT	Horizontal tab	STX	Start of text
IFS	Interchange file separator	SUB	Substitute

SYN	Synchronous idle
UC	Upper case
VT	Vertical tab

Figure 5-2. EBCDIC is used by IBM's mainframe computers.

Character	Standard BCD interchange code	Character	Standard BCD interchange code	Character	Standard BCD interchange code
0	00 1010	A	11 0001	N	10 0101
1	00 0001	B	11 0010	O	10 0110
2	00 0010	C	11 0011	P	10 0111
3	00 0011	D	11 0100	Q	10 1000
4	00 0100	E	11 0101	R	10 1001
5	00 0101	F	11 0110	S	01 0010
6	00 0110	G	11 0111	T	01 0011
7	00 0111	H	11 1000	U	01 0100
8	00 1000	I	11 1001	V	01 0101
9	00 1001	J	10 0001	W	01 0110
		K	10 0010	X	01 0111
		L	10 0011	Y	01 1000
		M	10 0100	Z	01 1001

Figure 5-3. BCD Code. BCD is one of the oldest and simplest computer codes.

Just as with numbers, we have a series of 0's and 1's to use for symbols. However, humans want to see conventional symbols like the letters *A, B, C, . . . Z*.

A *code* is used to represent symbols and numbers that are used for display rather than computation. For example, for printing numbers on a report, a computer might have a coded representation of the number 6. This code might not be one that is suitable for computation. For simplicity's sake, the 6 for printing will occupy an entire byte, whereas for computation the numbers are represented in hexadecimal, two to a byte.

Remember our earlier discussions about how many symbols can be represented by a certain number of bits. If we have two bits, we can assign a code to four distinct symbols as follows:

00   N
10   S
01   E
11   W

Four symbols are not very many, so it is unlikely that anyone would use a two-bit code. If we move to six bits, we have 2 to the sixth, or 64 different patterns that we can assign to different symbols. In the second generation of computers, a six-bit code was common; by the third generation, we had moved to eight bits, to give us 256 different possible symbols. Then, computers could display upper- and lower-case letters along with many special symbols.

The IBM 360/370 uses an eight-bit code called **EBCDIC** (see Figure 5-2) for display and internally, but not for computation. Many computers use the **BCD** (binary-coded decimal) to present data to the outside world. One can use a four-bit BCD for just numbers, as shown in Figure 5-3. Each digit is represented by its binary equivalent rather than the whole number. For example 14 in binary is 1110, but in BCD it would be 0001 0100.

0001   0100
 1   4

If we expand BCD to six bits in order to add capital and small letters, two zone positions are added to the four numeric bits, giving a code that looks like

ASCII CODE

	Bit Position			7 6 5	0 0 0	0 0 1	0 1 0	0 1 1	1 0 0	1 0 1	1 1 0	1 1 1
4	3	2	1									
0	0	0	0		NUL	DLE	SP	0	@	P	\	p
0	0	0	1		SOH	DC1	!	1	A	Q	a	q
0	0	1	0		STX	DC2	"	2	B	R	b	r
0	0	1	1		ETX	DC3	#	3	C	S	c	s
0	1	0	0		EOT	DC4	$	4	D	T	d	t
0	1	0	1		ENQ	NAK	%	5	E	U	e	u
0	1	1	0		ACK	SYN	&	6	F	V	f	v
0	1	1	1		BEL	ETB	'	7	G	W	g	w
1	0	0	0		BS	CAN	(	8	H	X	h	x
1	0	0	1		HT	EM	)	9	I	Y	i	y
1	0	1	0		LF	SUB	*	:	J	Z	j	z
1	0	1	1		VT	ESC	+	;	K	[	k	{
1	1	0	0		FF	FS	,	<	L	\	|	:
1	1	0	1		CR	GS	–	=	M	]	m	}
1	1	1	0		SO	RS	.	>	N	∧	n	~
1	1	1	1		SI	US	/	?	O	—	o	DEL

ªACK Acknowledge	DEL Delete	FS File separator	SOH Start of heading
BEL Bell, or alarm	DLE Data link escape	GS Group separator	SP Space
BS Backspace	EM End of medium	HT Horizontal tab	STX Start of text
CAN Cancel	ENQ Enquiry	LF Line feed	SUB Substitute
CR Carriage return	EOT End of transmission	NAK Negative acknowledge	SYN Synchronous idle
DC1 Device control 1	ESC Escape	NUL Null, or all zeros	US Unit separator
DC2 Device control 2	ETB End of transmission block	RS Record separator	US Unit separator
DC3 Device control 3	ETX End of text	SI Shift in	VT Vertical tab
DC4 Device control 4	FF Form feed	SO Shift out	

Figure 5-4. Each unique combination of 7 bits represents a character or control action in ASCII.

BA1234. Now we can code 64 symbols, which give us 10 digits and 26 capital letters plus a few special symbols for punctuation.

The last code of interest is the American Standards Code for Information Interchange, or *ASCII*. This code has seven bits plus a check bit. The check bit is used to check for errors as described in the next section. This code is used by a large number of computers, including almost all micros. It is also used heavily in data communications. (See Figure 5-4 for a description of the ASCII code.)

Error Checking

Usually, codes have some sort of error checking, for example, a seven-bit code with one bit for checking, using a scheme called *parity checking*. The **parity bit** may be used to keep all of the bits in the charac-

Figure 5-5. An Example of Odd parity for Error Detection.

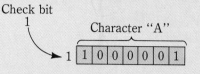

ASCII code for character "A"

7 bits: 1 0 0 0 0 0 1

Number of 1's is 2 ie, even, so need to add a 1 to obtain odd number of ones.

Check bit
1

Character "A"

1 1 0 0 0 0 0 1

Representation of character "A" in computers using ASCII coding scheme and odd parity checking:

8 bits: 1 1 0 0 0 0 0 1

ter either even or odd. In the case of odd parity, a character string of 1000001 would have a single parity bit added because it has an even number of 1's. If the receiving unit found an even number of 1's, it would mean that there had been an error because every string should have odd parity. This rather simple scheme will find an error of one bit, three bits, and so on. If two bits are missing, the parity will still be odd and the error will go undetected (see Figure 5-5).

There are many more sophisticated coding schemes, but these usually require us to take a byte or two every so many characters to code additional information. The code is usually computed in some way by the sending unit and is recomputed by the receiving unit. If one wants to send enough information, it is possible to use error-correcting codes that not only alert the receiver that something is wrong, but that try to provide information to fix the error.

MOVING ON TO SOFTWARE

We have now explained the major parts of a computer and how it represents numbers. The only thing missing is how we command the computer to do work. Software and programs represent instructions that control the computer.

The numbers and symbols discussed in this chapter can all be stored in computer memory. The implications of this fact might be that the symbols are all data. However, the last chapter pointed out that computers store both data and instructions in memory. What then is an ***instruction?*** It is a series of symbols that, when put into the CPU, is examined by electronic circuits, is decoded as to what the instruction means, and then is finally executed.

Suppose that the symbols 1CF01234 meant, "Add what is at location 1234 in memory to a register in the CPU." If this instruction were placed in the instruction register in the CPU, circuits in the CPU would interpret 1CF as an ADD, and would cause the data at location 1234 to be fetched and then added to the register implied by the instruction. Programs and data must be kept separate and must be identified in computer memory. If a computer tries to treat data as if they were instructions, the results are unpredictable but are likely to cause the program to stop.

In Chapter 8 we shall explore this aspect of computers further and find out about the elaborate languages that have been built with simple instructions.

Application

Figure 5-6. The Reservations Terminals at the Hilton Hotel in Disney World, Orlando, Florida.

Computers were invented to process information. In this chapter, we have studied how they are able to perform computations on the data. The example of a system at Ramada Inns illustrates well how computers are used for calculations and for the manipulation of symbols.

Ramada Inns is an international chain of hotels and motels headquartered in Phoenix, Arizona. Each inn is like a separate small business. One service provided by headquarters is a centralized reservations system. A traveler can call a single number and make a reservation at any of the Ramada Inns using the system. The central computer is an IBM mainframe located in Omaha, Nebraska.

A few years ago, Ramada Inns decided to improve the services provided to the local inns. Each inn had a terminal connected to the mainframe through the regular phone network. The terminal had no local logic and hence was useful only for mainframe applications like making reservations.

Ramada Inns replaced these "dumb" terminals with microcomputers. The Ramada Inns programming staff developed a communications program that runs all the time on the personal computers. The micro can be connected to the mainframe and vice versa so that they can share data. For example,

when a reservation is made for a particular inn, the central computer in Omaha looks up the phone number of the local inn, dials it on the phone, and downloads the information on the reservation to it.

One of the major advantages of installing the local microcomputers is the ability of each inn to control its own processing for systems that have no need for central coordination. Thus, a steady stream of new applications to aid the local inn should be forthcoming. For example, it would be very useful to have a local computer that kept track of all room charges for each customer. This kind of system is certainly one that should be local to each inn.

Figure 5-6 shows a computerized reservation application. How does this application illustrate computations and symbol manipulation? Calculations are done to figure out when a room is reserved, the number of people in the room, and the rate. In addition, much of the information processed on the system is symbolic. The local inn must have the name of the person making the reservation; other symbols are found in the messages transmitted between the micros and the mainframe. As in most commercial applications, the computational and symbol-manipulation powers of the computer are used heavily at Ramada Inns. ∎

Review of Chapter 5

REVIEW

This chapter has covered the mathematical basis of computing. We have seen that the binary number system features just two digits, a 0 and a 1. It is relatively easy for the computer to represent two states electronically. Engineers are also able to build circuits that perform arithmetic on binary numbers. Because we know how to convert binary numbers into their decimal equivalents, the computer can operate in binary and report its results back to us in the familiar decimal notation. We have seen that computers can add and subtract in binary, and we have observed the distinction between fixed-point and floating-point numbers.

However, arithmetic is only part of the story; we also want to process other kinds of data such as symbols, for example, the symbols in your name and address.

The computer must use 0's and 1's for this purpose, too. The solution is to establish codes in which different patterns of bits are assigned to a symbol. The chapter contains an example of the bit patterns associated with the popular EBCDIC, BCD, and ASCII codes. With this base, we can continue learning about how the computer works for us.

KEY WORDS

ASCII	Fixed point
Base	Floating point
BCD	Hexadecimal
Binary number system	Instruction
Bit	Machine language
Code	Memory
Complement	Octal
CPU	Parity bit
EBCDIC	Position
Error checking	Rounding off

BUSINESS PROBLEMS

5-1. One major change in the way we approach information systems today is that we recommend that companies first think about buying a package before programming a system from scratch themselves. The costs of labor are increasing, and it seems to take an inordinate amount of time to program new applications. (We shall talk more about this kind of advice in Chapter 13).

A package is a program that has been written by a firm for sale to others. The idea is that many applications of computers are quite similar across companies; a single program that can be adapted to each company might make the development process a little easier and certainly faster.

One company in the cruise ship business wanted to replace an aging reservations system with a new one. They found a package but were concerned about whether the package would perform fast enough for them. That is, would the reservations agent have to wait only a few seconds for a response from the computer, or would the computer take ten or more seconds to answer each request for service? The company also wondered what changes would be necessary to make the package fit its environment, whether the changes were possible, and how much they would cost.

The package was in use at another cruise line. How would you suggest that the company try to answer its questions? Describe a plan of the activities necessary to answer the company's questions satisfactorily.

5-2. One of the key questions in looking at microcomputers (or almost any computer today) is compatibility. This term means many things to different people. There is something called *hardware compatibility,* which means that the same machine-language instructions can be executed by two compatible computers.

The issue of software compatibility is a more difficult one. We shall see in Chapter 8 that there are actually layers of software; a control program called an *operating system* is at the top of the hierarchy. Underneath it are problem or user programs. Even though two computers may be compatible from a hardware standpoint, differences in the operating systems or in the way in which certain features are implemented may make them incompatible as far as software is concerned.

What is the importance of compatibility to a user? Why does a vendor want either to encourage or to discourage compatibility? Will the vendor always provide compatibility within its product lines? Why or why not? What makes compatibility difficult to achieve?

REVIEW QUESTIONS

1. Write the number 34256 in positional-notation base 10.
2. Convert the number to its binary equivalent.
3. Add the number to 110101101.
4. Now take the sum and subtract 101101, using

the 2's complement and adding.

5. What is 7 + 6 in octal?
6. What is the difference between floating-point and fixed-point numbers?
7. What is BCD coding used for?
8. What is EBCDIC?
9. What are the uses of ASCII?
10. What does *error detecting* mean? *Error correcting?*
11. How can a computer keep data and instructions straight if both are in memory?
12. What are the steps followed by the CPU in executing an instruction?
13. Explain parity checking.

THOUGHT QUESTIONS

14. Why is the binary number system so natural for a computer?
15. Why do computers subtract by adding?
16. Why are floating-point numbers harder for a computer to process?
17. What are the advantages of having floating-point hardware on a computer?
18. Why do we use hexadecimal instead of binary notation?

19. What is the round-off problem in a binary computer?
20. How do modern computers get around the round-off problem?
21. Why do codes for display represent data differently from codes for computation?
22. What should a computer do if it detects a parity error in moving data from memory to the CPU?
23. What is the disadvantage of using software to simulate floating-point instructions?
24. How do you think a computer handles floating-point multiplication?
25. What is the purpose of the instruction register in the CPU?

RECOMMENDED READINGS

Bohl, M. *Information Processing with Basic* (4th ed.). Palo Alto, CA: SRA, 1984. A book with a great deal of detail on how computers work.

Kronke, D. *Business Computer Systems*. Santa Cruz, CA: Mitchell Publishing, 1981. This book has many details on the mathematical basis of computers.

Sanders, D. *Computers Today*. New York: McGraw-Hill, 1983. A book with many good illustrations of computers and their components.

Chapter 6

Having mastered how a computer is able to calculate, we now go on to the different types of computers. The principles of operation are all the same, but just as with many other products, a range of options is available.

The choice among computers has become more complicated, if anything, in recent years. When there were just seven or eight vendors, all selling a line of mainframe computers, the buyer was limited to choosing among very similar products. Now, we have a proliferation of computers. The first to be developed were mainframes, followed by minicomputers. Then came the computer on a chip, the microcomputer. Finally, some minis grew up and became superminis.

Now we have two kinds of overlap that generate confusion. First, the high end of one type of computer overlaps with the low end of another: some superminis are more powerful than small mainframes. Further confusion is introduced because each generation of computer becomes more powerful. The microcomputer of today has more power than the mainframe of twenty years ago.

We shall try to clarify some of the issues in this chapter and to provide an indication of how different types of computers are used.

After reading the chapter, you should be able to:

- Describe the development of mainframe computers.
- Explain how minicomputers came into being.
- Describe the difference between personal computers and other types of machines.
- Describe a supermini.
- Explain the uses for supercomputers.

SO MANY COMPUTERS: MAINFRAME, MINIS, AND MICROS

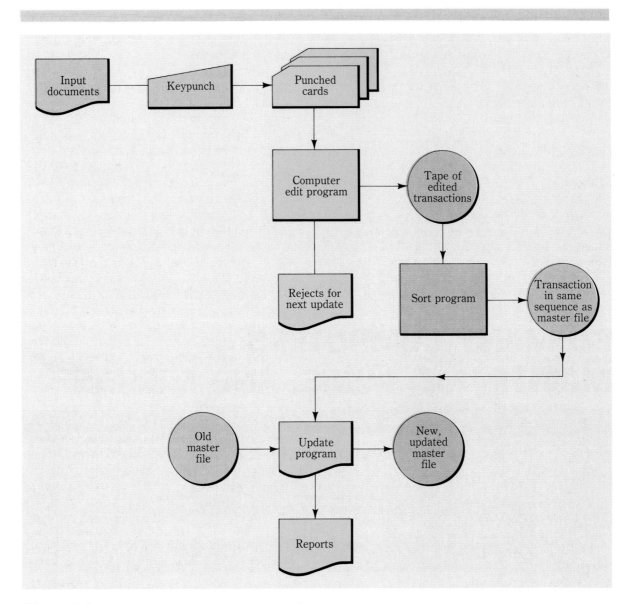

Figure 6-1. The flow of data through a typical batch processing computer application.

INTRODUCTION

For those of us who began careers early in the computer field, today's array of computers is quite remarkable. However, for someone beginning to satisfy her or his curiosity about computers, the situation must be overwhelming. In this chapter, we shall try to differentiate among some of the many different types of computers available today.

Because organizations and individuals are purchasing computers at such a rapid pace, the consumer needs to become educated quickly about how to proceed. What are the different kinds of computers? Is there one computer that is best for a particular job? There is probably no one best computer, but some knowledge of the alternatives can help narrow down the choices.

TYPES OF PROCESSING

To understand the development of minicomputers and microcomputers and to prepare for systems analysis and design, we need to be sure that we understand the different types of processing on computers. There are three categories of applications, though, of course, sometimes we find a mixture of processing types with the same application.

We began with *batch* processing (see Figure 6-1). Almost all input was through punched cards. The user submitted transactions like payments to the keypunchers in a large batch. The keypunch operators keyed the input and turned a deck of punched cards over to computer operations. The computer operators loaded files containing historical data on a tape and then input the cards. The program read the cards, updated the tape, and produced output reports.

Note that all the processing occurred in distinct stages:

1. All input was given to a keypunch operator.
2. All input was keypunched to provide a deck of cards.
3. The deck of input cards was processed in its entirety.
4. The data files were updated at one point in time.
5. Reports were produced at one point in time.

Batch processing is rather inflexible; we cannot request a special run several times a day to update a file. Because programs are written and debugged in the same way, it can take days for a programmer to get a few runs of his or her program.

Remember from our discussions of computer history that frustrated programmers pushed for the development of *time-sharing*. How does time-sharing differ from batch processing (see Figure 6-2)? First, the user does not submit input to a keypunch group. The user is responsible for entering data through a terminal connected directly to the computer. Other users are also entering input at the same time. The computer does not work on just one job at a time; instead, it must keep track of the jobs of User 1, User 2, and all of the other users connected to the computer. As data can be input at the discretion of the user, there is no need to update files all at one time, so we have much more flexibility. Time-sharing, at least on early systems, gave the user the ability to write and debug programs. At first, this ability to enter and modify programs quickly was the major motivation for time-sharing.

On-line processing is similar to time-sharing in the sense that each user has a terminal connected to the computer (see Figure 6-3). However, the term *on-line* generally refers to computers that are dedicated to business applications as opposed to program development, a characteristic of time-sharing systems. The user cannot write a program using the on-line system; instead, the user interacts with a program written by someone else, usually a professional computer programmer.

An airline reservations system is an example of an on-line system. We do not want ticket agents writing programs. Instead, the agent has access to a number of commands that deal with his or her responsibilities: making a reservation, changing a reservation, issuing a ticket, and so on.

It is important to understand these broad classes of processing as they will be discussed further throughout the text. All of these modes are still in use, and new applications are being developed that feature these three different types of processing.

HOW WE ARRIVED

Chapter 3 presented a history of computers but did not really go into detail about the types of computers now offered. We began with computers of basically one type; the manufacturers offered a family of machines from small, limited computers to more capable, more expensive models.

What distinguished among the computers of the

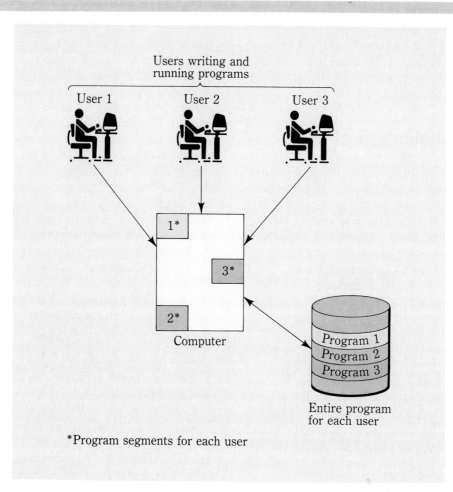

Users writing and
running programs

User 1   User 2   User 3

1*

3*

2*

Computer

Program 1
Program 2
Program 3

Entire program
for each user

*Program segments for each user

Figure 6-2. In time-sharing, many users share the computational capabilities of the computer. The system gives each user a slice of time on the CPU, alternating repeatedly among users.

first and second generation? Less expensive computers had slower CPUs, limited memory, few I/O (input/output) devices, and not much data storage. Larger computers gave the customer more of everything. However, the technology used to build all of these computers was virtually the same.

Minicomputers

In the late 1960s, companies like Digital Equipment Corporation (DEC) developed ways to manufacture the previously expensive CPU for far less money than in the past. Using large-scale integration (*LSI*), DEC and others came out with computers that were less powerful than mainframes, but that were substantially better in terms of cost and performance. That is, a **minicomputer** that cost one fourth the price of a mainframe and had half its performance, had a **cost–performance** advantage of 2. LSI is the ability to put more components on a chip. If more circuits and/or memory will fit on a chip, fewer chips are needed to make a computer, and there is less

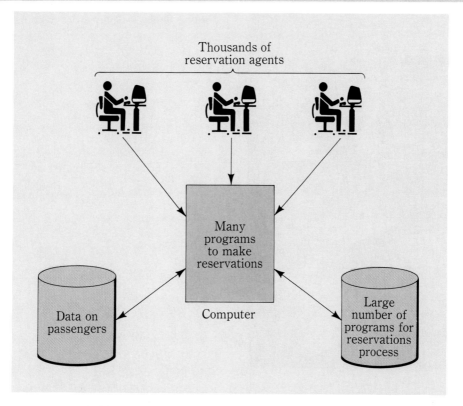

Figure 6-3. On-line processing is similar to time-sharing. An on-line application, however, is dedicated to a particular business problem like making airline reservations whereas a time-sharing user can actually write programs.

labor involved in building the machine.

Most of these computers had word lengths of 16 **bits,** compared to the 32 bits of mainframes. Why be concerned about word lengths? Word length is something that affects the speed of the computer. With a longer word length, more data move between the CPU and memory at one time. If the computer can do arithmetic on 32 bits at a time instead of 16, processing is faster as well. The minis might have 16,000 to 256,000 bytes of primary memory, whereas the mainframe ran from that number to the millions of bytes (megabytes) of main memory.

Minicomputers had programs that made them very good for time-sharing, a market that the large mainframe manufacturers had not addressed with strong software products. Remember that time-

sharing is created through an operating system that allocates the computer's resources among groups of users working on terminals; it looks as if each user has his or her own computer (see Figure 6-4).

Thus, the relatively inexpensive mini might perform better than a mainframe for time-sharing. How was this possible? Until this time, the mainframe manufacturers had concentrated on machines that were very good at batch processing, that is, running jobs like a payroll or an inventory control system. The input appeared all at one time, and the job started and ran to completion.

A time-sharing system usually needs less power for straight computations; instead, it has to be clever in the way the operating system handles interaction with the terminals. Much of the workload on a time-

Figure 6-4. A Sperry Minicomputer.

sharing system involves processing input and output from terminals, a task that does not take much computer power (i.e., many computer instructions). A batch-processing program that updates several files and has complicated processing requirements needs a powerful CPU. Several of the minicomputers used for time-sharing actually had two CPUs. The main CPU handled the computations, and the second one was responsible for interaction with the terminals, handling I/O in an efficient manner.

ORIGINAL EQUIPMENT MANUFACTURERS

Small entrepreneurs saw a bonanza in these minicomputers, with their time-sharing operating systems. These firms bought minicomputers and used the time-sharing operating system to build a *dedicated application* for some industry (*dedicated* means that the computer is used for one task, like airline reservations). These firms are sometimes known as original equipment manufacturers (OEMs) because the computer vendors classify them under this heading when giving discounts on the purchase of computer systems.

One such company was founded by a group of individuals who had spent many years in the garment business. Using the time-sharing operating system, these managers developed a very comprehensive set of programs to be used by a garment manufacturer. This service company offered its product two ways: as a service on its own computer or for sale as a hardware–software *package.* A small garment firm could run the programs on the vendor's computer; when the customer reached a certain size, the vendor sold both a computer and the software for installation on the customer's site.

How can one make a time-sharing system like an on-line application? Most time-sharing systems give the user the ability to write and execute programs using a terminal. An application that is on-line does not provide programming facilities for the user; for example, an on-line system that answers police offi-

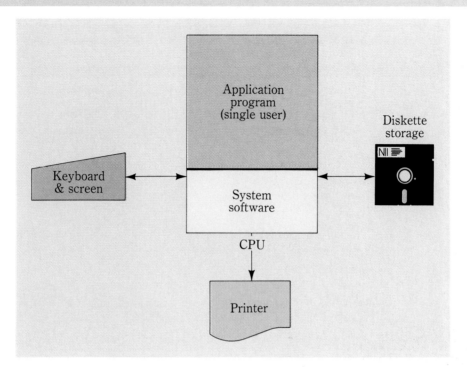

Figure 6-5. A Schematic of a Microcomputer.

cer inquiries from a terminal about automobile license numbers does not provide a programming facility for the user.

Using time-sharing, a programmer can write a program that interacts with a user at a terminal. As far as the user can tell, the only functions available are those provided by the program; he or she does not know that it might be possible to write a program himself or herself, using the computer. In some operating systems, it is even possible to give users, each of whom is identified by an account, the ability only to execute programs, not to write them. Thus, the time-sharing operating system helps the programmer to develop the system and then handles all of the terminals and other aspects of a dedicated on-line application.

For the user of large mainframes, it actually might take longer to develop an on-line application. The operating systems for these computers evolved from batch processing; they did not offer all of the features necessary to handle communications and the interface of the computer with a large number of remote terminals. Soon, however, the mainframe vendors saw the trends in computing and began to develop new software that would make it far easier to develop on-line applications for their computers. For a few years, the small firm that could use a minicomputer was actually ahead of the larger users that had traditionally been the leaders in the field.

Microcomputers

All types of computers have steadily become more powerful, and the basic distinction between minis and mainframes held pretty well until the *microprocessor* came along. A micro is basically a computer on a chip, though it really consists of several chips. One chip usually contains the CPU, and other chips furnish memory, I/O capabilities, and so on (see Figure 6-5).

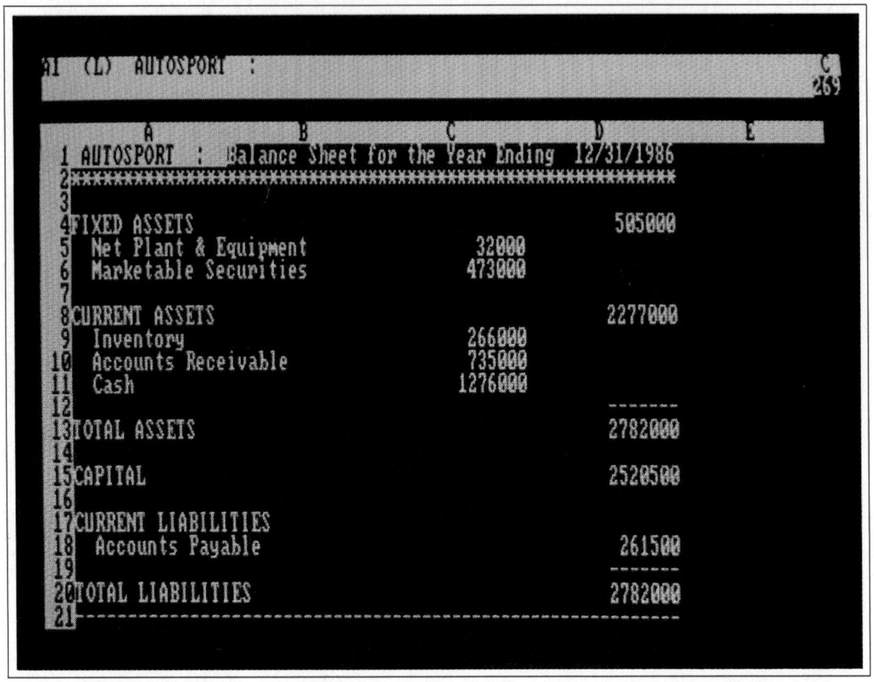

Figure 6-6. Visicalc Example. Visicalc was the first electronic spreadsheet program and was responsible for the sale of many microcomputers.

The previously expensive CPU now came on a chip! The first micros had four- or eight-bit data-access paths and were not particularly fast. At first, they were used to provide *local intelligence.* This term means that some device remote from the computer actually has logic capabilities. An example would be a remote banking terminal, which might contain the logic for updating a passbook for savings. The terminal could check the balance through a connection to a large mainframe computer. However, all of the local processing could be done in the terminal.

The advantage of this approach is that the local terminal can work exclusively on the task at hand, providing a fast response. The local terminal can also execute some of its functions even if something happens to the main computer of the communications lines. The microcomputer made it economical to provide this kind of intelligence in devices other than the main computer.

The chips were not used just for computing de-

vices; product designers saw advantages in incorporating them into many different kinds of goods. For example, the automobile industry is one of the largest consumers of chips: a small microprocessor can be used to sense the critical parameters of a car's operation and to balance fuel consumption against emissions. The microprocessor can adjust the spark advance and meter the fuel provided to the engine.

Consumer products like microwave ovens also use chips to control themselves. One colleague remarked that his washing machine has more logic in it now than the first computer he used.

In 1977, when the Apple II computer appeared, a whole new type of computing was introduced. The developers of the Apple used a series of chips, not for a dedicated task like engine control, but to create a small personal computer.

Because the computer would be used by one person at a time, its operating system could be fairly simple. It needed a language compiler, or *inter-*

Figure 6-7. The IBM Personal Computer or PC has been so successful that many call any microcomputer a "PC."

preter, and a few applications programs to get started. (An interpreter does not actually produce code; it looks at each statement in the program and executes it.)

Then an MBA student watching a professor construct a huge spreadsheet to analyze a finance case came up with an idea. Why wouldn't it be possible to program a computer to do these spreadsheets? He and a partner created a program called *Visicalc.* Visicalc was the first ***electronic-spreadsheet program***, and it contributed greatly to the success of the personal computer: the buyer response cards for the Apple indicated that a significant number of them had been purchased just to run Visicalc. Today, no manufacturer would offer a new microcomputer without having an electronic spreadsheet package ready for it (see Figure 6-6).

The Lines Blur

In 1981, IBM entered the personal computer market and began to take a major market share. IBM's first

personal computer used a sixteen-bit chip, whereas existing micros used eight bits (actually, the IBM chip, an Intel 8088, fetches eight bits at a time from memory but does computations on sixteen bits at a time) (see Figure 6-7). There is a large number of microcomputer manufacturers, some designing unique computers and others stressing their compatibility with existing machines like the IBM personal computer (***PC***). Several manufacturers are now offering microcomputers with thirty-two-bit processors.

The minicomputer vendors did not sleep through all of this rapid development of microcomputers. They pushed ahead to produce the ***"supermini,"*** generally a microcomputer with a thirty-two-bit processor. In fact, some of the superminis actually have more capacity than mainframes.

Now we have complete confusion, a great blurring of lines. There are eight- to thirty-two bit microcomputers, sixteen- to thirty-two-bit minis, and mainframes with thirty-two bits or more. Figure 6-8 shows the broad overlap and cost performance of

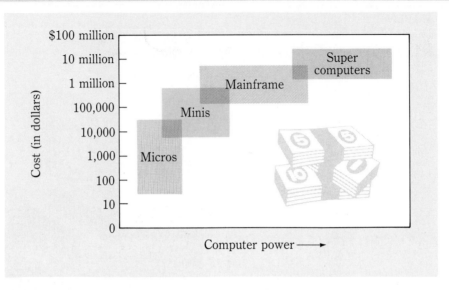

Figure 6-8. Computer Overlap. Computer models overlap each other in both cost and power.

the different options. It is very difficult today to place a computer in a category. Some of the characteristics one might use include:

- Cost
- Processor speed
- Data fetch size
- Arithmetic word size
- Primary-memory size
- Secondary-memory size
- Number of users
- Type of I/O

MICROS

We begin with the smallest computers, though they happen to be the newest:

- Cost: $100 to $30,000
- Speed: 0.001 to 0.5+ MIPS (million instructions per second)
- Data fetch: 4, 8, 16, 32 bits
- Primary memory: 16K to 512K (K is either 1,000 or 1,024)

- Secondary memory: 128K to 30 megabytes (million bytes)
- Number of users: 1 (generally)
- Type of I/O: Keyboard, CRT, diskette, disk

The instruction set for the Intel 8088, the chip in the popular IBM PC, was shown in Figure 4-7. The micro has helped create a movement toward workstations for various types of users. A workstation is a computer with many functions; for a manager, it might provide a spreadsheet package, work processing, and access to the corporate mainframe to extract data. The micro has extended computers to far more users and is proliferating rapidly.

Some organizations are eliminating word processors and substituting microcomputers because they can be used for other tasks as well. We shall discuss the logic of work processing in detail in Chapter 16. Electronic spreadsheets have made the micro an important computer for all types of professionals; we shall learn more about this type of package in Chapter 15.

Although this discussion has stressed business uses of micros, there is a substantial market for

Figure 6-9. A minicomputer complex at the University of New Hampshire at Durham in the Electrical and Computer Engineering Facility.

home computers as well. At first, most of these computers were used for game playing. Now there is more interest in packages that help the consumer with taxes, accounting, and personal filing systems. The reaction to these computers for other than playing games has been mixed; it is not clear how much need for computation the average consumer has. Certainly professionals and the self-employed can gain a great deal from having a computer at home. Whether others can or not will depend on the creativity of software designers in coming up with useful and compelling programs for this market.

MINICOMPUTERS

Minicomputers are generally found in the following range:

- Cost: $30,000 to $500,000
- Processor speed: 0.1 to 1+ MIPS
- Data fetch: 8, 16, or 32 bits
- Arithmetic: 8, 16, or 32 bits
- Primary memory: 16K to 1 megabyte
- Secondary memory: 10 to 1,000 megabytes
- Number of users: 1 to 100
- Types of I/O: All

As already mentioned, minis are very popular for time-sharing and are heavily utilized in companies, high schools, and universities. These computers have also found a place in laboratories for all types of scientific work. A mini may be the only computer in a medium-sized company. Independent vendors, as in the garment industry example described earlier, offer a number of packages and complete systems for specific industries (see Figure 6-9).

Figure 6-10. A Prime 9955 high end super-minicomputer introduced in 1985.

The superminis with thirty-two bits are used in scientific and engineering work. These systems overlap with small mainframes and can be used for some of the same applications (see Figure 6-10).

MAINFRAMES

We used to call a large computer's CPU and primary memory the *mainframe;* it was surrounded with peripherals and other devices. Now we generally use the term to refer to a large computer (see Figure 6-11).

- Cost: $250,000 to $4 million
- Processor speed: .5 to 40 MIPS
- Data fetch: 32+ bits
- Arithmetic: 32 bits
- Primary memory size: 500K to 32 megabytes
- Secondary memory: .5 to 50 gigabytes (billion bytes)

- Number of users: 100 to 1,000's
- Type of I/O: All

The problem with this description is that the mainframe often is not a single computer; it may have more than one CPU, or there may be a center with multiple computers in it.

Software allows these computers to be tied together, so the user actually has the power of several mainframes working at once. A large computing complex with many different computers might support thousands of users, such as a worldwide airline reservations system.

What does one do with a mainframe? Virtually anything imaginable. The applications range from processing all the transactions for users of a credit card to providing production planning for a factory. A university might use a mainframe for registering students and administering student accounts. For example, the following functions might be included in a comprehensive university administrative system:

Figure 6-11. A Burroughs A9 Mainframe Computer. Computers in this series have main memories for 6 to 24 million bytes and larger models handle up to 144 data communication lines.

- Admissions
- Financial aid
- Registration
- Bursar's office processing
- Grade reporting
- Transcript maintenance

All of these packages could be designed to operate on-line from a series of terminals located in different administrative offices of the school.

We also find mainframes used heavily in all kinds of business firms. One manufacturing firm uses a large mainframe computer to support batch processing, on-line applications, and time-sharing, all on the same CPU. This company's manufacturing system is very complex because of the nature of the production process, the large number of parts it manufactures, and the presence of multiple plants.

The firm manufactures electronic components, devices that are used in making electronic circuits. The company has multiple plants, but it wants its customers to be able to call a single number to place an order and not to worry about which plants make the parts that the customer is ordering. Therefore, order entry is run centrally at the largest plant.

The orders are used in conjunction with a master scheduling program. This program looks at forecast demand and orders that have already arrived and tries to fit the demand for products to the capacity of each manufacturing line. The orders have to be "exploded" into their components. That is, if product A requires one ounce of raw material 12, then an order for 16 A's will take one pound of raw material. The finished product must be traced back through all the required manufacturing steps so that the demands on each work center can be determined.

The system decides when it must release an order for production and issues the required shop papers. A routing document goes with the goods as they are produced, telling the supervisors in the factory what each step is in manufacturing the product. As each job moves through the factory, data entry

Figure 6-12. The Cray I Supercomputer. Note the compact design to minimize the distance signals must travel and to maximize cooling.

personnel work on terminals in the factory to update movements. Thus, the system knows the status and location of each job in the shop. The system processes over seventy-five thousand transactions per day on-line and then has substantial batch processing at night to update the production data kept on files in the computer.

A system like this, featuring highly centralized ordering and a large number of terminals, requires the capacity of a mainframe computer. We find mainframe computers in environments where there is a large volume of data to be processed and where a large number of terminals need access to centralized data.

SUPERCOMPUTERS

Very large computers used generally for scientific calculations are called *supercomputers.* Only a few organizations can afford these machines or have problems that need their capacity (see Figure 6-12):

- Cost: $8,000,000+
- Processor speed: 50 to 100 to 500+ MIPS
- Data fetch: 64+ bits
- Arithmetic: 64 bits
- Primary memory: to 32 megabytes
- Secondary memory: 256+ megabytes
- Number of users: 50+
- Types of I/O: CRT, printer, disk, tape

These computers may be controlled by a smaller machine that handles I/O, leaving the supercomputer to compute. The system supports a relatively small number of users because of its specialized nature.

How many supercomputers are there? It is estimated that at the end of 1985 there were about one hundred sixty supercomputers worldwide. Most of the U.S. supercomputers were found in government

Figure 6-13. Marathon Oil Company Geophysics Manager and Geophysicist examine a computer generated contour map from a 3-D seismic plot. Using computers, geophysicists are now manipulating seismic data to create accurate pictures of the depth and breadth of subsurface structure.

Figure 6-14 (below). Weather is analyzed at the National Severe Storms Laboratory using data gathered from the echo radar: (a) A scientist at the NSSL works at the computer terminal as radar imaging is displayed at right. (b) A tornado formation is depicted in this color-code wind-speed display from the echo radar; the highest speed winds are indicated by red.

laboratories; the private sector owners tended to be oil and automobile companies.

What kind of problem needs a supercomputer? Government laboratories involved in nuclear physics make use of them, as do several oil companies for the analysis of seismographic data (see Figure 6-13).

In Europe, a supercomputer is being used by weather forecasters.

Why is so much power needed? As an example, to forecast the weather, meteorologists create models of the atmosphere above the earth (see Figure 6-14). The variables in the model are calculated for three-dimensional blocks of atmosphere stacked on the earth's surface up to fifty thousand feet. The smaller the block, the greater the accuracy of the forecast and also the more computations required of the computer. A supercomputer makes it possible to have smaller and smaller blocks, thereby improving the accuracy of the forecasts.

Eight oil firms have purchased supercomputers, generally for processing seismic data to determine the likelihood of a particular area's containing oil. Supercomputers are also being used to simulate petroleum flows in underground locations to determine how to increase the yield of oil after primary recovery techniques have been exhausted.

IMPLICATIONS

One theme should be obvious: over time, computers have become considerably more powerful and less costly, a trend we do not see in many other products. These dramatic improvements in cost–performance ratios have had two major impacts:

1. Computers are proliferating rapidly.
2. We can afford to use hardware less efficiently today than in the past.

The first implication means that all of us will make use personally of computers in out daily lives, both on the job and at home. This technology will become increasingly important in improving the productivity of individuals in office jobs and all of those who process information. (By the way, the U.S. government estimates that over 50 percent of the work force is involved in primary information-processing tasks.)

The second implication means that we can afford elaborate programs that might use a lot of the computer's resources, possibly inefficiently, to make life easier for the user of the computer. We shall see many examples of this trend in later chapters, particularly in Chapter 7, as we see how computer software has developed.

Application

A Computer for Southrest

Southrest, a division of Multicorp, is in the throes of trying to choose a new computer system. The company has identified three major applications:

- Financial control and modeling
- Accounting
- Project management

Remember that Southrest develops resort properties. It has to determine whether a new project is financially sound by developing a financial model of costs and revenues over time. While a project is under construction, Southrest must perform project accounting. Of course, it also has to keep its own accounts. Finally, Southrest has found that it needs to help monitor and schedule projects to be sure that they are completed on time. Delays in construction can be very costly.

Southrest has developed a framework for analysis of the alternatives before investigating various processing alternatives. It is interesting to see how the firm has approached this problem of evaluating different computer systems. In the spreadsheet that follows, the company has set up a series of criteria on which to judge the different vendors. A weight attached to each criterion reflects its relative importance in evaluation. This weight is multiplied by a rating for each vendor on each criterion. For example, the score for Vendor 1 on cost is Vendor 1's rating of 8 multiplied by the weight of .15, giving a score of 1.2.

Criterion	Weight	Vendor 1		Vendor 2	
		Rating	Score	Rating	Score
Cost	.15	8	1.2	4	.6
Time-sharing	.10	4	.4	5	.5
Number of terminals	.10	5	.5	6	.6
Packages	.25	6	1.5	5	1.25
Modeling languages	.10	2	.2	3	.3
Expansion	.20	5	1.0	5	1.0
Vendor support	.10	6	.6	5	.5
Total score			5.4		4.75

The scores in the spreadsheet are hypothetical and indicate how the scoring scheme works; Southrest has yet to undertake the actual research.

The criteria reflect an implicit choice already. The firm has decided that it needs a multiuser system; it has decided that one or a series of microcomputers is not sufficient for its needs. Given this basic decision and the amount of money the firm wants to spend, it has a choice between a minicomputer and supermini. A large part of the evaluation will involve examining the software packages and the modeling languages available with the proposed systems. The firm also is interested in expansion: Can it increase the power of the computer in small increments? How much additional work load will the machine take before reaching its capacity?

Southrest has a lot more work to do before choosing a computer. However, they have taken a well-structured approach to their decision. They are ready to send a request for a proposal (RFP) to different vendors. Then Southrest will attend demonstrations and contact existing users of the vendors' systems, visiting at least one site for each vendor. Finally, they will make a decision, place an order, and plan for the installation of the system.

Review of Chapter 6

REVIEW

In this chapter, we have tried to clear up some of the confusion that surrounds the computer industry's offerings. The first computers were mainframes. They were followed by minicomputers and then micros. Superminis came about as minicomputers expanded, and supercomputers are dedicated to jobs that require great computational power.

There is a lot of overlap among computers as we have seen. The following general guidelines at least help in our thinking about the alternatives:

- Supercomputers: Used for highly complex computations like weather forecasting, nuclear physics, and seismic analysis.
- Mainframes: Good for high-volume transactions-processing systems and for maintaining large, centralized databases.
- Superminis: Time-sharing is a specialty, especially for scientific and engineering users.
- Minicomputers: Good for general-purpose time-sharing and dedicated on-line applications.

- Microcomputers: Excellent for the individual workstations of managers, engineers, and professionals.

In the chapters that follow, we shall continue to explore the ways in which different kinds of computers can be applied to the solution of information-processing problems.

KEY WORDS

Batch	Megabyte
Bits	Microprocessor
Cost–performance ratio	Minicomputer
	On-line
Dedicated application	Package
Electronic spreadsheet program	PC
	Primary storage
Interpreter	Secondary storage
Local intelligence	Supercomputer
LSI	Supermini
Mainframe	Time-sharing

BUSINESS PROBLEMS

6-1. There is a vocal community in the United States that argues the government should support research in supercomputers. Many of the supporters of this view are academics in areas, like physics, that use computers extensively. The argument is that we must not fall behind or become dependent on foreign manufacturers for supercomputers.

There are several U.S. companies that make supercomputers, but in Japan there is a great deal of government support for building computers. The Japanese electronics industry looks at supercomputers as a prestige item. Firms in the United States, lacking government support, must make a profit and find it difficult to invest in manufacturing supercomputers, for which there is a relatively small market.

How big is the market for supercomputers? Is it in the interest of U.S. national policy to encourage the domestic manufacture of these giant computers? Why have more mainframe vendors not developed supercomputers?

6-2. This chapter maintains that we will continue to use hardware inefficiently in order to develop systems faster. What are the different ways in which one could use hardware inefficiently? How would this kind of policy contribute to reductions in the length of time required to develop a computer application?

One component of your answer should deal with something called *end user programming*. This term does not mean that the end user actually writes programs using the same language as the computer professional, at least in most instances. Instead, the user works with something called a *fourth-generation language,* a very-high-level language that is much closer to the way we think about problems than is the typical programming language COBOL. Why do you think these languages might be inefficient from a hardware standpoint? Is there any justification for the professional computer staff's using these languages as well? What will the cost be of such a policy?

REVIEW QUESTIONS

1. List the major types of computers discussed in this chapter.
2. Why is the number of bits fetched an indicator of computer power?
3. Why is I/O important for the user of a computer?
4. What advances led to the development of minicomputers?
5. What led to the development of Visicalc?
6. What is the significance of an electronic spreadsheet package?
7. What advances in the manufacturing of electronic components made the microcomputer possible?
8. What did the term *mainframe* originally describe?
9. What kind of organizations can use a supercomputer?

THOUGHT QUESTIONS

10. Why do you think minis first came out with sixteen-bit words?
11. Can you explain how a time-sharing system operates.
12. Why did small entrepreneurs adopt time-sharing minis to develop applications for sale to others?
13. Why do users often prefer on-line access to batch processing?
14. Can you think of advantages of batch processing?
15. Describe the applications of micros in consumer products like automobiles.
16. Describe products that do not use micros but that might in the future. How would the products be different from today's versions?
17. Why is software so important to the buyer of a microcomputer?
18. An accounting firm has purchased microcomputers for all of its partners to aid in audits. How do you think these computers will be used?

19. Could a small business use a micro as its only computer?
20. Why are minicomputers good for time-sharing?
21. Why might an organization not purchase any more word processors but substitute personal computers instead?
22. Why do firms sometimes group several mainframes together into a computing complex?
23. Take an application like student-record keeping and describe the various steps involved in the process.
24. If the market for a supercomputer is relatively small, why are vendors (and some countries) interested?
25. We saw in Chapter 3 that vendors underestimated the demand for mainframes in the first generation. The demand for personal computers also exceeded estimates. Why does the industry have this problem?
26. What are some of the implications for firms of the rapid proliferation of microcomputers? For students?
27. Why should we want to use hardware inefficiently?
28. Does a supercomputer need a lot of secondary storage? Why or why not?
29. What applications can you think of for a home computer?
30. What use would a student make of a personal computer?

RECOMMENDED READINGS

Byte, published by McGraw-Hill, is one of the leading popular magazines on microcomputers.

Computer is one of the journals published by the Institute of Electronics and Electrical Engineers; although occasionally technical, it gives a good picture of current computer advances and research.

Computer World, published by Interactive Data Corporation, is a weekly newspaper describing major news plus feature articles each week.

Sanders, D. *Computers Today.* New York: McGraw-Hill, 1983. Contains a good chapter on the different types of computers.

PC World is a magazine devoted entirely to articles about the IBM PC.

Chapter 7

In order to be useful, the computer must be able to accept input data and produce some kind of output. The hardware devices that are used for input and output (I/O) are called *peripherals*. In addition, there are devices that store large amounts of data outside primary memory; sometimes these devices are also called *peripheral storage units.*

There is a tremendous mismatch between the internal speed of the CPU and memory and the speed of input/output devices. Input and output have long been a bottleneck in computation. Part of the trend toward on-line processing is aimed at solving some of this problem. Instead of many individuals filling out forms that are then sent to be keyed as batch input, we find terminals in the locations where data originate. The individual at the source of the data inputs them, saving handling and getting information into the computer more quickly.

Input still has to be keyed into the machine. Some new types of input are aimed at making this task easier. Personal computers feature graphics input devices and touch screens, and a few have very limited voice input. In most instances, however, data enter the computer through some keying operation.

For output, there are a number of devices that present hard copy, that is, output on paper. Also popular for inquiry work is a cathode ray tube (CRT). A good language that lets a user ask questions about data stored in the computer can reduce the amount of printed output needed. If a user has a terminal and the ability to ask questions directly of the computer, it is hoped that the user will not need large printed reports any longer.

The ability of computers to store massive amounts of data in secondary storage is crucial to business systems. There are different kinds of devices for this purpose; traditionally, we have used magnetic tapes and disks. However, there are new technologies that may change the way some information is stored and disseminated.

After reading this chapter, you should be able to:

- List the major input devices for computers.
- List the major output devices.
- Describe the important secondary-storage devices.
- Explain the reason that I/O is a bottleneck.
- Describe how data are stored on tapes.
- Explain how data are stored on disks and what makes disks direct-access devices.
- Discuss some new approaches to peripheral devices.

COMPUTER PERIPHERALS

Input		Storage	
Paper tape	Inexpensive, difficult to use	Magnetic tape	Sequential access, high capacity, good for off-line storage, backup
Punched cards	Staple for many years; gradually being replaced	Magnetic disk	Random access, good for on-line storage
Key to tape or disk	Batch input; limited editing	Floppies	Inexpensive, removable, used heavily on microcomputers
Terminal	On-line editing, immediate feedback, collect data at the source	Streamers	Designed for backing up hard disks
Voice	Emerging technology; increasingly important	Bubble	Used for some terminals, future uncertain
Other	Touch screen, menus, graphics	Mass	Archival data
OCR	Good for high-speed document processing	Optical	High volume, read only

Output	
Paper reports	A variety of printers: line, matrix, laser
Terminal	Interactive, on-line queries
Plotters	Good for graphics, engineering work
Voice	Synthesis of words for audio response to queries

Figure 7-1. Summary of the Three Types of Peripherals Discussed in This Chapter.

INTRODUCTION

Attached to the CPU and primary memory of computers are many different types of devices called **peripherals.** These devices provide ways to input data, store them, and present the results of processing. We have to be able to enter data into a computer to have them processed. After processing, the user wants to see the results, so some form of output is needed. Finally, to avoid keying data over and over again and to make the data available to a large number of users, we use secondary storage.

This chapter explores the three major classes of peripherals. We shall look at some of the original devices in each category, a surprising number of which are still in use today. We shall also explore some promising new technologies, which should be playing a more important role in computing in the near future. Figure 7-1 is a summary of the devices we shall discuss; it lists each device and a few of its major characteristics.

INPUT

Computers process data in the range of nanoseconds (billionths of a second); one of the biggest bottlenecks is providing the data to be processed. Data originate in many different places and forms; a variety of techniques are used to enter data for computer processing.

The Old Ways

The earliest computers used a medium called *punched paper tape;* holes punched in a long strip of paper tape represented characters. The tape was

Figure 7-2. A 1963 Photograph of Paper Tape I/O. Photoelectric devices read the characters represented by holes in the tape.

Figure 7-3. A key punch operator keying data around the time of the IBM 360 computer in the mid 1960s.

bulky, hard to handle, and very difficult to correct. Fortunately, paper tape is rarely found today (see Figure 7-2).

The punched card has been around since it was developed by Hollerith; it was the predominant form of input for the first twenty-five years of computers. Rooms full of operators used devices called *key punches* to prepare cards for computer input (see Figure 7-3). As the industry moved toward more on-line systems, the use of punched cards dropped dramatically. Cards are still found in industry and also in universities, where they offer a flexible medium for data analysis tasks. Survey forms, questionnaires, and other research instruments are punched on cards for entry into a computer. However, on many computers, it is easier to key the data directly into the machine from a terminal.

Cards are compatible and can be read by a variety of computers. Almost any minicomputer or mainframe can read the familiar eighty-column punched card. (There are some small, older computers that use a ninety-six-column card, so it is important to check before assuming that a particular computer can read your cards.)

Key-Driven Input

There are several alternatives to keying data on a card short of actual on-line input into the computer. Key-to-tape and key-to-disk devices represent the evolution of the old key punch. These devices resemble the punch, but the keystrokes are recorded on tape or disk rather than on cards. Because the operation is electronic, the devices can provide some features to ease the input task. A good example is a device capable of storing a line of input before writing it onto the tape or disk so that it can be reviewed for errors. The input device has a buffer, an area of storage in which the **input** record is **keyed.** The record is not written until the end of the input, so the operator can check the results before recording them. With a punched card, an error requires the preparation of a new card.

We should observe that this kind of key-driven

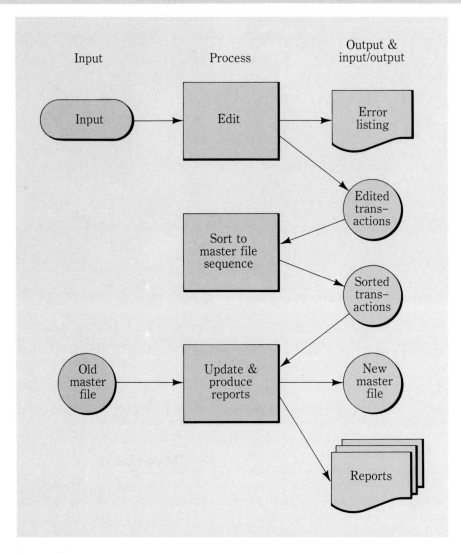

Figure 7-4. Batch Processing. Batch processing is characterized by the completion of input forms, keying of data, and processing of data at one point in time. Retrieval is often very limited.

input is suitable only for batch processing; all of the data are collected at one point in time and then processed by the computer (see Figure 7-4). For many kinds of processing, this is an adequate approach. Even on-line systems may have certain aspects that are updated in batch. For example, consider the program that computes the payroll. We would really not want to have the payroll computed at a different time for each employee. For control purposes, we want to calculate the payroll all at one time; then someone reviews the results to be sure that everything balances, that all employees have been paid that no one has been paid more than once, and so on. Figure 7-5 shows payroll processing.

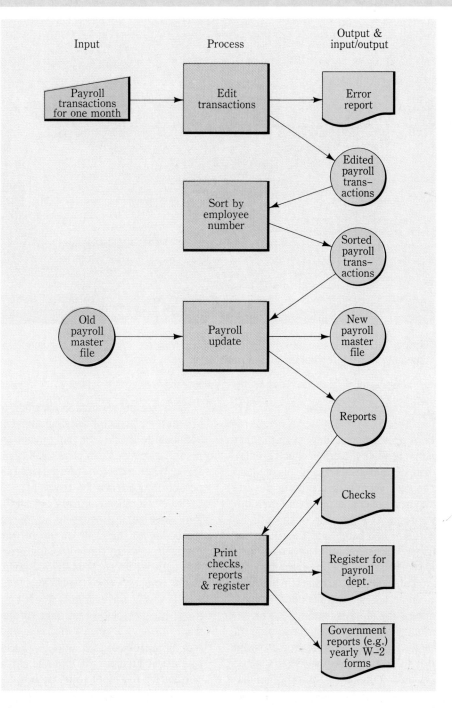

Figure 7-5. Payroll Processing. Payroll is frequently a batch application since it is run periodically, needs good security and controls, and payroll data should probably not be available on-line all of the time.

Figure 7-6. An insurance agent in Portland, Maine uses a computer to enter insurance claim information into a data bank.

On-line Input

Most organizations are designing new systems that have on-line input. The ability to edit is much greater with this form of input, and the user controls input so that is not the responsibility of the computer department. On-line input is usually faster than batch because data are entered at their source; there is no need to collect them in a batch and then wait for key-driven entry and later computer processing.

On-line input requires that the operator be connected to the computer directly, so that the program accepting input can access various files on the computer to determine if the input is legitimate. For example, an order entry clerk might key the number of a customer placing an order. The computer program uses this number to retrieve the customer's name and address from a computer file. The program displays the name and address so that the input clerk can check it against the name typed on the order. The full power of the computer can be used to check the input.

As a second example, consider a program that processes claims for an insurance company. A person insured by the company might have a policy for medical expenses that pays for X rays and laboratory tests. When a doctor orders these tests, the insured person files a claim for payment.

If the insurance company's claims-processing system uses batch processing, an operator keys all of the codes for the claim on a card, tape, or disk. (In batch processing the computer processes all input and updates its records at one point in time.) The claims adjusters code the claim on a form in the field; a code of 7A, for example, might be an X ray, Z121 might mean a blood test, and so on. The company wants to have a record of claims and also wants to use the history of payments in developing insurance rates (see Figure 7-6). For these reasons, it is important for the input to be accurate. Unfortunately, the claims agents do not always use the correct codes, and sometimes they put the codes in the wrong places. With batch input, the operator keys what is on the form; he or she has no knowledge if

Figure 7-7. A Bank of Virginia Autoteller in a Shopping Center Parking Lot in the Norfolk, Va. Area.

something is wrong. When an edit program preceding the file update executes, it examines the codes and produces an error listing. Then someone has to go back through the batches of forms and find the ones in error, correct them, and resubmit them to the computer.

With on-line input data are entered into the computer continuously during the day through a terminal. An edit program is written not to operate in batch, but to look at each form as entered by an operator. If there is something wrong, the program notifies the operator immediately; the operator can try to correct the error or turn the incorrect form over to someone who contacts the adjuster and clears up the problem. This type of input, then, is fast and improves the chances that accurate data enter the computer.

Terminal. The most frequently used device for on-line input is a traditional keyboard CRT. Under the control of a program, an input screen appears. The operator types in the data, sometimes filling in the blanks on what looks like a paper form. Another alternative is a *menu,* which allows the operator to select from a series of choices. (We shall see menus in a slightly different context when we cover word processing in Chapter 16 and electronic spreadsheet programming in Chapter 15.)

A menu might look like this:

1. View inventory status.
2. Request a part.
3. Update arrival of merchandise.
4. Make a physical inventory adjustment.

After a choice is made, another menu appears with the next selection. Menus are very good for making a selection when there are a lot of options, but they are slow for an experienced operator. Some on-line systems, like the ones used by the airlines for reservations, have codes that tell what kind of transaction is being entered. Because the reservations agents use the terminals all day long, it is not difficult for them to learn the codes, which are the command language for the application.

Special Terminals. A variety of industry-oriented terminals are available. Banks have been using automated teller terminals to reduce staff costs and to extend banking to a variety of locations. Many of these terminals are actually small computers; they can function alone. However, in order to check balances, they are often connected to a mainframe computer that has a record of each account and the funds in it. Figure 7-7 shows a *bank autoteller* machine.

You have probably seen point-of-sale (*POS*) terminals in a variety of settings. Retailers use these terminals to enter data on what has been purchased.

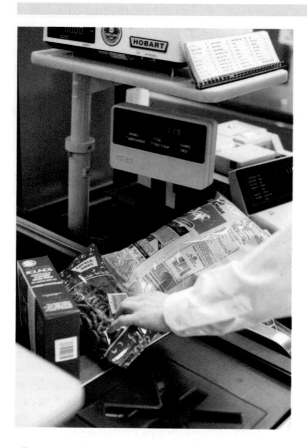

Figure 7-8. A grocery store scanner (bottom) reads price and product data from the bar code (Universal Product Code) on the product packaging in an automated grocery store in a Philadelphia suburb. The customer's receipt will identify each product by name and price paid.

Unlike the old cash register, which just recorded the amount of the sale, the POS terminal keeps a record of the specific stock number of the item sold. As a result, it is possible to maintain a very accurate book inventory. Buyers in the store know exactly what is in stock and can tell what to reorder.

A special-purpose point-of-sale terminal is the grocery store scanner. Most grocery items are marked with a funny code made up of a number of bars (Universal Product Code). An industry association developed this code, and all producers have agreed to follow its conventions. A separate set of bars identifies each product sold (see Figure 7-8).

In the grocery store, there is a computer that has the price of each separate item in its records. When the item passes over a slot in the checkout counter, a laser reads the product code. The code is transferred to the store computer, which looks up the price of the item; the computer prints the item iden-

tification and price on the register tape. The result is a much faster checkout and probably a more accurate recording of purchases.

Voice. If we could talk to the computer, there would be an explosion in the use of these machines. Think of having a speech typewriter; you would simply talk to a microphone and the typewriter would type out what you have dictated. Because we see a lot of examples of speech output, many people wonder why speech input is not widespread. Speech output by computer is relatively easy because a structured output message is all that is required. For a telephone information operator who uses a computer to "play" the number you have requested, there are only a few options. One has a message that says, "The number is . . . " and then a string of digits. How many possibilities? There are ten digits, so that total amount of recording required is small.

Figure 7-9. An ITT System that Allows Its Personal Computer, the XTRA, to Recognize Voice Input and Record and Playback Digitized Speech.

Also, there is no question about what is to be spoken: the information operator has indicated the proper number to the computer.

The current level of speech recognition, however, is fairly limited; understanding natural speech is a very difficult task for a computer. First, the computer has to translate the sounds that it hears into the actual words. Considering the different pitches, speed, and intonation of humans, just getting the words as spoken is very complicated. Figure 7-9 illustrates a voice input system.

Next, the computer has to understand the natural language used by the speaker. Again, it is a very difficult task to translate natural language because we understand a great deal from the context and the emphasis of the speaker. Consider the sentence "Time flies like an arrow." Does this mean that a special kind of fly is fond of an arrow? How can time, which is not a physical entity, fly? For a human, the interpretation of the sentence is easy; for a computer, it is not so clear.

Today, we have limited voice-recognition systems for input. These systems generally have to be trained by the speaker to recognize his or her voice. They require than an envelope of silence surround each word and therefore are known as discrete word systems (continuous speech recognition, described above, is still in the research stage). One system for integration with microcomputers claims that it made only thirty-four errors in a test to recognize more than fifty thousand words.

The first application of these systems has not been for the executive in an office talking to a terminal. Instead, voice input has been applied in situations where the input operator needs to have his or her hands available for another task rather than on a keyboard for data entry. Inspectors in plants and employees sorting packages for mail distribution, for example, occasionally use a voice input system today.

At General Electric, voice input is used by inspectors who look at the more than fifteen thousand range and oven parts that are manufactured daily. The inspector has a belt-mounted transmitter that sends data to a computer. The system recognizes up to one hundred words provided by the speaker; it has eliminated the previous form of data entry, which required some three steps.

Even though we are a few years away from continuous voice recognition, there is still much that can be accomplished with the limited systems available today. For example, it should be fairly easy to develop a voice recognition system for a spreadsheet program, at least for making the choices on a menu. Several microcomputer vendors are offering speech recognition chips as an option with their microcomputers, so many other applications should be coming soon.

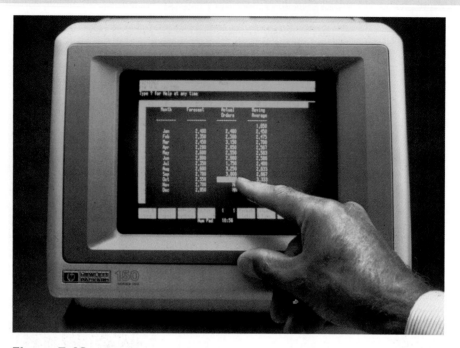

Figure 7-10. The Hewlett-Packard HP150 microcomputer features touch screen input.

Other Techniques

One personal computer now features a ***touch screen:*** the user puts his or her finger on the menu choice, actually touching the choice on the screen. One system uses a grid of infrared lights on the left side and the bottom of the screen. When something breaks the light (a finger or a pencil), the receivers on the right and the top do not receive light where the screen was touched. The electronic circuits of the screen interpret the absence of light and send the coordinates to the computer. The user can merely touch the menu; he or she does not have to type the response or remember the commands. This system is illustrated in Figure 7-10.

The American Stock Exchange (AMEX) is using a custom-designed touch-screen terminal to speed transactions. Brokerage house orders for stocks arrive at a rate of ten per second when the market is open. The trades are captured directly by a specialist or a market maker in the stock being traded, someone who buys and sells stocks sometimes from his or her holdings, to maintain an orderly market. The specialist uses a touch screen terminal in which the user touches a membrane instead of pressing a well-defined key. Using ***soft keys*** instead of a fixed keyboard like the one on a typewriter (the functions of soft keys change with the program being run), the specialist obtains the most recent sale price of the stock, executes the order, identifies the brokers on both sides of the trade, and sends the confirmation.

The system automatically makes a backup copy. There are no keystrokes or paper involved. Tests indicate that the system cuts the time needed to make a trade from five minutes to three seconds on the two thirds of the exchange's trades that involve less than three hundred shares of stock. Errors are expected to drop from 5 to .8 per 100 trades. There will be seventy touch screens connected to batches of Intel 8088 processors when the system is completely installed. Large Tandem computers process the incoming orders.

Graphics pads are also used for some applications, especially in drawing and engineering. The

Figure 7-11. Dr. Harold Kellogg of Mercy College in Dobbs Ferry, New York, works at his home office where he is devising computer graphics programs for teaching geometry. His hand rests on the digital pad and holds a stylus. The Vectrix monitor displays a geometric configuration which Dr. Kellogg is about to change: note the word ERASE on screen. Using a NEC graphics processor and a 15 megabyte hard disk (not seen) storage device, Dr. Kellogg has available a palette of colors totalling several million.

user has a **stylus,** a writing instrument like a pen, but with a point that has no ink, which he or she uses to make a drawing on a special board. Various electrical techniques are used to sense the location of the pen on the tablet. The X-Y coordinates are sent to the computer, and its program plots the line on the **CRT** (see Figure 7-11).

One device attracting a great deal of interest in the personal computer market is the **mouse.** A mouse is some type of device that the operator moves around to control the **cursor,** the bright spot of light on a CRT that shows where we are pointing on the screen. One mouse is placed on a flat surface; as the mouse is moved around on the pad, the cursor on the screen moves correspondingly. Two buttons on the mouse either select the choice on which the mouse rests or cause the screen to scroll, that is, move to a new screen to show different material. Whether the mouse will be faster than keying, and under what conditions, remains to be seen. Figure 7-12 shows a mouse and associated input.

The **joystick** is a similar kind of device, some-

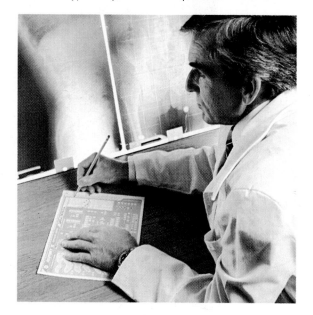

times found on computers used for games. The joystick can also be used for graphics work to select a line or a menu choice on a screen.

Character Readers

Some of the first character readers were used by banks and are known as magnetic ink character recognition (**MICR**) devices. The stylized numbers at the bottom of a check came from a banking industry agreement on placement and format. Data like the account number and the amount of the check are printed with a special ink that has magnetic particles in it. Machines in the bank are capable of reading the magnetic ink and sorting the checks into various groups based on the account number, which was printed on the checks before they were sent to the customer. The sort includes categories such as "checks on us" and those in transit to other banks. When checks arrive at the bank, an operator used a device that places magnetic characters on the check to record the amount of the check; this information, combined with the magnetically encoded unique account number at the bottom, is all the bank needs to process the check.

One reader that is not used extensively any longer is the mark sense reader. Here, a simple light is used to determine whether or not a small square on a piece of paper has been darkened with a pencil. Mark sense is still used for testing; the student darkens a choice in a multiple-choice exam. In reading, the dark mark reflects the light, and the light passes through the sheet where there is no mark. (See Figure 7-13 for an example.)

Figure 7-14. In the foreground is a storage rack for magnetic tape in use in a computer room. Note tape drives on the left.

Because there has to be a square for each answer, mark sense is rather limited. For example, think of how big a portion of the form was required for your name, as there had to be space for a long name and twenty-six choices for each possible letter.

More complex optical readers employing lasers can read carefully printed numbers and a variety of type fonts. A special optical character recognition (*OCR*) font is available for a variety of typewriters; this font is one of the easiest for a machine to read. Generally, as OCR equipment is able to read more fonts, it becomes more expensive.

STORAGE

Once we have data in a computer, we want to store it somewhere. **Primary memory** is the most expensive and is limited in size compared to the massive amounts of data stored by some firms. As with the payroll, we do not want all data in primary memory at one time, anyway. **Secondary storage** is available for the purpose of storing data, either off-

line for backup or on-line for immediate access.

Remember that the key distinction between primary and secondary storage is that the CPU cannot directly access secondary storage; the data must be moved from secondary to primary memory and then processed.

Magnetic Tape

One of the first secondary-storage media was magnetic tape. Like the tape used in home tape recorders, a computer tape features magnetic iron oxide to record data (see Figure 7-14). The direction of magnetization of the domains on the tape indicates whether the data are a 0 or a 1. Typically, the tape has nine tracks, and a bit is stored on each track. The first eight tracks represent a character and the ninth is present for error checking. Magnetic tape for mainframe computers can store data at 1,600 or 6,250 characters per inch.

Because we usually process a small amount of information at a time, tapes are designed to start, transmit a block of data, and then stop. The block transferred is known as a **physical record;** between these physical records is a **gap** to allow for the acceleration and deceleration of the tape.

When being read, the tape moves at a constant velocity of 120 to 200 inches per second. To reach this speed, it must accelerate quickly. Often, one sees a long strip of tape hanging down on each side of the read mechanism of the tape drive. The tape hangs in chambers that have a vacuum to isolate the tape from sudden acceleration. Tapes come in various lengths up to two thousand four hundred feet.

It is good practice to have two types of labels on tapes. We need some kind of adhesive label on the outside of the reel itself with the name of the tape and the date it was created. If there are a large number of tapes, labels are very important in identifying the tape we want. Large tape libraries usually use some kind of a computer program that associates a tape number with its contents. The computer operator looks up a topic heading like "payroll file" and finds the number of the payroll tape. The tape is filed in the library under this permanent reel number.

The second kind of label is written by the operating system under the direction of the program when a file is created. This label is the first record on the tape and identifies the contents of the tape and its creation date and may contain other information as well. It is a good practice to create labeled tapes in case it is ever necessary to figure out what is on the tape.

One firm supposedly fired its tape librarian but gave two weeks' notice. During that time, the librarian changed the external labels on all of the reels of tape in the tape library. It took many months for the firm to rectify the problems caused by this act.

Tape is known as a **sequential** medium; we can read only what is under the read or write head on the tape drive. To find some record at random, we would have to process half the tape, on the average, because we do not know where the item is located: sometimes the information we want will be in the first half of the tape, and sometimes it will be in the second half. We generally associate tape files with batch processing because it is not really feasible to ask for individual pieces of data stored on a tape from an on-line terminal: searching the tape for the requested data would be just too time-consuming.

Hard Disks

To provide access at random—that is, access to any piece of data stored on a device—within a reasonable time, we must use something other than magnetic tape. One of the most important of these random- or direct-access storage devices is a hard disk. A hard disk consists of a series of platters on a spindle. The platter looks like a long-playing record, except that it is coated with magnetic material, like that on a cassette tape rather than the grooves on a record. The spindle is like the spindle on a record player, and the platters are evenly spaced vertically on it. A read/write head moves in and out while the disk revolves. The heads actually fly a small distance above the platter on the air pressure created by the revolving disk. Because the heads move in and out and the disk rotates, we can locate any spot on the disk relatively quickly, at least in the range of 20 to 30 milliseconds (thousands of a second). This type of device is known as **random**- or **direct-access** because we can get to data on it much more quickly than with the sequential access of tape storage. The time taken to move to a new track is called **seek time:** the heads are seeking a new track (see Figure 7-15 and 7-16.)

How are the data actually stored? Each platter in Figure 7-15 is formatted in concentric rings on the surface of a platter. These rings are called **tracks,** and each track holds a certain number of data in terms of bytes (each holds the same number, even though the outer tracks are slightly larger than the inner ones). If the read/write head is positioned over a track, it must wait for the beginning of the track (called **rotational delay time**) and then it can begin reading or writing. As the platter revolves under the head, the head traces out a path directly over the track.

The top platter of the disk and the bottom platter do not record on their outer surfaces, as these surfaces are the most likely to be damaged. The other platters have a recording surface on both sides. If

Figure 7-15. A Seagate Technology ST225 Hard Disk Drive Without its Cover.

Figure 7-16. A drawing of the Seagate drive in Figure 7-15. The device stores 20.15 million bytes of data once a program has formated the disk. The disk rotates at 3600 RPM. The two disk platters are accessed by four read-write heads. Average access time is 85 milliseconds.

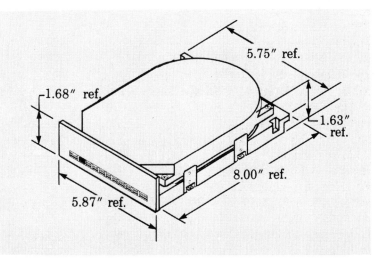

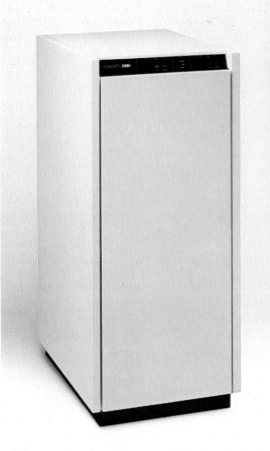

b

Figure 7-17. (a) The Memorex 3680 Disk Storage Subsystem can be configured with up to 10 gigabyte (10 billion bytes) and covers 26 square feet of floorspace. (b) A technician inspects a stack of rigid drives.

the read/write heads are left in one position, the revolving tracks on each platter form a cylinder. The capacity of the disk then depends on the number of bits per inch stored on a track, the number of tracks on each surface, and the number of platters that make up the cylinder.

Direct-access files are a requirement for on-line systems. You would not want to wait five or ten minutes on the phone when making a plane reservation for a computer to search a tape.

Some disks are removable; their entire pack of platters and heads come off the drive in a sealed compartment. A popular disk is called the *Winchester*. This disk is of the sealed variety, which eliminates alignment problems between the head and the

disk and reduces the exposure of the surface to dust and dirt in the air. The prototype unit contained two drives, each of which held 30 megabytes (30 million bytes) of data. As the old Winchester rifle was a 30-30, Winchester seemed like a natural code name. There are also disks with heads fixed over the surface of the disk; these drives are fast because the heads never have to move. The disks that come with personal computers are usually nonremovable.

Floppy Disks (Diskettes)

The hard disk is made of a rigid material; the heads do not actually come in contact with the magnetic media on the platters, (see Figure 7-17). With a

a   b

Figure 7-18. (a) A floppy disk being inserted into an Apple II disk drive. (b) A Macintosh 3½ inch plastic-encased disk.

floppy disk, on the other hand, the read/write heads touch the disk surface. The diskette itself is flexible (floppy); the diskettes come in several sizes, including 3.5, 5.25, and 8 inches in diameter. The diskette stores a relatively small amount of data, say 360,000 to 720,000 characters versus the tens and even hundreds of millions of characters stored on a hard disk.

The diskette, however, is much less expensive than a hard disk. The diskettes are easily removed and inserted, providing a quite convenient storage mechanism.

As shown in Figure 7-18, the diskette is in a protective envelope or a plastic case. (Never touch the exposed part of the disk where the read/write heads make contact with it.) The entire envelope or case goes into the drive, and the diskette rotates within the envelope. Because the head comes in contact with the diskette, there can be wear; diskettes eventually stop working. For this reason, it is always important to have a backup copy of key files or programs when a diskette is the primary storage medium in use.

Streaming Devices

A tape drive used for data recording, as described earlier in this chapter, must start and stop between blocks. Although this mode of operation is very appropriate for updating a file a transaction at a time, it is not particularly fast for backing up a disk by making another copy of its contents. A *backup* copy is a copy that is made and stored in case something happens to the original.

Personal computers are available with ten-megabyte hard disks that cannot be removed. Making a backup of the contents of these disks can take a long time with a cassette recorder. Backup using floppies takes a lot of disks and a lot of time.

One answer to this backup problem is to use a *streaming tape* drive. This drive, as the name implies, does not stop for physical blocks; its one purpose in life is to back up a hard disk. As a result the device can be relatively cheap. Making a backup tape of your disk and storing it off-site is a good policy.

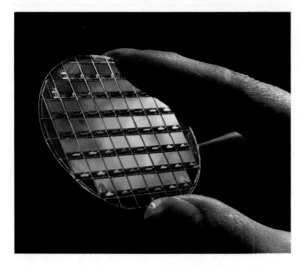

Figure 7-19. Bubble Memory Chips in a Wafer.

Bubbles

Bubble memory arrived with great expectations. This memory is solid-state and is nonvolatile; when the power is turned off, the contents of memory remain. Small bubbles are created by the application of an electric current to certain materials. Data can be stored and retrieved by a detector as tiny rings of bubbles circulate. Even though the bubbles are in sequential strings, there are many strings, and each can be accessed, so that this is a direct-access memory.

Bubble memory has been used in some terminals for portable storage. However, several major manufacturers have stopped making bubble devices, and the future is somewhat uncertain for this medium (see Figure 7-19).

Mass Storage

One can think of storage as a hierarchy: the faster the memory, the more costly it is. Therefore, we want to provide a range of storage. Primary memory is the most expensive and the fastest memory. Next comes the disk, and after that usually a tape. For huge masses of data, however, firms may need something that is larger but slower than a tape.

A *mass storage* device can hold 16 billion bytes of data; it consists of tape strips in cartridges. The cartridges are arranged in a honeycomb structure; a mechanism that resembles a juke box retrieves a cartridge under program control, moves it to a read/write area, and returns it when finished. The data are loaded from the mass store to a disk drive, and then the computer can access them there. This operation can take several minutes.

What is the advantage of this type of device? Billions of bytes of data can be stored inexpensively. A firm might even replace most of its tape library with a mass store; the program calls for the data far enough in advance and finds it available on a disk shortly thereafter.

Optical Storage

Optical storage offers great promise for high-density recording (more bits packed per square inch) and large volumes. The medium is called *optical* because storage is based on light instead of magnetics. The commercial optical products available today use a *laser* to make a change in the flat surface of a recording medium. For example, a small bump is all that is necessary to represent a 1. One device uses a laser that projects light from the bottom of the optical disk. Under high power (twenty or more milliwatts of power), it writes by creating a bubble on the surface. The bubble is one micron (millionth of a meter) or less in diameter. The disk reads under low

Figure 7-20. An OSI Laser Drive removable medium disk stores one gigabyte (1 billion bytes) of data on one side of a 12-inch diameter disk.

power of one to two milliwatts. The bubble created in writing causes reflected light to be altered in amplitude or phase, so that there is a difference from the light where there is no bubble. The altered light can represent a 1 and a normal reflection a 0.

Optical storage has extremely high capacities: a single-surface twelve-inch diameter disk will store 1 billion bytes (1 gigabyte) of data. Another advantage of this type of storage is the ease and low cost of reproducing copies of the disk; the process is similar to making copies of a phonograph record from a master record.

As you probably suspect, these optical disks are read only after the data are written the first time. In certain applications where archival data are needed, the inability to change data is not a limitation. Other applications might use the optical store and simply write changes in a new area and destroy the old copy. A major user of optical disks may turn out to be firms that offer proprietary databases (valuable data sold to users). A single disk can store over 400,000 ordinary typed pages of data. It may be

cheaper for a database service to put its data on an optical disk and send it by mail than to provide on-line access with a computer system. Figure 7-20 shows an optical disk device.

An optical disk that can be erased and rewritten will be a major storage breakthrough. Several companies are conducting research on this type of medium. Current optical storage units can place the equivalent of ten reels of tape on a videodisk with access time in the millisecond range.

OUTPUT

All of the input and processing of data are interesting only if they produce some results. Computer systems have many different ways of providing output.

The Product

For some types of processing, particularly transactions-oriented systems, the output may actually be

Figure 7-21. A Sperry Corporation Medium-speed Line Printer.

the results of processing. A bank processes thousands of checks a day to produce a statement. The statement is the printed product and is one of the major outputs of the system. All types of bills, statements, and notices are printed on paper and distributed.

Reports

The design of reports is a complex task; it is difficult to determine what information is needed and to arrange it in a convenient format. Systems analysis and design include the design of report formats. There is a growing tendency today to ask users to actually design their own reports.

A computer often has a *line printer;* with this device, a rotating chain with letters on it is used to print a line. When the letter desired falls under the appropriate position, a hammer presses the letter onto the ribbon and paper. Such printers can be very fast, up to two thousands lines per minute, and can make multiple copies using carbon paper (see Figure 7-21).

For smaller computers, there are serial printers like those using a *daisy wheel.* A serial printer

prints one character at a time, in contrast to line printers, which are capable of printing a line at a time. The same technology as that in an electronic typewriter is found in one of these printers (in fact, one can use an electronic typewriter as the output device for many personal computers). A wheel with letters on it spins to the appropriate letter, and a hammer presses it against the ribbon and the paper. This *impact* printer produces a letter-quality output, though it prints only one character at a time and hence is slower than a line printer (see Figure 7-22).

Matrix printers are very popular with small computers because they are relatively inexpensive and can do limited plotting and graphics. The printer has a matrix of wires; the appropriate wires in the matrix are selected to form a letter and are pressed against the ribbon to make an impact on the paper. By offsetting the head slightly and printing twice, we can make a fairly thick letter, though not as thick as the impact of a typewriter. The matrix printer is also serial; the head moves back and forth when printing. Figure 7-23 shows a matrix printer.

Nonimpact printers work in several different ways. They do not use any kind of hammer to press type against a ribbon and paper. We can have a dot

Figure 7-22. A Daisy Wheel from a Letter-Quality Printer Made by Juki.

Figure 7-23. (a) A Dot Matrix Printer Print Head. (b) A dot matrix printer from Epson which has a dot matrix of 24 points and a maximum speed of 200 characters per second.

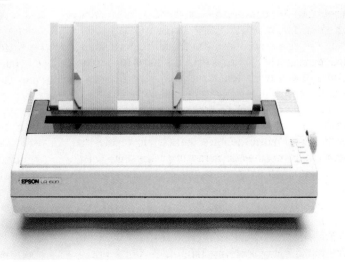

a   b

Figure 7-24. A product designer uses a CAD system from Computervision to visualize his design; to his right is the print-out of an earlier design.

matrix printer with no ribbon. Instead, the wires that form a letter are heated and come in contact with a heat-sensitive paper to make an image. In an ***ink-jet printer,*** charged droplets of ink are shot at the paper. As they leave the nozzle, they are deflected by a magnetic field to form letters. Ink jets produce good quality letters and some can use different color inks.

The highest-speed printers produce a page using laser technology. The approach is similar to the one used in photocopiers and produces a speed equivalent to twenty thousand lines per minute. The movement of paper becomes a problem at this speed, and the document must be printed twice (or photocopied) to produce multiple copies. However, the need for special preprinted forms is eliminated because forms can be set up by use of the printer. One major brokerage firm uses two high-speed page printers for a mainframe computer to help with all of the output it generates each day. Also available are lower-priced, slower laser printers for microcomputers and low-volume printing.

Interactive Output

Some of us feel that we produce too much paper. One way to reduce the amount of printed output is through more inquiry systems rather than producing bulky reports for reference. The CRT used for input is also a good medium for output; if the system is on-line, we can use the CRT to answer many questions, given the appropriate software support. If needed, a slow-speed printer is placed near the CRT to make a hard copy of the inquiry and its results.

For some applications, like engineering design, we want a graphics terminal, one capable of producing continuous lines and shapes. (We can do limited business graphics on ***alphanumeric*** printers, which print only characters and not continuous lines.) A variety of graphics terminals are available. These terminals are used extensively in design work, such as computer-aided design (CAD) for developing manufacturing components (see Figure 7-24). They are also a mainstay in the design of integrated circuits. Graphics are also very important for

a

b

Figure 7-25. (a) Hewlett-Packard six-pen plotter showing a bar graph and six-pen holder, right foreground. (b) A larger Hewlett-Packard plotter creates a complex integrated-circuit design in minutes.

some control applications, like running a power plant or an oil refinery. Well-designed graphics can make the flow of an operation very clear to an operator, certainly more clear than a large display full of gauges and meters.

Other

Plotters. The engineer may want a *hard copy* (a copy on paper) of a drawing, or the financial analyst may want a transparency of a graph. For these purposes, one uses a *plotter,* a device with different-colored pens that move across the paper drawing lines. There are relatively inexpensive one-color and multicolor plotters for business graphics on a small com-

puter, and there are very elaborate engineering plotters with accuracies in the thousandths of an inch (see Figure 7-25).

Voice. For many years computers have been able to provide voice answerback through the use of pre-recorded messages. Banks sometimes provide these systems so that a caller can inquire about his or her account balance. Today a variety of speech-synthesizing chips are available. The chips contain a small number of phonemes that must be strung together to form a word. Current technology produces some rather unusual sounds, and much research is being done to improve this form of output.

Microfilm. For archival data, microfilm can help

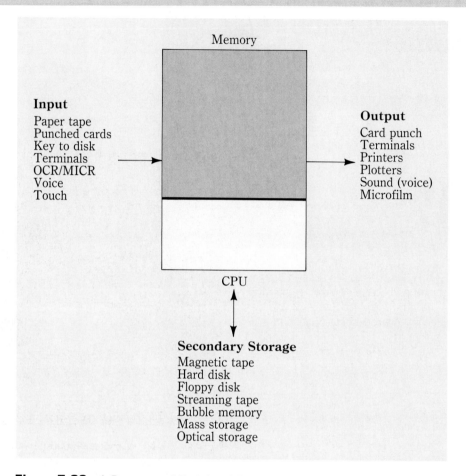

Memory

Input
Paper tape
Punched cards
Key to disk
Terminals
OCR/MICR
Voice
Touch

Output
Card punch
Terminals
Printers
Plotters
Sound (voice)
Microfilm

CPU

Secondary Storage
Magnetic tape
Hard disk
Floppy disk
Streaming tape
Bubble memory
Mass storage
Optical storage

Figure 7-26. A Summary of Peripheral Devices. What are the advantages and disadvantages of the different device for input, output and storage?

reduce a mountain of paper to manageable size. One insurance company enters all of the data from a policy application into the computer, microfilms the application, and destroys the original document. Microfilm is not as accessible as other computer data, but it can be very economical. Computer output can be placed on tape, and the tape can be processed by a device that will generate microfilm.

In the future, we may find optical-disk or videodisk technology taking over some of this archival function because data can be located more quickly on the disk than by the use of a microfilm reader.

SUMMARY

We have discussed the major forms of computer input and output. There are others as well and more are likely to be developed. I/O is a significant bottleneck in working with computers. There is a trend toward making more data accessible on-line in order to reduce the amount of paper produced. Of course, this trend creates a need for more on-line storage. We expect to see continued advances in the methods for storing and retrieving data and for communicating with computers. (See Figure 7-26 for a summary of peripheral devices.)

Application

Figure 7-27. A microcomputer-based engineering/scientific workstation with high quality graphics enhances the productivity of these professionals.

Computers are finding their way into a variety of jobs; one of the newest is in graphic arts. The latest equipment enables an artist to do layouts, draw freehand, or create standard forms such as pie and bar charts. There are simple systems for microcomputers and more elaborate systems to be used for laying out magazine pages.

Many of these systems can be linked to pen plotters, ink-jet printers, or film recorders to produce a slide, a transparency, or a paper copy of the results. Other devices let the artist use an electronic tablet for graphics input. Some of the software allows the artist to paint colors easily; he or she can enlarge or change the color of an image by moving a stylus over the input graphics tablet.

The systems have produced rather dramatic gains in productivity. One in-house graphics department felt that it was producing four times the amount of output with the system as opposed to using noncomputerized techniques.

This application illustrates all of the types of peripherals discussed in this chapter. There is a unique input, which is graphics; of course, there will be some keyboard entry, too, particularly for text. There is secondary storage to hold various drawings while they are being constructed. Also, a library of old drawings forms a series of building blocks for graphics to be created in the future. Finally, there is output in several different forms from printed to overhead transparencies.

Review of Chapter 7

REVIEW

This chapter has covered a lot of material; you may want to review Figure 7-1 again. We began looking at input techniques; today the most prevalent is the CRT capturing data at the source where they are created. What else would we like? It would be nice to develop reliable and easily used voice-input systems. The keyboard is still a stumbling block for a lot of potential computer users.

Voice input will first come in the highly structured format of today's systems. For example, the user will see a menu and tell the computer the number of his or her choice. The next step will be more free-form input, something that is called *natural language*. These input approaches require more research and more computing power than we have today.

Storage on the computer is what lets organizations keep vast amounts of data readily available; without secondary storage, computers would be far less useful. Firms have a growing need for storage, and the capacity of secondary devices has steadily increased. The current standby for mainframe and minicomputers is the hard disk, whereas floppies dominate the micro market. The optical disk offers tremendous potential for the future.

Output for business systems still involves massive numbers of printed data on reports. As we develop more on-line systems and languages to allow users to ask questions about the data in their files, we may be able to reduce some of the printing. Also, some of the approaches to designing new applications, like tying two organizations together via computer, should reduce the amount of paper. For inquiry purposes, the CRT is again the standard.

We have now completed a survey of the hardware; these are the components that we can physically see and feel. In the next few chapters, we shall see how all of this works by discussing software and how data are organized for secondary storage.

KEY WORDS

Alphanumeric	Cursor
Backup	Daisy wheel
Bank autoteller	Direct access
Bubble memory	Disk
CRT	Diskette

Floppy disk
Gap
Graphics
Hard copy
Hard disk
Impact
Ink-jet printer
Joystick
Keyed input
Laser
Line printer
Mass storage
Matrix printer
Menu
MICR
Microfilm
Mouse
Nonimpact
OCR

Optical storage
Page printer
Peripherals
Plotter
POS
Physical record
Primary storage
Random access
Records
Rotational delay
  time
Secondary storage
Seek time
Soft key
Streaming tape
Touch screen
Track
Voice

BUSINESS PROBLEMS

7-1. There is limited voice input for computer systems now. Some experts have argued that voice input will open up use of the computer to a large number of individuals, particularly those who are not comfortable with a keyboard.

On the other hand, a large number of new computer users have been created by the exploding sales of microcomputers. Many of these same individuals have studiously avoided computer terminals at work. The allure of the personal computer has attracted them to a keyboard without having voice input.

Where do you see voice input as being most likely to encourage new users of the technology? What kind of features will voice input have to provide to be successful?

Right now, we are limited to isolated, discrete words for voice input. Continuous speech recognition is an unsolved problem at the present. Will the widespread application of speech have to wait for continuous recognition? Why or why not?

7-2. Apple Computer has popularized the mouse as an input device. Two Apple models, the Lisa and the Macintosh, feature a mouse for input. The mouse moves a cursor around on the screen instead of using keys with arrows. The arrow keys move in discrete steps, whereas the motion of the mouse is continuous.

What are the advantages and disadvantages of this kind of input? Take a popular program like a word processor or a spreadsheet program and examine its commands. Where would the use of a mouse be most beneficial?

Try to find a demonstration of a MacIntosh or another computer with a word processor that uses a mouse. Can you compare the mouse with the alternative of keyboard input? Which do you prefer personally? How much extra would you be willing to spend for a mouse on a personal computer?

REVIEW QUESTIONS

1. Why is paper tape no longer used heavily for computer I/O?
2. What are the advantages and disadvantages of punched cards as an input/output form?
3. What is the difference between a keypunch and a key-to-disk device?
4. Describe batch processing. How does it differ from on-line processing?
5. List two advantages of on-line data entry over batch input.
6. What is a POS terminal? Give an example.
7. What is the Universal Product Code, and how is it used?
8. What are the major limitations on voice input for computers?
9. What are the major current applications using voice input?
10. How does a touch screen work? What are its advantages?
11. What is a graphics pad? A joystick? How are they similar?
12. Define MICR and describe how it is used.
13. What is OCR? What applications might make use of OCR?
14. What are the advantages of a mouse for input?
15. How are data recorded on a magnetic tape?
16. How does a streaming tape drive differ from conventional tape drives?
17. Why is error checking needed with a tape?
18. Why is tape described as a sequential medium?
19. How does a hard disk work?
20. What is the major difference between a tape and a disk?

21. For batch and on-line processing, describe the different types of storage most commonly employed.
22. What is the advantage of bubble memory?
23. What is the advantage of the matrix printer?
24. How does an ink-jet printer work?
25. What is the purpose of an interrecord gap?

THOUGHT QUESTIONS

26. Is there a role for tapes in an on-line system? If so, what?
27. How does a floppy disk (diskette) differ from a hard disk?
28. What is the reason one would want a removable as opposed to a fixed disk?
29. Define a storage hierarchy for computers.
30. Who might use a mass storage device?
31. What is the potential of optical storage? Where can it be used with today's technology?
32. Why do most batch systems produce large volumes of printed output?
33. Why would you want a letter-quality printer with a personal computer?

34. Who might make use of a laser page printer?
35. What are the applications for a graphics terminal?
36. Describe how a staff analyst might use a plotter on a personal computer.
37. Describe an application for voice input.
38. What are the advantages of microfilm? What is the biggest threat to this medium?
39. Why is input/output one of the biggest bottlenecks with computers?
40. Why do we need secondary storage?

RECOMMENDED READINGS

Bohl, M. *Information Processing with Basic* (4th ed.). Palo Alto, CA: SRA, 1984. A good discussion of the various kinds of computer input/output devices.

Minimicro Systems, published by Hayden Publishing, is a monthly magazine that has a number of articles about computer peripherals.

Sanders, D. *Computers Today.* New York: McGraw-Hill, 1983. The chapters on I/O and storage devices are very good.

Chapter 8

Software is the name given to the instructions that control the operation of the computer. Externally, we can see software in the form of listings of programs, but we cannot see a program inside the computer when it is running. This chapter is an overview of software and how it developed. We shall distinguish between the software used by a programmer and something called *systems software,* which controls the computer's resources.

Software is one of the most important topics of the day. When the industry began, hardware was key; it was the most expensive part of computing. Today, computers can be mass-produced very rapidly; circuits on chips are made through a photographic and printing process. The key is software, which makes the computer do useful work. Software is not produced as easily as hardware; writing a program is more like working in a craft shop than in a factory.

At the end of this chapter, you should be able to:

- Describe the history of software.
- Explain the motivation for assembly language.
- Discuss the difference between assembly and higher-level languages.
- Describe package programs and their advantages.
- Explain what a fourth-generation language is.
- List some of the common computer languages and tell for what purposes they are used.
- Describe the basic functions of an operating system.

SOFTWARE:
THE KEY TO PROCESSING

INTRODUCTION

In the preceding chapters, we have studied the components of a computer, and now we are ready to see how software makes it all happen. We begin with a very simple computer to explain the need for different kinds of programs. Then it is worthwhile to look at some more advanced languages. We shall observe a trend in which languages have grown to look more and more like English. Vendors are attempting to make the computer easier to use so that nonprofessional programmers can make the computer respond to their needs.

An important type of software is called the *operating system.* It is a type of systems software, software that controls the computer's resources. This program is superior to the kind of programs written by an *applications programmer* in a language like BASIC or COBOL. The operating system schedules these applications programs and assigns the resources of the computer to them.

Remember that software consists of instructions that tell the computer what to do; software is written by people, not machines. Software, as it is written today, is very labor-intensive. Many approaches are being taken to try to improve the productivity of the individuals who write programs, but creating a program still takes a lot of human effort.

MACHINE LANGUAGE

The first computers understood binary instructions and numbers. Programming in binary is not a particularly pleasant experience, as you would probably agree. Remember that we talked about grouping binary digits to use another number system for machine language like octal or hexadecimal. A good definition of machine language is that it can be directly executed by the circuits in the computer. You can see a machine language program by looking at a printout of the contents of the memory where the program is located.

Figure 8-1 shows the steps in the execution of an instruction by the CPU. In Step 1, the *CPU fetches* the instruction and brings it to an *instruction register (IR).* That is, the CPU sends signals that the contents of the location in memory where the instruction is located are to be moved into the CPU's instruction register. The IR is the place where the CPU decodes and interprets instructions. Decoding means that the CPU must figure out what the instruction says to do, such as add, subtract, or print. Interpreting means that the CPU does what the instruction says to do. If the instruction is "add," then the CPU must see that an addition takes place.

At the end of the fetch cycle, then, a copy of the instruction resides in the instruction register; the contents of the memory holding the instruction are unchanged. Step 2 is the *execute* cycle. Assume that the instruction points to data in memory. Execution causes the data to be moved, in this case to an arithmetic register. The actual arithmetic, remember, occurs in an arithmetic register. The instruction register has its job, which is decoding and seeing that the instruction is executed. The execution of the instruction causes the arithmetic register to take action for an arithmetic instruction.

Now the instruction fetch and execute cycles are over for this one instruction; the CPU will begin another cycle, fetching the next instruction in sequence in the program and executing it. What instruction is taken next? There is another register in the CPU called the *instruction location counter.* This register points to the address of the next instruction in memory to be executed; in most instances, it is the next instruction after the one just completed. In the case of a branch or jump in the program, the instruction location counter is changed to point to the new place in the program where execution is to begin.

A Simple Computer

To illustrate how a computer might work we shall invent an illustrative machine (see Figure 8-2). There are a few simple instructions in this computer. An instruction must have two components for our computer: First, it needs an instruction code to say what the instruction is, like "add," "subtract," or "multiply." We shall make the instruction code two digits, and the format of the instruction is a two-digit

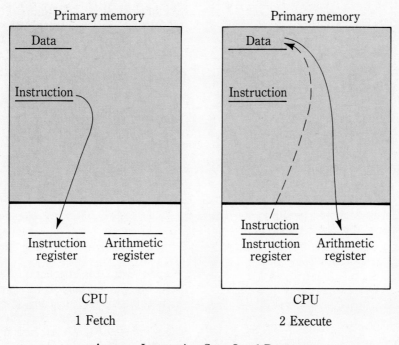

Primary memory | Primary memory

Data

Instruction

Instruction register   Arithmetic register

CPU

1 Fetch

Data

Instruction

Instruction
Instruction register   Arithmetic register

CPU

2 Execute

Assume Instruction Says Load Data
into Arithmetic Register

Figure 8-1. Instruction Execution. Assume instruction says load data in arithmetic register. The instruction is moved to the CPU during the fetch cycle. During the execute cycle, the CPU moves the data at the location referenced by the instruction into the arithmetic register.

instruction followed by an address. Remember that the address is the location in memory where some data of interest are located. An instruction for our computer of 014174 would mean input and put the data at memory address 4174.

Our machine has a very simple set of instructions. In fact, the first two input/output instructions really would not be in machine language (a lot of software is needed for input and output). However, as this is an imaginary computer, let's pretend that we do not have to be concerned with I/O.

Each instruction may have a reference to a memory address and/or a reference to an arithmetic register. The memory address reference usually means the location in memory where there are data on which the instruction wants to operate. If the reference to the arithmetic register is assumed, for example, then an "add" instruction means, "Take the data from the address location referenced in the instruction and add it to the contents of the arithmetic register." (This machine has one arithmetic register that performs all arithmetic calculations.)

A Program

We shall write a program to add two numbers together. First, the data will be placed in Location 9999, and the first statement in the program will be

			Instruction Code	Memory Location	Arithmetic Register
I/O	INP	Input	01	Y	
	DIS	Display	02	Y	
Arithmetic	ADD	Add	03	Y	Y
	SUB	Subtract	04	Y	Y
Control	JMP	Jump	05	Y	
Logic	J +	Jump + (1)	06	Y	Y
	J −	Jump − (2)	07	Y	Y
Memory	LDA	Load	08	Y	Y
	STO	Store	09	Y	Y

(1) Jump if arithmetic register is positive.
(2) Jump if arithmetic register is negative.

Figure 8-2. (a) Instruction Set. This simple instruction set is representative of the types of instructions found in real computers. (b) Instructional Computer. Our simple instructional computer with 10,000 memory positions, one arithmetic register, and an instruction register.

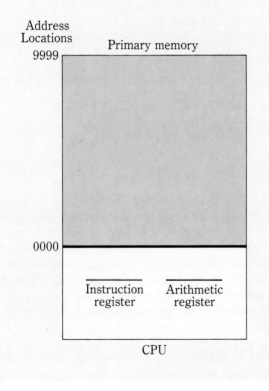

at Location 1. (See Figure 8-3 for the program.)

The first instruction at Location 1 is 019999; this instruction, when executed, will read data and place them in Location 9999. The second instruction is 019998; it also reads data and places them in Location 9998. The instruction at Location 3 in memory says to take the data in Location 9999 and move them to the arithmetic register; whatever was in that register before is now erased (written over).

The instruction 039998 says to add the contents of Location 9998 to the contents of the arithmetic register. The direct reference is to Memory Location 9998, the implied reference for an "add" instruction in this computer is always the arithmetic register. This means that the "add" instruction expects to find one addend in memory at the address in the instruction and the other addend already in the arithmetic register. How did the second addend get to the arithmetic register? An instruction before the

Location	Contents	Memory
1	019999	Input addend 1 to location 9999
2	019998	Input addend 2 to location 9998
3	089999	Load arithmetic register with contents of location 9999
4	039998	Add contents of location 9998 to contents of arithmetic register
5	099997	Put contents of arithmetic register in 9997
6	029997	Display contents of location 9997

Figure 8-3. A Simple Program.

Figure 8-4 (below). Execution of a Program. Execution begins at the lower left and proceeds to the top right where we end up with 641 in location 997.

9999		462	462	462	462	462	462
9998			179	179	179	179	179
9997						641	641
⋮							
6	029997						←
5	099997					←	
4	039998				←		
3	089999			←			
2	019998		←				
1	019999	←*					
Instruction register		019999	019998	089999	039998	099997	029997
Arithmetic register				462	641	641	641
Execute instruction at location		1	2	3	4	5	6

*Arrows point to instruction in program being executed at each step.

"add" instruction, like the "load" instruction, must have put it there.

The instruction at Location 5 says to take the contents of the arithmetic register (the answer) and store them in Location 9997, writing over whatever might have been in Location 9997. The last instruction says to display the contents of Location 9997, that is, to show us the answer.

Figure 8-4 shows the execution of the program.

Note that the various contents of memory do not change just because a number is moved to the CPU. The two numbers being added are 462 and 179; note that once they are in memory, they remain in their respective memory locations. At each step, the line opposite "IR" shows the instruction being executed, and just below it, the contents of the arithmetic register are visible. Study Figure 8-4 until you understand how the program works.

```
INP   X
INP   Y
LDA   X
ADD   Y
STO   Z
DIS   Z
```

Figure 8-5. Assembly Language Version. Note how mnemonic codes replace numbers for operation codes and symbols replace memory locations.

ASSEMBLY LANGUAGE

Programming in machine language is not much fun. The users of first generation computers actually invented a language that was easier to use and called it *assembly language.* The idea was to substitute simple codes or mnemonics for the numbers in machine language. Instead of using a number to mean "add," the programmer would like to be able simply to type *ADD*. It is a lot easier to remember *ADD* than some number that stands for addition in the machine's instruction set.

We would also like to substitute variables like X and Y for the actual storage locations, so that we do not have to try to remember where the data are stored. The programmer would like to be relieved of memory management to the greatest extent possible. By giving the programmer the ability to use names that mean something like *RATE* or *PAY,* we should make the programming job easier. Figure 8-5 shows the machine language program of Figure 8-3 written in assembly language. Does it look easier to understand assembly language?

How do we get from assembly language to machine language? After all, the computer understands only machine language. The programmers who invented assembly language had the answer: they would write a program in machine language that would translate assembly language into machine language. The program that does the translation is called the *assembler.* Its input is a program in *assembly language,* and its ouput is the *machine language* translation of that program; the computer can execute the output (see Figure 8-6).

As the figure shows, the programmer writes a program using assembly language. The results of the programmer's efforts become the input into the assembler, or translator. The translator processes the program and generates machine language, which carries out the commands of the programmer's assembly-language program. The assembler lets the programmer think at a higher and more convenient level than machine language, leading to greater productivity in programming.

Very few of us (fortunately) will ever program in machine or assembly language. These topics are included here to provide an idea of how the computer actually works. The principle of building languages that are easier for humans to understand and then translating them into machine language is an important one, and it started with assembly language. We shall see it used further to build even higher-order languages.

HIGHER-LEVEL LANGUAGES

FORTRAN

In 1957, a group of users developed the *FORTRAN* language. The language is oriented to computation, and the intended user group included scientists and engineers. These individuals certainly did not want to bother with assembly languages; a scientist wanted to think and compute at the level of:

$$X = Y + \text{SQRT}(A * B)/136.5$$

The translation of a language at this level is more complicated than going from assembly language to machine language. The developers of the language also put together the first *compiler,* a *translator,*

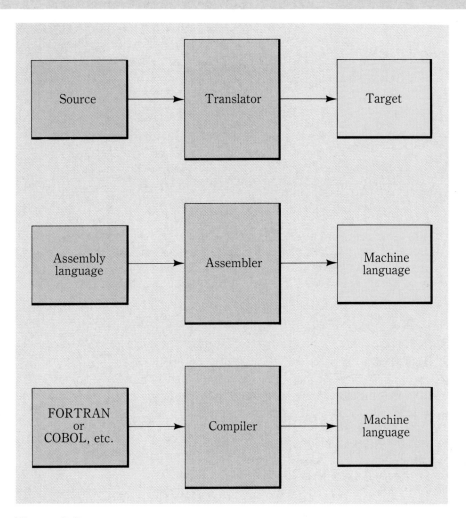

Figure 8-6. The Translation Process. Top: the general translation of a source to a target language; middle: translation for assembly language, and, bottom: a compiler for a high-level language.

that takes FORTRAN and prepares it to run on the computer. Because so little was known about translation at this time, the first compiler actually translated a FORTRAN program into assembly language; then the operator of the computer took the output of the compiler and ran it through the assembler to get machine language.

Today, the field of computer science has developed very efficient techniques for writing compilers. One does not go through several steps; instead, the compiler produces machine language directly from the input or source statements in the program.

FORTRAN marked another step in bringing the computer closer to the end user who was not a professional programmer. The scientist or engineer who wanted to learn how to program did not have to learn assembly language; instead, she or he had a language that was reasonably well-suited to the problem to be solved. (See Figure 8-7 for an example of a short FORTRAN program.)

```fortran
C This program determines the annual economic order quantity for a particular inventory item.

      REAL DEMAND, SUCOST, UTCOST, CRCOST, QNTITY
      INTEGER I

      WRITE (5,5)
5     FORMAT (' ')
      WRITE (5,10)
10    FORMAT (' AUTOSPORT ECONOMIC-ORDER QUANTITY SYSTEM')
      WRITE (5,5)

      WRITE (5,15)
15    FORMAT (' Enter the annual demand of the product in units')
      READ (5,20) DEMAND
20    FORMAT (F5.2)
      WRITE (5,5)

      WRITE (5,30)
30    FORMAT (' Enter the set-up costs for manufacturing the item')
      READ (5,20) SUCOST

      WRITE (5,5)
      WRITE (5,35)
35    FORMAT (' Enter the cost of manufacturing the item')
      READ (5,20) UTCOST
      WRITE (5,5)

      WRITE (5,40)
40    FORMAT (' Enter the annual carrying cost of the item, as a %')
      READ (5,20) CRCOST
      CRCOST = CRCOST/100
      WRITE (5,5)

      CALL EOQRTN (DEMAND, SUCOST, UTCOST, CRCOST, QNTITY)

50    DO 55 I = 1,3
55    WRITE (5,5)
      WRITE (5,60) QNTITY
60    FORMAT (' The annual economic order quantity is:', F8.2)
      STOP
      END

C     ****************************************************************************
      SUBROUTINE EOQRTN (DEMAND, SUCOST, UTCOST, CRCOST, QNTITY)

C     This procedure calculates the economic order quantity for an
C     inventory item, using the basic formula:
C
C
C                      Q + SQRT (2DS/UC)
C
C
C     where, Q = annual economic order quantity
C            D = annual demand of item in units
C            S = cost of machine set-up
C            U = cost of manufacturing the item
C            C = annual cost of carrying the item

      QNTITY = SQRT ((2.0 * DEMAND * SUCOST) / (UTCOST * CRCOST))
      RETURN
      END
```

Figure 8-7. Example of FORTRAN Program—Economic Order Quantity Computation.

COBOL

The business answer to FORTRAN is *COBOL;* it was designed with the needs of business in mind by a committee sponsored by the U.S. Department of Defense. The committee, known as the CODASYL committee, represented computer vendors, government bureaus, business organizations, and universities. The first version of COBOL was published in 1960. COBOL is the most widely used commercial programming language today, though the trend is to move toward even higher-level languages.

Commercial programmers need to manipulate data rather than to perform complex calculations. The typical commercial program accepts input and edits it extensively. The editing is relatively simple compared with the computations required to solve a problem in physics. A commercial program is also likely to process data files, a task that requires a lot of input and output, but again little computational power. Figure 8-8 is an example of a COBOL pro-

gram. Notice that this language is quite wordy; one has to enter a lot of verbiage with COBOL.

A COBOL program is divided into four parts, the first of which is an identification division that identifies the program. Much of the information contained in a COBOL program is used to document it, that is, to describe what the program does. In a commercial environment, it is frequently the case that one programmer writes a program and several others maintain it over its lifetime. Maintenance involves fixing errors as they are found and making changes to enhance the system.

The second division of COBOL is the environment division; it identifies the hardware on which the program is to be run.

The third division describes the data; it is divided into file and working storage portions. This division presents in complete detail all input data, the storage locations needed during processing to hold the results of the computations, and the format to be used for all output.

```
IDENTIFICATION DIVISION.
Program-Id.    Commis.
Author.        K.S. Mann.
Date-Written.  8-3-1986.


* * * * * * * * * * * * * * * * * * * * * *
*                                         *
*  This program produces a report of the salesmen  *
*  monthly commission earnings listed by branch,    *
*  as well as branch and company total commission   *
*  earnings, for a given month.            *
*                                         *
* * * * * * * * * * * * * * * * * * * * * *


ENVIRONMENT DIVISION.
CONFIGURATION SECTION.
Source-Computer.  DECSYSTEM-20.
Object-Computer.  DECSYSTEM-20.
```

```
INPUT-OUTPUT SECTION.

File-Control.
        Select Salesman-File assign to DISK
             Recording Mode is ASCII.
        Select Commission-Report assign to PRINTER
             Recording Mode is ASCII.

DATA DIVISION.

FILE SECTION.

FD  Salesman-File
        Value of ID is "SALES DTA".
01  Salesman-Record.
        03 Salesman-Number.
             88 END-of-FILE value HIGH-VALUES.
           05 Branch -Code        PIC 99.
           05 Salesman-Id         PIC 999.
        03 Salesman-Name          PIC X(20).
        03 Monthly-Sales          PIC 9(5)v99.
        03 Commission-Rate        PIC 999v99.
        03 Year-to-Date-Sales     PIC 9(8)v99.
FD  Commission-Report
        Value of ID is "COMMS REP".
01  Comm-Report-Line              PIC X(80).
```

Figure 8-8. Example of COBOL Program—Report of Sales Representative Earning (continues on next page).

WORKING-STORAGE SECTION.

```
01   Report-Heading-1.
     05 Filler              PIC X(15) Value Spaces.
     05 Filler              PIC X(46) Value
          "AUTOSPORT SALESMEN MONTHLY
          COMMISSION REPORT: ".
     05 Report-Month        PIC 99.
     05 Filler              PIC X(3) Value "19".
     05 Report-Year         PIC 99.
     05 Filler              PIC X(12) Value Spaces.

01   Report-Heading-2.
     05 Filler              PIC X(12) Value
                      "    SALESMAN#".
     05 Filler              PIC X(34) Value "    NAME".
     05 Filler              PIC X(14) Value "SALES".
     05 Filler              PIC X(20) Value
                      "    COMMISSION".

01   Report-Total-Line.
     05 Filler              PIC X(36) Value Spaces.
     05 Filler              PIC X(25) Value
          "TOTAL COMMISSIONS EARNED ".
     05 Report-Total        PIC Z(7).99.
     05 Filler              PIC X(9) Value Spaces.

01   Report-Ending-Line
     05 Filler              PIC X(32) Value all "*".
     05 Filler              PIC X(15) Value
                      " END OF REPORT ".
     05 Filler              PIC X(33) Value all "*".

01   Branch-Total-Line.
     05 Filler              PIC X(36) Value Spaces.
     05 Filler              PIC X(7) Value "BRANCH ".
     05 Branch-Ind          PIC 99.
     05 Filler              PIC X(18) Value
                      " TOTAL COMMISSION ".
     05 Branch-Total        PIC Z(5).99.
     05 Filler              PIC X(9) Value Spaces.

01   Report-Detail-Line.
     05 Filler              PIC X(3) Value Spaces.
     05 Report-Number       PIC 9(5).
     05 Filler              PIC X(6) Value Spaces.
     05 Report-Name         PIC X(32).
     05 Report-Sales        PIC Z(5).99.
     05 Filler              PIC X(9) Value Spaces.
     05 Report-Commission   PIC Z(5).99.
     05 Filler              PIC X(9) Value Spaces.

01   Report-Blank-Line      PIC X(80) Value Spaces.

01   Accumulators.
     05 Branch-Total-Comm   PIC 9(5)v99.
     05 Report-Total-Comm   PIC 9(7)v99.
     05 Commission          PIC 9(5)v99.

01   Current-Date.
     05 Current-Year        PIC 99.
     05 Current-Month       PIC 99.
     05 Current-Day         PIC 99.

01   Current-Branch         PIC 99.
```

PROCEDURE DIVISION.

```
          Perform 10-Initialization.
          Perform 20-Produce-Comm-Report
                until End-of-File.
          Perform 30-Termination.
          Stop Run.

10-Initialization.
          Open Input Salesman-File
                Output Commission-Report.
          Perform 11-Print-Report-Headings.
          Move zeros to Report-Total-Comm.
          Perform 12-Read-Salesman.

11-Print-Report-Headings.
          Accept Current-Date from Date.
          Move Current-Year to Report-Year.
          Move Current-Month to Report-Month.
          Write Comm-Report-Line from Report-Heading-1.
          Write Comm-Report-Line from Report-Heading-2
                after advancing 2 lines.

12-Read-Salesman.
          Read Salesman-File, at end
                move High-Values to Salesman-Number.

20-Produce-Comm-Report.
          Move Branch-Code to Current-Branch.
          Move zeros to Branch-Total-Comm.
          Write Comm-Report-Line from Report-Blank-Line.
          Perform 21-Process-Branch
                until Branch-Code not = Current-Branch.
          Perform 22-Print-Branch-Total.
          Add Branch-Total-Comm to Report-Total-Comm.

21-Process-Branch.
          Move Salesman-Number to Report-Number.
          Move Salesman-Name to Report-Name.
          Move Monthly-Sales to Report-Sales.
          Compute Commission = Monthly-Sales *
                Commission-Rate / 100.
          Move Commission to Report-Commission.
          Add Commission to Branch-Total-Comm.
          Write Comm-Report-Line from Report-Detail-Line.
          Perform 12-Read-Salesman.

22-Print-Branch-Total.
          Move Current-Branch to Branch-Ind.
          Move Branch-Total-Comm to Branch-Total.
          Write Comm-Report-Line from Branch-Total-Line
                after advancing 2 lines.

30-Termination.
          Write Comm-Report-Line from Report-Blank-Line.
          Move Report-Total-Comm to Report-Total.
          Write Comm-Report-Line from Report-Total-Line
                after advancing 2 lines.
          Write Comm-Report-Line from Report-Ending-Line
                after advancing 2 lines.
          Close Salesman-File, Commission-Report.

40-Exit.
          Exit.
```

Figure 8-8 (continued).

Figure 8-9. The Structures of a COBOL Program.

IDENTIFICATION DIVISION
program identification date of creation
ENVIRONMENT DIVISION
hardware identification
DATA DIVISION
description of data used —external to program (from files in secondary storage) —internal to program (primary storage)
PROCEDURE DIVISION
action statements to be carried out by computer

Finally, the procedure division presents the statements that are executed by the computer. A paragraph in COBOL contains sentences that are related to each other; they each are required to perform some task. A selection contains a group of related paragraphs that constitute the program (see Figure 8-9).

COBOL was designed to be closer to English than existing programming languages. In 1960 it most certainly was, but in today's environment, programming all applications in COBOL has proved to be quite a bottleneck. We shall explore how to help reduce the backlog created by our inability to develop as many programs as users are able to demand.

BASIC

Professors Kemeny and Kurtz at Dartmouth developed BASIC for time-sharing as described in Chapter 3. Each user thinks that he or she has a private computer. In Chapter 18, we shall discuss BASIC in more detail. This language has been significantly

enhanced and expanded from original versions and is far more capable now. BASIC is the major language of time-sharing; minis and personal computers are also often programmed in BASIC (see Figure 8-10).

Pascal

Pascal is a superb language for teaching programming concepts. It was developed by computer scientists rather than engineers or business programmers. Because it is a relatively new language, Pascal reflects experience with the shortcomings of other languages. Figure 8-11 is an example of a Pascal program.

Pascal is available in a fairly standard form for a variety of computers. It is more transportable than some other languages; that is, it is easier to move a program from one computer to another without making major changes.

Figure 8-12 shows the development concept for one version of Pascal. Given a standard description of the language, one writes a compiler to translate

```
 10 REM      This program determines the economic order quantity of a
             particular inventory item.
 20 PRINT
 30 PRINT    "  AUTOSPORT ECONOMIC ORDER QUANTITY SYSTEM"
 40 PRINT
 50 INPUT    "Enter the annual demand for the item in units"; DEMAND
 60 PRINT
 70 INPUT    "Enter the set-up-costs for manufacturing the item"; SET.UP.COST
 80 PRINT
 90 INPUT    "Enter the cost of manufacturing the item"; UNIT.COST
100 PRINT
110 INPUT    "Enter the annual carrying cost of the item, as a %"; CARRYING.COST
120 CARRYING.COST = CARRYING.COST / 100
130 GOSUB 180   'subroutine to calculate the economic order quantity
140 PRINT
150 PRINT USING   "The annual economic order quantity is: ######.##"; QUANTITY
160 END
170 REM      * * * * * * * * * * * * * * * * * * * * * * * * * * * * * * * * * * * * * *
180 REM   This subroutine calculates the economic order quantity for an inventory
190 REM      item, using the basic formula:
200 REM                                        Q = SQRT  (2DS/UC)
210 REM
220 REM   where,
230 REM      Q = annual economic order quantity
240 REM      D = annual demand of the item in units
250 REM      S = cost of the machine set-up
260 REM      U = cost of manufacturing the item
270 REM      C = annual cost of carrying the item.
280 REM
290 QUANTITY = SQR ((2 * DEMAND * SET.UP.COST) / (UNIT.COST * CARRYING.COST))
300 RETURN
310 REM      * * * * * * * * * * * * * * * * * * * * * * * * * * * * * * * * * * * * * *
```

Figure 8-10. Example of BASIC Program—Economic Order Quantity Computation.

the language into an intermediate language called *P code,* instead of generating machine code.

To move Pascal to another computer, one writes an interpreter for the P code that will run on the new computer. In Figure 8-12, an interpreter for Computer Two might be written in Computer Two's assembly language. It interprets correct P code so that the compiler at the top of the figure can be used for other machines. We have one standard compiler, a difficult program to write, that is created only once for a variety of computers. The only thing we have to do to move Pascal to another computer is to write an interpreter for that computer to execute P code.

An *interpreter* looks at each statement in the P code and executes it directly (remember that a compiler usually generates actual code). The interpreter must execute several statements to interpret a line of the P code, so interpreted programs should be a little slower than those compiled. Here we are trading off program execution speed for portability and for having a language whose features are the same across a number of computers.

APL

APL is an unusual language as it follows mathematical notation more closely than any other programming language (see the sample APL program in Figure 8-13). APL was designed for time-sharing, and its goal was to make it easy for the programmer to reason at a very high level. Many operators and operations that would take a long list of instructions in another language may require only one statement in APL. APL has a structure that is similar to mathe-

```
      program ECONOMIC-ORDER-QUANTITY (input, output);
/*    This program determines the annual economic order quantity                      */
/*    for a particular inventory item.                                                */

var DEMAND,                            /*         annual demand for the item in units     */
    SET-UP-COST,                       /*         cost of machine set-up for the item      */
    UNIT-COST,                         /*         cost of manufacturing the item           */
    CARRYING-COST,                     /*         annual cost of carrying the item         */
    QUANTITY : real;                   /*         economic order qty to be determined      */
/  * * * * * * * * * * * * * * * * * * * * * * * * * * * * * * * * * * * * * * * * * * */
      procedure ECON-ORDER-QTY (var DEMAND, SET-UP-COST, UNIT-COST,
                                CARRYING-COST, QUANTITY : real);

/*    This procedure calculates the economic order quantity for                        */
/*    an item, using the basic formula :                                               */
/*                                                                                     */
/*                            Q = SQRT (2DS/UC)                                        */
/*                                                                                     */
/*                                                                                     */
/*    where: Q = annual economic order quantity                                        */
/*           D = annual demand of item in units                                        */
/*           S = cost of machine set-up                                                */
/*           U = cost of manufacturing the item                                        */
/*           C = annual cost of carrying the item (decimal)                            */

begin;                                            /* ECON-ORDER-QTY procedure          */
   QUANTITY := SQRT (( 2.0 * SET-UP-COST)
             / (UNIT-COST * CARRYING-COST))

END;                                              /* ECON-ORDER-QTY procedure          */
/ * * * * * * * * * * * * * * * * * * * * * * * * * * * * * * * * * * * * * * * * * * */
begin                                             /* Main body of program              */
   writeln;
   writeln ('                         AUTOSPORT ECONOMIC-ORDER-QUANTITY SYSTEM');
   writeln;

   writeln ('Enter the annual demand of the item in units');
   readln;
   read (DEMAND);
   writeln;

   writeln ('Enter the set-up costs for manufacturing the item');
   readln;
   read (SET-UP-COSTS);
   writeln;

   writeln ('Enter the cost of manufacturing the item');
   readln;
   read (UNIT-COST);
   writeln;

   writeln ('Enter the annual carrying cost of the item, as a %');
   readln;
   read (CARRYING-COST);
   CARRYING-COST := CARRYING-COST/100;
   writeln;

   ECON-ORDER-QTY (DEMAND, SET-UP-COST, UNIT-COST,
                   CARRYING-COST, QUANTITY);

   writeln;
   writeln ('The annual economic order quantity is : ', QUANTITY:1:2)
   end.                                 /* Program * /
```

Figure 8-11. Example of Pascal Program—Economic Order Quantity Computation.

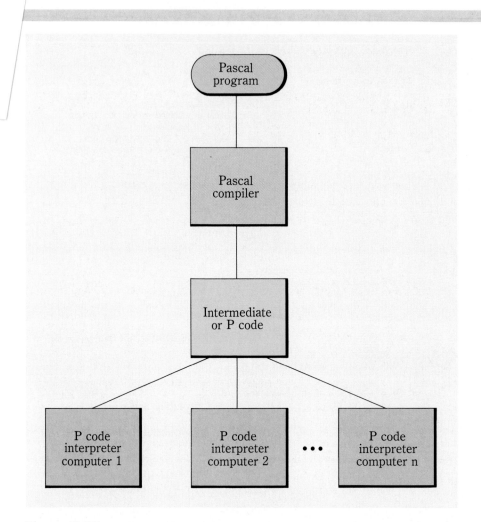

Figure 8-12. A Pascal Compiler translates a program into intermediate or P-code. To run on a different computer, one needs to write an interpreter program in the target computer's language that interprets intermediate P-code and executes it on the new computer.

matical notation, and it is quite popular for getting a program up and running quickly.

The extreme power and terseness of the language is also one of its major drawbacks. Because each statement does so much processing, it can be very hard to read and understand an APL program. If a programmer cannot read and comprehend code, it is very difficult to make changes in a program when they are needed.

PACKAGES

A *package* is a program written by a vendor for sale to someone else. In their infancy, packages were often crude and did not work well. Today, the package business is booming. Personal computer packages have set new standards for the quality of their user interfaces and the functions that they make available.

```
          ▽ PGM[□]▽
      ▽    PGM
[1]       A THIS PROGRAM ACCEPTS INPUTS FOR FINDING THE ECONOMIC
[2]       A ORDERING QUANTITY
[3]         ' '
[4]         'AUTOSPORT ECONOMIC ORDER QUANTITY SYSTEM'
[5]         ' '
[6]         'ENTER THE ANNUAL DEMAND FOR THE ITEM IN UNITS'
[7]         DEMAND←□
[8]         ' '
[9]         'ENTER THE SET UP COSTS FOR MANUFACTURING THE ITEM'
[10]        SETUPCOST←□
[11]        ' '
[12]        'ENTER THE COST OF MANUFACTURING THE ITEM'
[13]        UNITCOST←□
[14]        ' '
[15]        'ENTER THE ANNUAL CARRYING COST OF THE ITEM, AS A PCTG'
[16]        CARCOST←□
[17]        CARRYINGCOST ←(CARCOST ÷ 100)
[18]      A CALLS SUBROUTINE FOR CALCULATION OF EOC
[19]        CALC
[20]        ' '
[21]      A OUTPUTS RESULT
[22]        'THE ANNUAL ECONOMIC ORDER QUANTITY IS          ';QUANTITY
      ▽

          ▽ CALC[□]▽
      ▽    CALC
[1]       A THIS PROGRAM MODULE CALCULATES THE ECONOMIC ORDER QUANTITY
[2]       A FOR AN INVENTORY ITEM, USING THE BASIC FORMULA:
[3]       A
[4]       A                         Q = SQRT (2DS/UC)
[5]       A
[6]       A WHERE:
[7]       A        Q = ANNUAL ECONOMIC ORDER QUANTITY
[8]       A        D = ANNUAL DEMAND OF THE ITEM IN UNITS
[9]       A        S = COST OF THE MACHINE SET-UP
[10]      A        U = COST OF MANUFACTURING THE ITEM
[11]      A        C = ANNUAL COST OF CARRYING THE ITEM.
[12]      A
[13]        QUANTITY←(((2xDEMANDxSETUPCOST) ÷ (UNITCOSTxCARRYINGCOST))*0.5)
[14]      A
[15]      A TO ROUND QUANTITY TO TWO PLACES:
[16]      A
[17]        QUANTITY←((⌈((QUANTITYx100) − 0.5)) ÷ 100)
      ▽


          PGM
AUTOSPORT ECONOMIC ORDER QUANTITY SYSTEM
ENTER THE ANNUAL DEMAND FOR THE ITEM IN UNITS
    □:      4
ENTER THE SET UP COSTS FOR MANUFACTURING THE ITEM
    □:      4
```

Figure 8-13. Example of an APL Program—Economic Order Quantity Computation (continues on next page).

```
ENTER THE COST OF MANUFACTURING THE ITEM
□:        8

ENTER THE ANNUAL CARRYING COST OF THE ITEM, AS A PCTG
□:        25

THE ANNUAL ECONOMIC ORDER QUANTITY IS  4



        PGM

AUTOSPORT ECONOMIC ORDER QUANTITY SYSTEM

ENTER THE ANNUAL DEMAND FOR THE ITEM IN UNITS
□:        23500

ENTER THE SET UP COSTS FOR MANUFACTURING THE ITEM
□:        30000

ENTER THE COST OF MANUFACTURING THE ITEM
□:        200

ENTER THE ANNUAL CARRYING COST OF THE ITEM, AS A PCTG
□:        20

THE ANNUAL ECONOMIC ORDER QUANTITY IS  5937.17
```

Figure 8-13 (continued).

Dedicated Packages

The first kind of packages produced were generally *dedicated* to a particular application. For example, one might want to purchase an accounts receivable program. Accounts receivable is a common business application; almost all firms that offer a product or service must bill their customers.

A company sells a service or a product; when a customer buys that service, the customer creates a receivable for the firm. Having shipped its product, the company now wants to bill the customer, usually on some basis like the beginning of each month. Depending on the kind of business, the receivables operations vary considerably: think of the differences between Cray selling supercomputers and Apple selling microcomputers. Their respective accounts receivable applications will look considerably different from each other.

One vendor's package for accounts receivable handles the following tasks:

1. Creation and management of data files.
2. Daily entry of invoices and product returns.
3. Daily posting of cash receipts.
4. Daily listing of sales and the cash journal.
5. Aged accounts-receivable reports, customer statements, salesperson commissions, and so on at the end of each month.
6. Information reports for sales analysis and credit determination.

The buyer of the package sets up master files (data on secondary storage devices) about the firm; the system then creates transactions files as the data are entered. The particular package being discussed here operates on-line; all input is from CRT terminals.

Why would anyone buy such a package rather than program the application herself or himself? The answer is time and money. If one can use a package like this without having to make many modifications to the package or to one's own internal procedures, it can save both time and money. Developing an application can take a long time, at least a year for a system like this one. Depending on the cost of the package, it is likely to be cheaper to buy than to build. The package vendor hopes to have many sales so that it does not have to charge the full development price to each customer.

General-Purpose Packages

General-purpose packages are designed to assist in the solution of a problem; they are not a solution themselves. The user of the package works with it to create a solution. The best example of this type of package runs on personal computers. Electronic spreadsheet applications, which we have seen and which we shall study in detail in Chapter 15, are such packages. They are oriented toward the solution of the broad class of problems that can be placed in the context of a spreadsheet.

These general-purpose packages have done a great deal to extend the power of computers to end users. Individuals who would never have considered working with a computer are now avid users of spreadsheet programs, graphics packages, word processing, and personal file systems.

In Chapter 13, we shall explore packages in further detail as an alternative to building custom systems in a language like COBOL. Just as hardware has advanced, so has the design of packages. Twenty years ago, many packages were crude, and as a result, packages still have a bad reputation with a number of professional computer departments. However, times have changed and packages are now a very appealing option.

Fourth-Generation Languages

Fourth-generation languages have grown from early package developments. The purpose of fourth-generation languages is to make programming far easier and to extend the computer to the end user, too. Vendors claim that the use of one of these programs can expedite the process of systems analysis and design by making it possible to program something faster, to obtain feedback quickly on the re-

sults, and to change the design more easily than with conventional languages like COBOL.

A number of these languages are sold like other packages, including FOCUS, RAMIS, and NATURAL (see Figure 8-14 for a sample program in one of these languages). As you can tell from the illustration, fourth-generation languages are at an even higher level than FORTRAN or COBOL; that is, each statement in a fourth-generation language would require several statements to do the same processing in FORTRAN or COBOL. We expect to see more end users writing programs to access data and to produce reports using this type of language. There is no time wasted while waiting for a professional programmer to be assigned, to write and debug the program, and to produce results. (See chapter 17 for more information on a fourth-generation language.)

Firms are developing consulting offices to help users work with these languages. The consultants may locate the desired data in corporate files and quickly write a program to extract the data and put it on a file for the user. The user works with the fourth-generation language to produce the analysis desired; the professional computer staff provides consulting but does not do the work. In this way, the user obtains quick results at the cost of doing the work himself or herself.

OPERATING SYSTEMS

In the earlier discussion of the history of computers, we first mentioned the ***operating system.*** Remember that it is the control program that manages the resources of the computer such as memory, the CPU, and the peripherals; it provides facilities for the programmer and is always superior to the user's program. (Because of this superiority, the operating system is often called the *supervisor*.) Basically, an operating system handles resources:

1. It assigns the CPU to different tasks.
2. It manages primary memory.
3. It manages secondary storage.
4. It controls input and output.
5. It provides security and control.

```
0010   INPUT // 'Enter the date you wish to check for (YYYYMMDD): ' #IN-DATE
0020   WRITE TITLE "DAILY COMMISSION VS PROCEEDS REPORT' //
0030   READ TRADE-FILE LOGICAL BY ENTRY-DATE = #IN-DATE
0040        AT END OF DATA DO SKIP 1
0050                    WRITE 'TOTAL COMMISSIONS: ' SUM(COMMISSION)
0060                      / 'TOTAL PROCEEDS:   ' TOTAL-PROCEEDS
0070                    DOEND
0080        IF COMMISSION = O THEN DO
0090                    COMPUTE PROCEEDS = QUANTITY * PRICE - COMMISSION
0100                    ADD PROCEEDS TO TOTAL-PROCEEDS
0110                    DISPLAY COMMISSION QUANTITY PRICE PROCEEDS
0120                    DOEND
0130   END
```

DAILY COMMISSION VS PROCEEDS REPORT

COMMISSION	QUANTITY	PRICE	PROCEEDS
220.14	500.00	39.00	19279.86
354.00	5900.00	29.87	175908.50
348.00	5800.00	30.00	173652.00
675.00	4500.00	50.00	224325.00
500.00	10000.00	17.18	171370.00
192.00	600.00	37.75	22458.00
368.00	4600.00	18.00	82432.00
1000.00	10000.00	42.00	41900.00
260.00	2600.00	25.62	66365.00

TOTAL COMMISSIONS   3917.14
TOTAL PROCEEDS   977690.36

Figure 8-14. An Example of a Natural Program.

Some of the features of a popular microcomputer operating-system should help to illustrate what this piece of software does.

1. *The processor*
    Starts a program.
    Helps debug the program (gets the errors out).
    Manages the BASIC interpreter.
    Manages the BASIC compiler.
    Starts the user's program running.

2. *The Editor*
    Provides a text editor (a program that accepts and manipulates text) for entering programs and data.

3. *Diskette Operations*
    Formats a diskette (prepares it for data or programs).
    Compares two diskettes to see if they are the same.
    Copies a diskette onto another one.

4. *File Operations*
    Produces a directory listing of what files are on a diskette.
    Erases or destroys a file.
    Copies files among diskettes.

5. *Input/Output*
    Provides all software necessary for input and output.

The operating system for a personal computer is relatively simple; those for larger computers can take hundreds of thousands of bytes of memory. In a large computer, the system may have multiple programs and multiple processors to manage all the executing instructions at one time. Much of the

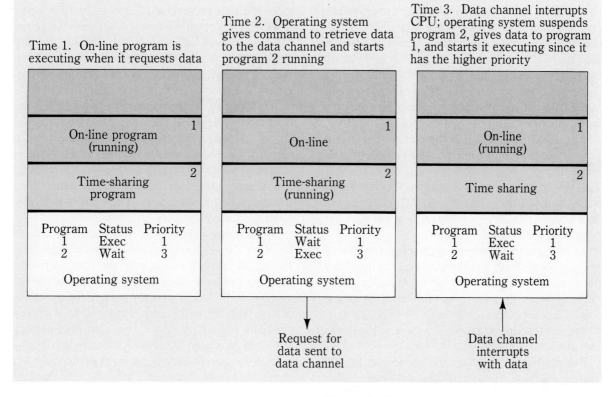

Time 1. On-line program is executing when it requests data

Program	Status	Priority
1	Exec	1
2	Wait	3

Operating system

Time 2. Operating system gives command to retrieve data to the data channel and starts program 2 running

Program	Status	Priority
1	Wait	1
2	Exec	3

Operating system

Request for data sent to data channel

Time 3. Data channel interrupts CPU; operating system suspends program 2, gives data to program 1, and starts it executing since it has the higher priority

Program	Status	Priority
1	Exec	1
2	Wait	3

Operating system

Data channel interrupts with data

Figure 8-15. The operating system manages the execution of several programs that are active in the computer at the same time.

power of a computer today comes from the features provided by the operating system.

Mainframe Operating Systems

The microcomputer operating system just described illustrates the principle of such a program. The first operating systems were not as complex as the one described, though they were for mainframes because there were no other computers at the time.

Soon, however, mainframe operating systems grew in complexity. Remember from our discussion of computer generations that the third generation marked the first time that the user had to work through an operating system.

What do we find in a mainframe operating system that is not present in the micro's system? First, the mainframe operating system manages a lot of things; we have described mainframes in which the system simultaneously runs batch jobs, time-sharing, and on-line applications. How can all of this happen at once?

The actions of the operating system make possible this apparently simultaneous set of activities. The operating system manages the computer's resources, which consist of processors (assume a single CPU for discussion purposes), primary and secondary memory (disks, tapes, and so on), and input/output devices.

For now, we shall concentrate on three of these resources: the CPU, the primary memory, and disk storage (see Figure 8-15). The operating system keeps a list of tasks that are waiting to be executed. One of these tasks might be the request of an on-line program for a piece of data on a disk file. The operating system commands the data channel to get that data record; then the operating system looks at its list of tasks and decides to answer a time-sharing request for computation. Priorities can be assigned to the different tasks, so that some jobs or users get better service.

When the data channel has the data for the on-line program, it interrupts the CPU. This interruption is serviced by the operating system, which notes that now the on-line program is ready to be processed again. If its priority is higher than the priority of the time-sharing job, the operating system will start the on-line program again.

All of this activity happens so fast that the user of the on-line program and the time-sharing user may not even be aware that the other person has been serviced while they were working on their terminals. The operating system has scheduled and controlled the resources to provide service to the different users.

The programmer invokes the services of the operating system through a language, sometimes called *JCL* for "job control language." Computer operators also monitor the execution of the operating system and respond to its requests. We usually think of the operating system as providing a number of programs, called *utilities,* for example, a program that sorts data into a different order. Operating systems also work with language compilers like COBOL and FORTRAN; the programmer calls for a program compilation, and the operating system sees that it happens.

Virtual Memory

One important feature of many modern computers is something called **virtual memory.** Virtual memory is usually created through a combination of hardware and software techniques. The motivation for virtual memory came from programmers, who always seem to need more memory for their programs.

In this approach, a user's program is broken up into various equal-sized pieces called *pages;* the com-piler accomplishes this task. The pages for each program are kept on secondary storage, usually a disk drive. The operating system is responsible for bringing the pages of the program needed into primary memory for execution (see Figure 8-16). Note that a number of different pages from different users' programs are all in memory at one time.

What happens when memory gets full? Then the operating system has to decide to remove some pages; it usually chooses the ones that have been in memory the longest without having been used. The operating system writes these pages back onto the disk if there have been any changes in them. Then the operating system brings in new pages that have been demanded by other programs.

If you study Figure 8-16, you should be able to see that a user's program can be much larger than the actual primary memory of the computer. The program can have many pages on disk storage because only the pages actually needed for execution at one time are in memory. Rarely is all of a large program needed at once, so virtually memory systems generally work well. The term, by the way, refers to the fact that a programmer now has virtually infinite memory available for writing programs.

STRATEGY

We have discussed a lot about software in this chapter, and all of the material is important because it is software that makes the computer do work. How should you proceed when selecting software? What language should you learn? What packages should you buy?

Today, the first step is generally to look for a package. However, whether a dedicated or a general-purpose package, we must define what we need. (For a dedicated package, one should do a high-level systems design; see Chapters 12 and 13.) Even for a spreadsheet package, the potential buyer should decide how it will be used and what features are important.

Next, look for a package. Where? Try magazines for personal computers, as they often have product

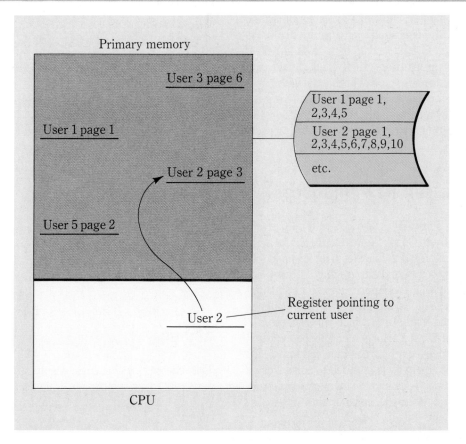

Figure 8-16. Virtual Storage. In a virtual memory system, the user's program is broken into a series of pages by the compiler. The operating system manages these pages so that only the ones needed are in memory. The sum of the space required for all pages can exceed physical memory size by many times.

comparisons or surveys of packages for a particular task, like producing graphics. Go to a retail computer store and look at the manuals for the software they sell.

For a dedicated package, look at trade journals for the industry. One manufacturer of clothing found a garment package in a trade journal for the garment industry, not a computer magazine. For information on a dedicated package, you can also call computer vendors to ask if they know of a package that runs on their equipment. There are various loose-leaf services to which one can subscribe to obtain listings of the available software.

If there is no package available, then consider a custom system, either one that you program yourself or one that is programmed by professionals in the field.

What language should you adopt? This is a very difficult question. The best language is one supported by your organization; for example, do not be the only Pascal user in a company that promotes BASIC.

If you are a nonprofessional, someone not writing computer applications for a living, you should probably choose from among BASIC, Pascal, and APL, at least for microcomputers and time-sharing. For a mainframe computer, hopefully your organization will have a fourth-generation language or a high-level query language for extracting data from its files.

Packages have matured greatly and should continue to help users to solve problems with computers. When a package is not available or does not seem to fit the requirements, then the options involve the different ways of developing the applications oneself.

SOFTWARE FOR NEW PRODUCTS

The world of software is broad and multifaceted. Dun & Bradstreet Corporation (D&B) has been in the financial information business for almost 140 years. Today, computer hardware and software are the key to providing this information to its customers. How successful is the firm? It is the leader in almost all of the markets in which it competes.

The company has a management philosophy that stresses interdepartmental communications. D&B recognizes that creativity is required to conceive and develop its products. A number of successful products have come from the collaboration of two or more departments that pool their resources.

The product roster has increased by 150 new offerings in the past few years. D&B answers some 30 percent of its credit inquiries electronically, up from zero in 1977. Two departments worked together to create Keypoint, a service that provides on-line information on some 500,000 Canadian businesses. D&B has also created new products by reformulating existing data bases. Dun's Financial Profiles provides detailed balance-sheet and income data on 800,000 companies. This service cost $200,000 to develop; it brought in $2 million in revenue in its first full year of operation and is expected to reach $5.5 million in Year 2.

Software and hardware combine to create new products and new markets for companies. Managers at a company like D&B have to understand the technology because it is a part of what they do. In the future, most other companies will also find a lot of their success depending on information processing, and that means software.

Review of Chapter 8

REVIEW

This chapter has discussed software, the instructions that make the computer do useful work for us. We began by looking at machine language, the first language available for programmers. Soon it was realized that only a few professional programmers would ever learn to program in machine language. Assembly language extended the power of the computer to more individuals; less skill was required then for straight machine-language programming.

This trend has continued; higher-level languages like COBOL, FORTRAN, and BASIC have all made it possible for more individuals to program computers. Now we see software at higher-level, so-called fourth-generation languages. Where will it all stop? Hopefully, we will get to the point where programming a computer will take no more skill than driving an automobile. We are not there yet, and much more work is needed to achieve this goal.

We also discussed operating systems as an example of a class of programs known as *systems software*. The operating system controls the computer; it allocates the resources of the computer and provides many important services for the user. All computer systems used today to process information have operating systems, from the simplest micro to the largest mainframe.

Software is truly the key to unlocking the potential of the computer; the hardware cannot do work alone. The tremendous advances in hardware technology have made it possible to use higher and higher level languages. These languages take more computing power to translate and to execute, but we know that the cost of computing power is dropping while performance is increasing. Thus, we should look for even more software that makes it easier for users to work with computers.

KEY WORDS

Address	Fetch
APL	FORTRAN
Assembler	Fourth-generation
Assembly language	language
BASIC	Instruction location
COBOL	counter
Compiler	Instruction register
CPU	(IR)
Dedicated	Instruction set
Execute	Interpreter

Higher-level	Pascal
language	P code
Machine language	Translator
Operating system	Virtual memory
Package	

BUSINESS PROBLEMS

8-1. The senior vice-president of a large company in New York has issued a decree that managers shall not write programs on personal computers. His feeling is that executives who are highly paid should employ a less expensive computer staff member when programs are to be written. He is afraid that personal computers will turn executives into "hackers," people who spend all of their time trying to make a computer do some particular task.

The manager charged with trying to enforce this policy has real problems. Consider an electronic spreadsheet package. Is the user programming when he or she enters data? How about when the rules are input to manipulate the data?

Can you come up with a policy that clearly states what is programming and what is just use of a package when dealing with microcomputers? How about with mainframes? Is the distinction any more clear here? Is the use of a fourth-generation language programming in your opinion?

8.2. With the huge number of software products being announced each month for microcomputers, users are faced with a significant problem in deciding what packages to acquire. As each package used in the organization is likely to require some support from a consulting group, the decision is not to be taken lightly.

There are a number of ways to find out about packages, but none of them is guaranteed to be exhaustive. One can visit a computer store and talk with the sales representatives, though often these individuals do not use the products they sell. Another source is the directories that vendors publish of available software. The drawback with this method is that the descriptions can be very terse. Finally, one can look through the trade magazines for the industry and watch for product comparison tests.

Given these alternatives, what would you say to a superior who came to you looking for advice on the best spreadsheet package to buy for your department? Would your answer be any different if the request was for word-processing packages?

REVIEW QUESTIONS

1. What is machine language?
2. Why was assembly language developed?
3. What happens during the fetch cycle of the CPU?
4. What happens during the execute cycle of the CPU?
5. What is an address in memory?
6. How does an instruction reference different parts of the computer?
7. What is a compiler?
8. Describe a software package.
9. What is the difference between a dedicated package and one that is general-purpose?
10. What is a fourth-generation language?
11. What is an operating system?
12. What functions does an operating system perform?

THOUGHT QUESTIONS

13. Explain why assembly language is easier to use them machine language.
14. What is the major difference between FORTRAN and COBOL?

15. How does Pascal differ from the other languages discussed in the chapter?
16. For what kind of problems is FORTRAN intended?
17. For whom was BASIC intended?
18. For what kinds of tasks would you choose APL?
19. How can an organization support users who want to work with a fourth-generation language?
20. What problems do you see potentially with a virtual computer operating system?
21. What are the differences between a personal-computer operating system and one for a mainframe?
22. Why do we recommend looking for a package before trying to develop a custom program?
23. Where does one locate packages?
24. Having found a package, how would you evaluate it?
25. Why is it important to develop some preliminary specifications of what you want before looking for a package?
26. Why are packages more popular now than they were twenty years ago?
27. Why might one computer have more instructions in its instruction set than another?

28. How do fourth-generation languages actually run? Are they compiled or interpreted or both?
29. What kinds of problems are amenable to solution by means of an electronic spreadsheet package?
30. What industries do you think are the most natural users of a set of dedicated applications packages?
31. Why do you think computer vendors have developed a great interest in packages?

RECOMMENDED READINGS

Byte, published by McGraw-Hill. You will find a number of packages advertised in this magazine, plus product comparisons.

Computer Decisions. This journal contains a regular column discussing the software available for a different task each month.

Datamation. Another trade journal, but one that is aimed more at mainframes and minis than just at micros.

Martin, James. *Applications Development Without Programmers.* Englewood Cliffs, NJ: Prentice-Hall, 1982. A book that describes fourth-generation languages and the rationale for using them.

Chapter 9

Primary memory in the computer holds programs and data. Although computers, especially mainframes, may have 4 million, 8 million, 16 million, or more characters of this main memory, it is not enough to hold all of the data that a large company might need to access. Not only is primary memory too small for all of these data, often billions of characters, but it would not be a good idea to keep these data in primary storage. Why? Because they are not needed all of the time.

An insurance company might need access to data on all of its policyholders; it is important for the data to be available when a policyholder calls. However, on any day, only a very small percentage of the total number of customers actually calls. It would be wasteful to try to keep all policyholder data in primary memory at all times; most of them will not be used on a given day. Secondary storage makes it possible to process large numbers of data on a computer at a reasonable cost.

In this chapter, we shall discuss two major types of secondary-storage data organization: sequential and direct. Given these two kinds of organization, we shall see how to develop elaborate data structures.

After reading this chapter, you should be able to:

- Describe the difference between primary and secondary storage.
- Explain how data are stored in logical records.
- Distinguish between a physical and a logical record.
- Describe sequential file processing.
- Discuss the difference between sequential and direct-access processing.
- Describe how and when to use each type of processing.
- Explain how to create different data structures.

DATA STORAGE AND RETRIEVAL

INTRODUCTION

Secondary storage is one of the components that makes a computer so useful. Without storage, we would have to input data each time we needed them for computations. Large secondary storage units provide a user with access to massive numbers of data. For example, Merrill Lynch has over 1 million cash management accounts. Each CMA has a status and history of recent transactions; the status shows what stocks and bonds are held in the account. Transactions can include stock purchases and sales, checks written on the account, and the use of a credit card. Imagine how many data, then, exist and and must be processed for this type of account.

We use secondary storage for a number of reasons. First, there is not enough room in primary memory for all of the data that we might want to store even if it were desirable to keep them there. Second, primary memory is the most costly form of storage; it is much less expensive to keep data on secondary storage. Also, we may want to remove data from active storage and keep them off-line in a room away from the computer as a backup file in case some disaster strikes the computer center.

What is the price we pay for this convenience and this large-capacity storage? Basically, it is speed; it is more time-consuming to access data on secondary storage than data in primary memory. In fact, the access time for primary versus secondary storage is a classic example of the computer trade-off of cost versus speed.

Remember that primary memory operates in nanoseconds (billionths of a second). The CPU can directly access data that are stored in primary memory; it cannot do the same for data on secondary storage. Data on tapes or disks must first be moved to primary memory; then the CPU can access them. In a sense, we have double work. As a result, it takes longer to reach these data, and the price we have paid is access time.

OPERATIONS

A Manual Example

Assume that you have just been hired to prepare the payroll for Multicorp's headquarters. As the headquarters operation is relatively small, it has not been computerized. Instead, a file cabinet contains all of the information needed to calculate the payroll.

In the cabinet, there is a file folder for each employee. Written on the inside of the folder is the name of the employee, his or her social security number, the monthly pay, and information about withholding taxes and insurance deductions. Also listed is the number of dependents. The outside tab of the folder contains the employee's name, written with the last name first. Finally, inside the folder, filed with the most recent stub on top is a copy of the paycheck showing pay and deductions (see Figure 9-1).

To compute the payroll, you must take the time sheet filled out by each employee and match it with the file folder that constitutes her or his permanent record. As the file folders are in alphabetical order by last name, you sort the weekly time sheets into alphabetical order and go through both the time sheets and the file folders one at a time. There is a form for you to use to record the information to be typed on the check by the payroll secretary.

To figure the payroll, look first to see if the employee is paid on an hourly basis or is salaried. This information is noted on the file folder by a colored tab, green for hourly and blue for salaried. If the employee is salaried, you write on the check form the weekly pay and then compute the deductions. The file folder tells you what to deduct for company plans like health insurance. A table provided by the Internal Revenue Service shows the amount to be withheld from each check for taxes, based on the employee's weekly pay.

You follow the same procedure for an hourly em-

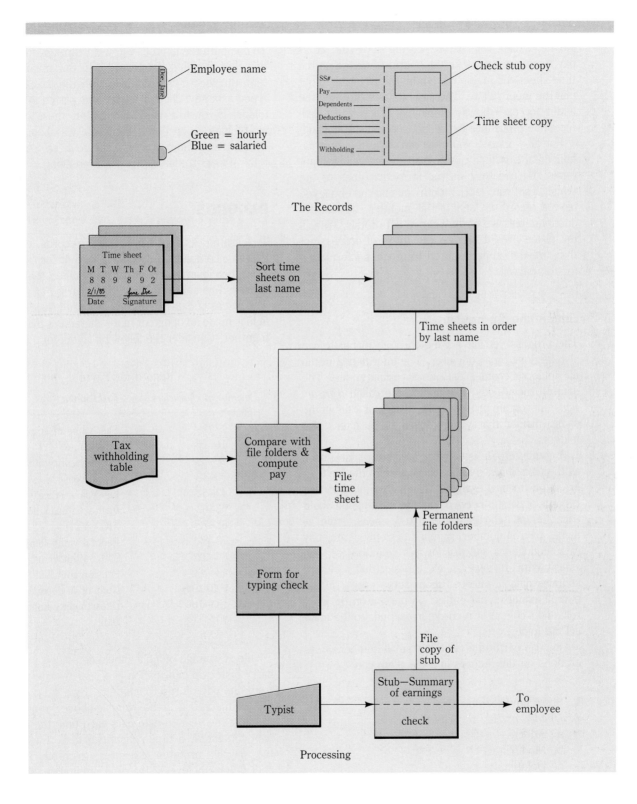

Employee name

Green = hourly
Blue = salaried

SS#
Pay
Dependents
Deductions

Withholding

Check stub copy

Time sheet copy

The Records

Time sheet

M T W Th F Ot
8   8   9   8   9   2
2/1/85   Jane Doe
Date   Signature

Sort time
sheets on
last name

Time sheets in order
by last name

Tax
withholding
table

Compare with
file folders &
compute
pay

File
time
sheet

Permanent
file folders

Form for
typing check

File
copy of
stub

Typist

Stub—Summary
of earnings

check

To
employee

Processing

ployee, except that before writing down the gross pay, you first must take the hours submitted on the time sheet and multiply them by the pay rate to obtain the month's pay. The pay rate is written on the folder for each hourly employee. Then you follow the same procedure for deductions and withholding.

For all workers, you must also take the information on the last pay stub that shows year-to-date totals and update it on the form that goes to the typist. That way, each month you and the employee have a record not only of this month's pay and deductions, but also of the year-to-date totals. We call the procedures described the *logic* of processing; they are the steps required to process information for the payroll.

Enter the Computer

The process you have gone through manually can also be done by a computer. The information in the file folders becomes data on a computer file. The data on the weekly time sheets are called *transactions;* a program processes them against a file in the same manner that you matched them against file folders.

A computer *file* is some related set of data, such as the payroll file, which is analogous to the file folders in our manual example. The payroll file contains records of data; a *record* contains information about each person who is to receive a check, such as name, payroll number, number of dependents, pay rate, deductions and pay for this year to date, and similar data. In general, we can say that a record contains data of interest about some entity; in the payroll example, the entity is a person on the payroll, and a computer record corresponds to the manual file folder.

One can perform a relatively small number of operations on the records in a file. One can

1. Store new records.
2. *Update* existing records through
   a. Adding.
   b. Modifying.
   c. Deleting.
3. *Retrieve* records.

To compute the payroll, you went through an operation that modified the records. In this manual system, the record was modified after the checks were typed as a new check register was placed in the file folder. If you had used a computer, these changes would have been done as the file was being processed. By computer, it is easy to keep a running total of year-to-date pay as you go along.

RECORDS

To learn more about the details of records, we shall look at a computerized version of Multicorp's rather small headquarters payroll. Remember that a file consists of a set of records. But what is in a record? The pieces of data in a record are called *fields.* Each field is made up of one or more characters that group together. Consider the following layout for a record:

Record for Payroll

Position in characters	Field name
1–15	Last name of employee
16–25	First name
26–34	Social security number
35–42	Weekly pay
43–52	Pay year-to-date (YTD)
53–62	Insurance deduction YTD
63–72	FICA YTD
73–82	Federal withholding YTD
83–92	State withholding YTD
93–102	Pension contribution YTD
103–104	Number of dependents
105–106	Department number
107–112	Date

One advantage of a file should be evident; we can carry historical information like year-to-date figures from one payroll run to another. If we did not have files, someone, as in the example above, would have to enter the year-to-date data each time the payroll was computed, a time-consuming task. Each time the payroll program executes to produce new checks for employees, the program updates the historical figures to reflect the addition of the current period's amounts. For example, if an employee is paid $2,000 per month the year-to-date figure will begin with 0 on January 1. When the January payroll is run, the figure will be $2,000. The February payroll will increase this figure to $4,000 and so on until the end of the year, when year-to-date pay should be $24,000. The year-to-date figures must be reset to zero at the beginning of the next year.

The record above is of **fixed length** and fixed position; even if there are blanks (say if a name does not take fifteen characters), we would still have a field that is fifteen characters long. We do waste some space, but the amount wasted is minimal. Fixed records like this are the easiest to use; there are fewer chances of errors.

However, in some processing situations, it is desirable to have different record structures. We shall not try to deal with these more advanced structures except to mention that it is possible to have **variable-length** records. These records can have different lengths to reflect a complex problem. Consider, for example, a medical clinic. One does not know in advance what tests the doctor will order; some tests produce a lot of data for the patient's record, whereas others result in only one or two numbers. In this situation, the designers would probably elect variable-length records to accommodate the differing lengths of test results.

UPDATE

Remember that the early discussion on different types of storage media pointed out that a computer can have **sequential** or **direct-access** files. The structure of these two types of files is quite different, leading to different strategies for processing them.

Sequential Files

It is easiest to visualize a sequential file on tape. The tape is continuous: one record follows another in order (see Figure 9-2). In the case of the payroll, the records are in order by social security number. Although in theory one could find a particular record by searching the file, it would be very inefficient to do

so. Why? Some records are at the end, some at the beginning, and some in the middle. For random searches, we would have to move the tape forward and backward continually. For this reason, we process the entire file at one time, reading each record and making modifications.

In a sequential update of a payroll, the computer reads an entire **master file** (the permanent collection of records about payroll), makes changes as indicated by incoming transactions, and writes a new file. A master file is saved from run to run, and the old versions become the backup for the most recently updated master file (see Figure 9-3). The logic of this update depends on the records' being in sequence on some field called the *key field* or the **key,** for short. For the Multicorp payroll, the social security number is the key.

Figure 9-3 shows the old master file (the one being updated) in sequence by social security number. The computer **sorts** new **transactions** into the same sequence. This means that a new transaction must be identified by the employee's social security number. What is a transaction? For the payroll file, it would be the data on the employee's time sheet. However, there are other transactions as well, for example, the addition of a new employee who has just been hired, the deletion of an employee after the end of the year in which the employee left, or a change in the number of dependents. These latter transactions are called **maintenance** and correspond to setting up a new file folder in the manual system or making changes in the "permanent" information kept in an employee's folder.

The process described requires that the incoming transactions be placed in the same order as the master file, that is, in order by the employee's social security number. To accomplish this ordering, the computer executes a **sort program.** The sort program takes the input transactions in whatever order they occurred during the month and puts them in sequence by social security number. Generally, the sort program is purchased from the computer vendor or an independent software firm.

Data are sorted in the same way that you might sort a set of index cards that had social security numbers on them. You would sort from right to left; that is, you would sort first on the units position by

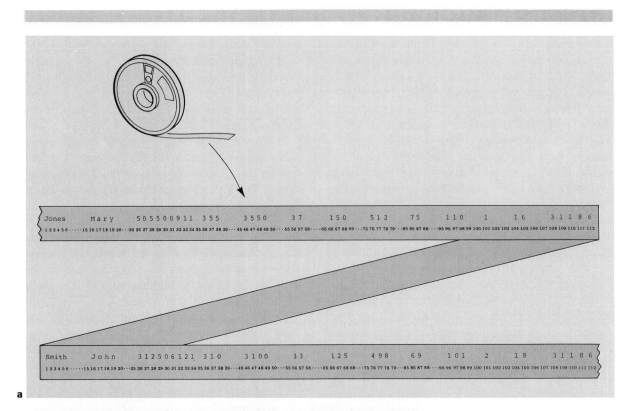

Jones   Mary   5 0 5 5 0 0 9 1 1   3 5 5   3 5 5 0   3 7   1 5 0   5 1 2   7 5   1 1 0   1   1 6   3 1 1 8 6
1 2 3 4 5 6 · · · · · 15 16 17 18 19 20 · · · 25 26 27 28 29 30 31 32 33 34 35 36 37 38 39 · · · · 45 46 47 48 49 50 · · 55 56 57 58 · · · 65 66 67 68 69 · · · 75 76 77 78 79 · · 85 86 87 88 · · · · 95 96 97 98 99 100 101 102 103 104 105 106 107 108 109 110 111 112

Smith   John   3 1 2 5 0 6 1 2 1   3 1 0   3 1 0 0   3 3   1 2 5   4 9 8   6 9   1 0 1   2   1 8   3 1 1 8 6
1 2 3 4 5 6 · · · · · 15 16 17 18 19 20 · · · 25 26 27 28 29 30 31 32 33 34 35 36 37 38 39 · · · · 45 46 47 48 49 50 · · 55 56 57 58 · · · 65 66 67 68 69 · · · 75 76 77 78 79 · · 85 86 87 88 · · · 95 96 97 98 99 100 101 102 103 104 105 106 107 108 109 110 111 112

a

b

Figure 9-2. (a) These two records are right next to each other on the tape. (The character position numbers on the first record are not actually on the tape.) Note that the fields are fixed length and that blanks are used to fill unused spaces. (b) An IBM Mass Storage Device which uses tape strips in carriers stored in these "honeycomb" cells.

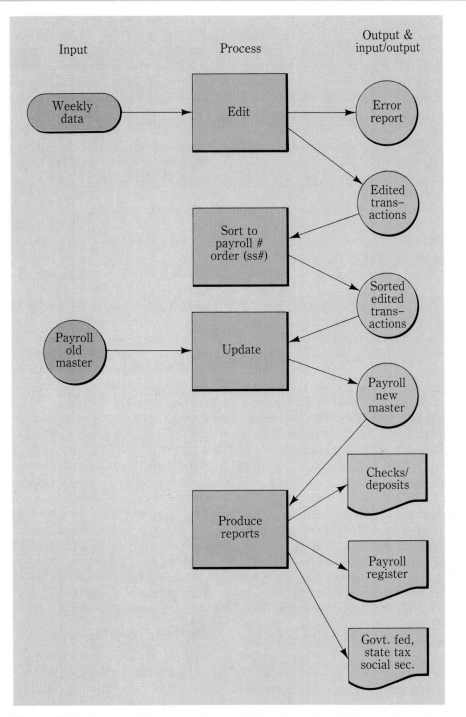

Figure 9-3. System Flowchart of Payroll Processing at Multicorp. Note the similarity between this flowchart and other examples of batch processing.

throwing the cards into piles 0 through 9. Then, you would pick up the cards in each pile and do the same thing again for the 10's digit. By the time you finished with the left-most digit, the cards would be in order by social security number.

Do you now see the logic of the sequential file update? The program reads a transaction and the first record from the old master file. It then compares the keys to determine what action to take. These are the possibilities:

Transaction key		Old file key	Action
5	>	3	Read old file
5	=	5	Change old file
8	<	10	Create new record

If the transaction file key is less than the key of a record from the old master file, the program has not reached the place in the old master file to which the transaction applies; therefore, the program keeps reading the old file. Consider the following simplified example. The computer is reading the transactions file and reads a record with a key of 5. The next record on the old master file is record 3. As the key of 5 is *greater* than the key of 3, the program has not reached the appropriate place on the old master file yet; it must read on.

In the second case in the table, if the transaction key *equals* the old master file key, the transaction must be some kind of a change in the old master file record; the program makes the change and continues. For example, the program reaches a record with a key of 5 in the old master file. As there is a transactions file record with this key, we must want to apply some transaction to record 5 in the old master file.

The final possibility is that the transaction key is *less* than the old master file key, and that the transaction is therefore a new record. Why? Assume that, in the table, we have made the changes in record 5 and have written this record into the new master file. Having read and processed the record from the transactions file and the master file, we now read new records from each. The transactions file gives

us a record with a key of 8. The old master file's next record has a key of 10. How do we deal with a transactions record with a key that comes before the next key in the old master file record? It has to be a new record. We have processed a transactions record with a key of 5 and an old master file record with a key of 5. The very next record on the old master file has a key of 10. There is no old master file record with a key of 8. Therefore, a transactions record with a key of 8 must be either a new addition to the file or an error.

Old master file:	3	5	10 . . .
Transactions file:		5 8	10 . . .
New master file:	3	5 8	10 . . .

We can see from the new master file that the transaction with a key of 8 has been added to the file; it was not present in the old master file and has been added as a transaction.

We use a code to identify the type of each transaction, like a "1" for a new person added to the file or a "9" to delete a record. If the code that identifies the transaction with the key of 8 is not a 1, then the program should print an error notification. It is likely to be an input error, but it could also represent an attempt by someone to make an unauthorized change in the system.

Why write the master file over again during a sequential file update? The program cannot anticipate what records might be added. For example, there could be many records between the numbers 45567 and 62231; it would be too difficult (and it would waste a lot of space) to try to decide how much room to leave. Also, it has been considered dangerous to try to move a tape around so that one can read and write different records on the tape.

Physical Records

There is one slight complication to the updating of sequential files, one that might best be ignored except for the fact that the complication may prove confusing if you ever try to access some data stored on a tape file.

In the discussion of tape drives, we noted that

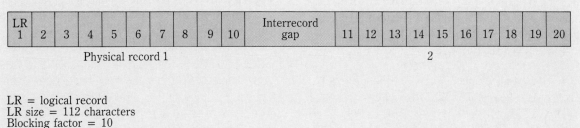

LR = logical record
LR size = 112 characters
Blocking factor = 10
Physical record size = 1120 characters

Figure 9-4. In blocking, a number of logical records are put into a physical record (in this case 10) to speed input and output and to save space. The tape drive reads and writes one physical block at a time.

these devices do a lot of starting and stopping; they transfer a block of data and then wait for the next command. The reason should be clear by now: The computer in a sequential file update reads a record from the old master file and one from the transactions file and then processes them for a while. The program is not really able to process all of the data at once; the approach is one record at a time.

The reading and writing of a tape take a long time when compared with the speed of the central processing unit. As a result, programmers try to make the physical block of data transferred with each read from a tape as long as possible. How can they do this trick? After all, the length of the record is set by the application.

The answer to this problem is to take a group of *logical records* and combine them into a *physical record* (see Figure 9-4). This act, called *blocking* the tape (making a physical block out of a set of logical records), saves time and space. The logical record in the Multicorp payroll is 112 characters long and would take a little over one sixteenth of an inch if the computer had 1,600-character-per-inch tape drives. The interrecord gap that separates physical records might be one-half inch long; the gap alone could hold nearly four logical records.

The space issue is important, but not as important

as speed. The computer has to read only one block to transfer all of the logical records in it to primary memory. If there are ten logical records in a block, the number of reads is cut down by a factor of ten.

This sounds like a lot of work for the programmer, but fortunately, blocking is a service provided by the operating system. The programmer notifies the operating system of the desired blocking factor and it takes over. The operating system reads the physical block and puts it in a *buffer* in memory (a buffer is a temporary storage location for data). When the program reads a logical record, the operating system determines which logical record is next and supplies it to the program. When the physical block is exhausted, the operating system gets another. (See Figure 9-4.)

Why this long-winded explanation? If you use a fourth-generation language to access sequential files someday, you will find that those files are probably blocked. You must tell the language or the operating system the length of the logical record and either the blocking factor or the length of the physical record (which is the blocking factor times the length of the logical record). If the file in the example were blocked, then you would have to specify that the logical record size is 112 and the physical size is 1,120.

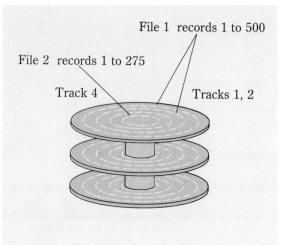

File 2 records 1 to 275

File 1 records 1 to 500

Track 4   Tracks 1, 2

File 1 takes tracks 1 and 2 on all platters (cylinders one and two)

File 2 takes ½ a cylinder starting at track 4

All files are addressed by logical record numbers in programs

Figure 9-5. Files on Disk. All of the logical records within a file are addressed by consecutive numbers, i.e., 1–n if there are n records in the file.

Direct-Access Files

Sequential file updates are relatively simple because all of the records are in the same order on some key. The major difficulty with sequential files comes in trying to modify only a particular record and in retrieving data a record at a time. Sequential files are fine for batch processing, but if a user wants on-line access to data, direct-access files are the answer.

A direct-access file still contains logical records, but they can be placed anywhere on the file. Each record has a logical address on the disk, so we can think of the file as having logical records 1 . . . n, where n is the last record in the file (see Figure 9-5).

For a concrete example, we shall take a simplified order-entry system at Autosport. Each order has an order number, which is the key. To simplify things, assume that only one item appears on an order (see Figure 9-6).

As the orders come in at random, there is no guarantee of their sequence. Where, then, should the program place them on the direct-access file? Once they are placed, how does the program find them for retrieval? There is a key, the order number, and an address of a logical record on the disk; somehow the two have to be related.

Figure 9-7 shows one way to accomplish this task. Remember that we do not want to search the entire disk for the order because that would take a lot of time. The disk operates at millisecond speeds (30×10^{-3}), whereas primary memory may have an access time of 50 nanoseconds (50×10^{-9}), which is about a million times faster than the speed of the disk.

The strategy for storing and then finding a record on a direct-access file is like the index of a book; in fact, the computer version is often called the index as well. If you look for a topic—say, direct-access files—in this text, you could begin in Chapter 1 and read all of the headings sequentially until you

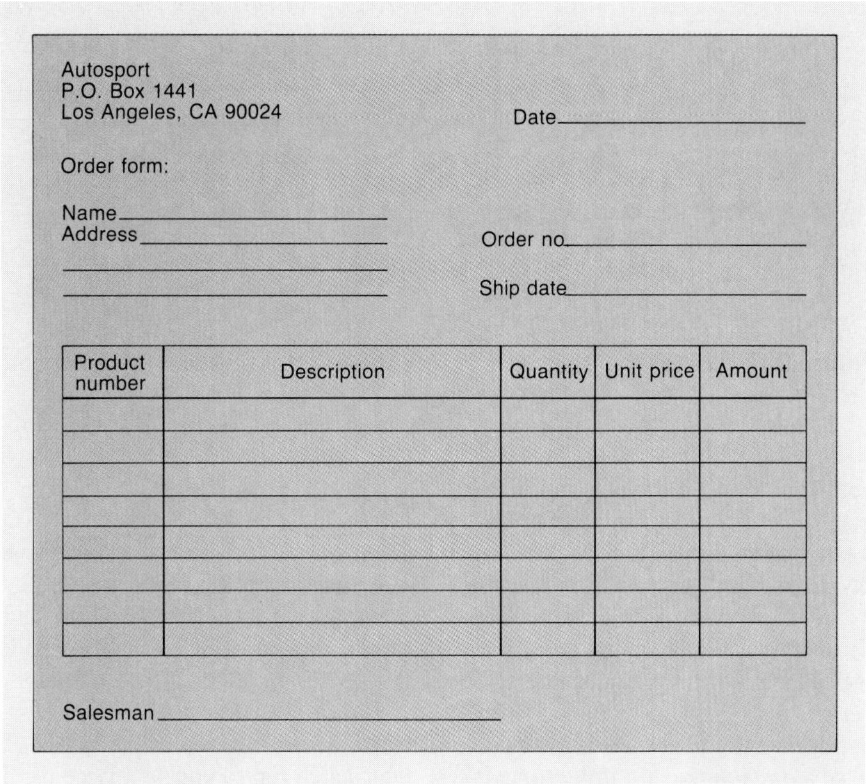
Autosport
P.O. Box 1441
Los Angeles, CA 90024

Date__________

Order form:

Name__________
Address__________

Order no.__________

Ship date__________

Product number	Description	Quantity	Unit price	Amount

Salesman__________

Figure 9-6. Example of an Order Entry Form for Autosport.

Figure 9-7. File and Index for Autosport. The primary key is the order number. The computer program searches the order number index at primary memory speeds and finds the address of the record for that order number on the disk. The program then reads the correct record for that order from the disk.

INDEX IN PRIMARY MEMORY		ORDER FILE ON DISK						
Key (order number)	**Address (record or disk)**	**Record**	**Order Number**	**Customer Number**	**Item Number**	**Quantity Ordered**	**Price Quoted**	**Deliver Date**
12341	2	1	12343	1111	1A276	5	10.	6/20
12342	3	2	12341	2222	1B704	15	.75	7/1
12343	1	3	12342	3333	1A402	1	50.	8/15
12344	4	4	12344	1111	1Z246	100	.80	6/30

	Batch	On-line
Sequential Files	Typical, e.g., Payroll	For backup and logging transactions
Direct Access Files	Often used for long updates, e.g., of an on-line production control system	Required

Figure 9-8. File Comparisons. Direct access files offer the most flexibility, but there is still an important role for sequential access.

reached this spot. That would be a long and time-consuming search. A better idea (if the author has remembered to put it in the index) is to look in the index for "direct-access files" and to find the pages on which they are discussed. You have looked through a much shorter list, the index, to get a pointer (the page number) to the topic of interest.

For a computer file, a program builds a small index to be kept in primary memory (if possible); the index is sometimes called a *dictionary* or a *directory.* It contains the logical key, in this case the order number, and the logical address where this particular order record is stored on the disk. The program that adds new records to the file updates the index when each new order record is processed. The program that retrieves a record searches the index at primary memory speeds, because the index is in primary memory, and locates the records with one access to the disk.

To update a record (say, to change the part number ordered), one can retrieve and change a single record; there is no need to read and recopy the entire file. This facility means that the files can be *on-line* all day and that individual records can be added, changed, or retrieved for inquiry at any time.

In summary, our strategy has been to search a small amount of information about the file (the index) at primary memory speeds in order to find the record desired. The search gives us the record's logical address on the disk, and the program has to access the disk only once to find it.

Application

The use of direct-access and sequential-access files in on-line and batch processing can be a bit confusing. Figure 9-8 tries to clarify the different possibilities. Direct-access files can be used for batch or on-line processing; they are required for on-line access.

Batch jobs may use direct-access files. For example, at night, one company uses a four- to six-hour batch run to update a large file on where parts are in its factory. All of the reports from the factory on the movement of parts are entered during the day on terminals, and these reports are used to update the location of each of the products in the factory. The data on part location are available on-line during the day, but because the update is so complex, the firm does not want to load the computer with the update and the on-line queries at the same time. Also, if the data are being updated, one would have to block queries about the records being changed to prevent access to information that is being changed.

There is also a role for sequential files in an on-line system. The first use is for logging transactions; usually, a tape is kept of each transaction to aid in reconstructing the database in case there is a failure. In addition to the **log** tape, there is a tape copy of the direct-access files. If there is a failure, the log tape is used to update the last dump tape of the direct-access files. (Data are "dumped" to tape from direct-access files to provide backup for the direct-access files.)

DIRECTORY	
Part Number	**Starting Address**
ABC111	4
EFG203	1
XK123	2

RECORD

Logical Address	Order No.	Part No.	Quantity	Link
1	1111	EFG203	10	
2	1234	XK123	8	
3	2222	EFG203	4	
4	2345	ABC111	11	
5	3333	EFG203	3	
6	4321	XK123	2	
7	5555	ABC111	16	
8	5678	XK123	11	
9	7777	EFG203	4	
10	8912	XK123	9	

Figure 9-9. Linked List Linked on Part Number. A linked list is formed by associating records with each other when they have the same value for a field. In this case, the common link is on the part number.

DATA STRUCTURES

For the direct-access order-entry file at Autosport, we have a simple or primary key: there is one order number per order. However, one could ask interesting questions about the data in this file that could not be answered through this one key. For example, the warehouse manager might want to know how many of part XK123 are to be shipped by the end of this month, based on orders received so far. The only way to answer this question with the current file structure is to search the file, reading every record, and printing those that contain an order for part XK123.

CHAINED OR LINKED LIST

We can use direct-access files to create logical **data structures,** in a sense to represent any picture we would like to have of the data. Figure 9-9 shows a simple data structure, a linked list on the part num-

	RECORD				
Logical Address	Order No.	Part No.	Quantity	Pointer	Ship Date
1	1111	EFG203	10	3	8/30
2	1234	XK123	8	6	7/31
3	2222	EFG203	4	5	8/30
4	2345	ABC111	11	7	7/31
5	3333	EFG203	3	9	7/31
6	4321	XK123	2	8	8/30
7	5555	ABC111	16	0	7/31
8	5678	XK123	11	10	7/31
9	7777	EFG203	4	0	8/30
10	8912	XK123	9	0	8/30

Figure 9-10. Physical Pointers. The links drawn in Figure 9-9 are actually created by record pointers. A pointer is simply the record address of the next record on the same chain. For example, XK123 is at record 2; the next location of XK123 is at record 6. So the pointer field for record 2 is a 6.

ber ordered. The various records are linked together if they have the same value in a particular field, in this case, the same part number.

How is the logical structure in Figure 9-9 implemented physically in the file? The first step is to set up an index or directory to locate the first instance of the part—in this case, XK123. Each record in the file for XK123 has a *pointer,* a number that is the record address of the next order for XK123 (see Figure 9-10).

Such a chain of pointers is necessary for every part number that has been ordered; with this data structure, it would not take long to answer the warehouse manager's question about any particular part. The program would first ask the manager for the part number in question, for example, XK123. Then it would check the directory to find the first logical record address having the requested part number, a

2 in Figure 9-8. The program reads the record at address 2 and keeps track of the quantity of the part on order. Then it takes the pointer, 6, as the address of the next record that it is to read. The program then reads the record at location 6. The pointer of this record tells the program the next one to read; in this case, the pointer is 8. The program would keep reading in this way until it reached the end of the list.

The manager now knows how many orders there are for part XK123. Next, he wants to know how many orders are to be shipped by the end of this month. He finds out by reading through the chain connecting all of the XK123 orders and looking for shipping dates that are for this month. An index could also be built on shipping dates that is analogous to the one for part numbers. Then the manager could ask directly for information about shipping

Part number	Addresses
ABC111	4, 7
EFG203	1, 3, 5, 9,
XK123	2, 6, 8, 10

Ship Date	Addresses
7/31	2, 4, 5, 7, 8
8/30	1, 3, 6, 9, 10

Figure 9-11. Inverted Directory. An inverted directory can speed retrieval; some questions can be answered by just processing the directory.

dates. However, the combined question of shipping date and part number would still require one of the chains to be searched since there is no index or chain on both ship date and part number.

Inverted Directory

A different kind of directory would make it easier to answer the question of how many of a certain part are to be shipped by a particular date.

In Figure 9-11, the various pointers in the file have been removed from the file records and placed in the index. The type of index created here is called **inverted** because it removes the pointers from the file with the linked list and puts them all in a directory.

Although the index itself becomes more complicated, the inverted index or directory does have a great deal of flexibility in implementing different kinds of data structures. It is also possible to do some processing in the directories without actually accessing the file. Figure 9-10 shows how we could answer the question of how many XK123's are to be shipped by August 30. We simply match the record numbers in the directory for the XK123 entry and the August 30 entry. Where the record numbers are equal, we have a record that contains XK123 and August 30.

CHANGES

We have emphasized so far the creation and accessing of various data records. There are two types of changes that an organization makes in these structures. First, think about an update in which one might add a record, change an existing record, or delete an existing record. Generally, when a data structure makes retrieval easy, it is harder to update, and vice versa.

A sequential file is not fast on retrieval, but it is easy to change. A new file is created with each update. In direct-access files, it is necessary to change the directory contents when a record is added or deleted.

When the direct-access file has linked lists running through it, deleting a record could destroy the chain of pointers on some field like "location at which each employee works" (see Figure 9-12). For this reason, the program often simply sets some character in the record to indicate that the record is no longer active; it remains in the file temporarily to preserve the list of pointers. Later, probably at night, the file will be reorganized and inactive records will be deleted.

If we want to add a record to a file with chains of pointers, all of the fields involved with pointers must be added to their appropriate chains. The file looks

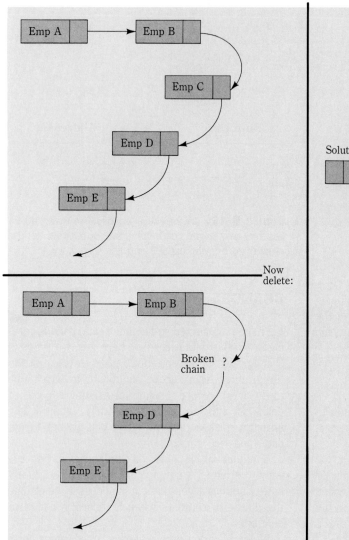
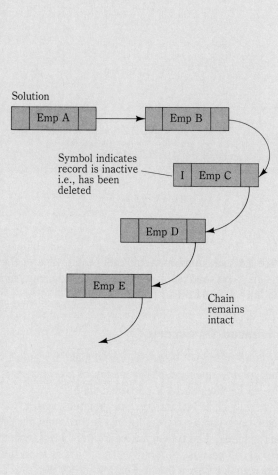

Figure 9-12. If we physically remove the record for employee C if he or she quits, the chain of pointers is broken. By setting a delete indicator, the chain remains intact, but the program knows to ignore employee C's record when processing data.

logically like the links of a real metal chain. If we wanted to add a new link in the middle of a metal chain, we would have to cut the chain apart at the links where the new link is to be inserted. Then we would insert the new link and fasten it securely. We must do the same thing in adding a new record to a logically linked list with a direct-access file (see Figure 9-13). In a file with inverted directories with

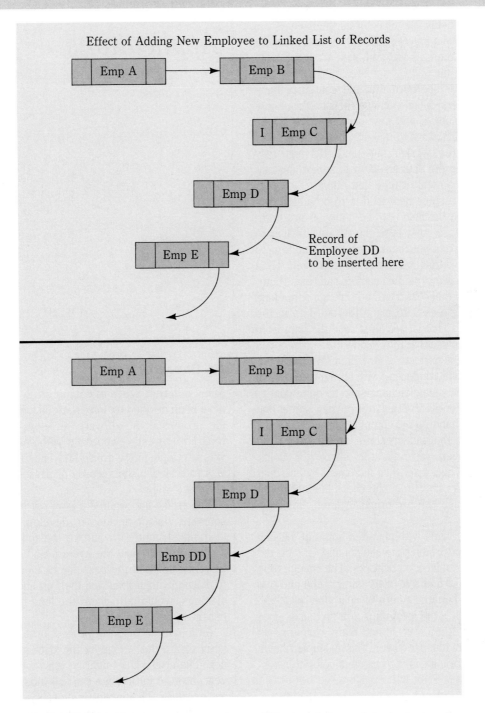

Figure 9-13. To insert a new employee, DD, the chain must be broken and a new link inserted.

keys on many fields, the directories themselves can become huge, and a great deal of time can be spent in processing them as we add, delete, and modify records in the file.

Such changes are normal in the course of business. Customers call and change their orders, some orders are canceled, and new orders arrive. Quite frequently, users want to make a change in the way the entire system works. This kind of change may involve altering the data structures, something that can take a great deal of time and effort.

Suppose that some new field is to be added to a record and that the field is to be a key. A programmer has to figure out where the data will originate for input, where to put them in a record, and how to process them during updating and retrieval. Then the programmer makes the changes and tests them. Finally, it will be necessary to go through some kind of conversion process to place the old data in the new structure. That is, we must read the data from the old files and see that they are written correctly in the new file that reflects a new data structure.

Even when we are dealing with straight sequential files, a seemingly simple change can be quite costly. The Social Security Administration has some one thousand two hundred old computer programs and a library of fifty thousand reels of tapes. When the benefits changed recently, the space for dollar amounts on a check had to be increased by one digit because, for the first time, the check amount might exceed the space that had originally been allowed in the file.

The Agency came with eighteen hours of missing the deadline for printing the checks and, in fact, did issue a number of incorrect checks. The change took twenty thousand hours of programmer time and two thousand five hundred hours of computer processing. Admittedly, the programs are in fairly poor shape because they are old and many changes had been made already. However, this example shows that it is not always easy to change a computer system!

Applications

An Ocean Cruise

Many different types of computer file organizations have been devised to solve various kinds of processing problems. A software development company took an interesting approach with a system that it was developing for a cruise-ship line. The application was to maintain the records of passenger bookings on cruise ships.

The cruise line wanted a low-cost system, so the software vendor decided to develop the most efficient file structure it could for the application. First, it was obvious that the system had to be on-line; travel agents and the passengers themselves, used to dealing with airlines and their on-line reservations systems, would not accept the long time delays inherent in batch updating.

Although the mode of processing to be used was fairly clear, the design of the data structures was not. The cruise line might accept reservations for a year into the future; we can call these reservations an *inventory*. This inventory consists of information about the cruise, the cabin to which the passenger was assigned, the names of the passengers in the cabin, and information about the travel agent who

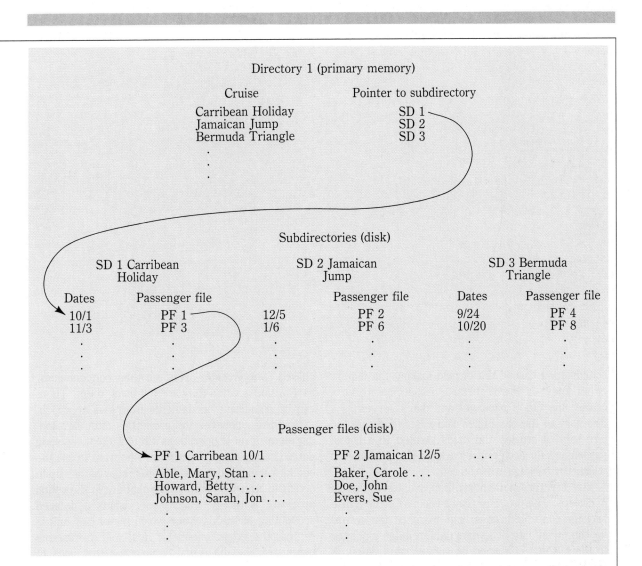

Directory 1 (primary memory)

Cruise	Pointer to subdirectory
Carribean Holiday	SD 1
Jamaican Jump	SD 2
Bermuda Triangle	SD 3

Subdirectories (disk)

SD 1 Carribean
Holiday

Dates	Passenger file
10/1	PF 1
11/3	PF 3

SD 2 Jamaican
Jump

	Passenger file
12/5	PF 2
1/6	PF 6

SD 3 Bermuda
Triangle

Dates	Passenger file
9/24	PF 4
10/20	PF 8

Passenger files (disk)

PF 1 Carribean 10/1

Able, Mary, Stan . . .
Howard, Betty . . .
Johnson, Sarah, Jon . . .

PF 2 Jamaican 12/5   . . .

Baker, Carole . . .
Doe, John
Evers, Sue

Figure 9-14. Cruise Line Data Structures. The first directory in primary memory points to a subdirectory on disk for each cruise package. This directory matches the date of the cruise and points to a file of passenger names.

had made the reservation.

The problem was to access data on cruises quickly, without spending a lot of time searching a large number of records. The solution chosen was to use a series of directories and small files to reach the passenger data (see Figure 9-14). The first directory contained information on the cruise tour, for example, "Caribbean Holiday." This directory pointed to a file that contained all of the various cruise packages and the dates on which the trip was scheduled. Because the person making the inquiry either knew or was requesting a specific date for a cruise, the file of packages and dates served as a directory to the passenger name lists. This second directory of cruises and dates pointed to a list of passengers for each cruise package for each date on which the package was offered.

The directory in memory, then, pointed to the file of cruises. The program read a record for the cruise package (one file access) and searched the record for the given date. The date data included a pointer to the file that contained passenger information. A single file access reached the appropriate list of passengers. Depending on the size of the ship, it was possible to read the entire file into primary memory and search it at primary memory speeds. If that was not possible, it did not take more than a few accesses to read the passenger information, which was maintained in alphabetical order.   ■

Help for Southrest

Southrest is a Multicorp subsidiary that operates several resorts. Most of the resorts consist of condominium housing units that investors have pur-

chased. The investors rent out their condominiums as a business when they are not using them. There can be significant tax benefits from this approach.

Southrest manages the properties after developing them. It must operate as a rental agent, booking dates into the future for renters who want to use the condominiums. Southrest accepts reservations up to a year in advance for the units that are in the rental program. Naturally, each owner wants a detailed accounting of the days for which his or her unit is rented, the gross amount of rent, and the various expenses, like the rental commission that goes to Southrest, cleaning fees, maintenance, and charges for the grounds.

Recognizing that some of its larger competitors have developed quite sophisticated computer systems for both reservations and accounting, Southrest is considering a system of its own. Management has decided that it makes the most sense to start with a reservations system because a reservation is the event that eventually results in rental income and the various transactions that are of interest to the owner. Can you suggest a possible file structure for a Southrest reservations system based on the material in this chapter?   ■

Review of Chapter 9

REVIEW

This chapter is concerned with an extremely important topic: the storage of data on files and in databases. For the application of computers to solving problems in organizations, file capabilities are extremely important. Some of the most valuable contributions of computers to organizations come from their ability to control and make available a small amount of important information from a large mass of data.

We have seen how data are represented by fields of characters, such as someone's last name. The fields are grouped together to form logical records, and the logical records are aggregated to become files. There are two major types of files: sequential and direct access. The sequential file is most associated with batch processing; the payroll file in the example is processed sequentially in batch mode.

Because we cannot retrieve a record at random from a sequential file, many applications of computers require direct-access processing. The major added complication here is to keep track of where records are located. We must be able to store and find a record according to some key field; this key must be associated with an address on the direct-access file.

Using data called *pointers,* which are really direct-access file addresses, we saw that quite complex data structures can be developed.

KEY WORDS

Batch	Logical record
Blocking	Master file
Dictionary	On-line
Direct-access file	Physical record
Directory	Pointer
Field	Query
File	Relational
Inverted directory	Sequential-access file
Key	Sort program
Logic	Transaction

BUSINESS PROBLEM

9-1. A company has asked your help in designing an accounts receivable system. The system keeps track of open items, that is, items for which customers have been billed but have not paid. For reference purposes, the system also maintains closed (paid) items for the calendar year.

When products are shipped to customers, the packing slip comes to a clerk, who enters the data into the computer. The computer system generates an invoice and at the same time creates a receivable for this customer.

Describe the files that will be needed if this type of system is to work. Explain each item in the file and its use. Then write a short narrative showing how the system will work. What are the major transactions? What kind of input screens would the clerk see on a CRT? What inquiries do you think the customers might make? What inquiries would the accounts receivable staff make?

REVIEW QUESTIONS

1. What are the fundamental operations that can be performed on files?
2. What is a physical record?
3. How does a physical record differ from a logical one?
4. What is a field?
5. What are fixed-length records? Why are they popular?
6. Describe a variable-length record.
7. When do we need variable-length records?
8. Explain how a sequential update works.
9. Why is an entirely new file created in a sequential update?
10. Why is the transactions file sorted in a sequential update?
11. How does a sort program work?
12. What happens if the transaction key is greater than the old master file key in a sequential update and the transaction is not an addition of a new record?
13. What is a blocking factor?
14. Why are physical blocks usually different from logical records?
15. How do we save space and time with record blocking?
16. What is the role of the operating system in record blocking?
17. What is the disadvantage of a sequential file in retrieval?
18. What is involved in transforming a record key

into an address in a disk file?

19. What does a file index do?
20. Why do we not want to make a sequential search of a file that is on disk?
21. For what purposes are sequential files used? Direct-access files?
22. What is a data structure?
23. Describe a linked-list structure.
24. How does an inverted directory differ from a linked list?
25. What is the difference between physical and logical data structures?
26. What is involved in making changes in a sequential file? A direct-access file?
27. How are direct access files used in a sequential application?
28. What is a key?
29. What is a pointer?
30. How are sequential files used in an on-line system?

THOUGHT QUESTIONS

31. What do computer files provide for us?
32. What are the advantages of each type of data structure?
33. For what applications would each major type of data structure be most suited?
34. Why is it seemingly more difficult to update a file structure designed for retrieval than a more simple file structure?
35. Do you see a solution to the problem of programmers' inventing access routines over and over again to store and retrieve data on direct-access files?

RECOMMENDED READINGS

Lucas, H. C., Jr. *The Analysis, Design and Implementation of Information Systems* (3rd ed.). New York: McGraw-Hill, 1985. Contains two chapters on files and detabase management.

Tsichritzis, D., and F. Lochovsky. *Data Models*. Englewood Cliffs, NJ: Prentice-Hall, 1982. An advanced book on data structures.

Chapter 10

In the last chapter, we studied various kinds of computer files. Remember that files are used to store and retrieve data. Files are called *secondary storage* because they cannot be directly accessed by the computer; the computer must initiate an input/output operation, move data from the file to primary memory, and access the data from primary data.

To use secondary storage, programmers must design and manipulate files. The development of sequential files is straightforward because what can be done with these files is limited. However, direct-access files present more of a challenge. The programmer must design and implement various kinds of directories in order to set up and process direct-access files.

Think about two different applications, one for answering information about what parts are in inventory and another for verifying that you are not over your limit on a charge card. In each instance, the query comes in with a key. In the first case, there is an inventory part number, like **AJ1234**. For the credit card, there is a long number like **4250 1099 4513**. An operator at a terminal receives each query over the phone. He or she then enters the number. In the inventory case, the computer responds with the balance in inventory of the part, its cost, and a short description. The credit card system returns the amount of credit outstanding and the customer's credit limit, plus a code that indicates the credit rating of the account.

In each of these instances, the program has gone through the same process. It has taken an incoming key, transformed it into an address on the disk, and retrieved information stored on a record on that disk. The recognition of duplication if the programmers for inventory and credit applications both program data access routines, plus several other problems led to the development of automated systems that help programmers to develop applications. This software is called a *database management system (DBMS)*.

After completing this chapter, you should be able to:

- Describe the three major data structures.
- Explain the motivation for creating database systems.
- Set up a simple relational database.
- Describe the features of a database management system (DBMS).
- Discuss the duties of a database administrator.
- Give an example of how a **DBMS** has helped an organization.

DATABASE MANAGEMENT

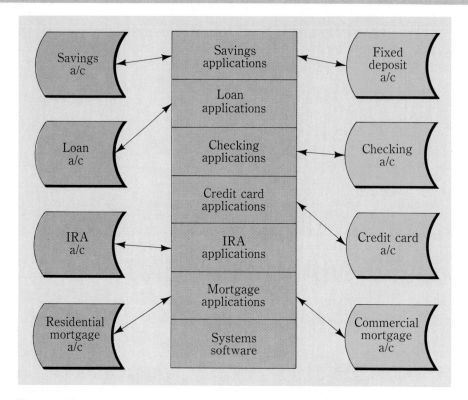

Figure 10-1. An Example of Bank Applications "Owning" Their Data. Much information is duplicated in the separate files.

INTRODUCTION

One reason for an innovative approach to developing **direct-access files** is the fact that so much file processing is similar. Another reason is a bit more complicated but is still quite important. In the early days of computing, when all we had was **sequential files,** each of the many programs in a sequential processing application set up its own files, updated them, and produced reports. Very little thought was given to one system's accessing another system's files; files were unique to each application. The same data might even be known by different names in different systems.

As an example, consider a bank at which you have several different kinds of accounts. The first might be a savings account, the second an auto loan, and the third a mortgage. In a sequential environment,

three separate computer applications would probably exist, each creating and maintaining its own files. If you wanted to change your address because of a pending move, you might have to fill out three change-of-address forms, one for each account, because the three systems duplicated the same information about you (see Figure 10-1).

All of this redundancy inhibited the ability of the bank to offer service; it did not seem to be well managed if customers had to go through an address change for each account. Of course, the bank could hire someone to take one form and translate it into three, but that would certainly destroy any idea that computer systems are labor-saving devices.

Another problem in the use of direct-access files comes in changing the system. Users often want to have new reports or to change the processing logic of an application. In a sequential application, the en-

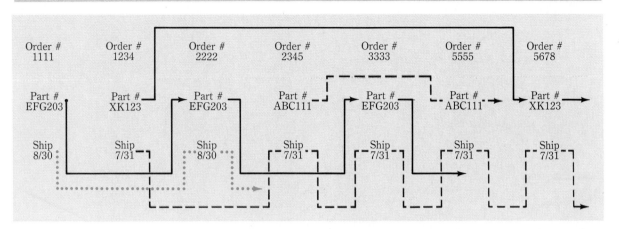

Figure 10-2. Data Structure for Part of File in Figure 9-10. The data structure is a diagram of the relationship between records with fields having the same value, e.g., the same part number or ship date.

tire format of every file that each program accesses is specified in its code. There is no way to work with a file unless the programmer names the fields in the file of interest in the program and describes the length of the record.

If it is necessary to change one *field* in a record or the structure of the record in any way, the programmer has to find each program that either read or wrote the file and change its description of the records in the file. Often a programmer misses one program, creating errors and problems in processing.

To summarize, we have mentioned three major problems connected with the use of the direct-access files described in Chapter 9:

1. Programmers must reinvent access techniques each time they create a directory and define a direct-access file.
2. Applications feature many redundant data; the same data exist in several places in different systems and are probably known by a different name in each.
3. It is difficult to change programs without affecting another program in the system.

The answer to these problems was to develop a piece of systems software, a series of programs that assist the systems designer and the programmer in using direct-access files. This set of programs is known as a *database management system,* which is the topic of this chapter. Before we explain what each component of a DBMS does, we will discuss data structures in a little more detail.

MORE DATA STRUCTURES

Review of the Basics

In the last chapter, we discussed the use of physical record pointers to lead us from one piece of data to another, for example, to find the records of all items to be shipped on the same day in a file of orders. The logical relationship is simply a chained list, as shown in Figure 10-2. The user and the analyst can think of the file as being connected in some way, so that if they ask for a certain key, like the date August 30, there is a way to quickly find all records having this date, for example as the shipping date.

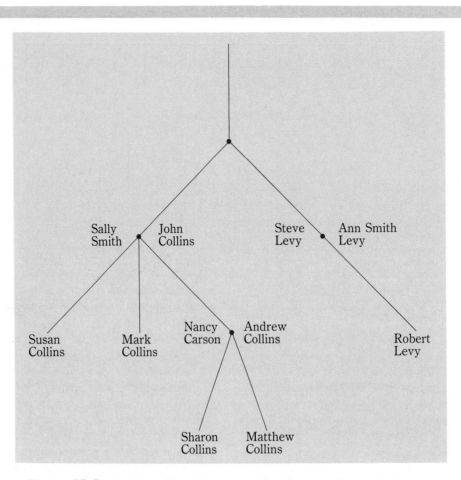

Figure 10-3. A Hierarchical Structure. The data look like a simple tree.

The physical pointers discussed in the last chapter implement the logical structure in a physical database. Before the kind of systems described in this chapter, the analyst and programmer had to worry about these pointers and the physical data. Today, we might find a specialist in the organization taking the responsibility for the physical design of the database; it is likely that the analyst and user will stay at the logical level.

There are many different types of **data structures.** The designer can create a variety of linkages among fields of data.

As an example, one could make the end of the list for the shipping date in Figure 10-2 point back to the first record with that date. The result is a circle or a ring; the linked list forms a chain. Where might such a structure be useful?

The Important Structures

There are three quite important types of data structures: **hierarchical, network** or **plex,** and **relational.** A hierarchical data structure resembles a family tree. There is a natural hierarchy in the data, so that they fit the hierarchical model quite well. For example, a bill of materials that contains the name of an item manufactured from various parts and all of the subassemblies and components of the subassemblies forms a hierarchical data structure. Other applications also seem to have an underlying

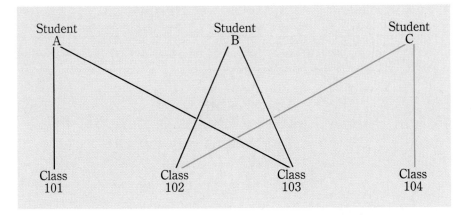

Figure 10-4. A Network Structure. Links among entities form a network.

structure that fits the hierarchy (see Figure 10-3).

The tree in the hierarchical file is composed of a set of nodes; the highest-level node is known as the *root*. Every node except the root is related to a node at a higher level, which is called the *node's parent*. In a hierarchical structure, a node can have only one parent, though it can have more than one lower-level node. These lower-level nodes are, as you might expect, known as *children*.

The second kind of structure is the plex, or network, and is shown in Figure 10-4. Here, there can be multiple links among the various entities in the structure. We can look at the network as being similar to the hierarchy, but now a child in the relationship can have more than one parent. In a simple plex structure, the child-to-parent mapping is simple; that is, the arrows go in only one direction. As you might imagine, the physical data structure that supports a complex network structure is difficult to develop, as the designer has to allow for arrows in both directions at the same time.

The relational structure in Figure 10-5 is the newest and most appealing because it is one of the easiest to understand. The data are set up in tables that represent relations among the columns of the table. These two-dimensional tables are easy for a user to understand and for an analyst to develop. Many of the newer database management systems described later, particularly those for microcomputers, are constructed around the relational model.

Another advantage of relational data structures is that they can be described more easily mathematically than other types. In addition, a number of well-defined operations can be performed on the tables—or relations, as they are known. For example, one can join two relations to form a new relation that contains the matching items in each of the joined relations. One can project over a field and select only the records having a certain value, such as the cities in which the people in a personnel file live. We would not want to list duplicate cities; the project command picks out each city in the relation only once.

The major point is that direct-access files provide tremendous flexibility in creating data structures for almost any application. There are firms with billions of characters of on-line data, and the design of data structures for their applications is a very important task.

We might want to distinguish again between physical and logical data structures. The logical structure is how the data appear to the user; as an example, the data in a family tree might look quite hierarchical to the user. However, the actual physical storage of data, the physical data structure, is not going to look hierarchical. The hierarchy on the disk file would be represented by data followed by a pointer to the next branch on the tree. There also might be a pointer back to the node on the family tree that im-

Order Relation

Order No.	Customer No.	Part No.	Quantity	Ship Date
1234	16702	XK123	10	8/30
9876	15407	ABC111	4	7/31
2222	13792	XK123	18	8/30
3456	16702	ABC111	8	7/31

Customer Relation

Customer No.	Name	Street	City	State	Zip Code
16702	Ball Mfg	1234 Maple	Summit	NJ	07901
15407	Autosport	18 Sepulveda	Los Angeles	CA	67320
13792	Alex Garments	1733 Broadway	New York	NY	10020

Figure 10-5. Relational Structure. The relational file is called a flat file. Can you figure out why?

mediately precedes the current node. For the most part, we are interested in logical data structures, that is, what the user sees.

DATABASE MANAGEMENT SYSTEMS

The answer to many of the problems connected with sequential file applications and early direct-access file systems is a database management system, a software package that provides a great deal of service to the computer staff and to the organization. The goals of this kind of system are to:

1. Create more independence of the data from the programs that access them, so that changes can be facilitated. This feature is sometimes called the *database concept,* the greater separation of data and programs.

2. Reduce the duplication of data, that is, the presence of the same information in many places, such as a bank's recording a customer's name and address separately in a checking, a loan, and a mortgage system.

3. Provide a facility for defining the logical and the physical characteristics of data.

4. Provide a file that accesses technique, that is, that establishes and manages directories and responds to requests for data.

5. Provide facilities that protect the integrity and security of data.

Figure 10-6 shows the components of a typical database management system.

Database Administration

Organizations using a DBMS usually add a new position, that of the ***database administrator (DBA).***

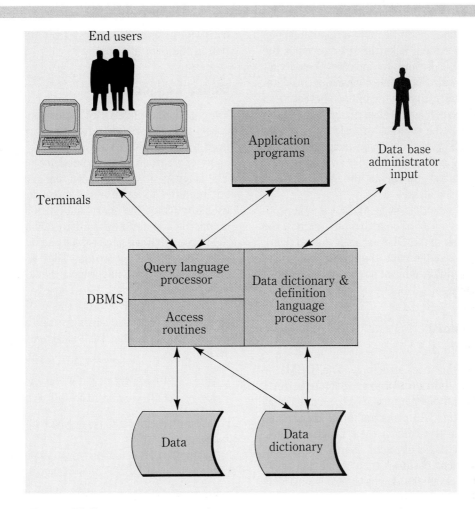

Figure 10-6. Database Management System. A DBMS consists of at least a data definition language and file access routine. It also may include a data dictionary and query language.

This individual works with systems analysts to take the logical views of the data and to create a physical structure to support them.

What are different logical views? Consider a cruise-ship reservation system: the reservations agent sees a passenger name record for a cabin on a cruise; the accounting department sees a set of fares for each individual on the cruise; and the ship's crew is interested in a map showing the cabins on the ship and the names of their occupants and any special requirements, like an extra bed.

Data Definition Language

The DBA must define the records and the relationship among them. In a hierarchical database system, the DBA provides a record description that looks very much like the kind of records we described in the last chapter. In addition, he or she also describes the relationship among the records; for example, this record is the child of a previous record.

In a **relational** database for a micro, the user might use only a simple command, like DEFINE

ORDERS to define the contents of a relation named ORDERS. The system asks the user to input the names of the fields and to indicate their type, whether numerical, alphabetic, alphanumeric, date, and so on. The user is given the option of creating an index on the relation and of describing initial values for data items. Some systems provide the ability to define ranges for valid data; for example, a field might have to be between 0 and 9999 when entered. If the data are outside this range, the DBMS refuses to accept them for input.

The data definition language (DDL) is unique to the DBMS. It is a way of describing the data to the system. The task of the DBA or analyst is to figure out the structure of the data; the task of translation into the DDL is not as difficult as the initial design of the data structures.

Data Dictionary

The DBA and the systems analysts agree on a database definition and structure. The DBMS is likely to have a *data dictionary,* which is an automated approach to keeping track of the names of all data in the system. All programmers then use the same names for the data in their programs. The DBA defines the data and places them in the dictionary. The dictionary becomes the central repository for information about the database; it contains data definitions and the structure of the data. The DBMS can access the contents of the data dictionary to obtain the information it needs to operate.

In its simplest form, the data dictionary might consist of the data entered using the data definition part of the DBMS. For the micro relational database manager, it would contain the names of the fields that the user has entered and their characteristics. The data dictionary is consulted as the system processes each command.

Many data dictionaries operate on-line; that is, the DBA can enter and retrieve data from a terminal. A good dictionary is dynamically linked to the programs; that is, during the execution of a user's program, the DBMS actually refers to the data dictionary to find out information about the database. This means that the DBA can make certain changes in the data without ever doing more than making an alteration in the data dictionary.

Query Language

The final feature of a DBMS is usually a query processor, a high-level retrieval language that can be used by individuals to ask questions, such as "How many of a certain part are needed by a given date?" The language is easy to learn, and a programmer is not required to write a statement for a user. The user formulates the query and types it on a terminal or microcomputer keyboard to obtain the answer.

Suppose that we have a database of magazine articles indexed by key words. That is, an article on computer hardware might have the key words *hardware, VLSI,* and *chips.* To retrieve articles about hardware, the user would employ the **query language.** Each of these languages has a different syntax or structure. One such language would require an entry like:

SELECT BIBLIO WHERE KEYWORD EQ HARDWARE OR KEYWORD EQ VLSI OR KEYWORD EQ CHIPS

if the name of the database is *biblio,* short for *bibliography.*

Examples of commands from a popular microcomputer relational DBMS query language are

- APPEND—add records from another relation.
- COMBINE—combine two relations.
- COMPARE—compare two relations on a field.
- COMPUTE—perform computations.
- COPY—make another copy.
- DELETE—eliminate a record.
- DESTROY—eliminate a database.
- ENTER—input data.
- INDEX—create an index.
- JOIN—join two relations with a common field.
- LIST—display the contents of a relation.
- POST—make changes by applying transactions.
- PRINT—print rows in a relation.
- PROJECT—project over a field picking unique values.
- RENAME—change the name of a relation.
- REORG—reorganize a relation.

- REPORT—create and print a report.
- SAVE—save a temporary relation.
- SELECT—select records based on some criteria.
- SORT—change the order of a relation based on a field.
- TABULATE—count the occurrences in a field.
- UPDATE—make changes in individual records.
- WRITE—create an output file.

Although the query language gives the user a great deal of flexibility in answering his or her own questions, there can be some problems. Some research has shown that users tend to ask questions, using the query language, that the database cannot answer. Although we would like to isolate the user from the structure of the data and certainly to remove the need to interact with a programmer to ask a question, it is difficult to accomplish these goals completely. To be successful with a query language, the user has to learn something about the data, their structure, and the kinds of questions the database can support.

Execution of the System

Figure 10-7 describes how the DBMS actually operates. The user enters a query in the query language (we assume that the database has been defined and created in advance). The query processor reads and interprets the query. The query processor passes the request that it has just interpreted to file-access routines in the database manager.

These access routines first look at the data definitions to be sure that the requested files and fields exist. If they do not, the request is aborted. If the request is all right, the access routines check with the data dictionary to determine the type of data and where they are located. If the data are indexed, the access routines will use the index to find the data as quickly as possible.

Next, the access routines locate the data and retrieve them. The access routines may pass the data to some kind of display routine, which then returns the answer to the user who entered the original query. All of these steps sound time-consuming, but fortunately, computers are fast. One does notice the time on a microcomputer, but mainframe database management systems generally operate with a good response time if the computer is not overloaded.

Types of DBMS

The first database management systems were developed for mainframe computers because mainframes were about the only computers around at the time. These first systems were rather crude by today's standards, but they were eagerly adopted by large organizations that needed to develop major applications.

With the advent of minicomputers, vendors began to develop database management systems to run on the minis. These systems tended to be simpler and began to automate more of the systems development task. At least one vendor built a data dictionary and a database management system as a part of the operating system for a computer, an approach that created a highly productive programming environment.

Naturally, software vendors have rushed to develop database management packages for micros. These packages are very complete; often, they come close to being applications generators. Several of the major DBMSs for micros have routines that allow the user to define a format for an input screen and to describe quite elaborate report formats for output.

One computer vendor offers a database computer, a machine whose instruction set has been designed to access data on secondary storage. The vendor claims that this machine is highly efficient in manipulating data and should be used as a go-between or path between a mainframe and its secondary storage.

Another vendor has designed database features into the actual hardware of the computer. The computer and its languages have features that automatically develop indexes. Special instructions facilitate the manipulation of data with very little effort required on the part of the programmer. This computer, too, has achieved a reputation for great programmer productivity in developing and changing applications quickly.

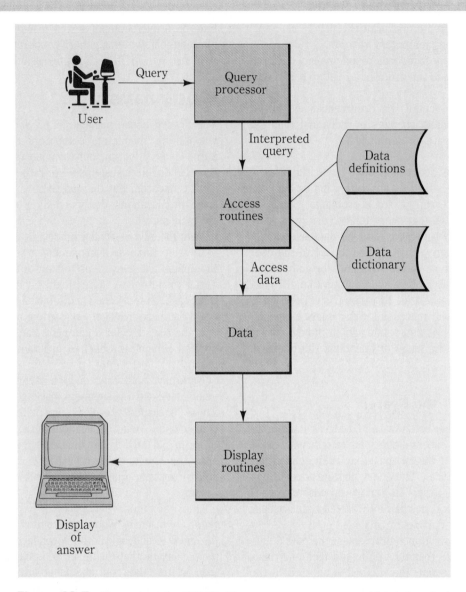

Figure 10-7. Execution of a DBMS. The user enters a query which is handled by the query processor. The interpreted query is passed to the access routines, which consult data definitions to determine where the data are located. Access routines locate the data and pass them to a display routine, which formats an answer.

Application

To illustrate the database concept, the following example shows two relations for Autosport using a relational DBMS for a personal computer. See Figure 10-8 for a definition of the file and its contents. The

Figure 10-8. ORDER and CUSTOMER relations from Autosport.

Order relation

ORDNO	CUSTNO	PARTNO	QUANTITY	SHIPDATE
1234	16702	XK 123	10	8/30
9876	15407	ABC 111	4	7/31
2222	13792	XK 123	18	8/30
3456	16702	ABC 111	8	7/31

Customer Relation

CUSTNO	NAME	STREET	CITY	STATE	ZIP CODE
16702	Ball Mfg.	1234 Maple	Summit	NJ	07901
15407	Autosport	18 Sepulveda	Los Angeles	CA	67320
13792	Alex Garments	1733 Broadway	New York	NY	10020

following queries show how to retrieve data from the database:

SELECT ORDER WHERE ORDNO EQ
SELECT ORDER WHERE SHIPDATE EQ
SELECT CUSTOMER WHERE CUSTNO EQ

There are several ways to combine files. A join is the most frequent operation: it creates a new relation for each matching line in the file. One would join "Order" and "Customer relations" to get information for an invoice (see Figure 10-9). ∎

Figure 10-9. Result of Join Operation on Order and Customer Relations. A join takes place in a common field of two relations. Here it occurs on CUSTNO, producing a new relation which combines information from the joined relations.

Order–customer relation

ORDNO	CUSTNO	PARTNO	QUANTITY	SHIPDATE	NAME	STREET	CITY	STATE	ZIP CODE
1234	16702	XK 123	10	8/30	Ball Mfg.	1234 Maple	Summit	NJ	07901
9876	15407	ABC 111	4	7/31	Autosport	18 Sepulveda	Los Angeles	CA	67320
2222	13792	XK 123	18	8/30	Alex Garments	1733 Broadway	New York	NY	10020
3456	16702	ABC 111	8	7/31	Ball Mfg.	1234 Maple	Summit	NJ	07901

Result of join operation on the ORDER & CUSTOMER relations (joined on common data item: CUSTNO)

Figure 10-10. The Cray Computer Facility at the Naval Research Laboratory is an example of a modern supercomputer system.

SUMMARY

Storing and retrieving data are complex, yet they provide much of the power of a modern information system.

Whether you work in an organization and need to access its large database (such as the case in Figure 10-10), or just want to set up a personal database, the concepts are the same. Data storage and retrieval are the foundations for a computer-based information system.

TWO EXAMPLES

Examples of how two organizations use database techniques should help to convey an idea of some of the things that can be done with computers and secondary storage.

Mobil Oil Company is the second largest U.S. firm, with sales of over $60 billion and over 200,000 employees. Much of Mobil's U.S. processing occurs at two major computer centers, one in Princeton, New Jersey, and the other in Dallas, Texas. Both centers use multiple IBM mainframes and a database management system called *IMS*.

The firm started a database administration department in 1976 on the basis of three major premises:

1. Data are important and are a shared resource that should be managed.
2. Information about data should be widely available.
3. Data quality should be controlled.

The database administrators (DBAs) use a data dictionary as a major tool in their job. It organizes the data and contains their description, characteristics, interrelationships, and structure. The dictionary shows where data are being used. In a firm as large as Mobil, it is very important to maintain control over data. The DBMS objective of preventing redundancy cannot be achieved if many separate applications use a piece of data and it is known by a different name in each application. In a large main-frame computer installation maintaining control of a DBMS requires a great deal of work.

Another example is drawn from the federal judiciary. Recent legislation defining what is meant in the U.S. Constitution by a "speedy trial" has forced the federal courts to do a better job of managing cases. If a defendant is not brought to trial according to a set schedule, the charges must be dismissed.

The courts established a judicial systems laboratory that has developed several database applications to help manage the judicial process. There are databases on each court, as courts are organized by district. The various databases are maintained on several DEC System-10 computers located in Washington, D.C., and access is provided through terminals and printers in the courts; the connections to Washington are via a telecommunications network.

The criminal docketing database is a key part of the system. The clerk of the court must maintain an official court docket for each case; this docket is a fundamental reference document used to determine case status and progress. The contents of the docket provide data pertinent to case tracking and reporting. The line items on the docket are known as *events* and correspond to a significant court transaction like arraignment.

The data for the docket come from a variety of sources, including open court proceedings. Filings by attorneys and other agencies, such as the U.S. Marshal, also generate entries on the docket. The database for docketing contains information on:

1. Parties to the case.
2. Offenses charged.
3. Docketed events.
4. Judges assigned to the case.
5. Attorneys associated with the proceedings.
6. Time constraints.
7. Related cases.

The database structure is complex and must represent the relationships that exist among entities; a network data structure is used. The system has significantly improved judicial administration and compliance with the speedy trial act.

Review of Chapter 10

REVIEW

This chapter has discussed the development of a powerful systems software tool that increases productivity in systems development: the database management system. DBMSs were developed to eliminate the need for programmers to program directories and access routines that are common across applications, to reduce data redundancy, and to make programs easier to change. The database management system presents the concept of data as something separate from the programs that access data, the idea of data independence.

Because the creation and manipulation of data structures is quite similar from one computer application to another, vendors realized that they could market software to accomplish these tasks. These database management systems have been extremely successful and have helped reduce the length of time it takes to create, and especially to modify, a computer application. Whether you are working with a mainframe or a micro, database management is a key concept to understand.

KEY WORDS

Batch	Field
Data definition language	Hierarchical
Data dictionary	Network
Data structure	Plex
DBA	Query language
DBMS	Relational
Direct access file	Sequential file
Directory	

BUSINESS PROBLEMS

10-1. Your employer is trying to decide whether to acquire a package called a database management system (DBMS) to help develop direct access file applications. The firm knows that it is inefficient to keep creating direct-access file routines, but the cost of the DBMS is discouraging.

One employee who is opposed to the idea has presented a number of arguments against the system. First, he thinks that it will be too costly. "Not only do we have the purchase price," he argues, "we must also think about training. I bet it will end up costing us twice the price of the package."

The negative case also includes fears that the sys-tem will be too complex: "What if we change ven-dors for hardware? We are locked in to this DBMS. Besides, this kind of software is very inefficient; our programmers can do a better job than any package like this. What will the users gain? How will the company be better off?"

You have been asked to prepare a memorandum with counterarguments to the negative ones presented. What positive features of a database management system do you see? Why would you recommend one to your firm?

10-2. With the explosion of microcomputers in business, a major problem is choosing software for applications like database management. There are probably twenty or more packages that advertise that they are the best DBMS for users. Most organizations do not have the time nor the resources to evaluate all of these claims. How might a firm go about choosing this kind of software?

What are the important issues in comparing and contrasting DBMSs? Where should one start? What is the first step, what are the key evaluation criteria, and who should do the analysis? Develop a plan for determining the needs in a firm for a micro DBMS and describe how you would conduct the analysis.

Once the system has been selected, how would you prepare users to work with it? Is a database management system more difficult to understand and use than a spreadsheet package? Why or why not?

10-3. One of the major design tasks with a DBMS is to learn how different users view the data. Although this may sound a bit obscure, the problem of views is not very difficult to understand, even if it is hard to resolve. Different users have different views of data. For example, a manager of accounting may be primarily interested in history, whereas the marketing analyst wants to forecast trends. The database administrator and the systems designer have to understand the different views and then model them, that is, develop a data structure to support both views. When the analysis is completed, the DBA must figure out the best structure for entry into the database management system.

What do you think the criteria are for picking the "best" structure? What are the different factors that the DBA will try to trade off in coming up with a design? What are the possible costs of selecting an inappropriate design?

REVIEW QUESTIONS

1. What are the major reasons for developing a DBMS?
2. What is a data redundancy?
3. How does a physical data structure differ from a logical one?
4. What is a DBA?
5. What is a data structure?
6. Describe a linked list.
7. What is the difference between a hierarchical data structure and a network structure? A relational structure?
8. Explain how a ring differs from a linked list.
9. What is data independence?
10. Why were programmers reinventing a lot of programming before the development of a DBMS?
11. How does a data dictionary help the DBA?
12. What is a data definition language?
13. What is a database management system?
14. What are the goals of a DBMS?
15. Describe the various components of a DBMS.
16. What is the role of a data base administrator?
17. How does a user work with a query language?

18. What does a join operation do?
19. What is involved in making changes in a sequential file? A direct-access file?
20. What is the database concept?
21. What are access routines provided by a DBMS?

THOUGHT QUESTIONS

22. What are the advantages of a relational database?
23. Why does Mobil Oil need a DBA department?
24. How has a DBMS helped the federal judiciary?
25. In what ways is a DBMS more than just a way to access data?
26. Is a firm likely to place all of its data in a DBMS?
27. What applications do you see for a DBMS on a micro?
28. What features would a micro DBMS need to be useful in developing a complete application?
29. Would a firm be well advised to develop its own DBMS instead of buying one?
30. Design a relational database that keeps track of a professor's list of students in each class taught.

RECOMMENDED READINGS

Allen, F. W., M. E. S. Loomis, and M. V. Mannino. "The Integrated Dictionary/Directory System," *Computing Surveys,* Vol. 14, No. 2 (June 1982), pp. 245–286. A very good article, though somewhat advanced, on data dictionaries; it also provides information on DBMSs in general.

Lucas, H. C., Jr. *The Analysis, Design and Implementation of Information Systems* (3rd ed.). New York: McGraw-Hill, 1985. Contains two chapters on files and database management.

Martin, James. *Computer Data Base Organization* (2nd ed.). Englewood Cliffs, NJ: Prentice-Hall, 1977. A little old, but still a very clear explanation of databases.

Chapter 11

The first computers operated in batch mode in one room of the firm. There were no terminals or connections outside that location. Soon, organizations began to transmit punched cards and magnetic tapes over normal telephone lines using special equipment. The American Airlines Sabre system was the first nationwide on-line application featuring terminals. For this system, communications became a major issue.

Today, computers communicate in a variety of ways. There are several major networks that tie together universities in the United States and abroad. Firms have huge networks spanning the world. A number of communications companies offer their services as common carriers. With the divestiture of AT&T, there is much more competition in the communications business. As this aspect of computing is becoming more and more important, we need to understand the fundamentals of telecommunications.

After reading this chapter, you should be able to:

- Describe how two devices communicate.
- Understand the different types of communications (e.g., synchronous versus asynchronous).
- Describe what is involved in actually sending and receiving data.
- Explain how a network can be formed.
- Contrast a worldwide network with a local area network.

COMPUTER COMMUNICATIONS

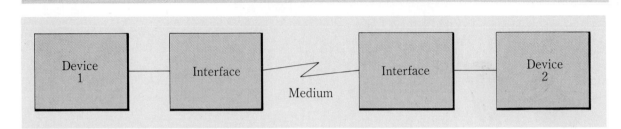

Figure 11-1. General Communications. Communications between devices usually require some kind of interface between the device and the communications medium.

INTRODUCTION

Communications is a fundamental part of organizations; we could not coordinate work or interact with each other without communications. Before the invention of the telephone, communications required messengers to deliver spoken or written messages. The telegraph represented a quantum leap in speed and distance; once there were telegraph wires, humans could communicate across thousands of miles in a few minutes.

The telephone again increased the ease of communicating; it was faster than the telegraph because there was no need to code or decode the message. In addition, people could talk with each other and communicate information by the tone of their voices.

Business today thinks of the telephone as an essential part of the office; it would be hard to imagine working in an industrialized nation without easy access to a high-quality telephone system.

DATA COMMUNICATIONS

As we have discussed, the first computers processed data in batch mode at one point in time. As some organizations had data at one site that were needed at another, vendors invented devices that would send the information on a deck of punched cards electronically over the phone line to a receiving terminal that punched a duplicate set. One central office, for example, might accept orders from customers. That office punched the orders on cards and sorted the cards according to the factory that produced the item ordered. At night, the computer operator at the central office would call the computer center at each of the factories and transmit its cards. Compared with what is done today, this approach seems rather crude, but it is an example of early data communications.

When the first systems appeared that featured remote terminals connected directly to a computer (the on-line reservations systems), a whole new era in data communications began. (Technically the first on-line systems were for air defense, but of course these were not seen by the general public.) At about the same time, users began to connect terminals to time-sharing computers over phone lines.

Today, a tremendous volume of data is transmitted over a variety of communications paths. Not only do terminals communicate with computers, but there is much communication between computers. A clear industry trend is for this kind of communication to increase. The U.S. will soon have a greater volume of data communication than voice communication.

In this chapter, we shall discuss some of the fundamentals of data communications. Figure 11-1 is a basic diagram of communications among machines. The area is highly specialized; a company that has extensive data communications needs a staff of individuals who are expert in this field. All that we can do here is explain the general concepts involved in this important area.

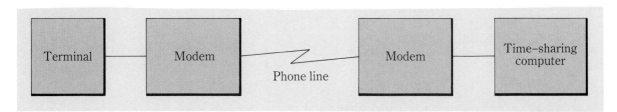

Figure 11-2. Example of Communications. For a terminal connected to a time-sharing computer we could use a device called a modem as the interface and a voice-grade phone line as the medium.

FUNDAMENTALS

In the simplest kind of communications, a terminal is connected to a computer. The transmission line for, say, a time-sharing system may just be an ordinary pair of twisted wires from the terminal to the central computer. Such a terminal is directly wired, or "hard-wired," to the computer. Figure 11-2 shows a terminal connected over a regular phone system to a computer. How do we actually send the data? We must discuss several aspects of communications to answer this question, including the aspects of coding data, transmission, and signaling.

Coding

A *code* must be used to send data over the communications line. As early data communications made use of existing networks, the transmission code was often the same one used by teletypes. (In fact, the early terminals were teletype machines.) The computer may use one code internally and a different one for data transmission. However, as it is important for different computers to be able to communicate, we want a standard transmission code. Unfortunately, there is more than one code, but the number of codes is reasonably small.

The most frequent code used for exchanging data is called *ASCII* (American Standard Code for Information Interchange), which is discussed in Chapter 4. This code has seven bits for data and one bit for error checking. Early computers used BCD (Bi-

nary Coded Decimal), a six-bit code. Finally, IBM uses its EBCDIC code for transmission.

All codes must use a sequence of 1's and 0's for the different symbols in the code, just as in the coding of data in the computer itself. The ASCII code for the letter L is 0011001. The sending unit translates the L into a string of bits for transmission, and the receiving end translates the string of digits back into an L. There may be a relationship between the code used for transmission and the internal code of the computer, but there does not have to be. A great deal of data communication involves code translation.

As an example, using IBM equipment, one communicates with an IBM mainframe using EBCDIC. However, it is possible to place a minicomputer in front of the mainframe that runs a program which accepts ASCII code and translates it into EBCDIC for the mainframe (see Figure 11-3).

When communicating, it is not possible just to send a string of digits over a wire; somehow the encoding device must define what constitutes a *character* and also must provide some error-checking capabilities. A very simple approach to sending one character at a time includes a start bit and a stop bit to delimit the beginning and the end of the character. The start and stop bits tell the receiving unit that what is between them is the character.

For error checking, we can use the same type of parity checking that was discussed with secondary storage in Chapter 9. One extra bit is used to keep the number of bits in the character transmitted ei-

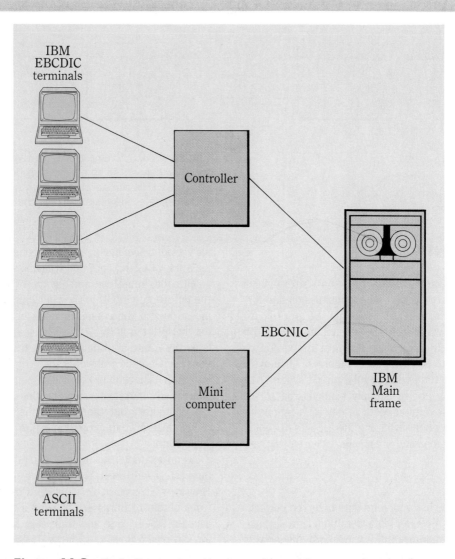

Figure 11-3. Code Conversion. Hardware (the minicomputer) and software make it possible for ASCII terminals to communicate with a mainframe that expects to see EBCDIC code.

ther all even or all odd. If the receiving station finds a parity error, it can ask for a retransmission from the sender. Remember that a simple one-bit parity-checking scheme can detect errors if only if an odd number of bits is missing. More elaborate schemes have been invented not only to signal the presence of an error, but to allow the receiving station to correct the error. These error-correcting codes carry enough redundant information for the receiving end to reconstruct what was sent, even if the message has a large number of erroneous bits.

Transmission

Data are usually transmitted in one of two forms: character or block mode. The simplest is character

Figure 11-4. Summary of Transmission Modes.

TYPE	
Serial	**Block**
One character at a time with start and stop bits	One block at a time
Asynchronous sender and receiver	Synchronized sender and receiver

LINES	
Simplex	one direction
Half duplex	both directions, but one at a time
Full Duplex	both directions simultaneously on 2 lines

mode; here, the data are transmitted as single characters as they are typed on a terminal. This scheme does not require terribly complicated hardware or software.

Block mode transmission requires that the sending device have a **buffer,** that is, a separate memory for the temporary storage of data. The data to be sent are accumulated in the buffer. The sending unit surrounds the block of data with characters that indicate the beginning and the end of the block and with characters for error detection (and possibly correction). If the receiving unit detects an error that it cannot correct, it signals the sending unit to retransmit the message.

When data are sent in character mode, the transmission is known as **asynchronous** because the characters are sent as entered. The method is slow because extra bits are attached at the beginning and the end of the character to delimit it.

Synchronous transmission is used for **blocks** of data that can be sent together. The blocks are of equal length, and one follows the other. There is no need to signal characters by start and stop bits, so

that considerable overhead is saved. Of course, one does have to identify the beginning of a new block. This approach requires that the sending and receiving units be synchronized; they must operate together and at the same speed.

There are a number of other ways to send data over communications lines as well. In simplex transmission, the data are sent only in a single direction, an approach that is relatively rare today. In **half duplex** transmission, data travel in two directions, but not at the same time. **Full duplex** is the most convenient form of interactive transmission, as data are transmitted simultaneously in both directions. Of course, this approach requires two lines because the same line cannot carry signals in two directions at once. Figure 11-4 summarizes the transmission modes.

Signals

Historically, signals were sent in analog form; the electrical signal had a shape that was analogous to the way people communicate by voice. The **voice-**

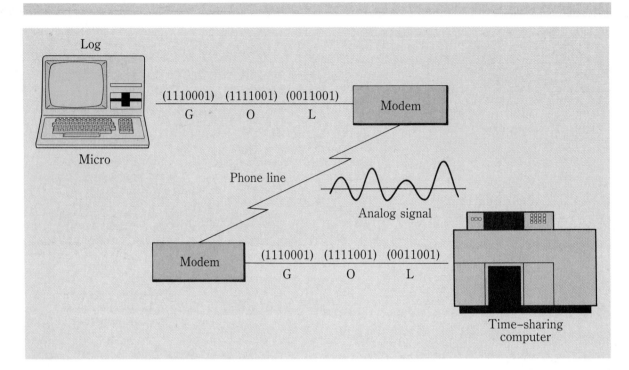

Figure 11-5. A modem changes digital signals from the microcomputer to analog signals for transmission over phone lines. Decoders at the time-sharing computer site change the phone signals back to digital code. When the time-sharing computer sends data to the micro, the operation is reversed.

grade telephone system is **analog** to match the characteristics of the human voice. Because computers communicate using digits, their signal must be converted if conventional phone lines are to used.

The conversion process is called **modulation:** the digital signal is placed on an analog signal for transmission and then demodulated (changed back to a digital signal) at the receiving end. A **modem** (Figure 11-5) is the device that converts the digital signals to analog form and vice versa. Figure 11-6 presents two examples of how modems are used.

In Figure 11-7, we can see how the encoding is done with **amplitude** modulation. The top wave in the figure is the **carrier,** a uniform sine wave that we will alter in some way to encode data. The analog

signal is continuous in the form of a sine wave. When different amplitudes are used to represent a 0 and a 1, the digital data can be encoded for transmission over the analog line. In addition to amplitude modulation, it is possible to encode signals by varying the frequency of the wave or by changing its phase to represent a 0 or a 1.

Now that data transmission has become so important, phone companies and private communications carriers have developed digital transmission networks. In a digital network, there is no need for a modem to transmit digital data. Nevertheless, we do have to have an interface device that is not as elaborate as a modem to connect the communications devices with the line.

a

b

Figure 11-6. (a) A traveling journalist uses a portable computer equipped with a modem to transmit his stories via public telephone to his publisher. (b) A portable computer on a desk communicating with another office via a modem and telephone.

Figure 11-7. Amplitude Modulation. The amplitude (height) of the sine wave is modulated (modified) to encode the presence of a 0 or 1 bit.

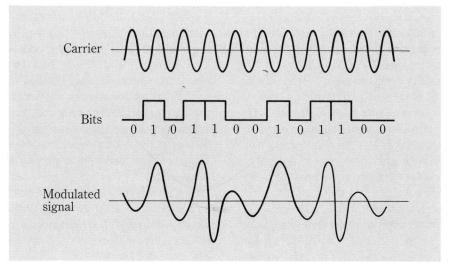

However, if one wants to send voice data, a *vocoder* must be used to digitize the human voice for transmission. This device works by sampling the analog signal at a high rate (thousands of times a second). Each second, the encoder examines the analog wave and represents it using a digit, for example, a digit that represents the amplitude of the analog wave at the point in time when the device observed the wave. The digit is transmitted in binary form, and thus the device has converted an analog signal to a digital one.

Line Speed

Transmission takes place at different speeds; the communications specialist uses a measure of speed called a *baud*. A baud is the number of times per second that the signal changes. It is far easier to think in terms of *bits* or characters *(bytes)* per second transmitted.

Lines that are of subvoice grade transmit from 45 to 150 bits per second, whereas voice-grade lines can transmit a little over 14,000 bits per second, with 9,600 being a popular speed. *Wideband* transmission can reach 230,400 bits per second.

PROTOCOL

When we talk on the phone, we have a simple *protocol.* The person receiving the call usually answers the phone and says, "Hello," to indicate that the phone has been picked up and that the recipient of the call is ready to talk.

The person calling generally says, "Hello, this is so and so calling." Now, both parties know who is on the line and the conversation can go on. Because it is difficult to hear when someone else is speaking, the phone protocol is usually to let the other party finish a thought before beginning ourselves. At the end of the call, the protocol is that one party after the other says, "Good-bye."

If we did not have these social conventions, it would be difficult to use the phone; we would not know, at first, who has called us, nor would we know when the conversation was over. Similarly, when machines communicate, they need some kind of a protocol.

Both the sending and the receiving stations must adhere to the same procedures. If blocks are being transmitted, then both stations must agree that the transmission is to be in block mode. Protocols also increase efficiency of transmission by reducing the control data needed.

Typically, a protocol helps to set up a session, to establish a path from one transmission node to another, to correct and detect errors, to format messages, to control lines, and to sequence messages (see Figure 11-8).

SUMMARY

Computers and computer devices need to be able to communicate with each other. Communication takes place over lines of some type. There may be different modes for transmission, and communication can occur at different line speeds. Digital transmission is efficient for computers, but often analog transmission is used because it is readily available through the phone system.

NETWORKS

There is a great deal of current interest in *networks.* The simplest definition of a network is that it consists of a series of devices and some type of communications capability that allows the devices to communicate with each other over some distance. The network might include only two devices, but usually we think of some number of devices over two. Not all of the devices are necessarily in use at one time. The telephone network is one of the largest networks we encounter every day. All telephones in the country are connected to it in some way, though certainly not all phones are in use at one time.

In a computer network, the devices include some computer(s). The first computer networks were developed when a few *terminals* were connected to time-sharing systems over phone lines. Designers of on-line systems also wanted to have wide-

TERMINAL	COMPUTER

① Terminal sends a message whose text is a single control character—ENQ. This means "I have some data to send to you."

② Computer receives ENQ.

③ Computer acknowledges presence of terminal by responding with a "go ahead" message (ACK0).

④ Terminal receives "go ahead" (ACK0).

⑤ Terminal sends block of data.

⑥ Computer receives block of data and checks for parity errors. If no error, jump to 8.

If an error has occurred, the computer sends a control character (NAK or negative acknowledgement) which says "please retransmit last message."

⑦ Terminal receives NAK and retransmits last message.

⑧ Computer responds with an acknowledgement message (ACK) which says "I received that OK—send me the next message."

⑨ Terminal sends next block of data or, if transmission is complete, sends a control character (EOT—for end-of-transmission) which says "I am finished."

⑩ Computer receives EOT message and terminates its RECEIVE sequence.

Figure 11-8. Typical Data Exchange Using the BISYNC Protocol Between a Terminal and a Computer. A protocol is necessary to coordinate sending and receiving devices.

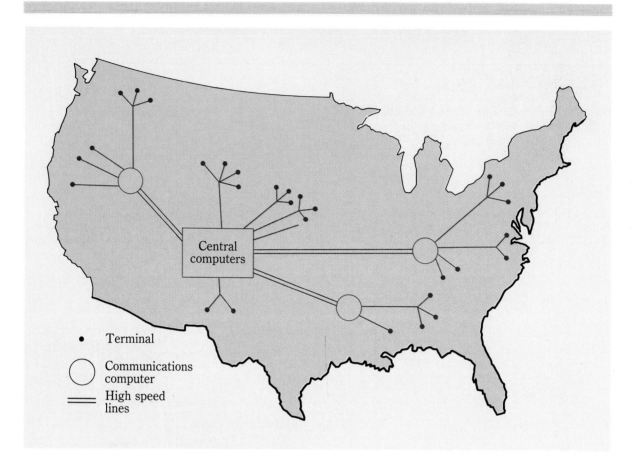

- • Terminal
- ◯ Communications computer
- ═══ High speed lines

Figure 11-9. (a) A Centralized Network. A centralized network with local computers to make communication more efficient.

spread access to their computers, so they constructed a network using leased phone lines across the country connecting terminals to a large central computer. As the number of phone lines grew, designers installed local computers at various places in the network to handle communications with the mainframe, or host. Suddenly, we had many growing networks consisting of computers and terminal devices. See Figure 11-9 for examples of centralized and distributed computer networks.

There are a number of alternatives for creating a network. The simplest is the public, switched network, the one used for carrying most voice traffic. Every time we wish to hold a session (i.e., connect to the computer), we must dial a phone number and make the connection. Telephone, telex, and private **carriers** provide switched service.

Leasing lines is an option when the traffic between points is high. By paying a flat fee, the lessor can use the line as much as is desired for any purpose, voice and/or data transmission. There are also firms that provide something known as **packet switching** (see Figure 11-10). These firms have a network of lines leased from common carriers like AT&T; the

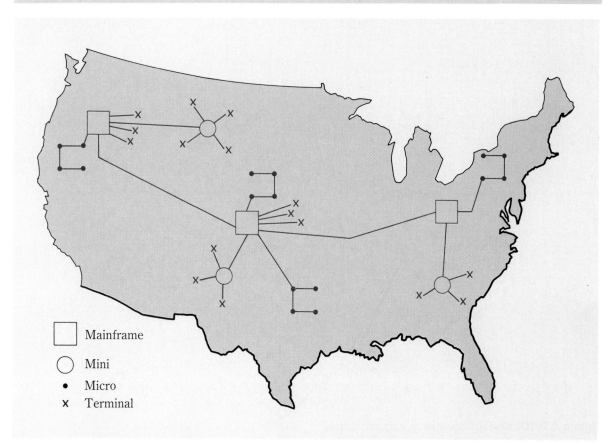

Mainframe

Mini

Micro

x Terminal

Figure 11-9. (b) Various mainframes, minis, and micros are connected with leased communications lines to form a distributed computer network.

user sends a stream of data that the network splits into packets. Each packet has routing instructions, and the network sends it to a destination.

Structure

Given various communications options, we can configure a network of computers and terminal devices in a wide variety of ways. Figure 11-11 shows some popular structures. In a hierarchical scheme, one computer controls a series of subordinate computers; an example of this approach might be a central computer controlling local retail-store com-

puters. The local computers, in turn, control point-of-sale terminals for sales clerks.

A star configuration is similar, but it features a single host computer that can communicate with remote computers. The local computers communicate with each other only by sending messages through the central host.

In a loop or ring all processors can communicate with an immediate neighbor. With the addition of cross-links, the ring can be set up so that any processor can talk to any other processor.

As you can see, there are a lot of options. Given a variety of carriers, as well as tariffs and design con-

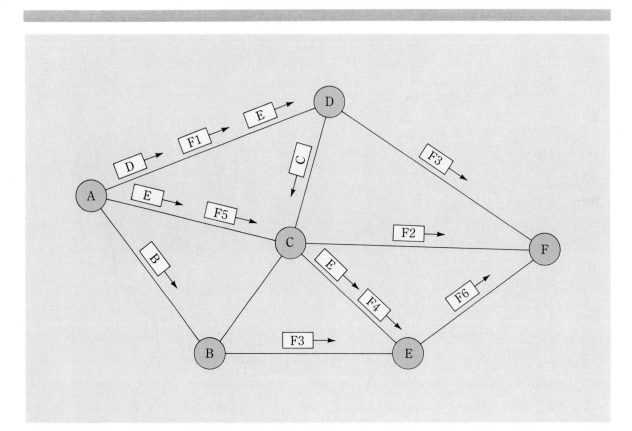

Figure 11-10. Packet Switching. Assuming one-way flow for simplicity, location A has a message for location F. A routes this message over various links. Each node looks at the message address and accepts or forwards the message on the best route at the time. F, the receiving node, must put the message together in the proper sequence.

siderations, firms generally rely on a specialist to help configure a network.

Local Area Networks

A *local area network (LAN)* is a topic of considerable current interest. LANs can be used to connect various devices that need to communicate with each other and that are grouped together (see Figure 11-12). A LAN might be used in a single office building, for example (as shown in Figure 11-13). Devices on the network include not only computers and termi-

nals, but also copying machines, communicating work processors, building alarm sensors, television, and facsimile devices (see Figure 11-14).

LANs have high data rates, in the range of .1 million to 100 million bits per second, but they cover short distances, say, .1 to 50 kilometers. They are expected to have low error rates in transmission.

One of the major advantages of local area networks is resource sharing. With a group of microcomputers connected in a LAN, it is possible for all users to share a high-quality printer and a plotter.

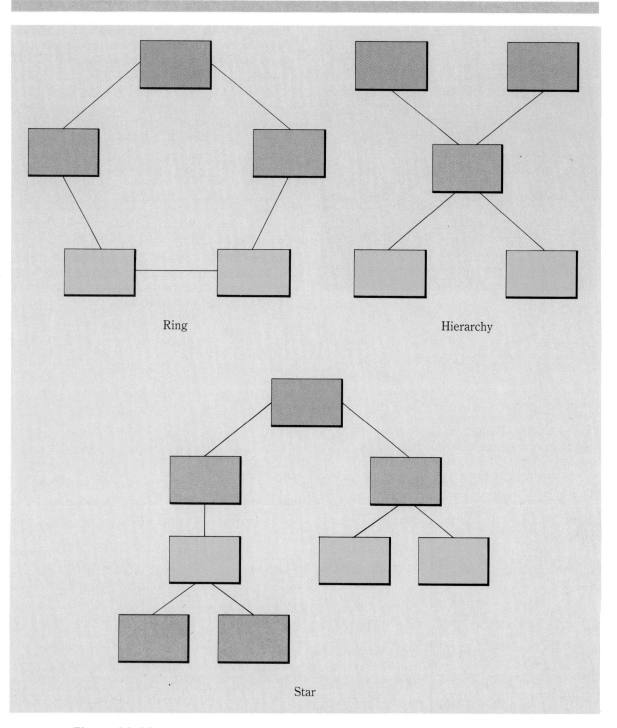

Ring

Hierarchy

Star

Figure 11-11. Network Configurations. This figure presents the most popular network configurations, but there are many combinations and variations possible.

Figure 11-12. A Sytek Corporation LocalNet device which, when combined with appropriate software, can be used to link a network of IBM PCs together.

Figure 11-13. (below) A diagram of how an office might be wired for a local area network. Ethernet is one LAN standard for hardware connection and a protocol for data transmission.

Ethernet is basically a coaxial cable and communications protocol that can be easily installed in a building through ceilings, walls or in existing ducts.

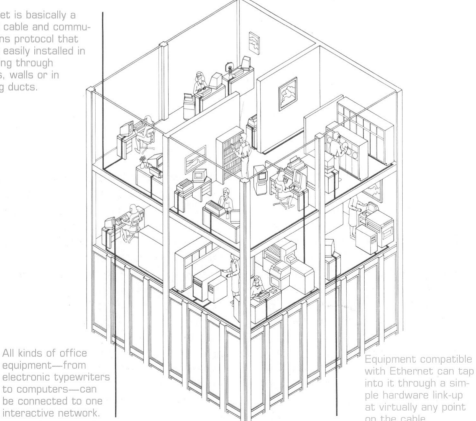

All kinds of office equipment—from electronic typewriters to computers—can be connected to one interactive network.

Equipment compatible with Ethernet can tap into it through a simple hardware link-up at virtually any point on the cable.

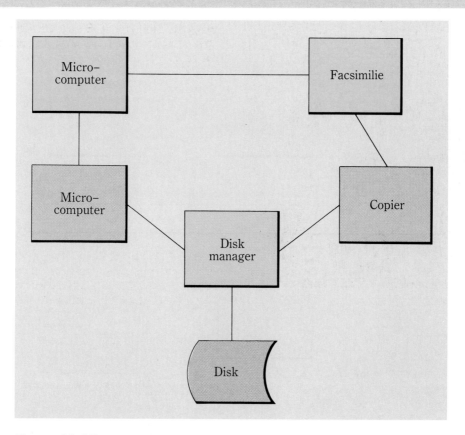

Figure 11-14. Local Area Network. One function of the LAN is to allow several micros to share devices.

There is no need to have one device for each user; instead, the network provides a single device that is shared by all users. For the user, the local area network provides redundancy; if there are ten personal computers and one fails, nine more are available. If we have ten terminals connected to a time-sharing system that fails, all ten users are without service.

Local area networks can be connected to form a pattern that is similar to other communications networks. We can have a star, in which a central device is connected to all other device, or a ring, where each device is connected to its immediate neighbors. Some LANs use a bus (Figure 11-15), which is a single pathway with various devices connected to it. Finally, we can have a tree structure.

Two major types of LANs are discussed today:

baseband and **broadband.** Baseband systems use digital signaling and a bus. (Remember that a bus is simply a transmission path with which various devices are connected.) The length of the network can be a few kilometers. A simple baseband system might consist of twisted paired wires, a very inexpensive cabling approach. This low-cost system also features low performance (say, a data rate of 1 million bits per second) and is connected to up to ten devices over a distance of say, one kilometer. A baseband system using coaxial cable might support a hundred devices with a data rate of 10 million bits per second; devices called *repeaters* are used to extend the length of the network.

A broadband system can stretch up to tens of kilometers. It uses a bus or tree, and all signaling is

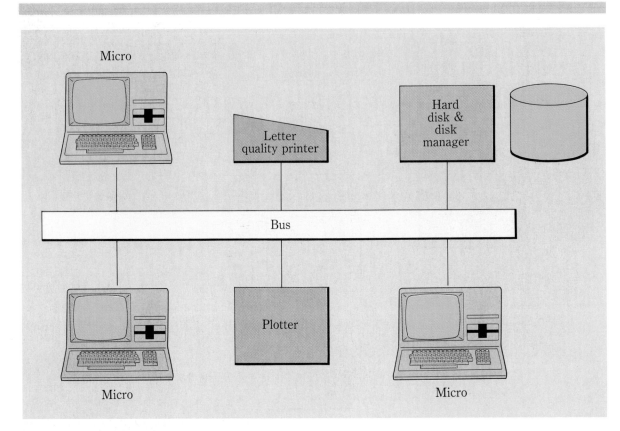

Figure 11-15. A LAN Using a Bus. The bus is a central communications pathway for all of the devices on the network.

analog. These LANs employ frequency-division multiplexing. The frequency spectrum of the cable is divided into channels or sections with various bandwidths. Separate channels are used to support data transmission, for example, TV and radio signals. For certain channels that are reserved for the exclusive use of two devices, transfer rates of 20 million bits per second are possible.

A rapid expansion is expected in the number of local area networks developed in the future. Groups of LANs may be connected to other networks through *gateways*. A user on a local area network could then access data and systems on other, longer-distance networks in addition to sharing devices with other users of the LAN.

Some experts think that the *private branch exchange (PBX)* will be a major competitor of LANs. These exchanges were developed for voice communications only and are used by many firms. The vendors of PBX equipment have designed new models that can transmit digital data as well as voice; thus, they are becoming competitors for the LAN. As most buildings already have phone lines, if the PBX is good at handling digital signals it offers an alternative to running the lines for a LAN.

New PBXs therefore feature digital transmissions so that modems are not needed for the sending of data. Some of these units digitize voice at the PBX,

Figure 11-16. Advertisements from Sytek for its broadband LAN.

and newer systems digitize voice at the telephone instrument itself.

New buildings may be constructed with cables for a local area network and wiring for a PBX. The occupants will have to decide which alternative is best for them. Figure 11-16 presents some suggestions for developing networks from one vendor!

SOURCES OF SERVICE

There is a large number of sources for transmission services. We have already mentioned the public switched network, in which phone lines on the local level connect with AT&T Telecommunications. There are now a number of alternative long-distance carriers besides AT&T. An organization can lease a line or pay by the time the line is in use.

Land lines, **microwave,** and satellites, or a combination of the three, may be used to carry data. Microwave stations were developed after World War II to carry telephone conversations; this high-frequency transmission can carry a great many data on a line-of-sight basis. Microwaves are not reflected by the atmosphere as AM radio signals are; thus, a microwave path consists of a series of towers each of which receives a signal from a previous tower and transmit it to the next tower in line. Each tower must have a straight-line, unobstructed view of the next and previous towers; the towers are in each other's line of sight. One can see microwave antennas on many buildings and repeater stations in rural areas.

Packet-switching companies use leased lines and are known as *value-added carriers* because they add a service or value to the lines leased to carry packets. The customer is likely to be charged by the number of packets sent, rather than by the distance involved. This is a quite different philosophy from the traditional approach of charges for time and distance.

One large bank in New York City has invested tens of millions of dollars in its own private network, expecting to recoup the investment in a few years. This network will carry most of the bank's data and voice traffic, at least within the organization. The bank uses a satellite transponder leased from a provider of satellite channels.

With the deregulation of communications in the United States, there will be many changes in voice and data transmission. Firms like the New York City bank will create private networks, and other organizations will configure a wide variety of networks from the services of different common carriers.

SOFTWARE

The transmission of data depends on software and hardware that work together. The hardware components include terminals, computers that combine signals and transmit them (concentrators and multiplexors), special communications processors, mainframes, minis, and micros.

Software is needed to control the network and the traffic flow, to convert speeds, to convert codes, to detect and correct errors, to format messages, and to perform similar functions. Much of the software for communications can be purchased today in the form of packages. In the mainframe computer, there is usually a piece of systems software known as a **telecommunications handler.** This software takes care of the communications process between terminals and the computer to which they are connected. The programmer has to worry only about the applications software, not the systems functions involved in telecommunications.

Similarly, communications carriers are offering services to attract customers. The carrier would like a customer to be able to connect any device to any computer using the carrier's communications network. To accomplish this task requires a great deal of software to set up communications and control them. It is also necessary to worry about code conversion, so that an ASCII terminal can communicate with an EBCDIC computer without the customer's having to write special software.

There are many options in building a communications network, and more appear every day. Communications are becoming an increasingly important part of the computing environment.

SOME EXAMPLES

Computer vendors are all interested in communications. Hewlett-Packard (HP), a leading maker of minicomputers and microcomputers, has developed a **satellite**-based private network service that it is pricing substantially below competing terrestrial microwave facilities. This satellite service allows HP customers with a particular series of minicomputers to communicate through earth stations (supplied by a company called Vitalink) through a satellite channel provided by Western Union's Westar IV satellite.

The HP computer in question can emulate IBM mainframes, so that users of IBM mainframes can also transmit voice and data over the network.

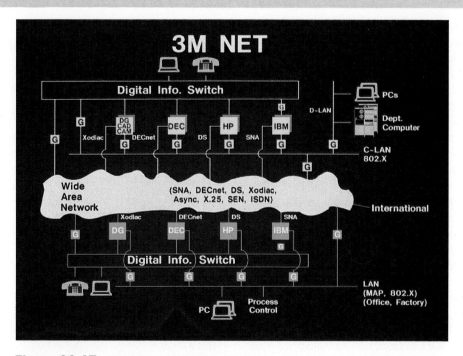

Figure 11-17. Schematic Showing the 3M Company's Corporate Networking System in Overview. Encompassing operations in the United States and 50 subsidiaries outside the U.S., this total information processing system provides communications links via telephone lines, satellite, and long-haul fiber optic networks. Utilizing the private and public switching networks world-wide, the major emphasis of the system is linkage between 3M corporate headquarters in Minneapolis, Minnesota and all other 3M operations so that instantaneous communications can allow access to data entry and acquisition processing systems electronically. This photo is a computer-generated graphic which as of July, 1985 indicates the direction 3M sees its data processing networking to be headed.

Vitalink is a manufacturer of earth stations and a supplier of satellite-based private networks; it has negotiated similar joint ventures with Tandem Computers and Electronic Data Systems, Inc.

Why is HP interested in this kind of arrangement? Vendors want to make it easy for customers to use their products. As there is considerable demand by customers for telecommunications, HP can gain a marketing advantage by providing such a service.

Our next example illustrates how a large firm uses data communications. Minnesota Mining & Manufacturing (3M) is a diversified manufacturer headquar-

tered in St. Paul, Minnesota. The firm began in the sandpaper business in 1902 and now produces goods in more than forty-five product lines; it is the forty-fourth largest U.S. corporation, with sales over $6 billion and eighty-seven thousand employees worldwide.

The firm has a long-range plan to create a unified worldwide computer network (see Figure 11-17). Four systems will be included in the network. The first type will be the mainframe systems. Four large IBM mainframes serve the centralized portion of the company, some twelve thousand workers in St. Paul and ten thousand others in the rest of Minnesota.

3M's second type of computer is a distributed system consisting of more than ninety HP 3000 minicomputers. These computers may be found in plants and branches across the United States. The distributed system handles local processing and communicates with the mainframes in St. Paul.

A third type of system for the network is in-house time-sharing service. For this application, the firm uses eleven DEC 20 mainframe systems. Users control these computers.

The last component of the network, as you might expect, is the company's growing inventory of personal computers. The firm has micros from IBM, HP, and DEC.

Plans call for all four of these computer environments to be connected through a communications network to facilitate the sharing of data and programs.

Another illustration of the importance of communications is M&C Electronics, a subsidiary of Multicorp. M&C has a series of terminals in its stores that are used for inventory control and stock replenishment. As sales are made during the day, the local store uses a dial-up phone line to connect the terminal to a computer in each M&C warehouse. The local store sends the sales that have been recorded by the microcomputers in the cash registers.

The warehouse minicomputer keeps track of the store inventory, as it has a list of all sales and keeps track of the goods that are shipped from the warehouse to the stores. The warehouse computer updates its records of each store's inventory and automatically determines what goods to send to the store to replenish stock.

Because there is no need for continuous updating, the store does not have to transmit more than once a day. The volume of any one store is small enough so that a daylong connection to the warehouse computer would not be justified. Although not a sophisticated network, the system serves M&C quite well.

Review of Chapter 11

REVIEW

Because organizations have adopted computer technology with enthusiasm, we find a need for communications. There are massive amounts of data on-line in files, and there are many individuals who have a need for data at various locations. Users also employ computers to communicate with each other, so that networks become an important part of a firm's control system.

This chapter has presented the fundamentals of communications. We began with a simple terminal connected to a computer and saw how communications took place. The terminal operated asynchronously and in serial mode, sending a character at a time. Block mode transmission is much faster, as larger groups of characters are sent, and the sending and receiving nodes are synchronized. A protocol is required to coordinate communications. Also, software is needed to handle the logic of encoding data at the sending end and decoding it at the receiving end.

Various combinations of communications are built into networks, both worldwide networks and local area networks. Software is needed for networks to control the transmission and routing of messages. A number of common carriers provide communications services. The choice of a carrier and of the services that it offers makes a difference in the hardware and software needed by the organization installing a network. Communications is expected to be one of the fastest growing parts of the computer industry.

KEY WORDS

ASCII	Modulation
Amplitude	Network
Analog	Node
Asynchronous	Packet switching
Baseband	Private branch
Baud	exchange (PBX)
Block	Protocol
Broadband	Satellite
Buffer	Synchronous
Carrier	Telecommunications
Character	handler
Code	Terminal
Local area network	Vocoder
Microwave	Voice grade
Modem	

BUSINESS PROBLEMS

11-1. What is the difference between distributed and decentralized processing? How are they similar? Suppose that a firm features decentralized processing. Is there any need for central coordination of the decentralized locations?

If we allow each local area to make its own decisions on hardware and software, what are the risks? How does decentralized processing change into distributed processing? What are the reasons that a firm might want to develop a network from decentralized sites?

What advantages does a network have for you as a user of computer services? Can you think of any technical problems in making the network operate properly? Make a list of the issues that you think important in building a network and including the computers of a decentralized firm in the net. Given your observations and the list, what recommendations would you give to a company that is not yet ready to develop a network, but that will probably want to configure one in the next four or five years?

11-2. A $2-billion a-year division of a major corporation in the United States just decided to split into eight smaller divisions. The ostensible reason was to provide for more local control over the entire business. Each division head is now like the president of a smaller company.

The first thing that one division president has decided on is to try to become independent in computer processing. Her staff has moved several small systems to local computers. However, the majority of the processing is done at the same large computer center that processed work when the eight divisions were just one.

The problem is that these systems were never designed with the idea of eight divisions. There are plants that make products, for example, for more than one division. No one is sure whether it is possible to move these large systems to the local plants.

How would you approach the problem of helping this firm? What are the steps that the firm should take in conducting research about the systems? What role does company management in this process? What kind of technical questions do you think will arise?

REVIEW QUESTIONS

1. Why did the phone system originally use analog transmission?
2. Why do computers communicate digitally?
3. Define *protocol*.
4. Describe a communications protocol.
5. What is the difference between synchronous and asynchronous transmission?
6. How does block mode transmission differ from serial transmission?
7. What are the advantages of the block mode?
8. Describe the various components of a communications network.
9. What are simplex communications? How are they different from full duplex?
10. What is a PBX?
11. Name two functions of software in communications.
12. What is modulation? Why is it needed?
13. What is a LAN?
14. Explain how data are coded for transmission.
15. What is the difference between the public switched network and a private network?

THOUGHT QUESTIONS

16. How does batch processing differ from on-line computing?
17. How can you use a time-sharing computer to develop an on-line, dedicated application?
18. What are the advantages of an eight-bit code?
19. Draw sine waves of different amplitude, frequency, and phase.
20. Why might we use serial communications for a time-sharing terminal?
21. What are the advantages of voice-grade lines for time-sharing?
22. Draw one network configuration and describe an application for it.
23. What is the difference between a LAN and a PBX?
24. Why might a firm develop its own private communications network?
25. Why can a local area network do without a host computer?
26. How might a university use a LAN?
27. What are the advantages and disadvantages of satellite communications?
28. Why do we need communications specialists?
29. What are the advantages to the user of a computer network?
30. What is the role of a personal computer in a large network?
31. What is the role of the mainframe in a network?
32. What does a personal computer need to be able to connect to a network?
33. How can a home computer take advantage of communications?

RECOMMENDED READINGS

Houseley, T. *Data Communications and Teleprocessing Systems.* Englewood Cliffs, NJ: Prentice-Hall, 1979. A basic book on communications.

Loomis, M. *Data Communications.* Englewood Cliffs, NJ: Prentice-Hall, 1983. This introductory book has an interesting history of the industry.

Stallings, W. "Local Networks," *Computing Surveys,* Vol. 16, No. 1 (March, 1984), pp. 3–41. An excellent paper, though somewhat technical and advanced, on the types of local networks.

Part III

Now, as experts on the technology, we can think about how to apply computers to solving business problems. It sounds easy, but we leave the certainty of hardware and software and move into the more nebulous and creative area of design.

Information systems process information, a simple statement. However, information itself is abstract, and so are the procedures that one uses to process it. For this reason, the approach to designing a computer system must be imaginative and creative. We must work with individuals to find out what their processing needs are and then try to develop new ways to accomplish that processing. Because creativity is needed, the systems design task is best accomplished through a project team.

Chapter 12 presents the systems life cycle and describes what has to be accomplished at each step. You will probably find the life cycle and the design process vague. Do not expect the precision you would find in a cookbook; the recipe for systems analysis and design is not as well formulated as the one for your favorite dish.

We will advocate structuring the process to the extent possible. Some of the tools we introduce, called *data flow diagrams* and *top-down design,* will help in this structuring process. However, there is still a great deal of creativity involved in design, and it is very difficult to teach creativity.

We have found that systems designed following the classic life cycle take a long time; often, they are over budget and do not meet the original specifications when finally finished.

The time and resources required to build systems in the conventional way have created a huge bottleneck. Users are waiting several years just to have an application started, much less finished. Not only is there a long list of applications waiting for attention, there are many applications that have yet to be suggested because the users are so discouraged.

Chapter 13 presents several modern approaches that attempt to circumvent the custom systems-designed process presented in Chapter 12. Many systems require the conventional approach. However, the trend

SYSTEMS ANALYSIS AND DESIGN

today is to try first to find an alternative, and then to turn to custom development if it is the only answer.

To make this section as concrete as possible. Chapter 14 presents in some detail an example of the logical design (a description of how the system works) of an application. The system is for a chain of Multicorp computer stores. It focuses on inventory control and runs on a personal computer in each store. The application is an example of something called *distributed processing* because the personal computer communicates with a larger computer in the company's warehouse once or twice a day.

The data flow diagrams and input screens seen by the users should help make clear what is meant by the logical design of an information system. We firmly believe that users should be able to participate in systems analysis and design. They should be able to understand and communicate at the level of detail presented in Chapter 14.

Chapter 12

We have seen numerous examples of systems up to this point. Some systems have helped airlines control reservations and other aspects of their businesses, and others have aided the federal courts in complying with laws requiring a speedy trial. All of these systems have one thing in common: they were developed by human beings working together. There is no magic to the design process; it is an intellectual, creative human task.

This chapter should help you to develop an understanding of what is required to build a system. However, do not expect that reading about it will make it easy. There is no substitute for being involved in the design of a system to learn what it is all about. We can talk about it, provide some checklists, and make recommendations. Only participation in design will prepare you for the number of details involved and provide an appreciation of how important human considerations are in this process.

After reading the chapter, you should be able to:

- Describe the steps in the systems life cycle.
- Explain the differences between some of the alternatives for a system.
- Describe how systems design impacts the four components of a system presented earlier.
- Discuss the role of the user in systems design.
- Explain why feasibility studies are not as important as they once were.
- Describe the results of each stage in the life cycle.
- Explain why several alternatives should come from the process of constructing specifications.

BUILDING A SYSTEM

INTRODUCTION

We have seen a lot of systems, but it is probably a good idea to review the definition of a **system** before proceeding. A system is a set of interrelated components that work together to accomplish some goal. In a computer-based information system, the computer is used to help control or analyze data for the organization.

It is difficult to avoid confusion with the term *computer system,* which can be either a collection of hardware or an application, such as the processing of a payroll. It is unfortunate that the terminology is used so loosely, but the context of the discussion is usually adequate to disclose its meaning. This chapter generally discusses applications systems; the application makes use of a computer system to help in processing data.

The term *system* is confusing for another reason as well. There are really hierarchies of systems. For example, consider the transportation system as a whole; it is made up of numerous subsystems like ground transportation, railroads, and airlines.

Depending on our focus, we might actually define the system of interest as being rail traffic, and we might consider passenger train travel a subsystem. The point is to keep clearly in mind the environment and the system under discussion.

COMPONENTS OF A SYSTEM

Very early in the book, we discussed the four major components of computer-based systems (see Figure 12-1). How does the process of building a system create or impact each of these components? The **organization** is usually given; it provides the environment in which the system will be designed. In many ways, it is the key to the design process, yet the designer may not have much influence on it. The organization provides the need for the system and the resources to build it. Unfortunately, the organization can also provide resistance to the new application and can offer conditions that are not conducive to design.

As an example, suppose the firm is terribly understaffed, so that key individuals are working sixty hours a week. How can these people contribute to the design of a new system? How can the designer interview them and obtain their input if the designer needs twenty hours a week of their time? The organization may also say that it needs a major computer system to remain competitive, but it may then provide too little in the way of funds for computer equipment and staff.

In the design process, the designer interacts with the organization and depends on it. This person, or team, has a tremendous impact on the firm, at least on certain types of systems. We shall discuss this impact further in Chapter 19. Do not forget to assess the **environment** in which a system is being designed before beginning work.

Next in Figure 12-1 we find the **user.** One task is to identify the individuals who will interact with a system because they are crucial to its design. Although this identification does not sound complicated, as a system is designed and various pieces are added to it new users appear. We might begin with an inventory system that involves warehouse personnel and accounting. Then, the design team decides that the system should really be tied to order entry as well, so all of the staff in order processing suddenly become potential users.

We have found that the more heavily users are involved in the design of a computer system, the more successful the system is. Therefore, it is very important to form a design team on which the users having a significant representation. In fact, some firms actually place a user in charge of the design process, demonstrating again why non-information-systems-specialists need to understand systems design.

Users also have to define and follow procedures for a system to work. If an order entry application replaces a manual process, using paper forms, with a computer-based system and CRTs, a large number of procedures will be new and different. The design team must consider these changes and prepare the users for them.

The third component of a computer system is the **application,** the use of a computer to solve some information-processing problem. The application is

COMPONENTS	SYSTEMS ANALYSIS AND DESIGN
Organization	Usually given

User
   Individuals
   Procedure
	Must be identified
	Include in design, to be specified and
	   possibly redesigned

Application
   Logic
	What has to be designed
	Core of the program design process
	Key part of human system
	
	May be given or acquired
	Must specify where processing takes
	   place, where data are located, what
	   software is used

...onents of an Application and the Design Process.

...rforms, for ...the payroll, ...r that plans ...the context ...h the appli-

...n to create ...-processing ...application ...f computer programs, however; it also includes all of the manual procedures and the tasks of the user. Sometimes, systems designers think only of the application and the technology; it is very important to look at all the components of our model and not to forget the organization or the user.

The fourth component of our systems model is the underlying *technology*. Technology may be a given; management may say that a new system is to operate on existing computer hardware and with current software. Although a constraint, such a requirement might actually be a blessing. Why? Because there are so many ways of undertaking processing. However, in most instances, the design team has to decide what kind of technology is appro-

priate. Existing hardware and software will be available, as will the alternative of acquiring new hardware for the system being developed.

THE SYSTEMS LIFE CYCLE

It is helpful to think of a system as having a life consisting of different stages. Normally, one talks about the systems life cycle, from inception through maturity. (Systems rarely seem to die.) The life cycle has the following steps:

Inception. A user determines that the potential exists to solve a problem using a computer-based system. There is a *preliminary needs analysis* at this point that shows whether the idea is worth pursuing.

Feasibility Study. Many organizations require a formal study to determine if a system is feasible or not, that is, whether there will be a payback, including intangible benefits, that exceeds costs. With today's technology, one can almost always find some way for a computer to help. The issue is which alternative for processing is the most advisable.

Systems Analysis. The first task in systems analysis is to understand present processing procedures. Once the current of processing information has been digested, we enter the requirements analysis phase, which is when systems analysts and users work together to specify the logic of the system.

Specifications. The requirements analysis gradually evolves into a series of specifications for a new computer-based system. The specifications must show the processing logic, the database contents, the input and output required, the structure of the major programs, and the manual procedures associated with processing.

Programming. If the system involves custom programming, it is undertaken during this stage.

Testing. The system must be tested; the users provide the data, and the computer staff attempts to test all aspects of the system. Testing involves locating errors and correcting them.

Training. Systems require new procedures; if the changes are major, then effort must be devoted to training the users, who will have to learn new ways of doing their work.

Conversion. When all is ready, it is time to convert to the new system, to begin using it for regular processing.

Operations. When the computer operations staff accepts a new system, it becomes operational. The operations staff has to agree that the major errors are repaired and that they can maintain the system. *Maintenance* involves some fixing of errors, but its major function is actually enhancing the system, adding new features as the users see the need for improvements.

Figure 12-2 shows the results that one might expect from each stage in the life cycle; this illustration provides an idea of what has to be accomplished as design proceeds.

If a potential new system is brought up informally in a meeting, the results from the inception phase may be nonexistent. More likely, a memorandum will make a broad suggestion for some type of computer application. This initial idea leads to the feasibility study.

Instead of a formal analysis of whether a system is feasible, we recommend that the organization sketch several different alternatives and comment on the desirability of each. We shall discuss how to construct the alternatives later. Each alternative is compared on what it will cost and on the benefits it will provide, particularly the way in which it will accomplish the goals of the users who asked for the system in the first place. Often, we do find a formal document here.

Systems analysis means understanding what the system does. The flowcharts and data flow diagrams discussed in this chapter and in Chapter 14 are one way of documenting the operations of the present system. The analysis of the system generally includes the information flows, the data storage requirements, the volume of data, the format of the data, and the structure of the existing relationships among data items.

We will also include in the analysis a list of desired features for the new system. These features will probably be rough at this point, possibly a list of requests for processing and some new reports or the ability to access data in new ways. Some of these requests will be quite detailed; for example, the accounting department may want a list of all items in inventory that have been declared surplus. Later, the designers will have to figure out how to provide such a report; at this time, it goes on the systems wish list.

Specifications are developed as a part of the design of the new system. This stage of the life cycle and part of the analysis stage are often called *requirements analysis* because the designers are determining the requirements for a new computer application. This stage is the creative part of design; this is where the designers build a new system, at least in the form of some written specifications.

The systems analysts develop a complete set of specifications for the programmers. For the users,

STAGE	RESULTS
Inception	Memorandum on need for a system
Feasibility Study	Becoming optional; comparison of several alternatives, costs vs. benefits
Systems Analyses	Informal memos and reports documenting information flows, data storage, volume, format, structure, processing (who does what, when?), desired features
Specifications (Requirements)	Creative part of design: What functions are included? What is the logic of processing? Database logic Manual procedures
Programming	Prepare program and/or purchase package, monitor progress, manage project
Testing	Program modules, Acceptance tests
Training	Prepare documents
Conversion	Plans for cutover to new system
Operations	Maintenance, change requests

Figure 12-2. Results of Design.

the specifications are more likely to be at the functional level. What functions is the system to perform? What is the logic of each one? An example might help us to understand what is meant by *logic.*

Suppose that we are developing a new order-entry system. The specifications for entering an order might look like the following:

1. A clerical staff member opens orders arriving in the mail and edits them for completeness. A staff member adds up the total number of items ordered and the dollar amount of the order.
2. The order is transmitted to an operator at a CRT. The CRT has several functions shown on a menu.
3. The CRT operator chooses the menu item for entering an order.
4. The operator enters the customer's number.
5. The system responds with the customer's name and address, which the operator checks against the order.
6. The operator enters the item number of each item on the order and the quantity ordered.
7. The system looks up the price on a file and prices out the item, displaying the results on the order form on the screen.
8. At the completion of the processing of the order, the operator enters the total computed by the staff member in Step 1 for the number of items ordered and the dollar amount.
9. The computer checks the manually computed total with the total it computed from the order when it was entered.
10. The operator corrects any discrepancies before going on to the next order.

Note that specifications show system logic and manual procedures. The specifications would also include details on the design of the *database:* What are the contents of the files? What are the sizes of the data items? Where do they originate? How are they related? What queries will users make? We shall see an example of rather complete logical specifications for a system for Multicorp in Chapter 14.

If the system to be designed will be programmed, there is a need to prepare program specifications and/or to purchase a package. The programming task will generate a great deal of output beyond the programming specifications. Usually, the task of turning the design team's logical design into programming specifications is done by a systems analyst.

During programming, the programmers should develop documentation for their programs. *Documentation* refers to written information on how the program works. There is no industry standard for such documentation, and the extent to which it is prepared varies widely from organization to organization.

In testing, the programmers prepare documents that specify how the programs are to be tested and what test data are to be used. The results of the tests should also be documented; that is, a record should be maintained of what programs have been tested and how. The user should also be heavily involved in developing the specifications for and carrying out the *acceptance tests.* These tests, as the name implies, are designed so that the users can evaluate the system. If the system passes the tests, it means that users find the system acceptable.

During programming and testing, the systems analyst in the Computer Department responsible for the system must monitor progress. This individual may use some kind of formal project-management system or tool such as the *critical path method.* This project-management approach represents a project as a network; various events are represented by nodes and lines showing what event has to precede and follow each other event. The manager uses a program to calculate what activities will take the longest, and this becomes the "critical path" through the network, or diagram. The manager watches the critical activities carefully because if they fall behind schedule, the project will definitely be delayed.

A number of project management tools are available. Basically, analysts and programmers working on the project provide estimates of the time required for each task in the design and then indicate their weekly progress toward completing the task. The project management system alerts the project manager to problems so that he or she can reallocate resources to provide extra help where deadlines will not be met.

During training, we will need documents to be used as training materials. Also, it is helpful to have procedures manuals so that the users can consult them when a question arises. However, newer systems that are on-line often feature "help" keys, so that questions can be answered from the terminal. Designers have become more skilled in developing on-line menus and input forms, so that users require less training and questions arise less frequently than with some older systems.

The conversion stage usually includes a plan for the *cutover* to the new system. To use a new system, it is often necessary to collect data to go into the new system's files and to train users on new procedures. An organization often converts to a new system gradually, one geographic area at a time.

During operations, a whole set of procedures is specified by the Computer Department for requesting maintenance and enhancements. Remember that operational systems usually have to be changed while they are being used. Of course, the better the design, the fewer the change requests.

TRADE-OFFS

The discussion of hardware and software in Chapters 4 and 8 covered the topic of trade-offs. A *trade-off* exists when two variables have to be balanced against each other. The task of designing a system is replete with trade-offs, often some feature being traded off with cost. For example, we might want a very fast response time for an application. However, programming the application for a mainframe may be very expensive compared to the use of a slower system on a microcomputer.

Such a trade-off is at a fairly high level; it will de-

Where do the data originate? Where is the data processed? Who needs access to data? At what locations?		
Centralized	**Distributed**	**Decentralized**
Data originates in many locations. Access needed on-line	Some local and some centralized data processing	Data originates and is processed locally, limited sharing with other locations. Special packages

Figure 12-3. Generating Alternatives for Processing. One of the most difficult management decisions today is how much local control to allow over information processing.

termine what computer will be used in processing. Trade-offs also exist at the very detailed design level. An experienced user might want to have very terse commands, whereas the novice wants complete instructions in the system menus. Here, trade-off exists between efficiency of use and the degree of explanation provided. Designers and users must decide what to provide for the user interface, the interaction between the system and the user, in such a case.

The actual practice of design, then, involves developing ideas, features, and functions and then discussing various alternatives. We would expect to find compromise, negotiation, and probably a number of changes as the design process proceeds. For most of these decisions, there is no "right" answer; instead, the designers and the users pick a compromise that they can all accept.

HARDWARE AND SOFTWARE CONSIDERATIONS

Processing Configurations

One of the very difficult decisions in design today is what kind of technology to employ and where it should be located. Chapter 11, on communications,

described different ways of configuring computers. The design team has to select the appropriate organization and technology for the system. The range of organizational alternatives is outlined in Figure 12-3.

The basic questions for the design team are these: Where do the data originate and where are they processed? Who and at what locations needs access to the data? A centralized configuration makes sense when the data originate in many locations and access is needed on-line from a lot of different places. A good example is a centralized airline-reservations system.

On the other hand, we might find that the data originate and are processed locally and that there is only limited sharing among locations, as in a holding company with a number of local businesses. All the holding company cares about is a monthly set of financial statements. Such an environment suggests decentralized processing. Another reason for decentralized processing would be to purchase a software package or a combined hardware/software solution to a unique problem. One manufacturing company bought a complete minicomputer system for quality control for a single plant. There was no need to share data or to use the system at another location.

Distributed processing occurs when there is a combination of centralized and decentralized computing and some kind of communications is involved.

Number of users	Number of simultaneous users	Number of transactions	Number of file accesses to process transactions	Response time requirements	Communications requirements	Data base size

Figure 12-4. Hardware Capacity Considerations. These demands have a significant impact on the performance of a computer system.

Because this configuration provides some of the advantages of both centralized and decentralized processing and a lot of flexibility, it has become very popular.

Is there always a right configuration? The answer is most assuredly "no." With so many options available, from supercomputers to micros, it would be difficult to claim that one particular plan is better than all others. Instead, just as implied in the discussion of trade-offs for design features, the designers will have to generate some different processing alternatives and reach a consensus on what looks as if it will work best. Given the trends in computing, the most likely configuration of hardware in the future will consist of large mainframes in a network with smaller computers; the smaller local computers will have significant processing power and will do a lot of work locally. Data will be shipped around the network where they are needed for processing. For many users, the location at which computing is done will not be apparent in the future; processing will simply happen someplace on the network.

Capacity

Once the desired configuration for processing is decided on, one key question remains: How much capacity does the technology have to provide? Figure 12-4 is a list of some of the things that one must

consider in coming up with adequate capacity for the technological component of a system.

The number of users influences how large and powerful a system is needed. Of course, what the users will be doing is also important. For example, how many of them will use the computer simultaneously? For what tasks? Will they be updating files or just making inquiries? What kind of a load will the users place on the system?

In acquiring a computer to process transactions for a company, the buyer has to consider the number and types of transactions that the system will have to process. An important determinant of the size necessary for a system is the number of file accesses required to process each transaction. How fast a computer do we need in order to have fast enough disk files to process the work load?

Performance is often viewed by users as being synonymous with *response time.* What is the objective: 90 percent of responses within four seconds, six seconds, or ten seconds (slow)? What are the communications requirements of the applications running on the computer? How large is the database? Some small computers have a maximum amount of disk space; if the planned use for the new computer suggests more data than it can store, a larger-capacity machine will be needed.

In the early days of computing, we were concerned with raw hardware speed and size. Today,

ALTERNATIVES

Criteria	Weight	Mainframe Package		Local Microprocessor		Local Micro Connected to Microframe	
		Score	Result	Score	Result	Score	Result
% User needs met	.35	6		5		7	
Cost	.15	3		5		4	
Time to implement	.20	6		5		4	
Expansion capacity	.30	4		6		6	

Figure 12-5. Alternative Systems Architecture. One way to compare alternatives for a particular application is with a numerical weighting scheme. The final totals should not be automatically accepted. Instead, review the scores to see where each alternative seems best.

the performance of a computer system depends heavily on both the underlying hardware and the software. Computer vendors and the buyer's professional computer staff can help estimate the demands that will be placed by a system on the underlying technology of hardware and systems software.

Capacity is a major issue for on-line systems, where a lack of capacity can mean that work will not be done and/or that response times will degrade to unacceptable levels. (The response time is the time that elapses between the user's pressing a key and the computer's response.) As Figure 12-4 indicates, response time and performance are influenced by the number of users and transactions that the system is supposed to process. Also important in determining capacity is the size of the database and the complexity of inquiries and updates. A system that does mostly retrievals with limited updates, like one that answers information queries on telephone numbers, makes a relatively light demand on a processor. Updating is very simple and does not happen often in this telephone application. A system that updates information constantly, like one that processes airline reservations, has a quite different set of processing demands.

PROVIDING ALTERNATIVES

Throughout the design discussion, we have stressed alternatives and trade-offs. For many years, design teams and users have been faced with the choice of taking a large, comprehensive new system or keeping their old procedures. With so many ways of processing information today, the question is not whether the proposed system is feasible, but what approach to helping the user seems best.

There is no one answer to this question because circumstances are always changing. Remember that one important component of a system is the organization and its environment. It is very possible that whereas the user would like a very comprehensive new application, the organization cannot supply it. Possibly, the systems staff is already committed to other projects, so our user will have to wait two years before work on her or his project begins. Under these conditions, the user may well opt for an application that is far less comprehensive, but that can be implemented quickly.

Figure 12-5 shows how a design team might go about describing and evaluating different options for a system. The criteria on the left indicate what the users see as being important considerations, and the weights indicate how important each criterion is. For example, the percentage of user needs met has received the highest weight, .35.

Across the top of the figure are three ways in which a proposed application might be implemented. The first is a mainframe package, the second a local microcomputer, and the last a local microcomputer connected to the mainframe. Each alternative is scored on the criteria in a range of 1 to 7 points. To get a score for each alternative, the weights are multiplied by the score, and the totals are summed for each alternative.

The design team would not use the final scores as the absolute decision. Rather, they would use the analysis as a decision aid to call attention to places where one alternative looks superior to another. At the end of this exercise, the objective would be for the design team to develop a consensus on which alternative to implement.

A NEW VENTURE

We could continue with more details on the design process. However, at this point, it would be more interesting to look at some users actually trying to design a system. Their efforts illustrate what managers and users must do in the design process. We expect that most readers of this text will work with computers as users and managers, rather than as computer professionals. You will probably want more details on the system being designed here, and they will appear in Chapter 14.

Multicorp has decided to use its knowledge of systems to develop a new business, a chain of retail computer stores selling microcomputers and software. The first stores will be on the East Coast, and there is to be a warehouse on the outskirts of Philadelphia in Cherry Hill, New Jersey.

The cast of characters in the new venture includes Mary Hardy, a systems analyst for the new division, which is called Computerware. The VP and manager of operations for Computerware is Jon Martin, and the president is Kathy Levin. Dave Adams is the warehouse manager of the Cherry Hill location.

To illustrate the process of systems analysis and design, we shall follow discussions at Computerware as these individuals work on developing a system to serve their new business.

Inception

The group is meeting to discuss what kind of systems they will need in order to run the new business.

Kathy began, "I asked the four of you here because we need a system in place before we can begin operations. That means we have to hurry."

Mary responded, "It also means that we do not have an existing system to analyze."

"What do you mean?" asked Dave.

"Nothing is in place now, so we will have to work on past experience and new ideas. When we have an existing system to analyze it is a little easier to figure out what everyone will want in a new one."

Dave interjected, "That's not completely true. We have begun to develop procedures, and I just came from another company where I was the assistant manager of a distributor's warehouse for electronic products. I have a pretty good knowledge of our problems and information needs there."

Jon added, "We shall just have to be creative."

"One good thing," said Mary, "is that this kind of situation will keep you all involved."

"OK, but where do we start?" asked Jon.

"First we need to specify the boundaries of the system. What should it encompass?"

"Let me start," Dave began. "I want to record goods as they arrive, review orders, and ship the goods. That means a system has to tell me what the orders are. I also have to know what to reorder and when."

"It sounds to me as if we need an order entry system," thought Jon aloud, "and if we are doing that, then let's also add accounts receivable to keep track of what our customers owe us."

Mary sighed, "That's a lot of systems. Are you sure you need it all, at least right away?"

Kathy entered the conversation: "Yes, we need it, but I am not sure it has to be ready for us to open for business."

"Why don't we concentrate on inventory? Our orders will be small, and they will come only from our own stores. That should be easy to handle. I just want to be sure that we can control stock."

"OK," Mary said, "I see a compromise coming. Let's work on specifications for the inventory system, and we'll look for a package at the same time for order entry, and even later for accounts receivable."

The group has been trying to set a boundary on what will be done in total, and then to put priorities on the various components. Unless they are very lucky and find a quite comprehensive software package, it will be necessary to attack the problem a subsystem at a time. One of the hard things to learn in developing systems is that we cannot do it all, at least not all at one time.

Feasibility

Several weeks later, Mary, Jon, and Dave met. Mary spoke first. "Jon, for a system like this, do we need a formal feasibility statement?"

"What do you mean?"

"Something showing costs and benefits and a sketch of the system. You know, to impress management that there will be some return from investing in the system."

"No, we are on our own," replied Jon. "We all feel that we need a system. I suppose each of us has a point at which it would be too costly, but quite frankly, given the technology, we have to be able to find something to help the stores at a reasonable price. Anyway, we want to create the image of being a high-technology marketing organization. We can't do that if our stores feature all manual systems."

"What we see today are very few systems that are not feasible. Just how much do you want to include? How fancy and complete you want to be will determine the final cost."

"I would like options, you know, bare bones with so many features versus Plan B with so much more added to the base."

"That we can do, but first we need some analysis and specification of what the system is supposed to do."

"OK, where do we begin? Don't you just design something?" asked Dave.

Mary responded, "No, that doesn't seem to work. I guess I'm just not that smart. What I want to do is to teach you how to draw some logic charts because you understand the business process better than I do."

"I don't like that. We shouldn't have to work that hard!"

Jon added, "Well, it makes some sense; you and I know warehouse management, at least we're supposed to."

Flowcharts

The earliest type of documentation for a computer application is the *flowchart.* Figure 12-6 shows flowchart symbols; Figure 12-7 shows a flowchart of a process. The idea is to make it easy for someone to understand complex procedures by drawing a flow of information and indicating the major processing done on it.

In newer approaches, the charts are more structured; one of these is something called a *data flow diagram (DFD).* This approach uses a relatively small number of symbols (see Figure 12-8). With the DFD, the person making the chart tries first to develop a very high level diagram and then to move to more details at each step. Figure 12-8 shows a first-level chart for inventory, and Figure 12-9 goes to one more level of detail. Jon and Dave prepared these charts after brief instructions from Mary.

The advantage of working from the top level down is that it makes the system easier to follow. It is very difficult to plunge into a highly detailed design. Consider an architect designing a building. The building plans do not begin at the greatest level of detail. Instead, the drawings usually show a view of the entire building. The next page might be side views, followed by a floor plan. Finally, we get to details on plumbing, ventilation, and electrical wiring.

Data flow diagrams are a part of a recent approach to building systems called *structured design.* The objective is to place some constraints on the design process to make it more disciplined and less chaotic.

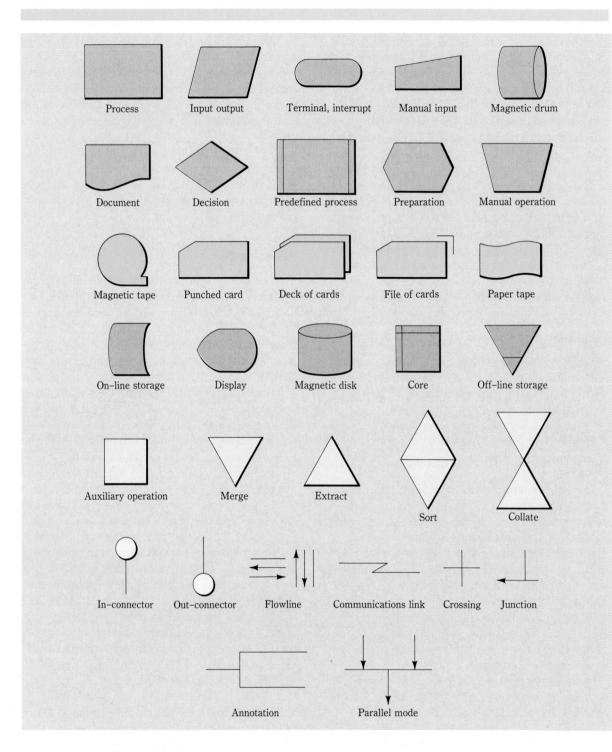

Figure 12-6. Examples of Flowchart Symbols (from the ANSI Standard).

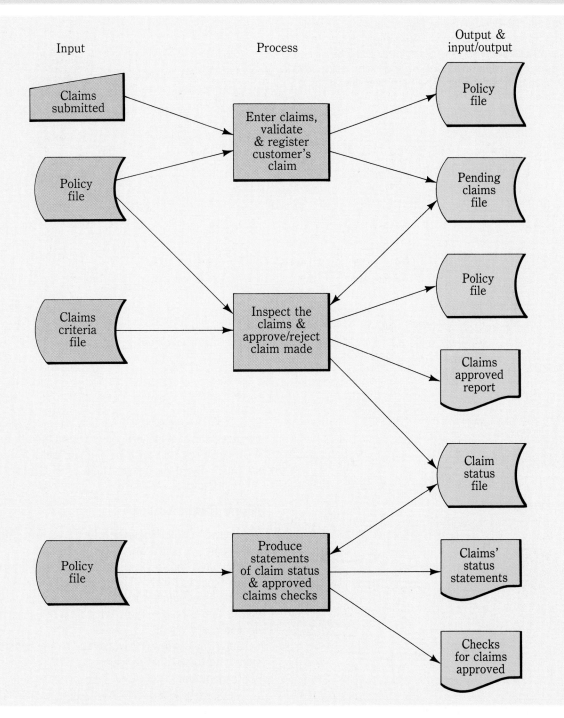

Figure 12-7. Example of a Flowchart—Safehaven Claims Processing. Flowcharts are very helpful for describing information flows and processing.

Figure 12-8. (a) Data Flow Diagram Symbols. Data flow diagrams have been recommended over flowcharts because they contain fewer symbols and encourage "top-down" design. (b) High Level Data Flow at Computerware. The first overview of processing.

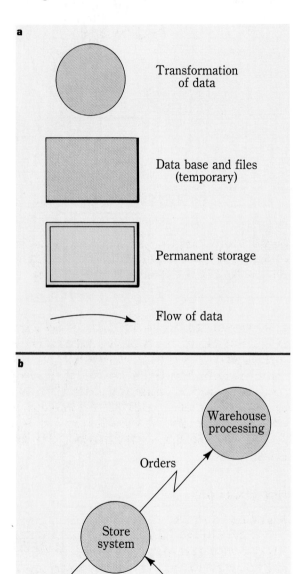

By keeping the number of symbols on each page to a manageable number and going from top to bottom, we can always back up a page if confused. We shall see many more data flow diagrams in Chapter 14.

More Requirements

We attend another meeting with Dave, Jon, Mary, and Kathy.

"You have done a great job with the data flow diagrams," began Mary. "They help me to understand the process a whole lot better. Now I want to ask you to think about output. What kind of information do you really need?"

Kathy replied first, "I would like to see inventory value and turns, that is, sales."

"How often?"

"Daily on sales. I also want this year-to-date."

"Do you want a printed report or just to be able to see it on a display screen—you know, a terminal in your office."

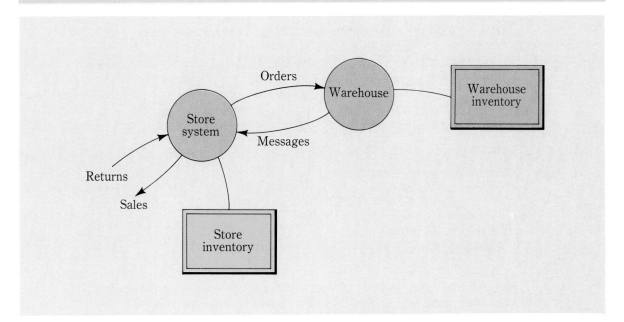

Figure 12-9. Next Level of Data Flow Detail for Computerware. A more detailed view; one can always back up to the previous level if confused.

"That's a hard question. Maybe you should do both for now, and then we can drop the printed report if I don't use it."

Mary turned to Jon. "How about you?"

"Basically the same information, but let me have inventory by class if you can."

"How will we know the class?"

Dave answered, "That's easy. We'll make it part of the item number."

Mary asked, "Could I get you to rough out the format of those reports and other output—you know, packing slips, reorder forms, and so on."

See Figure 12-10 for samples of some of the reports that will be in the system, including:

- Sales query
- Inventory by class
- Reorder report
- Reorder notice
- Labels/picking slips
- Daily sales

The key to Mary's approach is to let the users design their own reports because the user is in the best position to rough out what is wanted. She knows that if the designer develops the report, it will reflect only what the designer wants. Mary can use a computer program to develop a pro forma report, a simulation of the user's design. The user can then revise this rough draft several times until he or she is happy with it.

Specifications

Jon asked, "How are we doing?"

"Great," responded Mary. "We have a fairly high-level design, but I have a question or two. First, we need to review the files. I would like each of you to develop his or her own files and see that the data you need are in them."

She showed the others Figure 12-11, which has the contents of the files so far, and Figure 12-12, a diagram of the logical structure of the data.

COMPUTERWARE INVENTORY CONTROL SYSTEM: Sales Query

* *

ITEM NO: H-8600   CLASS: Hardware
DESCRIPTION: Letter Quality Printer
UNITS: 1
QUANTITY ON HAND: 130   REORDER POINT: 200
QUANTITY AVAILABLE: 330   REORDER QUANTITY: 500

Further information is available on:
1. the SUPPLIER
2. pending PURCHASE ORDERS from suppliers
3. incomplete ORDERS from the retail stores.

Enter your selection digit ____
or press the ESCAPE key to return to the Main Menu.

Figure 12-10. (a) Example of Computerware Sample Application Screen for Queries into Sales of an Item. [Note: (i) Quantity Available = Quantity on Hand + Quantity on Order − Quantity on Incomplete Orders. (ii) Although the Computerware warehouse makes no direct sales to customers, serving merely as an intermediary for retail stores selling directly to the public, common usage refers to warehouse inventory issues as "sales." We will continue this convention.]

Figure 12-10. (b) Example of Computerware Inventory Control System Application Report (continues on next page).

COMPUTERWARE INVENTORY CONTROL REPORT

* *

PERIOD: May 1, 1986 – May 31, 1986

CLASS: Hardware — CPU

Item Number	Description	Units	Unit Cost	Opening Balance	Receipts	Issues	Quantity on Hand	Value on Hand
H-1400	System Unit	1	2500	430	250	310	370	925000
Total Inventory Value of Hardware: CPU Class				$925,000				

CLASS: Hardware — Terminals

Item Number	Description	Units	Unit Cost	Opening Balance	Receipts	Issues	Quantity on Hand	Value on Hand
H-2020	USA Keyboard	1	200	621	400	585	436	87200
H-2280	RGB Color Monitor	1	900	705	200	580	325	292500
H-2300	Grn. Phos. Monitor	1	300	480	320	554	246	73800
Total Inventory Value of Hardware: Terminal Class				$453,500				

CLASS: Hardware — Peripherals

Item Number	Description	Units	Unit Cost	Opening Balance	Receipts	Issues	Quantity on Hand	Value on Hand
H-3100	128kb Memory Md.	1	400	413	200	350	263	105200
H-3300	256kb Memory Md.	1	700	502	180	390	292	204400
H-6000	Dual Disk Drive	1	800	312	150	290	172	137600

Total Inventory Value of Hardware: Peripherals Class $447,200

CLASS: Hardware — Printers

Item Number	Description	Units	Unit Cost	Opening Balance	Receipts	Issues	Quantity on Hand	Value on Hand
H-8050	LA50 Pers. Printer	1	600	3082	3000	4050	2032	1219200
H-8500	Letter Qlt. Printer	1	2400	4118	4000	931	87	10048800

Total Inventory Value of Hardware: Printers Class $11,268,000

COMPUTERWARE DAILY SALES REPORT

DATE :   August 11, 1986

Class : HARDWARE

Item#	Description	Units	Unit Cost	Sales (units)	Sales (value)
H-2280	RGB Color Monitor	1	900	4	3600
H-2300	Grn Phos. Monitor	1	300	5	1500
H-3300	256kb Memory Module	1	700	4	2800
H-8050	LA50 Personal Printer	1	600	10	6000
			TOTAL HARDWARE SALES		$17,500

Class : ACCESSORIES

Item#	Description	Units	Unit Cost	Sales (units)	Sales (value)
A-0100	LQP Printwheels Pica 10	6	30	15	450
A-0130	LQP Printwheels Elite 12	6	30	5	150
A-0200	LA50 Ribbon Cartridges	6	25	20	500
A-0400	8 inch Diskettes	10	40	100	4000
A-0800	Printer Standshelf	1	150	4	600
			TOTAL ACCESSORIES SALES		$5,700

Class : SOFTWARE

Item#	Description	Units	Unit Cost	Sales (units)	Sales (value)
S-2010	BASIC Compiler	1	300	8	2400
S-2020	COBOL Compiler	1	600	5	3000
S-2030	BASIC Compiler	1	300	14	4200
S-8000	Sort Facility	1	150	3	450
			TOTAL SOFTWARE SALES		$10,050
			TOTAL DAILY SALES		$33,250

Figure 12-10(b), continued.

SUBJECT FILES
* * * * * * * *

INVENTORY
Item Number
  - first character denotes
      class, i.e. 'H' = hardware
              'S' = software
              'A' = accessories
  - next four characters indicate the item number
      within class
Description
Units
Unit Cost
Quantity on Hand
Reorder Amount
Reorder Point
Supplier Identification
STORES
Store Identification
  - 2 character value identifying each store
      e.g., 'BN' = Boston
            'MN' = Manhattan
            'PH' = Philadelphia
Manager Name
Address
  - Street
  - City
  - State
  - Zip
SUPPLIER
Supplier Identification
  - 3 character mnemonic value identifying each
      supplier, e.g. 'APP' = Apple
                    'DEC' = Digital
                    'IBM' = IBM
Name
Address
  - Street
  - City
  - State
  - Zip
Credit Terms

TRANSACTION FILES
* * * * * * * * * * *

ORDERS (received from retail stores)
Order Number
Date Order Made
Store Identification
Delivery Date
Item Number
Description
Units
Unit Cost
Quantity Ordered
Total Value of Order
Status of Order
ISSUES (inventory sent to retail stores)
Item Number
Order Number
Store Identification
Date Delivered
Quantity Delivered
RETURNS (inventory returned by retail stores)
Item Number
Order Number
Store Identification
Date Returned
Quantity Returned
PURCHASE ORDERS (made to suppliers)
Purchase Order Number
Date Order Made
Supplier Identification
Item Number
Quantity Ordered
INVENTORY RECEIVED (from suppliers)
Item Number
Purchase Order Number
Supplier Identification
Date Received
Unit Price
Quantity Received
Total Value of Inventory Received
INVENTORY RETURNED (to suppliers)
Item Number
Purchase Order Number
Supplier Identification
Date Returned
Unit Price
Quantity Returned
Total Value of Inventory Returned

Figure 12-11. Note the large amount of information that must be kept on file even for a relatively simple application.

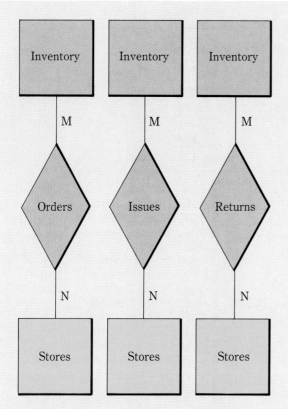

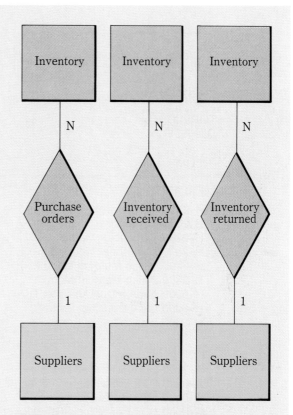

Each Subject file or *Entity* of Figure 10-8, represented here by a rectangular box, has logical associations or *Relationships* with other entities. As shown here, Inventory has 3 separate relationships with Stores (Orders, Issues and Receipts) and 3 separate relationships with Suppliers (Purchase–Orders, Inventory Received and Inventory Returned).

In the Inventory–Stores relationships, the associations are many to many (M:N), e.g. any store can order many inventory items, and any inventory item can be ordered by many stores. In the Inventory–Suppliers relationships, the associations are many to one (N:1), e.g. any supplier can supply many inventory items, but any inventory item can only be supplied by one particular supplier. [For simplicity, we have assumed that Computerware only gets its items from the original source].

Figure 12-12. The Logical Structure of Data in the Computerware Example Showing Relationships Among Entities.

"Looks OK to me," said Dave.

Kathy added, "I'm no expert, but it seems to have what I want."

"Hmm. All right for now, but can it be changed?" asked Jon.

"Yes, of course. But I would like each of you to take copies and think a little more. Check them against your reports—they're attached, too—if you would, please."

Jon asked, "How will you prevent chaos in the warehouse with this system? I mean, most order-entry systems sort orders in sequence by some warehouse location so that the pickers don't have to run all over the place. I don't see that in here."

ORDER FORM

COMPUTERWARE

STORE ID: *N.Y.*
ADDRESS: *40 West 4th Street*
             New York, N.Y.
Attention: *Dan*

Order No:
Date: *July 8, 1986*

REQUESTED
Delivery Date: *July 26, 1986*

HARDWARE

- [ ] H–1400 System Unit
- [ ] H–2020 Keyboard
- [2] H–2280 RGB Color Monitor
- [10] H–2300 Grn. Phos. Video Monitor
- [ ] H–3100 128kb Memory Module
- [ ] H–3300 256kb Memory Module
- [ ] H–6000 Add on Dual Diskette Drive
- [ ] H–8050 LA50 Personal Printer
- [10] H–8500 Letter Quality Printer

ACCESSORIES

- [ ] A–0100 LQP Printwheels Pica 10
- [ ] A–0120 LQP Printwheels Courier 10
- [50] A–0130 LQP Printwheels Elite 12
- [ ] A–0150 LQP Printwheels Greek/Math
- [ ] A–0200 LA50 Ribbon Cartridges
- [ ] A–0210 LQP Loop Ribbon
- [30] A–0400 8 inch Diskettes
- [ ] A–0450 Double Density Diskette Pack
- [ ] A–0500 Mouse
- [2] A–0800 Printer Stand Shelf

SOFTWARE

- [ ] S–1020 Accounts Payable
- [ ] S–1030 Accounts Receivable
- [ ] S–1040 General Ledger
- [40] S–1050 Payroll
- [ ] S–1600 Spread Sheet
- [ ] S–1700 Word Processor
- [ ] S–1880 Typing Lesson
- [15] S–2010 BASIC Compiler
- [ ] S–2020 COBOL Compiler
- [20] S–2030 PASCAL Compiler
- [ ] S–4010 Data Management
- [ ] S–4020 Query Language
- [ ] S–5000 Games
- [ ] S–8800 Sort Facility

Figure 12-13. Sample Order Form for Computerware.

Dave responded, "Well, here is our situation. We don't have very many products, so we'll have pre-printed order forms. The items will appear on the form in the sequence in which they are located in the warehouse. The picker can just follow the order form directly and trace an efficient path through the warehouse." Figure 12-13 is a draft order form.

"That's good," Mary observed, "and when we get an order-entry-system study started, we can look at doing the sorting and changing the form if you want to. Now we have to make a hard decision. We should stop at this point in my opinion and develop a requirements document that looks at alternatives for doing this job."

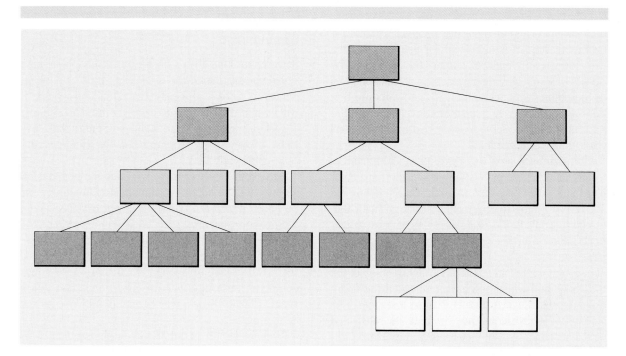

Figure 12-14. A diagram of the structure of a program showing the relationship among modules.

"Like what?"

Mary went to the flip-chart in the corner and began writing:

- Custom programming
- A package
- A generator language

"What are each of these all about?" asked Jon.

We shall attempt to answer his question in Chapter 13. For now, assume that Computerware chose **custom programming.** What steps would be required?

First, Computerware would have to hire staff and then develop even more detailed specifications that could be programmed. This task involves breaking the system down into programs and the programs into modules.

A **module** is a small piece of a program. We want to have modules isolated from other modules to make the system easy to change. Thus, a module that is responsible for computing a reorder quantity would be further broken down into smaller modules, say, one to check balances, one to compute an economic (least cost) order quantity, and one to report items that need to be reordered. The idea is to make modules small enough to be easily understood and to have only one purpose or function. They should also have a minimal impact on other modules (see Figure 12-14).

Programming

Given the kind of specifications described, Computerware programmers (or programmers from Multicorp or from a consulting firm) would develop modules. The firm might decide to acquire a database management system to use for this application and future applications. Either Mary or someone newly hired would have to serve as the database administrator. The programming staff would then use the DBMS in writing their programs.

Programmers test the modules they write with

their own data and then put the modules together for further testing. It is important for users to provide data for various kinds of testing and to check the results. The users should present unusual conditions to the editing routines and error checks to see that they are working. It is also necessary to test the system at a high volume to show that everything will work under a heavy load.

One insurance company developed a new system to edit input; the new system was much more complete in its checking than the old. The company did not run a volume test but simply assured itself that the edits would work. With the stringent new conditions imposed by the program, the new system rejected several hundred thousand transactions. (The old system would have accepted the logical errors in the codes and would still have processed the financial data, which were correct in most instances.) As a result, the firm could not compute its sales, and senior management did not receive the financial reports it expected. Testing with a day's full transactions would have identified this problem.

User acceptance tests, then, are a key event in the life of a system. The users provide both realistic and highly erroneous data to be sure that the system works correctly. Remember that it is the user who lives with the results; the programmers go off to another assignment and do not use the system.

At Computerware, the users will have to develop some sample orders and be a bit creative because the firm has not yet really started business. They will have to input some inventory data, and possibly there will be some real inventory around in preparation for the start of business that can be entered for the test.

Training

Having users involved in the design of a system helps in training. Because the users have worked on the system, they should have some understanding of its functions. It is still important for the users to have enough formal training so that they understand how to use the system. A number of disasters have happened when information systems were installed without employees' being trained to use them.

Conversion

If we have done things correctly to this point, then *conversion* should go smoothly. It is important, however, to have a plan for the actual conversion. It will be necessary to begin using the new procedures associated with the system. Files of data often have to be created to start the system; this can be a very time-consuming task.

At Computerware, there will have to be a physical inventory. The data from the physical inventory will be entered into the computer inventory file. Then, the program will print this "book" inventory, and the warehouse staff will take the report to the warehouse and count again to be sure that the book and the physical inventories match. If there are errors, someone must key in corrections and then check again. This process will continue until all of the counts agree.

If business has begun before the system conversion, the conversion would probably have to take place over a weekend when there is no picking in the warehouse. It would be very hard indeed to get counts to agree if employees were selecting stock from the shelves and preparing it for shipping while one was attempting to reconcile the book and the physical inventories.

Operations

If a system is successful and is used, there will always be some changes requested as the users see new opportunities. However, most computer departments spend 40 to 80 percent of their time on maintenance, which seems a bit excessive. Most of the maintenance is enhancements (as opposed to fixing errors), features that were not included in the original design. As has already been mentioned, there will always be some, but how many of these changes occur because we failed to design the system well?

The heavy involvement of the users in the design process stressed here should help reduce the need for later enhancements. If the users understand the system before they begin to use it, hopefully they will suggest some features that they want when it is

Figure 12-15. An Implementation Failure? A secretary uses her old, familiar tools while a microcomputer remains unused in the shadows.

relatively easy to incorporate them into the design. The key to success is to spend time and effort in the design process and not to design the system after it has been programmed and installed.

A REAL EXPERIENCE

There are millions of different types of computer applications, and each design effort probably generates as many stories as programs. This tale is true, but the company will remain anonymous to protect those involved in the development effort. There is a lesson to be learned from this experience.

The firm is a large mining company with an old system for keeping track of goods in the spare parts inventory. Because mining takes a lot of specialized equipment, the spare parts are numerous. They are also very important because a mining operation can be shut down for lack of the appropriate part. The firm in this example had fifty-two thousand items in spare parts inventories.

There are four divisions in the firm, all performing the same tasks at different locations; one division is as large as the other three put together. A design team spent one year meeting with the users at the large division and developing specifications for the features of a new spare-parts-inventory system. The new system would incorporate a sophisticated forecasting routine to predict the demand for critical parts. In addition, there would be calculations to de-

termine the optimal order quantity and the best re-order point. None of these features existed in the old system.

At first, the company officials did not want to review the design document with the other three divisions, even though they were supposed to adopt the system once it was completed. The design team persisted, and a long trip to the other divisions resulted in another six months of work and a considerably more detailed systems specification.

After a lengthy programming period, the system was finally implemented at the largest division. A year later, the assistant controller, who had been the chief user on the design team, spoke glowingly of the system and the money it was saving. When asked about the other three divisions, he indicated that though he could show them cost savings, the division managers were successfully resisting the implementation of the system in their divisions.

Why? The reason was the organizational environment problem that we mentioned earlier. The firm had a long history of not involving users in design and of building systems for the large division and forcing them on the other three units. The inventory system was a technological success, but an organizational failure. By bringing the other division managers in on the decisions and involving their staff members in the design, the design team would have increased its chances of success.

See Figure 12-15 for an example of problems with implementation.

Review of Chapter 12

REVIEW

Systems analysis and design is a key activity in the organization; it requires creativity and human intellectual effort. The task is difficult and demands attention to detail. The systems designed today determine the kind of information processing that the organization will enjoy for at least the next five and possibly ten years.

This chapter has presented the systems life cycle, the stages through which the design of a new application progresses. We have stressed the need for heavy user involvement on the design team for a new system. There is a role for the user in each stage of the life cycle.

It is also important to think about the trade-offs inherent in the design process and to realize that there is no one best design for a particular application. Similarly, there is no one best way to provide the technology to run an application. We have discussed some alternatives and considerations in terms of centralized, distributed, or decentralized processing. We have also presented some charting techniques that help to document a system and to communicate things about it.

Finally, the chapter followed some design meetings at Multicorp's newest venture. The users are trying to take advantage of the technology to help a start-up business begin. Chapter 14 will present the results of the team's effort in great detail, as their system illustrates well what we mean by logical specifications for a computer application.

KEY WORDS

Acceptance tests	Flowchart
Analysis	Inception
Application	Logic
Conversion	Maintenance
Critical path	Module
method	Operations
Custom programming	Preliminary needs
Cutover	analysis
Database	Programming
Data flow diagram	Requirements
(DFD)	analysis
Documentation	Response time
Environment	Specifications
Feasibility	Structured design

System	Trade-off
Systems analysis	Training
Technology	User
Testing	

BUSINESS PROBLEMS

12-1. The analogy often used with systems analysis and design is that of an architect constructing a building. The architect works with an idea provided by the client. He or she sketches the building and then reviews it with the client. Each meeting further refines the view of the building. Finally, the last blueprints are approved, and building commences. The architect then manages the project and coordinates the various groups working on the building.

Compare this process with the systems life cycle. How are they similar? Where do the processes differ? Consider the types of reviews that take place and the tools for representing a building. For example, how does the architect often give the client an idea of the external appearance of a building? Is there a similar part of systems analysis and design?

What are some of the things that designers could learn from looking at the model of an architect? What is the role of the client in the design process? What should the role of the client, or the user, be in systems analysis and design?

12-2. One company decided to replace a ten-year-old order-entry system with a new one. The firm had used its first system to gain a competitive advantage in its industry. It could respond to customer requests and orders faster than any competitor.

Now, the system was out-of-date; new approaches to design would make it substantially better. The management of the firm wanted to take advantage of the need for a new system to make a number of changes in policy. For example, it wanted to form a new customer-services department by merging individuals in two separate areas that currently dealt with customers. Management also wanted to change some inventory and forecasting policies.

Management communicated these desires to the design team, which set about the task of systems analysis and design. After extensive interviews with the users, the design team produced a very comprehensive specification, about four hundred pages long in a loose-leaf binder. This document was sent to twenty-five managers, including the president of the firm.

At this point, management became worried because no one could understand the document. In addition, the users who the design team said had been involved were critical of the system and did not seem to understand if very well.

What do you think went wrong? What could have been done instead? What would you recommend to management?

REVIEW QUESTIONS

1. Define *system*.
2. Describe the steps in the systems life cycle.
3. Why do we say that it is usually feasible to use a computer in some way to help solve an information processing problem?
4. What are the boundaries of a system?
5. What factors are important in trying to set the boundaries?
6. What is the purpose of a flowchart?
7. What is the purpose of having diagrams at differing levels of detail?

8. What is a program module?
9. What are the desirable characteristics of a module?
10. Why should the users develop the data for testing?
11. What might be in a conversion plan for a new system?
12. Why might Computerware want to use a database management system?
13. What is a volume test?
14. Why do we need to present extreme values to a system in testing?
15. What is an acceptance test?
16. Why is there so much maintenance of existing systems?
17. What can be done to reduce maintenance?

THOUGHT QUESTIONS

18. Describe a system with which you are familiar. What are its major subsystems?
19. What is the difference between an applications system and a computer system?
20. Why does Computerware seem most inter-

ested in an inventory system?

21. Describe a trade-off in the Computerware example in the chapter.
22. Describe the functions of an order entry system for Computerware.
23. Define the file contents for order entry.
24. Describe the input and output of an order entry system.
25. Why would a company sort the items on an order into a bin sequence for their warehouse?
26. How do inventory, shipping, and billing all tie together?
27. What is the relationship of accounts receivable to shipping?
28. Draw a flowchart of the student registration process at your school.
29. How does a data flow diagram differ from a flowchart?
30. How could a package program facilitate the installation of Computerware's system?
31. How does a database management system contribute to maintenance?
32. Why do users request changes in a system?
33. Will we ever have a system in which no changes are desired? If so, what does the lack of changes say about the system?
34. What is the difference between systems analysis and design?
35. Why is it said that design is a creative task?

RECOMMENDED READINGS

Burch, J., F. Strater, and G. Gruditski. *Information Systems Theory and Practice* (2nd ed.). New York: Wiley, 1979. A good introductory book on systems.

Lucas, Henry C., Jr. *The Analysis, Design and Implementation of Information Systems* (3rd ed.). New York: McGraw-Hill, 1985. This text is written for design students and contains more details on the topics covered in this chapter.

Martin, J., and C. McClure. *Software Maintenance*. Englewood Cliffs, NJ: Prentice-Hall, Inc., 1983. An excellent discussion of the maintenance problem with some suggested solutions.

Semprevivo, P. *Systems Analysis* (2nd ed.). Palo Alto, CA: Science Research Associates, 1982. A good introduction to systems analysis by a practitioner in the field.

Chapter 13

You should have obtained the impression from the last chapter that systems analysis and design is a time-consuming task. We are continually seeking ways to reduce the time and effort required for design and to enhance the quality of the systems that result from the design process. This chapter presents some new alternatives to the custom-tailored systems-design approach we just studied.

Even with the techniques described here, it is unwise to eliminate all the traditional activities in systems analysis and design simply because the design team feels one of these alternatives is superior. Each approach still requires thinking about the functions that a system should perform. There is no shortcut to doing systems specification at a high conceptual level.

The first alternative discussed in this chapter is the use of a package. Packages are very appealing; many managers think that the solution to all computer problems is to buy a package and run it. Such a view is a bit of an oversimplification. There may be an instance where such a purchase is possible, but we need to look at the classes of packages and the differences among them.

Another way to improve applications development is through the use of software tools. In this category, one finds applications generators and very-high-level languages, the so-called fourth-generation languages.

Two final approaches are to build a prototype of a system and/or to encourage the end users to do some of their own programming.

After reading this chapter, you should be able to:

- Distinguish among different kinds of packages.
- Describe the analysis that is needed before looking at a software package.
- Explain how general-purpose packages can be used to help develop a system.
- Define an applications generator.
- Describe the characteristics of a fourth-generation language.
- Define a prototype and describe how it can be used.
- Describe end user programming and how it reduces systems design efforts.

ALTERNATIVES
TO TRADITIONAL DESIGN

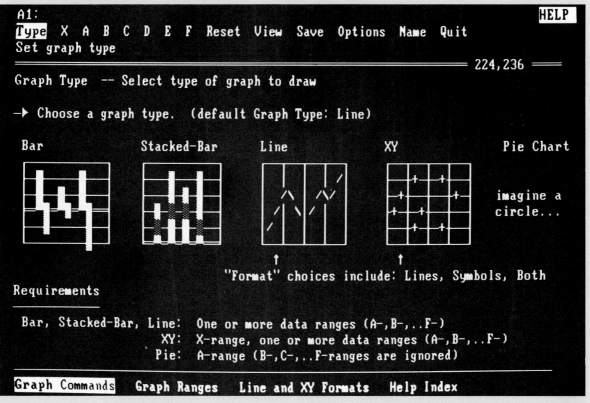

```
A1:                                                                    HELP
Type  X A B C D E F  Reset  View  Save  Options  Name  Quit
Set graph type
══════════════════════════════════════════════════ 224,236 ══════

Graph Type  -- Select type of graph to draw

─▶ Choose a graph type.  (default Graph Type: Line)


Bar                Stacked-Bar        Line             XY              Pie Chart



                                                                      imagine a
                                                                      circle...



                                ↑                 ↑
                         "Format" choices include: Lines, Symbols, Both

Requirements
────────────
  Bar, Stacked-Bar, Line:  One or more data ranges (A-,B-,..F-)
                     XY:  X-range, one or more data ranges (A-,B-,..F-)
                    Pie:  A-range (B-,C-,..F-ranges are ignored)
  ─────────────────────────────────────────────────────────────
 Graph Commands   Graph Ranges   Line and XY Formats   Help Index
```

Package Type	Characteristics	Example
Very high level of Fourth generator languages	Easy–to–use; user solves own problem	Focus NATURAL, RAMIS
Systems Software	Computer–oriented task like terminal management Possibly DBMS	CICS ADABASE, DBASE,
Problem–Oriented	Language fits problem type like statistical analysis	SPSS, SAS, LOTUS 1–2–3 MULTIPLAN
Dedicated	Focused on one application area	Production control COPICS, accounts receivable

Figure 13-1. A Framework for Classifying Packages.

INTRODUCTION

The previous chapter describes a traditional approach to design: A design team develops the specifications for a system. The programmers write a code and test it with the users. The programmers test the programs and convert and install the system. This approach has encountered a number of difficulties. First, it seems to take a long time to complete the system, usually much longer than has been forecast. Second, it is often found that some of the features of the system have to be sacrificed; either they are too difficult to include, or they add too much to the time required to complete the system.

Because design is a creative task, it resembles research-and-development efforts. It is very hard to predict how long it will take from beginning to end to develop a system. One manager of a computer department will make forecasts only for the next stage in the development process; at the beginning of the project, he will not give a complete forecast of how long it will take to complete the whole system.

One of the reasons that forecasting is so poor is that at each stage in the life cycle, we find out more about the system. At first, we may see only the tip of the iceberg; the other 90 percent is not apparent yet. At each stage, more of the requirements will unfold.

There is general dissatisfaction with these conditions. The relatively poor performance of systems designers creates a lot of user dissatisfaction. Are there alternatives to the traditional model? There are some alternatives today to producing a custom system, and in addition, there are some new software tools that help to cut down the development time if a custom system is selected. We shall discuss the following:

- Alternatives to custom design
  Packages
- Software tools that improve custom design
  Applications generators and nonprocedural languages
  Prototyping and end user programming.

PACKAGES

A *package* is generally thought of as a piece of software, a program developed by one organization to be sold to others. That is true, but the package may be a combination of hardware and software. We can think of a package as a problem solution that is partially or completely ready to be implemented. The package almost always includes computer programs and may also include hardware.

The purpose of a package is to reduce the time required to install a system by saving part of the design effort and most of the programming required. Although these are the goals of the package, it is not always possible to achieve these savings because firms frequently want to modify the package to fit their particular circumstances.

The advantages usually listed for packages include the following:

1. The total development time should be less because of less programming and less design.
2. The total costs of a package should be lower because one piece of software is being sold to a number of firms. No customer has to pay the full development cost.
3. A package may have more functions than a system we develop ourselves.
4. If the package has already been sold and is in operation, we are buying programs that already execute. There should be fewer errors in them than in new programs that we might write ourselves.

There are disadvantages with packages, too:

1. A package may not have all of the functions we want.
2. The package may have to be extensively modified. Sometimes, vendors do not want to change their packages; it can be hard for an in-house staff to understand the package's programs and make changes.
3. Companies sometimes have to change their procedures to use the package because they do not want to pay for changes in the package.

4. The company buying the package depends on the package vendor for support.

The vendor has to construct a general-purpose program that will fit many customers. Usually, the package comes with a lot of input parameters, data values that the customer must supply to make the package work in his or her environment. For example, the user would have to enter the numbers used to label his or her accounts in order to use a package for the general ledger of the firm.

Some packages have different *modules* for the same task and the customer selects the one that is appropriate. For example, we could have an accounting package with modules for two or three types of depreciation. The customer chooses the depreciation module that reflects the way in which the company handles depreciation.

Package Types

There are many different types of packages that are intended for different purposes. Some packages are really like languages; the user works with the package to build an *application.* Other packages are really *dedicated* to a particular application, like accounts receivable, material requirements planning for manufacturing, or inventory control (see Figure 13-1).

Very-High-Level Languages

We have called these programs fourth-generation languages. They have statements that are at a higher level than BASIC, COBOL, or FORTRAN. That is, a fourth-generation language has statements that would require many individual statements in a compiler-level language. For example, suppose that Computerware had a file of items in inventory and a *very-high-level language.* Jon could produce a report by entering something like the following:

SELECT INVENTORY PARTNO EQ 1234 THRU 7788

This kind of package is not used for a specific application; rather, the user solves a particular problem using the package's language. Some languages

Figure 13-2. Example of Output from an SPSS Run.

```
*  *  *  *     CROSSTABULATION OF     *  *  *  *
*  *  *  *  *  *  *  *  *  *  *  *  *  *  *  *  *  *
```

		SEX		
Count % : Row % : Col % : Total % :	FEMALE :	:	:	Row Total
MAJOR ——— :	——— :	MALE : ——— :		
ACCOUNTING: :	4 : 40.0 : 11.8 : 5.7 :	6 : 60.0 : 16.7 : 8.6 :		10 14.3
INFO. SYSTEMS :	6 : 75.0 : 17.6 : 8.6 :	2 : 25.0 : 5.6 : 2.9 :		8 11.4
ECONOMICS :	6 : 50.0 : 17.6 : 8.6 :	6 : 50.0 : 16.7 : 8.6 :		12 17.1
FINANCE :	5 : 35.7 : 14.7 : 7.1 :	9 : 64.3 : 25.0 : 12.9 :		14 20.0
MANAGEMENT :	10 : 62.5 : 29.4 : 14.3 :	6 : 37.5 : 16.7 : 8.6 :		16 22.9
MARKETING :	3 : 30.0 : 8.8 : 4.3 :	7 : 70.0 : 19.4 : 10.0 :		10 14.3
Column : Total	34 : 48.6	36 : 51.4 :		70 100.0

4 out of 12 (33.3%) of the valid cells have expected cell
  frequency less than 5.0.
Minimum expected cell frequency = 3.886
Chi square = 6.09069 with 5 Degrees of freedom;
  Significance = 0.2975
Cramer's V = 0.29497

are designed for special types of problems, such as financial modeling, and others are more general-purpose. A growing number of these languages is available for mainframes, minicomputers, and microcomputers.

The example above may appear to be very similar to a *query language* used to extract data from a file or a database. In fact, the statements in a query language are often at the same high level as the statements of a *fourth-generation language.* Both of these types of languages try to present the user of the computer with an interface that is closer to natural language than to a computer language.

A fourth-generation or *very-high-level language* has to feature retrieval statements, but it also must offer a lot more. This very-high-level language must make it possible to process data once they have been retrieved, to process transactions against data files, to define input forms, and to define and format output reports. A very-high-level language, then, should contain many of the features of a query language plus many more capabilities.

Systems Software

There are software packages for specific purposes, such as controlling the interaction between a computer system and its terminals. This particular ter-

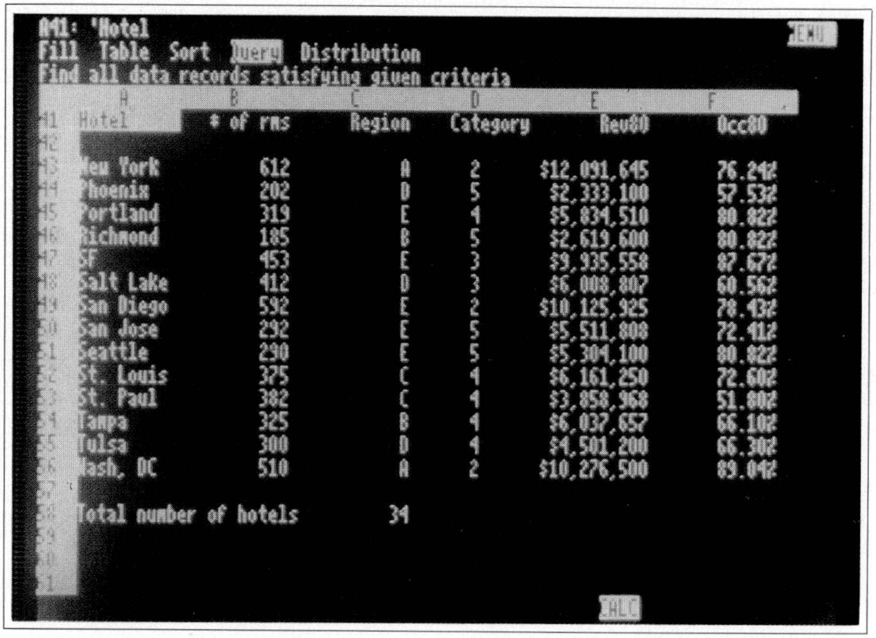

Figure 13-3. Part of a Lotus 1-2-3 Spreadsheet. (Chapter 15 will discuss spreadsheets in more detail.)

minal-handling program is called a *telecommunications monitor*.

Some would include database management packages in this category of systems software. A program for a personal computer that managed diskettes and a hard disk would be a piece of systems software.

Problem-Oriented Packages

These packages are like higher-order languages but are aimed at a specific problem. A good example of this type of package is SPSS (Statistical Package for the Social Sciences); this program is used by nonprogrammers who have data that they wish to analyze statistically. The user of the package does write a program, but in a very-high-level language that is oriented toward someone with a knowledge of statistics. Figure 13-2 shows the results of the SPSS run on seventy student records, given the following input program:

VARIABLE LIST	AGE,SEX,MAJOR
INPUT FORMAT	FIXED(I2,A1,I2)
VALUE LABELS	SEX('F')FEMALE ('M')MALE
VALUE LABELS	MAJOR(20)ACCOUNTING (30)INFO. SYSTEMS(45) ECONOMICS(50)FINANCE (65)MANAGEMENT(90) MARKETING
N OF CASES	70
INPUT MEDIUM	DISK
CROSSTABS	TABLES=MAJOR BY SEX
OPTIONS	1
STATISTICS	1,2
READ INPUT DATA	
FINISH	

Two of the most popular packages in this category are Visicalc and Lotus 1-2-3. We shall go into much greater detail on how one of them works in Chapter 5 (see Figure 13-3).

Dedicated Packages

The problem-oriented packages, remember, are all used to solve a particular processing problem. The packages we call *dedicated* are very different because the buyer is focusing on a single function. The package is not used to create a solution; it is the solution (at least according to the vendor).

Consider a function like accounts receivable. A firm must keep track of the funds that its customers owe it. The vendor of a package for this function will try to create a system that can be used by a large number of firms. Think of the possibilities.

There are companies that sell many small items repeatedly to the same customers, say, a sweater manufacturer selling to various kinds of clothing stores across the country. The package vendor would also like to be able to sell to a different type of company, maybe one that sells airplanes. Such a company probably has one customer that does business with the firm every few years, if that often (see Figure 13-4).

Each of these diverse firms would keep a different kind of accounts receivable. It is possible that one dedicated package with different options could satisfy each of them. The sweater company will have a large number of transactions listed for each customer; it will want to match each payment with the different invoices that it has sent to its customers, probably one for each shipment. The aircraft sales firm's receivables will be fairly simple but will represent a large amount of money. Here, financing, working capital, funds flow, and late payments will be of concern because the manufacturer must be able to finance production and meet its payroll with large, irregular payments from its customer. It sells many fewer airplanes than the garment manufacturer does sweaters. In fact, it is quite possible that a manual ledger is all that the airplane manufacturer will want until it becomes quite large.

On the surface, it probably looks as if all accounts-receivable applications are the same: "If you've seen one, you've seen them all." However, the example of the sweater and airplane manufacturers should demonstrate that all applications for the same function, such as accounts receivable, are not identical.

For this reason, the user should define the requirements of his or her system before looking at packages. One cannot assume that because the package is designed to handle accounts receivable it will necessarily work in one's own environment.

There is also a considerable difference between packages intended for the user to construct his or her own solution and packages that are the solution to the problem themselves. The packages used to construct a solution are general-purpose and will not, in general, be modified by their vendors. The user is expected to figure out how to apply the package to his or her problem. Implementing a dedicated package may involve modifications in the software and/or changes in the buyer's procedures.

Acquisition

Choosing a package is a difficult task. The step often forgotten is determining what one wants. It is very important, in the choice of any kind of package, to determine the requirements of the application. In the case of a problem-solving tool like Visicalc or Lotus 1-2-3, the buyer should consider the features that he or she will actually use before selecting a product. This specification will be fairly simple because certain generic functions are performed by all packages in this category.

Where does one find information about packages? There are numerous magazines that report on new microcomputer software; in addition, a prospective customer can visit one of the many stores that sell computer hardware and software. For larger computers, it will probably be necessary to contact the vendors of the computer to see if they have or know of a package for the task at hand.

The preparation for acquiring a dedicated package is even more demanding than for a general-purpose package. It is necessary to develop a preliminary systems design at a high level before actually looking for the package. Why? Because the users need to think about the kind of system they want before being influenced by package vendors.

The buyer needs to have a benchmark, a plan with which she or he can compare the features of various packages. With such a plan, it is possible to estimate

Figure 13-4. An Accounts Receivable Department at a Suburban Philadelphia Newspaper, the Pottstown Mercury.

what modifications will be required to use the package. It is unusual not to make some modifications in a dedicated package, at least for large organizations with established procedures. It may be simpler and certainly less expensive for the small firm to accept a package as is and change its own procedures.

Whatever is decided about changes, it is important for the users to be heavily involved in the selection of a dedicated package. They should be sure to see the package work and understand what it will and will not do. For the actual selection, the kind of procedure advocated for selecting alternative systems in the last chapter is appropriate: ranking and evaluating the various packages and then choosing the one that appears to be the best. The package can also be compared with alternatives such as a custom system on the same criteria.

An Example

Warren Communications is a $10-million manufacturer of power supplies used in telephone systems; the firm is a subsidiary of General Signal Corporation. Several years ago, more than half the company's shipments were late, a circumstance leading to irate customers, some of whom canceled their business with Warren. In addition, costs were out of control. Because of written guarantees of product delivery, customers were assessing the firm late-charge penalties.

At one point, only 47 percent of the firm's orders were being filled on time. Inventories of raw materials were confused, and key parts were out of stock. Sometimes, shipments of finished products were delayed for up to three months.

The purchasing of raw materials was always done on a rush basis at premium prices. The inventories of goods in the process of being manufactured (in-process inventories) were overflowing; items were piled up in the aisles. New production managers felt that something had to be done to improve operations. The solution was to invest about $160,000 in a package for the firm's computer, which was already in use for payroll and production expediting.

The package is an example of a manufacturing control system called *Materials Requirements Planning II* (MRP II). In the Warren case, the computer sets up a master production schedule. Lists (bills) of materials showing what raw materials and subassemblies are needed for final assembly are associated with each product. Inventory records are also included, and they are linked with bills of materials.

The system takes a production forecast and actual orders; it then produces a production schedule, taking into account due dates and the capacity of each line in the factory. For example, if a certain subassembly takes five weeks to produce, it can be started into production no later than five weeks before the shipping date for the final product, plus the time needed for final assembly.

MRP explodes the bill of materials to get the requirements for raw materials. (The process of breaking an assembly down into all of its component parts in manufacturing is called a *piece parts explosion*.) As a result, it can alert purchasing to the need for more inventory well before it is needed for production. By encouraging steady, planned production, the system reduces work-in-process inventories and rush orders for raw materials.

At Warren, the results have been dramatic. The firm is planning to expand plant capacity by 50 to 100 percent. The first year, the system saved the firm $850,000; it has nearly eliminated late delivery penalties. The company used to need fifteen people for an annual physical inventory that took four days to complete. Now, the inventory takes an hour. Manufacturing overtime was reduced from 12 percent of total payroll to 3 percent. Customers are beginning to come back now that they can count on Warren to deliver on time.

Implementing a dedicated package can take time. Warren required two years to plan and install the software. One needs commitment from senior levels of management. In this case, the vice-president of manufacturing and engineering was behind the project. It is also important to plan and to train employees to use the new approaches. Some companies have installed MRP only to use it as a way to streamline their old ways of doing business. At Warren, the time was taken to obtain the maximum that the system had to offer.

GENERATORS AND NONPROCEDURAL LANGUAGES

The kind of language described in this section is at a higher level than a language like COBOL or FORTRAN. Basically, the higher the level of a language, the fewer the statements in the language required to accomplish some task. With the use of BASIC, it takes only a single statement to compute the following formula:

$$A1 + B2/(A1*2 + C1-56)$$

Many more statements in assembly language would be necessary to perform this computation. Very-high-level languages accomplish tasks in fewer statements than a language like BASIC. For example, to sort a series of data records into a new order—say, to change from an order by social security number to one by last name—would require a number of statements in BASIC or FORTRAN. In a very-high-level language, we could say something like:

SORT STUDENTS by LAST NAME

Compiler-level languages are considered procedural because the programmer has to specify quite detailed procedures for solving his or her problem. A *nonprocedural language* requires many fewer details. Of course, very-high-level languages are not quite at the level of being able to say, "Compute payroll," but some of these languages are very powerful.

End User Programming

A major trend is toward more programming on the part of end users. This programming, however, does not closely resemble the traditional code produced by professional programmers. Instead, users work with a variety of special languages and packages on different types of computers.

In Chapter 15, we shall see how an electronic spreadsheet package works; you will have difficulty calling the use of this package "programming," particularly if you compare it with programming in BASIC in Chapter 18. Instead, the user works with a tool to solve his or her own problem. This kind of package runs on a microcomputer; there is a great deal of micro software available for use by the end user. One of the great appeals of these computers is that, for the most part, a systems professional is not required to make it work.

For mainframes, some of the packages described later make it feasible for end users to develop some of their own problem solutions. Using these tools may approach conventional programming, but they are used for such tasks and in such a way that the end user can rapidly learn how to apply the tool. It is

Figure 13-5. Example of an RPG Program. RPG is intended to be an easy-to-use programming language. What do you think? (Figure continues on next two pages.)

This program prints a formatted report that contains heading information and a list of the records from the input file DETORDL (detail orders), which is described externally. The output file, which is a program described file, is named QPRINT. Only the input fields QTYORD, ITEM, DESCRP, and EXTENS are to be printed in the detail output record. No calculations are to be performed on the data in the input record.

To write the specifications for this job, you need to:
· Refer to the description of the externally described file DETORDL so you can use the correct field names and field lengths in describing the output file.
· Design the format of the printed report by completing a printer layout form.
· Code the file description specifications.
· Refer to the printer layout form to code the output specifications.

probably more accurate to say that end users are solving their own information-processing problems rather than to say that they are programming.

Report Generators

Some of the first attempts to develop easy-to-use languages resulted in *report generators.* Specifying a report in a conventional programming language can be a very tedious process. These report generators helped the user to define the layout of a file, to extract records based on logical criteria (for example, "Salary greater than $1,000"), to manipulate the data, and to format a report.

Some report generators actually evolved into languages and included the ability to update a file. Theoretically, one could develop an entire application using just a report generator. (See the example in Figure 13-5.)

Report generators first appeared for sequential files. They are particularly good for extracting data from different files. In one instance, an insurance company used a generator to combine a master rec-

ord on losses by policy and another file of details for each claim for its auditors. The report generator sorted both files into the same sequence (policy number) and produced a report of each policy's total losses and a detailed history of claims.

Report generators have been provided with more capabilities to take advantage of the widespread use of direct-access files and database management systems. Sometimes, the report generators are called *retrieval languages,* and they are frequently sold to users in an organization who want to develop reports quickly without the need of a programmer.

Query Languages

Database management systems usually come with some kind of query language for retrieving data from the database without the intervention of a programmer. Remember that a query is some question that the user wants to ask of the database. The user enters statements, which the query language processor interprets. A typical statement for a microcomputer relational DBMS would be

Printer Layout

POSITION

```
        1-10              11-20              21-30              31-40              41-50              51-60              61-70              71-80
```

```
H  06                          O R D E R
H  08  QUANTITY          ITEM        DESCRIPTION                              COST
D  10  XXX              X,XXX        XXXXXXXXXXXXXXXXXXXXX              X,XXX.XX
   11  (QTYORD)         (ITEM)       (DESCRP)                          (EXTENS)
```

16   Double-space heading
17   lines and single-space
18   detail lines

IBM International Business Machines Corporation   **DATA DESCRIPTION SPECIFICATIONS**   GX21-7754 UM/050*
                                                                                                                   Printed in U.S.A.

| File | | Keying | Graphic | | | | Description | Page 1 of 1 |
| Programmer | Date | Instruction | Key | | | | DETORDL | |

Form Type	And/Or/Comment (A/O/*)	Name	Length	Decimal Positions	Functions
A*		DETAIL ORDER FILE -- DETORDL			
A	R ORDDTL				PFILE(DETORDP)
A		CUST	5		TEXT('Customer Number')
A		ORDER	5	0	TEXT('Order Number')
A		LINNUM	3	0	TEXT('Line Number on Invoice')
A		ITEM	5		TEXT('Item Number')
A		QTYORD	3	0	TEXT('Quantity Ordered')
A		DESCRP	18		TEXT('Item Description')
A		PRICE	5	2	TEXT('Price per Unit')
A		EXTENS	6	2	TEXT('Extension of QTYORD x PRICE')
A		WHSLOC	3		TEXT('Warehouse Location')
A		ORDDAT	6	0	TEXT('Order Date')
A		CUSTYP	1		TEXT('Customer Type')
A		STATE	2		TEXT('State Abbreviation')
A					

Figure 13-5 (continued).

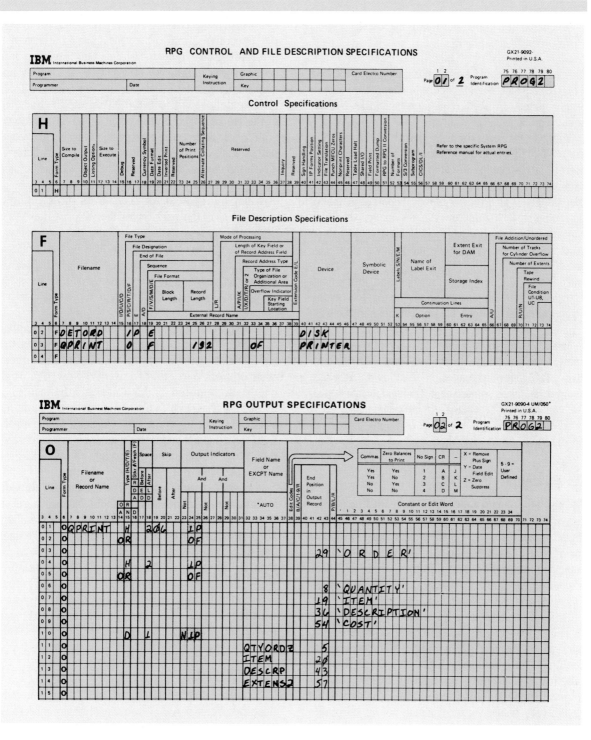

Figure 13-5 (continued).

SELECT STUDENT WHERE NAME EQ SMITH
OR JONES OR ANDERSON

This command would search the database file called STUDENT and select records where the names Smith, Jones, or Anderson appear in the NAME field.

The query processor first looks for the relation (file) STUDENT in a dictionary, to be sure that there is a field called NAME. Then it accesses the data and looks at each row in STUDENT for one of the names. The system moves records matching the request to a temporary file. Finally, the user can print the contents of the temporary file to see what records satisfy the original request (see Figure 13-6).

To use a query language, a person must have knowledge of the database. She or he must know the structure of the various files or relations in the system.

Most database management systems feature some type of query language. Computer vendors also offer query languages of their own. Although using them takes some training plus an awareness of the contents of the database, these languages are a good example of how the power of a computer can be extended to an end user.

An Example

Filene's is a department store chain with headquarters in Boston, Massachusetts; it is a unit of Federated Department Stores. The company has twelve main stores, six basement stores, and about seven thousand employees. Its sales are over $350 million a year. The traditional stores sell ready-to-wear fashions, and the basement stores sell off-price and off-season products at a discount.

The stores' buyers need to monitor sales and to spot trends quickly; they want a fast response to requests. The information-processing department felt that it could not keep up with the buyers' requests for information. Some of the information that the buyers wanted was available in the corporate data files, but there was no convenient way for the buyers to access it.

To provide access to these data for the buyers, the executives, and others, the firm purchased a natural-language query system. This program lets users access data using terms with which they are familiar. The program allows the user to type free-form sentences in English; it interprets the meaning of the words based on the program's built-in knowledge of English and a special dictionary. The computer staff at Filene's developed the dictionary, which contains a description of the fields in the files being accessed.

When the system has a problem interpreting a query, it asks the user for further explanation. As a first application, the store chose a well-defined database: its personnel records. It took about fifteen working days for two employees to create the terms in the dictionary. The file consists of 120 fields for seven thousand active and eight thousand inactive employees.

On the first day of the system's use, the number of requests for information from employees in the personnel department to the computer department dropped from thirty-four to twenty. Now, almost all queries are entered by the users directly, instead of by making a request to the computer department for a special run or program. One of Filene's main objectives is being achieved: the users are doing some of their own programming, though, if asked, they would probably not call it programming.

A query language can help the user to get immediate answers to a question without having to get in line and request help from a computer staff member. Of course, the data must exist already, and the user has to be given help in accessing it. Still, the more work a user can do, the more the computer staff is freed to work on new applications. Not only is more work done in total, but the users tend to be more satisfied because their requests are answered much more quickly through their own initiative.

Generators

The *generator* programs of today are generally used by professional systems analysts or programmers to create a new application. The analyst describes the desired system to the generator pro-

STUDENT RELATION

NAME	FIRST NAME	SEX	AGE	MAJOR SUBJECT
Abrahams	Jane	F	22	Finance
Anderson	Shirley	F	24	Economics
Baron	Christopher	M	23	Operations Research
Berger	Mark	M	24	Information Systems
Groves	Carol	F	22	Accounting
Groves	Claude	M	23	Management
Hopkins	Ian	M	21	Management
Jones	Vicky	F	22	Accounting
Jones	William	M	23	Information Systems
MacGregor	Alice	F	24	Operations Research
Murphy	Phyllis	F	21	Finance
Pullman	Michael	M	23	Marketing
Roberts	Susan	F	24	Accounting
Robertson	Tom	M	21	Management
Smith	Alfred	M	23	Operations Research
Smith	Beverley	F	22	Information Systems
Smith	Dave	M	24	Finance
Smith-Brown	Lucian	M	22	Marketing
Stein	Joan	F	23	Accounting
Walters	Trevor	M	22	Information Systems

RESULTING RELATION

NAME	FIRST NAME	SEX	AGE	MAJOR SUBJECT
Anderson	Shirley	F	24	Economics
Jones	Vicky	F	22	Accounting
Jones	William	M	23	Information Systems
Smith	Alfred	M	23	Operations Research
Smith	Beverley	F	22	Information Systems
Smith	Dave	M	24	Finance

Figure 13-6. Example of a Base Relation: STUDENT and the Result of a Query "SELECT STUDENT WHERE NAME = ANDERSON OR JONES OR SMITH."

gram, which, in turn, creates the database and the programs necessary to operate the application. Although this process sounds simple, a great deal of information must be put into the generator. The generator is actually a number of very complex programs that a firm must purchase if it wishes to adopt this approach to building applications.

A complete generator should assist with the definition of input transactions, the editing of transactions, the creation of a database, file updating, report generation, and query processing (see Figure 13-7). Most of these programs are constructed as part of a database management system because the definition and creation of a database is critical in the design process.

The generator is aimed at reducing the time required in the programming and testing stages. One organization reported reducing the time needed to develop transactions-oriented applications by a factor of four to five by using a generator available for a popular DBMS. This time saving means that users quickly see the results of the design; they do not

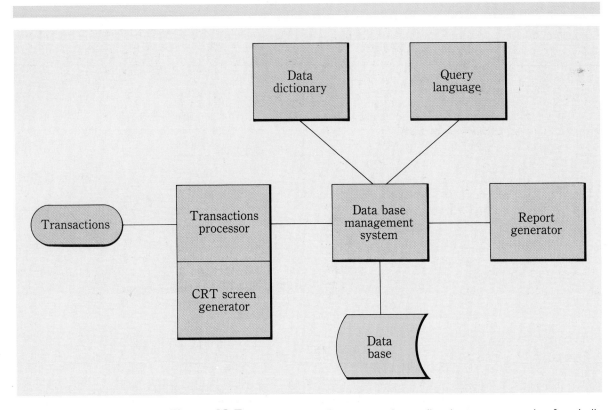

Figure 13-7. Applications Generator. An applications generator is often built around a database management system. A transactions processor generates code that processes input transactions and updates the database. A report generator is also a part of the package.

have to wait for the laborious coding of programs in a language like COBOL.

Even with a generator, it is still necessary to design a system. A specification is needed before a generator can be used. The generator cuts down on programming time and can help in giving users feedback on a preliminary basis. One has to know what the application is supposed to do, however, before it makes sense to generate a system.

PROTOTYPING

It is fairly common in many fields to build a model of a product, or ***prototype,*** before assembling the finished version: prototypes of automobiles are almost always constructed, and an architect often builds a scale model of a building before developing final plans. In creating a system, some experts advocate building prototypes where possible. The prototype may be not for the entire application, but for only a part of it.

The objective of a prototype is to reduce the time before the user sees something concrete from the systems design effort. Too often in custom development, the user does not understand system specifications when approving them. As a result, the first real picture he or she gets is at testing. A long time, possibly years, has elapsed between the idea for the system and the first tests of the system.

With a prototype, the user can given the designer rapid feedback, as there is something for the user to see fairly soon after design has started. The prototype becomes a focal point for discussing the system and completing its design. Examining the prototype can force the user to become involved in the design process.

Time-sharing systems and microcomputers are excellent tools to use in developing prototypes. One company used a microcomputer database-management system to develop a comprehensive personnel system. Using the database management system, the original development effort on the micro took a week; that week produced a sample to which managers could respond. The prototype became a living specification that programmers then converted so that it could be run on the firm's mainframe. When satisfied that the system worked as desired, the company had its computer staff reprogram it in BASIC to make it run faster on a mainframe.

Another firm is trying to use tools like report generators and applications generators to make prototyping a part of every development project. The idea is to have some kind of sample system for a user within two weeks of a request. It remains to be seen if this approach will succeed, but it is certainly worth trying. We must do something to reduce user frustration levels over systems development and to be more responsive to requests for new computer applications.

SUMMARY

This chapter has presented some ideas for supplementing the traditional approach to developing a system. The goal is to reduce the labor-intensive and time-consuming systems analysis and design task. Through the intelligent use of packages, nonprocedural languages, generators, and prototyping many organizations have been able to achieve impressive results. The use of these modern techniques need not be mutually exclusive; one can envision using a generator to quickly prototype an application. Because the traditional approach takes so long and requires a lot of scarce human resources, it is a good idea to use whatever alternatives can improve on this process.

Review of Chapter 13

REVIEW

In this chapter, we have seen that advanced approaches are making a dent in the huge applications backlog that exists today. The most traditional approach is the use of an applications package, at least, a dedicated package. These hardware/software solutions to very specific problems have been around for twenty or more years. Today, because the costs and time involved in custom development are large, packages of all types have become more appealing. Also, many packages have gone through several generations themselves, so they are much improved over their earliest versions.

It is important to distinguish between the dedicated package, which is designed for one function like accounts receivable, and the general-purpose package, which is more like a language to be used in developing an application. The general-purpose package is used to help solve a problem; the dedicated package purports to be the solution itself. In either case, the user should still go through systems analysis and requirements definition so that the firm knows what it wants a system to do.

Applications generators and nonprocedural languages help to produce a custom application more quickly than programming in a language like COBOL. These approaches also require a systems analysis and a set of specifications; otherwise, what should be generated? Analysts and programmers work with generators, whereas some users may be able to develop applications in nonprocedural languages.

Our final strategies are prototyping and end user programming.

A prototype is a model, a vehicle that provides a rapid response to a user and that obtains feedback from him or her. The prototype may be a model for the development of a totally new application, or the prototype may grow into the final system.

End user programming brings more hands to the development task. With today's tools, like query and fourth-generation languages, end user programming is probably best suited to giving users access to data that already exist on computers. These languages should make it possible for users to easily access data that they feel are theirs already.

All of these approaches can help improve productivity during the development life cycle. There has been too little success with convention; bold new ideas are needed if systems development is to be responsive to users.

KEY WORDS

Application	Package
Database management system	Problem-oriented packages
Dedicated	Prototype
Fourth-generation language	Query language
Generator	Report generator
Module	Systems software
Nonprocedural language	Very-high-level language

BUSINESS PROBLEM

3-1. There is real debate among computer programmers and systems analysts about the use of fourth-generation languages. The adherents point to reduced programming time because the programmer is working at a much higher level of detail. Much less in the way of procedural detail has to be programmed.

For example, if you were giving a driver instructions on how to get to a building several blocks away, you would like to be able to say, "Go to the next intersection, turn left, go one block, and turn right at the light." That is a level of detail that would be necessary and not overburdening. However, what if it were necessary to say, "Put the car in gear, slowly let out the clutch; as you approach the next intersection, take your foot off the accelerator and put it on the brake" and so on. It would take a long time to give these instructions, and in the process, you might even have forgotten your main objective.

The proponents of fourth-generation languages, then, say that one can develop systems faster, thus helping to break up the bottleneck in systems development. It should also be easier to maintain systems and to make modifications because there are fewer details to worry about.

Those opposed to these languages argue that they make terribly inefficient use of the computer, and that the programs are likely to run very slowly. The organization using them is likely to need additional computers.

What is your opinion in this argument? What are the pros and cons of each position? What do you recommend?

13-2. A small nonprofit economic-development agency is trying to decide whether it needs a computer. The agency has only ten staff members, but it seems that there is a tremendous amount of paperwork in their jobs. First, the agency needs elaborate budgets, not just for its own organization, but for the businesses it is helping to get started. Financial statements are also needed for external funding agencies.

The agency must also manage projects, or at very least, it must furnish consulting help to its clients with their projects. Project management requires keeping a lot of records and frequent checking on each stage of progress. Consequently, the agency finds its already-scarce staff resources tied up in these tasks.

Because this is a nonprofit agency, the senior managers are concerned about the cost of computers. They know that a mainframe is probably not at all necessary or feasible. However, they are not even sure how to proceed. They have heard about minis, personal computers, programmers, and packages.

Under the circumstances, what advice could you give the senior management of the agency? How should they proceed to decide whether a computer system can help them and, if so, how to use a system to solve their problems?

REVIEW QUESTIONS

1. How do packages reduce development time for a system?
2. How does a package vendor provide a system that will fit into different organizations?
3. What is the user's role in making a decision on a package?
4. Why should the user prepare a specification before considering a package?
5. What is the primary motivation behind applications generators?
6. What functions does a typical report generator fulfill?
7. How is a query language generally used?
8. Why are some very-high-level languages called *nonprocedural?*
9. How can an applications generator be used in prototyping?
10. What are the best tools for developing a prototype?
11. What are the reasons for prototyping?
12. How does a prototype secure user involvement in design?
13. How does prototyping relate to higher-order languages?

THOUGHT QUESTIONS

14. How can packages lower development costs? Do they always?
15. Does one always get debugged programs when buying a package?
16. Why should we insist on a demonstration when buying a package?
17. Under what conditions might a firm be willing to make changes in its procedures in order to use a package?
18. What areas do you think can make best use of a problem-oriented language?
19. Describe how you think implementation might differ between a custom system and a package.
20. How does the user identify the required changes in a dedicated package in order to use it in her or his organization?
21. What is the difference between an applications generator and a query language?
22. Why can it be faster for a user to write a program using a report generator than for the user to have a programmer produce the desired output?
23. Why is a database management system an integral part of most applications generators?

24. Why must a user understand the structure of a database in order to use a query language?
25. Under what conditions would one want to develop a custom application using traditional approaches?
26. What actions are necessary on the part of the computer staff to support the use of report generators by users?
27. Where do the techniques in this chapter impact the systems life cycle?
28. How does a prototype of a computer system differ from the architect's model? How are they similar?
29. What kind of help does an end user need to work with a query language?
30. If generators become more prevalent, will there be a need for applications programmers?

RECOMMENDED READINGS

Martin, James. *Applications Development Without Programmers*. Englewood Cliffs, NJ: Prentice-Hall, 1982. An excellent book showing a number of alternatives to tradition.

Mason, R. E. A., and T. T. Carey. "Prototyping Interactive Information Systems," *Communications of the ACM,* Vol. 26, No. 5 (May 1983), pp. 347–354. A good discussion of the reasons for prototyping.

Nauman, J., and M. Jenkins. "Prototyping: The New Paradigm for Systems Development," *MIS Quarterly* (September 1982). A thorough discussion of prototyping.

Nie, N., et al. *Statistical Package for the Social Sciences* (2nd ed.). New York: McGraw-Hill, 1975. An excellent example of package documentation; the discussion of statistical procedures is often more enlightening than that in a statistics book.

Chapter 14

One of the best ways to gain an appreciation for systems analysis and design is to study a single system in some detail. This chapter presents the Computerware retail-store example to demonstrate what is meant by the logical design of a system.

Remember that design is always arbitrary; there is no one best way for a system to function. The designers look at different alternatives and then compromise on what seems like the best choice, given present resources and constraints. Good designers also think about the future; they would like to have a system that will last for as long as possible with small changes. Sometimes a designer includes more capacity and features than are required in an attempt to anticipate future as well as present needs.

After reading this chapter, you should be able to:

- Understand and draw data flow diagrams.
- Explain how the Computerware system functions.
- Develop the design of a simple microcomputer application.
- Design the on-line menus for a system.
- Design report formats for an application.
- Describe what is meant by *logical design*.

AN EXAMPLE OF AN APPLICATION

INTRODUCTION

In this chapter, we develop an application in detail in order to provide the reader with a good understanding of a business use of computers. The chapter uses the data flow diagrams discussed in Chapter 12 to describe the application. See Figure 14-1 for an explanation of the symbols used in this chapter. Remember that these diagrams are drawn in a top-down manner; that is, they move from a high level of conceptualization to more detailed levels. You will note in this chapter that each diagram fits on a single page. When another level of detail is needed, a portion of the current diagram is "exploded" into more detail on a succeeding page.

This chapter is a very important part of the text, as organizations have applied computer technology to develop hundreds of thousands of systems such as the one shown in Figure 14-2. What you see in this chapter is not something that only a professional systems analyst should be able to understand; the specifications in this chapter could be prepared, with assistance from a professional, by a design team with heavy user representation. An educated person today needs to understand how computers are used in a business setting, and the Computerware story offers a good vehicle for developing that kind of understanding.

THE ENVIRONMENT

The system described here is to be used in Computerware retail stores. Remember that these stores are relatively small establishments selling various computer components and software. At least for the present, Multicorp views these stores as autonomous businesses, run by the store manager. The philosophy at headquarters is that local store autonomy will encourage better management,

as the store managers will feel able to make their own decisions. Also, the store managers will be able to respond to the unique conditions in their locations better than headquarters can.

The system will focus on in-store inventory and reordering. It is very important for the local stores to have the merchandise that customers want, or at least to be able to obtain it quickly if it is out of stock. The operations of the retail store with respect to inventory are fairly simple. The store has a certain number of items in stock. Items are sold from this stock. When the inventory of an item is low, it should be reordered. The flow into the inventory comes from reorders; reductions in inventory result from sales.

Multicorp will provide central warehousing and ordering to take advantage of quantity discounts when buying merchandise for the stores. It is quite common for suppliers to offer quantity discounts. The supplier can justify a lower price for a large order because the supplier's expenses for processing the order are less per unit ordered. If the order involves setting up machinery and making the product, the setup costs are also lower per unit produced.

With central purchasing, all of the goods needed by all stores will be ordered at one time by Multicorp, a procedure that should produce the maximum possible volume-purchase discounts. The retail stores will keep their own books and records, but they will have to obtain all of their supplies from the Multicorp warehouse.

Design Strategy

This chapter concentrates on the design of the system. Can the designers sit down and generate something like the specifications in this chapter on the first attempt? The answer is definitely "no." It is not feasible, nor would it be particularly clear, to present

Legend

⬤ Check validity   Transforms or transformations of data

Inventory records ➚   Data flows of data elements

⊛ "AND" operator i.e., both data flows required

⊕ "OR" operator i.e., either one of the 2 data flows is required

Inv DB   Databases (permanent) and files (temporary) stored at the retail store

Warehouse files   Files stored at the warehouse

Message   Data transmitted along a dial-up connection between the store and warehouse

Figure 14-2. A Grocery Store Re-order Application.

(1) A store employee uses a bar code scanner to obtain product information from the store shelf as the first step in re-ordering the cereal product from the store's central warehouse.

(2) The bar code reader is connected via modem to the telephone line which transmits product orders to the warehouse. A tone notifies the manager when his order is registered.

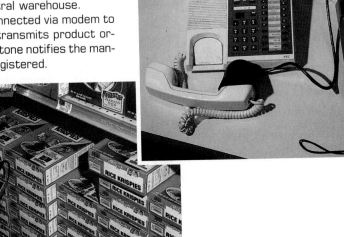

2

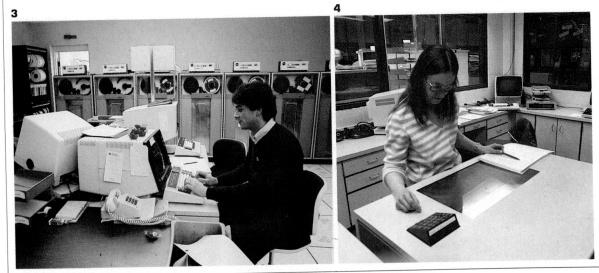

1

(3) At the central processing area of the warehouse, the order from the retail store has been received and the computer stores the data on a file.

(4) In the mainframe computer room a clerk watches a hard copy of store's order being printed.

3

4

5

(5) The warehouse receives the order from the computer and prepares a print-out of the order for warehouse workers, including labels for cartons and an order check-list.

(6) A warehouse worker locates a commodity to be shipped to the store, and places it on a pallet.

6

(7) Back at the retail store loading dock, the receiving clerk checks the computer print-out against merchandise.

(8) A store employee scans the product bar code to verify pricing.

7

8

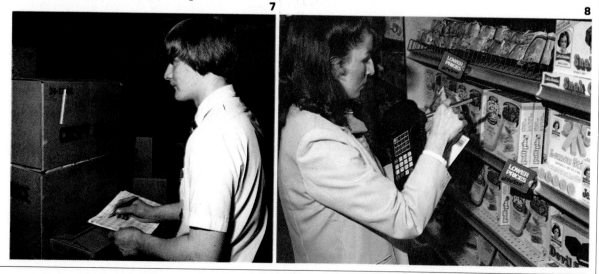

all of the false starts and crumpled pieces of paper. The design presented here looks fairly complete. However, just as an architect's final plans look far different from the original sketches, there were various versions of the system prior to the one presented here.

In a design effort of this type, Multicorp forms a design team consisting of several store managers, warehouse managers, and professional computer-staff members. The design reported here is the result of their deliberations and discussions. Everything that looks finished about the system requires discussion. There are trade-offs at every point in the design; that is, there are many different ways of accomplishing inventory control. The designers had to balance the options and come up with a satisfactory solution, considering variables like system cost, convenience, and ability to do the required processing.

An early decision made by the design team was that the application would take advantage of the personal computers in the stores. There would be no need for a large, centralized computer system with terminals on-line all day in the stores. An operation in which most of the processing is done locally is possible because the need to communicate with the warehouse is infrequent. Once or twice a day is probably sufficient for most of the stores, at least at this early stage in the development of the business. In a similar manner, the design team made other decisions about the application.

The basic processing is envisioned as occurring during the day, when someone has time to input data. There will be a routine to start up computer operations in the morning and shut them down in the evening at the close of business.

During the day, sales personnel will write sales tickets when items are sold. A copy of the sales ticket will then be filed for input into the computer, either by one data-entry person or by each sales representative. The tickets must be entered sometime during the day they are written.

Similarly, when items to replenish inventory are received from the warehouse, someone will be designated to input this information into the local store's personal computer. At the end of the day, the system will display the inventory items that it recom-

mends for reorder; a manager will ratify these recommendations and will actually instruct the system to produce a reorder for transmission to the warehouse.

A system must also take into account the possibility of **returns**. There will be two types of returns for Computerware. First, a customer may return an item purchased to the store. Second, Computerware stores may, on occasion, return items to the warehouse.

It is important to keep in mind the various **keys** that will be needed to identify information in the system. A key is a field that is used for an index, that is, a field used as the basis for retrieving or updating the data on a file.

First, there will be an item number for every item in inventory; the warehouse will assign this number when a new product is to be stocked. The local computer system will generate an order number that will be unique to the store and to each order. Finally, Computerware will have to assign a sales representative number to each sales person in the store.

The following is a summary of the major design decisions:

1. The system will focus on **inventory control**.
2. Multicorp management has determined that it will provide a **warehouse** and central purchasing to take advantage of quantity discounts.
3. Local store managers are to have **autonomy**.
4. The system does not need to be on-line all day.
5. The system is to run on a local store microcomputer, which will also support other applications.
6. The manager will review and approve reorders; they will not be made automatically by the system.
7. The system will be able to transmit messages between the stores and the warehouse.
8. Orders are to be entered at least once a day.
9. The warehouse will attempt to ship on the day after the order arrives.
10. The system will keep track of **sales** for the store manager and will produce sales **reports**.
11. The system will have inquiry facilities.
12. Local store management will be responsible for

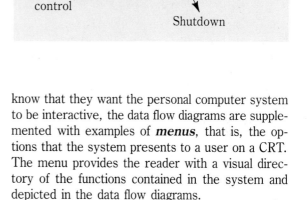

file backup (making copies of the files to save in case the main copy is damaged).

Please remember that the design represents a series of compromises and trade-offs. A different group of designers would produce a different design, but it would probably provide most of the same functions.

System Overview

Figure 14-3 shows the major functions in the proposed system to control inventory at the Computerware stores. Because the stores sell *microcomputers*, one of the demonstration computers can easily be used to help keep track of store inventory. As shown in the figure, the major application is inventory control. In order to know what is in inventory and to actually place *orders*, the retail store's personal computer system must be able to communicate with a computer at the warehouse.

Design Strategy

As advocated in previous chapters, the design team takes a top-down approach to design. Figure 14-2 is at a high level of conceptualization; in the rest of the chapter, we shall consider parts of the system in increasing levels of detail.
Data flow diagrams are helpful in communicating how a system works. Because the designers

know that they want the personal computer system to be interactive, the data flow diagrams are supplemented with examples of *menus*, that is, the options that the system presents to a user on a CRT. The menu provides the reader with a visual directory of the functions contained in the system and depicted in the data flow diagrams.

THE BEGINNING AND THE END

The top half of Figure 14-4 shows the main menu that appears after the user has booted the system (loaded the operating system from the system diskette and turned on the computer). There are three options at this level: *retrieval* of messages from the warehouse, inventory control, and system *shutdown*.
The bottom half of Figure 14-3 shows a data flow diagram for processing this first menu. The first task is to check the *validity* of the entry; the system must be designed to catch any possible *error* that the user might make. The system must *check* for the entry of the numbers 1, 2, or 3; anything else is an error, and the system requests that the user reenter the number.

Messages

The application includes a messaging capability; the warehouse staff may want to send a *message* to all

Figure 14-4. Main Menu. This DFD shows the processing to execute the menu in the top half of the figure. Note that the validity of input must always be checked in case a user makes an error.

COMPUTERWARE SYSTEMS

1. Retrieve messages from warehouse
2. Inventory control
3. Shutdown

Make your selection by typing the corresponding digit ___

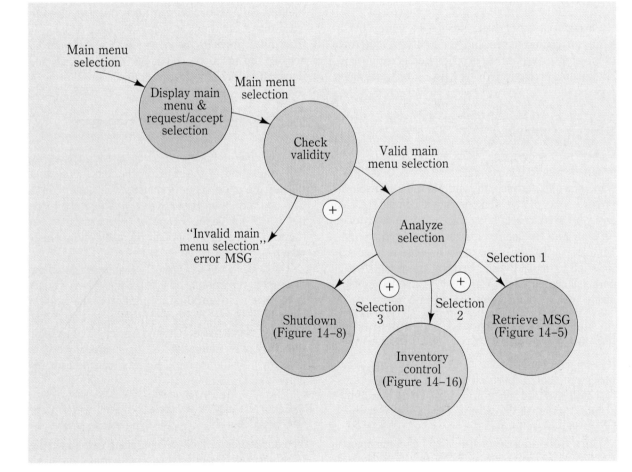

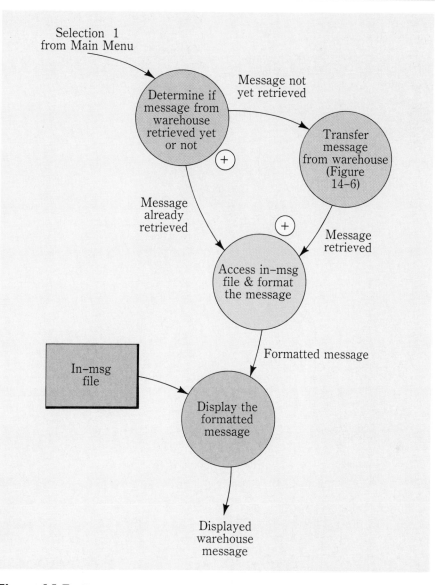

Figure 14-5. Retrieve Message from Warehouse. The system contains a simple electronic mail facility. This DFD describes the processing necessary to read messages from the warehouse in the local store.

stores or to one individual location. The local store should, at least once a day, see if there are any messages for it. Figure 14-5 shows how the system retrieves a message from the warehouse.

The main question for the system is whether the message has been transferred yet from the warehouse to the local store computer that day. Figure 14-5 contains a check to see if the message is available locally, and if it is, the computer formats and **displays** the message.

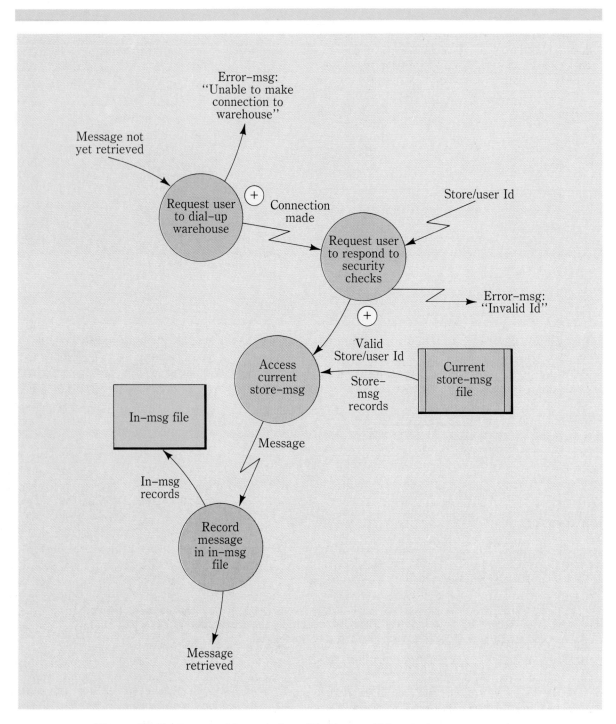

Figure 14-6. Transfer Message from Warehouse. This step is necessary when the warehouse messages have not yet been transferred to the store.

Figure 14-7. There are a number of options available to shut down the system. The local store manager checks orders to go to the warehouse and then sends them. Daily sales are compiled and the manager must backup the database by making a copy of it.

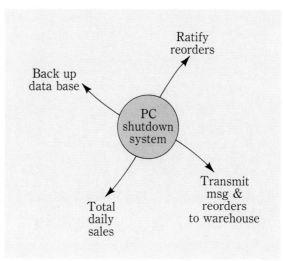

Figure 14-6 shows the logic for retrieving a message from the warehouse computer if this has not yet been done. One design decision was not to be on-line all day; as communications with the warehouse are limited, *dial-up* lines are the preferred mode of transmission. In Figure 14-5, the user must dial up the warehouse using a modem or a communications board in the computer. The warehouse computer checks security and then transfers the appropriate store-message-file contents to the local personal computer.

Shutdown

Figure 14-7 contains the logic for system *shutdown*. A number of options are available. The designers envisioned that during the day when there is time, someone in the local store will enter copies of sales tickets into the local computer. As this is an inventory control application, the computer is expected to recommend when it is time to reorder merchandise from the warehouse because local store stocks are running low.

At the close of business, part of the shutdown procedure is to transfer these orders to the warehouse so that the items can be picked and distributed the next day. However, because the computer is automatically generating candidates for reorder, the local manager should review the reorders before transmitting them. For example, the local manager may want to phase out a product, in which case the reorder, although correct from the standpoint of the computer program, is not desired. The manager can override the delivery date and the quantity ordered if desired. He or she may also add items that have not yet reached the reorder level.

The system will also total daily sales for the manager so that he or she can judge the business for the day. Finally, it is important to *back up* the database; key data on inventory and sales should be kept off-site. Why? Because there is always the possibility that a fire or some other disaster may strike the store, or just the diskette with the inventory on it. (One story is that a computer installation found that the bottom shelf of tapes in its tape library was being erased. Having an off-site backup would keep this problem from causing serious damage. What was the cause? An all-night vigil found that the custodian's floor polisher was to blame.)

For a small operation like a local Computerware store, the store manager could probably take the backup file copy home in a briefcase and keep it under the bed!

Figure 14-8 presents the shutdown menu in the top half and a data flow diagram for processing the menu in the bottom half.

The following SHUTDOWN MENU is displayed in response to selections ③ SHUTDOWN from the Main Menu.

COMPUTERWARE SYSTEMS

SHUTDOWN MENU :

1. Ratify Reorders
2. Transmit MSG/reorders to warehouse
3. Total daily sales
4. Back-up database

Make your selection by typing the corresponding digit __
PRESS ⟨ESC⟩ to return to the MAIN MENU

Figure 14-8. This menu and DFD implement the shutdown procedure.

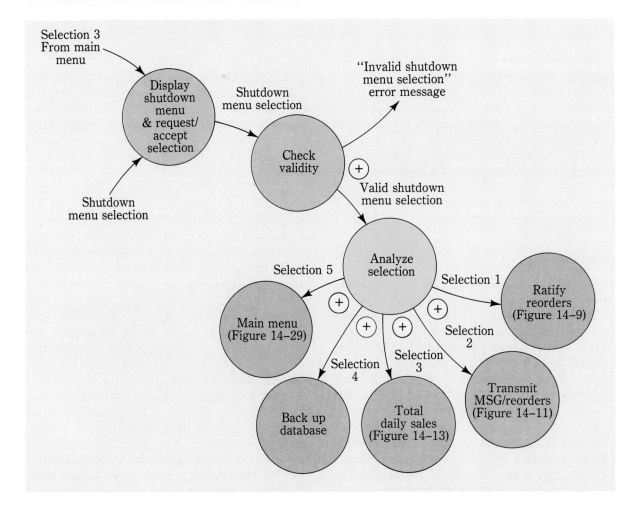

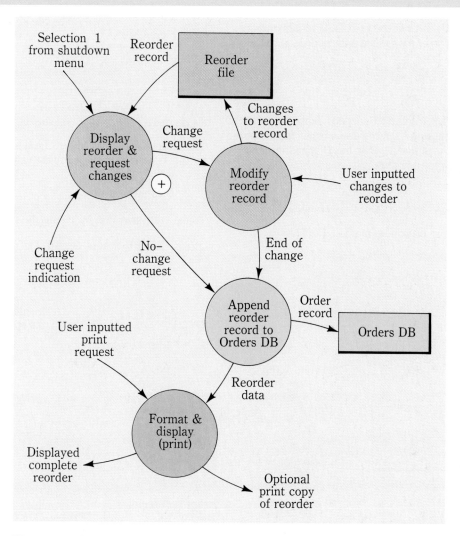

Figure 14-9. Ratify Reorders. The System recommends orders automatically when stock reaches too low a level. However, the store manager reviews the recommendations and ratifies (approves) them before orders are transmitted to the warehouse.

Ratifying Reorders

The process in Figure 14-9 looks a bit complex, but the basic purpose is to allow the user to modify a reorder before it is sent to the warehouse. The system retrieves each reorder record that it is recommending; the user approves or modifies the record (including possibly deleting it). The completed records are then added to the order **database**. If the

user wishes, he or she can print a copy of the order for future reference.

Transmission

Figure 14-10 shows the menu for actually transmitting messages and reorders to the warehouse as a part of the daily shutdown procedure. The process-

Figure 14-10. This is the first DFD to implement the transmission of messages and recorders to the warehouse.

Figure 14-11. Transmit/Reorders. Note that the system checks to be sure the same order file is not sent twice by mistake! Then it builds message and reorder files which are transmitted as shown in Figure 14-12.

The menu appears in response to selection ② TRANSMIT/MSG REORDERS from Shutdown Menu

COMPUTERWARE SYSTEMS

TRANSMIT MSG/REORDERS Menu :

This procedure allows you to transmit information to the Warehouse. Do you wish to transmit :

1. A Message
2. Current Reorders

Make your selection by typing the corresponding digit ___
Press ⟨ESC⟩ to return to SHUTDOWN MENU

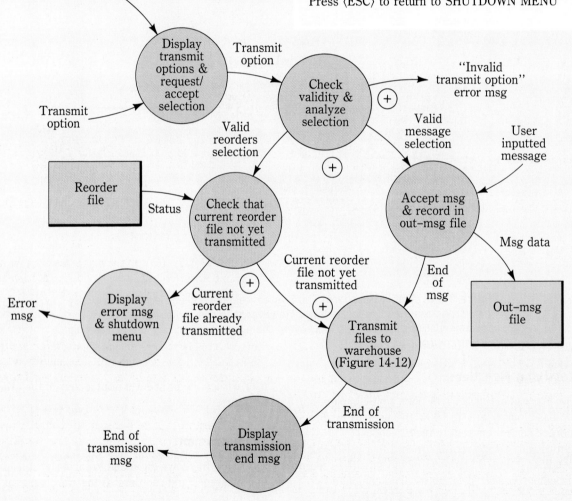

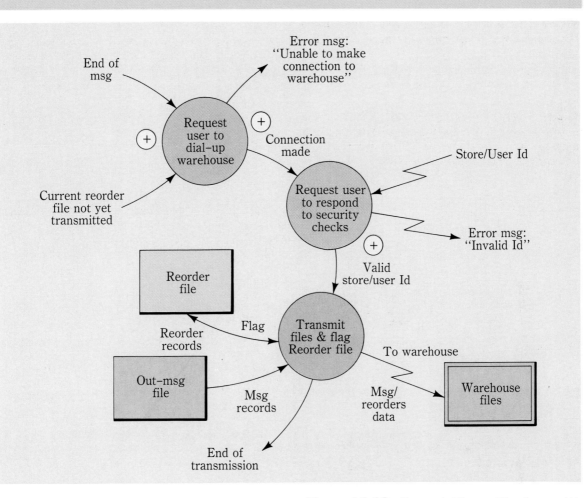

Figure 14-12. Transmit Files to Warehouse. We will want some kind of security check to allow only authorized entry to the warehouse computer.

ing for reorders and messages is explained further by the diagrams in Figures 14-11 and 14-12.

Because there are two types of data to transmit to the warehouse, both are included in the same procedure. The program will have to provide the option to send messages as well as reorders. The program accepts messages and records them in a message file. For reorders, the system must check to see that the file of orders has not been transmitted successfully already. If a file were transmitted twice, it could easily result in double orders being shipped to

the store. This is another example of the need to consider what can go wrong in designing a system and to design a procedure to prevent it from happening.

Figure 14-12 is similar to what we saw in retrieving messages from the warehouse. The user must dial up the warehouse and log into the warehouse computer. Software in the warehouse computer then accepts the files transmitted from the store microcomputer and copies the files into the warehouse computer's disk storage. The warehouse

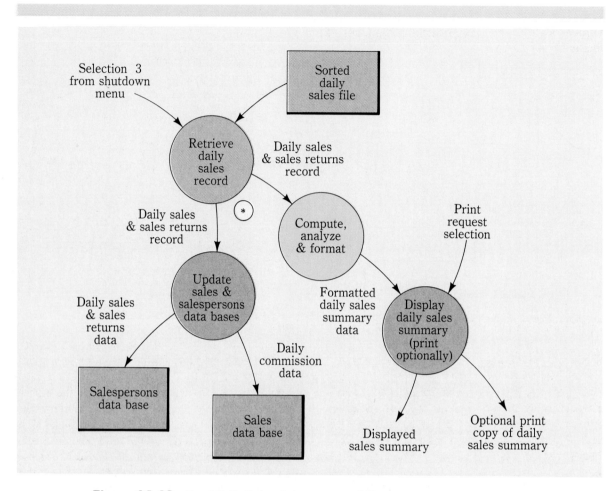

Figure 14-13. Total Daily Sales. It is not very difficult to total daily sales as a byproduct of processing.

computer puts a flag (character) in the reorder file to indicate its receipt so that it will not be accepted again.

Daily Sales

Reporting daily sales is a by-product of the system. Although not really a major consideration in design, it is almost free. Why? Because the system requires the store to enter sales tickets so that the inventory control program will know what items have been withdrawn from inventory and sold. It takes very little additional effort to enter and total the dollar values and returns (which have to be entered any-

way to update inventory records, just as sales must be entered).

Although the sales information exists, it is still necessary to set up some files and programs to process it. Figure 14-13 shows a small subsystem that keeps track of sales and returns plus sales by salesperson for the purpose of computing **commissions**. The temporary file into which the daily sales and returns are written **updates** the weekly sales database at the end of each day.

As the weekly sales file is large, random updates in it during the day would be time-consuming. It is probably better to avoid this constant file access by using a small, temporary daily-sales file.

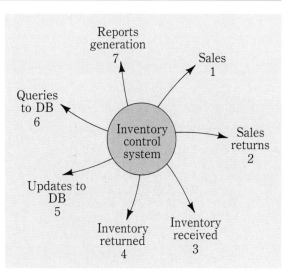

Figure 14-14. Inventory control is the heart of the system.

THE INVENTORY CONTROL SYSTEM

The heart of the Computerware system is inventory control (see the overview of the inventory control subsystem in Figure 14-14). Basically, few transactions affect inventory. Sales reduce inventory as items are removed and sold to the customer. If the store sends any inventory back to the warehouse, then that transaction, too, reduces store inventory. Inventory is added that comes from the warehouse and from merchandise returned by customers (hopefully, a very infrequent entry).

The store personnel may want to ask questions like "How much do we have of a certain item in inventory?" There also will be some inventory reports, primarily to show the status and value of the inventory. Finally, it must be possible to update the database itself, for example, to add new items that are being carried for the first time by the store.

Figure 14-15 is the inventory control menu and Figure 14-16 is a data flow diagram of its processing.

Sales and Returns

Someone in the store enters sales from the tickets filled out by the sales representatives at the cash register. During the day, when there is time, either a single person or each salesperson enters the sales into the computer system.

Figures 14-17 and 14-18 depict the logic of recording both a sale and a return. Basically, the validity of the entry must be checked. E.g., is it a valid item, and is the salesperson assigned to the store?

These sales transactions affect several important files. First, the inventory database tells whether the item sold is a legitimate product, and the salesperson database allows the system to validate the salesperson's number. The program has to update the daily sales file and the inventory database.

Whenever anything is subtracted from an item's record in the inventory database, a program looks to see if the reorder point has been reached. (You may want to examine the file contents in Figure 14-32.) The reorder point is set by the store manager, with recommendations from the warehouse that consider the demand for the product, the need for safety stock (the amount that should remain in inventory for sale before the arrival of reordered goods), and the lead time for obtaining the item. There are mathematical models that allow one to choose an optimum *reorder point* and *quantity*. The reorder point is stored in each inventory record along with an allowance for a reasonable delivery date from the warehouse. All of these values can be changed by the store manager.

The reorder routine compares the quantity on

On selecting INVENTORY CONTROL (selection ②) from the Main Menu, the following menu is displayed:

COMPUTERWARE SYSTEMS
INVENTORY CONTROL:

Do you wish to:

1. Record SALES
2. Record SALES RETURNS
3. Record INVENTORY RECEIVED
4. Record INVENTORY RETURNED
5. Update the Database
6. Query the Database
7. Generate Reports

Make your selection by typing the corresponding digit __
Press ⟨ESC⟩ to return to the MAIN MENU

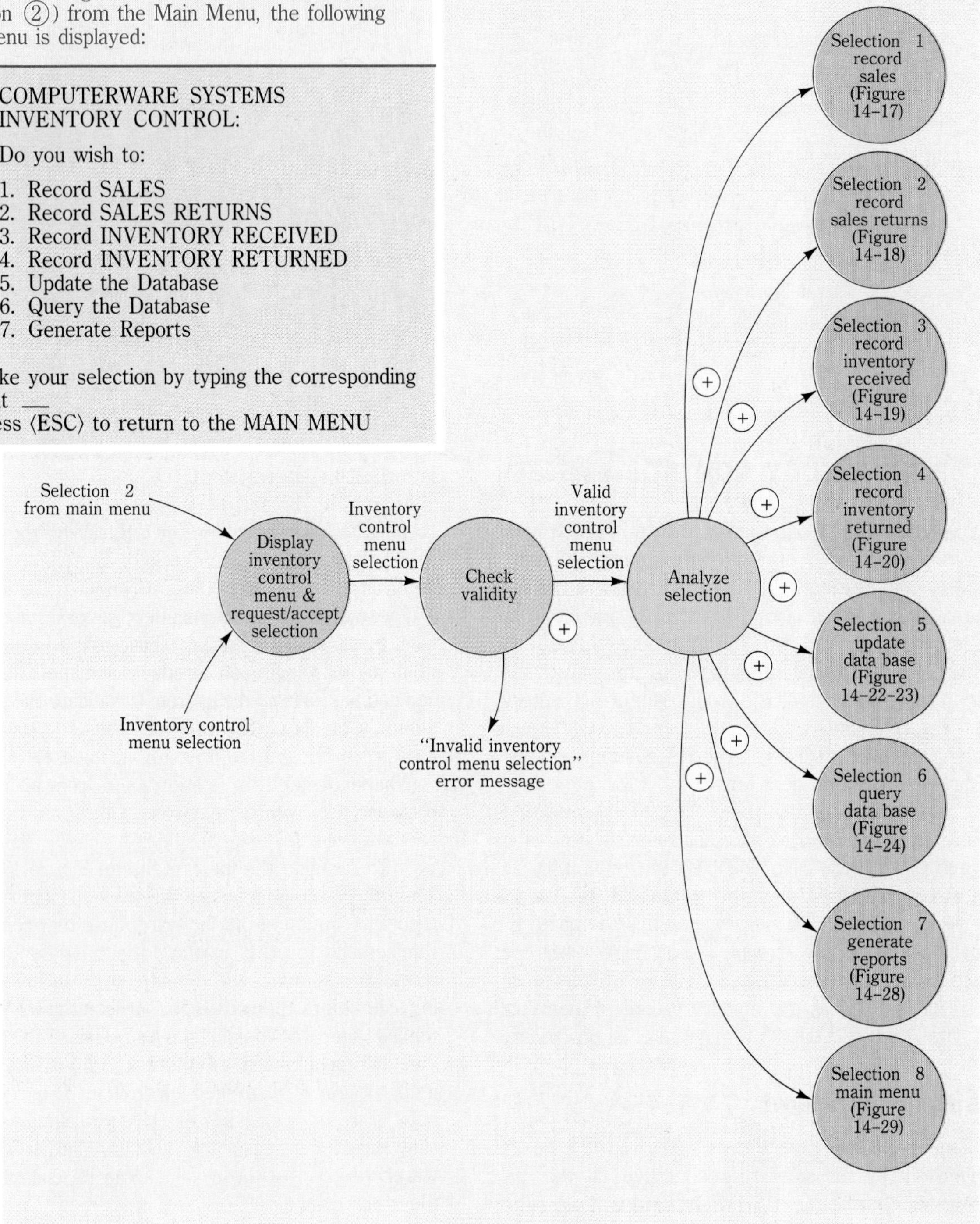

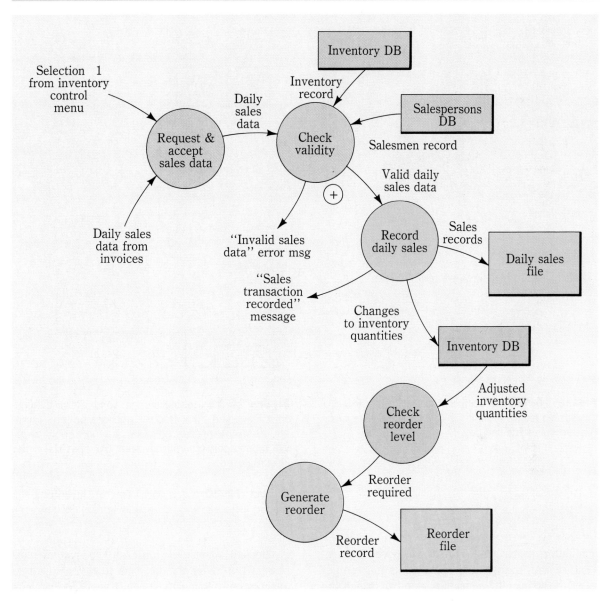

Figure 14-17. Record Sales. The daily invoices filled out for each store sale provide the data for accumulating sales information and subtracting the items sold from the computer's inventory records.

Figure 14-15 (inset on opposite page). The Inventory Control Menu. Here are the seven options for inventory control.

Figure 14-16 (opposite). Inventory Control. Implementation of the menu of Figure 14-15.

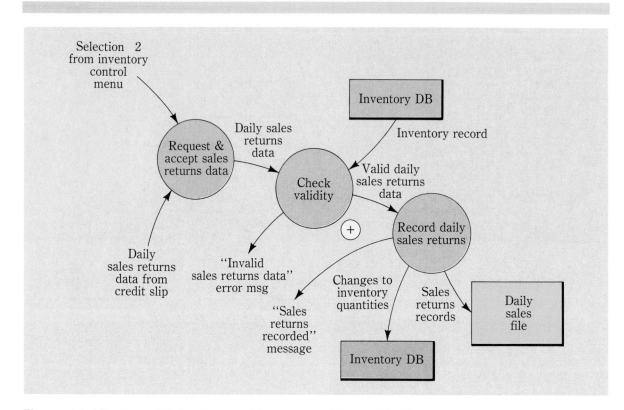

Figure 14-18. Record Sales Returns. Unfortunately, some items will be returned. The returns reduce sales for the day.

Figure 14-19 (opposite page, top). Record Inventory Received. The flow of goods from the warehouse to inventory completes the ordering cycle. We must update inventory and note that the order is completed.

Figure 14-20 (opposite). Record Inventory Returned. The system adjusts inventory for returns.

hand after merchandise has been removed from inventory with the quantity specified as the reorder point. If the quantity on hand is less than or equal to the reorder point, this program writes that information into a reorder file. You may want to review at this point the discussion of system shutdown when orders are ratified and sent to the warehouse.

Inventory Receipts

Figures 14-19 and 14-20 show the logic of processing inventory received by or inventory returned to the local store. As always, the validity of the receipt

is checked against the orders. The system must change the inventory database to reflect the new quantity on hand and must adjust the order database to show that the order has now been received. Similar logic applies to items that, for some reason, are returned to the warehouse after having been accepted for inventory.

Database Update

In any application, the user must have the ability to update the database independent of incoming transactions. Can you think why? First, there can be er-

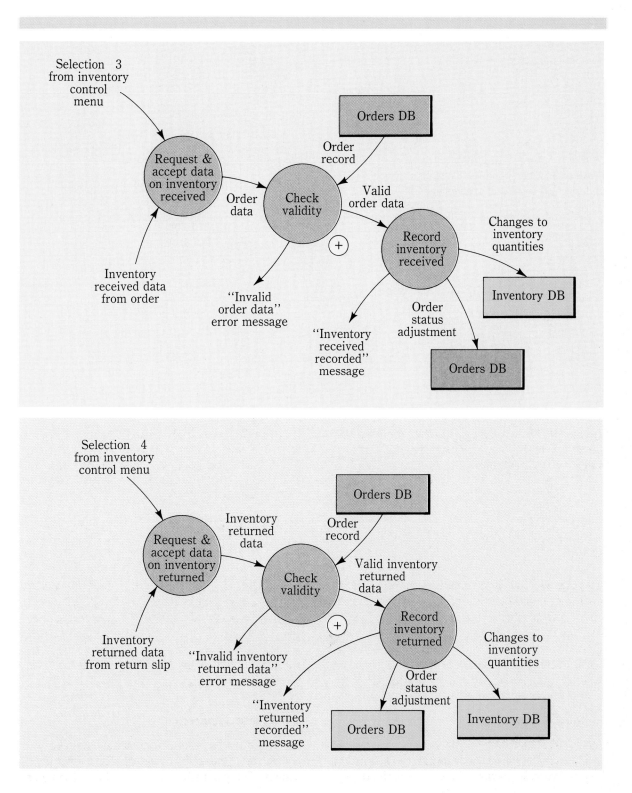

Figure 14-21. Update of Databases. Users must be able to update the database to correct errors.

Figure 14-22. Update Database. The DFD for updating (maintaining) the database.

On selecting UPDATE DATABASE (selection ⑤) from the Inventory Control Menu, the following menu is displayed:

COMPUTERWARE SYSTEMS
INVENTORY CONTROL : UPDATE THE
DATABASE

Which of the following databases do you wish to update:

1. INVENTORY Database
2. ORDERS Database
3. SALES Database
4. SALESPERSONS Database

Make your selection by typing the corresponding digit ___
Press ⟨ESC⟩ to return to the INVENTORY CONTROL MENU.

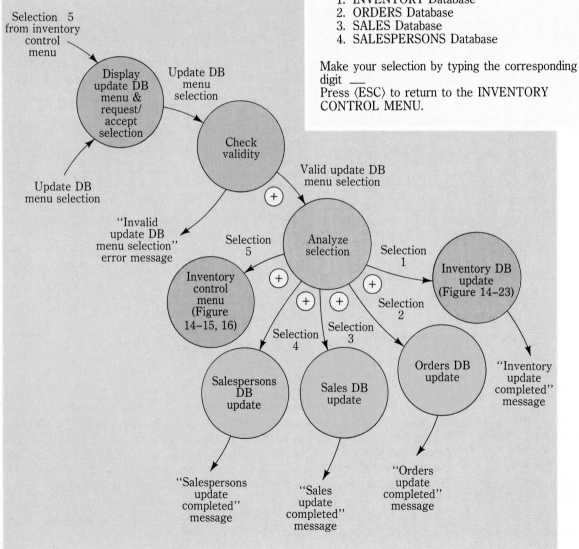

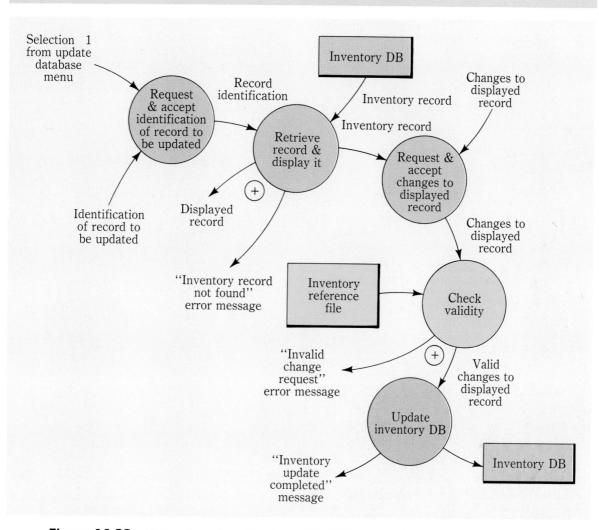

Figure 14-23. Update Inventory Database. The DFD for the inventory database update.

rors that are not checked by the system. In the inventory example, the system cannot know if the quantity sold is two when the person entering the data errs and types a 4. The answer could legitimately have been four; there is no way to check.

Obviously, the system should ask the user to verify that the data entered are correct before accepting them, but errors still occur.

There is also a need to make additions to the files; in this case, it must be possible to add new products to inventory and to delete items that are no longer to

be sold. Finally, it is occasionally necessary to take a *physical inventory* (to count what is actually in the store on the shelves) and to compare it to the inventory recorded on the computer (the book inventory). Where there are discrepancies, the store should record the physical amount as the new book figure and adjust its inventory value accordingly.

Figure 14-21 is the menu for updating the databases for the Computerware system, and Figure 14-22 is the logic for menu processing.

Figure 14-23 displays the inventory database up-

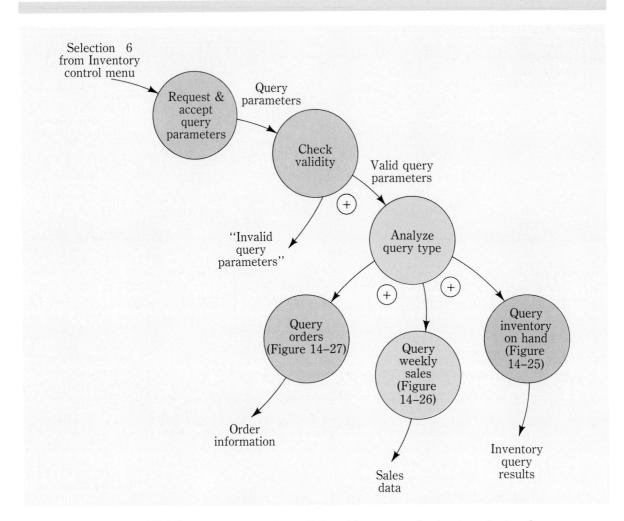

Figure 14-24. Query the Database. Being able to query the database is one of the major benefits of a system like this. The DFD represents the high-level menu.

date. The user must input the identification of the record to be updated. The program then retrieves that record and displays it for the user. The user is given the option of changing the various fields in the record, and the system asks the user to accept the changes before updating the inventory database. (The system checks for valid data, for example, to be sure that the user has entered numeric data in fields that have been defined as numeric.)

The logic for updating other databases is identical; these procedures are not diagrammed in the text.

Inquiry

The local store computer supports inquiries about the status of the items in inventory (the quantity on hand), sales, and orders (see Figure 14-24). Figure 14-25 shows how the system processes inquiries about the quantity on hand. The user must supply the inventory item number so that the system can retrieve the inventory record and display it.

The same logic is shown in Figure 14-26 if the inquiry is about the weekly sales of the item. In this

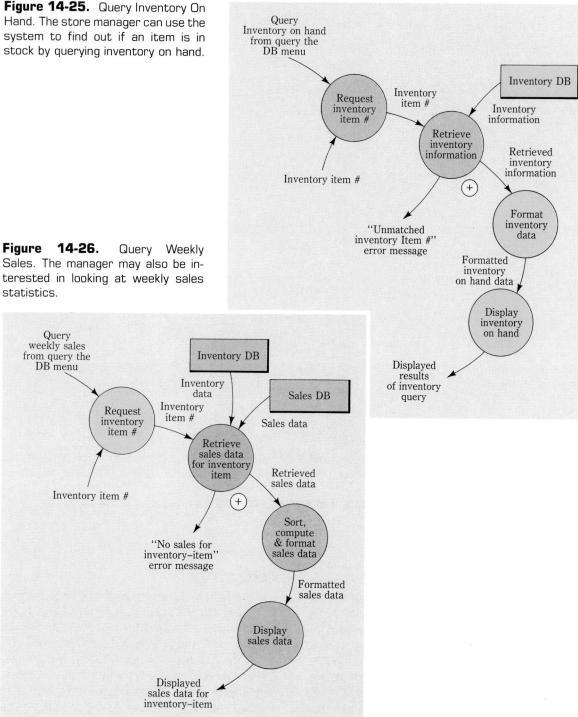

Figure 14-25. Query Inventory On Hand. The store manager can use the system to find out if an item is in stock by querying inventory on hand.

Figure 14-26. Query Weekly Sales. The manager may also be interested in looking at weekly sales statistics.

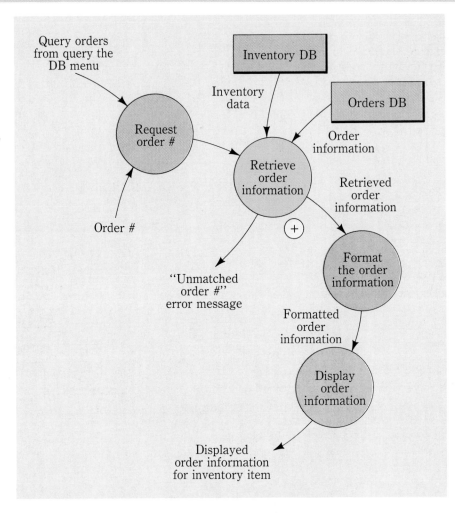

Figure 14-27. Query Orders. Finally the manager can review orders placed by the store.

case, the system retrieves the data for weekly sales. A sort is shown in the figure to allow a change of sequence on retrieved records, for example, if the user wants to display sales for an item number in order by date or by salesperson number.

Similar logic is followed in Figure 14-27 for inquiries about orders. In this case, a customer may wonder when a product is expected to arrive that is not currently available. Store personnel can also see if a shipment is overdue and contact the warehouse.

REPORTING

Queries (individual questions about what is in the files) are good for answering an immediate question about sales, an item's availability, or the status of an order. For a number of purposes, however, one may want hard-copy printed reports from the database (see Figure 14-28). For example, Figure 14-28 shows an option to generate a weekly sales report, which allows store management to analyze its busi-

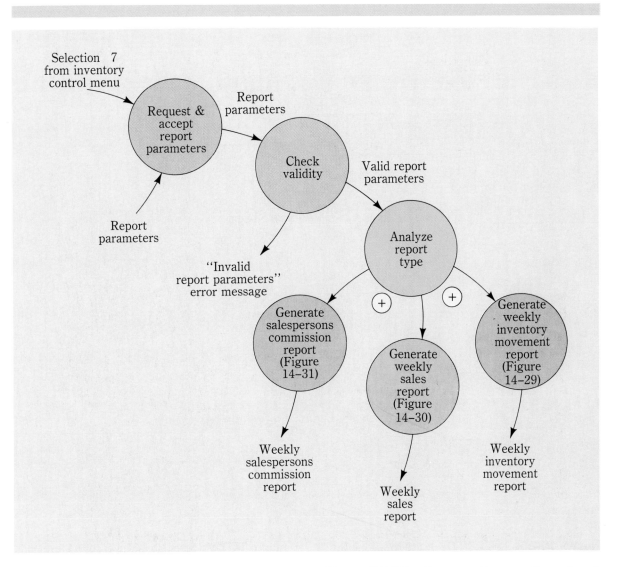

Figure 14-28. Generate Reports. Even though the system is essentially on-line, a user may still want to obtain hard copy printed reports. This DFD is for a report-generation menu.

ness. Should there be a promotion for certain items? Should some product be closed out? Should there be an increase in the order quantity based on recent experience with some item?

Similarly, an inventory movement report can be valuable to management in determining how many times the items in inventory are turning over; that is, if average inventory is fifty items and five hundred are sold in a year, then inventory is turning over ten times during the year, or less than one time

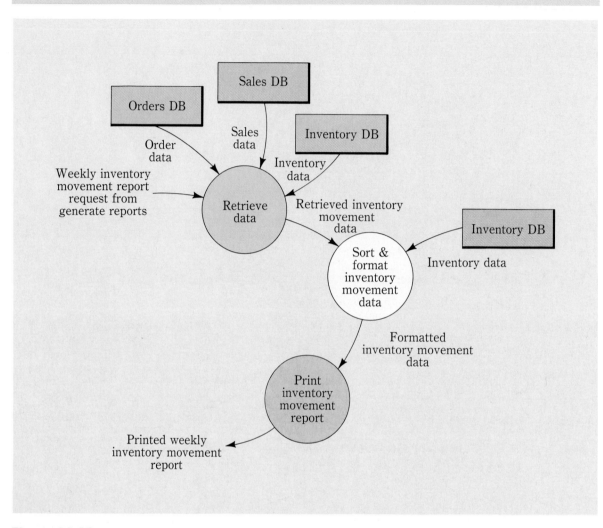

Figure 14-29a (above). Generate Weekly Inventory Movement Report. An inventory movement report helps the store manager know which products are selling well and which are selling poorly.

Figure 14-29b (opposite). Inventory Movement Report. Example of the Computerware system's weekly store inventory movement report.

a month. Managers are interested in inventory turnover because a high turnover means that items spend less time in inventory, and inventory carrying costs are reduced. An extremely low-turnover product is a candidate for discontinuation. Finally, a sales commission report is needed for the purpose of paying the sales staff their commissions.

Figure 14-29a is the data flow diagram for generating the weekly inventory-movement report (Figure 14-29b). This report requires the program to access data in the order, sales, and inventory databases.

Note that the program will have to merge and sort the data into an acceptable format for printing.

MOVEMENT REPORT :

Item	Description	Unit	A	B	C	D	E	F	G	H

A = Qty on hand from previous week
B = Sales to customers during current week
C = Sales returns from customers during current week
D = Net sales/returns to customers $(B - C)$
E = Inventory received from warehouse during current week
F = Inventory returned to warehouse during current week
G = Net receipts/returns from warehouse $(E - F)$
H = Qty on hand at end of current week $(A + G - D)$
    Should correspond to qty on hand value in the Inventory Record

COMPUTERWARE STORES INVENTORY MOVEMENT REPORT

PERIOD: August 17, 1986 – August 24, 1986

CLASS: Hardware — CPU

Item Number	Description	Units	Opening Balance	Net Sales	Net Receipts	Quantity on Hand
H-1400	System Unit	1	430	250	100	310

CLASS: Hardware — Terminals

Item Number	Description	Units	Opening Balance	Net Sales	Net Receipts	Quantity on Hand
H-2280	RGB Color Monitor	1	200	80	50	170
H-2300	Grn. Phos. Monitor	1	220	96	100	224

CLASS: Hardware — Peripherals

Item Number	Description	Units	Opening Balance	Net Sales	Net Receipts	Quantity on Hand
H-3100	128kb Memory Md.	1	350	240	200	310
H-3300	256kb Memory Md.	1	180	130	160	210

CLASS: Hardware — Printers

Item Number	Description	Units	Opening Balance	Net Sales	Net Receipts	Quantity on Hand
H-8050	LA50 Pers. Printer	1	300	250	275	325
H-8500	Letter Qlt. Printer	1	240	118	140	262

CLASS: Accessories

Item Number	Description	Units	Opening Balance	Net Sales	Net Receipts	Quantity on Hand
A-0100	LQP Prnt/wh Pica10	6	920	725	400	615
A-0200	LA50 Ribbon Cartr.	6	505	312	400	593

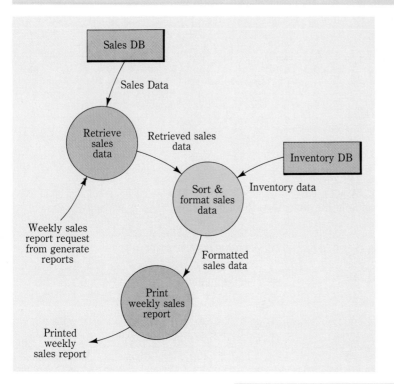

Figure 14-30. Generate Weekly Sales Report. The sales report also can be used to judge store performance. Now the manager is looking at revenue rather than products alone.

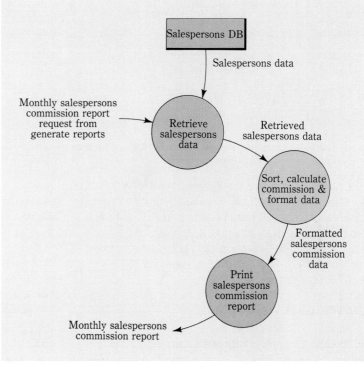

Figure 14-31. Generate Monthly Salesperson's Commission Report. The commission report is very important for sales clerks in the store.

DATABASES

INV DB	*SALES DB*
Item# (Category, Number)	Inv#
Description	Item#
Qty on hand	Date
Units	Qty sold
Unit price	Price
Reorder point	Discount
Reorder qty	Tax
	Invoice total
ORDERS DB	Salesman#
Order#	Returns Ind.
Date	Monthly Sales : JAN–DEC
Item#	
Qty ordered	*DAILY SALES FILE*
Delivery date	Same as SALES DB
Status	but without the
	monthly sales data
REORDERS FILE	
Order #	*SALESPERSONS DB*
Date	Salesperson # (Dept, ID#)
Item #	Name
Qty ordered	Value Sold (to date for week)
Delivery date	Monthly value sold:
	JAN–DEC
IN-MSG/OUT-MSG FILES	Commission Rate
Date created/sent	
Header	
Text	

Figure 14-32. Computerware System Databases. A lot of data is required for a system like this!

Figure 14-30 and 14-31 show the parallel logic for the sales reports and the salesperson commission report. The sales report requires access to the sales database and the inventory database, and the monthly commission report requires only sorting and calculating from the salesperson database.

DATABASE CONTENTS

Figure 14-32 contains the minimal contents of the various database files in the system. You may want to think of other items that could be added to the files because they would provide useful information for the local stores or the warehouse.

SUMMARY

We have presented a high-level logical design for a relatively simple system. This exercise has required a full chapter and a large number of diagrams. At this point, a programmer could use one of the database management systems that comes close to being an applications generator to produce at least a prototype.

For such a system, designers would try the prototype in one store (a small one) to see how it works. Then they would make refinements and modifications before trying it elsewhere. If the prototype is acceptable in terms of the functions it provides and its mode of operation (for example, dial-up access to the warehouse twice a day), the designers and users would have to assess performance. If the database system is too slow, then the programming staff could use the prototype system as a living specification for developing the system in a conventional programming language. However, the hope is that the database system is fast enough to prevent this last step.

There are several things that the reader should try to remember about this chapter:

1. The logic for a computer system has to be described unambiguously and in great detail.
2. There are many trade-offs and different ways of doing things with computers. It is unlikely that there will be a "right" answer; we try to find an acceptable solution.
3. Using techniques such as menus and data flow diagrams is critical in communicating about information systems.
4. Design is a creative process, best done with a team of designers because it is very difficult for one person to think of all the possible contingencies.
5. It is vital for the user and the manager to become involved in the design process because even some of the detailed decisions in design will affect their jobs.

The use of computers for applications like the one developed in this chapter has brought a new era to business. A knowledge of how the computer can contribute to the firm and of how to apply the technology is of great importance to individuals who expect to be a part of an organization.

Review of Chapter 14

REVIEW

Studying the detailed design of an application is the next best thing to participating in the design of a system. This chapter has attempted to provide the reader with a feeling for what is involved in design. Thousands of alternatives must be considered and decisions must be made about the design of a system.

Design is creative because there is no magic formula for making decisions. Both users and professional designers must be involved because these decisions need the input of the individuals who will use the system. The professional designer does not use the system in most instances; he or she fades away at the completion of the design to begin work on another system for a different group of users.

The example of Computerware also illustrates the use of data flow diagrams and menus to provide documentation for a system. Both users and designers can draw and understand these symbols, which document the system and serve as a vehicle for communications about design progress and decisions.

We have designed an application that is resident on a local microcomputer, though it ties to a larger mainframe at the warehouse. This type of design is becoming more common; in past chapters, we have seen examples for Ramada Inns and Resorts International that employ local personal computers communicating intermittently with central mainframes. The logic diagrams included here are just as well suited to the design of a mainframe application. It is the logic that is of interest, not the computer on which the application runs.

KEY WORDS

Autonomy	Physical inventory
Backup	Queries
Commissions	Report
Database	Reorder point
Data flow diagram	Reorder quantity
Dial-up	Retrieval
Display	Returns
Error checking	Sales
Inventory control	Shutdown
Key	Transmission
Menu	Update
Message	Validity
Microcomputer	Warehouse
Order	

BUSINESS PROBLEMS

14-1. There is no one way to design a system. The design process is creative and represents a series of trade-offs. The designers make the best decisions possible given the situation at the time that the system is designed and the available technology.

A good example is point-of-sale systems. Some companies that were waiting for scanners in grocery store checkout counters to be developed for scanning product codes used alternative technology. One such alternative was a cassette recorder. An employee went through the store after closing and keyed into the cassette recorder the items and quantities to be reordered. Then the recorder was attached to the telephone, and a central computer was called during the night to retrieve the data and prepare orders for the main warehouse to send to the grocery store.

This technology was not extremely costly, so the stores could convert without much trouble when the scanners became available.

But what about Computerware? The system in this chapter is being developed as a simple one limited in power and scope. Is the firm making a mistake? Will it be too costly to expand the system?

Consider what increases in volume might do to the system and discuss how they can be handled in the present design. Then make a list of the functions that you think it might be desirable to add to the system, and estimate whether they could be undertaken with this system or whether a complete redesign would be necessary. What are your conclusions about this system? Is it viable, given these new considerations?

4-2. One expert in the systems field has developed a design methodology called *critical success factors* (CSFs). The idea is that senior management makes a list of the factors that it considers to be the most critical in the success of the organization. Then the designers try to develop systems to monitor and report on these factors.

As an example, the head of an insurance company likes to look at sales and an unaudited balance sheet each week. She has learned to manage by using these tools. To her, sales and the balance sheet are critical to success, and so systems should reliably provide this information each week.

Place yourself in the position of a store manager at Computerware. What do you think the critical success factors will be in a business like this? Which of these factors can the store manager influence? Can an information system support these CSFs? If so, what additional features should be a part of the system designed in this chapter?

REVIEW QUESTIONS

1. What is the purpose of the keys in the system, for example, the inventory item number?
2. What is top-down design? What are its advantages?
3. Why is it necessary to check the validity of every input for an on-line system?
4. What is the purpose of keeping a copy of the database off-site?
5. What kind of messages might flow between Computerware stores and the warehouse?
6. Why does the store manager need to ratify the order recommendations made by the system?
7. How can one develop reorder quantities and reorder points? Do they need to be set by the warehouse?
8. Why is it necessary to be able to update the database independently of transactions?
9. Why would one want a database management

system with a query and report-writing capability for this application?

THOUGHT QUESTIONS

10. Why is a microcomputer system a better candidate for Computerware than a centralized on-line application?

11. At what point is the microcomputer system likely to have performance problems?

12. Would a Computerware store ever need to make inquiries at the warehouse?

13. Under what conditions is the inquiry on inventory item number likely to be used in the store?

14. What procedures should be installed to assure that the daily shutdown is completed each day?

15. Why not have a leased line between each store and the warehouse for data transmission? That is, why consider dial-up service?

16. Why might physical inventory differ from book inventory?

17. Would this kind of computer application work in a grocery store? Why or why not? What alternatives are there for such a store?

18. Why would one prototype such a system using a microcomputer database-management system?

19. What would keep the prototype from becoming the finished product?

20. What would be required for the system to print checks for the sales staff? Why might one not want to include this feature?

21. Is it likely a package exists for this kind of application? What would be its unique characteristics?

22. What criteria would you use to decide if the prototype was complete and successful?

23. How would you go about implementing this system in all of the stores after it had passed acceptance tests in one or two?

24. What are the opportunities of expanding this system in terms of the functions provided to the stores?

25. If input volume becomes burdensome, what options are there for automatic data collection, at least on sales? On inventory replenishment?

RECOMMENDED READINGS

Please see the Recommended Readings for Chapters 10 and 11.

Part IV

The text to this point has been very descriptive. Now you have the opportunity to try it yourself. This section of the book is concerned with actual hands-on experience. Hopefully, you will have access to some kind of computing resources.

Chapter 15 presents an example of electronic spreadsheets. These popular programs have found a myriad of uses in business and at home. They are the reason that many people bought the first Apple computers on the market.

We shall go through an example in some detail using the currently most popular spreadsheet package. After reading this chapter, you will hopefully understand the reasons for the excitement that this kind of software generates. It has been a major force in extending computing to more end users, for removing the need for the services of a computer professional.

Chapter 16 looks at another extremely popular package for personal computers: a word processor. Word processing assists the user in preparing documents. The program has modes for text entry, editing what has been entered, and running off a final copy of the document. A word processor makes it possible to avoid constant retypings as a document goes through various drafts. Word processing enhances productivity and improves the quality of the output product.

Spreadsheets and word processing, then, are two extremely popular uses of personal computers. For the individual planning a business career, these packages will become very familiar. We have discussed how the computer will be the engine, the capital equipment base behind the office worker. These two applications will probably continue to be among the most common uses for all of us whose work involves processing information.

Chapter 17 is a portfolio of hands-on applications; it contains a number of examples of how different microcomputer programs appear on the CRT to provide an idea of the capabilities of different kinds of software.

HANDS-ON COMPUTING

The last chapter in this section, Chapter 18, presents a higher-level programming language, called **BASIC**. The language offers an interesting contrast with spreadsheets and word processing. It should be clear after completing the chapter that the programs discussed in Chapters 15 and 16 are at a much higher level than **BASIC**.

BASIC offers flexibility; the other two programs are oriented toward specific types of problems. The first was developed for problems that involve computations and that can be cast in the framework of a spreadsheet. The second is good for processing documents. **BASIC** can be used to construct a program for almost any purpose. It has been used by students and home computer fans to write simple programs; vendors have written quite complex business applications in **BASIC** for minicomputers. The language should help to put different types of software into perspective.

Chapter 15

We have seen electronic spreadsheets as early as Chapter 1 with our first example of a computer problem at Multicorp. These programs have taken a great deal of the drudgery out of business analysis. They are responsible for much of the phenomenal sale of microcomputers; many of the first Apples were sold just to use Visicalc, the first of the spreadsheet programs.

What is it that makes these packages to appealing? Basically, they make it possible to construct a model using the computer as the worksheet. The model is a representation of some phenomenon, for example, a representation of the results of making and selling a new product. The "model" is a series of numbers, which include projected sales, the costs of the goods sold, total revenue, expenses, and profits. Different assumptions about sales and costs can be tried in the model, so that one can estimate the impact of changing the assumptions on, for example, profits and cash flow.

To think about a spreadsheet as a model, picture a sheet of paper divided into columns and rows. The intersection of each row and column is a cell; the cell can hold a number or a label that consists of text. If the cell holds a number, the number can be either entered directly or computed by a formula that includes other rows or columns.

It is the ability to enter a formula that makes these packages so useful. By constructing the spreadsheet with formulas, we can immediately see the impact of changing a single number in the analysis.

Managers involved in decision making always want to consider different alternatives. They like to ask "what if" questions, for example: What if the prime interest rate goes up a point? A well-constructed spreadsheet model can answer that question in seconds.

In this chapter, we describe how to use one of the most popular of the spreadsheet packages, Lotus 1-2-3. The exact commands used differ from package to package, but the concept remains the same. There are rows, columns, and cells in all of the systems. One can enter numbers, formulas, or text in the form

ELECTRONIC SPREADSHEETS

of labels. The ability to use one of these packages is essential for students, managers, and professionals of all types.

At the completion of the chapter, you should be able to:

- Explain the worksheet or spreadsheet concept.
- Describe the row and column components of a spreadsheet.
- Distinguish between the two types of data that can be entered on a spreadsheet.
- Describe how a formula works to relate different columns and rows on a spreadsheet.
- Describe the importance of a variable in spreadsheet construction.
- Explain how copy commands help speed model construction.
- Pick up the manual for a spreadsheet package and figure out how to solve a simple problem.

GENERIC FEATURES

Before beginning an actual example, we shall discuss some of the generic features that one would find in most spreadsheet programs. Remember that there is a large number of different programs that perform electronic worksheet calculations.

Environment

In previous chapters, you have seen examples of electronic *spreadsheet* packages. You might want to review the opening scene in Chapter 1 to refresh your memory. The basis of these packages is a worksheet on the CRT; the sheet is divided into columns and rows. Each column has a letter or number designation, and each row usually has a number. The intersection of a row and a column is a *cell*, which is the location for entering a value or a letter.

Letter or word entries are called *labels* because one does no computations with them. Labels are very important for documenting the worksheet so that you will remember the logic behind your calculations later on.

Values come from two sources. First, you may enter them directly as a number, say, 62845. One of the powerful features of these packages, however, is the ability to use a *formula*. We can say that the contents of a particular cell are computed from a formula that takes values from other cells as part of the computation. The example later in the chapter will make this clearer.

Commands

A package provides various *commands* to be used in constructing the worksheet. Remember, the commands generally involve using the cursor as a pointer to a cell or a group of cells on the spreadsheet, or the command requires the user to type the cell coordinates for the cells affected:

- ERASE—erase a cell or a group of cells.
- CLEAR—clear or erase the entire worksheet.
- DELETE—delete the contents of a column or a row.

- EDIT—edit the contents of a cell.
- FORMAT—format the cell, for example, to contain currency, percentages, or scientific notations.
- GLOBAL—make modifications in formats, calculation order, column width, and so on that affect the entire worksheet.
- INSERT—insert a new row or column.
- MOVE—move a row or column to a new location.
- PRINT—print the worksheet.
- COPY—copy the formulas from one cell(s) to another, adjusting for relative position if necessary.
- FILE—retrieve an existing worksheet or save a new one.
- WINDOW—create a window so that two parts of the worksheet are shown on the CRT at once.

As you might expect, these commands all have subcommands to take the particular action desired. For example, in a *file* storage operation, one must designate whether a worksheet is to be loaded or stored.

Other Features

Generally, a package provides a number of functions to be used in computation, for example, trigonometric functions, logic functions, and functions that search for values such as those found in a tax table.

Different vendors' packages have additional features that are best discovered by use of the programs. The example in this chapter involves one of the most popular of the spreadsheet programs, Lotus 1-2-3.

Popularity

Why are these packages so powerful? The example in Chapter 1 and the example to follow should help explain the power of these packages. These spreadsheet programs make it possible to perform analyses that were not feasible before their development. Consider a bank loan officer trying to figure out different ways to provide the funds to finance a company. Before the advent of these packages, he or she performed all of the calculations manually. Why?

Because even though we had computers, it was too difficult to arrange for a programmer to use a conventional language to perform the analysis. The software available was too complex and intimidating for the bank officer to use, so the calculations were done manually.

Enter the spreadsheet program. Now it is easy for someone who is not a computer expert to use the computer. These packages are quite easy to use; in a few hours, you can become proficient enough to solve a large problem. In many managerial situations, the volume of data is not great. The user can construct a spreadsheet model and enter the data himself or herself. There is no reason to call on a professional programmer and then wait for service and for a system to be developed. The packages are very powerful and provide the user with a new tool for problem solving.

AN EXAMPLE

Basics

In this chapter we shall use another example from Multicorp, this time a forecast for the sale of a new engine additive at Autosport. This engine additive helps to clean the engine and is used when a mechanic suspects that the engine's valves are sticking. Autosport is trying to decide whether to negotiate for the rights to sell the additive in its stores and wants to determine the potential profit at various selling prices over the next few years.

A user builds a spreadsheet by drawing a rough sketch on paper of the analysis that he or she desires. Then the user enters the sketch into the spreadsheet program, specifying the relationships among the various numbers through the use of formulas. Finally, after checking to see that the calculations have been input correctly, the user can change different numbers and see the impact of these changes on the analysis.

This type of application is helpful for answering *"what if" questions*, for example, "What if sales increase by 15 percent next year instead of 10 percent?" or "What will our income statement look like

for next year if the inflation rate is 5 percent, 10 percent, or 15 percent?" Systems that answer this type of question are called *decision support systems* because they aid the decision maker in solving a problem. Often, the analysis is ad hoc; that is, the model is built and used only once. Decision support systems using spreadsheet programs represent one of the most popular managerial uses of microcomputers.

Cells

As we saw in Chapter 1, an electronic spreadsheet presents the user with a large table of columns and rows; each of these columns and rows has a designation. The system we shall use designates rows by arabic numbers and columns by letters.

The intersection of a row and a column is described by the column letter followed by the row number. Thus, in Figure 15-1, the intersection of Column C with Row 5 is designated as Cell C5. We can think of each of these cells as a bucket that will hold various contents at different times.

We can reference a particular cell in several different ways, for example, by typing the address of the cell or by using the *cursor*.

The cursor is a bright spot of light, which is in Cell C5 of Figure 15-1. The cursor is extremely important because it is the primary method that the user employs to point to different locations in the spreadsheet. It is very important to be able to move the cursor around the spreadsheet. Usually, there are a series of keys with arrows on them. Pressing the arrow will move the cursor in the direction indicated; every time the left arrow is pressed, the cursor moves one cell to the left. On most computers, you can hold down the arrow and the cursor will keep moving; it is not necessary to press the key for each cell move.

If you experiment by moving the cursor a long distance to the right (say, past the letter H in Figure 15-1), you will notice that there are a lot more columns than appear on the screen. For the spreadsheet used in this chapter, 256 columns and 2,048 rows are available for use. The screen on the monitor, then, is a single view of a piece of the spread-

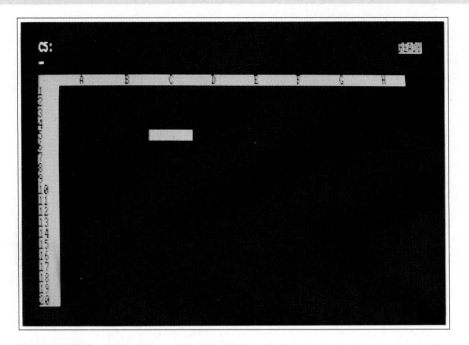

Figure 15-1. The electronic spreadsheet frame shows the cursor in position C5. Note the cursor position is identified at the top left part of the screen.

sheet. Moving around the spreadsheet with the cursor gives us different views of what is on the sheet; cursor movement alone, however, will not change the contents of any cell. Nor will having a cell move off the screen change its contents. Just because a cell does not appear on the screen does not mean that it is empty.

Label Data

What does one put in the cells of the worksheet? There are two basic kinds of information that we might want to place in a cell. The first is extremely important, a label. A label is a set of characters that describes something. In Figure 15-2, Column A contains a series of labels like "Sales," "Cost of Goods Sold," and "Profit." How did they get there? First, the user selects the cell where the label starts (in this case, Cell A5 for "Sales") by moving the cursor to that cell. Then the user types the label on the keyboard. It is very important to use a lot of labels in setting up a spreadsheet so that both you and others who read the sheet will be able to understand the figures contained in the nonlabel cells.

In the spreadsheet package that we are using, the labels have a specific feature: we can actually type a label that is longer than the width of one of the columns. The label will then spill over into other columns. However, if we enter something in one of the adjacent columns, it will obliterate that part of the label. The label in Row 2, Column A of Figure 15-2, "AUTOSPORT PROFIT FORECAST FOR X-12 ADDITIVE," stretches over four columns.

How does the program know when we want to enter a label? It assumes that if the first character entered is an alphabetic character, the information we are entering is a label. If we want to enter a number as a label, such as a year like "1986," we want to be sure that the year is treated as a label rather than as a number. Otherwise, at some point, the year might look like $1986.00.

To enter something that might not look like a label, such as the year, simply begin the entry with a quotation mark: "1986 will work beautifully.

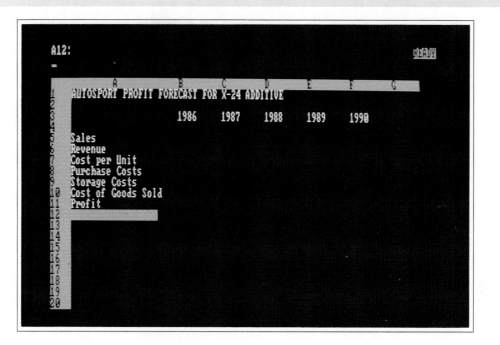

Figure 15-2. A Framework for the Hands-on Problem. The data here are all labels.

Numeric Data

Labels tell us what is going to appear on the spreadsheet; generally, we want to place various **numbers** on the sheet to build a model of some activity. As we have just seen, if we just type in a number, it will appear on the spreadsheet. For example, under "1987 sales" in Figure 15-3, we simply typed 25,000. For many of the cells, numbers are entered directly in this manner.

Formulas

If all we do is enter numbers, then we have used the spreadsheet package as little more than a calculator connected to a typewriter. The real power in this kind of software comes from the ability to enter a formula. What is a formula? Exactly what you studied in a beginning algebra course.

A formula relates one or more cells in a spreadsheet. In Figure 15-3, the cursor is on Cell B6. In the **scratch area** (a place for symbols that do not appear on the final spreadsheet) on the top of the

screen at the left, we see the cell identification and what is in that cell. It is the following formula: +B5*4.95. (The * is used to denote multiplication; a / signifies division.) This formula takes the number of units sold from Cell B5 and multiplies it by the unit price of $4.95. Why do we indicate a +B5? Do you remember in entering the labels that any input beginning with a letter is considered a label? The plus sign tells the program that we are going to enter a number or a formula.

The formula can actually be read as B6= +B5*4.95. Thus, the ability to enter a formula means that we can calculate the number that should be in one cell from any combination of other cells, a very powerful feature of the package.

What kind of calculations can be performed? A large number of formulas can be expressed by most spreadsheets. Just as in conventional programming languages, the symbols used for operators (multiply, divide, add, and so on) differ from package to package. The spreadsheet used here has the following mathematical operators:

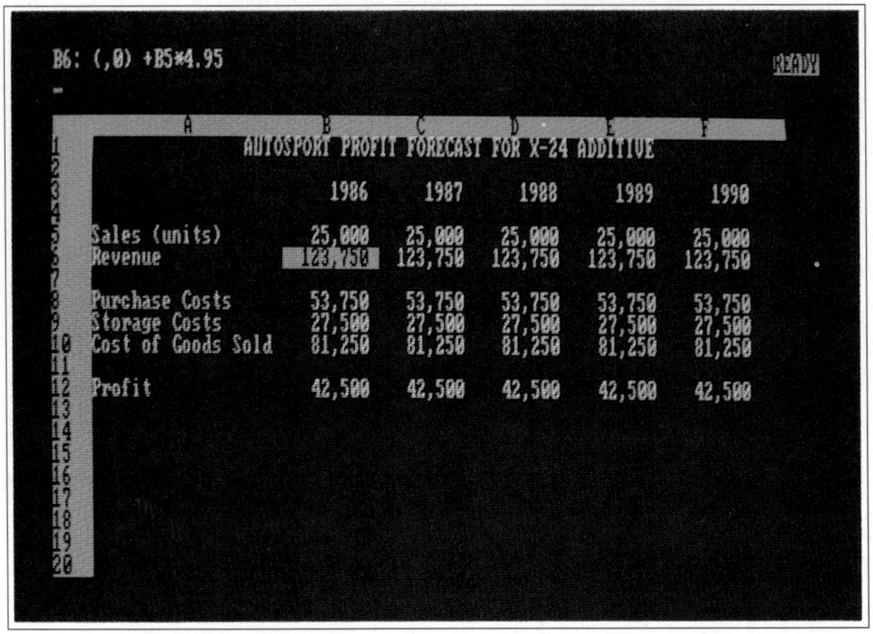

Figure 15-3. Now we add some numbers and formulas.

∧   Exponentiation
+,− Positive, negative
∗,/   Multiplication, division
+,− Addition, subtraction.

The operators are applied in the order of precedence given in the list. Thus, to take B5 to the third power and add C6, we type +B5∧3+C6, as exponentiation takes precedence over addition. However, to take the sum of B5 and C6 to the third power, we must use parentheses: (+B5+C6)∧3. Formulas are evaluated left to right, and you should always use parentheses if in doubt.

Variables

In the example, we entered the price of $4.95 directly in the formula. There is nothing wrong with this practice, but there is a better way. Let us take two cells that we do not plan to use, like A15 and B15, and put the price there. In A15, we would type "Price" and in B15 the entry is "4.95." Now, in cell B6, we would replace "+B5∗4.95" with "+B5∗B15," so that the price will be whatever number we put in Cell B15 (see Figure 15-4). We might call the price in B15 a *variable,* a cell that is used to contain a value that we will want to change during our analysis to see its impact on the worksheet.

Note also in Figure 15-4 that in each year, the same calculation is repeated of unit sales times unit cost. Suppose that one of the parameters we have to decide on in the analysis for Autosport is cost. Then it would be very nice to explore alternatives for sales and profits by changing the price in one place, Cell B15, and making each year's calculation include B15 as the price rather than $4.95. As shown in Figure 15-5, a new price of $6.15 in B15 results in quite different profits for each year once we have entered the new formula across Row 6 from 1987 to 1990.

Formulas, then, give the spreadsheet its power of answering "what if" questions. We should always endeavor to use formulas whenever we are building such a spreadsheet. It is also a good idea to use

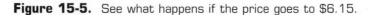

```
B6: (,0) +B5*B15                                                      READY
-
            A              B          C          D          E          F
                 AUTOSPORT PROFIT FORECAST FOR X-24 ADDITIVE
1
2
3                          1986       1987       1988       1989       1990
4
5   Sales                 25,000     25,000     25,000     25,000     25,000
6   Revenue              123,750    123,750    123,750    123,750    123,750
7
8   Purchase Costs        53,750     53,750     53,750     53,750     53,750
9   Storage Costs         27,500     27,500     27,500     27,500     27,500
10  Cost of Goods Sold    81,250     81,250     81,250     81,250     81,250
11
12  Profit                42,500     42,500     42,500     42,500     42,500
13
14
15  Price                   4.95
16
17
18
19
20
```

Figure 15-4. Making price a variable contributes to an analysis of results given different prices. All the user has to do is change 4.95 in cell B15 to a new figure.

```
B15: 6.15                                                             READY
-
            A              B          C          D          E          F
                 AUTOSPORT PROFIT FORECAST FOR X-24 ADDITIVE
1
2
3                          1986       1987       1988       1989       1990
4
5   Sales                 25,000     25,000     25,000     25,000     25,000
6   Revenue              153,750    153,750    153,750    153,750    153,750
7
8   Purchase Costs        53,750     53,750     53,750     53,750     53,750
9   Storage Costs         27,500     27,500     27,500     27,500     27,500
10  Cost of Goods Sold    81,250     81,250     81,250     81,250     81,250
11
12  Profit                72,500     72,500     72,500     72,500     72,500
13
14
15  Price                   6.15
16
17
18
19
20
```

Figure 15-5. See what happens if the price goes to $6.15.

```
C5: (,0) +B5*1.1                                                    MENU
Worksheet Range Copy Move File Print Graph Data Quit
Global, Insert, Delete, Column-Width, Erase, Titles, Window, Status
           A            B         C         D         E         F
               AUTOSPORT PROFIT FORECAST FOR X-24 ADDITIVE
 1
 2
 3                      1986      1987      1988      1989      1990
 4
 5  Sales              25,000    27,500    25,000    25,000    25,000
 6  Revenue           153,750   169,125   153,750   153,750   153,750
 7
 8  Purchase Costs     53,750    59,125    53,750    53,750    53,750
 9  Storage Costs      27,500    30,250    27,500    27,500    27,500
10  Cost of Goods Sold 81,250    89,375    81,250    81,250    81,250
11
12  Profit             72,500    79,750    72,500    72,500    72,500
13
14
15  Price               6.15
16
17
18
19
20
```

Figure 15-6. Our model after using a formula to increase 1987 sales by 10% over 1986 sales.

```
C5: (,0) +B5*1.1                                                   POINT
Enter range to copy FROM: C5..C5
           A            B         C         D         E         F
               AUTOSPORT PROFIT FORECAST FOR X-24 ADDITIVE
 1
 2
 3                      1986      1987      1988      1989      1990
 4
 5  Sales              25,000    27,500    25,000    25,000    25,000
 6  Revenue           153,750   169,125   153,750   153,750   153,750
 7
 8  Purchase Costs     53,750    59,125    53,750    53,750    53,750
 9  Storage Costs      27,500    30,250    27,500    27,500    27,500
10  Cost of Goods Sold 81,250    89,375    81,250    81,250    81,250
11
12  Profit             72,500    79,750    72,500    72,500    72,500
13
14
15  Price               6.15
16
17
18
19
20
```

Figure 15-7. The First Part of the Copy Command.

variables where possible, so that we will have the option of changing the parameters easily. For these reasons, it is a good idea to sit down and draft the spreadsheet on a piece of paper before entering it. See how long it will be and then find a convenient area for keeping your variables. Do not forget to label them, or you will forget what they are the next time you look at the model.

MAKING LIFE EASIER

One can build almost any model using the basics described. However, much of the data entry for a model would be rather tedious. Most spreadsheet packages have some features that make things a little easier for the user. In this section, we shall review some of the most common features that aid the user.

Copying

In the example in this chapter, we will find essentially the same computation in several places. Look across Row 5, where the annual sales in units appear. Suppose that instead of putting in a number for each year, we want to put in 25,000 for the first year and then have a 10 percent annual increase in succeeding years.

In Figure 15-6, the cursor is on Cell C5, the first year of sales after our base sales of 25,000. The formula appearing in this cell is +B5*1.1, which gives us a 10 percent increase in the second year. Suppose that this same formula—that is, a 10 percent increase from the previous year—is to apply each year. Given what we know now, it would be necessary to type in the formula for each year, that is, D5=C5*1.1 and so on. However, the package that we are using gives us a series of commands. You will note a line of commands across the top of the screen in Figure 15-6. Whenever the user types a /, or slash, the command line appears.

To select a command, we can either use the arrow keys to move the cursor until the command we want is highlighted and press the return, or we can more simply type the first letter of the command. The

command that we want from this menu is the "*copy*" command, so we type c, which results in the display shown in Figure 15-7.

Note that now the message line asks us the "from" range for the copy command. For many of the commands we use, it is necessary to indicate the range of cells that are to be affected by the command. The range can be a single cell, a row of cells, or a block of cells. In this instance, we want to copy from one cell only, the formula in Cell C5, so we press the return key to designate C5 as the "from" range.

This action creates a display that asks for the "to" *range* of the copy, that is, where we want the formula to appear. Our cursor is still resting in Cell C5 because that was the place we copied from; now we move the cursor to Cell D5, which is the first location into which the formula should be copied. Then we type a period to indicate that the first cell of the range has been indicated; the message line from the program will now look like "D5 . . . "; it is waiting for the end of the range. We could type the ending cell here; instead, we move the cursor across the other years to position F5.

Figure 15-8 shows the results of the cursor movement; the range we are interested in is highlighted in its entirety, so that it is easy to check for errors. Now the message line shows that we are copying from C5 . . . C5 to the range D5 . . . F5, which is correct. Pressing the return produces Figure 15-9.

Note that each year's sales represent a 10 percent increase over the prior year's sales. What happened? The "copy" command is quite powerful; it looks at the formula and changes the references from the old range to the new. Thus, it automatically changed the formula C5=B5*1.1 when it copied to Cell D5, so that this cell equals C5*1.1, and so on.

The copy command will also copy an entire range of cells to another range, and it can also be used to copy labels, numbers, and formulas. This command is one of the most helpful in constructing and changing a spreadsheet.

The example shows relative copying, that is, the formula cell *references* are changed by one column as the formula is copied to each new column. This relative copying is what we want because each col-

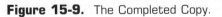

```
F5: (,0) 25000
Enter range to copy FROM: C5..C5        Enter range to copy TO: D5..F5            POINT

            A         B         C         D         E         F
              AUTOSPORT PROFIT FORECAST FOR X-24 ADDITIVE
 1
 2
 3                  1986      1987      1988      1989      1990
 4
 5   Sales        25,000    27,500    25,000    25,000    25,000
 6   Revenue     153,750   169,125   153,750   153,750   153,750
 7
 8   Purchase Costs 53,750  59,125    53,750    53,750    53,750
 9   Storage Costs  27,500  30,250    27,500    27,500    27,500
10   Cost of Goods Sold 81,250 89,375 81,250    81,250    81,250
11
12   Profit        72,500   79,750    72,500    72,500    72,500
13
14
15   Price          6.15
16
17
18
19
20
```

Figure 15-8. The copy in process with the "to" range highlighted on the screen.

```
C5: (,0) +B5*1.1                                                              READY

            A         B         C         D         E         F
              AUTOSPORT PROFIT FORECAST FOR X-24 ADDITIVE
 1
 2
 3                  1986      1987      1988      1989      1990
 4
 5   Sales        25,000    27,500    30,250    33,275    36,603
 6   Revenue     153,750   169,125   186,038   204,641   225,105
 7
 8   Purchase Costs 53,750  59,125    65,038    71,541    78,695
 9   Storage Costs  27,500  30,250    33,275    36,603    40,263
10   Cost of Goods Sold 81,250 89,375 98,313   108,144   118,958
11
12   Profit        72,500   79,750    87,725    96,498   106,147
13
14
15   Price          6.15
16
17
18
19
20
```

Figure 15-9. The Completed Copy.

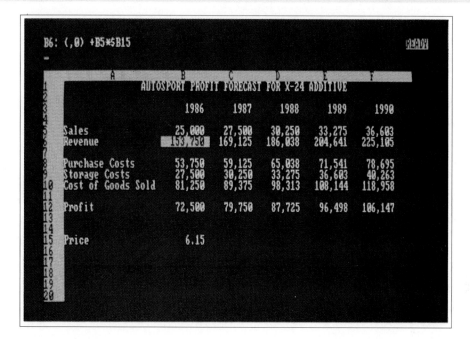

Figure 15-10. Sometimes we have to use an absolute instead of a relative reference. Note the $B15 in the formula for cell B6 at the top of the screen.

umn takes its value from the immediately preceding column.

There are instances where we do not want to have the cell references changed as we copy formulas. Looking at Row 6 in our example in Figure 15-10; the computation is to take the price in Cell B15 times the quantity sold in Row 5 to arrive at revenue for the year. If we used the same formula and copy command as in our first example for annual sales, the package would change B15 to C15 in Column C, D15 in Column D, and so on. In this case, we do not want a relative reference; instead, we need an absolute reference. (The first time we put the formula in referencing B15, we typed it for each column; here we will save work by using the copy command.) That is, we want the price as specified in B15, not a price whose cell reference is changed by 1 when the formula is copied. A relative reference is changed when we copy a formula to reflect the new rows and columns into which the formula is copied. An absolute reference keeps using the same cell in the work-

sheet while formulas are copied into different cells in the worksheet. In this particular package, the difference is shown by typing a dollar sign in front of a cell reference that is to be absolute.

The formula shown in Figure 15-10 for Cell B6 should be as follows: +B5*B15. Now, if we use the copy command, each succeeding cell in Row 6 will be taken times the sales in Row 5 and the single price figure in Cell B15 (see Figure 15-11).

Windows

Suppose now that we want to extend the analysis in our example to ten years. The last few years are going to be out of our view. Of course, with the arrow keys, we can move to the place that we shall be working, but in the process, the labels on the left-hand side of the spreadsheet will *scroll* left off the screen. To prevent this from happening, we shall use another command to create two *windows* on the spreadsheet.

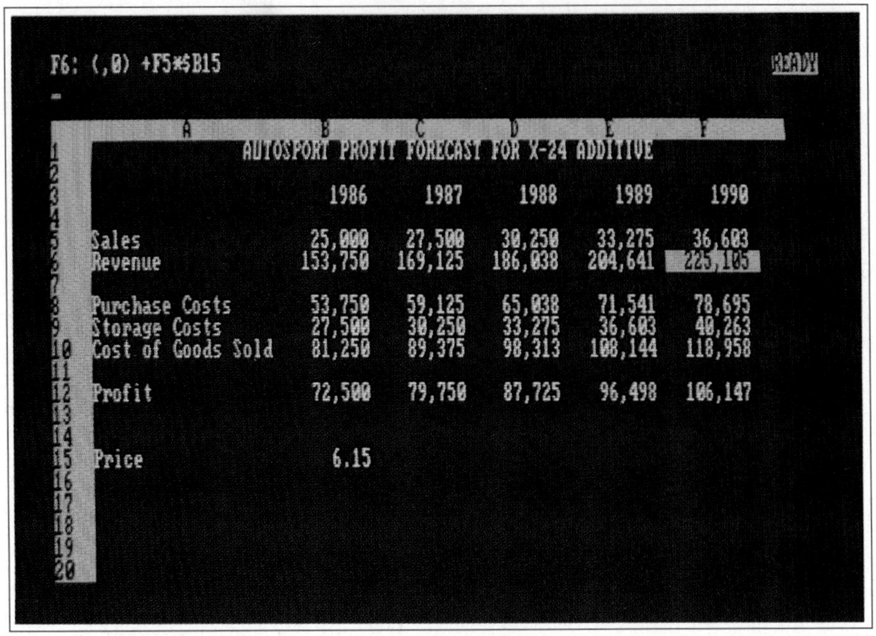

Figure 15-11. Completed Copy with an Absolute Reference.

Typing the slash brings up the menu, and we select *W* for "worksheet" and then *W* again for "window." The result will be a submenu of "Horizontal, Vertical, Sync, Unsync, and Clear" (see Figure 15-12). If we choose horizontal, the spreadsheet will be split horizontally at the cursor location. In this instance, we want a vertical window in Column C, so that we will keep the labels in Column A and can see the set of numbers for our first year's projections. The results of choosing the vertical window and then scrolling the right window to the new work area are shown in Figure 15-13.

To move the cursor between windows in this system, we use a function key, F6. The normal mode of operation is for the windows to be synchronized; that is, the windows scroll together so that they are aligned on rows. Thus, if we were to scroll the right window down, the left window would be in synchronization with it. For this application, synchronized scrolling is what we want; however, there could be other instances where we would not want to synchronize. Suppose that we have a very large spreadsheet and there is one area around Row 500 that

contains a long list of variables. During our work with the sheet, we might want a two-column window that contains a variable like the dollar price per unit in our example. We might put the variable in an unsynchronized window so that we could manipulate it separately from the rest of the spreadsheet.

Using the clear option in the window menu eliminates the window when we no longer need it.

Functions

To add up a series of numbers in a row or column, the user can type each cell reference. For a long spreadsheet, such a process can be quite tedious. Suppose we wanted to add up all of the yearly sales figures in order to come up with the gross sales during the time of the analysis. Figure 15-14 shows what we would type using the sum function; note that it is simply "@sum(range)," where range is the set of cells to be included in the sum. Figure 15-15 shows the results after we hit the return.

Some of the spreadsheet packages provide a number of **functions** for **mathematics**, including the

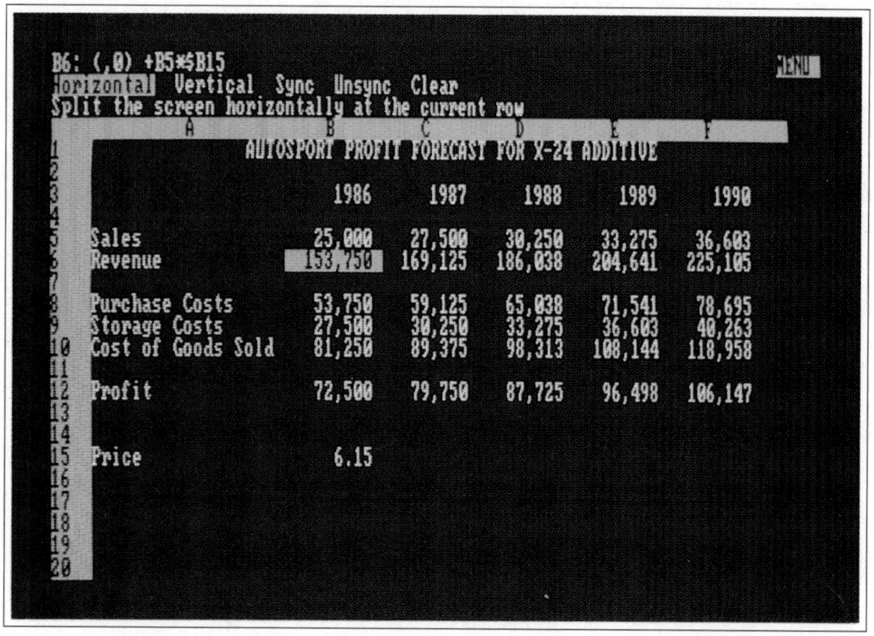

Figure 15-12. In the Middle of Creating Two Windows.

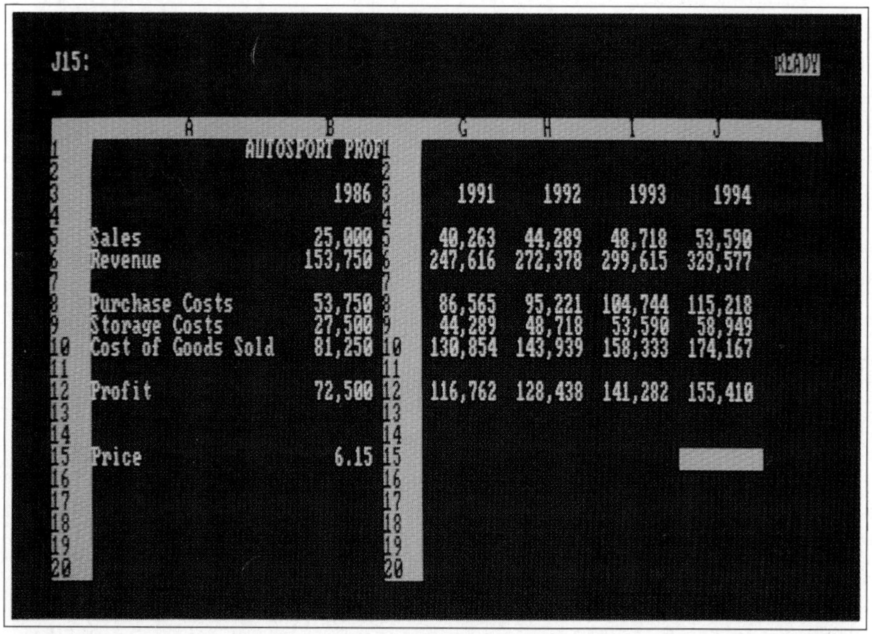

Figure 15-13. A window can be helpful in working with a spreadsheet that is larger than the screen.

Figure 15-14. The Use of the @Sum Function.

```
B17:
@sum(b5..j5)_                                                    VALUE

          A              B         C         D         E         F
               AUTOSPORT PROFIT FORECAST FOR X-24 ADDITIVE
1
2                       1986      1987      1988      1989      1990
3
4  Sales              25,000    27,500    30,250    33,275    36,603
5  Revenue           153,750   169,125   186,038   204,641   225,105
6
7
8  Purchase Costs     53,750    59,125    65,038    71,541    78,695
9  Storage Costs      27,500    30,250    33,275    36,603    40,263
10 Cost of Goods Sold 81,250    89,375    98,313   108,144   118,958
11
12 Profit             72,500    79,750    87,725    96,498   106,147
13
14
15 Price               6.15
16
17 Gross Sales
18
19
20
```

Figure 15-14. The Use of the @Sum Function.

```
B17: (,0) @SUM(B5..J5)                                           READY


          A              B         C         D         E         F
               AUTOSPORT PROFIT FORECAST FOR X-24 ADDITIVE
1
2                       1986      1987      1988      1989      1990
3
4  Sales              25,000    27,500    30,250    33,275    36,603
5  Revenue           153,750   169,125   186,038   204,641   225,105
6
7
8  Purchase Costs     53,750    59,125    65,038    71,541    78,695
9  Storage Costs      27,500    30,250    33,275    36,603    40,263
10 Cost of Goods Sold 81,250    89,375    98,313   108,144   118,958
11
12 Profit             72,500    79,750    87,725    96,498   106,147
13
14
15 Price               6.15
16
17 Gross Sales       339,481
18
19
20
```

Figure 15-15. The use of the sum function speeds spreadsheet construction.

trigonometric functions, logarithms, random number generation, and exponentiation.

There are also other classes of functions; the package we are using includes some logical functions where the value of 0 is "false" and of 1 is "true." It provides an "IF" function to test if something is true or false, giving the user some of the capabilities of a programming language. The user can examine various cells and make computations contingent on whether some condition exists.

Our package also has *financial* and *statistical functions*. These include rate of return, present values, and payment functions, along with sums, averages, standard deviations, and variances, among others.

Table Look-Up

One very valuable function allows us to look up values in a table. If the additive for Autosport had a discount structure so that the price differed based on quantity, we could put the different prices in a table in an unused part of the spreadsheet. For example, one can might cost $4.95, two cans $4.50 each, three to eight cans $4.25, and so on.

The table look-up function would allow us to use the number of cans as an index and to select the price depending on the number of cans sold. We would, of course, have to break down the sales figures into more detail, that is, estimate the number of sales of one can at a time, two cans, three to eight cans, and so on. We would probably not go into this much detail, but the example does show how table look-ups can be used.

Storage

It is crucial to be able to *save* work and to *retrieve* it later. At some point, we will also want to access data that have come from some other source. Thus, a package must be able to save and retrieve files.

The package that we are using has file commands. "Save" allows us to name a file and place it on a storage device, and "retrieve" selects and loads a file from storage. There is also a "combine" command that allows us to incorporate part of a separate spreadsheet file into the current spreadsheet.

OTHER FEATURES

Different packages have different features. The package used in the illustrations in this chapter (Lotus 1-2-3) is one of the most popular; it contains a number of other commands that are quite useful in setting up a spreadsheet. We shall list some of these commands.

Worksheet

We have seen one worksheet command, the "window" command. Other commands in the program let us set the overall format of the worksheet, such as the format for numbers, the alignment or justification of labels, and the width of columns.

Two important commands are "*insert*" and "*delete*." Often, in constructing a spreadsheet, we find the need to add a row or a column. In Figure 15-16, we have decided to improve the appearance of the sheet by adding a row of dashes. Using the "insert" command as shown in the figure, we generate a worksheet with a blank row and insert dashes there, as shown in Figure 15-17. The important thing is that the insertion of the row changes all of the relative addresses automatically. Thus, when everything is moved down, the package changes the various formula references to correspond to their new locations.

Range and Move

The package allows one to specify a *range* of cells and to give them a name. The range can be manipulated; for example, it can be protected against changes. We can also *move* sections of the spreadsheet to a new location. If a row or some part of the spreadsheet should really be somewhere else, the "move" command makes it possible to restructure the spreadsheet.

Print

Naturally, we shall at some point want to *print* the results of our work. The package provides a number of "print" commands to facilitate hard copy output.

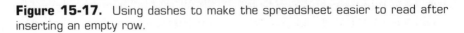

```
B4:                                                              MENU
Column Row
Insert one or more blank columns to the left of the cell pointer
         A         B         C         D         E         F
          AUTOSPORT PROFIT FORECAST FOR X-24 ADDITIVE

                    1986      1987      1988      1989      1990

     Sales          25,000    27,500    30,250    33,275    36,603
     Revenue       153,750   169,125   186,038   204,641   225,105

     Purchase Costs 53,750    59,125    65,038    71,541    78,695
     Storage Costs  27,500    30,250    33,275    36,603    40,263
     Cost of Goods Sold 81,250 89,375   98,313   108,144   118,958

     Profit         72,500    79,750    87,725    96,498   106,147


     Price           6.15

     Gross Sales   339,487
```

Figure 15-16. In the Middle of the Insert Command.

```
A20:                                                            READY
-
         A         B         C         D         E         F
          AUTOSPORT PROFIT FORECAST FOR X-24 ADDITIVE

                    1986      1987      1988      1989      1990
     ----------------------------------------------------------------

     Sales          25,000    27,500    30,250    33,275    36,603
     Revenue       153,750   169,125   186,038   204,641   225,105

     Purchase Costs 53,750    59,125    65,038    71,541    78,695
     Storage Costs  27,500    30,250    33,275    36,603    40,263
     Cost of Goods Sold 81,250 89,375   98,313   108,144   118,958

     Profit         72,500    79,750    87,725    96,498   106,147


     Price           6.15

     Gross Sales   339,487
```

Figure 15-17. Using dashes to make the spreadsheet easier to read after inserting an empty row.

Figure 15-18. The graphic representation of data is very easy with a program like this one.

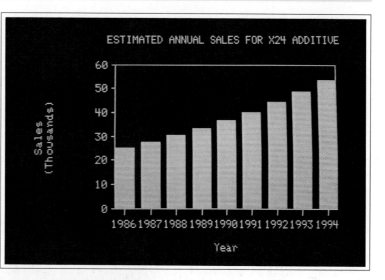

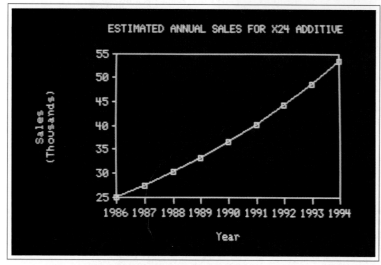

We can specify the format of a page, include header and footer comments (comments at the top and the bottom of the page), and even display the spreadsheet with the formulas (rather than the results of calculations) in the cells.

Graph

Not all spreadsheet packages have graphics routines built into them; the one we are using has graphics integrated with the other commands. With some packages, there is a separate program that produces graphics.

We select a **graph** type (line, bar, circle, or stacked bar) and then set the ranges for the data. The first range is an optional one for labels. In our example, we shall use the years as the labels. Then we can point out up to six data ranges for graphing. Figure 15-18 shows a line graph and a bar graph created from the anticipated annual sales in our example. Other graphics commands let us set a legend and add titles. With a color monitor, the graph can be viewed in color.

There is also a way to save the graph as a file and then load another program that will print the graph on a dot matrix printer. Because the printer is black-and-white, the graph should be stored in black-and-white rather than in color.

Data Management

The package that we are using has a rudimentary data-management capability. We can define a range of cells as a *database* and perform operations on them. For example, each row defined in the database is treated as a record. We must name each field on the row above the data records. Then we can apply record-oriented operations to the data, such as sorting the records on some key field. It is not necessary to mention each field; rather, the entire record is specified at one time. We can also use the various statistical commands on the database and calculate frequency distributions for different fields in the record. There is a way to highlight various records that meet certain inquiry criteria, but this feature is difficult to use.

SUMMARY

Spreadsheets are one of the major applications of microcomputers; their power has motivated many end users to work with computers for the first time. The packages can be used for stand-alone applications, where we enter and control the data ourselves, and they are also being used increasingly to access data from public data banks or from corporate computer files.

A spreadsheet package is easy to learn and to use; it is strongly recommended that the reader spend at least a few hours working with this type of software. Many organizations assume that a professional employee knows how to work with a spreadsheet package and that he or she will use it as a tool for increasing the productivity and the quality of his or her work.

Review of Chapter 15

REVIEW

This is our first chapter about "hands-on computing." The ability to use a spreadsheet program is an important part of anyone's business education.

To construct a spreadsheet, we should first draw on paper a rough sketch of how the output should appear, labeling the columns and rows as they should look on the finished worksheet, and then indicating the relationships among the data to be entered.

With the rough sketch completed, we load the spreadsheet program and begin to enter the labels. If we have forgotten something, we just use the "insert" command to give ourselves another row or column. We must remember to reserve a block of cells for variables that will be used in formulas, variables for items like prices or interest rates.

The next step in building the model is to enter the data and formulas. We put in a few of the numbers and then complete the worksheet using formulas and the "copy" command. After the worksheet looks complete, it is probably a good idea to print a copy and sit down with our old calculator just to be sure we typed and copied everything correctly.

If we have constructed the spreadsheet well, using variables and formulas, we are now ready to perform the analysis, changing data to see the impact on the rest of the spreadsheet. We try out new assumptions, even making changes in the formulas and studying the results.

Spreadsheet packages have brought microcomputers to end users and have demonstrated that computers can, in fact, help a large number of professionals.

KEY WORDS

Cell	Number
Command	Print
Copy	Range
Cursor	Reference
Database	Retrieve
Delete	Save
File	Scratch area
Financial functions	Scroll
Formula	Spreadsheet
Graph	Statistical functions
Insert	Trigonometric
Label	functions
Mathematical functions	"What if" questions
Move	Window

BUSINESS PROBLEMS

15-1. Electronic spreadsheet packages, like Visicalc, Multiplan, and Lotus 1-2-3, have been responsible for many of the sales of microcomputers. These packages have been used by countless staff members and managers to build their own decision support systems. These DSSs contain rudimentary models, models formed by expressing arithmetic and algebraic relationships among figures on the worksheet.

There are many uses for these systems. One that a department manager might find helpful is a salary administration spreadsheet. Suppose that your department is given a percentage raise for a year applied to the sum of the salaries in the department. If your department were given a 6 percent raise and had a total of $500,000 in salaries, then you, as the manager, could distribute up to $30,000 among all your employees.

You would want to see a column for the existing wages of each employee, the sum total of that column, and a column for raises. You would also probably want to have a column that gave the percentage raise planned and another column for the final new salary.

Using formulas to compute the percentages, you could see the impact of each change on the total percentage raise for the area. By adjusting each person's salary, you could converge on the 6 percent total raise and still give a range of raises to different individuals.

Construct the worksheet for this application. In other words, draw a picture of the columns and indicate the formulas that you would use to produce this application.

15-2. Spreadsheets have been used for a number of applications that do not require great computational power.

One engineer used Visicalc to lay out circuit diagrams with dashes and bars in the various cells. There are probably better programs available for this purpose now.

The president of the textbook division of Macmillan, the publisher of this text, has developed an application using Lotus 1-2-3 to keep track of authors (a notoriously unreliable group) and their progress on books.

He uses columns to represent the significant dates for the various stages of completion of a manuscript, for example, the receipt of the first draft,

revisions based on outside reviews, copy editing completed, and galley proofs returned. The dates are then placed in the columns opposite the author's name.

Draw a worksheet for this example and describe how it would be used. What other kind of package might be appropriate for such an application? What are the advantages of the spreadsheet format for showing project status?

REVIEW QUESTIONS

1. What is the primary use of spreadsheet packages?
2. What is the difference between labels and numbers?
3. Why are labels used in a spreadsheet?
4. What is a formula?
5. Why should we use formulas wherever possible in a spreadsheet model?
6. What is the difference between a relative cell address and one that is absolute?
7. Why should we use as many variables as possible in the spreadsheet?
8. How do we distinguish an absolute reference

for the "copy" command in the package used in this chapter?

9. Why do we need commands in a spreadsheet package to insert and delete rows and columns?
10. What is the purpose of a "format" command?
11. What is the "window" command? How do we use windows in building a spreadsheet?
12. What is the use of a table look-up function?

THOUGHT QUESTIONS

13. Why do managers often have "what if" questions?
14. What is a model?
15. How does a spreadsheet package contribute to the development of a model?
16. What is the value of graphics for managerial decision-making?
17. How do functions like "@sum" help in constructing a spreadsheet?
18. Why is the "copy" command so useful?
19. How does "move" differ from "copy"?
20. What use can you think of for having an integrated database system with a spreadsheet package?

21. The package in this chapter has a number of functions assigned to special keys on the side of the keyboard. How does this feature help the user?
22. What is the advantage of using the cursor to indicate ranges? Where is it a disadvantage? What alternative is there to the cursor?
23. Why is it important to save a spreadsheet?
24. Why might you want to copy only a portion of another spreadsheet stored on a file to your present model?
25. How can Autosport use the model in this chapter to make a decision on whether to sell the new product?

RECOMMENDED READINGS

Lotus 1-2-3 Manual, Lotus Development Corporation, 1983. The manual for the most popular spreadsheet package and the one used in this chapter as an example.

Using 1-2-3. Indianapolis: Que Corporation, 1983. A very good book on how to work with Lotus.

Visicalc Manual, Visicorp, The original spreadsheet program.

Chapter 16

It is difficult to know if electronic spreadsheets or word processing represents the most popular use of microcomputers. *Word processing* is the name given to programs that assist the user in preparing a document. There are many different word-processing software packages offering various functions, and each seems to have a different way of invoking its functions. (There are also dedicated machines which do only word processing; they do not have general computational capabilities; we shall not discuss such word processors.)

In this chapter, we shall demonstrate some of the elementary functions that one can perform with a word processor. We are using a word processor that is fairly capable, but not too demanding of the user for simple tasks. You may encounter easier word processors, but the major functions are similar among systems.

The basic functions of a word processor are to accept text, to facilitate making changes (editing), and to help in preparing a finished document. Each of these functions can be simple or quite comprehensive. As an example, consider the format or appearance of finished text: we can simply produce printing that is single- or double-spaced, or we might want to have combinations of underlining, boldface words, and even tabular material.

This chapter concentrates on the basics—text entry and editing—as these functions are found in all word processors. Extra features, and particularly the commands for formatting (determining the appearance of text), depend on the software used and have to be learned from the program instruction manual.

After reading this chapter, you should be able to:

- Explain the major functions of a word processor.
- Understand the difference between input, editing, and output preparation.
- Read the manual for a word-processing package and begin using the program.
- Describe how word processing contributes to improvements in document quality.

366

WORD PROCESSING

INTRODUCTION

Word processing is one of the major uses for microcomputers. In fact, word processing on microcomputers is rapidly replacing dedicated word processors because one can do many other things with the micro when it is not being used for word processing. (Dedicated word processors are devices that include logic, but are designed only to perform word processing.)

What is word processing? Haven't typists and others been processing words for years? The name comes from the fact that a computer is working primarily with words rather than numbers. If we were to enter numbers in a document being processed on most word processors, all the software could do would be to print the numbers; it could not calculate with them. Thus, we have computer software that primarily processes words rather than other types of data.

Word processing has a number of advantages. It can improve productivity and quality at the same time. As the user enters the text, the material is stored on a computer file or in primary memory until final storage on a file.

We use a regular computer keyboard; there is no mechanical connection with any kind of typing element. What we type appears in one form or another on the computer display as it is typed. As a result, entry is very fast compared to that with traditional typing. There is no waiting for a type element to strike a piece of paper, and it is virtually impossible to jam keys.

When the document is completed, it is possible to go back through it and make changes. We can edit as many times as we like to eliminate errors and misspellings. When satisfied, we print a copy of the document. There are no erasures, correction fluid, or misalignment of the words. With these features, we produce better-quality documents.

Is it faster? For a single short document like a letter, a good typist is probably faster if he or she is very accurate. The letter may not look quite as attractive as one generated with word processing, but it will probably be acceptable.

All we have so far, then, is improved visual quality. Increases in productivity come from the ability to store and retrieve documents and to edit them. Consider the preparation of this book. Actually, I used three different word-processing programs in order to test their features so that I could write about them in this chapter.

Each chapter was stored as a file on a diskette. The rough draft could be edited and run off on a draft-quality printer (with a dot matrix as opposed to a daisywheel printer) for review. As comments arrived, changes could be made and a clean copy prepared easily. As a result, the manuscript never had to be completely retyped after initial entry. For these reasons, word processing is used heavily by individuals who have to draft long documents that may have to be revised, for example, attorneys who write legal contracts.

Another use of word processing to increase productivity is for documents that are highly repetitive. Although no one likes a form letter, there are many instances where using a form letter is necessary because of the volume of mail. One can select different paragraphs from files saved on a word processor to compose a new document. There is no need to write an original letter as long as pieces that can be used to construct the document already exist.

In this chapter, we shall look at word processing in some detail. There is no clear winner among word processors. One computer center manager feels that the choice of a word processor is a matter of taste, much as in art and music. A user becomes accustomed to one package, and the resistance to change is high.

In general, the more features provided by the package, the more difficult it is to learn and use. The trend today appears to favor word processors that produce a display on the screen that is very close to the appearance of the final document. For example, Microsoft Word, the processor used as the example in this chapter, actually draws an underline on the screen under the text that is to be underlined. Another popular processor only highlights the text, and the user cannot tell if the highlight means an underline or boldface type.

AN EXAMPLE

A relatively sophisticated word processor has been chosen as the example here, because it provides an idea of the range of features possible in such software. The manual accompanying the software package is almost four hundred pages long, so we can touch on only the high points of the package. Almost anyone who is responsible for preparing written documents can make use of a word processor. The Word program presented in this chapter has been adopted as a standard by one of the largest accounting firms in the world. It will be used on over 7000 Macintosh microcomputers by professional workers and secretaries.

First, let us look at the functions that one can usually perform with a word processor:

1. Enter text to create a document.
2. Select various parts of the document for review and editing.
3. Make actual editing changes in the document.
4. Alter the format or appearance of the text.
5. Save the text on a file.
6. Print a copy of the document.
7. Retrieve a stored document.

It would be nice to be able to say that all these steps happen in sequence. In actuality, the sequence of steps taken by the user depends on the design of the package. It is typical to enter a document, to save and print it, and then to review the printed draft to make corrections. Then we retrieve the document, edit it further, file a new copy, and print a final draft. Even within the entry process, we shall notice errors and edit them as we go.

Entry

The first thing we want to do is to enter the *text* shown in Figure 16-1. Figure 16-2 is the *entry* screen of our word processor. Note the ruled square; this is a picture of the document. Just as with the spreadsheet, we can think of the square as a picture *window* moving through the document.

With the system we are using, there are keys on the right side of the keyboard labeled "Pg Up" and "Pg Dn" (Page Up and Page Down). Depressing these keys *scrolls* (moves) the document through the window. "Page down" brings the next page into view, and "page up" backs up one window full of text. We can also scroll a line at a time by using the cursor movement keys.

The command lines below the window provide various commands to be used in entry, editing, formatting, and printing. We shall review these commands as we need them in working with the document.

First, we start typing the document. The title can be typed flush with the left-hand margin. At the end of the word "NOTICE" we press the *return* key and then type the title. At the end of " . . . PROCESSING" we type another return. The return key tells the word-processing package that we want to end a paragraph. Now, we begin typing the text: "We are happy to present . . . " Notice that we do not have to press the return key at the end of the line; the software features something called *word wrap*. Words that do not fit on a line are moved to the next line. This feature is another reason that word processing is fast: there is no need to worry about where the line ends; the system does that for us.

Figure 16-3 shows the document immediately after entry. It is not particularly pretty, so we shall do a little formatting before editing. There are two ways to *format* with this package; the simplest is to use keystrokes to change the appearance of a paragraph or the whole document.

If we move the *cursor* to any character of the first line of the title and hold down the key labeled "alt" while pressing the letter *c* for "*center*," the first line of the title will be centered. We shall do the same for the second line. Now, we hold down the "alt" key and type *o*, and the system will open up the paragraphs, putting a blank line between each one. Now the document looks a lot better. We can improve it further by aligning the right-hand margin using "alt j" for "*justification*." Figure 16-4 shows the revised document.

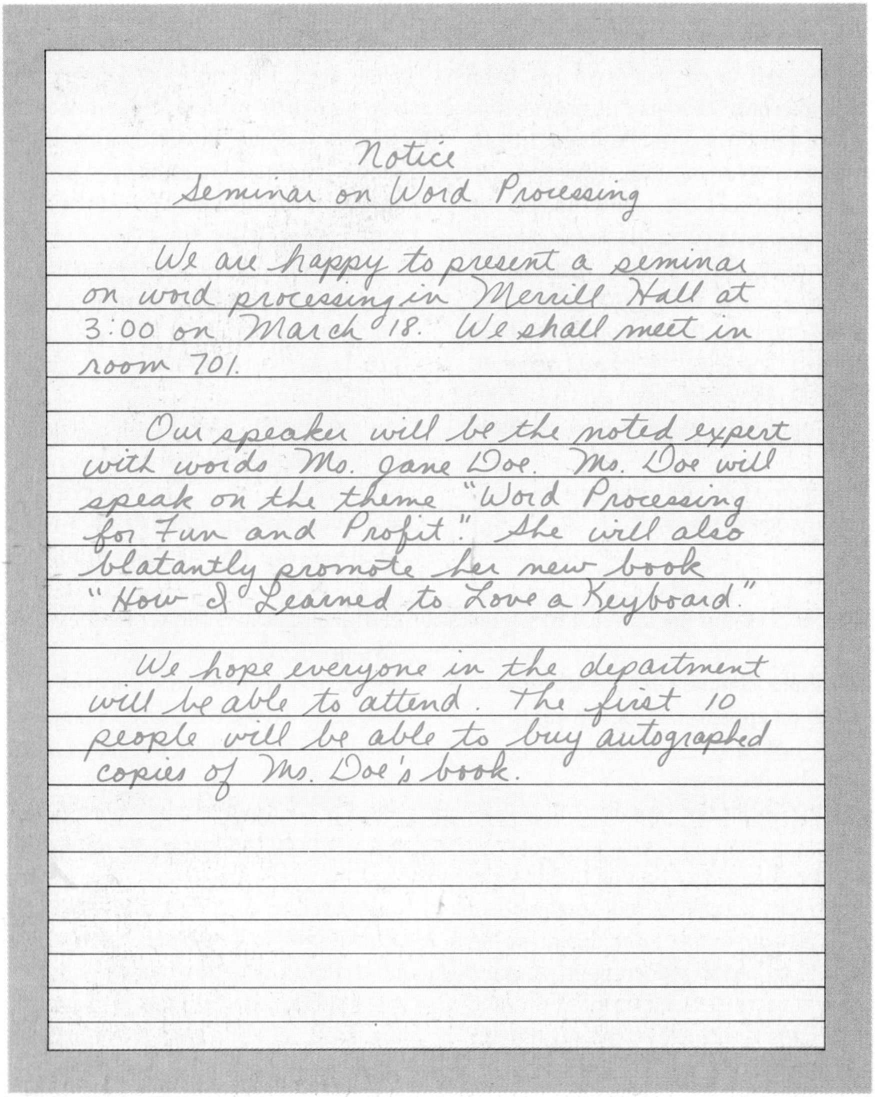

Figure 16-1. Notice to Be Entered. Here is the input for our example.

Some Editing

Having improved the appearance of the text, we look for things that might be in need of correction. After a change of heart, we have decided that the speaker will not blatantly promote her book but will do so subtly. We move the cursor to *blatantly* and press the "F8" key to select the word; it will now appear highlighted. If we press the delete key, the word will disappear, almost. It is no longer in the text, but it appears in brackets in the bottom line of the screen by the word "EDIT." Now, we type *subtly* and see how the line looks. If we are not happy with the change, we press the "Esc" (escape or cancel) key and the letter *U* for "**undo**." The original text, which was saved in the brackets, will be put

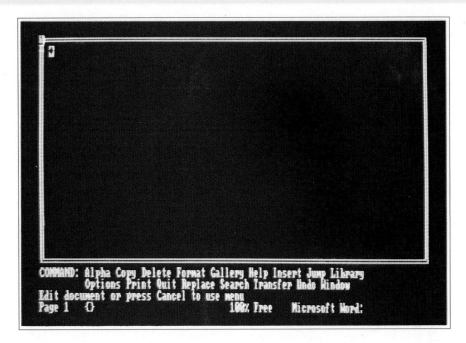

Figure 16-2. The Entry Screen of the Word Processor Used in this Chapter.

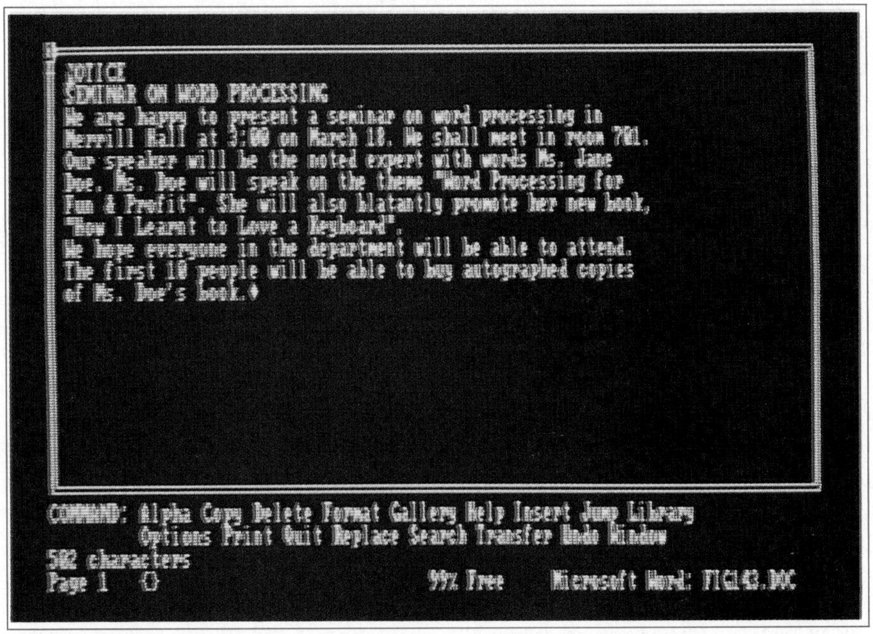

COMMAND: Alpha Copy Delete Format Gallery Help Insert Jump Library
            Options Print Quit Replace Search Transfer Undo Window
Edit document or press Cancel to use menu
Page 1   {}   100% Free   Microsoft Word:

NOTICE
SEMINAR ON WORD PROCESSING
We are happy to present a seminar on word processing in
Merrill Hall at 3:00 on March 18. We shall meet in room 701.
Our speaker will be the noted expert with words Ms. Jane
Doe. Ms. Doe will speak on the theme "Word Processing for
Fun & Profit". She will also blatantly promote her new book,
"How I Learnt to Love a Keyboard".
We hope everyone in the department will be able to attend.
The first 10 people will be able to buy autographed copies
of Ms. Doe's book.

COMMAND: Alpha Copy Delete Format Gallery Help Insert Jump Library
            Options Print Quit Replace Search Transfer Undo Window
502 characters
Page 1   {}   99% Free   Microsoft Word: FIG143.DOC

Figure 16-3. The Input as Typed Using the Word-Processing Program.

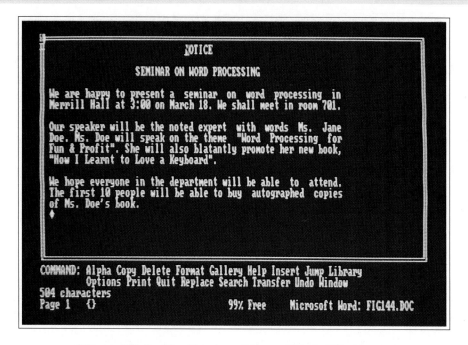

Figure 16-4. The Results of Some Simple Formatting.

back into the text. Now we are back to blatant promotion!

The **deleted** text that appeared in the bottom line brackets is in a place known as the **scrap**. It is a place where we can store things temporarily or throw them away for good. For example, to move text, we shall delete it to the scrap, move the cursor to a new location, and insert from the scrap.

Now we decide that we should really **underline** the title of Ms. Doe's book. We move the cursor to the first word in the title *How* and press the "F8" key to select that word; it will be highlighted. Now we hold down the "F6" key to repeat the action and depress "F8" until the entire title is highlighted. Next, we hold the "alt" key down and press *u* for "underline."

When we move the cursor again, the text will appear underlined. To highlight the date, we select March 18 with the cursor, press "F8" to select the word, "F6" and "F8" to extend to the *18,* and then "alt b" for **boldface**. When we move the cursor next, the text will appear in boldface type.

Our notice looks pretty good at this point (see Figure 16-5). However, we have just found out that a terrible mistake has been made. Jane Doe is married and likes to be called Mrs., not Ms., Doe. Fear not, it will not be necessary to retype the entire notice.

We shall use the "**replace**" command; first, we type *Esc* to get into the **menu** and then *R* for replace. We are asked to type the text to be replaced; in this instance, we type *Ms.,* then the "tab" key and the text to replace it: *Mrs.* We are given the option of seeing each instance of *Ms.* that the system finds and of confirming that it is to be replaced by *Mrs.* We choose "yes" here, so that we can be sure each change is all right. Most of the time, we will not worry about whether the words have upper- or lowercase letters in them. In this instance, because we are working with a capitalized title, we should be case-sensitive. We will also choose "whole word," or the search will locate *ms.* anywhere that it might appear, even embedded in some other word. The final results of our changes appear in Figure 16-6.

Now, we want to save the notice on a file in case

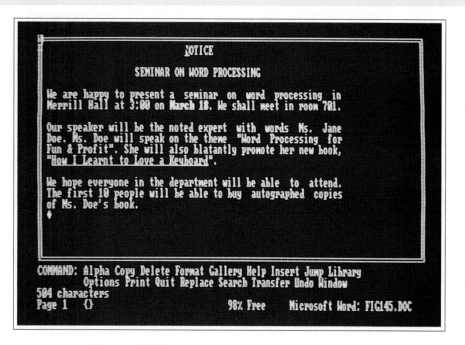

Figure 16-5. Adding Emphasis and Underlining.

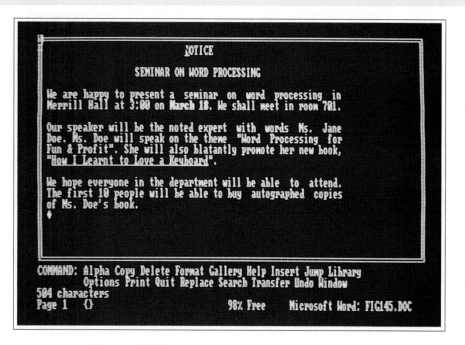

Figure 16-6. Search and Replace Ms. with Mrs.

```
                         NOTICE

                 SEMINAR ON WORD PROCESSING

We  are  happy  to  present  a  seminar on  word processing  in
Merrill  Hall  at  3:00 on  March 18. We shall  meet  in room 701.

Our speakers  will be  the noted expert with words Mrs. Jane
Doe. Mrs.  Doe will  speak on the theme "Word Processing for
Fun & Profit". She will also blatantly promote her new book,
"How I Learnt to Love a Keyboard".

We hope  everyone in  the department will be able to attend.
The first  10 people  will be able to buy autographed copies
of Mrs. Doe's book.
```

Figure 16-7. Printing the Notice.

there is a need to revise the notice sometime in the future. We press "Esc" and "T" for "transfer." Then, we select "*Save*" in the submenu and finally type a file name like "notice." Now the file is saved, and we can proceed to print it.

Again, we type *Esc* to get into the menu and then choose *P* for "***print***." The last selection is *P* again to print on the printer. The results of the entire effort can be seen in Figure 16-7.

MORE FEATURES

We can do a lot with what has been demonstrated so far. However, there are many additional features that make this word-processing package very powerful.

Scrolling

On a large document, we shall want to move around in the text more quickly than by pressing the arrow direction keys. We can use the "Pg Up" and "Pg Dn" (page-up and page-down) keys for this purpose. By holding the control key and pressing the "Pg Up" key, we return to the beginning of the document. The control key plus "Pg Dn" moves us to the end of the document. Depressing these keys without the control key moves the previous or the next page onto the screen.

```
FORMAT DIVISION break: Cont Column Page Odd Even
         page length:            width:            gutter width:
         pg #: Yes No        from top:         from left:
         numbering: Cont Start      at:          format: 1 l i A a
         margin top:           bottom:          left:          right:
         # of cols        space between:        footnotes: Same-page End
         running head pos      from top:        from bottom:
```

Figure 16-8. A Division Level Format Specification.

```
FORMAT PARAGRAPH alignment: Left Centered Right Justified    keep: Yes No
         left indent:            first line:          right indent:
         line spacing:           space before:        space after
```

Figure 16-9. A Paragraph Level Format Specification.

We can also use the *"Search"* command to find text that we want to locate. If we know there is a unique string of text, we use *Esc* and "Search," enter the text, and let the program find its location.

Formats

In our sample document, we did some formatting using the "alt" key and single-letter commands. For a simple format, such as the notice, these commands are sufficient. However, there are times when we will want to have more sophisticated formatting capabilities.

The division-level format gives us a great deal of control in describing the document (see Figure 16-8). We can choose a page length and width, whether to have page numbers, the position of footnotes and running heads, and the number of columns of text. For example, we might want to have a two-column format for a magazine or newspaper article.

We can define multiple divisions or segments of the document, and give each different part a different appearance. In addition, there can be special formats for paragraphs within divisions. Each division or paragraph format holds for the succeeding text until a new format is encountered.

Figure 16-9 shows the options for **paragraph** formatting. We can specify the same kind of formatting that we did with the "alt" and the single keystrokes. The paragraph can be aligned left or right, centered, or justified. We can specify the spacing within the paragraph and between paragraphs along with left or right indentation.

Beyond division and paragraph formats, the user of this package can actually create a **style sheet**. The style can specify the format of characters, paragraphs, and divisions. The user creates the style sheet and then inserts it into something called the *gallery*. Setting up style sheets is an advanced feature of this package; not many users will need to make use of it. However, the feature is there if needed. Figure 16-10 is a document processed with

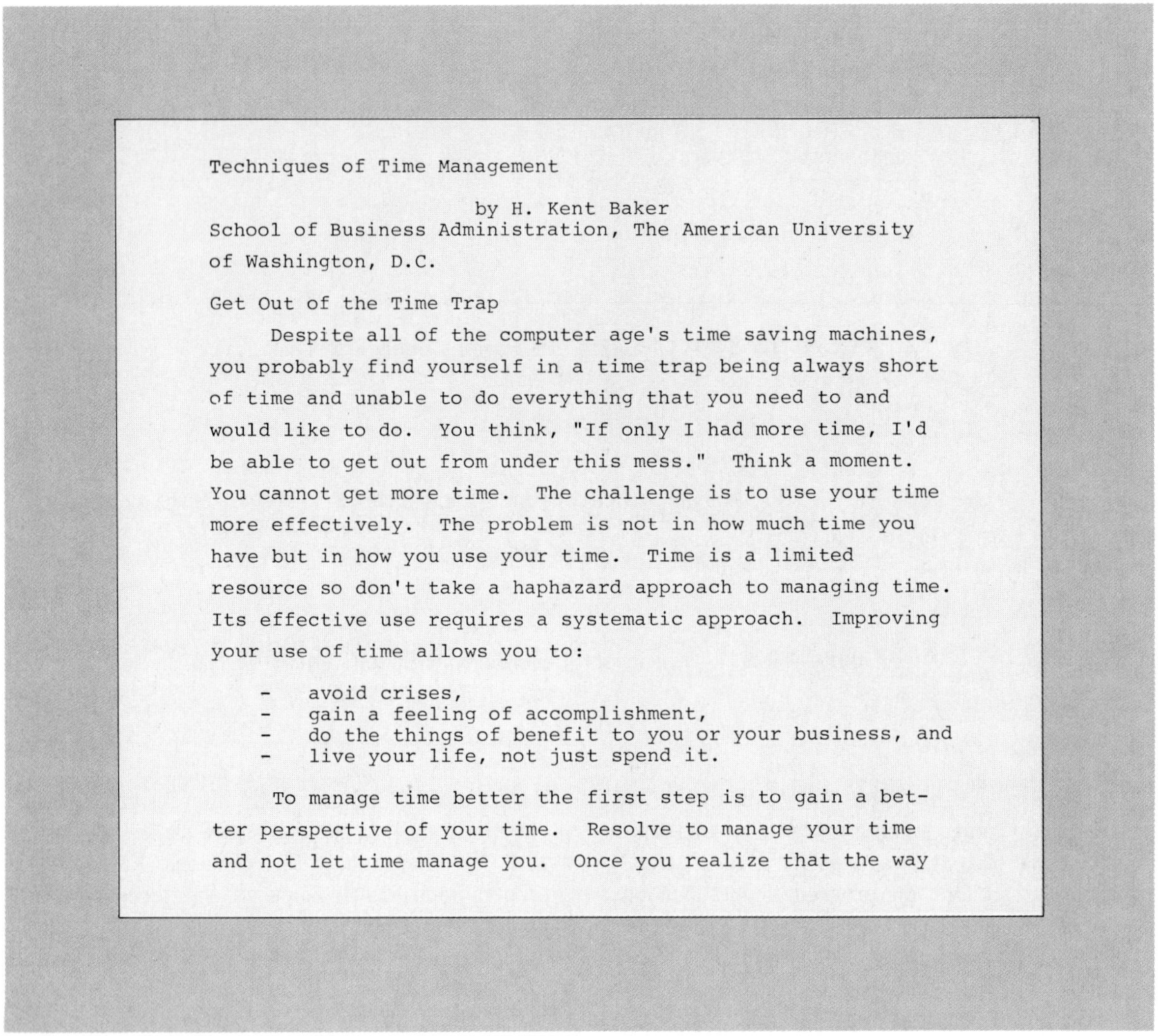

```
Techniques of Time Management

                         by H. Kent Baker
School of Business Administration, The American University
of Washington, D.C.

Get Out of the Time Trap
      Despite all of the computer age's time saving machines,
you probably find yourself in a time trap being always short
of time and unable to do everything that you need to and
would like to do.  You think, "If only I had more time, I'd
be able to get out from under this mess."  Think a moment.
You cannot get more time.  The challenge is to use your time
more effectively.  The problem is not in how much time you
have but in how you use your time.  Time is a limited
resource so don't take a haphazard approach to managing time.
Its effective use requires a systematic approach.  Improving
your use of time allows you to:

         -   avoid crises,
         -   gain a feeling of accomplishment,
         -   do the things of benefit to you or your business, and
         -   live your life, not just spend it.

      To manage time better the first step is to gain a bet-
ter perspective of your time.  Resolve to manage your time
and not let time manage you.  Once you realize that the way
```

Figure 16-10. A Document to Be Processed with a Draft Style Sheet.

a draft style sheet, and Figure 16-11 is the same document with an article style.

Windows

The package used here provides us with multiple windows. The manual suggests that we put our outline in one window and refer to it while writing a document. We can also open another window and use it to store citations for the bibliography or footnotes.

Windows are also useful for moving or copying text from parts of the document that are too far apart for both parts to fit in the main window.

Techniques of Time Management

by H. Kent Baker

School of Business Administration.
The American University of Washington, D.C.

Get Out of the Time Trap

Despite all of the computer ages time saving machines, you probably find yourself in a time trap, being always short of time and unable to do everything that you need to and would like to do. You think, "If only I had more time I'd be able to get out from under this mess." Think a moment. You cannot get more time. The challenge is to use your time more effectively. The problem is not in how much time you have but in how you use your time. Time is a limited resource so don't take a haphazard approach to managing time. Its effective use requires a systematic approach. Improving your use of time allows you to

- avoid crises.
- gain a feeling of accomplishment.
- do the things of benefit to you or your business, and
- live your life, not just spend it.

To manage time better the first step is to gain a better perspective of your time. Resolve to manage your time and not let time manage you. Once you realize that the way you handle time causes some of your time problems, then you can begin to develop a time management strategy.

In devising this strategy, keep two thoughts in mind. First, it takes time to learn how to use time effectively. Second, the principles of time use are not universally applicable. Although

This strategy of learning how to make your time of greater benefit involves investigating three important questions

1. Where does my time go?
2. Where should my time go?
3. How can I use time better?

By systematically answering each question, you will be better able to control your time.

Where Does My Time Go?

Frequently time management problems stem from poor work habits, so analyze how you spend your time. Find out how you waste time. Realize that *you* are the probable cause of most of your own time problems and the painful task of changing your habits is required.

Using a Time Log

A common technique for determining how much time is consumed on various tasks throughout the work day is to keep a **time log**. This procedure consists of maintaining a diary in which every 15–20 minutes you record what you have done. After several days of listing your activities you will have a sufficient number of observations for analysis. The time log should then be summarized and analyzed to determine what could have been done to make better use of your time.

In analyzing your time log, you should ask yourself several questions

1. What are the major activities or events which cause me to use my time ineffectively
2. Which of these tasks can be performed

Figure 16-11. The Document of Figure 16-10 with an Article Format Style.

OTHER COMMANDS

There are more commands for this word processor; we shall mention them briefly for completeness' sake:

- ALPHA—return to the entry mode from the menu to insert text.
- COPY—copy selected text into the scrap or a glossary.
- DELETE—delete selected text; the deleted text

can be placed in the scrap or in a named glossary for later use.

- FORMAT—we have discussed the formatting of divisions and paragraphs.
- GALLERY—used to specify formatting attributes for style sheets.
- HELP—used at any point to get a *help* screen explaining a command.
- INSERT—*insert* in front of the selected location text from the scrap or from a named glossary.
- JUMP—move quickly to another place in the document.
- LIBRARY—reserved for additions to the package.
- OPTIONS—sets various options, like the audible warning signal.
- PRINT—used to control the printing and actually print a document.
- QUIT—leave the word processor.
- REPLACE—replace all instances of one text string with another.
- SEARCH—locate a text string.
- TRANSFER—store or *retrieve* a file, process gallery entries, clear the current document, and so on.
- UNDO—undo the latest editing change.
- WINDOW—create and control windows on the screen.

SUMMARY

Word processing is an extremely popular use of microcomputers. Students, professionals, and others can enjoy the benefits of greater productivity and higher-quality written documents. For the nontypist, there are typing tutor programs to prepare one to use word processors.

Word processing and the spreadsheet packages described in Chapter 15 are two applications for personal computers that almost all of us can use. Together, they have stimulated the sale of many computers and are likely to be prerequisites for the professional in the coming decades.

Some Applications

A Law Case

A law firm was recently retained to help a company with a very serious problem. The company had retained a consultant for a number of years. One day, the consultant decided that a very important product that he had developed for the company really belonged to him; the firm had the right only to use it.

The consultant's logic was that he had always charged the firm for each modification in and enhancement to the product, so that it actually belonged to him. The company saw things differently: it had paid the consultant to develop a product that belonged to it.

Enter the attorney, who tried to prevent a lawsuit. The consultant had taken the plans for the product, and they could not be duplicated without great expense. The company was stuck, as it feared the consultant might destroy the plans or leave town with them.

The attorney sought help from an adviser who knew something about the product. It was technologically based, and the company lacked expertise in how it worked.

The adviser met several times with the consultant to try to negotiate a settlement. It turned out that the consultant was actually disgruntled about how he had been treated by the company. The seeds of a compromise began to grow.

At this point, the attorney entered into the negotiations with the consultant and the adviser. A formal draft contract was prepared to improve the arrangement between the consultant and the company and to state clearly that the product in dispute belonged to the company.

What about word processing? There were four parties involved in developing the contract: the firm's officers, the consultant, the adviser, and the attorney. The attorney's firm handled the document preparation using a word processor. As the negotiations became more intense, revised draft contracts could be prepared in a short period of time and sent by messenger to all involved for their approval. Rather than lengthy negotiations, which might have led to misunderstandings or individuals' changing their minds, the word-processing capabilities of the law firm kept the process timely. ■

The Congress

One of the major users of word processing is the Congress of the United States. Senators and Representatives are deluged with mail on various topics. It is very impressive to answer this mail with personalized letters. Before word processing, an army of typists and composers was required to answer the mail.

Using different types of word processors, congressional staff members can compose paragraphs that represent the Congress member's view on an issue. When a constituent sends a letter, the staff member composes a letter of response by indicating which paragraphs should be included in what order in the reply.

Programs that maintain mailing lists are a useful adjunct to word processing. In the case of Congress, a Senator or Representative can maintain a list of their constituents who have written on a particular issue. Using the program, a staff member can send a mailing to everyone who has written on a particular topic, like arms control or tax reform or the environment.

The computer and word-processing software help the member of Congress maintain the appearance of a personal answer while coping with a huge volume of mail. As a constituent, you must decide whether this is a good application of word processing and computing. ■

A WORKSTATION

We have now seen two major applications of personal computers: spreadsheet programs and word processing. Today, many experts in the field are talking about the managerial **workstation**, a powerful local computer that supports the manager in his or her job. The microcomputer with these two software packages is the nucleus of such a workstation; some of us would say that such a tool exists today.

An example of what is coming may be found at Merrill Lynch, the nation's largest stock broker. There is an ambitious project at Merrill Lynch to install personal computers capable of displaying multiple windows at the same time. Each window is a separate area on the screen, usually ruled off from other windows and often of a different color from other windows. One window might show ticker tape readouts of the latest stock prices; another, client data; and a third, research reports.

The broker will be able to use standard business software, such as a spreadsheet package, to analyze data in one of the windows. The firm wants to supply software so that the personal computers will be able to automatically update a client's portfolio. In fact, each broker can indicate a price that, if reached, means that the broker should notify clients of the new price. When the price hits this low or high level, the broker will be notified. The broker can then arrange for a letter to be produced automatically for all clients holding that stock. The workstation's components are here already. What remains is to integrate them into a package and combine the micro with a network to access large mainframe databases.

The skills that you have gained in this and the previous chapter will be very important in your functioning as a productive member of an organization.

Review of Chapter 16

REVIEW

In this chapter, we have learned about word processing through an example and a discussion of some of the advanced features of word-processing software. Word-processing and spreadsheet programs account for a great deal of the popularity of microcomputers.

How can the student use a word processor? It is a natural adjunct to classes whenever papers are assigned. It is possible to write the paper and make many drafts without having to reenter the text. Compared to the old methods of writing, typing, cutting, and pasting sections, it is a vast improvement.

For the professional, the impact is much the same. We can do many drafts of a document, hopefully improving it each time. The finished results can be typed without erasures or corrections, so that a higher-quality product is provided.

Some elementary schools are experimenting with using typewriters and word processors to help young children learn reading and writing skills. Children unable to write using a pencil find that they can press keys and put a story together.

Just as a firm today expects a managerial employee to be able to work with a spreadsheet program, the professional will soon be expected to be able to prepare documents on a word processor. Word processing is not something just for a secretary, it is a tool that helps in the writing of reports, memoranda, and books.

KEY WORDS

Boldface	Retrieve
Center	Return
Cursor	Save
Delete	Scrap
Entry	Scroll
Format	Search
Help	Style sheet
Insert	Text
Justification	Underline
Menu	Undo
Paragraph	Window
Print	Word wrap
Replace	Workstation

BUSINESS PROBLEMS

16-1. One computer-center manager muttered that he did not want to recommend word-processing packages to anyone because "It's like choosing art or music; word processing is a matter of personal taste." His fear was that no matter what was suggested, the user would probably be dissatisfied.

Why does word processing evoke such tremendous loyalties and emotional responses? In answering this question, consider the ways in which a word processor is used, the frequency of its use, and the individuals who are likely to work with it. Are there different types of processors that are better for different tasks?

A very frequent question, if you admit to any knowledge of computers, is "What word processor do you use?" Even though there seems to be a lot of loyalty, others are curious about your package, either because they want to think about switching or because they want to obtain confirmation that you, too, are using their package.

How do you give advice to someone asking such a question who is interested in obtaining a package and knows little about word processing on microcomputers? How should this person get started? What advice can you give so as to be helpful, but also so as not to get in trouble if your favorite does not turn out to be this person's?

16-2. A significant problem in using word processing with a microcomputer is final output. Because many micros are used for purposes other than word processing, they come with dot matrix printers to make graphing (say, from a spreadsheet package) possible. Unfortunately, dot-matrix-graphics printers do not produce letter-quality output.

There is now a new category known as *near letter-quality,* which is quite good, but not as attractive as an impact letter printer. Organizations and individuals face this problem. If a letter-quality printer is obtained, then the system will not be able to graph and produce special printouts. If the matrix printer is chosen, letter quality will not be possible.

Discuss some of the alternatives to solving this problem. You might want to consider the idea of shared printers or electronic typewriters that can be attached to a microcomputer. Try to develop suggestions for an organization with a number of microcomputers and for an individual professional who will have convenient access to only one microcomputer at home or in the office.

REVIEW QUESTIONS

1. What are the advantages of word processing?
2. How can word processing contribute to improvements in output quality?
3. How does text entry differ from editing?
4. What is word wrap? Why is it important?
5. Why do we need a command menu for word processing?
6. What is the purpose of the "alpha" command?
7. What is the use of the "copy" command?
8. What does the "delete" command do?
9. Describe the different kinds of formats discussed in the chapter.
10. What does a "help" function provide?
11. Why do we need an insert capability?
12. What is the scrap? What is its purpose during deletion? When moving text?
13. What function does a named glossary serve?
14. What does a "transfer" command do?

15. Why is it nice to have an "undo" command?

16. How is a style sheet used in word processing?

THOUGHT QUESTIONS

17. How does word processing contribute to the productivity of a knowledge worker?

18. What is the impact of word processing software for microcomputers likely to be on dedicated word processors?

19. Why would one want to have the direct format commands using the "alt" key?

20. How do "replace" and "search" seem similar?

21. What use can you see in having multiple windows for word processing?

22. What is the advantage of using a microcomputer for word processing instead of a dedicated word processor?

23. How can one reduce the expense of having a letter-quality printer for each microcomputer that does word processing?

24. For what kinds of work will we always probably prefer a "dumb typewriter," that is, a machine with no logic?

25. Why are users such supporters of the word-processing software that they use?

RECOMMENDED READINGS

Microsoft Word Manual. Microsoft Corporation, 1983. This is the manual for the word processor used as an example in this chapter.

Visiword Manual. Visicorp, 1983. This is a good word processor for the beginner, very simple to learn and use.

Chapter 17

Chapters **15** and **16** have presented examples of how the reader can work directly with a microcomputer. This chapter first shows how silicon chips, the "engines" that power computers, are made. Then the chapter describes how a number of individuals use computers in their jobs. Computers and the software that commands them have been applied to a myriad of different applications. Users, managers, and computer professionals have demonstrated tremendous creativity in finding new ways for computers to help organizations and individuals. We shall review a few of these applications in the pages which follow.

First we observe end-user computing in action: a user of information working with a computer staff member to define a report based on data in a main frame computer. The end-user is learning how to satisfy his or her own requests with minimal involvement from the computer staff.

Computers have tremendous power for graphics processing and several graphs were presented in the chapter on spreadsheets. A section follows on business graphics; it demonstrates the results of specialized programs for data analysis and graphic presentation.

Another important use of the technology has been in computer-aided design. Engineers and draftsmen use a computer to design and draw various parts for manufacture. At first these systems were limited to line drawings, but today there are versions that make it possible to model solids in three dimensions.

The next stage after design is computer-aided manufacturing. Some systems make it possible for the designer to generate instructions for numerically controlled machine tools to manufacture the part that has just been designed. In other settings, computers control robotic devices which automate the production process. Some companies are working on the development of completely automated factories. For example, General Motors has established a new division to manufacture a subcompact car in the United States called the Saturn. The new division is to show that an inexpensive car can be made profitable in the United States despite significant cost disadvantages com-

A PORTFOLIO OF TECHNOLOGY AND APPLICATIONS

pared with foreign companies. The key to success will be using computers to automate the entire production process.

Before presenting the various applications described above, we shall look at the manufacturing process for a computer chip, the component that makes all of these applications possible. The ability to manufacture chips with thousands of electrical circuits on them has resulted in computers that are increasingly powerful at steadily decreasing costs. The development of this technology is the reason why the applications in the rest of the chapter are possible.

After reading the chapter, you should be able to:

■ Discuss how a computer chip is manufactured.
■ Explain what is meant by end-user computing.
■ Describe how computers are important for graphics.
■ Explain the importance of computer-aided design.
■ Describe computer-aided manufacturing.

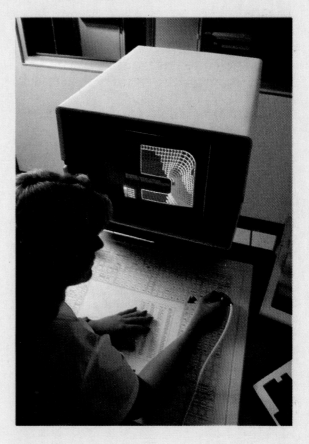

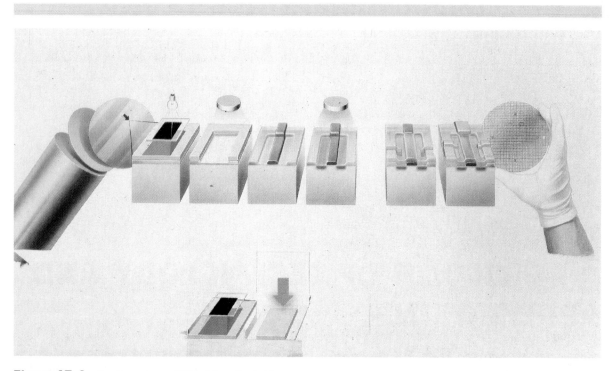

Figure 17-1. An Overview of Chip Manufacturing.

THE MAKING OF A CHIP

The heart of today's computer devices is an integrated circuit chip. As the name suggests, the chip contains a number of electronic circuits. These circuits can either store data and are used for memory, or they can process data and are used to provide the logic of computer devices. Remember that engineers and computer scientists can represent mathematical logic using electronic components and circuits. The physicist and materials scientist must develop ways to design and manufacture these circuits on chips.

Why are we continually trying to make circuits smaller and smaller? There are a number of reasons. First, the speed of computers is limited by how fast electrons move. While electrons travel theoretically at the speed of light, they actually move more slowly because of the resistance they encounter due to collisions with other elements. The smaller the dis-

tance electrons have to travel, the faster the computer. Small computers consume less power than their larger counterparts and also take less room in an office or on a user's desk. Smaller devices make it possible to use computers in places not possible before. Imagine trying to control an automobile engine with a first-generation vacuum-tube computer!

An Overview

Figure 17-1 presents an overview of the process of making a chip. Most chips today are constructed using silicon, but in the future it is expected that other elements will be used to obtain more speed, for example, gallium arsenide. In this chapter, we shall discuss silicon chip fabrication because it is the most common.

Silicon is the earth's most abundant element after oxygen. To make computer chips, silicon is refined from quartz rocks; it is melted and drawn into long crystals. After purification, the manufacturer slices the silicon into wafers as shown in step 1 in Figure 17-1. Next the wafers are insulated with a film of oxide, shown in tan, and then coated with a soft, light-sensitive plastic called photoresist, which is shown in purple. The manufacturer masks the wafer with a stencil that contains a pattern for each chip in the wafer. The wafer is flooded with ultraviolet light exposing the photoresist in areas not covered by the stencil.

In step 2 the photoresist, which has been exposed to light, hardens into the outline of the stencil. Acids and chemicals strip away unexposed photoresist and oxide, revealing the patterned silicon. In step 3 we see the wafer etched by superhot gases. More silicon is deposited, masked, and stripped as shown by the orange element in step 4.

The wafer is then implanted with chemical impurities or dopants, shown in green, that form negative and positive conducting zones. Step 5 shows that the manufacturer repeats these steps to build layers which are connected by "windows" as shown in step 6. Metal, like aluminum, shown in blue, is condensed onto the wafer filling the windows to form conducting pathways in step 7.

The manufacturer dices each chip, shown in red in step 8. The chip is then bonded with conventional wires and is ready for use in a computer device. Often the chips are placed in a package with pins as electrical leads to be plugged into a circuit board for a computer.

The Manufacturing Process

The photographs in this section show some of the steps and equipment used to manufacture chips at an IBM plant in East Fishkill, New York.

In this photograph we see the beginning of the process; here silicon chips are fabricated in a crucible inside a furnace. The furnace melts high-purity silicon at a temperature of 1400 degrees Centigrade. Under computer control, a "seed" crystal contacts the molten silicon, is rotated, and raised to produce a single rod-shaped ingot.

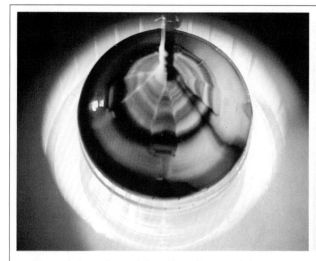

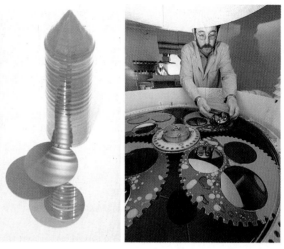

Above left, a view of the silicon ingot as it is growing inside the furnace. Center, the ingot as it is trimmed and ground to a uniform diameter, in this case, 82 mm. The ingot is sliced into razor-thin wafers and prepared for further processing. The wafers are polished to a smooth, flat uniform surface using a mechanical lapping process. The wafers in the right photograph are 125 mm thick.

The processing of wafers begins in a superclean room (pictured below) where filtered air removes fine airborne particles to minimize contamination. The air in clean rooms is many times purer than the air in a hospital operating room. The orange containers in the foreground contain batches of 82 mm wafers entering the production line.

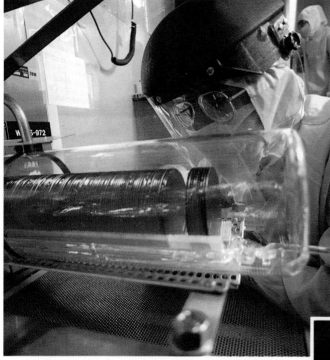

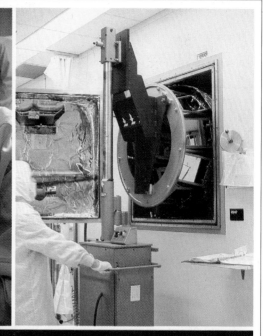

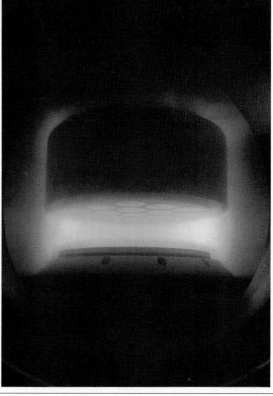

As manufacturing progresses, silicon wafers plus a source material like arsenic or boron are sealed inside a quartz tube and heated in a high-temperature furnace. As the arsenic or boron evaporates into a gas, its atoms diffuse into selected areas of the silicon wafers (above left). Areas that are altered by the diffused atoms or dopants become the transistors, resistors, and diodes (electronic components) in the individual chips on the wafer. Ion implantation (above right) is another means of injecting source materials into selected areas of individual chips on silicon wafers.

The photograph to the right shows radio frequency sputtering, which is performed in a vacuum chamber to deposit a protective insulating layer of quartz on selected areas of individual wafers. The quartz layer provides protection against metal corrosion and is an excellent insulator. Often as many as three layers of metal interconnection patterns are required to complete the integrated circuit product; quartz is used to insulate the layers separating the metal patterns.

Above left: a special, highly automated wafer-processing line controlled by computers. The purpose of this line is to interconnect transistors, resistors, and diodes via circuitry on top of the wafers. Electron beam tools are employed to generate the circuits in this QTAT (Quick Turn Around Time) wafer-processing line at IBM. Above right: wet chemical processing on the line is performed by computer-controlled tools. Grippers transport and immerse the wafers into select sectors of tanks containing liquid chemicals.

A photoresist apply-and-dry tool (right) monitors photoresist as it is applied to the wafer surface. Electron beam tools (below right) on the IBM line interconnect circuit elements in individual silicon chips on the wafers. In this fabrication process there are three levels of interconnections.

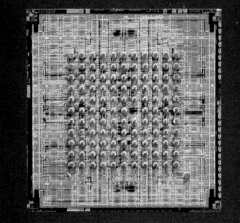

The completed silicon wafer containing logic chips is used in medium and mainframe computers (above). Inset: a dicing tool; a cutting head and abrasive slurry slice the wafers into individual silicon chips. Right: an individual logic chip after dicing. It contains some 700 logic circuits comprising upwards of 5000 transistors, resistors, and diodes.

The photograph below shows the testing of individual silicon chips under computer control. The machine has a preprogrammed series of electrical and functional tests to assure the operating integrity and reliability of individual chips.

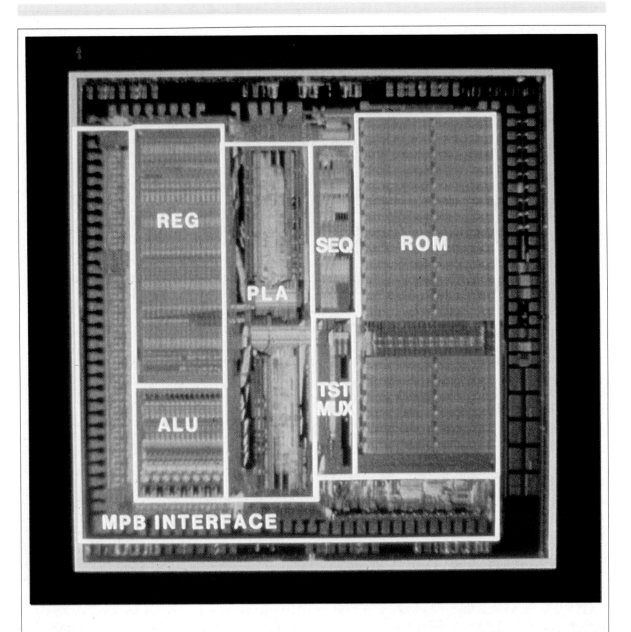

This is how far chip-making technology has progressed; the 6.35 mm-square chip in the photograph is a Hewlett-Packard 32 bit processor containing some 450,000 transistors and circuit elements. The various parts of the processor are highlighted in the photo. The chip contains 9,200 38-bit words of microcode ROM and is capable of executing 230 different instructions.

This series of photographs illustrates the high level of manufacturing sophistication required to fabricate logic chips and prepare them for use in computers. It is the success of the design and manufacturing process for chips that provides computers with tremendous power, power that we can use to process information and improve the effectiveness of individuals and organizations. ■

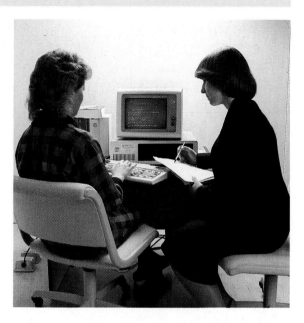

Figure 17-2. An End-user (left) and Computer Staff Consultant at MONY Financial Services in New York.

END-USER COMPUTING IN A FOURTH GENERATION LANGUAGE

One of the most significant recent developments in the information systems field is end-user computing. This term refers to the tendency for more and more individuals to work directly with computers. These people are *end-users* rather than computer professionals. What are the reasons for this trend? Most end-users are motivated by a desire to obtain information quickly without having to wait for a systems analyst or programmer to help them. There is a backlog of requests for help in most computer departments; the user who can help him or herself will obtain results more quickly than someone who has to rely on a computer professional for help.

Another good reason for the end-user to become involved directly in computing is communications. There have been many communications problems between the systems staff and users. An end-user working with powerful software can avoid some of the communications difficulties that arise from involving computer professionals in answering a request for service.

A User at Work

In this section we present some examples of the users of FOCUS, a very successful Fourth Generation Language that operates on IBM mainframe computers. There is also a version for a fairly *fully configured* personal computer, as well. Figure 17-2 is a photograph of two employees of MONY Financial Services in New York City. The end-user working at the computer is being assisted by a representative of the computer department.

The end-user makes use of a personal computer in New York City. This personal computer has a special interface board which provides direct access over phone lines to a mainframe computer in Syracuse, New York, several hundred miles from New York City. The personal computer is being used as a terminal in this application; it is connected to coaxial communications lines which run throughout the building. The actual data transmission to and from Syracuse occurs over telephone lines.

The end-user works in the Marketing Research Department and is interested in obtaining a new report. In Figure 17-2 the user is entering file numbers

Figure 17-3. The computer staff member points to the entry location for a file number.

Figure 17-4. The user consults a FOCUS Manual.

so FOCUS will know what files to access. The computer consultant is referring to a programmer's log to obtain the file numbers for the data the user would like to access. She points to the place where the file number is to be entered in Figure 17-3. While end-users can do much themselves, they need some help in learning how to use a language like FOCUS. They also must rely on the computer department to inform them as to where the data they want are located and how to identify files.

In Figure 17-4, the user is consulting the FOCUS User's Manual to learn how to create file layouts for entry. In Figure 17-5 we see an array of boxes or file segments appear on the screen showing the hierarchies of data entry and alerting the user to any errors in file names.

Figure 17-6 shows an error. The system has detected a file segment with a problem (the message on the screen reads "field name is not in the dictionary"). In Figure 17-7 the user corrects the problem by entering the right file name (the name of the file which contains the fields entered in the earlier steps). Figure 17-8 shows the successful results as FOCUS prints the report designed by the end-user.

Figure 17-5. The system displays file segments.

Figure 17-6. The system detects an error when it cannot find a field name in the dictionary.

Figure 17-7 (right). The user corrects the error.

Figure 17-8 (below right). The end of a successful session; FOCUS is printing the desired report.

SOME FURTHER EXAMPLES

The previous section demonstrates a user and consultant solving a problem with FOCUS. In this section examples are provided that give a better idea of the structure of the language and its power in generating reports. Figure 17-9 shows two simple files and their fields, a Sales file and a Supply file. Figure 17-10 is a FOCUS program to produce a listing from the files showing customer name, order amount, and order date for all order amounts over $1000. The listing is sorted by region and store code. The results of the request are shown in Figure 17-11.

Still working with the two files of Figure 17-9, we want to determine which customers placed the three largest orders during the year for each sales region. The FOCUS program for this request is shown in Figure 17-12. Note the RANKED statement which picks out the three largest orders. The results of the request appear in Figure 17-13.

In Figure 17-14 we use this fourth-generation language to produce a report which shows the distribution of units sold for each product across various regions, along with a total. The DEFINE statement is used to specify new data fields for a file. Figure 17-15 shows the results of running the program.

SALES FILE

FIELD NAME	MEANING
REGION	Marketing Region Code
SITE	Store Code
PONUM	Purchase Order Number
DATE	Order Date
NAME	Customer Name
AMOUNT	Total Amount of Order
TAX	State Tax on Order
FILLCODE	Indicator of Shipment Status
PRODUCT	Product Number
UNITS	Quantity Ordered

SUPPLY FILE

PRODUCT	Product Number
DESCRIPTION	Product Description
COST	Wholesale Cost
RETAIL	Retail Price
VENDOR	Supplier Code Number
QOH	Quantity on Hand in Warehouse

Figure 17-9. Two Files for a FOCUS Example.

```
TABLE FILE SALES
PRINT NAME AND AMOUNT
      AND DATE
BY REGION BY SITE
IF AMOUNT GT 1000
ON REGION SKIP-LINE
END
```

Figure 17-10 (above). A Program to Create a Simple Listing from the Sales File.

Figure 17-11 (right). The Report Requested in Figure 17-10.

PAGE 1

REGION	SITE	NAME	AMOUNT	DATE
MA	NEWK	ELIZABETH GAS	$2,877.30	82 AUG
	NEWY	KOCH RECONSTRUCTION	$6,086.23	82 APR
	PHIL	ROSS INC	$3,890.22	82 JUL
		LASSITER CONSTRUCTION	$1,120.22	82 SEP
MW	CHIC	BAKESHORE INC.	$5,678.23	82 OCT
		ROPERS BROTHERS	$2,789.20	82 AUG
	CLEV	BOVEY PARTS	$6,769.22	82 MAY
		ERIE INC	$1,556.78	82 JAN
NE	ALBN	ROCK CITY BUILDER	$1,722.30	82 JUL
	BOST	HANCOCK RESTORERS	$8,246.20	82 FEB
		WANKEL CONSTRUCTION	$2,345.25	82 JUN
		WARNER INDUSTRIES	$3,155.25	82 OCT
	STAM	ACORN INC	$2,006.20	82 MAR
		KANGERS CONSTRUCTION	$2,790.50	82 JUN
		DART INDUSTRIES	$7,780.22	82 MAY
		ARISTA MANUFACTURING	$4,295.90	82 FEB
SE	ATL	RICHS STORES	$1,345.17	82 AUG
	WASH	CAPITOL WHOLESALE	$3,789.00	82 JUN
		FEDERAL DEPOT	$2,195.25	82 MAR

```
TABLE FILE SALES
PRINT NAME BY REGION
RANKED BY HIGHEST 3 AMOUNT
ON REGION SKIP-LINE
IF DATE GE 8201
END
```

Figure 17-12 (above). A Program to Determine Which Customers Placed the Three Largest Orders During the Year for Each Sales Region.

Figure 17-13 (right). The Report Created by the Program in Figure 17-12.

PAGE 1 REGION	RANK	AMOUNT	NAME
MA	1	$75,120.22	LASSITER BUILDERS
	2	$56,086.23	KOCH RECONSTRUCTION
	3	$52,877.30	ELIZABETH METAL WORK
MW	1	$66,789.20	ROPER BROTHERS
	2	$56,769.22	BOVEY PARTS
	3	$54,978.34	COACH AND BODY WORKS
NE	1	$86,295.90	ARISTA MANUFACTURING
	2	$68,345.25	WANKEL BROTHERS
			WARNER CONSTRUCTION
	3	$68,246.20	HANCOCK RESTORERS
SE	1	$82,195.25	FEDERAL DEPOT
	2	$56,345.17	RICHS STORES
	3	$53,789.00	CAPITOL WHOLESALE

```
DEFINE FILE SALES
REGION/A12 = DECODE REGION(NE 'NORTH EAST'
                SE 'SOUTH EAST' MW 'MID WEST'
                MA 'MID-ATLANTIC');
END
TABLE FILE SALES
HEADING CENTER
"PRODUCT UNIT SALES ANALYSIS </1 "
SUM UNITS AND ROW-TOTAL AND COLUMN-TOTAL
ACROSS REGION
BY PRODNUM AS
'PRODUCT,NUMBER'
END
```

Figure 17-14 (left). Another Program, This Time to Show the Distribution of Sales by Product by Region.

Figure 17-15 (below). The Report Resulting from the Program in Figure 17-14.

PAGE 1 — PRODUCT UNIT SALES ANALYSIS

PRODUCT NUMBER	REGION MID WEST	MID-ATLANTIC	NORTH EAST	SOUTH EAST	TOTAL
10524	164	181	184	115	644
10526	40	126	150	45	361
11275	189	219	133	168	709
11302	179	130	288	172	769
11303	99	121	220	30	470
11537	90	260	110	124	584
11563	297	245	520	371	1433
11567	86	80	.	20	186
12275	.	.	.	30	30
12345	.	10	.	.	10
13737	.	.	29	.	29
13797	110	160	65	389	724
13938	324	186	441	164	1115
13979	.	12	.	.	12
14156	200	538	120	169	1027
15016	94	257	156	245	752
16394	252	210	187	40	689
16436	.	132	52	20	204
16934	.	50	.	.	50
17434	166	378	84	174	802
17905	164	70	108	199	541
34562	25	.	.	.	25
34567	100	.	.	.	100
56267	146	190	910	255	1501
TOTAL	2725	3555	3757	2730	12767

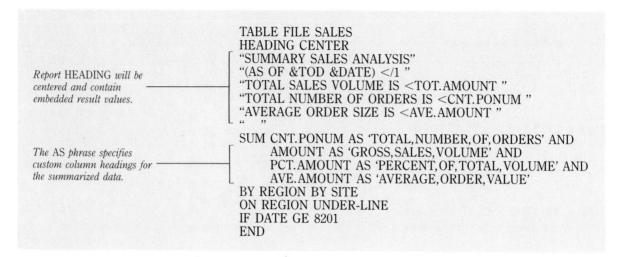

```
                              TABLE FILE SALES
                              HEADING CENTER
                              "SUMMARY SALES ANALYSIS"
Report HEADING will be        "(AS OF &TOD &DATE) </1 "
centered and contain          "TOTAL SALES VOLUME IS <TOT.AMOUNT "
embedded result values.       "TOTAL NUMBER OF ORDERS IS <CNT.PONUM "
                              "AVERAGE ORDER SIZE IS <AVE.AMOUNT "
                              " "
                              SUM CNT.PONUM AS 'TOTAL,NUMBER,OF,ORDERS' AND
The AS phrase specifies            AMOUNT AS 'GROSS,SALES,VOLUME' AND
custom column headings for         PCT.AMOUNT AS 'PERCENT,OF,TOTAL,VOLUME' AND
the summarized data.               AVE.AMOUNT AS 'AVERAGE,ORDER,VALUE'
                              BY REGION BY SITE
                              ON REGION UNDER-LINE
                              IF DATE GE 8201
                              END
```

Figure 17-16. A Management Report Program to Analyze Gross Sales.

Figure 17-17. The Report Resulting from the Program in Figure 17-16.

PAGE 1

SUMMARY OF SALES ANALYSIS
(AS OF 13.27.30 11/29/82)

TOTAL SALES VOLUME IS $2,576,655.45
TOTAL NUMBER OF ORDERS IS   3120
AVERAGE ORDER SIZE IS $,825.85

REGION	SITE	TOTAL NUMBER OF ORDERS	GROSS SALES VOLUME	PERCENT OF TOTAL VOLUME	AVERAGE ORDER VALUE
MA	NEWK	256	$195,869,80	7.60	$765.12
	NEWY	398	$234,424.20	9.10	$589.01
	PHIL	144	$175,978.96	6.83	$1,222.08
	PITT	126	$109,915.62	4.27	$872.35
MW	CHIC	416	$247,770.40	9.62	$595.60
	CLEV	387	$311,936.80	12.11	$806.04
NE	ALBN	215	$115,081.30	4.47	$535.26
	BOST	306	$283,277.75	10.99	$925.74
	STAM	416	$313,448.29	12.16	$753.48
SE	ATL	156	$224,785.69	8.72	$1,440.93
	RICH	195	$146,523.74	5.69	$751.40
	WASH	215	$217,642.90	8.45	$967.30

```
JOIN PRODNUM IN SUPPLY TO ALL PRODNUM IN SALES
TABLE FILE SUPPLY
SUM UNITS AS 'UNITS,ON,ORDER' AND
     ONHAND AS 'INVENTORY,LEVEL' AND COMPUTE
     SHORTAGE = UNITS – ONHAND;
BY PRODUCT BY DESCRIPTION
IF TOTAL SHORTAGE GE 10
IF FILLCODE NE 'Y'
END
```

The relational JOIN command is issued using PRODNUM as a variable common to both files.

A report is requested from the new relation.

UNITS data is from the SALES file.

ONHAND data is from the SUPPLY file.

SHORTAGE is dynamically computed.

The 'IF TOTAL' test enables screening of results prior to printing.

Figure 17-18. A Program to Join the Sales and Supply Files and Produce a Report of Shortage Conditions.

Figure 17-19. The Program of Figure 17-18 Generates This Report on Shortages.

PAGE 1

PRODNUM	DESCRIPTION	UNITS ON ORDER	INVENTORY LEVEL	SHORTAGE
11275	RADIAL ARM SAW (10 INCH)	570	489	81.00
13938	LATHE	735	689	46.00
14156	ENGINE ANALYZER	797	450	347.00
16394	ATERNATOR (3000 WATT)	533	367	166.00
17905	PAINT SPRAYER	421	344	77.00
56267	ARC WELDER	1251	244	1,007.00

Management also wants a report that analyzes gross sales on a store and region basis. Figure 17-16 contains the FOCUS program—note how easy it is to create totals and percentages compared with a language like COBOL! The report appears in Figure 17-17.

The most complex example arises from the need to know if there are any shortage conditions for products requested in unfilled orders. The data for this analysis is split between the Sales and Supply files and there are no pre-established linkages between the files. Using a relational JOIN command, FOCUS links the files together to create a new logical data structure.

Figure 17-18 shows the FOCUS program and 17-19 the resulting report.

Figure 17-20. Setting up a Business Graphics System: a Bar Chart.

BUSINESS GRAPHICS

The advent of easy-to-use computer graphics packages has encouraged business people to conduct more graphic analysis. While it is important to "know one's data," that is, to look at the numbers themselves, often a graph will help to highlight a subtle relationship in the data. Microcomputers have been particularly important in providing users with a graphics capability. For example, our spreadsheet program makes it possible to generate a number of graphs.

A Graphics Package

Figure 17-20 shows a user in the Actuarial Department at MONY Financial Services in New York working with a consultant from the Computer Department. They have just installed a high-resolution graphics CRT and graphics processing board in an IBM PC. They are working with the Statgraphics program, which in Figure 17-20 has generated a bar chart. Figure 17-21 shows a pie chart and 17-22 con-

tains a three-dimensional histogram analysis. This system can graph in up to sixteen colors.

Figure 17-23 is another example of the kind of graphics output available from the system, in this case the plot of the *bivariate normal distribution.* This plot shows the bivariate normal distribution. *Bi* means "two" and the figure shows the surface (the famous "bell" of the normal distribution) when we plot two normal variables that are related to each other. Figure 17-24 is a *least squares regression analysis.* In least squares a statistical procedure determines the slope and intercept of the regression line that minimizes the squares of the vertical distances of each data point from the line. Regression techniques are used extensively in data analysis.

Figure 17-25 is an example of a statistical quality control chart. This chart helps an employee in quality control to see if a production process is out of control. As long as the observed quality falls within the dotted lines, we cannot say statistically that there is anything wrong with the process. Figure 17-26 shows a plot of seasonal data, an analysis that is often used in forecasting.

Figure 17-21 (above). A Pie Chart Using the Color Graphics System.

Figure 17-22 (right). A Three-dimension Histogram Showing Relative Frequencies.

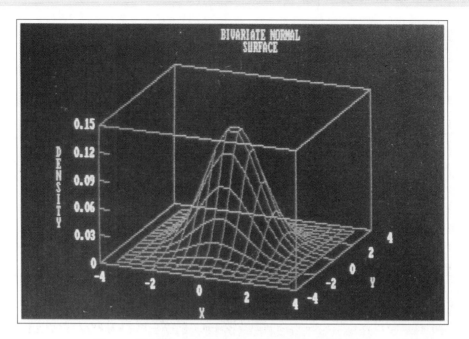

Figure 17-23. The Bivariate Normal Distribution.

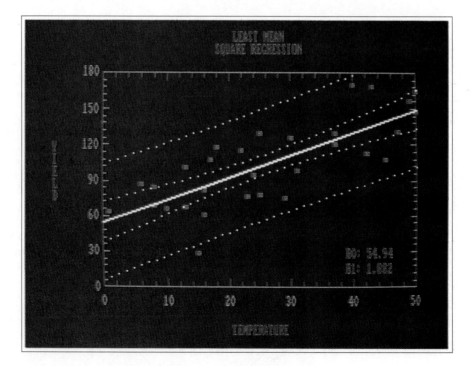

Figure 17-24. A Least Squares Regression.

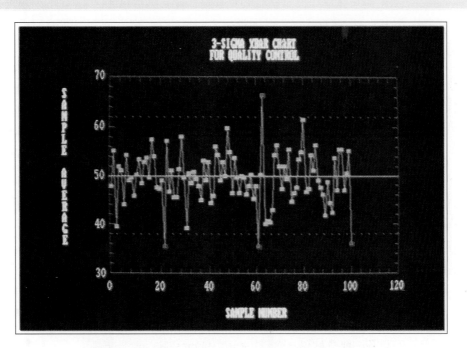

Figure 17-25. A Statistical Quality Control Chart.

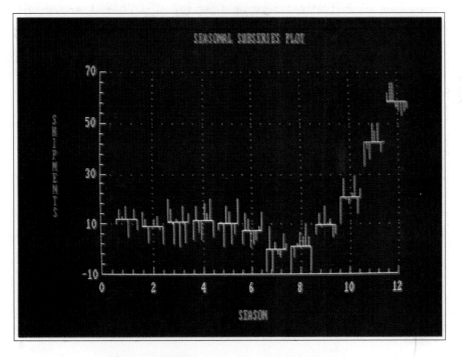

Figure 17-26. A Graph of Seasonal Data.

Figure 17-27. The Engineer at a CAD Workstation.

Figure 17-28. A Computervision CAD Workstation.

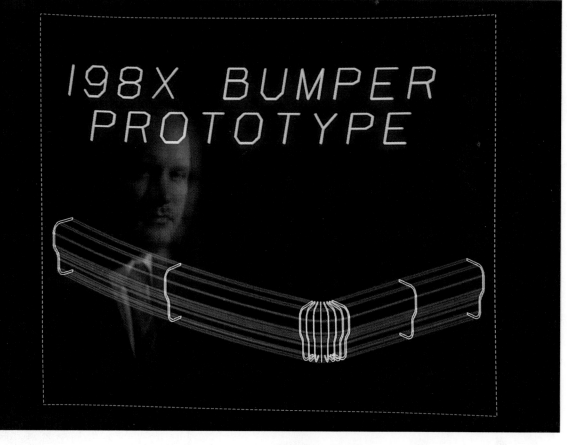

Figure 17-29. CAD Used to Develop an Automobile Bumper.

COMPUTER-AIDED DESIGN

The Engineering Workstation

The computer has provided the engineer with a powerful new tool, the engineering workstation and software for computer-aided design (CAD). When designing a manufacturing task an engineer might sit at a special terminal with added input keys and a light pen as shown in Figure 17-27. This particular engineer is working on the design of a tile for the Space Shuttle at Lockheed Corporation. Figure 17-28 shows a workstation offered by Computervision, one of the leaders in computer-aided design equipment. Figure 17-29 is the drawing of a bumper based

on a General Motors CAD system.

The first CAD systems were restricted to line drawings. Newer, more powerful hardware and software combinations make it possible to model solids as well. Figure 17-30 shows an engineer working with a Computervision solid drafting package. He might begin with a line drawing such as the one shown in Figure 17-31. From there, the package is capable of providing a shaded, exploded view of the part as seen in Figure 17-32. Figure 17-33 shows the paths that a numerically controlled tool would have to follow to manufacture the part. Figure 17-34 shows a tool handle that has been modeled with this system.

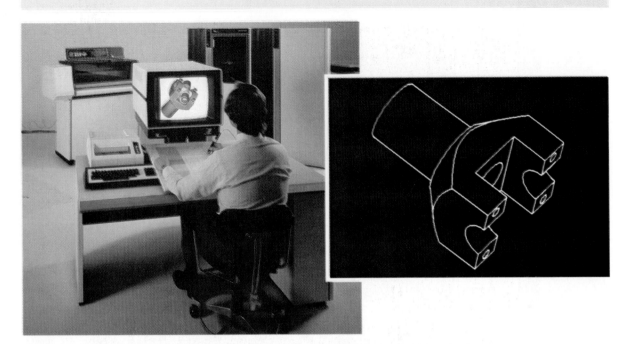

Figure 17-30. An Engineer Working with a CAD System with Three-Dimensional Capabilities.

Figure 17-31 (inset above). The engineer starts with a line drawing.

Figure 17-32 (left). A Shaded, Exploded View of the Drawing.

Figure 17-33 (below). The system displays paths for a numerically controlled machine tool to follow in manufacturing the part.

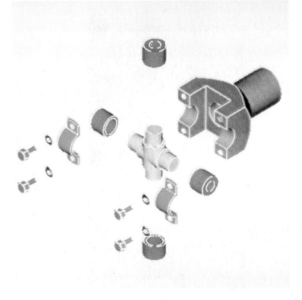

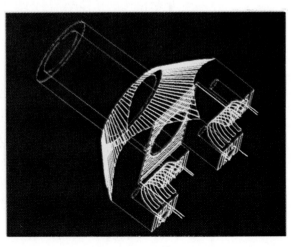

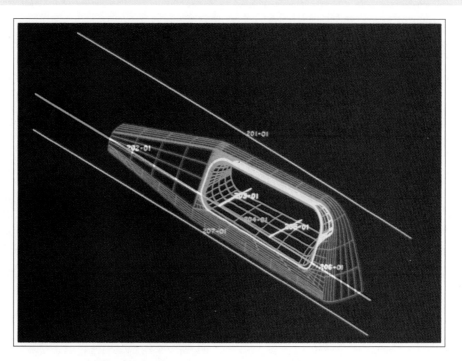

Figure 17-34 (a). The Design of a Tool Handle.

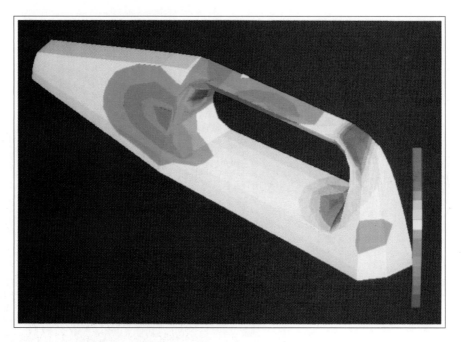

Figure 17-34 (b). A Stress Analysis of the Handle.

A CAD Session

We shall follow an engineer as he uses a computer-aided design system at work

In this photograph the engineer uses a digital pad and pencil to manipulate a wire frame drawing of a CRT screen enclosure.

Below, the engineer is consulting a technical drawing, and right, he develops the drawing using a mouse.

Labeling and programming with keyboard entry is shown above.

Based on a review of a drawing produced on a plotter, the engineer makes further changes in the drawing using a digital pad for input.

After the wire frame, the engineer wants to see a solid view from the CRT screen as shown below.

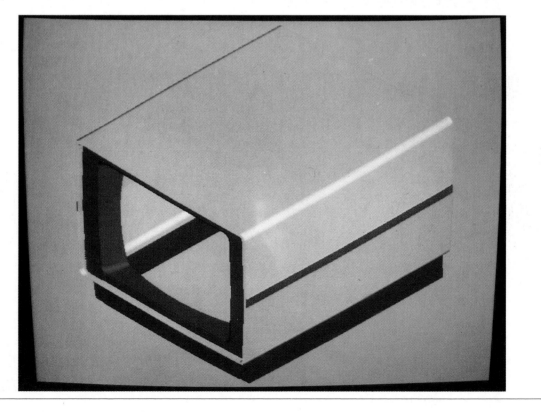

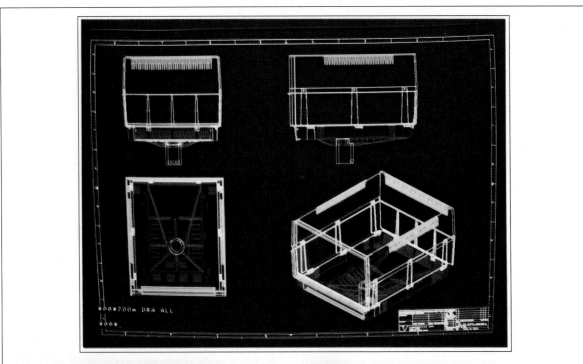

These are other wire frame diagrams on the CRT display above.

The updating of permanent storage of the design on tape shown to the left here.

The engineer has been able to recall a drawing, make changes, and generate a new drawing in a short period of time compared with previous manual techniques. CAD is an excellent example of how computers have contributed to productivity. The engineering workstation is also a good forerunner of the kind of managerial workstation we expect to see in the future. ∎

Application

A CAD Project

In 1983 the Ministry of Finance of France decided to move its offices out of the Louvre, freeing more space for the museum. Although it is the largest museum in the world, attendance at the Louvre is disappointing, with only 2.7 million visitors per year compared to some 8 million visitors at the Pompidou Center.

There have been a number of reasons advanced for the attendance problem: a hard-to-find entrance; long, dark hallways leading to visitor confusion; and insufficient space for workshops, gift shops, and rest rooms. Based on the recommendations of 15 museum directors world-wide, President Mitterrand of France personally called the renowned architect I. M. Pei to design a new entrance and ancillary space for the Louvre.

After six months of study, Pei suggested a 75,000 square meter underground space for parking, theaters, meetings, conferences, and museum shops. Above ground there would be four glass pyramids in the courtyard, three of which would be skylights to provide illumination for the new underground space. The largest pyramid would be a new visitor en-trance. Visitors entering the pyramid will descend by escalator to the lower level where they will have direct access to any of the three museum wings. A glass structure was chosen so that the visitor could see all of the wings of the Louvre and remain oriented to it. This entrance pyramid will be almost twenty meters high and will be surrounded by pools and fountains.

I. M. Pei turned to Computervision to model the entire building and courtyard. He was particularly interested in seeing how his design would look from various viewpoints. A joint team of architects and computers specialists used the computer to model and refine the design concept; the results of this effort were also used to present the concept to the French government.

It took about twenty-four hours of operator time to construct the computer model from manual plans for the building. The advantage of the computer system was that it allowed several different solutions to be studied at one time. Line or wire-frame drawings as well as surface and shaded perspectives made it possible to examine various sight lines. The photographs in this section display some of the computer models from this project.

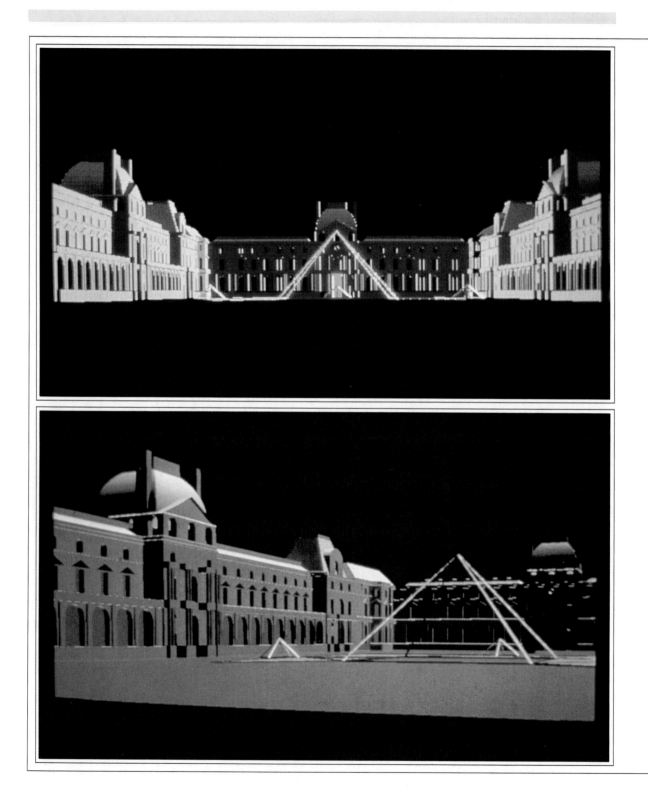

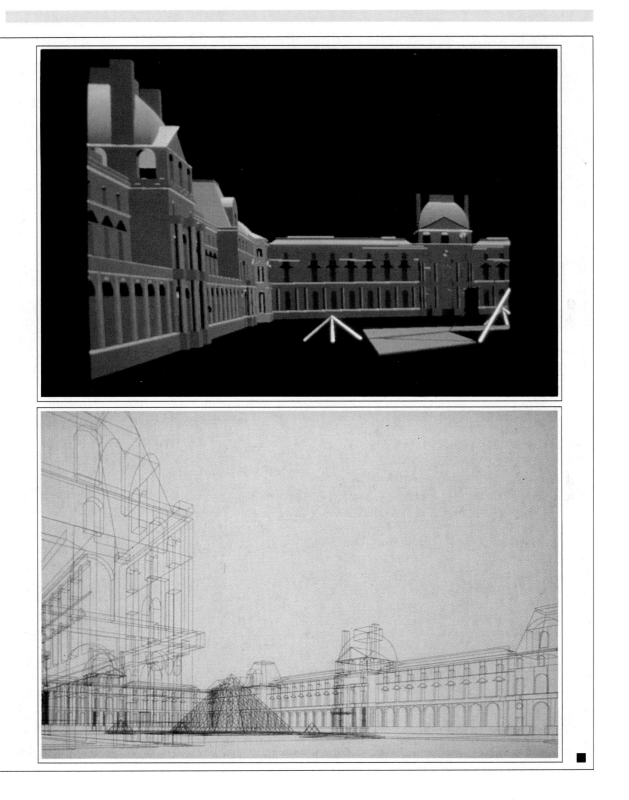

Figure 17-35. The GE Dishwasher Plant Control Booth.

SUMMARY

Computer-aided design has contributed markedly to productivity. Relatively inexpensive systems on personal computers are available to even the smallest manufacturing firm. No longer is there a need to redraw every part when there is a minor change; the computer makes all of the modifications and the engineer can quickly generate a new drawing on a plotter. The unique characteristics of the computer for modeling buildings and solids also provide a new tool. It would be very expensive to construct an example or physical model for many design projects; the computer provides this modeling capability as illustrated in the Louvre project.

COMPUTERS IN MANUFACTURING

Simple Robotics

Modern robots employ computer technology for a variety of tasks, from sensing to command and con-

trol. There are a number of advantages to robots, including their lack of sensitivity to a hostile environment such as a paint shop for automobile bodies. Robots do not need rest breaks and rarely go out on strike.

The Automated Factory

The field of robotics is moving in two directions. The first is to develop more intelligent robots, devices that will receive feedback on their performance in time to correct errors. For example, a welding robot might inspect its own weld and repair it if faulty. Robots with vision capabilities are under development that will be able to pick up different parts and assemble them.

Another direction in the development of robotics is to apply current technology to create more highly automated factories. Experience has shown that such a factory requires a rethinking of even the basics of how a product is made. For example, General Electric has constructed an automated dishwasher factory which required a complete redesign of the

dishwasher so that it could be built with available automatic equipment and robots. The number of parts in the dishwasher was reduced from approximately 5600 to 850 in order to use more automated manufacturing techniques.

The remodeled plant in Louisville, KY required an investment of over $38 million. GE has found that the average number of dishwasher customer service calls has been reduced by 53 percent since the new plant went into operation. The plant required five to six days to produce a dishwasher two years ago. It now requires only about 18 hours. Overall employee productivity has increased by more than 25 percent and production capacity at the plant is up by 20 percent.

The process of building a dishwasher including parts production, unit assembly, and warehousing is controlled and tracked by 34 Series Six programmable controllers developed by a GE division. Assembly operations are monitored from an overhead booth which contains three computer terminals connected to a Digital Equipment Corporation PDP 11/44 computer.

GE constructs the polypropylene tub and inner door using a proprietary process of injection molding. The tub mold weighs almost 22 tons; its injection machines are controlled by a Series Six programmable controller which monitors 32 different temperature points, 10 velocities, five gates, seven pressure points and a selection of counters.

While the tub is being constructed, metal structural and support parts are cut or stamped from steel coils. The plant makes 13 dishwasher models, each of which passes through a series of stations: 21 for tub assembly and 13 for the door.

The status of each unit is tracked through assembly by laser-scanned bar codes. An Automatic Camera Recognition System developed by another GE division aligns the door hinges and tub structure during fabrication. Proper door latching requires tolerances of several thousandths of an inch.

Figure 17-35 is a picture of the control booth which overlooks the dishwasher assembly line. Figure 17-36a is the tub structure assembly line while 17-36b is a closeup of the tub assembly line showing the tubs coming from the injection molding process.

Figure 17-37. Dishwasher Tub Inspection.

Figure 17-38. The Robot Handler Transferring Tubs from One Assembly Line to Another.

Figure 17-39. Tubs Being Fitted with Fasteners.

In Figure 17-37 we see the dishwasher tubs being inspected as they move. Figure 17-38 shows the robotic handler which takes the tub from the assembly line and transfers it to the next assembly point. In Figure 17-39 the tubs are fitted with fasteners for attaching doors and outer packaging.

Some portions of the plant require human manual dexterity, such as some of the final parts assembly process shown in Figure 17-40. Each operator has about 15 seconds to perform an assembly step, but can continue for up to 45 seconds if a problem develops. If the worker cannot finish, he or she logs a signal to the controller and the unit continues down the line for later repair.

In Figure 17-41 we see dishwasher doors passing a worker who handles the plant's point-of-use parts manufacturing data.

Before completed machines leave the plant, they are subjected to a rigorous quality audit which assures that the customer will receive a working dishwasher (see Figure 17-42).

This automated plant is the shape of manufacturing in the future. GE eventually would like to create a "closed loop" system in which communications will be shared throughout the entire production cycle and corrective action taken automatically. Information-processing technology is critical to improving the performance of manufacturing plants, as illustrated by GE's advanced dishwasher facility in Louisville.

Figure 17-40. Final Parts Assembly Requires the Dexterity of a Human.

Figure 17-41. Data Analysis in the Plant.

Figure 17-42. Quality testing is an important part of manufacturing.

SUMMARY

Computers in the early generations produced paper and reports. By the end of the second generation, we saw the first on-line systems; often the terminal was a typewriter-like device rather than a modern CRT. With the third generation, CRT's predominated for on-line applications. However, most interaction with the computer still involved text (including numbers) rather than graphics or other nontextual displays.

Today, as this chapter has tried to demonstrate, there are many different ways to work with computers and their output. The basic chip, with its very large scale integration of electronic components and circuits, has provided the power for a dramatic expansion in the way computers can be used.

This hardware combined with well-designed software provides end-users with the capabilities of a Fourth Generation Language like FOCUS. The same technology is used to develop engineering workstations to design various kinds of parts and buildings including the renovation of the Louvre in Paris. CAD will increasingly be linked with CAM (computer-aided manufacturing) so that the designer's efforts will flow into actual production. At the same time we shall see increasingly intelligent robots and more highly automated factories.

The purpose of this chapter has been to show the variety of ways in which computers interact with users and the numerous applications that exist for this technology. From the office to the factory floor, information-processing technology is improving the way business functions in countless ways.

Chapter 18

Why learn about a language like BASIC? Are there not enough packages so that someone should never have to write a program? For many of us, there probably will never be a need to write a program in BASIC to solve a problem. However, we cannot be sure; a package that can do a particular task may not be available, or it may be necessary to write a program to link the results of two packages together.

If you learn a language like BASIC, your knowledge of computing should be adequate for you to function as a user, certainly as a user of microcomputers. Knowing one programming language also facilitates learning a second.

Remember our discussions of end-user programming and fourth-generation languages. These languages are at a higher level than BASIC, but knowing BASIC will help you a great deal in understanding fourth-generation languages and query languages. Why? Because a feeling for BASIC provides an understanding of what these higher-level lan-

guages must be doing for the user. Writing a program in BASIC also teaches something about programming strategy and structure. All of this knowledge could prove very important in work with other systems, including minis and mainframes.

In this chapter, we present an introduction to BASIC. Because there are many versions of BASIC, the exact statements found here may differ from the BASIC you may be able to run on whatever computer is available to you. (This chapter uses Microsoft advanced BASIC for the IBM PC.)

In a book that covers computers and systems, we cannot really expect to have enough on a language for the reader to become an expert. Rather, this chapter should be viewed as an introduction and an overview. To become proficient in the language, it would be helpful to obtain a book that is devoted solely to BASIC and that has a lot of programming exercises. Going from this chapter to a complete text and having access to a computer should make it easy to learn BASIC.

BASIC: A HIGH-LEVEL LANGUAGE

After reading this chapter, you should be able to:

- Describe the components of a compiler-level language like **BASIC**.
- Explain the difference among types of variables in **BASIC**.
- Describe how to structure a program.
- Explain conditional statements in a language.
- Describe iteration statements in a language.
- Describe input/output in **BASIC**.
- Write a simple program in **BASIC**.

INTRODUCTION

In the last two chapters, we have looked at packages, one for spreadsheet analysis and the other for word processing. Before packages like these were available, it was necessary to write software in more traditional computer languages. BASIC was one of the first of these to enjoy widespread popularity among users.

As you may remember from Chapter 3, BASIC was developed by Professors Kemeny and Kurtz at Dartmouth as a time-sharing language. BASIC has been expanded dramatically from its early versions and now is much easier to use and more powerful than when it was first developed. Because BASIC is relatively easy to learn, it has been widely adopted on personal computers in addition to time-sharing systems.

Unfortunately, there are many different versions of BASIC, and there is little compatibility (i.e., ability to move a program from one computer to another with no changes). However, it is easier to move BASIC programs from one system to another than it is to move some other languages.

OVERVIEW

We shall introduce BASIC through an example that will be developed gradually, step by step, to show additional features of the language. Before we present the example, it is useful to think for a moment about the structure of a higher-level language. We can distinguish among three levels of programming.

The first level is the conceptual level, where the problem solver is designing the program. At this point, the program is very abstract; we are not at all concerned with implementation or even the language that will be used to solve the problem. At this level, the program consists of abstract data types, for example, the logical view of data that we saw in the section on data structures in Chapter 10.

The conceptual level also includes *algorithms;* an algorithm is an effective procedure, a series of steps, for accomplishing some task. A routine that sorts a list of names into alphabetical order uses a sort algorithm, a procedure that reorders the list. An algorithm is eventually converted into a computer program, but at the conceptual level, it can be stated in pseudo-English, that is, a highly structured series of statements.

The next level is implementation. Now, the problem solver expresses the abstract concepts from the first level in more specific programming-language constructs (i.e., a form closer to what must be coded in a program for the computer). The data structures become program variables of different types. Single-valued variables called *scalars,* tables of data called *arrays,* and file records are all examples of different representations of data. The algorithms are also translated into instructions in the programming language chosen to solve the problem.

The final level of the program is descriptive, the narrative version of computer code that constitutes the final program. This final level is put into the compiler and must be correct according to the rules (syntax) of the programming language. This program consists of statements in the programming language, of which there are several types:

1. *Declarations.* These statements are not executed; instead, they tell the BASIC translator certain things about the *variables,* for example, the size of a table.

2. *Control statements.* These statements control the flow of execution of the program; for example, they allow the program to perform loops (repetitive calculations or *iterations*) and to provide statements that let different decisions cause different parts of the program to be executed. Control statements also make it possible to divide the program into various components or routines.

3. *Assignment statements.* These statements assign new values to data types. A statement that $X = Y$ means that the current value of Y is assigned to the current value of X. Assignment statements can also be used to change data types, for example, to turn a decimal number into an integer.

4. *Input/output.* These statements are concerned with communicating with various other devices: the terminal, printers, and different kinds of secondary storage.

5. *Special features.* Added features are not neces-

sarily found in every language nor in every version of a language. The version of BASIC used here features a set of graphics commands for drawing various shapes on the monitor.

BASIC offers different types of variables that implement the abstract *data* structures which the programmer develops in first thinking about his or her program. (Remember that a variable is a name that holds a value, like the name *PAY,* which holds the computed value of someone's pay for the week.) The simplest variable is a scalar; it has a single value, like 432. This example is an integer, or a fixed-point scalar. We can also have floating-point scalars, like 432.567. A variable can also represent a character string like "PLEASE SELECT YOUR CHOICE."

An array is a variable in the form of a table that has more than one *dimension,* for example, a table on the cash register in a store that has one entry for the value of your purchase and a second entry for the amount of sales tax on a sale of that amount. Depending on the language, one can have arrays of more than two dimensions. Some languages also offer lists of items as a data type.

A GROWING PROGRAM

The example we shall build in this chapter is a simple payroll program for a Computerware store. As this new division of Multicorp is small, and as each store employs only a few people, the payroll program does not have to be complicated. (In reality, we would probably use a package program for such a payroll, but this is a good application to illustrate the use of BASIC.)

Problem Structure

The first thing to consider in writing a program is not to start too fast. It is very tempting to begin jotting down lines of code. Control yourself. Think first about what you want to do, and then write down something about the structure of the problem without even thinking about program statements.

What is our problem? The objective is to compute the payroll for a single employee. What are the various components of the problem? Eventually, we shall want to think about deductions, taxes, and government reports.

If we knew BASIC well, we would tackle the entire problem in a *top-down* approach; that is, we would first describe at the conceptual level what we need to do. Then, the problem would be broken down into smaller and smaller parts until we reached the lowest level of detail.

Finally, we would start programming. At first, we would develop the highest-level program and then fill in detailed routines at lower levels. Figure 18-1 shows the overall logic for a payroll application and the planned structure of a program to compute the payroll. The first high-level data-flow diagram shows that there is information about each employee, such as pay rate, number of dependents, year-to-date pay, taxes, and social security (FICA).

The steps involved are to:

1. Compute the gross pay.
2. Compute the withholding.
3. Compute the deductions.
4. Compute the FICA.
5. Calculate the net pay.
6. Update the year-to-date totals.
7. Produce reports.

Figure 18-2 shows some of the modules from Figure 18-1 broken down into further detail. Payroll processing involves the use of a file on secondary storage. To update year-to-date totals, the program will read the old totals for this year to date, like the total pay and taxes so far, and then add the results for the current pay period. The program writes the revised year-to-date figures back to the file for the next run of the payroll program.

A Beginning

Given the relative simplicity of the program, we could begin work at the highest level and follow the top-down programming approach advocated earlier. However, it is easier to introduce BASIC by beginning at the lowest level and working our way up.

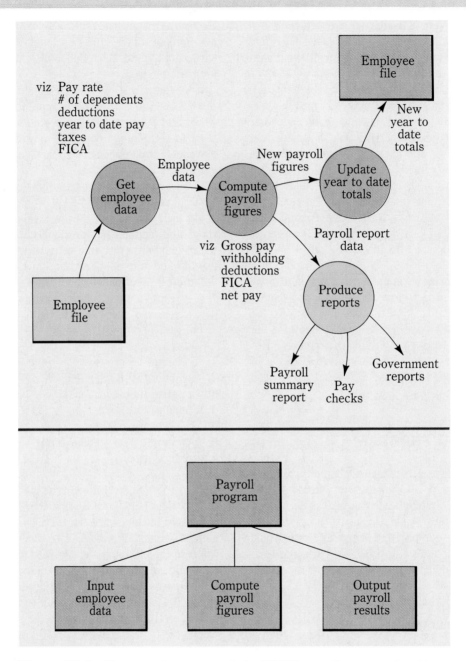

Figure 18-1. The overall strategy of the BASIC payroll program has three components.

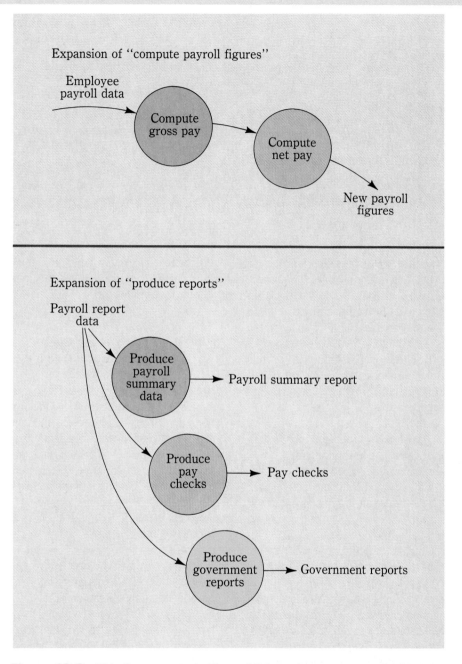

Expansion of "compute payroll figures"

Employee payroll data

Compute gross pay

Compute net pay

New payroll figures

Expansion of "produce reports"

Payroll report data

Produce payroll summary data

Payroll summary report

Produce pay checks

Pay checks

Produce government reports

Government reports

Figure 18-2. This figure expands Figure 18-1 to show more program details.

```
10 REM  * * * * * * * * * * * * * * * * * * * * * * * * * *
20 REM  *  This program accepts employee payroll data as input,    *
        *  computes net pay by deducting all taxes and deductions  *
        *  from gross pay and displays this result.                *
30 REM  * * * * * * * * * * * * * * * * * * * * * * * * * *
40 REM
50 INPUT "Gross Pay, FICA, Deductions, Income Tax";
         GROSS.PAY, FICA, DEDUCTIONS, INCOME.TAX
60 NET.PAY = GROSS.PAY - (FICA + DEDUCTIONS INCOME.TAX)
70 PRINT "Net pay is "; NET.PAY
```

Figure 18-3. A Simple Program to Compute Pay.

This approach is taken only for instructional purposes; it is not the best way to develop a program.

At first, let us address the problem of the computation of pay. We need to name some variables. In BASIC, a variable stands for some number or some string of characters. Variable names can be up to forty characters long in this Microsoft version of BASIC for the IBM Personal Computer. For this problem, we need a series of variables to represent different parts of the payroll program. The ones that are apparent right now are

- Gross pay, for gross pay earned for this period.
- FICA, for social security for this period.
- Deductions, the amount deducted for this period.
- Income tax, for this period's income taxes.
- Net pay, the pay left over after all taxes and other deductions.

BASIC offers a number of different variable types. We can have integer variables that can hold values in the range of $-32,768$ to $+32,767$ in this version of BASIC. There are also single-precision and double-precision floating-point numbers. **Single-precision** variables hold values of up to seven or fewer significant digits, and **double-precision** values have up to sixteen digits. Finally, there are string variables that contain character strings of up to 255 characters. A character **string** is simply a series of alphabetic characters than can be manipulated by program statements.

We need to let BASIC know what kind of variables

we are using. One way is to put a special character after each variable name. For example, Name$ would be a string variable because $ means a string. The other symbols are

% Integer variable
! Single-precision variable
Double-precision variable

If we fail to define a variable type, then BASIC assumes that it is a single-precision number. Computations are fastest on integers, then single-precision, and finally double-precision numbers.

There is another way to define the variables that we are using, for example, a statement that declares that variables beginning with certain characters are integers. To keep things simple, we shall use the initial character % to define integers and so on, as in the preceding list.

There are two modes of operation in the BASIC that we are using. The first is direct; statements are executed as soon as they are entered into the computer. Although this mode is useful for testing and debugging or when the computer is used as a calculator, we often want to write a program and save it for later use. For this purpose, we enter a line number preceding each BASIC statement. The line number sequence indicates the order in which the statements appear and are executed.

Figure 18-3 shows a simple program that computes pay. We shall actually introduce several different types of statements here. The first is relatively

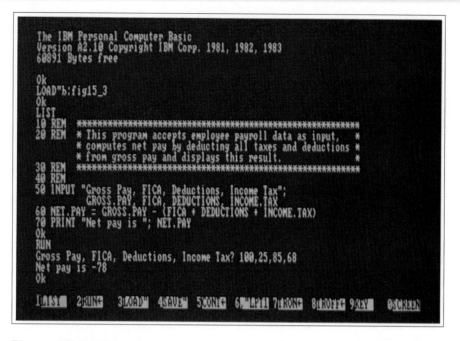

Figure 18-4. Execution of Program in 18-3. The first program which is basically computation of pay only.

simple: the "Remark" or "REM" statement. BASIC ignores remark statements; they are in the program to improve its readability. It is very hard for someone to look at another person's program and figure out what it does. It is even difficult for us to pick up a program that we wrote ourselves several months or years ago and remember what the variables do and how the program works.

In Figure 18-3, note that the first several lines are REM statements or remarks. A REM statement with nothing following it is used to provide spacing in the program and to make it more legible. The remarks or comments give the overall purpose of this piece of code and also the definition of the variables, like Gross Pay, FICA, Deductions, and Income Tax. Note that a variable can be only one word, so to use terms that are normally two words, like *Gross pay,* we must connect the two words with a character so that BASIC will see only one name, in this case "Gross.Pay."

The first executable statement is one that asks for input from the person at the keyboard. For this simple program, we must have a way to provide the computer with data. The "Input" statement accepts data from the keyboard; note the *prompt line,* so that we will know what to type.

The next statement is the computation of the payroll and is known as an *assignment statement.* We are assigning a value to net pay, which is gross pay minus all of the deductions. Finally, the last statement is a "print" statement that labels and prints the results. The program is executed in Figure 18-4.

Computing Pay

The next step in developing the program is actually to compute the pay. In our first program, we only input the pay; now we shall perform a computation. To compute pay, we need some more variables:

- Payrate, the rate of hourly pay.
- Hours.week, the hours worked this week.

The actual computation of "Gross.pay," then, is fairly simple: Gross.pay = Hours.week*Pay.rate. How can we modify the program to include this computation? We have here another example of the assignment statement, assigning a value to the variable "Gross.pay."

Just as we saw with the spreadsheet package, one can use a number of *operators* in BASIC:

$\wedge$	Exponentiation
$-$	Negation
$*, /$	Multiplication, floating-point division
$\pm$	Integer division
$+, -$	Addition, subtraction

These operators are listed in order of precedence. To change the order, one needs to use parentheses. If $A = 2$ and $B = 3$ and $C = 4$, then $A + B * C$ is 14 because multiplication takes precedence over addition. The expression $(A + B) * C$ would be 20 because the parentheses indicate that first A and B are to be added before multiplication by C.

It appears that we have a good solution to computing hours, except for one problem: if an employee works more than forty hours, we must pay overtime. This possibility gives us a chance to introduce one of the most powerful capabilities of a computer, the ability to make decisions. The *conditional* statement in BASIC is "IF *expression* THEN *clause* ELSE *clause*." An *expression* is any mathematical comparison or computation that evaluates to a zero (false) or a nonzero (true) value. *Clauses* are executable statements. The easiest way to illustrate this is with the actual computation for our example:

```
IF Hours.week <= 40 THEN
    Gross.pay = Pay.rate*Hours.week
ELSE
    Gross.pay = Pay.rate*Hours.week +
    (Hours.week-40)*Pay.rate*0.5
```

The first clause of this computation calculates gross pay as straight-time hours times the rate as long as the employee worked forty hours or less. The second clause calculates straight-time pay for all hours worked and then adds a 50 percent bonus for hours in excess of forty. The total effect, then, is to pay the first forty hours at regular time and the overtime hours at time-and-a-half.

Note that the "IF . . . THEN" statement can be written on one line. However, as a matter of programming style, we use separate lines and make the two computations as clear as possible. In this instance, clearly written conditionals contribute to good structure along with the comments that are found in Figure 18-5. The program also has some additional input to accept hours and rate data.

We also have seen in this example our first use of logical variables. This version of BASIC has a number of *logical* or relational *operators.* An expression that evaluates as true is assigned a value of -1, and a false expression is 0. The operators are

$=$	Equality
$<>$ or $><$	Inequality
$<$	Less than
$>$	Greater than
$<=$ or $=>$	Less than or equal to
$>=$ or $=>$	Greater than or equal to

These operators apply to numeric comparisons or to character strings, so that we can compare Able with Baker and find that Baker is greater than Able. For sorting names, we can compare string characters and place them in alphabetical sequence; names with a higher comparison fall later in the alphabet (e.g., Baker is greater than Able).

Loops

Another powerful feature of programming languages is their ability to *loop,* that is, to execute the same section of code over a specified number of times. This kind of execution is also known as an *iteration.* One of the most important things about loops is to be sure that they will end. We should always figure out how the loop will stop and be sure that the conditions for stopping will be reached. Almost every programmer has had the most unsettling experience of having a program loop that never stops!

Basic has a pair of statements that control loops. The format of the statements is

```
10 REM   * * * * * * * * * * * * * * * * * * * * * * * * * * * *
20 REM   *   This program accepts employee payroll data as input,      *
         *   computes the gross pay and computes and displays net pay.  *
30 REM   * * * * * * * * * * * * * * * * * * * * * * * * * * * *
40 REM
50 INPUT "Employee's pay rate, Hours worked, FICA, Deductions, Income Tax";
         PAY.RATE, HOURS.WEEK, FICA, DEDUCTIONS, INCOME.TAX
60 IF HOURS.WEEK < = 40 THEN
      GROSS.PAY      = PAY.RATE * HOURS.WEEK
    ELSE GROSS.PAY = PAY.RATE * HOURS.WEEK + (HOURS.WEEK - 40) * PAY.RATE * .5
70 NET.PAY = GROSS.PAY - (FICA + DEDUCTIONS + INCOME.TAX)
80 PRINT "Net pay is "; NET.PAY
```

Figure 18-5. The next version adds overtime pay calculations. Note the use of the conditional IF -THEN ELSE statement.

FOR *variable* = *x* TO *y* [STEP *z*]
loop body (statements in the loop)
NEXT *variable*

These statements control the number of iterations. The variable is any variable in the program; often, we use an integer counter of some kind like "Employee%," which in this case is a variable that will automatically be assigned values from *x* to *y*. For example, if there were 20 employees, the statement would be "FOR Employee%=1 to 20." The "STEP" is optional and is the value that is added to the counter each time. The default value is 1, so that the statement above would cause the loop to be executed twenty times, once for each employee. There are times when we want a different step, but not in our sample program.

"NEXT" simply tells us the location of the end of the loop. The statements between "FOR" and "NEXT" will be executed as many times as the loop is executed. From a style standpoint, it is a good idea to **indent** the statements that are in the loop body to make clear the beginning and the end of the loop, just as we indented the "IF" statement.

To use a loop in our sample program, we need to ask for input in the beginning on the number of employees. The program in Figure 18-6 now asks at the beginning for input to set the loop parameters, the number of employees—"Num.emp%." Note

also that we use loop indexes that are integers to speed up computations. The program then executes once for each employee, performing the payroll calculations and printing the results. Figure 18-7 shows the execution of the program.

More Thoughts on Structure

We have seen and discussed examples of programming style, namely, using comments, separating parts of conditional statements, and using indentation on conditionals and iteration statements. There is a lot more to program style.

The style concerns already discussed refer to local areas in the program; there is also the issue of the entire program and its **structure.** Remember that we stressed the top-down approach in systems design and in our introduction to the example problem in this chapter. We begin at a high-level view of the problem and then fill in the details subsequently. How do we accomplish that in programming? One way to produce a structure that is easy to read and easy to debug in BASIC is with different program **modules.** A module is a portion of the program that performs one task. We can think of a program as one master routine that calls a series of modules. The modules may, in turn, call other modules.

Figure 18-8 shows the hierarchical nature of a

```
10 REM   * * * * * * * * * * * * * * * * * * * * * * * * * * * * * *
20 REM   *   This program calculates the gross and net pay of each employee,   *
         *   accepting as input employee payroll data (hours worked, pay rate,  *
         *   FICA, deductions and income tax) and displaying net pay.           *
30 REM   * * * * * * * * * * * * * * * * * * * * * * * * * * * * * *
40 REM
50 INPUT "Number of employees to be processed"; NUM.EMP%
60 REM
70 FOR EMPLOYEE% = 1 TO NUM.EMP%
80      INPUT "Employee's pay rate, Hours worked, FICA, Deductions, Income Tax";
                PAY.RATE, HOURS.WEEK, FICA, DEDUCTIONS, INCOME.TAX
90      GROSS.PAY = PAY.RATE * HOURS.WEEK
100     NET.PAY   = GROSS.PAY - (FICA + DEDUCTIONS + INCOME.TAX)
110     PRINT "Net pay is "; NET.PAY
120 NEXT EMPLOYEE%
```

Figure 18-6. The original program with a loop or iteration. Look closely at how the FOR NEXT loop works.

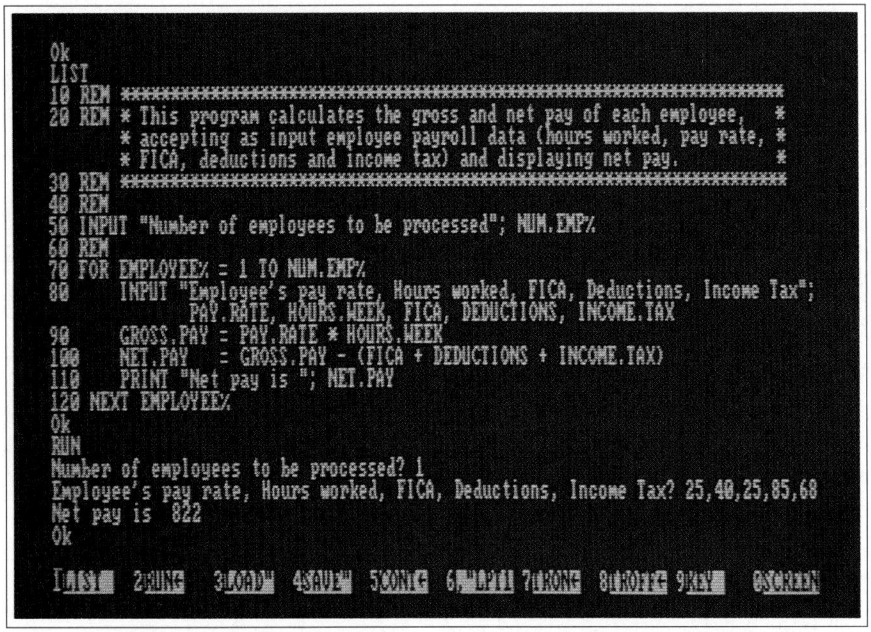

Figure 18-7. Execution of the Program in Figure 18-6.

Figure 18-8 (opposite). (a) The program can be viewed as a hierarchy of modules. Such a view organizes the programmer's thinking and also helps later in program maintenance. (b) Here the modules are more obvious in the structure chart.

a

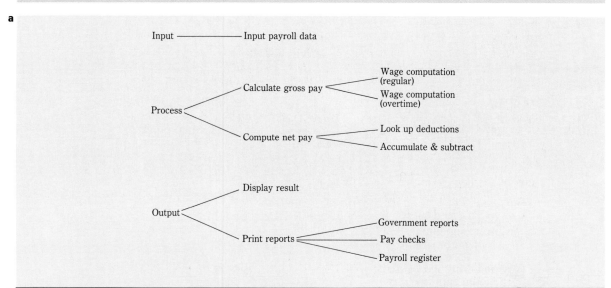

Input ——————— Input payroll data

Process
- Calculate gross pay
  - Wage computation (regular)
  - Wage computation (overtime)
- Compute net pay
  - Look up deductions
  - Accumulate & subtract

Output
- Display result
- Print reports
  - Government reports
  - Pay checks
  - Payroll register

b

Program structure as module

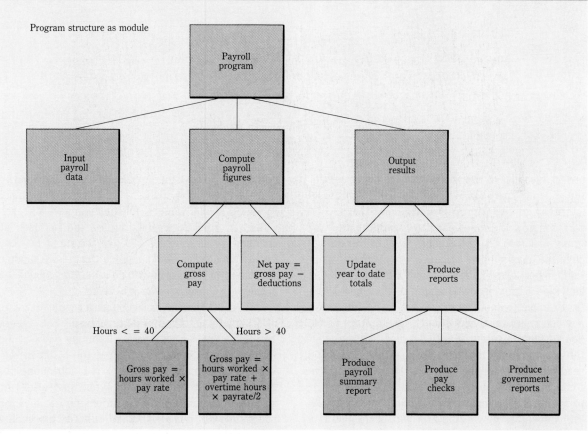

Payroll program

- Input payroll data
- Compute payroll figures
  - Compute gross pay
    - Hours < = 40: Gross pay = hours worked × pay rate
    - Hours > 40: Gross pay = hours worked × pay rate + overtime hours × payrate/2
  - Net pay = gross pay − deductions
- Output results
  - Update year to date totals
  - Produce reports
    - Produce payroll summary report
    - Produce pay checks
    - Produce government reports

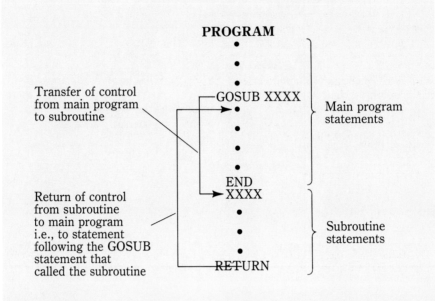

PROGRAM

Transfer of control
from main program
to subroutine

GOSUB XXXX

Main program
statements

END

Return of control
from subroutine
to main program
i.e., to statement
following the GOSUB
statement that
called the subroutine

XXXX

Subroutine
statements

RETURN

Figure 18-9. Diagram Depicting Transfer of Execution Control with Subroutines. Subroutines are very important; they are the way we do modular programming in BASIC.

program similar to the one constructed in this chapter. The first part of the figure shows the functional hierarchy of the payroll program, and the second part contains the modules that constitute the program structure. At the highest level of the hierarchy, the programmer thinks of three major functions: input, computation, and output. Each of these activities is broken down into further levels of detail; for example, computations involve calculating gross pay and subtracting deductions. The top part of the figure shows a series of very detailed functions that the program must perform. Some of these would be ready for programming, whereas others might have to be broken down into more detail. The bottom part of Figure 18-9 shows the program structure: how the conceptual view in the first part of the figure is broken down into program modules.

What constitutes a module? A module should be

dedicated to one task. A module should be small so that we can read it and keep its **functions** in mind. Modules should have a minimum impact on each other. In BASIC, all data values can be used or changed by all modules, so that we must be very careful about what data a module changes. A module might alter a piece of data used in another module by accident, causing a program error.

In BASIC, the way to accomplish modularity is to use something called a **subroutine.** See Figure 18-9 for a diagram of how a subroutine works. The main program transfers control to a subroutine. When execution is completed, the subroutine returns control to the main program just after the statement that called it. The statement that calls the subroutine is "*GOSUB* xxxx," where "xxxx" is a line number. The subroutine returns to the main program using a RETURN statement.

```
10 REM    * * * * * * * * * * * * * * * * * * * * * * * * * * *
20 REM    *    This program accepts employee payroll data as input,        *
          *    computes the gross pay and computes and displays net pay.    *
30 REM    * * * * * * * * * * * * * * * * * * * * * * * * * * *
40 REM
50 INPUT "Number of employees to be processed"; NUM.EMP%
60 FOR EMPLOYEE% = 1 TO NUM.EMP%
70         GOSUB 150        'subroutine to accept employee payroll data as input
80         GOSUB 220        'subroutine to calculate gross and net pay
90         GOSUB 300        'subroutine to print the required payroll results
100 NEXT EMPLOYEE%
110 REM
120 END        'stop program execution
130 REM
140 REM    * * * * * * * * * * * * * * * * * * * * * * * * * *
150 REM    *    This subroutine inputs the payroll data for each employee    *
160 REM    * * * * * * * * * * * * * * * * * * * * * * * * * *
170 REM
180 INPUT "Employee's pay rate, Hours worked, FICA, Deductions, Income Tax";
           PAY.RATE, HOURS.WEEK, FICA, DEDUCTIONS, INCOME.TAX
190 RETURN
200 REM
210 REM    * * * * * * * * * * * * * * * * * * * * * * * * * *
220 REM    *    This subroutine computes the gross and net pay of each       *
           *    employee, calculating overtime pay for hours in excess       *
           *    of 40 at time and a half.                                    *
230 REM    * * * * * * * * * * * * * * * * * * * * * * * * * *
240 REM
250 IF    HOURS.WEEK < = 40 THEN
           GROSS.PAY = PAY.RATE * HOURS.WEEK
      ELSE GROSS.PAY = PAY.RATE * HOURS.WEEK + (HOURS.WEEK − 40) * PAY.RATE * .5
260 NET.PAY = GROSS.PAY − (FICA + DEDUCTIONS + INCOME.TAX)
270 RETURN
280 REM
290 REM    * * * * * * * * * * * * * * * * * * * * * * * * * *
300 REM    *    This subroutine prints the payroll results for each employee    *
310 REM    * * * * * * * * * * * * * * * * * * * * * * * * * *
320 REM
330 PRINT "Net pay is "; NET.PAY
340 RETURN
```

Figure 18-10. The program is more logical and easier to read when structured as a series of modules.

Sometimes we will find it very useful, when writing an interactive program with a menu, to use a slightly different version of the GOSUB statement: "ON *expression* GOSUB *line* [,*line*] . . . " This statement chooses the subroutine beginning on a given line based on the value as calculated in the expression. If the value is 1, the subroutine line number listed first is chosen; if 2, the second line number listed is chosen; and so on.

Figure 18-10 shows our example program restructured. Now, the main program obtains the number of employees and then begins the iteration. The major parts of the program are now subroutines, one to input the data on each employee, one to compute the wages, and the last to print the results. With a simple program like this one, the advantages of subroutines may not be apparent. However, as we add features, it will be easier to read and modify the program.

Matrices

To this point, we have input the withholding tax information. However, there is no reason that a computer program cannot look at gross wages for the week and compute the amount of withholding. Withholding is figured from a table provided by the Internal Revenue Service (IRS). To figure the proper amount, we actually look up the data in the IRS table based on gross pay as the index.

To create a table in the program, we need to use a new data structure: an array, or **matrix.** In this case, we shall need two dimensions: one will be the gross pay amounts and the other the corresponding withholding amount. The table that we want to create in the program is shown in Figure 18-11. We must tell the BASIC translator the size of the table; for this purpose, we use the DIM statement for "dimension." (The DIM statement is an example of a declaration.) Given a greatly simplified table from the IRS, the dimensions are 15 × 2. (Actually, there are several tables for withholding, depending on the status of the taxpayer, for example, single or married. To simplify things we shall use an abbreviated form of the table for married persons who file jointly and who have no dependents.)

The strategy of the program is to find the row into whose range an employee's gross pay falls. As an example, if an employee has a weekly gross pay of $125, his or her gross-pay amount would be in Row 4, and we would search until we found the amount field in Column 2; the weekly withholding should be $9.80. This example shows how an entry in a matrix is referenced. The name of the matrix in the program is TAX.TABLE, and we have just seen that TAX.TABLE(4,2) = 9.80. The 4 is the row or

first dimension of the table's location, and the 2 is the column or the second dimension of the table's location. The intersection of the row (4) and the column (2) contains 9.8 as the entry in the table or matrix.

To add a withholding computation to our program, we need to put the matrix into the program and add a search routine. We shall set the value of the table in a subroutine that will be at the very end of the program, so it will be easy to find and change if the government decides to change withholding rates. A "GOSUB" to initialize this table will be inserted early in the program, before the program reads the number of employees.

The routine that actually calculates the withholding will use a loop to look through the table. Note also (in Figure 18-12) the error message in case, for some reason, the loop fails to find a number.

Data Statements

With a small number of employees, it is not difficult to sit at the personal computer and enter information about rates of pay and so on. However, that information is redundant unless we are giving raises each week.

One way to keep from entering repetitive information is to place it in DATA statements in the program (though a file would be the best way for the payroll application, as we shall see later). In BASIC, the READ statement is an input statement that takes data for its variables from the DATA statement. Reviewing the program in Figure 18-13 should help to make this clear. The READ statement will take the data beginning at the first DATA statement. The data are separated by commas, and BASIC reads one item from the DATA statements for each variable in the READ statement. It will be easier if we make a DATA statement contain only the data for one employee. Then, to add a new employee, we simply enter a new DATA statement for that employee. We change the DATA statement values to reflect changes in pay, number of dependents, or name. Because we shall want to make changes, the DATA statements are grouped in one spot near the end of the program.

Figure 18-11. A Simplified Tax Withholding Table.

Gross Weekly Pay		Withholding Tax
less than $	50	.50
	70	3.00
	100	6.80
	125	9.80
	150	13.10
	180	16.70
	200	20.10
	240	26.90
	270	32.00
	390	37.10
	320	40.50
	340	43.90
	360	44.00
	380	51.50
	400	55.90

Figure 18-12. Tables of data are found frequently in all types of programs. Here we implement a tax withholding table in our payroll program. (Figure continues on pages 436 and 437.)

```
 10 REM    * * * * * * * * * * * * * * * * * * * * * * * * * * * * *
 20 REM    *   This program uses subroutines to :                  *
           *      —initialize a table containing withholding tax information;  *
 30 REM    *      —input each employee's payroll data;             *
 40 REM    *      —determine each employee's gross pay (normal and overtime),  *
           *        withholding tax, and net pay;                   *
 50 REM    *      —display each employee's net pay.                 *
 60 REM    * * * * * * * * * * * * * * * * * * * * * * * * * * * * *
 70 REM
 80 GOSUB 600       'subroutine to initialize the withholding tax table
 90 INPUT "Number of employees to be processed"; NUM.EMP%
100 REM
110 FOR EMPLOYEE% = 1 TO NUM.EMP%
120        GOSUB 190      'subroutine to accept employee payroll data as input
130        GOSUB 270      'subroutine to calculate gross and net pay
140        GOSUB 370      'subroutine to print the required payroll results
150 NEXT EMPLOYEE%
160 END       'stop program execution
170 REM
180 REM    * * * * * * * * * * * * * * * * * * * * * * * * * * * * *
190 REM    *   This subroutine inputs the payroll data for each employee    *
200 REM    * * * * * * * * * * * * * * * * * * * * * * * * * * * * *
210 REM
220 PRINT
230 INPUT 'Employee's pay rate, Hours worked, FICA, Deductions";
          PAY.RATE, HOURS.WEEK, FICA, DEDUCTIONS
240 RETURN
250 REM
```

```
260 REM    * * * * * * * * * * * * * * * * * * * * * * * * * * * * * *
270 REM    *    This subroutine computes the gross and net pay of each      *
           *    employee, calculating overtime pay for hours in excess      *
           *    of 40 at time and a half.                                   *
280 REM    * * * * * * * * * * * * * * * * * * * * * * * * * * * * * *
290 REM
300 IF    HOURS.WEEK < = 40 THEN
              GROSS.PAY        = PAY.RATE * HOURS.WEEK
          ELSE GROSS.PAY = PAY.RATE * HOURS.WEEK + (HOURS.WEEK − 40) * PAY.RATE * .5
310 REM
320 GOSUB 440        'subroutine to lookup the withholding tax of an employee
                          given his/her weekly gross pay
330 NET.PAY = GROSS.PAY − (FICA + DEDUCTIONS + INCOME.TAX)
340 RETURN
350 REM
360        * * * * * * * * * * * * * * * * * * * * * * * * * * * * * *
370 REM    *    This subroutine prints the payroll results for each employee     *
380        * * * * * * * * * * * * * * * * * * * * * * * * * * * * * *
390 REM
400 PRINT "Net pay is "; NET.PAY
410 RETURN
420 REM
430 REM    * * * * * * * * * * * * * * * * * * * * * * * * * * * * * * *
440 REM    *    This subroutine uses the TAX.TABLE to lookup the withholding tax   *
           *    amount of an employee given his weekly gross pay.              *
450 REM    * * * * * * * * * * * * * * * * * * * * * * * * * * * * * * *
460 REM
470 IF NOT GROSS.PAY > TAX.TABLE (15,1) THEN 520
480 REM
490 PRINT "ERROR: Employee's weekly gross pay exceeds the range of tax table"
500 GOTO 150      'process next employee
510 REM
520 I = 1
530 WHILE NOT GROSS.PAY < TAX.TABLE (I,1)
540        I = I + 1
550 WEND
560 INCOME.TAX = TAX.TABLE (I,2)
570 RETURN
580 REM
590 REM    * * * * * * * * * * * * * * * * * * * * * * * * * * * * * * * *
600 REM    *    This subroutine initializes a two dimensional matrix, TAX.TABLE,   *
           *    that contains the current withholding tax data supplied by the IRS.   *
610 REM    * * * * * * * * * * * * * * * * * * * * * * * * * * * * * * * *
620 REM
630 DIM TAX.TABLE (15,2)        'specifying size of the withholding tax table
640 REM
650 REM    * * * * * * * * * * * * * * * * * * * * * * * * * * * * * * * *
660 REM    *    The following statements assign the relevant gross pay categories   *
           *    to the first column of the table, and the respective tax amounts    *
           *    to the second column.                                          *
670 REM    * * * * * * * * * * * * * * * * * * * * * * * * * * * * * * * *
680 REM
690 TAX.TABLE (1,1) = 50
700 TAX.TABLE (1,2) = .5
710 TAX.TABLE (2,1) = 70
```

Figure 18-12 (continued).

```
720 TAX.TABLE  (2,2)  =  3
730 TAX.TABLE  (3,1)  =  100
740 TAX.TABLE  (3,2)  =  6.8
750 TAX.TABLE  (4,1)  =  125
760 TAX.TABLE  (4,2)  =  9.8
770 TAX.TABLE  (5,1)  =  150
780 TAX.TABLE  (5,2)  =  13.1
790 TAX.TABLE  (6,1)  =  180
800 TAX.TABLE  (6,2)  =  16.7
810 TAX.TABLE  (7,1)  =  200
820 TAX.TABLE  (7,2)  =  20.1
830 TAX.TABLE  (8,1)  =  240
840 TAX.TABLE  (8,2)  =  26.9
850 TAX.TABLE  (9,1)  =  270
860 TAX.TABLE  (9,2)  =  32
870 TAX.TABLE  (10,1)  =  300
880 TAX.TABLE  (10,2)  =  37.1
890 TAX.TABLE  (11,1)  =  320
900 TAX.TABLE  (11,2)  =  40.5
910 TAX.TABLE  (12,1)  =  340
920 TAX.TABLE  (12,2)  =  43.9
930 TAX.TABLE  (13,1)  =  360
940 TAX.TABLE  (13,2)  =  44
950 TAX.TABLE  (14,1)  =  380
960 TAX.TABLE  (14,2)  =  51.5
970 TAX.TABLE  (15,1)  =  400
980 TAX.TABLE  (15,2)  =  55.9
990 RETURN
```

Figure 18-12 (continued).

Figure 18-13. Rather than enter data all of the time, one can use DATA and READ statements. (Figure continues on pages 438 and 439.)

```
10 REM    * * * * * * * * * * * * * * * * * * * * * * * * * * * * * * * *
20 REM    *   This program uses subroutines to :                         *
          *       —initialize a table containing withholding tax information;   *
30 REM    *       —input each employee's payroll data;                   *
40 REM    *       —determine each employee's gross pay (normal and overtime),  *
          *         withholding tax, and net pay;                        *
50 REM    *       —display each employee's net pay.                      *
60 REM    * * * * * * * * * * * * * * * * * * * * * * * * * * * * * * * *
70 REM
80 GOSUB 740      'subroutine to initialize the withholding tax table
90 INPUT "Number of employees to be processed "; NUM.EMP%
100 REM
110 FOR EMPLOYEE% = 1 TO NUM.EMP%
120        GOSUB  190    'subroutine to read employee payroll
130        GOSUB  410    'subroutine to calculate gross and net pay
140        GOSUB  510    'subroutine to print the required payroll results
150 NEXT EMPLOYEE%
160 END       'stop program execution
```

```
170 REM
180 REM   * * * * * * * * * * * * * * * * * * * * * * * * * *
190 REM   *    This subroutine reads the payroll data for each employee   *
          *    from DATA statements, found at the end of the subroutine.   *
200 REM   * * * * * * * * * * * * * * * * * * * * * * * * * *
210 REM
220 READ PAY.RATE, HOURS.WEEK, FICA, DEDUCTIONS
230 REM
240 REM   * * * * * * * * * * * * * * * * * * * * * * * * * *
250 REM   *    The following data statements contain the payroll data for   *
          *    the organization's employees                                 *
260 REM   * * * * * * * * * * * * * * * * * * * * * * * * * *
270 REM
280 DATA 5, 50, 50, 50
290 DATA 6, 30, 25, 60
300 DATA 4, 45, 55, 80
310 DATA 5, 40, 60, 60
320 DATA 6, 45, 50, 45
330 DATA 7, 50, 30, 45
340 DATA 6, 35, 60, 40
350 DATA 7, 50, 60, 35
360 DATA 6, 45, 50, 35
370 DATA 7, 30, 50, 40
380 RETURN
390 REM
400 REM   * * * * * * * * * * * * * * * * * * * * * * * * *
410 REM   *    This subroutine computes the gross and net pay of each   *
          *    employee, calculating overtime pay for hours in excess    *
          *    of 40 at time and a half.                                 *
420 REM   * * * * * * * * * * * * * * * * * * * * * * * * *
430 REM
440 IF   HOURS.WEEK < = 40 THEN
             GROSS.PAY      = PAY.RATE * HOURS.WEEK
         ELSE GROSS.PAY = PAY.RATE * HOURS.WEEK + (HOURS.WEEK - 40) * PAY.RATE * .5
450 REM
460 GOSUB 580       'subroutine to look up the withholding tax of an
                      employee given his/her weekly gross pay
470 NET.PAY = GROSS.PAY - (FICA + DEDUCTIONS + INCOME.TAX)
480 RETURN
490 REM
500 REM   * * * * * * * * * * * * * * * * * * * * * * * * * *
510 REM   *    This subroutine prints the payroll results for each employee   *
520 REM   * * * * * * * * * * * * * * * * * * * * * * * * * *
530 REM
540 PRINT "Net pay is "; NET.PAY
550 RETURN
560 REM
570 REM   * * * * * * * * * * * * * * * * * * * * * * * * * * *
580 REM   *    This subroutine uses the TAX.TABLE to look up the withholding tax   *
          *    amount of an employee given his weekly gross pay.                   *
590 REM   * * * * * * * * * * * * * * * * * * * * * * * * * * *
600 REM
610 IF NOT GROSS.PAY > TAX.TABLE (15,1) THEN 660
620 REM
```

Figure 18-13 (continued).

```
630 PRINT "ERROR: Employee's weekly gross pay exceeds the range of tax table"
640 GOTO 150      'process next employee
650 REM
660 I = 1
670 WHILE NOT GROSS.PAY < TAX.TABLE (I.1)
680         I = I + 1
690 WEND
700 INCOME.TAX = TAX.TABLE (I,2)
710 RETURN
720 REM
730 REM    * * * * * * * * * * * * * * * * * * * * * * * * * * * * *
740 REM    *   This subroutine initializes a two dimensional matrix, TAX.TABLE,   *
            *   that contains the current withholding tax data supplied by IRS.    *
750 REM    * * * * * * * * * * * * * * * * * * * * * * * * * * * * *
760 REM
770 DIM TAX.TABLE (15,2)      'specifying size of the withholding tax table
780 REM
790 REM    * * * * * * * * * * * * * * * * * * * * * * * * * * * * *
800 REM    *   The following statements assign the relevant gross pay categories   *
            *   the first column of the table, and the respective tax amounts to    *
            *   the second column.                                                  *
810 REM    * * * * * * * * * * * * * * * * * * * * * * * * * * * * *
820 REM
830 TAX.TABLE (1,1) = 50
840 TAX.TABLE (1,2) = .5
850 TAX.TABLE (2,1) = 70
860 TAX.TABLE (2,2) = 3
870 TAX.TABLE (3,1) = 100
880 TAX.TABLE (3,2) = 6.8
890 TAX.TABLE (4,1) = 125
900 TAX.TABLE (4,2) = 9.8
910 TAX.TABLE (5,1) = 150
920 TAX.TABLE (5,2) = 13.1
930 TAX.TABLE (6,1) = 180
940 TAX.TABLE (6,2) = 16.7
950 TAX.TABLE (7,1) = 200
960 TAX.TABLE (7,2) = 20.1
970 TAX.TABLE (8,1) = 240
980 TAX.TABLE (8,2) = 26.9
990 TAX.TABLE (9,1) = 270
1000 TAX.TABLE (9,2) = 32
1010 TAX.TABLE (10,1) = 300
1020 TAX.TABLE (10,2) = 37.1
1030 TAX.TABLE (11,1) = 320
1040 TAX.TABLE (11,2) = 40.5
1050 TAX.TABLE (12,1) = 340
1060 TAX.TABLE (12,2) = 43.9
1070 TAX.TABLE (13,1) = 360
1080 TAX.TABLE (13,2) = 44
1090 TAX.TABLE (14,1) = 380
1100 TAX.TABLE (14,2) = 51.5
1110 TAX.TABLE (15,1) = 400
1120 TAX.TABLE (15,2) = 55.9
1130 RETURN
```

Figure 18-13 (continued).

Employee.Number
Employee.Name
Pay.Rate
Hours.Week
Dependents
FICA
Deductions
Yr.To.Date.Gross
Yr.To.Date.Tax
Yr.To.Date.FICA
Yr.To.Date.Ded
Yr.To.Date.Net

Figure 18-14. Record Structure for a Sequential Payroll File.

Figure 18-15 (opposite). The program is quite a bit longer than when we started! Now the program works the way an application should: it uses files to store and update historical data. What is missing? (Hint: think about errors.) (Figure continues on pages 442–444.)

Files

The use of DATA statements to contain the values for each employee is probably all right for a small payroll run by the manager of a Computerware store. However, we would not really develop a computer application that depends on someone's changing the program, possibly every week, to reflect changes in data. Instead, we try to have programs in which it is easy to change the data without going to the trouble of modifying a program, a process that can lead to errors.

As discussed in Chapter 9 on files, it would be more professional to put employee data on a file and process it each week. The file is also needed if we are to provide year-to-date figures for later reporting to the IRS and the employee.

Changing our sample program to use files is a little bit more complicated. Unfortunately, the different versions of BASIC all have different file-accessing conventions. All that we need here is a simple *sequential file.* BASIC requires us to "OPEN" the files before using them. For a sequential file update, remember that we use two files: the old or existing file and a new file that is created during the update.

We shall open the old file for reading and create a new file that will be opened for writing. The program will ask the user to input the file names first and then

will continue execution from there. The record structure for the file is shown in Figure 18-14.

With DATA statements, it was relatively easy to add, delete, or modify the data for an employee. Storing values like the pay rate on a file complicates this process a little bit. We want to run the program interactively rather than in batch mode because this is a small application for a personal computer. To save the complexity of direct-access files in BASIC, we shall create a bit of a hybrid system, one that is very suitable for a Computerware store.

The strategy is for the program to read an employee's data from the file and to display it on the screen for changes. Note that the program in Figure 18-15 has an INPUT #1 statement that is very similar to past input statements, except that it now refers to a file number. Then, we are given the option of deleting an employee's record. (A more complex program would be required to allow modifications in each record.) The program calls routines to compute pay and FICA and to accumulate year-to-date totals. Then, the program calls a routine to write the data on the new payroll file.

We also want to be able to add employees to the file and to pay them. At the **end of the file** (which the program determines through the WHILE NOT EOF (1) statement, Line 120), the main program sets a **switch** (New.emp.switch) on, and from that

```
10 REM    * * * * * * * * * * * * * * * * * * * * * * * * * * * * * *
20 REM    *    This program uses subroutines to :                   *
          *       —initialize a table containing withholding tax information;   *
30 REM    *       —read each employee's payroll data from the Payroll File;     *
35 REM    *       —display each employee's payroll data;            *
40 REM    *       —allow the deletion of employee records, if desired;          *
50 REM    *       —determine each employee's gross pay (normal and overtime),   *
          *          withholding tax, and net pay;                  *
60 REM    *       —update the year to date totals with the new payroll values   *
          *          for each employee;                             *
70 REM    *       —write each employee's updated payroll data to the new Payroll *
          *          File, being created this run;                  *
80 REM    *       —print a register with year to date totals for each employee. *
90 REM    * * * * * * * * * * * * * * * * * * * * * * * * * * * * * *
100 REM
110 GOSUB 720                   'subroutine to initialize the withholding tax table
120 GOSUB 340                   'subroutine to set up the screen and ready the files
130 WHILE NOT EOF (1)
140        INPUT #1, EMPNUM, EMPNAME$, PAY.RATE, HOURS.WEEK, FICA, DEDUCTIONS,
                     YR.DATE.GROSS, YR.DATE.TAX, YR.DATE.NET
150        GOSUB 1420           'subroutine to display employee record values
160        GOSUB 1590           'subroutine to delete employee record, if desired
170        IF DELETE.IND$ = "Y" THEN 200    'process next employee
180        GOSUB 450            'subroutine to calculate gross and net pay, and
                                accumulate year to date totals
190        WRITE #2, EMPNUM, EMPNAME$, PAY.RATE, HOURS.WEEK, FICA, DEDUCTIONS,
                     YR.DATE.GROSS, YR.DATE.TAX, YR.DATE.NET
200 WEND
210 REM
220 NEW.EMP.SWITCH = 0      'switch initially set to off
230 WHILE NEW.EMP.SWITCH = 0
240        GOSUB 1140           'subroutine to accept new employee data
250        GOSUB 450            'subroutine to calculate gross and net pay, and
                                accumulate year to date totals
260        WRITE #2 EMPNUM, EMPNAME$, PAY.RATE, HOURS.WEEK, FICA, DEDUCTIONS,
                     YR.DATE.GROSS, YR.DATE.TAX, YR.DATE.NET
270 WEND
280 CLOSE                       'close the old and new Payroll Files
290 CLS : KEY OFF
300 GOSUB 1670                  'subroutine to print year to date payroll register
310 END                         'stop processing
320 REM
330 REM    * * * * * * * * * * * * * * * * * * * * * * * * * *
340 REM    *  This subroutine initializes switches and readies the  *
           *  files used by the program for processing.        *
350 REM    * * * * * * * * * * * * * * * * * * * * * * * * * *
360 REM
370 INPUT "Old Employee File Name"; OLD.EMP$
380 INPUT "New Employee File Name"; NEW.EMP$
390 OPEN OLD.EMP$ FOR INPUT AS #1
400 OPEN NEW.EMP$ FOR OUTPUT AS #2
410 CLS : KEY OFF
420 RETURN
430 REM
440 REM    * * * * * * * * * * * * * * * * * * * * * * * * * * * *
450 REM    *    This subroutine computes the gross and net pay of each   *
           *    employee, calculating overtime pay for hours in excess   *
           *    of 40, at time and a half.                     *
460 REM    * * * * * * * * * * * * * * * * * * * * * * * * * * * *
```

```
470 REM
480 IF   HOURS.WEEK < = 40 THEN
          NEW.GROSS    = PAY.RATE * HOURS.WEEK
      ELSE NEW.GROSS = PAY.RATE * HOURS.WEEK + (HOURS.WEEK − 40) * PAY.RATE * .5
490 GOSUB 570      'subroutine to lookup the withholding tax of an employee
                    given his/her weekly gross pay
500 NET.PAY = NEW.GROSS − (FICA + DEDUCTIONS + INCOME.TAX)
510 YR.DATE.GROSS = YR.DATE.GROSS + NEW.GROSS
520 YR.DATE.TAX   = YR.DATE.TAX + INCOME.TAX
530 YR.DATE.NET   = YR.DATE.NET + NET.PAY
540 RETURN
550 REM
560 REM  * * * * * * * * * * * * * * * * * * * * * * * * * * * * * * *
570 REM  *   This subroutine uses the TAX.TABLE to look up the withholding tax  *
         *   amount of an employee given his weekly gross pay.                  *
580 REM  * * * * * * * * * * * * * * * * * * * * * * * * * * * * * * *
590 REM
600 IF NOT NEW.GROSS > TAX.TABLE (15,1) THEN 640
610 LPRINT "ERROR : "; EMPNUM; SPC(5); EMPNAME$;
620 LPRINT " Above employee has a gross pay that exceeds the tax-table. Maximum
     gross pay is assumed."
630 NEW.GROSS = (TAX.TABLE (15,1) − 1)    'maximum gross pay assigned
640 I = 1
650 WHILE NOT NEW.GROSS < TAX.TABLE (I,1)
          I = I + 1
670 WEND
680 INCOME.TAX = TAX.TABLE (I,2)
690 RETURN
700 REM
         * * * * * * * * * * * * * * * * * * * * * * * * * * * * * * *
710 REM  *   This subroutine initializes a two dimensional matrix, TAX.TABLE,  *
720 REM  *   that contains the current withholding tax data supplied by IRS.   *
730 REM  * * * * * * * * * * * * * * * * * * * * * * * *.* * * * * * * * *
740 REM
750 DIM TAX.TABLE (15,2)      'specifying size of the withholding tax table
760 REM
770 REM  * * * * * * * * * * * * * * * * * * * * * * * * * * * * * * *
780 REM  *   The following statements assign the relevant gross pay categories  *
         *   to the first column of the table, and the respective tax amounts   *
         *   to the second column.                                              *
790 REM  * * * * * * * * * * * * * * * * * * * * * * * * * * * * * * *
800 REM
810 TAX.TABLE (1,1) = 50
820 TAX.TABLE (1,2) = .5
830 TAX.TABLE (2,1) = 70
840 TAX.TABLE (2,2) = 3
850 TAX.TABLE (3,1) = 100
860 TAX.TABLE (3,2) = 6.8
870 TAX.TABLE (4,1) = 125
880 TAX.TABLE (4,2) = 9.8
890 TAX.TABLE (5,1) = 150
900 TAX.TABLE (5,2) = 13.1
910 TAX.TABLE (6,1) = 180
920 TAX.TABLE (6,2) = 16.7
930 TAX.TABLE (7,1) = 200
940 TAX.TABLE (7,2) = 20.1
```

Figure 18-15 (continued).

```
 950 TAX.TABLE (8,1) = 240
 960 TAX.TABLE (8,2) = 26.9
 970 TAX.TABLE (9,1) = 270
 980 TAX.TABLE (9,2) = 32
 990 TAX.TABLE (10,1) = 300
1000 TAX.TABLE (10,2) = 37.1
1010 TAX.TABLE (11,1) = 320
1020 TAX.TABLE (11,2) = 40.5
1030 TAX.TABLE (12,1) = 340
1040 TAX.TABLE (12,2) = 43.9
1050 TAX.TABLE (13,1) = 360
1060 TAX.TABLE (13,2) = 44
1070 TAX.TABLE (14,1) = 380
1080 TAX.TABLE (14,2) = 51.5
1090 TAX.TABLE (15,1) = 400
1100 TAX.TABLE (15,2) = 55.9
1110 RETURN
1120 REM
1130 REM  * * * * * * * * * * * * * * * * * * * * * * * * * *
1140 REM  *   This subroutine accepts as input from the screen,   *
          *   payroll data for new employees.                     *
1150 REM  * * * * * * * * * * * * * * * * * * * * * * * * * *
1160 REM
1170 CLS ; KEY OFF      'clears the screen
1180 LOCATE 2,10 : PRINT "MULTICORP PAYROLL SYSTEM : New Employees"
1190 LOCATE 20,5 : PRINT "To end new employee record input, enter a blank
         employee number"
1200 REM
1210 LOCATE 5,5      'positions the cursor on the screen in specified location
1220 INPUT "Employee# ", EMPNUM
1230 IF NOT EMPNUM = 0 THEN 1260
1240 NEW.EMP.SWITCH = -1
1250 GOTO 230
1260 LOCATE 5,40
1270 INPUT "Name ", EMPNAME$
1280 LOCATE 7,5
1290 INPUT "Pay Rate ", PAY.RATE
1300 LOCATE 7,40
1310 INPUT "Hours Worked ", HOURS.WEEK
1320 LOCATE 9,5
1330 INPUT "FICA ", FICA
1340 LOCATE 9,40
1350 INPUT "Deductions ", DEDUCTIONS
1360 YR.DATE.GROSS = 0
1370 YR.DATE.TAX   = 0
1380 YR.DATE.NET   = 0
1390 RETURN
1400 REM
1410 REM  * * * * * * * * * * * * * * * * * * * * * * * * * * *
1420 REM  *   This subroutine displays the payroll data of existing   *
          *   employees, as read from the Payroll File.               *
1430 REM  * * * * * * * * * * * * * * * * * * * * * * * * * * *
1440 REM
1450 CLS : KEY OFF
1460 LOCATE 2,20  : PRINT "MULTICORP PAYROLL SYSTEM"
1470 LOCATE 5,5   : PRINT "Employee# "; EMPNUM
```

Figure 18-15 (continued).

```
1480 LOCATE  5,40  : PRINT "Name "; EMPNAME$
1490 LOCATE  7,5   : PRINT "Pay Rate "; PAY.RATE
1500 LOCATE  7,40  : PRINT "Hours Worked "; HOURS.WEEK
1510 LOCATE  9,5   : PRINT "FICA "; FICA
1520 LOCATE  9,40  : PRINT "Deductions "; DEDUCTIONS
1530 LOCATE 12,5   : PRINT "Year to Date Gross Pay "; YR.DATE.GROSS
1540 LOCATE 12,40  : PRINT "Year to Date Tax "; YR.DATE.TAX
1550 LOCATE 14,5   : PRINT "Year to Date Net Pay "; YR.DATE.NET
1560 RETURN
1570 REM
1580 REM    * * * * * * * * * * * * * * * * * * * * * * * * * * * *
1590 REM    *   This subroutine allows for the deletion of an employee record.  *
1600 REM    * * * * * * * * * * * * * * * * * * * * * * * * * * * *
1610 REM
1620 LOCATE 18,5
1630 INPUT "Delete the displayed employee record, Y/N "; DELETE.IND$
1640 RETURN
1650 REM
1660 REM    * * * * * * * * * * * * * * * * * * * * * * * * * * * *
1670 REM    *   This subroutine prints a Payroll Register, showing year to date    *
            *   totals for each employee, as read from the updated Payroll File.   *
1680 REM    * * * * * * * * * * * * * * * * * * * * * * * * * * * *
1690 REM
1700 OPEN NEW.EMP$ FOR INPUT AS #1
1710 REM
1720 REM    * * * * * * * * * * * * * * * * * * * * * * * * * * * *
1730 REM    *   The following statement defines the formatting specifications   *
            *   for the output of each detail line.                             *
1740 REM    * * * * * * * * * * * * * * * * * * * * * * * * * * * *
1750 REM
1760 FORMATS$ = "  ####     " + "\                   \" + " #####.## " +
                "  ####.##" + "  #####.## "
1770 REM
1780 FOR I + 1 TO 10
1790      LPRINT       'prints 10 blank lines on the printed page
1800 NEXT I
1810 REM
1820 LPRINT "MULTICORP PAYROLL REGISTER for the Week Ending "; DATE$
1830 LPRINT
1840 LPRINT "NUMBER "; "NAME"; SPC(23); " GROSS PAY "; "  TAX  "; "  NET PAY "
1850 LPRINT
1860 WHILE NOT EOF (1)
1870      INPUT #1, EMPNUM, EMPNAME$, PAY.RATE, HOURS.WEEK, FICA, DEDUCTIONS,
               YR.DATE.GROSS, YR.DATE.TAX, YR.DATE.NET
1880      LPRINT USING FORMAT$; EMPNUM, EMPNAME$, YR.DATE.GROSS,
               YR.DATE.TAX, YR.DATE.NET
1890 WEND
1900 LPRINT
1910 LPRINT "                       END OF PAYROLL REPORT
1920 RETURN
```

Figure 18-15 (continued).

```
                    MULTICORP PAYROLL SYSTEM

        Employee# 1001                  Name ANDREWS

        Pay Rate 5                      Hours Worked 45

        FICA 50                         Deductions 32


        Year to Date Gross Pay 10000    Year to Date Tax 2090

        Year to Date Net Pay 6700



        Delete the displayed employee record, Y/N ? _
```

Figure 18-16. The Results in the Middle of Running the Program in Figure 18-15.

point on, the program does not read from the old file but instead goes to the subroutine that reads new employees from the terminal. It also must compute their pay for the week, if any.

When there are no new employees left, the program goes to a reporting routine, which prints checks, a payroll register, and year-to-date information for the employee. (See the execution of this program in Figure 18-16.)

OTHER FEATURES

We have seen a lot of BASIC in the example developed throughout the chapter; however, there are many features beyond what has been shown. BASIC has been expanded considerably beyond its early versions; there are a number of quite elaborate business systems programmed in BASIC for minicomputers and micros. In fact, the package program for the garment industry discussed in Chapter 6 is an example of a system programmed in BASIC.

Depending on the computer and the BASIC version in use, there will be a number of **commands,** such as those required to load the BASIC compiler, to load a program, to save a program, and to run it. There may also be trace commands that help us to see the program while it is executing. Because of the direct execution function in the BASIC we are using, anytime the program stops for some reason, we can look at the value of variables by typing PRINT and the list of variables that we want to see. (This approach works as long as no lines in the program are changed after stopping, as such changes cause the BASIC translator to initialize the value of variables in preparation for another execution of the program.)

BASIC also has a large number of functions, and there are statements that allow a user to define his or her own function. There are functions to compute all of the trigonometric values, logarithms, and random numbers; to raise a variable to a power; and to process integers, to name a few.

There are also a variety of statements and functions that help in processing strings. Particularly for interactive use from a keyboard, strings of characters are very important for carrying on a dialogue with the user.

Advanced versions of BASIC for a personal computer with **graphics** output have a variety of commands for generating color graphics. There is a statement that will produce a circle or an oval and a general statement that causes the program to construct a line on the screen. There is also a "COLOR" command that sets foreground and background colors for the display monitor.

To create very large systems, there is a "CHAIN" command that lets one program call another one from a file and start the called program in execution. It is also possible to pass variables to the called program through a common data-storage area.

In summary, BASIC provides a very powerful high-level language for users of computers. It is more detailed and requires more programming knowledge to use than a very-high-level package like a spreadsheet program. However, with a little patience and with the use of good programming style, one can create quite elaborate systems with BASIC.

Review of Chapter 18

REVIEW

This chapter has presented an introduction to BASIC, one of the most popular user languages for minicomputers and microcomputers. It is important to study a language like BASIC to prepare for writing programs in case a package is not available. A language like BASIC is also an excellent background for using fourth-generation languages and query languages on minis and mainframes.

We have stressed the importance of planning a program, of thinking about it first at a conceptual level before getting down to the details of the descriptive level, which is the code presented to the computer.

BASIC has a number of statement types, including declarations, control statements, assignment, and input/output statements.

The original version of BASIC was fairly simple. More elaborate versions exist today that have been used to develop quite comprehensive business applications on microcomputers and minis. At this stage in the development of computers, it is well worth one's time to become familiar with BASIC.

KEY WORDS

Algorithm	Loop
Array	Matrix
Assignment statement	Module
Clause	Open
Commands	Operator
Conditional	Prompt line
Data	Read
Dimension	REM or remark
Double-precision	Scalar
End of file	Sequential file
Expression	Single-precision
Function	String
GOSUB	Structure
Graphics	Subroutine
IF-THEN-ELSE	Switch
Indentation	Top-down
Iteration	Variable
Logical operator	

BUSINESS PROBLEMS

18.1. BASIC is a language that allows the user to develop quite elegant programs that do a number of different tasks. There are very few limits on what can be accomplished using a language like BASIC. Minicomputer business applications have been developed exclusively in BASIC, and numerous applications that run on microcomputers have been programmed in this language.

One of the programs that has not used BASIC is Lotus 1-2-3, a very popular electronic spreadsheet program (see Chapter 15). Remember that the spreadsheet system is a program; your data and formulas are put into the program, which then processes them.

Lotus is written in assembly language, a formidable task. BASIC would have been far easier, because it is a development tool rather than assembler. In this text, we have downplayed the importance of assembly language because very few readers will ever have occasion to use it.

Why do you think Lotus found it desirable to program its spreadsheet package in assembler? Why might this strategy be justified for the kind of program and market that Lotus address?

18.2. In at least one major company, the senior financial executive does not want managers writing programs. There may be some debate about whether putting data into a spreadsheet system is programming, but there can be little argument that writing something in BASIC is programming.

The executive is probably right that highly paid managers who are not computer professionals should not spend a lot of time writing complex applications in BASIC. When such programs are needed, the firm should provide professional programmers to write the programs.

Unfortunately, this strategy is at odds with the purpose of having a personal computer. We want to be independent of professional programmers, so that we do not have to wait for our applications.

Can you come up with some guidelines for when the BASIC language should be considered? How can the organization be responsive in providing programming support? What must this executive do to carry out his policy successfully?

REVIEW QUESTIONS

1. What does an assignment statement do?
2. What is the purpose of a conditional statement?
3. How do conditionals give a computer so much flexibility?
4. What is a matrix or array?
5. Why does BASIC need a "DIM" statement for arrays?
6. What is a loop or iteration? How is it used?
7. Why indent loops and conditionals?
8. What is a program module?
9. How does one create modules in BASIC?
10. What does the "GOSUB" statement do?
11. Why do we recommend top-down design and programming?
12. What are the major classes of variables in BASIC?

THOUGHT QUESTIONS

13. What is the difference between BASIC and a spreadsheet program?
14. How would you go about sorting a list of names in BASIC?
15. In the sample program, the tax withholding tables were placed in the program. What is the disadvantage of this approach? What are the alternatives?

16. Design the structure of a program that would compute the grades for a college course.

17. Why are we interested in package programs in addition or as an alternative to programming in BASIC?

18. What applications can you think of for the graphics commands in BASIC?

19. Write a program in BASIC to balance your checkbook. Was it worth it?

20. Would you ever write a word-processing program in BASIC? Why or why not?

21. An interpreter looks at each statement in a program and executes it, taking several instructions to do so. A compiler actually produces machine language code that runs the program. BASIC comes with both, though most of us use just the interpreter. What is the advantage of the compiler?

22. What would the disadvantage of the compiler be (see Question 21)?

23. How would the payroll program be redesigned for direct-access files?

24. What are the characteristics of a good program module?

25. How could one write very large systems? (Hint: Think about the "CHAIN" command.)

26. How would a language like BASIC be used in prototyping during systems analysis and design?

27. Look at a programming book for a language like COBOL. What is the difference between this language and BASIC? How are they similar?

28. Why are there so many versions of BASIC?

29. If you were asked to use a personal computer to prepare a budgeting system, would you do it in BASIC? Why or why not?

30. What if you were asked to develop an inventory control application? Would BASIC be appropriate?

RECOMMENDED READINGS

Basic Manual. Boca Raton: IBM, 1981. Advanced BASIC for the IBM personal computer.

Sutherland, Robert F. *This Is BASIC*. New York: Macmillan Publishing Company, 1984. An introduction to computer programming.

Part V

Now that we have studied the technology and its applications, we next look at the impact of the computer revolution.

In Chapter 19, we examine the effect of computers on organizations. The chapter begins with positive impacts; in particular, we discuss some exciting applications that have made information processing a part of a firm's corporate strategy. The firms in the examples have used the technology to gain and protect their market share and, in at least one instance, to create a whole new product and market.

Other positive impacts from computers include improved quality of work and the ability to do jobs that would have been impossible before the technology. How could the Social Security Administration process 40 million payments a month totaling billions of dollars without computers?

Of course, computers can have a negative impact, too. We need to consider how the users view a new application, what the costs of using the system are, and what the benefits are to the user. Computers may have an impact on corporate structure and on how individuals do their jobs. It is up to management to plan carefully for the introduction of this powerful technology.

The theme of management action is treated in detail in Chapter 20, where we concentrate on the organizational environment of information systems. Managers have a key role, if not the most important role, in the development of systems and in the entire systems effort. Managers must be aware of the issues; they have to control information processing in the firm.

Chapter 20 presents a framework, a structure for management to use in controlling the technology. Managers must be leaders in showing others what they should do to contribute to successful systems. Managers also have to provide resources so that systems can be developed. Finally, managers have the critical job of evaluating the success of information-processing systems and taking action if there are problems.

Chapter 21 elevates our focus from the organization to society as a whole. We see, for example, how computers are being used to help the handicapped. It is possible that someday individuals who are paralyzed will walk again with the help of microcomputers and a variety of other equipment.

In addition to the positive contribution of computers to society, they raise a number of questions: Is it wise to rely on computer systems for nuclear defense? Is it a good idea to force the Soviet Union to rely on its inferior computer technology for its defense? What are the implications of the use of computers as a part of both sides' nuclear policies?

Computers also have implications for individual privacy. What constitutes legitimate use of personal information, and what is really misuse? We shall discuss the issues and offer a few remedies. One answer lies

COMPUTER BUSINESS AND SOCIETY

with careful and thoughtful systems design.

Chapter 22 looks at what may be coming in the future. It is helpful to understand trends in the technology in order to plan. If the future really holds a trend toward computer networking, we will save time and trouble later if we plan equipment acquisitions with networking in mind.

We have not assumed any particular career orientation on the part of the reader. Chapter 23 explains the different careers in the computer field. What are the options if one wants to work directly in the information-processing field? What kind of educational background is expected for different positions? What is the career path in the profession, that is, what job advancement is possible as one's career progresses?

There are many opportunities in information processing. Whether one enters the field specifically or works in some other area like finance, marketing, or accounting, all of us will increasingly make use of computers and information systems. Computer technology and information systems are our greatest hope for improving the productivity of the vast majority of the labor force that works with information. Individuals who are comfortable with this technology and who integrate it with the way they work will be at a decided advantage in the coming years.

Chapter 19

In Parts II and III of this text, we learned about how computers work and how to design systems. Part IV provided some insights into our personal use of computers. In this important chapter, we see how computers have affected modern organizations. The chapter concentrates on business firms, but government agencies and even volunteer organizations have also used the computer to create changes in the way they operate.

Information systems are used to consciously change operations, the management of a firm, and even corporate strategy. These systems also have an impact beyond their intended use. Systems have affected the structure of the organization and the individuals who work with computers. In some cases, the impact has been positive; in others, the changes seem negative.

Part of the responsibility of a manager and a systems designer is to plan for these changes and to anticipate the impact of computer systems. This chapter reviews some of the creative ways in which computers have contributed to organizations, and it raises issues that should be considered in the design of new systems and the management of the entire systems effort.

After reading this chapter, you should be able to:

- Describe how several firms have used systems to gain a competitive advantage.
- Explain how computers can help firms by saving money.
- Describe how some systems contribute to better quality work.
- Cite an example in which computer processing is the only way to do a job.
- Discuss the impact of computers on the structure of organizations.
- Describe office automation and its potential impacts.
- Explain some of the impact of computers on individuals and suggest how to motivate users to work with systems.
- Explain why it is important to involve users in the process of systems design and management.

THE IMPACT OF COMPUTERS ON ORGANIZATIONS

INTRODUCTION

How do computer-based information systems change the organization? How do conditions change for the users? What is the impact of having computers? Information systems have a great deal of potential, much of which has not yet been realized. In the future, business success will increasingly depend on our skills in building systems and in implementing change in the organization to take advantage of them.

THE ORGANIZATION

Organizations are very complex entities. What happens when designers attempt to build new systems in organizations? Organizations consist of individuals, all of whom have different interests, ways of behaving, and goals. It is important, but difficult, to predict the impact of computers on organizations and the individuals who work in them.

Strategy

A Brokerage Firm. A number of organizations have used computers to gain a competitive edge; they have developed creative applications ahead of the competition. Merrill Lynch is the largest stock brokerage firm in the United States. Its employees buy and sell stock for clients through one of the major stock exchanges, such as the New York Stock Exchange or the American Stock Exchange. There are also other regional exchanges, as well as exchanges that trade in commodities, like pork bellies and precious metals. Finally, there are unlisted (or over-the-counter) stocks.

A broker earns money from fees or commissions on the exchange of stock. Brokers try to win business from the public and from other firms' brokers. The brokerage firms have large research departments that provide information for brokers and for clients of the firm. Some individuals maintain accounts at several different firms in order to take advantage of the research or specialization of a particular broker.

Several years ago, most brokerage accounts (the clients' accounts with the broker) earned little or no interest on idle cash. There is cash in an account when stocks are sold; cash also comes in the form of dividends.

During one period of very high interest rates, **Merrill Lynch** developed an idea for a new kind of service, something it calls its *cash management account* (CMA). A bank in Columbus, Ohio, agreed to do some of the processing for such accounts and to furnish individuals subscribing to the accounts with a bank credit card.

The innovation in the CMA was to invest the idle funds from the brokerage accounts in Merrill Lynch's liquid assets funds. This kind of fund was developed to let the small investor take advantage of high interest, which until this time had been available only to large investors. The fund managers buy large-denomination securities with short maturities (e.g. a $100,000 certificate of deposit from a bank that is due in six months), and then the fund sells shares, usually at a $1 a share, to the public, with some kind of minimum investment, say, $1,000 (see Figure 19-1).

The fund holder earns interest from the day of purchase until the day of redemption. An attempt is made to keep the par value of the shares (the value at which shares are bought and sold by investors or users of the fund) at $1 and to reflect any changes in the interest rate earned. Because the securities have a short maturity, it is generally possible to keep the fund's return fairly close to current market rates.

The CMA approach is to automatically invest the client's idle cash from the brokerage fund (plus any that he or she wishes to supply in addition) in the liquid assets fund. The idea was slow to catch on, but within three years, Merrill Lynch had over a million CMA holders. Although some of these people had already been Merrill Lynch customers, it is estimated that some 450,000 new customers were attracted to the plan.

In addition to gaining customers, the plan has helped to make the Merrill Lynch liquid-assets fund one of the largest. Merrill Lynch succeeded in patenting the idea of a CMA and settled a suit for $1 million charging a competitor with having infringed

Figure 19-1. An Advertisement for Merrill's Cash Management Account.

on a Merrill Lynch patent and with having hired a Merrill Lynch employee to copy the system.

The only way the CMA could work is with computer processing. There would simply not be enough time to record manually the data needed to move money from one account to another for a million customers. The brokerage firm has used information processing to gain a competitive advantage.

Hospital Supply. *American Hospital* Supply Corporation is a $2-billion firm supplying hospitals with much of the material they need to function. American Hospital has put terminals in many hospital purchasing offices to make it easier for purchasing agents to enter orders. With a terminal connected to the American Hospital computer, those hospitals quite naturally order from American Hospital.

The system has grown to include one hundred twenty-two regional computer centers serving U.S. hospitals. Because the orders are entered directly, rather than being sent by mail, there is no resupply delay. American Hospital ships 95 percent of the orders the day they are received, so that a hospital can reduce its inventories and save money.

After setting up the ordering application, American Hospital offered hospitals an inventory control system to track the movement of supplies, disbursements, and stock levels. The data are also related to projected inventory levels. American Hospital has a management service that tailors the programs to each hospital (see Figure 19-2).

Has this strategy been successful? American Hospital has an average order of 5.8 items, compared to 1.7 for the industry and 2.4 items on conventional American Hospital orders (paper order forms instead of terminal entry). Customers that have the automatic terminal system are spending as much as three times more at American Hospital than before the terminals were installed.

American Hospital has gained a ***competitive advantage*** by using the technology to offer a service to its customers. In the process, it has linked

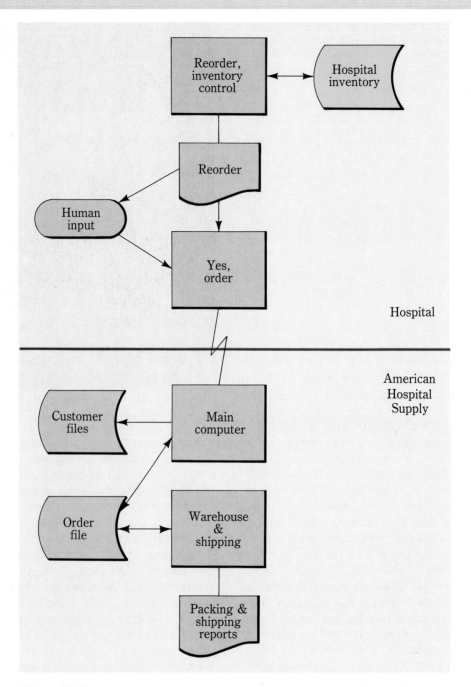

Figure 19-2. Schematic of American Hospital System. An order entry system at American Hospital becomes a strategic application.

Figure 19-3. A druggist studies the Economost system, a McKesson on-line ordering system for hospitals and pharmacies.

itself more closely to its customers and has increased its market share. To do so, it had to invest heavily in information-processing technology and to take a long-term view of its investment. American Hospital had to spend money on systems and computers with no guarantee that the expenditure would pay off, though the investment paid handsome returns in the final analysis.

Drug Supplies. *McKesson* Corporation is a San Francisco corporation that distributes drugs, foods, chemicals, and alcoholic beverages. Its annual sales exceed $4.5 billion. Drugstores are the primary customers for its products.

In the mid 1970s the company developed an information system called Economost for the purpose of increasing and protecting its market share. In the first version of the system, McKesson customers used hand-held terminals to key product codes into the terminal. The drugstore clerk checked the shelves, and when a product was out of stock or the stock was low, he or she entered the product code printed on the shelf label.

Then the drugstore used a modem to transmit an order to the McKesson central computer; the cen-

tral computer arranged for shipment.

The system has expanded over the years; now, there is a bar-code scanner that picks up the product code from a bar code on the shelf label. The system also has data on what products are shelved in which aisles in each of the drugstores; the computer-generated packing list is arranged so that products shelved on one aisle are packed in the same box.

McKesson also offers an insurance claims service for customers of drugstores whose prescription purchases are covered by programs like Medicare. The customer has a plastic card like a credit card; he or she pays a nominal amount, like a dollar, toward the price of the prescription. The card is used to prepare a claims form through which the drugstore receives the rest of the payment. A McKesson subsidiary processes the claims, and this service helps to bring customers back to the drugstore.

McKesson tries to provide as much service to drugstores as possible. It provides price stickers for products and a gross margin report (profits before expenses are subtracted) (see Figure 19-3).

The firm has tied its purchasing system directly into the order entry systems of its forty largest suppliers. This means that McKesson can enter orders directly, reducing the amount of time required for restocking its warehouse. This tie-in has allowed McKesson to reduce the number of employees who buy from its suppliers from 120 to 14 and the number of drug distribution warehouses from 85 to 55. While all of this has happened, volume has doubled.

This distribution firm has succeeded in using the technology to serve its customers better; better service has given McKesson a competitive edge. Even though some of these applications look operational and are aimed purely at efficiency, they are strategic in the way they make McKesson a leader and help it gain and keep its market share.

Merrill Lynch, American Hospital Supply, and McKesson have used computers creatively as a part of their corporate *strategies.* The firms have gained a competitive advantage because they have been able to make information-processing technology work for them.

A Decision Support System. The vice-president of marketing for *Marine Terminals* uses a personal computer for *decision support systems.* Marine Terminals operates ship terminals and provides stevedores at ports in California and Alaska. The VP had had experience with time-sharing and in 1979 bought an Apple II computer for $2,500.

One important decision-support system (DSS) involved a decision to build a new supply-base terminal. The staff looked at the financial effects of different configurations for the marine terminal. The variables included the number of ships that could be loaded or unloaded and the work schedule; a design featuring fewer berths would have produced a less expensive terminal, but labor costs for working around the clock to provide enough capacity to unload and load all ships would have been higher with a small number of berths. (A berth cost about $2 million to build.) Basically, the analysis had to balance the fixed cost of building a terminal with a lot of berths and the variable cost of labor to man the berths.

The analyses were numerous and included the net present value of fixed costs, income, and operating costs. The analysis also considered net income after taxes and investment tax credits. The terminal was planned for a scenic part of California, so the computer was used to compute the financial impact of various approaches to minimizing the visual and environmental impact of the terminal.

The staff used the Apple to display the results of the analysis with color graphics. Marine Terminals then made 35-mm color slides of the displays generated on the CRT, which were used in presentations to other managers and potential investors in the project. The project was approved, and the terminal is being built.

This application was successful because a single manager at a high level in the firm realized that hands-on computing would contribute to the quality of the analysis and to better decisions. He was willing to be the innovator and to bring the first micro into the firm. Furthermore, he demonstrated its value by using it to support an important decision.

Revenue

The firms described turned a competitive advantage into increased revenue. Creating more revenue from information-processing technology is another positive major impact of computerization. A number of firms have found ways to market information-processing systems directly and to earn money from these services; the computer systems become products themselves.

McDonnell Douglas is a large aerospace organization. Building on its own expertise in the technology, it has created a division called the Information Services Group that offers computer services and consulting to various clients. The firm has used the technology to enter into a new line of business: computer services.

Other firms have made their information-processing products available through computer systems. There are a number of financial data bases to which one can subscribe. It is possible to obtain hundreds of pieces of data about companies and their financial position. With a personal computer, one can dial a computer, gain access to its database, and have the data of interest transferred to the diskettes of the personal computer, all for a fee.

Mead Data Central offers a system called Lexis

that contains the full text of caselaw citations and court decisions (see Figure 19-4). The system is installed in major law offices where attorneys and their assistants can search for past decisions that may be relevant to the legal problem at hand. The firm saw an opportunity to offer a new product through information-processing technology and has been quite successful in its efforts.

All of these firms have used the technology to create products and services that they can sell to customers. The technology becomes a revenue producer when applied in this manner. The purpose is not necessarily for the firm to gain an edge on competition; rather, it is to offer a new product or service that will generate profits.

Savings

The traditional impact of computers on organizations has always been the expectation, at least, of *cost savings* because of computer applications. Companies have automated clerical tasks to reduce processing costs. For example, insurance companies and banks have automated the production of bills, notices, bank statements, renewals, and so on that are sent to customers.

Although possibly not reducing the number of employees, computers in these industries have very likely contributed to *cost avoidance;* fewer additional staff members have had to be hired than might otherwise have been required.

Firms have also saved money with computers by controlling their *inventories* better. The computer calculates the appropriate balance between the cost of carrying inventory and the cost of ordering items. These *economic order-quantity* models (EOQs) have been in existence for many years, but they are difficult to apply to an inventory of many items unless a computer is available to process the data.

Better Quality

Computer systems can improve a process in addition to automating it. Computer-aided design is a good case in point. Designers or engineers use a computer terminal to create drawings of a part. The system stores the drawing, so that it can be recalled later for easy modification. The system makes it possible to make a hard copy, usually on a plotting device. A line or section of the drawing can be changed and redraw in minutes. The system reduces much of the drudgery of design work and, in the process, probably reduces the need for drafters.

Word processing, which we explored in Chapter 16, also contributes to *quality.* With word processing, it is easy to make changes and to store and reprint the document. This process is more efficient than retyping the document manually with each change. The output will always be attractive, and there will be no erasures, correction fluid, or other marks. Word processing improves quality and the speed and ease of doing the typing task as well.

No Other Way

Systems have allowed the organization to do processing that is just not practicable any other way. Without a computer system, how could an airline associate a passenger name with all of the legs of a trip and have that information available anywhere in the world in a few seconds?

By the early 1960s, American Airlines had projected the failure of its manual reservations systems and began to develop Sabre, the first on-line commercial application. Sabre began working just in time and set a new standard for service in the industry. A major airline would be unable to operate today without such a system.

SUMMARY

A system can contribute to the organization in a number of ways. Most organizations find cost savings or better-quality work as a result of developing a system. Some of the most exciting results come from using a system to create a new source of revenue or from incorporating information-processing technology as a part of corporate strategy. The successful firms in the future will be those able to achieve the potential of their computer-based systems.

Figure 19-4. (a) An advertisement for Mead Data Central's Nexis/Lexis systems. (b) An attorney accesses the Lexis system in his law office on a PC. (c) A CRT screen display of a Lexis menu. (d) Nexis allows the user to access information from hundreds of newspapers and periodicals. (e) The computer room at Mead Data Central where Nexis and Lexis databases are maintained.

a

For the first time in a long time you can hold all the law in your own two hands.

b

ORGANIZATIONAL STRUCTURE

The impact of computers in the examples given has been very positive; the example firms have benefited greatly from the technology. However, computer systems can have unintended consequences. It is important to think about how systems can impact the organization and the people working in it.

In the early days of computers, many experts predicted that layers of management would be replaced. In one early military system, one level of command was no longer necessary, but the evidence of widespread changes of this type is slim.

We do expect the relations among departments in organizations and organizational units to change as a result of bringing in computer systems. The firm can organize departments in a number of ways to deal with its business environment. Since departments often depend on each other to process information, computer systems may make it possible to redefine the tasks assigned to a particular department.

One important variable in the design of organizations is centralization. The firm can centralize data or have information widely available in the corporation. If information is highly centralized (for example, if the only computers at Multicorp are at headquarters), then management can keep track of all operating decisions and control the organization from one place. On the other hand, Multicorp could be highly decentralized by requiring reports to be sent to headquarters only after a local manager has made a decision. This style of operation allows local management a high degree of discretion; it helps managers to learn how to make decisions. Also, local management can respond quickly to local situations.

In this discussion, note that the physical location of computers is not really important. A centralized on-line system can provide information at remote sites. A distributed computer system can be rigidly controlled from a central site that does all programming and downloads programs to the distributed computers; that is, the central site places programs on the disk file of the local computer for the local computer to execute.

Thus, there are many ways for the firm to organize itself and its information-processing activities.

The important point is to plan for the impact of computers. What kind of an organization do the managers want? How do they design systems to produce that kind of organization?

Interdependence

Information systems have an impact on the structure of the organization that has not yet been well measured. When a system is developed, departments become dependent on other departments in new ways. For example, a department with a new application now depends on the computer department for service.

In other instances, a department may depend on another one that has new information. In one firm, the customer services department adopted a new order-entry system. Before, this department had merely copied orders manually and sent the results to be keypunched. Customer services filed copies of the orders, but it was not easy to retrieve them.

With the new system, the staff in customer services enters orders using an on-line terminal. The orders are instantly accessible to authorized employees in customer services and others in the firm. The new system makes everyone highly dependent on customer services and, in addition, makes their work more visible.

Some departments do not notice increased interdependence; for others, it will become a source of friction, particularly if one department is perceived as having let down the other. This type of conflict is particularly noticeable in relations between the computer department and the users, as the users are almost always dependent on the computer department for service. It is very difficult to provide high-quality service, and the users tend to be very critical of computer departments.

New Structures

Opportunities exist to create new types of organizational structure with information systems, but there are few published cases in which a new *structure* has been a conscious goal of management in developing a new application.

In one company, management did use a new computer-based system to facilitate achieving some of its goals:

1. Management wanted a single forecast throughout the company at the level of individual items, including their color and style. Before the system was put in, marketing had made a forecast at the grade level (a grade contains many individual items) and had given it to production. Production had thrown it away and had made its own forecast at the level of individual color and style within grade. Management wanted one detailed forecast that everyone would use.

2. Management wanted to have three classes of inventory. The classes were to reflect the degree of sales activity, and there would be different rules for restocking items in the slowest-moving class.

3. There would be a single customer services department. Before the system was put in, retail customers had dealt with one department and contract, and wholesale customers with another. Yet, both departments needed some of the same information in order to promise delivery times.

A new computer system was necessary to achieve the last goal, and it certainly eased achieving the first two. A single system was needed to provide information to both retail and wholesale customers from a new, unified customer-services department.

Office Automation

One of the greatest areas for potential changes in organizational structure brought about by computers is *office automation.* Usually, office automation consists of *electronic mail,* word processing, and personal systems like calendars and reminders.

We have already discussed the advantages of word processing for the quality of output, for sending similar letters to a variety of individuals, and for storing text that is used over and over again.

Electronic mail is one of the features of office automation that can change organizational structures. Each individual on the system has an electronic mailbox, and a simple program is available for sending and reading mail. The program generally allows one to reply to a message directly, to forward a message to others, or to file it for later retrieval (see Figure 19-5).

There are a number of advantages in this kind of system. About 70 percent of business phone calls do not go through the first time they are dialed. The called individual is out or the line is busy. With electronic mail, communications do not require the recipient to be on the line; the person receiving the message can look at his or her electronic mail whenever it is convenient (see Figure 19-6). Of course, for the system to work, the users have to check the computer system regularly for messages.

Because copies are sent to a distribution list electronically, the time and cost of reproducing multiple copies and sending them to the recipients is eliminated. Thus, electronic mail makes it easy to communicate with individuals in text form. Because much of our communication does not need immediate discussion by phone or in person, an electronic medium is well suited to taking some of the communications burden from existing media.

In our department of the university, we use electronic mail extensively. It is possible to contact all members of the faculty and all graduate students with a single message. A faculty member can work at one of two campuses or at home and still stay in touch with a secretary and with colleagues. We can input a document at one location and have it printed at another. The system reduces the number of interruptions from phone calls.

Figure 19-7 shows two publicly available mail services offered by common carriers. With these services, the user is not limited to communicating with people who can access his or her computer.

If individuals do not have access to terminals when they are away from the office, or if the staff does not like the idea of typing on a keyboard, there are several types of voice mail available. *Frito-Lay,* with headquarters in Dallas, Texas, sells over $2 billion a year of snack food. The firm has forty-three manufacturing plants and is the only national snack-food firm that delivers directly to store shelves. There are some twenty-six thousand employees in the company.

Frito-Lay employees use a system that allows them to send spoken messages to others. Do not

```
@mm
NYU20.#DECnet MM–20 5.3(1051)
   Last read: 4–Sep–86 13:01:56, 8 messages, 4 pages

MM > send
   To: b20.M–PALLEY
   cc:
   Subject: re Assignment 5
   Message (End with ESCAPE or CTRL/Z.)

Mike, Hi!

Help! I am stuck on Assignment 5 of Prof. Lucas'
course. Have you any idea how to do it? I would really
appreciate some help with it. Perhaps we can meet
some time to discuss it, if you have any ideas.

Thanks,
Wanda

S > SEND
   B20.M–PALLEY@NYU20.#DECnet — queued
```

```
MM > read

   Message 10 (515 characters):
Mail–From: B20.M–PALLEY created at 4–Sep–86
            10:26:02
Date: Fri 5 Sep 86 10:26:02–EDT
From: Mike Palley <B20.M–PALLEY@NYU20 >
Subject: Re: re Assignment 5
To: B20.W–ORLIKOWSKI@NYU20
In-Reply-To: Message from "Wanda Orlikowski" of Thu
            4 Sep 86 15:22:47–EDT

As you probably guess, I have already finished
Assignment 5. Try the textbook, pages 120–135. If this
doesn't help, maybe I can find time to help you.
Next time, don't leave things to the last minute.

Mike
```

```
R > reply
   Message (End with ESCAPE or CTRL/Z.)

Thanks very much, Mike. I appreciate your help.
Next time I will really try and keep up to date
with the assignments.

Wanda

S > SEND
   B20.M–PALLEY@NYU20.#DECnet — queued
```

```
MM > read

   Message 12 (338 characters)
Mail–From: B20.M–PALLEY created at 8–Sep–86
            18:03:31
Date: Mon 8 Sep 86 18:03:31–EDT
From: Mike Palley <B20.M–PALLEY@NYU20 >
Subject: Re: re Assignment 5
To: B20.W–ORLIKOWSKI@NYU20
In-Reply-To: Message from "Wanda Orlikowski" of Sat
            6 Sep 86 9:40:10–EDT

That's what friends are for.

Mike

R > quit
MM > exit
```

Figure 19-5. Examples of Electronic Mail. This example of electronic mail shows how one can communicate without the missed calls and interruptions of the phone.

confuse this application with a telephone-answering system because the users can perform a variety of functions with the system.

The firm began its use of **voice mail** with the pilot test of a service bureau that rents "voice mailboxes" for $150 a month. The first use was with the vend sales division; its district managers were hard to reach, and the districts covered two or three states. Weekly status reports were always late in reaching headquarters. During the test, the district managers phoned voice reports to the regional managers' voice mailboxes; these managers added their own comments and forwarded the voice reports to headquarters. At headquarters, clerical personnel transcribed the reports, which were then available on Monday morning instead of on Thursday.

The number of missed calls dropped, and memos were reduced by 75 percent. (Of course, the increased phone charges and the mail system rental were additional costs.) Frito-Lay also found that its credit-approval cycle dropped from ten to two days. Two thirds of the users wanted to keep the system after the test. Another pilot test convinced the company to become a regular subscriber to voice mail.

Figure 19-6. An Office Worker Reading his Electronic Mail at the Beginning of Work.

Figure 19-7. Advertisements for Two Common Carrier Electronic Mail Systems.

Figure 19-8. An Example of an AT&T Teleconferencing Center.

Figure 19-9 (opposite). Examples of Computer Conferencing. Computer conferencing is similar to electronic mail, except that messages are oriented around one particular topic or conference. The conference is asynchronous; participants do not communicate at the same time. Source: Hiltz and Turoff, *The Network Nation.* (Figure continues on page 468.)

From these examples, it appears that at least some organizations have been very successful in using office automation. What is its impact, though, on organizational structure? Departments generally group together individuals who need to communicate. Project teams work together physically or travel to meet each other. It appears that if the individuals know each other, much of this kind of costly face-to-face communication can be replaced with electronic mail.

Teleconferencing

In a teleconference, a group of individuals meets with another group in a remote location. TV cameras

and telephone links are used to let each group see and talk with the other (see Figure 19-8).

There are also computer conferencing systems that are similar to a teleconference, except that the participants work independently of each other. The computer organizes comments about a topic and makes them available whenever a participant in the conference logs onto the computer and asks for them. Figure 19-9 shows an example of a computer-conferencing dialogue.

With these systems, management has a new communications tool, and **communications** are an important consideration in developing the structure of an organization. These tools can be used to develop new structures or to supplement existing ones.

14530 M BARRY WELLMAN (BARRY, 720) 4/1/77 5:13 PM
  Hi, Barry Wellman here ready to join real-time party. How do I get in???

14541 M ROBIN CRICKMAN (ROBIN, 730) 4/1/77 5:25 PM ROXANNE
  Like Barry, I am confused exactly how to proceed at this point. Am I supposed
to respond to specific items? Which ones? Maybe an item or group message from
you would be timely just now. RC

14551 M ROBERT BEZILLA (ROBERT, 213) 4/1/77 5:38 PM
  This seems to be one of those parties where everyone stands around waiting
for someone to say something.

162 C JACQUES VALLEE (704) 4/1/77 5:42 PM
  I just realized I would not be able to participate if I listed the messages waiting,
so I had to bypass the earlier discussion. I hope what I am going to enter will not
be too out of context.

14570 M ELAINE KERR (ELAINE, 114) 4/1/77 6:05 PM
  Private message: Roxanne, this is awful, please be dictatorial, seems nothing's
being accomplished.

14577 M ROXANNE HILTZ (ROXANNE, 120) 4/1/77 6:18 PM
  I am simply not going to try to tell you what to do or say, so please stop
asking me, people!

14620 M ANDY HARDY (719) 4/1/77 7:09 PM
  Roxanne when I said I wanted to see who was there I meant in conference 72
or with Group 72. I also by mistake discovered that everyone was interacting
through the message system, not the conference system as I had assumed. Kind
of like going to the wrong house when you're trying to get to a party.

M 14797 ROBIN CRICKMAN (ROBIN, 730) 4/4/77 12:01 PM
  An open letter to Roxanne on the "cocktail party" experience
  I have one observation I wanted to try out on you to see if you also think this
would help group activities. When I was using a computer conference in Michigan
to collect the opinions of citizens on recombinant DNA research, I found it
necessary to structure the interaction highly. This was initially resented as being
constricting and stifling creativity, but was later accepted (in retrospect) as the
only way to get a group of neophytes into the activity quickly and to keep the
discussion active.
  Just as the hostess of a cocktail party must see that most guests are introduced
to people and that new topics are suggested when conversation lags, I think it
becomes necessary for a CC organizer to accept a heavy burden when
simultaneous or mission-oriented activity is contemplated. The subject needs to be
broken into some series of questions and each person must understand how they
are to contribute to those subjects. The organizer must undertake to summarize
positions and suggest what each person is to do next. Some amusement or other
diversion has to be suggested for participants who are waiting until the system is
ready for them to take the next step. Some sort of closing convention is needed . . .
  I know we are all grown people who don't need to be led by the hand but I
also think that when a new technology is evolving, more structure should be
evoked for interaction. I learned how to greet people at f-t-f cocktail parties
several years ago, when to break off conversation and when the party was over
and I should go home. These were carried as implicit cues of the environment
and interaction. I don't have the cues in a CC cocktail party, and so I hope for
structure to replace them . . . .
CC: ROXANNE   (GROUP 72)

C 963 CC3 STEVE (2,962) 6/28/77 3:44 PM
  My name is Steve. What's yours?

C 963 CC5 JOANNE (5,965) 6/26/77 3:48 PM
  Hello Steve. I find this type of machinery interesting.

C 963 CC9 STEVE (2,962) 6/20/77 3:59 PM
   Hi Joanne. What year are you in?

C 963 CC11 JOANNE (5,965) 6/26/77 4:03 PM
   I am a biology major hopefully going on to physical therapy afterwards. I am there for the summer taking organic chemistry which find difficult if you do not do the work entail. Hello again Steve, I am in the third year.

C 904 CC7 JUDY (5,905) 6/21/77 1:22 PM
   Hi my name is Judy. I am a part time student at Upsala and a full time mother of three. I am also employed in an alcoholic rehab. center. My typing is terrible so please excuse my mistakes. Thank you. Hi Cindy. Hi Anne.

C 904 CC9 CINDY S (6,906) 6/21/77 1:24 PM
   I am Cindy and I am a mother of a 6 year old boy. I am here today for a group experiment that I am sure we will all enjoy.

C 904 CC11 ANNE (2,902) 6/21/77 1:27 PM
   The weather today is partly cloudy.
   Hi, my name is Anne and i am a mother of four, two daughters in college, one boy in high school and one boy in junior high. i am presently enrolled in the para-legal program here at Upsala. i used to teach chemistry and physics in the high school, but i am changing my career. My husband is an attorney.

C 904 CC12 CINDY S (6,906) 6/21/77 1:28 PM
   Is there anyone there who also speaks Spanish or Italian? Anyone there who is a music buff?

C 904 CC15 DAVID (3,903) 6/21/77 1:33 PM
   Is this how we are all going to spend the next two hours of our time? Well, I say that if they want to pay for it, then by all means it is okay with me.

C 904 CC18 ANNE (2,902) 6/21/77 1:36 PM
   I once took a short course in conversational Italian because I took a trip to Italy two years ago, but I cannot speak it. Does anyone play tennis?

C 904 CC19 CINDY S (6,906) 6/21/77 1:36 PM
   I still didn't get any answers folks, how about it? Dear David you are right. This is exactly how we are going to spend the next two hours. Have fun. Cindy.

C 904 CC21 JUDY (5,905) 6/21/77 1:37 PM
   Sorry Cindy. I do not speak any languages. I do enjoy good music: when I have the time. Anyone out there sports orientated?

C 904 CC25 CINDY S (6,906) 6/21/77 1:41 PM
   Sorry Judy, I am not into sports. Anne would you consider teaching me to play tennis? That is about the only thing athletic I might be able to handle.

C 904 CC27 JUDY (5,905) 6/21/77 1:42 PM
   Yes Anne. I play tennis every chance I get. Lucky me. I have a tennis court one half block from my house.

C 904 CC32 ANNE (2,902) 6/21/77 1:46 PM
   Wow. We all could get together for tennis at my house. I persuaded my husband to pave our backyard and we put in a makeshift tennis court. It is a lot of fun. So Cindy, I'll be glad to show you some of the fundamentals. But, I'm still working on my backhand and serve.

C 904 CC34 CINDY S (6,906) 6/21/77 1:48 PM
   Thanks Anne. I would like that. By the way folks, I am a senior here and a music major. So if anyone takes an intro. course to music and has problems, I will gladly help out.

Figure 19-9 (continued).

INDIVIDUALS

Individuals have exhibited the greatest fears of computers. Will I be replaced? If I am not replaced, will I be able to cope with the new technology and do my job?

Data on **unemployment** as a result of computerization are hard to gather and analyze. For thirty years, experts have predicted a decline in the number of managers because many would be replaced by computers. However, middle management and staff appear to be as numerous as ever. Computers are being used by these individuals to try new alternatives, to reduce uncertainty and risk, and to perform more thorough analyses than were possible before computers.

More than half of the U.S. work force can be classified as information workers. These individuals do not manufacture a tangible product; instead, information workers process data in some way. The government classifies such workers as entertainers, financial services employees, and educators, as primarily involved in information work. Computers are the major form of capital investment for information workers.

There will undoubtedly be reductions in factory jobs as more plants automate and install sophisticated robots. However, it is expected that this reduction in factory workers will be a gradual one over many years. There are also likely to be reductions in some clerical jobs, but again, here the impact will probably occur over a number of years. As we have seen, some of the impact will come simply from avoiding hiring more clerical staff rather than from outright reductions in staff.

A major problem is training and motivation. It is hard to find a new vocation for a middle-aged industrial worker. The challenge for government, education, and industry is to retrain and reequip such workers to be part of the economy.

Motivation

Fears of job loss, our adequacy to cope with computers, and general uncertainty due to change can have a serious negative impact on systems development. If potential users resist the system, it will be difficult or impossible to get the input needed to design it.

The designer and management need to motivate the users to participate in design, to overcome their fears, and to join in the development process. The users have to be shown that the benefits of a system overcome its costs.

The typical costs to the individual are:

1. Change.
2. Uncertainty.
3. Fears of not being able to cope.

There are usually some benefits from an application:

1. The user experiences less drudgery.
2. The user can often do a better job.
3. The system can be fun to use.
4. The user may have more confidence in the results.

Too often, the user pays all the costs and receives no **benefits** from a system. For example, a clerical worker may spend a fatiguing day at a terminal entering data but may never see or use the results. The benefits from the system accrue to management, which now has information not available before. The clerks are unhappy, and management does not understand why.

In the new order-entry system described earlier, the customer services staff found its job changed in a number of ways:

1. Clerks now typed the orders on a CRT.
2. They did not have to copy the information onto a sheet for keypunching.
3. The staff had instant access to data they had entered; there was no need to search files when the customer called.

The benefits of this new approach more than offset the costs of **retraining** and relearning. All of the order entry personnel are enthusiastic about the system, which has helped the system to succeed.

Designers and users need to assess these costs and benefits and to try to design systems that motivate the users to cooperate.

Involvement

Chapter 12 advocates that the users play a significant role in the development of systems. There are several reasons for this suggestion:

1. The users are knowledgeable about the existing system.
2. The users are knowledgeable about their needs.
3. Involvement can increase commitment to a system.
4. The users can improve the quality of a system with their ideas.
5. Involvement is an investment in training.
6. Involvement can be intrinsically satisfying.

Resistance to change can be reduced if the users are involved and have a real influence on design. The features desired by the user have to be carefully considered and included where at all possible. If they are not included, the designers should explain clearly to the user why not. Involvement itself is satisfying; people like to have an influence on things that affect them. Finally, involvement means that the users will be knowledgeable about a system, so that training will be easier.

How do you bring about involvement? The approach in Chapter 12 is intended to encourage involvement; the philosophy is that the user takes charge of design. The systems analyst acts as a tour guide, describing what has to happen next. The designer provides technical input and structure decisions for the design team, which decides on alternatives.

The users and the designers meet frequently to discuss the system and its features and status. Together, they choose among the alternatives and select the trade-offs. This approach requires some help from management, which provides leadership, time, and resources. We shall explore this role further in the next chapter.

Review of Chapter 19

REVIEW

The experiences of the firms described in this chapter demonstrate that computer systems can make a vital contribution to the organization. Companies have used information systems to develop new products and services and to create a market where none existed. By improving service, two of the companies in the chapter captured an added market share.

We have stressed that systems analysis and design is a creative activity; so is the generation of ideas for high-payoff applications. In our examples, managers and users thought carefully about what made their business successful, and they developed systems that enhanced that success. In addition, the managers were able to develop successful applications and to manage computing in their firms.

Other firms have reaped significant benefits from computers through better quality and enhanced revenues. Many computer applications do jobs that would be impossible without a computer, such as keeping track of the reservations for a rental car firm nationwide.

There is one cautionary note: we need to think carefully about how systems impact the structure of the organization and the individuals working in it. If these issues are ignored, then systems may be unsuccessful because individuals will resist changes that they perceive as having a negative impact.

Information technology does have the potential to make a positive contribution to the structure of organizations, but careful planning is required. Office automation is a good example of how technology provides a lot of options for structuring the organization. We can truly think of various alternatives for the place and time at which work occurs, given the flexibility of computer technology.

KEY WORDS

American Hospital
Benefits
Communications
Competitive advantage
Cost avoidance
Cost savings
Decision support
   system (DSS)
Economic order-
   quantity
Electronic mail
Frito-Lay
Interdependence
Inventory
Involvement

Marine Terminals
McKesson
Merrill Lynch
Motivation
Office automation
Quality
Retraining
Strategy
Structure
Unemployment
Voice mail
Word processing

BUSINESS PROBLEMS

19.1. We have spoken about strategic opportunities, but a firm today has to be vigilant for strategic threats. As an example, Merrill Lynch, the largest stock broker in the United States, and IBM are developing a system to run on personal computers that will provide stock prices for brokers.

Currently, a company called Quotron supplies terminals and quotations to numerous brokers around the country. Up to this point, Quotron has had a virtual monopoly on this business. In fact, Merrill Lynch was its major customer and accounted for a significant percentage of their business. Quotron stock suffered a dramatic drop on the day the IBM–Merrill Lynch joint venture was announced.

Quotron uses central computers and terminals; the IBM–Merrill Lynch system will use personal computers. What might the advantages of this approach be? What can Quotron do to meet this challenge? In general, can you devise a strategy for a firm so that it will be prepared for and can counter strategic threats fostered by the technology?

19.2. Managers and workers are extremely concerned about whether there are any health hazards in working with CRTs all day. A large number of individuals, about 90 percent of whom are female, spend a significant portion of their day working with these devices.

There are some who believe that the low-level radiation from the CRTs is a health hazard. There have been cases of claimed birth defects, and an abnormal number of these workers have had miscarriages. However, there is little scientific evidence about whether the devices constitute a health hazard. Another school of thought is that the jobs involved in data entry are boring and demeaning, and that complaints about the CRT and its possible impact on health are really symptoms of problems in the job itself. These individuals say that we would be wasting our time concentrating on radiation; instead, we should look at the quality of the system, its user interface, and the nature of the data entry task.

If you were a manager confronted with a group of angry data-entry operators, how would you try to solve their problems? Some labor unions have used this issue to become bargaining agents for CRT operators.

REVIEW QUESTIONS

1. What is your definition of *competitive strategy?*
2. How did Merrill Lynch use technology to gain an edge on its competition?
3. What was American Hospital Supply's computer strategy?
4. Was American Hospital Supply successful in using the technology? What evidence is there to support your answer?
5. How can a company obtain revenue from its computer systems?
6. Why would an attorney be interested in the Mead Data system?
7. How have firms saved money with computers?
8. Give an example of quality improvement through the use of computers.
9. How can computers affect the interdependence of departments?
10. What is office automation?
11. How does electronic mail work?
12. What are the advantages of electronic mail?
13. What are the best features of word processing?
14. What are the advantages of user involvement?

THOUGHT QUESTIONS

15. What is necessary for a strategy based on information processing to succeed?
16. What advantages are there to having your ter-

minals in a customer's location?

17. How can one avoid future costs by investing in information-processing technology?
18. Give an example of two systems that could not work without computers.
19. Why do you think computers have not replaced large numbers of middle managers?
20. Is there an association between where hardware is located and where information is available?
21. Why might one want to have decentralized decision-making?
22. What is the advantage of centralized control?
23. Why is there friction between the computer department and the user departments?
24. Why should one forecast the impact on the organization of a new system before developing it?
25. How could a student use a personal computer?
26. What applications are there for electronic mail in a university setting?
27. What is teleconferencing? How does it differ from computer conferencing?
28. What are the greatest fears of individuals about computers?
29. What does a typical information worker do?
30. How can we motivate users to cooperate in developing a system?

31. What are the typical costs and benefits of a computer application?
32. What are the costs of involvement in systems design to the user?
33. What does management have to do to support user involvement?
34. Should managers themselves be involved in design? If so, how?
35. How would you approach systems design to encourage the involvement of the users?

RECOMMENDED READINGS

Lucas, Henry C., Jr. *Implementation: The Key to Successful Information Systems*. New York: Columbia University Press, 1981. A monograph with a number of studies of implementation and an integrating framework.

Mumford, E., and D. Henshall. *A Participative Approach to Computer System Design*. London: Associated Business Press, 1979. A philosophy of user involvement in system design and an excellent case study.

Porter, M. *Competitive Strategy*. New York: Free Press, 1980. A good text on various approaches to competition.

Chapter 20

The successes of the last chapter create a lot of optimism about what can be accomplished with computers and information systems. For all of the positive examples we have seen in the text, there are dozens of organizations that are highly dissatisfied with information processing.

If the technology is so powerful, why are there so many problems? What can be done to help improve the chances of developing successful computer applications and operating them? The responsibility for information processing, just as for all other activities in the organization, lies with management.

This chapter offers suggestions for how to manage information processing in the firm. Without guidance and support from the top, it is virtually impossible to develop creative and successful computer applications, whether on a mainframe, a mini, or a micro.

After reading this chapter, you should be able to:

- Explain why it is difficult to manage information processing.
- Discuss the role of the end user in processing.
- Describe what a user should do in systems analysis and design.
- Explain the manager's role in design.
- Describe the need and contents of a plan for information processing.
- Explain what a manager should do to control information processing in the firm.

THE MANAGEMENT ISSUE: DEALING WITH COMPUTERS IN THE ORGANIZATION

INTRODUCTION

Information processing is one of the least successfully managed parts of a modern organization. Why do users and managers feel uncomfortable with the technology? There is no simple answer to this question, and there are probably many reasons why non-computer-professionals are not motivated to manage information processing.

1. The **technology** is **invisible.** A manager can go to a factory and see how a part is manufactured; the same is not possible with a program executing inside a computer.
2. Many individuals do not understand at all how a computer works and, as a result, may fear it.
3. Popular press accounts sometimes border on science fiction, creating unrealistic expectations (and fears) about machines.
4. Users have experienced a lack of success with many systems. These computer applications have not worked or lived up to their potential.
5. No one has explained to the users of systems or to managers what they need to do in designing systems and managing information processing.

THE END USER

Why is the **end user** important? First, there are not enough computer professionals to answer every request for information processing in the organization. If users want to answer questions, they will have to do some of the work themselves. The idea of end user computing is to equip the user to interact directly with the computer without needing a programmer. Second, the more end users know about information processing, the better decisions they will make about the design and operation of systems. Managers who are knowledgeable will be able to provide effective leadership for the systems function.

Several activities are included in the category of end user computing. The first is the hands-on use of computers to solve a particular problem. The second role of the user is in **systems analysis and design.**

End User Computing

This text has stressed the use of microcomputers for solving problems. The microcomputer is, in many instances, attached to a larger computer network; the users access data from that network for local analysis at the microcomputer. The end user, then, has to know the following:

1. *An electronic spreadsheet package on the micro.* The user works with the spreadsheet for a variety of tasks. Financial analysis may be the most frequent, but these packages can be applied to a number of assignments. An official at Macmillan, the publisher of this text, uses a spreadsheet program to keep track of the various dates on which manuscripts and other materials are due from authors; in this case, the spreadsheet system has been applied to project management.

2. *Word processing.* The next highly popular option for micros is word processing, which can be used for all types of documents. In our department at the university, almost everyone writes papers and books using a word processor on a home microcomputer or one on a large central minicomputer. The original author may revise the document or have a secretary put in the finishing touches. Papers, books, reports, proposals, and correspondence can all be prepared with the use of word processing.

3. *A personal filing or database system.* What do we need to record? From senior managers to students, we all have data that we would like to keep on file. My first personal file system is used to keep track of research articles, which are indexed on as many key words as necessary. When writing, I can query the database on a number of keys. The dean's office uses a simple file system to keep faculty records. There are a myriad of uses for this kind of application.

Beyond the tasks already mentioned, the user will want to connect to a network of computers, so he or she will need to understand:

1. *How to access the network.* Access is highly dependent on the computers in the network and the connections among them. In simple dial-up networks, a "smart modem" dials the computer and makes the connection; the user needs only to log in

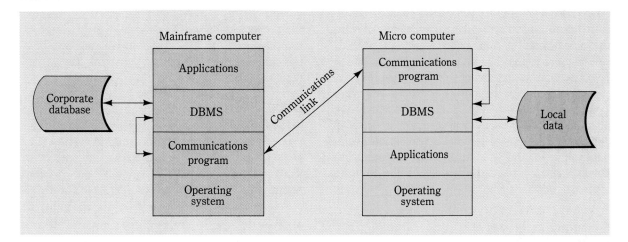

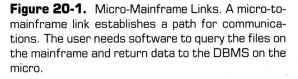

Figure 20-1. Micro-Mainframe Links. A micro-to-mainframe link establishes a path for communications. The user needs software to query the files on the mainframe and return data to the DBMS on the micro.

(establish a connection with and begin to use) the computer being accessed.

2. *How to access the files and the databases stored on the network.* The access to data on the network is far more complex than just getting on the network. The problem is that different users will have stored data on the network, quite possibly using different kinds of database management systems with different query languages. The user wanting to access the data will have to know the structure of the database being searched and the commands in that database. Computer staff members may write special programs to help the user in accessing diverse data (see Figure 20-1).

A related problem is how to transform the data extracted from another computer into the format required for analysis by means of programs like electronic spreadsheet packages on the micro. Some organizations have developed special software to make this transformation possible; without programs or help from the computer staff, it may be very difficult to figure out how to use the extracted data.

3. *How to run programs to download data from the*

network to the microcomputer. In addition to data, users will want to take advantage of programs on other computers. To the extent that these programs are easy to use, the user will be able to work with them. However, often it is not obvious how to use a program, and the user will require support from some kind of consulting group in the computer department.

Finally, the micro will be used as a "dumb" terminal using none of its local processing power. Here, the user will have to:

1. *Understand the database structure (with help from the computer department staff).* This problem is similar to the one of accessing data and downloading it for further analysis. The user must know what data are available and how to access them.

2. *Use a query language to answer requests for information.* This problem is similar to the one just described. There may be several database management systems in use in the organization, each having its own query language. Some dedicated applications packages come with their own query languages as well, and there is not necessarily a similarity among them.

3. *Work with a fourth-generation language to develop reports and ad hoc systems.* The user must learn the language and become adept at working with it. The computer staff has to provide extracts of the database or clear instructions on how to access the data to be run with the fourth-generation language.

Although the knowledge requirements may appear formidable, users will acquire it through courses, books, and help from the professional computer staff. Each day, the use of the computer becomes easier as we learn more about how to make systems "user friendly."

Systems Analysis

Chapters 12 and 13 discussed systems analysis and design and the user's role in this process. In the following paragraphs are the various stages in the systems life cycle and the responsibilities of the user at each stage.

Inception. Users should initiate the system; they determine that something new is needed and sketch their ideas for the systems professionals. At this point, the users want to take control of the project and maintain it. If they show early interest and commitment, the project will be off to a good start.

Feasibility. Users help assess the feasibility of a system. As almost any information-processing problem can be helped by a computer in some way, the feasibility study may focus on various alternatives for providing information-processing assistance. Users should insist on generating alternatives for how a particular application might be developed, and they should have a major say in choosing which alternative will be implemented. Remember that it is the user who is left with the system; the computer staff will always move on to the next project, whereas the user has to live with the results of the design effort.

Analysis. The analyst will depend on the user to help analyze the existing system and to develop the requirements for a new system. Here, it is important for the user to be able to describe how informa-

tion processing is currently accomplished. What are the procedures? How do different individuals process the data? The user needs to communicate how the system works so that the systems analyst understands it completely.

Design. In some organizations, the user actually helps in the design stage by developing some of the processing logic and report formats and even by suggesting file contents. At a minimum, the user must work with the analyst to understand and carefully review what the system will do. We have advocated that the user actually design the system. The background you have from Chapters 10 through 12 should make it possible for you to develop data flow diagrams and to describe what a new system should do.

Specifications. It is imperative for the users to understand the specifications for a system; if not, the users will be unsure of what the system will do. The computer professional also has a responsibility to communicate clearly to the users, so that they can respond to the specifications. Hopefully, by having had a part in the development of the design, the users will already understand what the system is to do. The exercise of drawing up documentation is a good vehicle for learning about the system.

Programming. Here, the user monitors progress, provides data, and sees that the project stays on schedule. Users are not expected to write programs, unless the alternative chosen is for a quick microcomputer application using a special language or package or the alternative is a fourth-generation system on a mainframe. If the computer staff is doing the programming, about all the user can do is monitor the status of the project.

Testing. The users must review the results of tests to be sure that the system works and that errors are caught and corrected to the greatest extent possible. The users participate in generating test data. Reviewing the results is also a user responsibility. Users should control acceptance testing: the users develop the test data and accept the system based on its performance on the user-designed tests.

Training. If the users understand a system well by virtue of having worked on its design, they are in a natural position to help train others in the use of the application. Some organizations encourage the users to write the training manuals because they can explain the system in simple terms.

One company even hired English majors from college and had them do the user manuals for a system. The analysts had to explain the system to these individuals. As the English specialists knew nothing about computers, the explanations had to be very clear. The result was good, easy-to-understand user manuals.

Conversion and Installation. The users must help in planning for conversion and installation; they can forecast the likely impact of the new system and can suggest the best approach to converting to it. There are costs and benefits for individuals working with a new system. Users and designers need to plan for the impact of a system and take care to see that employees are prepared for the installation of the new application. Conversion is best done gradually, with careful testing to prevent creating a major breakdown in the organization.

Operation. Hopefully, at this point, the users will be working with the system, and it will be in frequent use. It is likely that there will be new suggestions for enhancements and changes, but if the design is done properly, requests for changes should be reasonable. In Figure 20-2 one can see the importance of a computer system, one that tracks prices, for a commodities broker.

Although the preceding description may seem like a great deal of work, one is developing a set of computer and human procedures to process information for a minimum of five years. We used to think of the life cycle of a system as encompassing five to seven years; now it is probably at least ten years. In many instances, systems will evolve but will probably never be completely replaced. After all, an on-line reservations system for airline reservations costing

$200 million is unlikely to be discarded in favor of a completely new system.

If there is a two-year development time, we are planning for at least seven to ten years in the future, and possibly beyond, every time that a new system is developed. Given the crucial importance of information processing to the information worker, the manufacturing sector, and the service industry, users have to devote some of their energy and their time to systems as a necessary investment in the future.

Management Actions

Commitment on the part of users is far more likely if management takes part in systems analysis and design and encourages the users to do the same. The following are some of the areas in which management should be active:

Selecting Alternatives. Managers must insist on having several alternatives to consider for a given application. They must follow a consistent evaluation scheme, using the same criteria from system to system. A range of choices is necessary to the effective use of scarce development resources.

User Design. Managers must encourage a central user role in design. It may be necessary to hire additional employees so that key users can spend time on the system. Managers will also have to attend design *review meetings* to show their subordinates that participation is important. In attending these meetings, managers also obtain substantive feedback on the design decisions being made. They learn the concerns of others involved in the design effort. It is also important for the manager to review the policy-level implications of a system and its overall logic. Managers have many *objectives* in seeing a system developed.

Understanding. As the system will operate in the manager's area of responsibility, the manager should understand its basic functions and logic. The manager may see important implications that others miss in reviewing the system.

Figure 20-2 (opposite). Computerized charts of prices and volumes are important for commodities brokers.

Policy Objectives. It is vital for managers to state clearly the policy decisions that have already been made. In one company, management did not inform the employees of the fact that it wanted certain changes in the way the firm operated. The users blamed the system for the changes and refused to cooperate with the developers until management held a meeting and explained why the changes were necessary.

Resources. Managers control the resources of the organization. If a system is starved for resources (including user participation), the system has little chance of succeeding. Managers have a lot of options here. They can authorize overtime, bring in additional individuals to work on the project, or hire substitutes to free key subordinates to participate in design. Too often, managers do none of these but simply expect subordinates to complete their regular jobs and contribute to the new system as well. The results are usually that the individual's normal job is completed, and the system is given inadequate attention.

Rewards. Users can be encouraged to work on systems by being rewarded for their role in design. A successful system might bring an above-average raise, a promotion, or a bonus.

Impact of the System. Managers need to think about the likely impact of the system on their areas and on the firm. If the conversion is not carefully planned, it can have a disastrous effect on an organization. Planning and training are key elements in preparing for a new system. When a system has an adverse impact, the fault does not lie with the computer. Rather, the design is poor, and this problem is a management responsibility.

Project Management. A systems development project can be managed just as can any other project

in the firm. The user area management cannot rely solely on the computer professional to see that a project is completed on time and within budget. Instead, the user manager must review progress and influence resource allocation decisions to keep the project on schedule.

These suggestions will help to provide leadership to a project. If a manager follows these steps, he or she will encourage subordinates to play a role in design as well. The manager makes a direct contribution and an equally important indirect contribution by serving as a model for subordinates.

MANAGEMENT OF INFORMATION PROCESSING

Managers have the responsibility for the success of the organization. They must plan, set goals, and see that the resources of the organization are used to achieve these goals. In performing their functions, managers play a number of different roles in the organization:

1. Managers are *leaders.* Managers set the direction of the firm. What is its mission? How do managers motivate employees? Compensate them? What are the firm's responsibilities to society, customers, and suppliers?

2. Managers are figureheads. Senior managers, in particular, represent the firm to the outside world. The president talks to stockholders, securities analysts, and the press. Managers represent the business both to fellow employees and to customers and suppliers.

3. Managers are *decision makers.* Managers are always looking for new opportunities to improve the organization. They negotiate as well with various customers and with other managers in the firm. Managers also do a lot of "fire fighting" in handling and resolving various crises as they occur.

4. Managers are implementers. Managers must

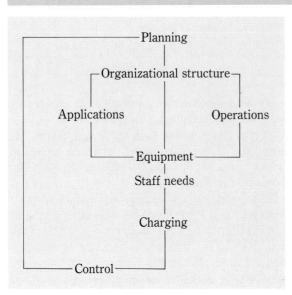

Figure 20-3. Management Control of Information Processing. Source: Lucas, *Coping with Computers* (New York: Free Press, 1982).

monitor the progress of specific projects and see that the firm implements the decisions made by management.

How do managers apply these roles to the management of information processing in the organization?

A Framework

Figure 20-3 is a framework for the management *control* of information processing. The framework's overall purpose is to aid in the planning and controlling of information-processing activities. Planning helps the firm to make today's decisions while giving consideration to their likely impact on the firm's future. Control allows information processing to be well managed and the firm to achieve its plans. In the following discussion, we shall cover each component of the framework.

Planning. The key to managing information processing is to start with a *plan.* A plan is a road map indicating what steps are to be accomplished. It also shows how resources are to be allocated and used during the planning period. One such planning document for an insurance company had the following contents:

1. *Executive summary.* This section described briefly the rest of the contents of the plan in summary form.

2. *Goals.* In this firm, there were several goals, the most important of which was to "turn around" information processing to make it work better and be more responsive to users.

3. *Assumptions.* In order to achieve the objectives of the plan, it was necessary to make certain assumptions about the growth of the firm and its willingness to invest in information systems.

4. *Scenario.* To encourage the users to support the plan, a scenario or a short story was included that depicted the environment that a typical division would encounter after the plan had been implemented.

5. *Applications.* This part of the plan was very important: it contained a list of all the planned and promised applications. The purpose was to create a list and to show what resources would be required to develop all of the proposed applications.

6. *Operations.* This section of the plan contained a projection of what kind of hardware and software was needed to operate existing systems and new, planned, systems. It also showed the requirements for the total number of staff members needed in operations.

	Centralized	Distributed	Decentralized
Equipment	Multicorp Headquarters	Manufacturing plants	Computerware stores
Operations	Headquarters	At plants	Store personnel
Development	Headquarters	At plants and central consulting	In store systems

Figure 20-4. Multicorp exhibits a variety of processing structures, like many modern organizations.

7. *Maintenance and enhancements.* Here, the plan explained what resources would be devoted to maintenance. The plan estimated how many changes could be accomplished within the current budget for information processing and suggested a mechanism for allocating the resources to the tasks.

8. *Organization structure.* The plan described the major processing centers and the communications connections among them. It also presented staffing plans to indicate what applications could be developed locally and what central policy would be needed.

9. *Impact of the plan.* The major effect called for in the plan was expected to have a significant impact on the firm. This section attempted to anticipate that impact and to make suggestions for reducing any negative results.

10. *Risks.* The risks were also included in this plan; the proposals were substantial, and a number of factors could inhibit execution of the plan.

While the plan was under development, the chairman of the firm became increasingly impatient and eventually replaced the manager of information processing. The new manager was not interested in picking up the plan, so it was abandoned. We cannot claim that the plan would have solved all problems, but it should have helped bring some order to the chaotic management of information processing experienced by the firm.

A good plan is a good road map. It tells the organi-

zation which direction it is going in information processing, and it gives the computer department a chance to prepare for orderly changes and growth in hardware, software, and staff.

A plan is not an attempt to predict or change the future; instead, the plan sets a direction. It anticipates the coming environment and tries to position the information-processing function so that it will support the firm no matter what the future brings. Obviously, the plan will be less successful in a turbulent and chaotic industry or firm than in a more stable environment.

Organizational Structure. We have stated that a firm can organize its computers so that they are centralized, distributed and decentralized. These forms of organization can also be applied to hardware, development, and operations.

Multicorp's structure for processing is shown in Figure 20-4. Like that of most organizations, Multicorp's structure can be classified as mixed. There is a computer at headquarters with its own operations staff and development group. The manufacturing plants tend to be distributed, with communications back and forth to the headquarters machine. At first, when a new venture like Computerware Stores starts up, processing is decentralized, and each store owner develops his or her own systems. At some time in the future, a common set of applications may be developed by a central staff for the stores, and the individual store owners encouraged to trade their own systems for the set of applications developed by the central staff. Headquarters personnel must stay aware of what is going on in the stores in order to prevent a lot of duplication and wasted effort.

There is no reason why the structure of the computer organization has to match the structure of the firm. A local division whose management is highly decentralized may not want to bother with the headaches of managing a computer department. The head of this division may want to purchase services from the firm's centralized computer department. Managers have to decide what is right for each part of the firm and develop a structure for computing that fits. A typical computer department structure is shown in Figure 20-5.

Applications. The plan identifies applications areas. For example, as a high priority, assume a firm wants to install a field terminal system. This system will have terminals in the distributors' offices so they can enter orders directly into our order-processing system.

The plan should list applications areas first and then show the various alternatives under consideration for the most important areas. A rough budget estimate is then made, based on the high-priority systems, to arrive at an idea of what the total development effort will be during the planning horizon (the length of time of the plan, e.g., five years).

This section of the plan is crucial. There is a huge backlog of demand for new applications in most firms. Management needs to see what is being requested and to determine what resources of the firm will be devoted to new systems. Managers also have to assign priorities and decide which applications will receive the organization's scarce resources.

Operations. Existing systems must be operated. As these applications exist and are currently in use, their processing demands are known. For example, we know what hardware, software, and staff are required for current operations. It is also necessary to estimate the growth in the volume processed by the existing systems so that hardware and staff in-

creases keep up with demands for service.

It is more difficult to estimate the impact of new applications on existing operations because it is hard to predict the processing required for a system that has yet to be designed. The need for hardware, software, and staff applications under development, however, must be considered if the firm is to come up with a plan for routine operations that has adequate computer capacity.

As long as the firm wants to continue running existing systems, there is little discretion in operating budgets. A certain number of individuals is necessary to operate a given number of computers, regardless of the applications they are running. Eliminating one application does not necessarily mean that a computer can be turned off; many other applications may use the computer.

Equipment Needs. To meet planned growth in applications and operations, the firm needs an orderly plan for acquiring new equipment. Why does the firm always need more? Hardware is cheaper each year, yet the total bill spent on computing seems to go higher and higher:

1. Users and managers want new applications, yet they rarely eliminate an existing application and replace it with a new one.

2. End user programming means that there are many more computer users. As we work with languages that are at higher and higher levels, we use more hardware cycles (i.e., more of the computer's resources). End users represent a new demand on computing resources, and capacity will have to expand to accommodate them. Firms have reported dramatic increases in the need for new mainframe computers as a result of encouraging end user programming.

3. Because of applications generators, database management systems, query languages, and fourth-generation languages, computers are used less efficiently than they might be if all programming were in assembly language. It is a conscious strategy to use more hardware to increase productivity and to reduce human labor. It is not clear that all approaches to design, e.g., a DBMS, are actually less efficient in execution on the computer; it is more likely that

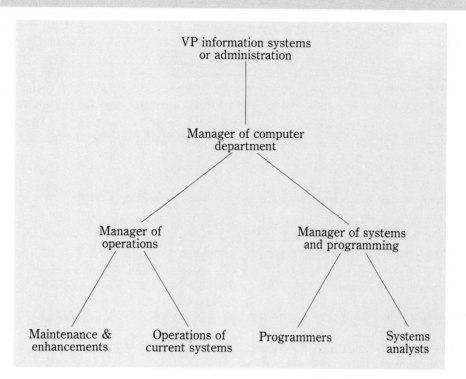

Figure 20-5. Structure of Information Processing. There are many ways to organize an information processing function. The one shown here is fairly typical.

extra computer resources are needed because so many more applications are being run owing to higher human productivity.

4. Firms are expanding access to their computers to customers and other organizations. Adding terminals in the field creates more users and more demands for service. The kinds of systems that interconnect with suppliers and customers generally involve a large number of new users. Hardware and software are needed to provide adequate computing; poor response times and systems that do not work are a great disaster if their impact falls on customers.

Staff Needs. Most of the staff required for operations is determined by current hardware. The applications scheduled for development during the next year also set requirements for systems analysts and programmers. Typically, 50 percent of the programming staff is tied up with maintenance and enhancements (mostly enhancements). Only 10 percent of the total computer department may be working on new applications. If major new systems are to be developed, it is necessary to plan for increases in staff. One cannot hire five or ten analysts and programmers and make them instantly productive.

Charging. One method for controlling the use of computers is to charge user departments for computing services. If users can control charges, this approach can be helpful in rationing computer use. However, if the user has no control over charges (for example, if there is a lot of overhead that continues regardless of usage levels), charging the user will be seen only as a nuisance, and spending money to compute charges will be seen as wasteful.

	Jan	Feb	March	April	May
Average response time (seconds)	5.1	6.2	4.8	4.9	5.0
Maximum average response time (seconds)	10.1	8.6	12.2	9.8	9.9
% on-line system available prime shift	98.0	97.5	98.1	98.2	97.3
No. of transactions processed per day (000)	75.0	80.0	76.0	82.0	79.0
Time spent on maintenance and enhancements (person months)	3.1	4.5	5.1	6.0	5.5
Backlog of maintenance (person months)	10.0	15.2	11.0	7	5.0
Development projects % on schedule by person months	75.0	60.0	70.0	73	76.0
Systems completed and accepted by users	2.0	0	1.0	0	2.0

Last user satisfaction questionnaire	**April**	5.6 out of 7 possible
	November (last year)	5.4

Figure 20-6. Report Card for Computer Department. Historically managers have had trouble evaluating the performance of a computer department. The measures above are one suggestion for what criteria are meaningful.

Charging to overhead encourages people to use the computer. This strategy is recommended when a firm is trying to increase use and when management feels that greater integration of the computer into the firm will be a benefit beyond the cost.

Control. One way to control an operation is to compare plans with actual performance. Plans should cover three to five years, and an annual review will allow management to evaluate whether the computer department is likely to achieve the goals set forth in the plan.

The review needs to go beyond the goals of the plan, however. Management should also look at user-oriented performance measures, such as the percentage of uptime (availability for use) on the computer for each shift, the distribution of downtime (time out of service) and its duration, and the computer's response-time distribution by shift. For ex-

ample, for different hours during the day, the average response time can be plotted from when a user hits a key on a keyboard to when the computer responds. These figures should be collected monthly by the computer department, which should publish them for users and managers (see Figure 20-6).

We also advocate using satisfaction questionnaires to assess users' perceptions of the quality of information-processing service. Such an instrument should be developed outside the computer department. Management then administers the questionnaire approximately twice a year to see how the users evaluate information processing (see Figure 20-7).

The last kind of control is project monitoring. Management will want to know for each development project whether it was completed on time and within budget, and whether it meets the original specifications.

MIS EVALUATION

Please complete the following questions by filling in the requested information or circling the appropriate answer. Questions 1–8 in this section are followed by a line with seven numbers on it. Please circle the number which best indicates how you feel about the question being asked. For example, if the question were

How hot is it today?

Cold 1 2 3 4 ⑤ 6 7 Hot

If you thought it was moderately warm, you might circle 5.

1. How important is the use of the computer to your job?

Not important 1 2 3 4 5 6 7 Extremely important

2. Please evaluate the input for your computer system(s) on the following criteria:

Ease of entry	Poor	1 2 3 4 5 6 7	Good
Quality of edits	Poor	1 2 3 4 5 6 7	Good
Accuracy of processing	Poor	1 2 3 4 5 6 7	Good

3. Please evaluate the output reports you receive from the computer on the following criteria:

Quality	Poor	1 2 3 4 5 6 7	Good
Accuracy	Poor	1 2 3 4 5 6 7	Good
Timeliness	Poor	1 2 3 4 5 6 7	Good
Usefulness	Poor	1 2 3 4 5 6 7	Good

4. How much use do you make of reports from the computer:

Little use 1 2 3 4 5 6 7 Much use

5. For the computer applications that you use (or of which you have knowledge), please evaluate their characteristics as follows:

Application (Transactions)	Extent of use	Quality of Application	Overall satisfaction (design, operation)
Order processing	Lo 1 2 3 4 5 6 7 Hi	Lo 1 2 3 4 5 6 7 Hi	Lo 1 2 3 4 5 6 7 Hi
etc.	Lo 1 2 3 4 5 6 7 Hi	Lo 1 2 3 4 5 6 7 Hi	Lo 1 2 3 4 5 6 7 Hi

6. To what extent have you been able to influence decisions about:

—Modifications to current systems:

No influence 1 2 3 4 5 6 7 Extensive influence

Figure 20-7. User Satisfaction Questionnaire. It is also important to learn how users subjectively evaluate computer services. This questionnaire is one way to obtain data on user satisfaction. (Figure continues on next page.)

—The design of new systems:

No influence   <u>1 2 3 4 5 6 7</u>   Extensive influence

7. To what extent does company management

    —support greater computer use

Little or no support   <u>1 2 3 4 5 6 7</u>   Extensive support

    —make use of your recommendations for improvements to existing systems?

Little or no use   <u>1 2 3 4 5 6 7</u>   Extensive use

    —encourage you to spend time helping design, test and install new computer applications

Little or no encouragement   <u>1 2 3 4 5 6 7</u>   Extensive encouragement

8. What is your opinion of the MIS staff:

Uninterested in the user	<u>1 2 3 4 5 6 7</u>	Interested in the user
Not too competent technically	<u>1 2 3 4 5 6 7</u>	Very competent technically
Not good in dealing with people	<u>1 2 3 4 5 6 7</u>	Very good in dealing with people
Do low quality work	<u>1 2 3 4 5 6 7</u>	Do high quality work
Design for benefit of the computer	<u>1 2 3 4 5 6 7</u>	Design for benefit of the user
Do not appreciate my knowledge of my job	<u>1 2 3 4 5 6 7</u>	Appreciate my knowledge of my job
Do not appreciate my problems	<u>1 2 3 4 5 6 7</u>	Appreciate my problems

Figure 20-7 (continued).

It is important for management to take action if processing is not in control. This action may involve changing work responsibilities, adding resources (including new staff), or changing objectives so that they are more feasible, given present resources.

Management Committees

A number of firms have formed management committees to help control information processing. One electronics manufacturer has a series of local steering committees. The purpose of these committees is to define the information-processing needs and priorities of each local division. As an example, the local committee might look at the major systems requested for its division and decide on which systems are the most important; these systems should be developed first.

An executive steering committee for the firm includes the chief operating officer of the company and the division heads. This committee reviews all projects and decides what resources are to be allocated to each. In addition, this committee has the responsibility for suggesting applications that cut across all divisions and are of corporate importance. An example would be a recent decision to place terminals in the offices of major customers to make it easier for these customers to place orders with the firm. Although it is a sales and order-entry function, this application has strategic consequences for the whole company.

In order to handle the maintenance requests that are of continuing annoyance to users, the company has a maintenance committee. The executive steering committee and the management of the computer department decide how many staff members to devote to maintenance and enhancements for the existing systems. The local committee reviews requests and determines which ones will be worked on each month.

There are disputes, and there never seem to be enough resources to go around, but the committee structure does seem to help. There has been much better management of information processing in the firm since the formation of the committees. They provide an opportunity for the users to be heard and to participate in the planning process. The committees also make clear the limitations on computer resources and the relative importance of each user's requests compared with the projects requested by other users.

Managerial Activities

The framework that has just been discussed is a conceptual approach to management. Given the activities described earlier, what does a manager do specifically to control information processing?

As a leader, the manager should

1. Think creatively about how to use information processing to gain a competitive edge.
2. See to it that there is a plan for information processing.
3. Create an executive steering committee to plan and evaluate information processing, to choose applications areas, and to set priorities.
4. Set objectives for the computer department and for specific systems.
5. Develop a conceptual understanding of how each system works.
6. Participate in the evaluation of the computer department each year.
7. See that others devote time to information processing.

As a figurehead, the manager can

1. Participate in systems analysis and design and review the logic of systems.
2. Be knowledgeable about the information-processing plan.

3. Be able to state the goals of information processing and the scenario for how information will be processed three years from now.

As a *decision maker,* the manager should

1. Decide on new applications areas.
2. Allocate resources to develop systems.
3. Help negotiate trade-offs among system features.

As a project manager, the manager should

1. Keep track of overall progress on projects.
2. Decide if more resources or external help is needed.
3. Encourage the use of modern techniques like packages and generators.

SUMMARY

Information processing can be managed. Organizations get the kind of computing that they deserve. Users and managers alike have responsibilities, and only if they and the computer staff do their jobs will information processing succeed. The management of computing is similar to any other management task; managers must learn enough to understand the phenomenon and to mange it as they do any other part of the business.

Review of Chapter 20

REVIEW

It is not enough for an organization to hire competent programmers and analysts or to provide the newest and most advanced computer equipment. Successful computing demands management leadership and support. This chapter has described appropriate action for managers and users.

In systems analysis and design, it is up to the user to see that a satisfactory design is produced. The user is the one who works with the system after its completion. The professional systems analyst can guide design efforts and delineate the alternatives for users. However, it is up to the users to decide what processing alternatives to pursue.

Managers play a key role in the development of a system. They must make decisions that involve company policies. For example, it is a management decision to change the way in which parts are classified in inventory or to change the firm's sales-forecasting techniques. Managers also need to understand the high-level logic of processing, particularly for systems that affect their areas of responsibility.

One way to control information processing in the organization is through a plan. The plan makes the goals of the computer department explicit and indicates what can be accomplished with a given level of resources. The decisions that arise can then be tied to the plan. For example, if our plan is to work toward a computer network, then the personal computers that we purchase should have compatible hardware and software. The plan is also a document for evaluating the computer department: Are objectives being achieved? Are projects completed on time and within budget? Are operations adequate?

The firms that take the time to manage and evaluate information processing and to take action if improvements are needed will be the leaders in the coming years. More and more, the firms that succeed are learning how to apply information-processing technology creatively to gain a competitive edge. The potential is tremendous; what is needed are creativity, new ideas, and a good dose of management leadership.

KEY WORDS

Applications	Control
Charging	Decision maker

End user	Plan
Equipment needs	Policy
Invisible technology	Project management
Leader	Review meetings
Objectives	Staff needs
Operations	Systems analysis and design

BUSINESS PROBLEMS

20.1. ABC Corporation has had a long history of poor computer service and conflict between the users and the computer department. Whenever business is off, the first suggestion is to cut the computer department budget. The manager of this department feels that such cuts are shortsighted: "If we lay off analysts and programmers, we reduce costs, but what about a year from now, when business turns around and everyone wants the systems we should be working on now?"

Management, however, feels that it is necessary to share the pain of cutbacks when they have to occur. The chief operating officer said, "Last year I had to lay off fourteen hundred employees. How can we treat the computer area any differently?"

One answer might be not to lay off programmers and analysts. The other options would be to lay off computer operators and data entry clerks. Is this a viable solution?

Now, just as predicted, business has improved, and users want systems that are not ready. Also, as ABC is in an unattractive area, it is not easy to re-hire programmers and analysts.

"No matter what happens, we always seem to end up losers," moans the computer department manager.

What policy can you recommend to management to get out of this dilemma? It is likely that there will be business downturns in the future. How should the company respond?

20.2 Let us continue with the example of ABC Company. Computer policy is almost nonexistent. The senior management of the firm spends very little time with the computer staff. There is a general feeling that the firm spends too much on computers and gets too little.

There are no plans for information systems beyond a one-year budget, and the most recent annual budget was not approved until almost the end of the first quarter. There are frequent delays in projects, and managers are very angry because they do not have the systems they need.

On the other hand, many emergency jobs come up. Given finite resources, the computer department manager has to delay an existing project to assign resources to the emergency jobs, particularly when they come from the most senior managers in the firm.

Do you have some suggestions for how ABC might manage information processing better? What can you recommend to senior management and to the manager of the computer department? What will your solution cost? How can it be implemented?

REVIEW QUESTIONS

1. Why do you think managers are often fearful of information processing?
2. What steps can be taken to help managers conquer their fears of computing?
3. What is the role of the end user in managing information processing?
4. What does a user need to know to use a microcomputer in the organization?
5. What must a user know to connect to a computer network?
6. What should a user know about using a mainframe?
7. Why do users have to understand the structure of corporate databases?
8. What should users do at the inception and feasibility stages?
9. What is the role of the user in analysis and design? In developing specifications?
10. How does a user contribute to programming and testing?
11. What do users contribute to training and installation?
12. What is the role of management in selecting alternatives for an application?
13. Describe what is in a typical plan for information processing.
14. How does a long-range plan function as a control tool?
15. Why is a complete list needed of the high-priority applications in a plan?

16. How are equipment needs determined?
17. How is a plan used to determine staff needs?
18. Under what conditions should computing be charged to overhead?
19. Describe various measures for evaluating the computer department.
20. List the various managerial activities that contribute to controlling information processing.

THOUGHT QUESTIONS

21. Why should maintenance be reduced if users are involved in the design of systems?
22. Why are systems designed to be used for such a long period of time?
23. How do managers contribute to user design?
24. Why do managers need to understand the high-level logic of an application?
25. Why do managers have to set the policy objectives for a system?
26. How can the reward structure influence users?
27. Why might a firm have different structures for computing and for the rest of the organization?

28. Why does more computing power always seem to be needed?
29. What is the single most important advice you would give a manager on controlling computing?
30. Why do so many firms fail to plan for information systems?

RECOMMENDED READINGS

Lucas, H. C., Jr. *Coping with Computers*. New York: Free Press, 1982. A book addressed to senior management and stressing their active role in controlling information processing.

Mintzberg, H. *On the Nature of Managerial Work*. New York: Harper & Row, 1973. A classic book describing the activities of and the different roles played by managers.

Nolan, R. "Managing Information Systems by Committee," *Harvard Business Review* (July–August 1982), pp. 72–79. A good article on how a firm can use senior management committees to control information systems.

Chapter 21

Questions of how computers are used to help individuals or how they can be used to harass citizens may seem remote; the stories are only about other people. Yet, the widespread use of computers means that we all may encounter some of the issues raised in this chapter.

First, we shall review some of the ways computers are being used to help individuals with special problems. There is promising research going on that will aid individuals who are paralyzed. Several projects are trying to use computer chips and electronics to restore functioning to limbs that a paraplegic can no longer control. In one instance, a quadriplegic is able to communicate with a microcomputer via voice; the micro provides its owner with a variety of services.

In addition to these positive uses for computers, a number of issues have arisen about how computers are being applied. One major issue is security and the prevention of unauthorized access to computers. Fears have also been raised about the reliability of computer systems in nuclear defense. Labor leaders are concerned about possible technological unemployment, particularly because of computer-controlled robots. We should all be interested in privacy and how it is affected by computer systems. These and similar issues are important for you to understand because you will have influence over how computers are used.

After reading this chapter, you should be able to:

- Identify applications of computers to help the disabled.
- Discuss how computers affect U.S. and USSR defense policies.
- Describe the implications of computer-based systems for privacy.
- Explain how to design safeguards into computer systems.
- Describe why security is an important consideration.

THE COMPUTER,
THE CITIZEN, AND SOCIETY

Figure 21-1. An Electronic Walker for Paraplegics.

INTRODUCTION

Computers are becoming increasingly pervasive in society. All of us are affected by these machines in our daily lives, both at work and at leisure. There are many ways in which computers improve living conditions and the economy. However there are also very important issues that a concerned citizen needs to consider about computers.

The solutions to some of the problems described in this chapter rest with systems analysis and design. We must think of the implications of applications when they are in design and ask penetrating questions about how the application can be misused. The designers of some systems need to question whether the whole premise of the application is sound. Individuals design systems, and they must take the responsibility for how the systems are used.

SOME USEFUL APPLICATIONS

A variety of computer equipment is being used to help people directly, particularly individuals who are handicapped. The computers used for these devices fit more into the category of process control than information systems applications. Instead of providing information in the form of a report or a response to a database query, these computers examine input signals and send an output to control an electrical or mechanical device. The application is similar to the use of a computer in a factory to control some production process; hence, the name *process control*.

Paralysis

Researchers at Case Western Reserve University have developed an electronic walker for paraplegics (see Figure 21-1). An engineer whose spine was

Figure 21-2. A student demonstrates the outdoor tricycle being developed at Wright State University. The tricycle uses a computerized electrical stimulation-feedback system to stimulate paralyzed muscles to pedal the tricycle.

shattered by a stray bullet demonstrated the walker at a recent medical conference. The engineer pressed a switch on the walker, which sent a series of electrical pulses from electrodes inserted into his leg muscles. A computer strapped to the engineer's waist controls the timing and the voltage of the signals. The signals cause first one leg and then the other to step forward.

Other researchers are working on ways to aid quadriplegics. By pushing a shoulder against switches in a shoulder harness, the patient can direct his or her hand to perform multiple grasping functions.

A group in Illinois has taken a different approach. Signals are generated by a patient's own muscles; no one has to press a switch. The patient has external *electrode sensors* on the upper part of the body and external electrode stimulators on the legs. These electrodes connect to a computer with a pro-

gram capable of recognizing various postures of the upper body. Given the posture, the computer signals appropriate responses for the lower body. One posture signals the computer to generate standing instructions, whereas another generates walking commands. The system is particularly effective because it recognizes postures and signals appropriate motions; as a result, there is less chance that the user will signal commands that will cause a fall.

At Wright State University , a research group has developed a tricycle for paraplegics (shown in Figure 21-2). The rider's paralyzed gluteus maximus and quadriceps muscles propel the vehicle at up to eight miles an hour. Computer-controlled electrical stimulation causes the muscles to respond. A sensor on the pedals keeps track of their position, and a sensor linked to the throttle on the handles instructs the computer to change the stimulation of the rider's muscles.

One of the most interesting systems was developed by a man for his brother, who at the age of seventeen became a quadriplegic in an automobile accident. The injured boy's brother built a remarkable patchwork of electronic parts, including an Apple II Plus microcomputer called "Hal" after the talking computer in the film *2001: A Space Odyssey*. By bothering various manufacturers, the pair of brothers was able to assemble $60,000 worth of free components.

The patient, Rob, is able to speak to the computer and command it by voice. For example, he might say, "Satellite search."

The computer's voice synthesizer responds, "What satellite do you want?"

Rob replies, "Satcom F3R."

Hal responds, "Yes, master."

Then Hal sends commands to a 13-foot parabolic dish antenna outside the house; it moves until focused on a communications satellite orbiting at 22,300 miles above the equator.

Hal asks, "What transponder do you want?"

Rob responds, "Atlanta."

The TV at the foot of the bed then comes on with a news broadcast from the all-news Atlanta station WTBS via the satellite.

Rob can search through satellite transponders and pick any of 150 TV channels. He can dial the phone, adjust the angle of his bed, dictate letters, play video games, and write computer programs on the Carnegie-Mellon University computer network. He can even take college courses using the satellite.

Artificial Limbs

An MIT team has developed a control system for a prosthetic leg so that it can echo the movement of a real leg after an appropriate time lag. Sensors on the wearer's real leg and the artificial leg feed information on their positions to a microcomputer. The micro, in turn, controls the motors of the artificial leg based on a mathematical model. The artificial leg is programmed to follow the steps of the real leg just as a natural leg would in walking.

A specialist in Utah uses a microcomputer to program an artificial arm. The arm is designed for amputees who have lost their real arms above the elbow. It has two movements: grasping with an artificial hand and up-and-down motions of the lower arm (see Figure 21-3). Electrical signals from the muscles in the arm stump activate the arm in either a slow or a rapid mode. Computers are expected to help provide the arm with more functions as well.

Other Applications

A doctor in New York has developed an approach to helping patients with spinal disorders like cerebral palsy, dystonia, and epilepsy. The doctor implants four tiny platinum electrodes along the upper spinal cord. These electrodes are, in turn, connected by stainless steel wires to a receiver implanted beneath the patient's skin on one side. It takes four weeks to tune the microcomputer that controls the system while hanging from the patient's belt.

A woman with dystonia musculorum deformans was confined to a wheelchair with no control over her bodily functions. After treatment, all catheters are gone, and she is able to walk without braces.

Another doctor, at Massachusetts General Hospital in Boston, has written a program that models the human eye. A doctor uses the model to help develop an understanding of a tumor in the eye; the program creates a graphic representation of the eye and the tumor. A doctor can determine the best method of attack and the dosage of radiation to use to treat the tumor. The program allows much more accurate treatment than before and reduces the risk of vision loss or eye damage because of the tumor. Some 90 percent of the patients treated have experienced successful results.

Computers, sensors, electrodes, and voice recognition and synthesis offer new hope to the handicapped. Some researchers are working to help the blind (see Figure 21-4); others are developing systems to let mutes communicate through eye movement that triggers a computer's voice synthesizer. The work is in its early stages, and there is great optimism that with computer-controlled equipment, many people with handicaps will be able to live relatively normal lives.

The applications that have been described are in

Figure 21-3. A Seattle victim of a powerline accident that claimed both arms and shoulders tries out his new electronic limbs, activated by motion sensors and electrical signals from the skin, at the University of Utah Center for Biomedical Design.

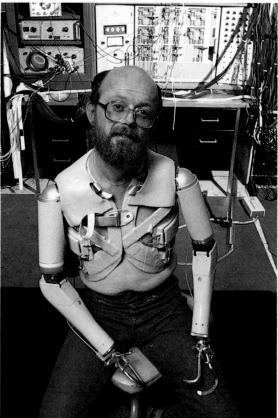

Figure 21-4. A blind person using a braille computer equipped with a braille-coded keyboard.

Figure 21-5. (a) Lifeline system is explained to an elderly person who wears the Lifeline system button, which alerts a nearby hospital in case of emergency, via the Lifeline call-in device under the patient's telephone. (b) A nurse in an emergency room can call the patient, a neighbor, or an ambulance when the Lifeline system alerts her to a problem.

the research-and-development stage. One very helpful system is available today: a home alert system. Some forty-two thousand people make use of the Lifeline Systems Inc. home medical-alert system (see Figure 21-5). This company sells a system to a hospital or some other health-care facility. Each customer who is at home has a two-inch-square transmitter that is attached either to a wristband or to a pendant worn around the neck.

If the customer, typically an elderly individual living alone, presses the button on the transmitter, the

device activates a home communicator attached to the phone. The communicator automatically dials the hospital. At the health-care facility, a computer sounds an alarm and flashes a number on the screen.

An attendant uses the number to retrieve the patient's card, which gives name and address. Then the attendant calls the patient to check for a false alarm. If there is no answer, an ambulance or a nearby friend is sent to check on the customer. The system also has a timer that can be set to automatically summon aid in twelve or twenty-four hours if it

Figure 21-6. Michael Patrick, who broke into Defense Department and other government computers from his microcomputer in his Wisconsin home, gives testimony to a legislative committee.

is not reset. This feature is a guard against the patient's falling or becoming unconscious without having a chance to press the call button.

The system helps people at medical risk to live at home instead of in the hospital. The customer is in familiar surroundings, and the costs are many times lower. (Typically the health-care facility charges $10 to $15 per month for the service.)

ISSUES FOR CONCERN

Computers are helping people in many different ways. The previous discussion focused on computers that are being used to improve health care. Other computers help doctors to see what is inside a patient's body through various types of scanners.

Computers also help companies and other organizations operate more efficiently. Think of how different air travel would be without computerized passenger-name reservations systems. How would we be able to carry on commerce at today's level of

transaction volume without bank and credit-card-company computers?

However, as with any technology, there are problems associated with computers. A citizen needs to be aware of the issues surrounding computers and to think about solutions to some very serious problems.

Security

Recently, a number of instances have been reported of unauthorized access to computers (see Figure 21-6). For example, a group of high-school students in Milwaukee used a national telecommunications network to access several computers around the United States. One of the computers contained patient radiation dosages at a major cancer hospital. Fortunately, the penetration was obvious, but imagine the life-threatening consequences of unknowingly altering a radiation dosage so that the patient is exposed to the wrong amount. The students did not intend to cause damage but could easily have done so.

Figure 21-7. Pershing Missiles on Their Way to Installation in West Germany.

Nuclear Defense

In the first chapter, we described control failures in the U.S. missile-alert system; because of a combination of human and technical factors, the computers have issued at least two false alerts.

U.S. defense policy has been to place nuclear missiles closer and closer to the Soviet Union, thus reducing the amount of time that the Russians would have for warning. That is, from the Russian perspective, there would be only about fifteen to twenty minutes from a missile launch in Western Europe to the explosion of a nuclear weapon somewhere in the Soviet Union. Some Russian targets are within six minutes of the Pershing missiles placed in Germany (see Figure 21-7).

Will this kind of strategy force the Soviets into what is called a *launch-on-warning policy?* **Launch-on-warning** means that instead of relying on human evaluation, computers decide that an attack by the United States is real and launch a Russian counterattack automatically. Launch-on-warning might be adopted by a country if its leaders fear that there will not be enough time after a warning of a launch of enemy missiles to evaluate the situation and to decide whether the warning is real (see Figure 21-8).

A group of concerned computer scientists is trying to educate legislators and the public about the danger of overreliance on computers in nuclear defense. Early-warning systems cannot be tested totally; designers cannot forecast all modes of potential system failures.

Communications systems for military command and control also rely heavily on computers. However, these communications networks might be rendered ineffective by a nuclear explosion, so that it would be very difficult, if not impossible, to stop a nuclear exchange before it became an all-out war. Thermonuclear explosions are known to cause electromagnetic pulses (EMP), which would send tens

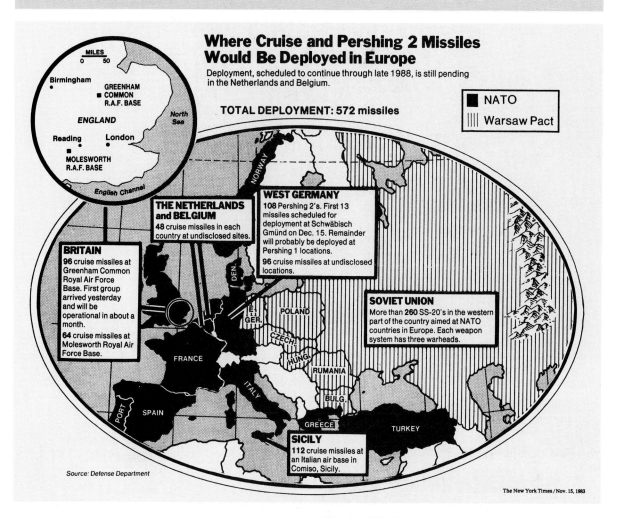

Figure 21-8. Planned Development Locations for Cruise and Pershing Missiles in Europe.

of thousands of volts through power lines; computers and other communications equipment that were not fully protected would be damaged or destroyed. Yet, it is impossible to test approaches for hardening communications completely because treaties ban the nuclear explosions that would be required for a test.

Many of us feel that launch-on-warning is very dangerous because computers and their sensors may not provide an infallible warning; there can be false alarms.

Dependence on computer and communications systems to send orders to nuclear defense forces might make it impossible to keep control of the situation in case of accident or a terrorist explosion of a nuclear device. The United States is far ahead of Russia in computer technology (Figure 21-9 shows how Russia is trying to obtain U.S. computers). If U.S. systems have failed on occasion, can we rely on Russian computers not to make a mistake and launch a nuclear counterattack when there really was no U.S. attack on Russia?

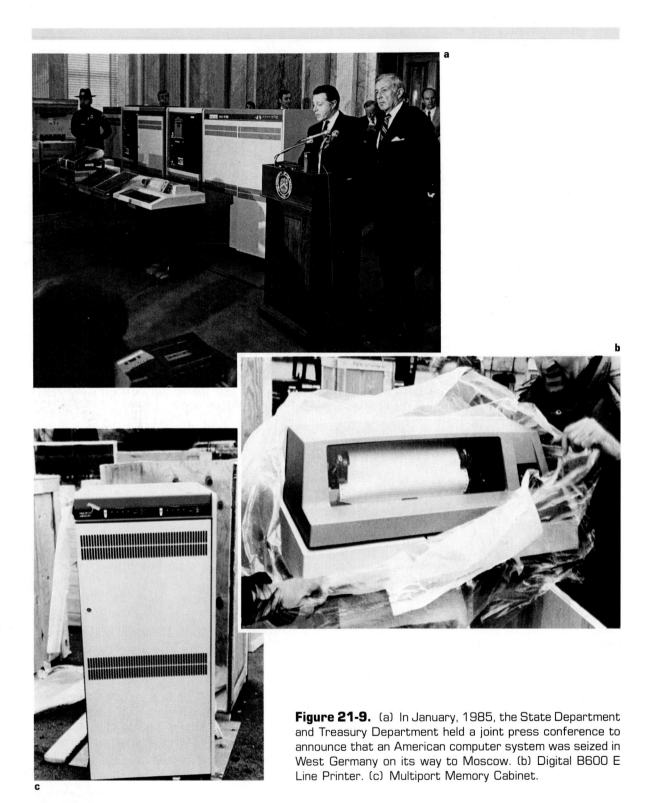

Figure 21-9. (a) In January, 1985, the State Department and Treasury Department held a joint press conference to announce that an American computer system was seized in West Germany on its way to Moscow. (b) Digital B600 E Line Printer. (c) Multiport Memory Cabinet.

Figure 21-10. An Instructional Robot in Kit Form.

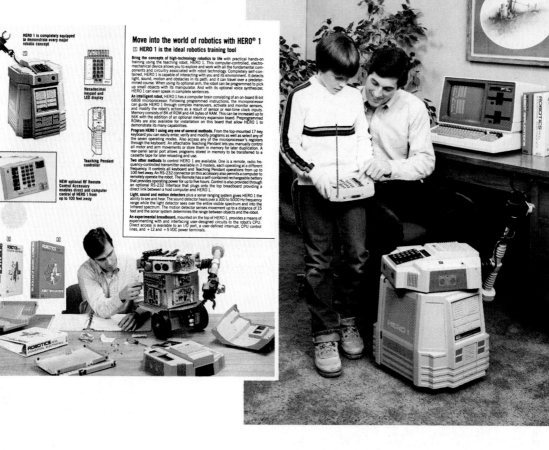

Automation and Unemployment

Computers are being used extensively in robotic devices. Figure 21-10 shows an example of a simple instructional robot. This robot, available as a kit, is designed for teaching students about robotics. The robot can move its arm and a gripper hand; it can also move around a room.

The user can program it or use a control mode in which the robot remembers a sequence of actions and then repeats them. The robot has a sonar sensor for sound and a speech synthesizer so that it can talk. Although relatively modest in strength and durability, the device does demonstrate many of the possible features of a robot.

Factories are employing **robots** extensively, often for jobs that humans do not like to do or that are hazardous.

For example, robots are very good for spray painting because they do not breathe paint. They are also used extensively for spot welding in automobile assembly (see Figure 21-11).

There is, however, an ominous side to robotics: the question of **unemployment.** Some experts have estimated that millions of operative jobs in factories will be taken over by robots. The implications for unemployment are not at all clear. Estimates have been made that blue-collar work will be divided into low- and high-skilled with no middle ground. If this happens, opportunities for advancement will be

Figure 21-11. Chrysler Corporation manufactures its Voyager mini-van using welding robots.

Figure 21-12. The aircraft engine parts plant, opened in 1983 in Bromont, Quebec, features GE technology, including this new Optomation II BinVision system. Consisting of seven GE robots, orchestrated by a programmable controller, the system automatically selects randomly positioned parts and processes the slugs from which airfoils are made.

limited. Early robots have taken jobs that many people do not want; more recent robots and those in the future will have more logic and dexterity, and they will thus be more competitive with human labor (see Figure 21-12).

What will the net impact be? The long-term trends show a decline in the number of workers in manufacturing. Even now, only about 20 percent of the work force is employed in this sector. Robots will further reduce this total, but will other sectors of the economy expand to offset the loss of manufacturing jobs? Employment forecasts for the future emphasize an expansion in service jobs and many unskilled positions, such as in the fast-food industry. There will also be a need for robot designers, programmers, and service personnel.

Regardless of long-term equilibrium, the economy will have to cope with short-term displacement as robots assume existing jobs. It is a national issue whether these displaced workers will end up on welfare or be **retrained** to continue as productive members of the economy.

Privacy

There is much concern over the privacy of the individual in American society. What is privacy? The term means many things to different people. For most of us, it means the right to be left alone and to determine ourselves what facts others will know about us. How, then, do computers affect privacy?

In 1974, Congress passed a law regulating federal data banks. This law gives people the right to see their own records in federal data banks, except for classified and law-enforcement files. One can object to errors and go to court if the errors are not acknowledged and corrected.

There is much information stored about individuals. It might be embarrassing for a bank to send one's employer all of the financial data on one's mortgage application. Such a use of data would be an invasion of privacy.

Similarly, there are many mailing lists that contain names and addresses. Companies buy and sell these lists routinely for use in phone and mail solicitations. One company used a list of 63 million licensed drivers to select the names and addresses of women 21 to 40 years old, under 5 feet 3 inches tall, and weighing less than 120 pounds. The company sells clothing and wanted a list of these women for promoting its petite line.

Targeting Systems is an Arlington, Virginia, firm that has ranked the individuals living in each of the nation's 240,000 census tracts on socioeconomic variables. There are forty classes. If a majority of those living in a census tract are, say, educated and affluent, the tract would be put into either Cluster 5 (furs and station wagons) or Cluster B (money and brains). For one customer that wanted to lobby Congress, the firm recommended different letters for four major groups. Two waves of letters were sent to half a million Americans, and telephone calls reached 60 percent of them. Half of those phoned offered to help in some way.

There is now a robot caller that will phone a series of numbers, play a recorded message, and wait to record the response. Forty-two companies now offer automatic phoning services in the United States. Are this device and the widespread use and sharing of mailing lists an invasion of privacy? Should our privacy be protected through legislation?

There have been proposals for large national data banks. One of these would contain a great many law-enforcement data, such as criminal records. Although there might be some benefits in having criminal information available, what are the costs? There are many opportunities for improper access to these records, for example, by a police officer who is an off-duty insurance investigator. One study of a sample of records showed an alarming number of inaccuracies, especially in criminal arrest dispositions. (See the tables in Figure 21-13.) Would not inaccurate data increase the threat to individuals from a national system?

Computer Matching

The government has used computer matching to find evidence of possible wrongdoing. In this kind of investigation, a file of individuals is compared with another file so that it can be determined whether someone has a record on both. As an example, the

DATA QUALITY OF FBI CRIMINAL HISTORY SYSTEMS NCIC-CCH AND IDENTIFICATION DIVISION CRIMINAL HISTORY RECORDS

	NCIC-CCH	Identification Division Criminal History Records
Arrests in sample	400	400
Positive Verification	256	235
Response rate	64.0%	58.5%
Arrests not verifiable because:		
pending or sealed	6	19
no record locatable*	54	37
no prosecution of arrest	10	7
fugitive	1	1
no arrest data	24	
	95(37.1%)	64(27.2%)
Total arrest cases verified	161	171
Characteristics of verified arrest case:		
No disposition reported	27.9%(45)	40.9%(70)
Incomplete record	.6%(1)	2.3%(4)
Inaccurate record	16.8%(27)	10.5%(18)
Ambiguous record	2.5%(4)	6.4%(11)
Combined problems	6.2%(10)	14.1%(24)
Complete, accurate, and unambiguous	45.9%(74)	25.7%(44)
Total	100.0%(161)	100.0%(171)

NOTES:

*in situations of "no record locatable" this generally reflected a police disposition of the arrest, e.g., person was released prior to presenting to a district attorney. This was removed from further analysis even though it might have been included as a "no disposition recorded"; hence, estimates of record characteristics are conservative.

1. If *no disposition* was reported ("record blank") the data analysis exempted the record from further consideration even though it might have other problems of accuracy and ambiguity. Estimates of these features are therefore conservative.
2. A record was *incomplete* if it failed to record conviction or correctional data.
3. A record was *inaccurate* if it incorrectly reflected the court records of disposition, charges, or sentence.
4. A record was *ambiguous* if it indicated more charges than dispositions but did not specify charges of conviction *or* if a record indicated more dispositions than charges *or* if for a number of reasons the record was not interpretable (see text).
5. A record had *combined problems* if it indicated more than one of the four logically possible permutations of incompleteness, inaccuracy, or ambiguity.

Figure 21-13. Audit Results of Quality of Criminal History Data at the Federal and State Levels. The data above suggest serious problems with data integrity and accuracy. They may be indicative of a faulty systems design. Why do you think more attention has been on examining the system than on fixing it? Source: K. C. Laudon, "Data Quality and Due Process in Large Interorganizational Record Systems," *Communications of the ACM.* (Figure continues on next page.)

CCH RECORD QUALITY IN THREE STATE SYSTEMS

	Western State	Mid-West State	Southern State
Individuals in sample	500	502	498
Total Prior Arrests	2733	985	1345
Total In-County Arrests	2172	739	1002
Arrest Not Verifiable Because:			
case pending	1	3	3
record sealed	0	0	0
docket not locatable	0	47	1
municipal court disp.	8	N/A	0
Total In-County Arrests Verified	2163	689	998
Characteristics of CCH Verified Arrests:			
no disposition reported	915 (42.3%)	107 (15.5%)	390 (39.1%)
incomplete	531 (24.5%)	93 (13.5%)	215 (21.5%)
inaccurate	16 (.7%)	91 (13.2%)	2 (.2%)
ambiguous	57 (2.6%)	22 (3.2%)	32 (3.2%)
combined problems	236 (10.9%)	35 (5.1%)	237 (23.7%)
complete, accurate, and unambiguous	408 (18.9%)	341 (49.4%)	122 (12.2%)
Total	2163 (100%)	689 (100%)	998 (100%)

NOTES:

1. Arrest were verified against local court records only if the arrest occurred within the prosecutional district where the sample of individuals was drawn See Task II for detailed analyses of coding sheets and samples.
2. If *no disposition* was reported on a CCH record ("record blank") the data analysis exempted the record from further consideration even though these records had other problems of incompleteness, inaccuracy, or ambiguity. Hence, estimates of these features of records are conservative.
3. A record was *incomplete* if it failed to record conviction or correctional data.
4. A record was *inaccurate* if it incorrectly reflected the court records of disposition, sentence, or charges.
5. A record was *ambiguous* if it indicated in response to multiple charges a single plea of guilty but did not specify of which charge (more charges than dispositions) *or* if more dispositions were recorded than charges *or* if the record was for a number of reasons not interpretable (see text for explanation).
6. A record had *combined problems* if it reflected one or more of the four logically possible permutations of incompleteness, inaccuracy, or ambiguity.

Figure 21-13 (continued).

government matched employee records of the Civil Service Commission with files of individuals receiving federal Aid to Families with Dependent Children for the purpose of locating fraud. The government has run over two hundred computer matches.

Some citizens are concerned about this use of data. A traditional law-enforcement investigation occurs because there is some evidence that a person is engaged in wrongdoing. In our society, and because there are limited resources, it is generally not possible to make sweeping investigations of thousands of individuals at one time. Also, we have a

Figure 21-14. At a computer camp grade-school children enjoy the fun of camp and learn about computing.

tradition that the government does not investigate individuals who are not suspected of committing a crime. A computer match is directed at an entire class of individuals. It is initiated not because an individual is suspected of misconduct, but because some class of citizens might contain individuals who are violating a law or regulation.

Government officials who defend computer matching feel that it is very useful for locating abuses of various government programs. In the long run, it should save the taxpayers' money. Do you feel that this is a good enough reason for computer matching? As a citizen and a taxpayer, what do you think are the pros and cons?

Errors and Harassment

Why is my credit-card bill wrong? How was I charged for this phone call? Who is putting money in my bank account?

Do computers make errors? If so, where do the errors originate? There are several ways in which things go wrong:

1. The input is in error.
2. The program is in error.
3. The hardware fails.

These error sources are listed in the order of their frequency of occurrence. Maybe the input edits are incomplete or an operator keying information is careless. An edit run can tell that $1 billion is too much to pay for a pencil, but it cannot easily tell that fifteen cents, instead of ten cents, is wrong. Many errors come from data entry or incorrect data submitted for entry.

Programs are also impossible to test completely; all programs are likely to have remaining "bugs" or errors. Some new combinations of data can cause a program to execute instructions in a different way

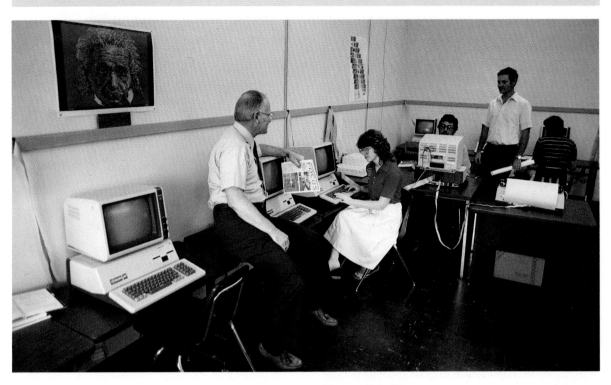

Figure 21-15. College Personal Computer Lab at the University of New Hampshire at Durham, a Part of the Computer Science Department.

from ever before, and instructions that are wrong cause an error in processing.

Occasionally, hardware fails, but rarely does the failure generate a processing error. There are a lot of checks built into the computer, and usually, although not always, a hardware fault is obvious. Processing stops until the computer is repaired.

The difficulty of having an error fixed is usually a function of the manual procedures that surround the computer system. The designer includes inputs to correct errors, but you must convince someone that the error exists, and that person must initiate a correction.

Often, it seems that an excessive number of approvals are required, and much time passes before things are corrected to your satisfaction. The problem here is usually with procedures and management more than with the computer system.

Education

All levels of schools are embracing computer education and *computer literacy.* Figure 21-14 shows microcomputers in use in a summer camp, and Figure 21-15 shows a college personal-computer laboratory. How are people who completed formal education years ago, before computers, to cope with the technology? What will happen to students in poor school districts that cannot afford computers and instructors? Some experts and politicians fear that a lack of knowledge about computers will force people into an economically and educationally underprivileged class.

Although some of these fears are probably extreme, there is great inconsistency in computer education. Because these machines will affect all aspects of our lives in the future, literacy in computing will be as important as literacy in written language and mathematics.

Crime

We discussed two examples of computer crime in the first chapter: the Federal Reserve employee's attempted theft of data and the Equity Funding fraud. There have been many other examples of crime involving computers.

What can be done to prevent crime? Normally, a firm's auditors will look at the potential for the fraudulent use of a computer system. There will probably always be crime. Do computers make it easier or harder?

It is probably easier for those who work with computers to cover their actions and to take large amounts of money. Using computers, banks routinely process billions of dollars a day in payments. A small percentage of this total would still be a large sum.

To counter these threats, designers will continue to build security and control measures into their applications. There will be more encrypting, or coding, of the data transmitted over communications lines. However, with the tendency toward on-line systems and providing access to a firm's computers to its suppliers and customers, it will be difficult to stay ahead of computer criminals.

Complexity

Many lists of policy issues concerning computers would contain the topics already discussed. However, experts frequently fail to include the issue of complexity. Computer systems are incredibly complex and are getting more so every day. Micros are simpler than mainframes, but software and hardware vendors are working to build more features and more complexity into these simple systems. As we find computers of all types in networks, complexity will grow even further.

Will the profession learn how to control this technology? Will we be able to find errors and correct them? How will we be sure that designers and users can cope with this complexity?

An Application

There is one recent application of computers that raises many of the issues discussed in this section of the chapter, the automated-teller machine *(ATM).* You probably have used one of these devices to withdraw money from a bank account. At first, these machines were located near the bank and provided an alternative to waiting in line for a teller.

Soon, banks placed ATMs in a variety of locations to make it easier for their patrons to make deposits and withdrawals. A small room in a shopping center could become a branch bank without the need of any staff.

The next step has been to form networks of ATMs, so that a customer can bank thousands of miles from home. In the space of three years in the early 1980s, the number of shared ATM networks went from 20 to over 150, and the number of ATMs from 10,000 to over 35,000. (One estimate is that there are nearly 50,000 ATMs currently in place.)

The oldest network is one run by American Express to provide traveler's checks. Credit card companies have or will soon have networks, at least one of which will cover thirty states with thirty-five thousand terminals.

What does the network provide? A customer of Chase Manhattan Bank in New York who runs out of money in San Francisco need only find a Bank of America ATM; from it, the customer can make a withdrawal from his or her account in New York. The networks of the two banks are linked together. If a Manufacturers Hanover customer from New York loses everything in Las Vegas, he or she can walk to the hotel lobby and use a networked ATM for a quick transfusion of cash.

What is the future? Some experts think that the networks could become the electronic funds system that has been suggested since the beginning of computing. Electronic Funds Transfer (EFT) would replace many of today's cash transactions. A bank card could become a debit card (a card that will immediately debit your account, unlike a credit card, for which you are billed once a month) used in various retail establishments. With a personal computer or terminal at home, you could handle all of your banking transactions without ever seeing the bank.

What are the issues for concern about ATMs?

The first is crime and security. In some large cities, criminals watch individuals leaving ATM locations and rob them of their withdrawal. There have also been fears that criminals would ascertain a customer's identification number and make withdrawals directly from the customer's account.

With the large number of cash transactions flowing across networks, the possibility exists of individuals' entering false information or tapping into a line and withdrawing huge amounts of money. There are ways to promote security, such as encrypting the data to make tampering more difficult, but these techniques add cost and complexity to the system.

Another social issue is errors and harassment. How do we prove that an error has been made? What are the limits of the bank's liability for an incorrect withdrawal? Finally, if ATMs do become a dominant factor in the payment system, how will customers' privacy be protected? It would theoretically be possible to track a significant portion of an individual's expenditures and travels through information that the network maintains on the place and time of each transaction. ∎

SUMMARY

Computers have tremendous potential for aiding society. As with any powerful technology, there is an opportunity for problems and abuse. The role of a responsible citizen is to stay aware of the issues and to have enough knowledge to influence policy. Many of the questions raised in this chapter can and should be addressed in the design of a system. We can assess the need for security precautions and ask if the information on file could compromise individual privacy. We can also critically examine proposals for national information systems to determine if they are really in the national interest.

Review of Chapter 21

REVIEW

Most of the applications in the text to this point have been oriented toward business. Generally, the systems that we have seen provide information that is used in the operation of the firm or in making decisions. This chapter offers a different view of what can be done with the technology.

In particular, we have examined how computer technology is being used to improve the quality of life for individuals with physical handicaps. Computerized systems may offer some hope to those who are paralyzed and can help to restore functioning to individuals who have lost a limb. Other experiments are using the technology to supplement lost neural functions.

Although such applications are exciting and offer great potential, we also looked at some issues that raise concern. One of these is the question how far U.S. defense policy should rely on computer-based systems. There are serious doubts among computer experts that a launch-on-warning policy for nuclear defense makes sense. We are particularly concerned if such a strategy is adopted by the Soviet Union because it fears insufficient warning time for a response by human decision-makers. Because Russian computer technology lags behind that of the United

States, forcing the USSR to rely on computers for a nuclear response is hazardous at best.

We have also looked at threats to individuals of violations of privacy. Many data banks contain information that is quite useful for the purpose originally intended. However, it turns out that others may have an interest in the data for other uses. If the use is only advertising, it may be an annoyance. On the other hand, some individuals' rights have been violated by the use of a database maintained on a computer.

There is no single solution to these problems. As citizens and as users of computer technology, we must remain vigilant. We must ask penetrating questions when confronted with the proposal for a system and take care in the design process. Awareness and citizen input are the best weapons against computer abuse.

KEY WORDS

Artificial limb	Computer match
ATM	Control
Automation	Crime
Complexity	Education
Computer literacy	Electrode
Errors	Retrain
Harassment	Robots
Launch-on-warning	Security
Medical applications	Sensors
Nuclear defense	Unemployment
Privacy	

BUSINESS PROBLEMS

21.1. As firms grow and computers become more pervasive, there is a desire to connect these devices over communications networks. Because the cost of a private network is very high, only a few organizations are likely to rent satellite transponders and to complete local loops from receivers to their locations in a city.

Most firms use some combination of leased lines and common carriers, for example, a packet-switched network. Recent penetrations of computers from remote locations have been on one of these networks. The organizations involved had good reasons for providing remote access to their computers. However, the damage from unauthorized access could have been considerable.

How can organizations defend themselves against these kinds of threats? Can you think of a series of measures that could be taken by the firm wanting to make access available, but also wanting to maintain security so that only authorized individuals can use its computer or access its data? What is the cost of your solution?

21.2. There have been proposals for many large national information systems. Some of these systems exist, and there are exceedingly large numbers of individuals who can access their data. The Internal Revenue Service is computerizing rapidly. There are proposals for keeping computerized criminal records centrally in Washington under the control of the FBI.

Studies have shown that there is widespread access to these systems and that unauthorized use is probably fairly easy. One study also showed that many of the criminal data are incomplete, misleading, or inaccurate.

There is a need for efficiency in government, and computers can do a great deal to control costs and to provide better service. On the other hand, some political scientists have claimed that a computer is the biggest blessing possible for a dictatorship, particularly one that wishes to rigidly control the population.

How would a computer assist a dictatorial government? What safeguards can be put in place to make that scenario less likely to occur? What actions in particular are appropriate in the United States?

REVIEW QUESTIONS

1. Sketch a system that would aid a paraplegic in walking.
2. How does the tricycle for paraplegics work?
3. Explain why a program that recognizes a person's upper-body posture aids in walking.
4. What is the role of electrodes and sensors in systems that aid the handicapped?
5. What is the key part of the system that Rob uses in place of his arms and legs?
6. How does the MIT artificial limb work?
7. What is a launch-on-warning policy?
8. What is the reason for most errors in systems?
9. Why can it take so long to have an error corrected?
10. Why is it not possible for programmed routines to catch all input errors?
11. Is it likely that hardware will cause a system error?

12. How does a citizen contribute to the solution of social problems concerning computers?

THOUGHT QUESTIONS

13. What kind of a computer system might aid the blind?
14. Name two ways to make a computer system more secure.
15. How do you think the Milwaukee gang penetrated so many systems?
16. How do missiles located close to an unfriendly country encourage it to rely more on computers for defense?
17. Can a system ever be completely error-free?
18. How do robots influence factory jobs?
19. Can the economy absorb workers displaced by automation? How?
20. What new jobs does the technology create?
21. What does privacy mean to you?
22. How should firms protect the data that they have about your personal life and finances?
23. Should there be legislation to prevent firms from using various mailing lists?
24. What are the issues in developing a national criminal-information network?
25. Why might arrest disposition information not be posted to computer files?
26. Where should education about computers begin?
27. Is crime easier with a computer?
28. Why are computer systems tempting and vulnerable targets for crime?
29. What is complexity? Why are computer systems complex?

RECOMMENDED READINGS

Laudon, K. "Data Quality and Due Process in Large Inter-Organizational Record Systems," *Communications of the ACM,* forthcoming. A good article containing data on the quality of some federal and state criminal-data systems.

Long, L. *Introduction to Computers and Information Processing.* Englewood Cliffs, NJ: Prentice-Hall, 1984. Contains a good chapter on social issues.

Office of Technology Assessment. "The Impact of Emerging New Computer Technologies on Public Policy," 1981. A good survey of information-processing policy issues.

Chapter 22

Business planners use economic forecasts to establish plans for the coming year. Short-term forecasts of the economy often play a role in a company's prediction of sales and its production scheduling. But what does one do with a technology forecast?

Very few inventions in history have had the impact of the computer. Not only have hardware and software advanced tremendously in a short period of time, but the creative applications of this technology are abundant. If the reader is planning a career that will span the next forty or so years, the only thing certain is that the environment halfway through that career will be substantially different from what it is today.

Looking at what is coming in information-processing technology will help us to prepare for the future. Advances in technology have made possible advances in the application of computers in two major ways.

First, computers are considerably more powerful today than when they were first invented. As computers become more powerful, it is possible to undertake new applica-

tions. An on-line system handling thousands of transactions a day would overwhelm most first-generation computer systems, even if the software existed to support the application. With today's computer, such systems are routine, and tomorrow's technology will make possible even more impressive applications.

The second way in which technological advances impact applications is through cost reductions. The cost (and power) of a second-generation computer precluded dedicating it to a single user. The personal computer that was used for word processing in the writing of this book is as powerful as a mid-range third-generation processor that cost many times more than the micro. As costs drop, marginal applications become feasible and computer applications continue to grow.

This chapter examines some of the trends to be expected in information processing. Hopefully, a glance at what is coming will provide further motivation to keep abreast of information processing. It is not clear that the marketing or financial departments of a

WHAT'S COMING

modern business will necessarily expand in the coming years. We can say with great confidence, however, that information-processing technology and the application of computers to the solution of business problems will continue their explosive growth.

At the completion of this chapter, you should be able to:

- Explain the significant trends in information systems.
- Describe expected advances in hardware and software.
- Discuss coming storage devices and approaches to input and output.
- Describe new applications opportunities like expert systems.
- Describe the likely information-processing environment in the coming years.
- Explain the significance of the trends in hardware and software for managers and users of computers.

INTRODUCTION

The computer field has witnessed tremendous growth and change in the last four decades. Predictions are always hazardous, but the giant strides in research and development and the number of innovative new products being developed provide hints on the coming computer environment. Although specific predictions may be in error, the overall trends are clear. More functions, more speed, and greater processing power will be available in the future at steadily declining costs. Figure 22-1 is an overview of the chapter.

HARDWARE

We discussed several categories of computers in previous chapters:

- Microcomputers
- Minicomputers
- Superminis
- General-purpose mainframes
- Supercomputers

Over time, each of these types of computers has become more powerful at a lower cost. For example, today's microcomputer is as powerful as and costs less than yesterday's mini.

One source of greater speed will come with new devices. Motorola has a processor chip that can handle thirty-two bits at a time and communicate with thirty-two bits. The processor is rated at a speed of 2 million to 3 million instructions per second, the speed of some mainframe computers today. This chip has evidently been constructed with current chip-making technology; there was no need for a technological breakthrough.

Another approach to increasing the power of the hardware is called *wafer-scale integration*. Currently, the manufacturer places many chips on a single wafer. After the chips are finished, workers cut the wafer on the chip lines and attach leads. The firm making a product with the chip then uses the wires to connect different chips together.

With wafer-scale technology, all of these circuits would be constructed on the chip. There would be no need to dice the wafer to obtain individual chips; work would be saved in attaching leads. More important, the circuits would be much faster because the electrons carrying information would not have to traverse wires; most of their travels would be confined to the wafer itself. If successful, this technology promises a supercomputer on a wafer. A few firms are working on developing wafer-scale technology; it is not commercially viable at the present time.

A current supercomputer's speed is measured in **megaflops** (a million floating-point instructions executed in a second), and a good number would be 200 to 500 megaflops for one of today's supercomputers. We expect to see complexes of processors forming a supercomputer system with a total speed of something like 1,000 megaflops achieved by the end of the 1980s.

The innovations in one class of computer will be adopted by other machines. It is likely that processors will be dedicated further to special tasks, as is characteristic of current microcomputers. For example, a typical micro has a processor that controls the CRT and one that controls the diskette drives. All of the processors communicate over a bus, that is, a path like a highway. The signals are sent along the bus to the appropriate unit.

Mainframe computers tend not to use a bus; instead, they have controllers for various functions. There is a storage controller, data channels (small computers themselves), and various controllers for peripherals. The channel has direct access to memory and takes its instructions from the CPU. The channel is connected to controllers for individual devices like disk drives and tapes. It is likely that higher-speed buses will be applied to mainframes; memory, the CPU, and secondary storage devices will all be connected to the bus. A **bus architecture** provides for more modularity than the present mainframe architecture, which features a direct connection between main memory and the CPU. One could offer different types of processors for different tasks and plug them into the system (see Figure 22-2).

TECHNOLOGICAL BASE	APPLICATIONS

Hardware
  Mainframe
  Minis
  Micros
  Networks
  Storage
    Magnetic
    Optical
  Communications
Software
  Professionals
    End users
Fifth Generators
  Expert systems
	Office Automation
	Factory Application
	Home Use

Figure 22-1. Chapter Overview.

There will be greater use of ***parallel processors*** in the future. Parallel processing means that several processors operate at once, each doing part of a task. Operating systems will assign tasks to free processors, each of which will be capable of doing a variety of operations. For example, there might be three or four processors capable of functioning as a CPU.

There will also be a growth in the use of highly specialized processors. Computers will routinely have extra processors, such as one that optimizes the handling of arrays; this processor will execute at high speed computations that can be cast into a matrix structure.

There will be increased interest in ***mass storage.*** We will be able to purchase storage subsystems in a variety of sizes and with differing levels of built-in logic, to the point of having one or more processors dedicated to controlling just the storage subsystem.

What emerges from this scenario is a picture of a computer complex, or network. We will think less in terms of a single computer and more of the range of resources available to us over the network (see Figure 22-3). There will be large mainframes and even a supercomputer at the heart of the network. Per-

sonal computers and local ***workstations*** will be connected to a local area network (LAN), which, in turn, will be a gateway into the network, where various minicomputers and mainframes will be interconnected. There will be specialized processors to handle storage and database management.

The user will work with packages on the personal computer/workstation, packages for electronic spreadsheet analysis, word processing, and personal file systems. Through a window, the personal computer will be logged onto the network and will be capable of accessing data on the mainframes. These data will be downloaded to local storage on the personal computer for manipulation by the "user-friendly" microcomputer software. For certain tasks, such as analyzing all of the firm's sales for this year, the user will simulate a terminal on the personal computer and employ a fourth-generation language to extract and analyze sales data on the mainframe.

Components

The late 1980s should see circuit ***densities*** of a million components on a chip using very-large-scale integration (VLSI). The chips will become faster and

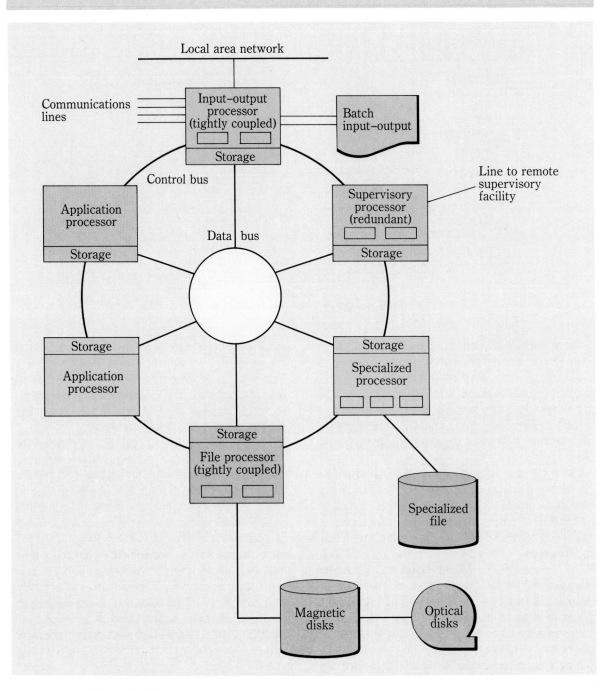

Figure 22-2. Future General-Purpose Computer System. A consulting company has prepared this forecast of a future computer system for a government agency. Source: National Bureau of Standards, "Future Information-Processing Technology," NBS Publication 500-103. From Arthur D. Little, Inc.

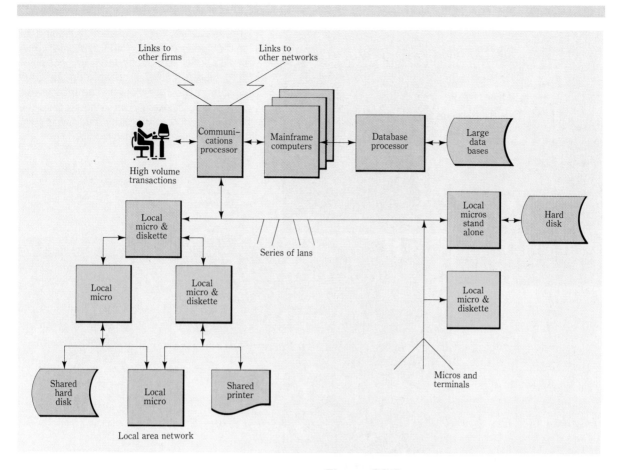

Figure 22-3. We predict that organizations will develop networks of mainframe mini- and microcomputers.

less expensive. Production is well under way on 256-K-bit memory chips, and million-bit chips are under test in laboratories.

There will also be progress in the custom development of logic chips. Computer-aided design of logic chips will reduce the cost of custom design and manufacture. Engineers will be able to afford to modify chips so that they are optimized for a specific task (see Figure 22-4).

Today's highest-performance **disk** drives use two sealed head/disk assemblies in a unit with a combined capacity of 1.26 **gigabytes** (billion characters). With the use of two head actuators per drive,

access time is 16 **milliseconds** (thousands of a second), and data are transferred to main memory at 3 megabytes per second. These drives have a density of 15,000 bits per linear inch, or 11 million bits per square inch (see Figure 22-5).

With the use of vertical recording (the magnetic domains, the elements that represent data, stand up instead of reclining on their sides), experts expect densities to rise to 100 to 400,000 bits per linear inch. In ten years, we might find 400 million bits per square inch for disk storage.

Video disk technology is used today to show viewers analogy scenes such as those found on television

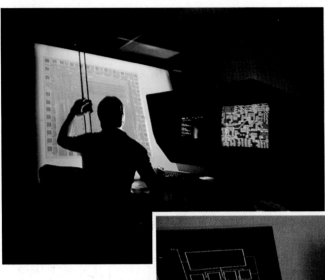

Figure 22-4. (a) Custom designing of logic chips is done on CAD systems. (b) A chip designer works at a large projection of his design, which was created on the CAD system in the foreground. The interactive design will ultimately be produced in the form of a photolithography mask which will be used to make the microchip.

or a videotape. See Figure 22-6 for an application of this technology. Video disks offer tremendous possibilities for recording data in digital form as well.

The use of video storage will increase, particularly for office systems. Current video-disk and optical-storage research is aimed at products that will both read and write. Today's commercial video-disk systems are generally nonerasable; once written on, the medium cannot be erased and rerecorded on. Such a medium is useful in office applications, where there is a need to store large amounts of data that do

not change, such as reports and correspondence. Also, large data-bank-information providers can make use of this technology.

One product available now can write data once and read them repeatedly during the estimated ten-year lifetime of the disk. The device stores up to 4 gigabytes (approximately 2 million typed, double-spaced pages) of data on a single 14-inch platter. The system transfers data at 3 megabytes per second.

We also find increasing attention to fail-safe com-

Figure 22-5. The head disk assembly for the Memorex 3680 storage subsystem.

Figure 22-6. An automobile retailer uses a video disk supplied by his auto supplier to train salesmen.

Figure 22-7. A Tandem "nonstop" computer being installed. This computer features duplicate hardware even including power supplies. Two processors work on the same program so that it can continue to run if one processor fails.

puters, machines that have redundant elements and fault-diagnostic routines (see Figure 22-7). The computers have components that can fail, but other parts should take over, allowing the machine to continue to operate in a degraded mode. Of course, software is required to determine the status of the program running on the failed component and to recover successfully. The idea is that the computer will be able to run when a component fails, and that it will be able to recover without being stopped by the failure.

Communications

Communications services are in a state of flux because of increasing deregulation and the divestiture of AT&T. From a market standpoint, we expect greatly increased competition. Certainly, more digital networks will be offered, and the costs for data transmission should begin to decline.

Long-distance communication is increasingly turning to *fiber optics.* A laser is used to modulate a signal, which is sent through fiber-optical cable (the cable is actually made of glass). The first such cable went into service between New York and Washington, D.C., in 1983. Large fiber-optics networks are being planned, including a transatlantic cable from the United States to Europe. Data are transmitted digitally at 90 megabits per second; fiber-optical communication has extremely high capacity. Other systems are planned or are under construction (see Figure 22-8).

High capacity will be needed for communicating among networks of computers. Bell Laboratory researchers have shown a new laser that can pulse its light beam 2 billion times a second. When a pulse is coded as a 1 and no pulse as a 0, tremendous transmission speeds are possible. Data that would take twenty-one hours to send over a copper telephone line can be sent in one second by means of the laser

Figure 22-8. (a) Seen through a special filter is a form from which lightguides will be drawn. Tests such as this help Bell Labs improve the glass fiber used in lightwave systems. (b) A team of researchers at AT&T Bell Labs set a new world long-distance lightwave record in 1983. Shown are a laser light source (bright spot near center) optical fiber (at left), and some of the electronics (at right) used to drive the subsystem. (c) High-capacity digital transmission is moving ever closer to customer premises through the Fiber SLC carrier system, here being installed in Chester Heights, PA. With such systems, data traffic can be more easily linked to the largely digital interexchange network, and voice traffic can be carried on fewer pairs of fiber lightguide.

and a fiber optics connection. By the end of this century, there may be no more use for copper wire in phone systems. It is possible that fiber optics will make land communications so cheap that there will be a decline in the number of communications satellites.

The Federal Communications Commission has allowed a doubling of the number of fixed, geostationary, orbiting communications satellites. (These satellites are in an orbit that keeps them in the same position, stationary, with respect to the earth as the earth rotates on its axis.) Broadcasters are interested in these satellites: first, to transmit television programs to affiliated stations, and second, to broadcast TV directly to home receivers. For data transmission, satellites offer a quick and inexpensive way to set up a private worldwide communications network.

Exotic Research

As circuits become smaller and smaller, we may have to replace silicon, the element on which chips are based, with another substance. The reason? As circuits shrink and are placed closer together, heat may cause the chip to melt. Shrinking circuits may begin to approach the size of a single molecule. Silicon transistors cannot be made that are only one molecule in size. Another technology will be needed to reduce components to this size and to increase the speed of computers.

One possibility is to replace silicon with organic compounds made of carbon, so-called biochips. One research group is looking at the photosynthesis process, which involves the flow of electrons. Could this flow be controlled and turned into the switching circuits needed for a computer?

Other researchers want to find ways to emulate the on–off switches of today's computers directly. For example, red blood cells in hemoglobin change from one shape to another when the cells' electrical charge is altered. Such a two-state cell could represent a 0 or a 1.

Devices made up of small molecules could probably not be manufactured by means of conventional techniques. One group of scientists would like to have cell-sized computers assemble themselves. These scientists hope to produce new molecules that, when combined by means of genetic engineering techniques, will form a known structure suitable for use as a computer circuit.

SOFTWARE

As always, software continues to be a bottleneck in computing. We expect programming in general to migrate to higher and higher levels of languages. More programming will be done in fourth-generation languages. Professional programmers will use applications generators to reduce the amount of COBOL programming required. Assembly language will be used by software and hardware vendors to build high-level systems. The average programmer will rarely program in assembly language.

The Professional

What will **professional programmers** who work in companies do in the future? First, there will still be custom systems. Although the trend is toward more packages, there are many special requirements and new opportunities for which packages will just not be available. However, we expect to see a decline in the amount of COBOL programming and more emphasis on systems requirements analysis.

The programmer will have a **workstation**, that is, a microcomputer connected to the mainframe. The micro will have software that facilitates the programmer's work; powerful text editors and function keys that generate language commands will be included. The programmer will have easy access to data dictionaries and graphic diagrams of database structure.

Most programming will be done with fourth-generation or higher-higher-level languages at a level above COBOL. Because of the features provided by the workstation, programmers should be more productive. The availability of generators and packages will encourage more prototyping, so that the users will be drawn into the systems analysis process and will be able to provide feedback based on a concrete representation of the system under development.

With a prototype, the user sees the results of analysis and design at each step; thus, the user will be forced to spend time on design. The results should be better systems completed in less time than with today's predominant approaches to custom applications development.

End User

The computer will become a more integrated part of the *end user's* environment. Knowledge or information workers and office workers will have their own workstations built around microcomputers. Major applications on the local machine will include:

- Spreadsheet analysis
- Presentation graphics (diagrams, charts, and so on)
- Word processing
- Terminal access to a network
- Electronic mail
- Computer conferencing
- Access to external databases

Hundreds of personal-computer software products are announced each month. There will be packages available for almost any conceivable task for the end user. However, this user will require considerable support. The computer department staff will acquire different packages and evaluate them; it will also help to train users and to update packages when new versions are developed.

The one clear trend of these advances is that the line between the end user and the computer professional will blur. The computer and its use will be even more pervasive than they are today.

THE FIFTH GENERATION

In Chapter 3, we mentioned the *fifth generation,* a term popularized by Japan in its search for a major advance in computing (see Figure 3-17 for a functional diagram of the system).

The hardware advances required to achieve the goals of the fifth generation are impressive. Circuits with considerably higher speeds than those of today, large memories, and low cost are necessary. Large amounts of external storage will also be needed.

The major difference between the fifth generation and conventional computers, however, lies in the *user interface,* the interaction between the user and the computer. The system features a "built-in" relational database, something not found today, at least not closely integrated with the computer.

Even more dramatic are the planned human interfaces using *natural language,* speech, and pictures. Supporting such interfaces is software consisting of a knowledge base and a problem-solving and inference mechanism. Finally, we see a new programming language called PROLOG.

Artificial Intelligence

Artificial Intelligence (AI) is a branch of computer science that focuses on computers as problem-solving and symbol-manipulating devices. In the 1950s, AI programs played games like chess and checkers in an attempt by researchers to learn how humans reasoned so that computers could exhibit "intelligence."

AI programs have two major parts: the strategy they follow and knowledge about the problem being addressed. Today, much of the knowledge is contained in rules that describe the decision situation. For example, we could think of building a system that tells a student whether he or she has completed the requirements to major in information systems in his or her business school. The program would consist of a series of rules about what constitutes a major. The highest-level rule might be in the form of:

> IS major consists of:
>   Course A and
>   Course B and
>   Course C or Course D and
>   One elective course

This rule would reference at least one other rule, the one defining an elective. The rules constitute knowledge about the problem domain, the qualifications for being an information systems major.

In order to ask this system if his or her program of study satisfied the major, the student would type in the courses taken or planned, and the system would check those courses against the rules that define the major. In evaluating the rule, the program would have to look as well at the definition of an elective course and determine whether one of the student's courses counted as an elective.

Expert Systems

Expert systems are a part of AI that focuses on capturing the decision rules of an expert and replicating them on a computer. The system can be used to help the expert remember certain rules and/or to make the expert's knowledge available to others.

Figure 22-9 is an example of a simple expert system written in the *PROLOG* language. PROLOG was developed in Europe and is designed for expressing a problem as a set of *rules* or goals. Built into the language is an inference mechanism, an algorithm that tries to prove each rule, that is, to satisfy each goal. The program searches for possible ways to satisfy each goal, and if it fails, it backtracks to take another approach until it runs out of options and reports back failure. The Japanese, having selected PROLOG as the basis of their fifth-generation system, now talk of machines whose power is measured in terms of the number of rules, rather than the number of instructions, they execute per second.

Expert-systems research has been applied extensively to medical diagnosis. One of the most ambitious of these programs is Internist, developed by Professor Harry Pople at the University of Pittsburgh. A sample dialogue with this system appears in Figure 22-10.

The expert-system part of the fifth generation is the base for its user interface and its intelligent behavior. A goal of the system is to understand natural language, the way we speak as opposed to the highly structured computer languages. AI approaches are generally employed in natural language systems and for speech recognition.

Pictorial input will require pattern matching, another AI research area.

Will the Japanese succeed in developing a fifth generation computer based on AI technology? (Several other countries have started similar fifth generation projects.) Since the major change from the second to the third generation in the mid-1960s, the development of computers has been evolutionary rather than revolutionary. We think that many of the features envisioned by the Japanese fifth-generation effort will appear before the 1990s. The concepts behind this effort will provide direction to designers. It is not likely that there will be an abrupt change from present approaches to a new generation. The ideas of the fifth generation will gradually be adopted along with other techniques for improving the utility of computers.

APPLICATIONS

There are thousands of applications for computers; imaginative users find new ones every day. There are several areas for new applications that are likely to have a significant impact on the organization.

Office Automation

Office automation involves the use of computers to support workers who primarily process information. The purpose of office automation is to provide tools to improve the effectiveness and the efficiency of knowledge workers, a group that constitutes over 50 percent of the U.S. work force.

Electronic mail is an important part of office automation systems. Also included are word processing, programs to accept and notify us of an event (reminder systems), and programs that help to keep an appointment calendar. The terminal or personal computer connects to a network, possibly an LAN. Usually, a central time-sharing computer is the repository for electronic mail.

With electronic mail, each user of a system has an electronic mailbox. Using a program, the sender composes a message and routes it to the electronic mailbox of the recipient. When the recipient logs on

```
/ * * * * * * * * * * * * * *
 *   CAIS student advisory system   *
* * * * * * * * * * * * * * * * * /

/ * * * * * * * * * * * * * * * *
 *   Test case for a hypothetical student   *
* * * * * * * * * * * * * * * * * * * /
takes(j on,b202310).
waives(j on,b202311).
takes(j on,b202312).
takes(j on,b203315).
takes(j on,b203316).
takes(j on,b203362).
takes(j on,b203160).
takes(j on,b203161).

/ * * * * * * * * * * * * * * * * * * * * * * * * * *
 / *   Definition of satisfying a required course: take the course or   *
 *   waive it                                                          *
* * * * * * * * * * * * * * * * * * * * * * * * * * * * * /

satisfies(S,X) :— takes(S,X).
satisfies(S,X) :— waives(S,X).

/ * * * * * * * * * * * * * * * * * * *
 *   Definition of taking a technical course   *
* * * * * * * * * * * * * * * * * * * * * /
techcourse(S,Y) :— takes(S,Y),
              member(Y,[b203316,b203321,b203334]).

/ * * * * * * * * * * * * * * * * * * *
 *   Definition of taking a managerial course   *
* * * * * * * * * * * * * * * * * * * * * /

mgtcourse(S,Z) :— takes(S,Z),
              member(Z,[b203362,b203364]).

/ * * * * * * * * * * * * * * * * * * * * * * * * * * * * *
 *   Definition of a cais elective                              *
 *   The first elective is a single course not already used for another   *
 *   requirement (checked in the caismajor rule). The second elective   *
 *   is for having taken any two minicourses.                   *
* * * * * * * * * * * * * * * * * * * * * * * * * * * * * * /

caiselective(S,Q,R):—takes(S,Q),
              member(Q,[b203314,b203316,b203318,b203321,b203322,
              b203331,b203334,b203360,b203362,b203364,b203361,
              b203368,b203370]).
caiselective(S,Q,R):—takes(S,Q),
              member(Q,[b203140,b203141,b203142,b203150,b203252,
              b203155,b203158,b203160,b203161]).
              takes(S,R),
              member(R,[b203140,b203141,b203142,b203150,b203252,
              b203155,b203158,b203160,b203161]),
              Q®==R.
```

Figure 22-9. Expert systems feature rules and symbolic instead of numeric processing. They are also able to explain the reasons for their recommendations. (Figure continues on pages 332–334.)

```
/ * * * * * * * * * * *
    *  Definition of member  *
* * * * * * * * * * * * * /

member(X,[X¶_]).
member(X,[_¶Y]) :— member(X,Y).

/ * * * * * * * * * * * * * * * *
    *  Description of the CAIS major  *
* * * * * * * * * * * * * * * * * /

caismajor(S) :-
      nl,
      write('working on 2310'),
      satisfies(S,b202310), !,
      nl,
      write('working on 2311'),
      satisfies(S,b202311), !,
      nl,
      write('working on 2312'),
      satisfies(S,b202312), !,
      nl,
      write('checking 3315'),
      takes(S,b203315), !,
      nl,
      write('looking at technical course requirement'),
      techcourse(S,TECH), !,
      nl,
      write('now for the management course'),
      mgtcourse(S,MGT), !,
      nl,
      write('at last the elective'),
      caiselective(S,E,F),
            E ®== TECH,
            E ®== MGT.

/ * * * * * * * * * * * * * * * * * * * * *
    *  Recommendations to nonmajors on Courses  *
* * * * * * * * * * * * * * * * * * * * * * * /

/ * * * * * * * * * * * * * * * * * * * * * *
    *  Only take 2310 or 2311, both are not required  *
* * * * * * * * * * * * * * * * * * * * * * * * /

satisfies10or11(M):-
      satisfies(M,b202310).
satisfies10or11(M):-
      satisfies(M,b202311).

/ * * * * * * * * * * * *
    *  Quant taking a minor  *
* * * * * * * * * * * * * /

recommend(M,Z):-
      satisfies10or11(M),
      satisfies(M,b202312),
      satisfies(M,b203315),
      member(Z,[quant]),
      write('The recommended advanced courses in order of priority are:'),
      nl,
      nl,
```

Figure 22-9 (continued).

```
           write('      1. b203334 on files and data base;there are good modeling '),
           nl,
           write('         opportunities both of file systems and from data stored on files'),
           nl,
           nl,
           write('      2. b203321 on decision support systems; a DSS is often a model'),
           nl,
           nl,
           write('      3. b203316 hardware and software is a good final choice').

/ * * * * * * * * * * * * * * * * * * * * * * *
 *  International business and management majors  *
 * * * * * * * * * * * * * * * * * * * * * * * * /
recommend(M,Z):-
           satisfies10or11(M),
           satisfies(M,b202312),
           satisfies(M,b203315),
           member(Z,[ib,management]),
           write('For a technical course, you should consider'),
           nl,
           write('      1. b203334 to learn about files and data bases or'),
           nl,
           write('      2. possibly b203321 for decision support systems'),
           nl,
           nl,
           write('For a more behavioral course there are three options:'),
           nl,
           write('      1. b203362 to learn about implementation issues'),
           nl,
           write('      2. b203364 for managing an information systems area'),
           nl,
           write('      3. b203360 to explore social issues like transborder'),
           nl,
           write('         data flows').

/ * * * * * * * * * * * * * * * * * * * * * *
 *  Finance, marketing, economics taking minor  *
 * * * * * * * * * * * * * * * * * * * * * * * /
recommend(M,Z):-
           satisfies10or11(M),
           satisfies(M,b202312),
           satisfies(M,b203315),
           member(Z,[finance,marketing,economics]),
           write('If you are interested in technical courses, the best choices are'),
           nl,
           write('      1. b203334 files and data base management for learning'),
           nl,
           write('         how to set up and access large data files for research'),
           nl,
           write('      2. b203321 decision support systems either alone or after'),
           nl,
           write('         the data base course—to learn how to build models.'),
           nl,
           write('      3. For a more behavioral interest in how to implement'),
           nl,
           write('         consider b203362, a course on implementation in organ-'),
```

Figure 22-9 (continued).

```
            nl,
            write('        izations regardless of the area of the application.')

    /*          */

            @prolog
            Prolog-10 version 3.3
            Copyright (C) 1981 by D. Warrren, F. Pereira and L. Byrd.

            ¶ ?- [proadv].

            proadv consulted      1380 words      0.53 sec.

            yes
            ¶ ?- caismajor(jon).

            working on 2310
            working on 2311
            working on 2312
            checking 3315
            looking at technical course requirement
            now for the management course
            at last the elective
            yes
            ¶ ?-

            recommend(jon,finance).
    If you are interested in technical courses, the best choices are
        1. b203334 files and data base management for learning
           how to set up and access large data files for research
        2. b203321 decision support systems either alone or after
           the data base course—to learn how to build models.
        3. For a more behavioral interest in how to implement
           consider b203362, a course on implementation in organ-
           izations regardless of the area of the application.
    yes
    ¶ ?-
```

Figure 22-9 (continued).

Figure 22-10. This expert system helps an internist diagnose what may be wrong with a patient. It is currently a research system. (Figure continues on pages 335–338.)

(DOCTOR)

This command is used to invoke the DOCTOR program, which embodies the interactive diagnostic procedure of INTERNIST-I;

INTERNIST-I consultation SUMEX AIM version

PLEASE ENTER FINDINGS.

After the initial prompt PLEASE ENTER FINDINGS, the person using the system enters whatever positive findings he chooses to divulge. The program prompts with "*" to request additional input until the re-

spondent types "GO"; after which INTERNIST-I commences the task definition procedure described in the previous section. Had the user wanted to enter negative findings during this initial exchange, he could have responded "DENY" to the prompt, causing subsequent entries to be interpreted as negative results.

```
*SEX MALE
*AGE 26 TO 55
*RACE WHITE
*ALCOHOLISM CHRONIC HX
*EXPOSURE TO RABBITS OR OTHER SMALL MAMMALS
*FEVER
*MYALGIA
*LEG <S> WEAKNESS BILATERAL
*LEG <S> WEAKNESS PROXIMAL ONLY
*PRESSURE ARTERIAL SYSTOLIC 90 TO 110
*PRESSURE ARTERIAL ORTHOSTATIC HYPOTENSION
*TACHYCARDIA
*JAUNDICE
*ANOREXIA
*DIARRHEA ACUTE
*FECES LIGHT COLORED
*VOMITING RECENT
*LIVER ENLARGED SLIGHT
*SKIN SPIDER ANGIOMATA
*SKIN PALMAR ERYTHEMA
*OLIGURIA HX
*UREA NITROGEN BLOOD 60 TO 100
*CREATININE BLOOD INCREASED
*WBC 14000 TO 30000
*PLATELETS LESS THAN 50000
*GO
```

Manifestations are expressed by means of precise sequences of terms in a controlled vocabulary; there are presently approximately 3500 vocabulary items that can be used to describe positive and negative findings.

DISREGARDING: EXPOSURE TO RABBITS OR OTHER SMALL MAMMALS, LEG <S> WEAKNESS BILATERAL LEG <S> WEAKNESS PROXIMAL ONLY, PRESSURE ARTERIAL ORTHOSTATIC HYPOTENSION, CREATININE BLOOD INCREASED, UREA NITROGEN BLOOD 60 to 100

CONSIDERING; AGE 26 TO 55, SEX MALE, ANOREXIA, MYALGIA, VOMITING RECENT, FECES LIGHT COLORED, FEVER, JAUNDICE, LIVER ENLARGED SLIGHT, SKIN PALMAR ERYTHEMA, SKIN SPIDER ANGIOMATA, WBC 14000 TO 30000, PLATELETS LESS THAN 50000

RULEOUT: HEPATITIS CHRONIC ACTIVE, ALCOHOLIC HEPATITIS, HEPATIC MILIARY TUBERCULOSIS, MICRONODAL CIRRHOSIS <LAENNECS>, HEPATITIS ACUTE VIRAL

At this point, INTERNIST-I reports concerning the initial differential diagnosis that will be the focus of problem-solving attention. Three lists are displayed, labelled respectively DISREGARDING, CONSIDERING, and RULEOUT. The CONSIDERING list identifies those positive findings whose differential diagnostic tasks were combined in coming to the differential diagnostic focus, which is described by the RULEOUT

Figure 22-10 (continued).

list. The DISREGARDING list tells what positive findings are not consistent with the differential diagnosis as formulated and are therefore being disregarded for the moment; they will, however, be attended to in due course. The keyword RULEOUT indicates what strategy INTERNIST-I is going to pursue relative to this task definition: in this case, as in any case when the differential list contains five or more alternatives, the program will try to find questions to ask which, if the response is negative, will serve to downgrade the score of one or more diagnoses on the list. While pursuing a RULEOUT strategy, the program limits the questions to be asked to items of information obtainable via history or physical exam.

Please Enter Findings of JAUNDICE HX
*GO

There are two formats used for asking questions. In the preceding line, the user is asked to provide any data that might be available within the specified category of findings. Actually, the respondent is free to enter whatever positive or negative data desired and is not constrained to the category mentioned in the query. In this case, the user chose to respond GO; this passes the initiative back to the program, which then typically follows up on the general question by asking about the specific finding of that category for which it particularly wants a YES or NO answer.

JAUNDICE INTERMITTENT HX?
NO

If the respondent did not have any information concerning this direct question, he could have answered N/A—meaning not available.

Please Enter Findings of APPETITE/WEIGHT
*GO

WEIGHT LOSS GTR THAN 10 PERCENT?
NO

The program asks a series of questions that have been selected in accordance with its problem-solving strategy, then repeats the scoring and partitioning of the task definition procedure.

DISREGARDING; EXPOSURE TO RABBITS OR OTHER SMALL MAMMALS, LEG <S> WEAKNESS BILATERAL LEG <S> WEAKNESS PROXIMAL ONLY, PRESSURE ARTERIAL ORTHOSTATIC HYPOTENSION, CREATININE BLOOD INCREASED, UREA NITROGEN BLOOD 60 TO 100

CONSIDERING; AGE 26 TO 55, SEX MALE, ANOREXIA, MYALGIA, VOMITING RECENT, FECES LIGHT COLORED, FEVER, JAUNDICE, LIVER ENLARGED SLIGHT, SKIN PALMAR ERYTHEMA, SKIN SPIDER ANGIOMATA, WBC 14000 TO 30000, PLATELETS LESS THAN 50000

RULEOUT: HEPATITIS CHRONIC ACTIVE, ALCOHOLIC HEPATITIS, HEPATIC MILIARY TUBERCULOSIS, HEPATITIS ACUTE VIRAL INFECTIOUS MONONUCLEOSIS

Except for the substitution of an acute process (infectious mononucleosis) for a chronic one (micronodal cirrhosis), this differential diagnosis

Figure 22-10 (continued).

is not significantly changed from the initial formulation. Note that the possibility of cirrhosis has not actually been ruled out; it has merely dropped out of sight because its score has fallen below the threshold used by the task definition procedure.

```
Please Enter Findings of PAIN ABDOMEN
*GO

ABDOMEN PAIN GENERALIZED?
NO

ABDOMEN PAIN EPIGASTRIUM?
NO

ABDOMEN PAIN NON COLICKY?
NO

ABDOMEN PAIN RIGHT UPPER QUADRANT?
NO
```

DISREGARDING: JAUNDICE, SKIN SPIDER ANGIOMATA, CREATININE BLOOD INCREASED, UREA NITROGEN BLOOD 60 TO 100

CONSIDERING: AGE 26 TO 55, EXPOSURE TO RABBITS OR OTHER SMALL MAMMALS, SEX MALE, ANOREXIA, DIARRHEA ACUTE, MYALGIA, VOMITING RECENT, FEVER, LEG <S> WEAKNESS BILATERAL LEG <S> WEAKNESS PROXIMAL ONLY.

PRESSURE ARTERIAL ORTHOSTATIC HYPOTENSION, PRESSURE ARTERIAL SYSTOLIC 90 TO 110. TACHYCARDIA, WBC 14000 TO 30000. PLATELETS LESS THAN 50000

DISCRIMINATE: LEPTOSPIROSIS SYSTEMIC, SARCOIDOSIS CHRONIC SYSTEMIC

The effect of the negative responses concerning abdominal pain has been to lower the scores of all of the hepatic disorders considered in the previous differential diagnosis. This time, when the partitioning algorithm is invoked the highest-ranking alternative is systemic leptospirosis; the only other diagnosis on the list capable of explaining substantially the same set of findings is systemic sarcoidosis. The keyword DISCRIMINATE indicates that the list of alternatives containing between two and four elements, the leading two of which are selected for comparative analysis. When engaged in a DISCRIMINATE mode of analysis, the program will attempt to ask questions serving to support one diagnosis at the expense of the other; more costly procedures may be called for in order to achieve this objective.

```
Please Enter Findings of VOMITING/REGURGITATION
*GO

HEMATEMESIS?
NO

HEMOPTYSIS GROSS?
NO

Please Enter Findings of TEMPERATURE
*GO

RIGOR <S> ?
YES
```

Figure 22-10 (continued).

Please Enter Findings of NEUROLOGIC EXAM CRANIAL NERVE <S>
*GO

NERVE PARALYSIS SEVENTH CRANIAL BILATERAL?
NO

SPLENECTOMY HX?
NO

The program is not actually interested in the answer to this question; what it wants to know is whether the spleen is enlarged. Because of the possibility of being misled by a negative answer, appropriate blocks have been created to prevent the program from asking about an increased spleen size in a patient whose spleen had been removed.

Please Enter Findings of PALPATION ABDOMEN
*GO

SPLENOMEGALY MODERATE?
NO

Please Enter Findings of XRAY LUNG FIELD <S>
*GO

CHEST XRAY HILAR ADENOPATHY BILATERAL?
NO

DISREGARDING: JAUNDICE, SKIN SPIDER ANGIOMATA, CREATININE BLOOD INCREASED, UREA NITROGEN BLOOD 60 TO 100

CONSIDERING: AGE 26 TO 55, EXPOSURE TO RABBITS OR OTHER SMALL MAMMALS, SEX MALE, ANOREXIA, DIARRHEA ACUTE, MYALGIA, VOMITING RECENT, FEVER, LEG <S> WEAKNESS BILATERAL, LEG <S> WEAKNESS PROXIMAL ONLY, PRESSURE ARTERIAL ORTHOSTATIC HYPOTENSION, PRESSURE ARTERIAL SYSTOLIC 90 TO 110, RIGOR <S>, TACHYCARDIA, WBC 14000 TO 30000, PLATELETS LESS THAN 50000

PURSUING: LEPTOSPIROSIS SYSTEMIC

The questions about rigors (shaking chills) is enough to separate the scores of these items so that now there is only one alternative left in the differential diagnosis. Before concluding that this diagnosis is actually correct, however, the program will now attempt to achieve a degree of separation between this diagnosis and its nearest competitor (now below the threshold and not printed out) that is twice the threshold value. The program invokes a PURSUING strategy, which calls for the identification and acquisition of clinching data; at this stage, the level of questioning is unconstrained so the program can ask about biopsies if useful, or other specialized procedures capable of providing pathognomonic data.

LEPTOSPIRA AGGLUTINATION POSITIVE?
YES

This finding is enough to clinch the diagnosis. However, the program proceeds to ask the additional questions that had been prepared for this round of information acquisition. As implemented in this program, the process of task formulation is too time consuming to have the procedure recycle after each new datum is entered.

Figure 22-10 (continued).

the computer, he or she can read the mail at leisure, file it, forward it to others, and/or reply to the sender's mailbox (see Figure 9-5).

At Digital Equipment Corporation (DEC), a multinational manufacturer of computers and electronic equipment, there is an electronic mail system with over six thousand active subscribers. This system is used internally by DEC employees, not by customers.

Electronic mail has several advantages over phone calls. Many phone calls are not completed because the party being called is not at the phone or the line is busy. Also, telephones interrupt the individual receiving the call, whereas an electronic message does not.

The mail system at DEC uses a series of computers that store messages and forward them. Each subscriber has a computer account and an electronic message file or mailbox. Individuals are addressed by name, and users work with terminals to enter and read messages.

The mail file does more than just hold messages; the user can treat it as an electronic filing cabinet. It is possible to go back and retrieve messages from a certain sender or messages on a particular topic.

Because the sender can send a single message to an entire distribution list, it is no more difficult to send mail to twenty people than to send it to one. This addressing capability is very important for project teams or for managers who wish to communicate with staff members who are in different locations.

DEC has found that 63 percent of its system's users are managers, 23 percent staff, and 14 percent secretaries. Some 62 percent of the users interact with the terminal, and the remainder rely on a secretary or an administrative aide to enter messages and to print hard copies of incoming mail.

The DEC users have been pleased with the speed and the effectiveness of communications. The system has been highly rated for broadcasting information, assigning a task, and following up on it. The distribution of information is more timely, and sending mail to multiple addressees in many locations is much simpler now. A majority of the users surveyed felt their productivity had increased by 5 to 15 percent.

The usual justification for electronic mail is not cost savings; rather, these systems are installed to improve productivity and communications. At DEC, an economic analysis showed that the break-even point on electronic mail versus traditional methods was one additional phone call or one extra copy of a message. DEC feels that for any copy after the second, electronic mail is significantly less costly than either a memo or a phone call.

The strongest indication of success came from the president of DEC, who said that he had become so dependent on the electronic mail system that he had forgotten what it was like before it was installed. Being able to communicate immediately with six thousand individuals around the world is so efficient that the president cannot conceive of working without electronic mail.

DEC is a leader in implementing electronic mail for its entire corporation. Other firms have electronic mail networks in a few locations or use one of the national services like Western Union and IT&T which offer electronic mail on systems for anyone with a terminal or a personal computer. In the future, firms will increasingly implement electronic mail systems because of the many communications advantages they provide.

Interorganizational Systems

Organizations are trying to gain a competitive advantage by extending computer systems to customers and the public. We have discussed several examples, such as American Hospital Supply's terminals in customer hospital purchasing departments. We also presented the McKesson nationwide system that provides services to drugstores, which make up much of the firm's customer base. These systems are interorganizational; that is, they tie two or more organizations together.

Given today's communications capabilities, what else is possible?

Think of how much paperwork and duplication could be eliminated if a link existed between a vendor's and a customer's computers (see Figure 22-11). An order for goods would be entered by the customer directly in the supplier's computer; the

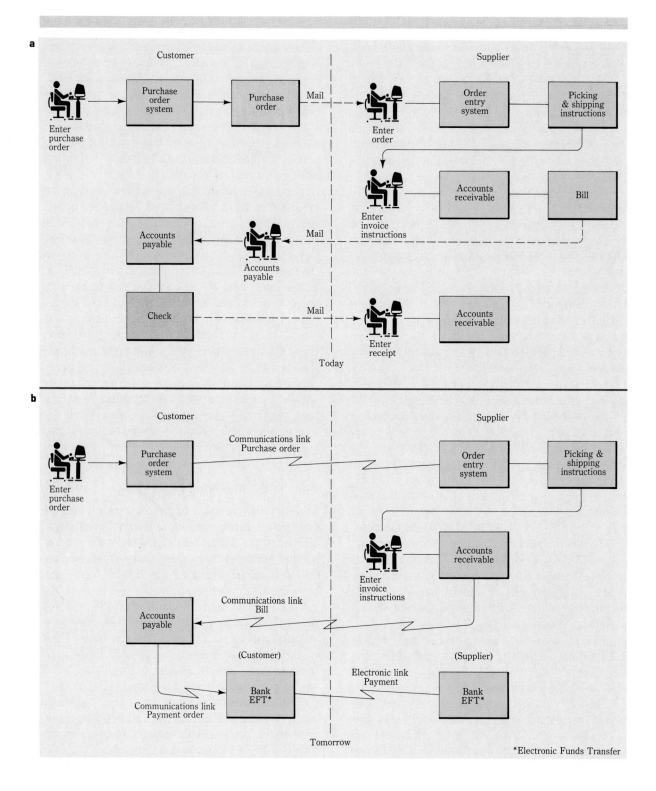

a

Customer | Supplier

Enter purchase order → Purchase order system → Purchase order — Mail → Enter order → Order entry system → Picking & shipping instructions → Enter invoice instructions → Accounts receivable — Bill

Accounts payable ← Mail ← Accounts payable ← Bill

Accounts payable — Check — Mail → Enter receipt → Accounts receivable

Today

b

Customer | Supplier

Enter purchase order → Purchase order system — Communications link Purchase order → Order entry system → Picking & shipping instructions → Enter invoice instructions → Accounts receivable

Accounts payable ← Communications link Bill

(Customer) | (Supplier)

Accounts payable — Communications link Payment order → Bank EFT* — Electronic link Payment → Bank EFT*

Tomorrow

*Electronic Funds Transfer

540 *Computer Business and Society*

Figure 22-11 (opposite). (a) Today: Electronic Connection Between Customer and Supplies. Today's environment includes a lot of duplicate effort, entering and printing data. (b) Tomorrow? In the near future, firms will establish direct computer-to-computer links to eliminate redundant operations.

order would trigger shipping instructions as well as an electronic invoice.

When the shipment arrives, the warehouse staff retrieves the purchase order and checks off the goods that have arrived. A clerk in the accounting department reviews the invoice and the purchase order to see that all items were delivered and that the prices are correct. Then the clerk approves payment. If the customer does a lot of business with the supplier, the payment could be combined with other payments and sent at the end of the month in one check. Alternatively, the customer could be connected to the supplier's bank and send payment electronically.

Such a system offers tremendous opportunities for efficiency. However, interorganizational systems raise a number of problems with security and backup. We must manage the technology well if these types of systems are to succeed.

Factory Automation

Computers are making major inroads into manufacturing, though the study of computers and factory automation is usually reserved for an engineering curriculum. Some of the factory computers feed data back to the digital computers used for information systems that control production and inventories.

Japan has built an almost completely automated factory, and the components exist to build others, given the right type of manufacturing. A key part of factory automation is *robots,* machines that are controlled by microcomputers.

The next advance in robotics will be *vision* systems and sensing robots (see Figure 22-12). A sensing robot can feel or sense things about the job; for example, it can sense the quality of a weld that it has just made and make repairs where necessary.

Vision systems may use a standard TV camera to scan objects and direct the robot. In one example, the robot receives orders from a TV camera on how to sort typewriter-key tops. Other vision systems identify different-shaped parts on a moving belt so the robot can select the appropriate part for assembly.

We expect continued growth and sophistication in this type of equipment as the manufacturing industry tries to cut costs and remain competitive.

There is also great interest in computer-aided design (CAD) and computer-aided manufacturing (CAM). We have seen some examples in Chapter 17. To aid in manufacturing, the computer-generated designs provide input into computers that produces the tooling for production. Computers then control the manufacturing process, too.

General Motors has developed sophisticated CAD/CAM systems to go directly from the design of an automobile to making the tooling. Blueprints are fastened on a wall and lasers scan them; the laser feeds digitized information directly into numerically controlled machines that make a clay model of the car. Later, the clay model can be scanned to provide information for the numerically controlled machines that produce the tooling for production (see Figure 22-13).

The newest trend in CAD is three-dimensional analysis as seen in Chapter 17. This approach was first developed several years ago, but the time required to generate and manipulate three-dimensional drawings was excessive. Recently, there have been breakthroughs in the design of algorithms for three-dimensional work; computers are also becoming more powerful and can better support this kind of processing. There is much interest in this technology for manufacturing.

One of the first applications of three-dimensional

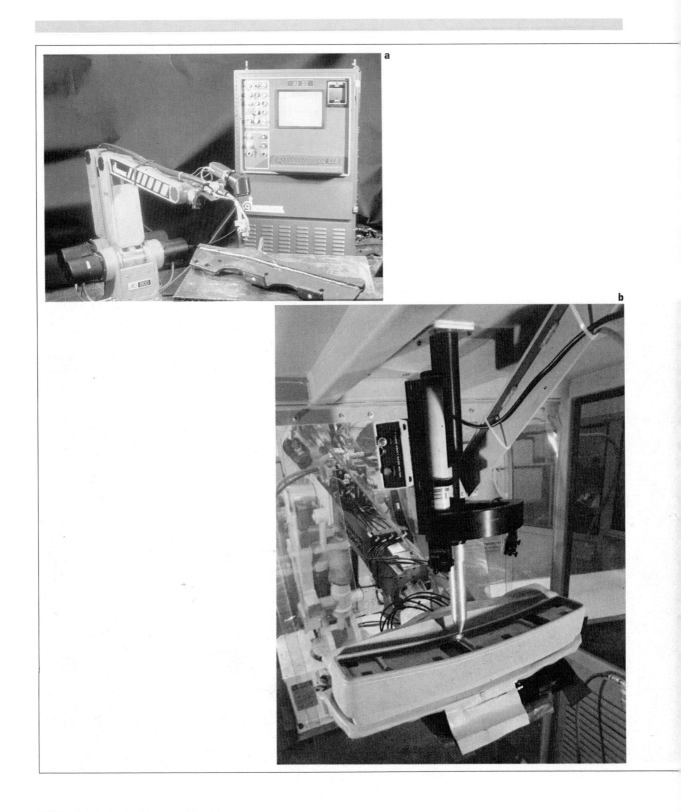

Figure 22-12. (a) Robovision II is a programmable Arc Welding System designed to increase welding productivity and to ensure consistently high quality welding. (b) A neon laser welding assembly, using a through-the-arc vision system to obtain quality welds, works in tandem with a Cincinnati Milacron robot on an auto-bumper assembly task. (c) A robot vision system used to give robots the ability to select specific industrial parts by shape from among dissimilar parts. At top are intense lights that provide high-contrast viewing of the part held by the robot arm, left. The video camera, lower left, obtains a picture of the part and this picture is digitized for analysis by the computer, right rear. The video displays show various interpretations of the video data.

c

Figure 22-13. A completely automated auto-painting room at General Motors.

modeling has been in medicine. A computer-aided tomography machine (CAT scanner) provides data taken every 5 mm on an object; these data are put into an image generator that stacks the slices to form a solid model.

A doctor at the University of Wisconsin uses a "trackball" controller to simulate an operation, such as one for reconstructing a crushed jaw. The doctor can cut through simulated tissue and remove bone fragments. He can also insert bone grafts and support pins. The computer checks whether the results of the operation would interfere with the patient's circulation.

From Home

Office automation and communications capabilities make it possible to change the place and time of work. In the future, it may be possible for a significant number of individuals to work either from their homes or from satellite offices. Communications and computer technology will be substituted for transportation.

Whereas some will be able to cut down on commuting, almost all of us will have access to a number of home services. Most homes will have personal computers or at least terminals. Through these devices, we can already reach a variety of services. There are companies that feature shopping at home through a personal computer. Compuserv in Columbus, Ohio, has a nationwide communications network that is available to personal computer users. These individuals converse with each other and maintain bulletin boards of messages and notices. The personal computer user can subscribe to services that will provide the closing stock averages.

Customers of Chemical Bank in New York City can use the Pronto banking service for twenty-four-hour banking from a microcomputer at home. The Pronto system provides information on balances and

Figure 22-14. An advertisement for the Chemical Bank Pronto home banking service.

the ability to transfer funds, to pay bills, to look at a register of checks, to obtain a statement, and to run a home budgeting program. The customer can set up automatic payments, such as a set amount on a certain day each month for rent or a mortgage. When the customer authorizes paying a bill, the bank's system takes over; the customer does not have to write a check or mail the bill to the merchant (see Figure 22-14).

A brokerage firm, C. D. Anderson in San Francisco, became the first broker to let a customer buy or sell stocks and options directly from home. A user from anywhere in the United States logs onto a value-added carrier, Telenet, and accesses the Trade*Plus system. The program asks the customer the form of the transaction (buying or selling), the company name, the number of shares to be sold or purchased, the price, and the status of the account (cash or margin). The system then requests a

password and redisplays the data for checking. Finally, after correction, the order is printed in Anderson's wire room and sent to the appropriate stock exchange. The system makes the customer's portfolio available when he or she is trading; the computer automatically updates the portfolio with each trade.

SUMMARY

There are many areas in which computers will be used in the future.

Research continues on making the machines faster, cheaper, and more friendly. As costs come down and power goes up, it becomes more feasible to use computers for new tasks. Educated and creative users and managers are needed to take advantages of the computer's potential.

Review of Chapter 22

REVIEW

This chapter has presented us with one scenario for the future. Improvements in technology are expected as competition and new discoveries lead to new devices. The proliferation of hardware and computers makes our job of applying the technology more difficult because there are so many choices.

We expect existing trends to continue for hardware: more power for processing and larger amounts of storage at declining costs.

The communications area is one of the most rapidly changing. Communications carriers are anticipating the desire for more networking of computers; fiber optics is one answer to increasing the capacity of the communications system.

For the user, more power means that the engines exist to process more information. Users will see more speed, larger storage, and software with more functions in their microcomputers and in the mainframes that process large volumes of transactions. The mainframes will keep huge databases that will need to be centralized, for example, a database of orders from customers.

Work on fifth-generation computers will begin to appear in products well before the 1990s. The idea of a more natural interface with a computer is most appealing to all of us. Both accurate voice recognition and natural language input would continue to extend the computer to end users, particularly to individuals who are opposed to keyboards.

How will you cope? The principles discussed in this text and the foundation that you have gained from earlier chapters should make it possible for you to incorporate new advances during your career. Examine the new technology to see if it really helps solve your problem. If it does not, then wait for someone else to be the pioneer. If the technology offers you a solution, then adopt it with enthusiasm, and work to make the application successful.

KEY WORDS

Artificial intelligence
Bus architecture
Communications
  satellite
Density
Disk
Electronic mail
End user
Expert systems
Fiber optics
Fifth generation
Gigabyte
Interorganizational
  systems
Mass storage
Megabyte

Megaflop	PROLOG
Millisecond	Robots
Natural language	Rules
Office automation	User interface
Parallel processors	Vision
Professional programmer	Workstations

BUSINESS PROBLEMS

22.1. As technology changes, the opportunities open to a firm also change. Systems that could not be justified suddenly become feasible. Plans that were once discarded can be considered again. The firms that will be successful in the future are likely to take advantage of the technology in formulating their strategies.

If the technology is a constantly moving target, how do you incorporate it into your planning? Take some examples of the advances predicted in this chapter and describe how they could change the type of applications undertaken by a firm. What will be the impact of declines in communications costs or at least improvements in service?

Given the changes you predict, what can a firm do to take changing technology into account in formulating its plans? Does the rapid advance in technology make planning a futile effort? What options are open to the firm that thinks planning is still worthwhile?

22.2. One possible future scenario includes a workstation for every manager and possibly every information worker. The workstation might be configured differently for the secretary and for the manager, but both would have computer power available.

The manager will want to have a powerful local processor and the ability to connect with a network. The network will offer access to corporate databases and to other workstations for sending mail and memoranda. Typical programs executed at the manager's workstation will include spreadsheet analysis, word processing, presentation graphics, and database applications. The workstation will be justified in the same way that a typewriter or a telephone is justified today.

How can the organization prepare for this environment? What steps should it take now to be able to enjoy the benefits of this kind of technology in the future? What are the implications for training managers and other professionals? Can you think of any technological breakthroughs that would facilitate the implementation of this environment?

REVIEW QUESTIONS

1. What is a megaflop? How does it differ from an MIP?
2. How does a bus architecture differ from one based on controllers?
3. What is a parallel processor? Why is it faster than a single processor?
4. What is an array processor?
5. What breakthroughs are expected in mass storage?
6. What is VLSI?
7. What is the major drawback to optical storage?
8. What applications can make the most use of optical storage?
9. Why is fiber optics used for communications?
10. What is the advantage of satellite communications?
11. Why is heat a problem for computers?
12. What are the goals of the fifth-generation computer project?
13. What is the user interface? What is new about the user interface planned for the fifth generation?
14. What is natural language?
15. What is an expert system? Where do you think one could be used in business?
16. What is Artificial Intelligence? Why is it important to the fifth-generation effort?
17. Describe an electronic mail system. What are its advantages?
18. How does electronic mail supplement other forms of communications?
19. What was the impact of electronic mail at DEC?
20. Define CAD/CAM and tell how it can improve the manufacturing process.

THOUGHT QUESTIONS

21. Which new computer technologies appear most promising?
22. What is the role of the operating system in a multiprocessor system?
23. Describe the kind of computer complex you expect to see in the future.
24. Why do we keep trying to shrink the size of logic circuits and memory chips?
25. What will happen when circuits are reduced the size of molecules?

26. Why would a company want a private communications network?

27. Do you think entire computers will ever be made of biological components rather than silicon chips?

28. Why does the programmer need all of the tools described in this chapter?

29. Why will there be less COBOL programming in the future?

30. What are the alternatives to COBOL programming?

31. Why do we advocate the use of prototypes? What are the advantages of this approach? The disadvantages?

32. Sketch the coming computer environment for the end user.

33. Can you think of any drawbacks to natural-language computer input?

34. How does PROLOG differ from a more conventional language?

35. What are the implications of interorganizational systems, especially for privacy and security?

36. Why is it useful for robots to be able to see and feel?

37. Why is General Motors interested in CAD/CAM?

38. Why will computers continue to proliferate?

39. What are the programs that an end user is likely to employ from a microprocessor workstation connected to a large computer network?

40. What are the major limitations in applying the technology?

RECOMMENDED READINGS

Feigenbaum, E., and P. McCorduck. *The Fifth Generation*. Reading, MA: Addison-Wesley, 1983. A book that you will find easy to understand as it addresses the goals and techniques of the Japanese fifth-generation project.

High Technology. A popular magazine that explains advances in technology for lay people.

IEEE Spectrum. See especially the annual January issues, which forecast the technology for the coming year.

Kay, P., and P. Powell (eds.). "Future Information Processing Technology-1983," Washington, DC: National Bureau of Standards, 1983. An interesting technology forecast.

Chapter 23

One observation in the text has been the great shortage of qualified computer professionals. For a reader thinking about a future career, this profession offers a lot of opportunities. The popular conception is that information systems is a highly technical and mathematical field. This chapter will try to place the profession in perspective. Yes, there are positions that probably do rely on mathematics and draw on a computer science background. Yet, the majority of individuals working to use computers to solve business problems do not come out of computer science programs.

If you think back to the chapters on systems analysis and design and the numerous examples of systems discussed in the text, hopefully you will agree that much of the development effort is managerial. Systems analysis and determining the requirements for a new application are very important activities; for the most part, they require personal interaction among members of a design team and an ability to reason logically. A good understanding of the functions of business is an excellent preparation for this kind of work.

In this chapter, we discuss some of the careers in the computer profession. The positions covered are general; a specific company might not have individuals with these job titles or descriptions. For the most part, however, a firm with mainframes, minis, and/or micros will have someone performing the functions discussed in the chapter.

At the completion of this chapter, you should be able to:

- Describe the work done by computer professionals.
- Explain the way in which a typical firm organizes its computer department.
- Describe the structure of a computer department itself.
- Explain the difference between systems design and operations.
- Describe career paths for individuals working in the computer field.

THE COMPUTER PROFESSION

INTRODUCTION

As more users work with computers and the line between the end user and the professional blurs, will there still be a computer profession? The answer is definitely "yes." In fact, more demands than ever will be placed on the professional, though his or her role will change from what it is today.

We expect that the systems analyst and the programmer who works on applications will become more consultants and teachers for users. The whole computer profession will be providing far more education, preparing users to do more processing. A single systems analyst can work on one or two systems at a time. At the same time, he or she could train ten or more users to make a contribution to the design process or to write programs as end users.

THE COMPUTER INDUSTRY

A number of computer professionals work in the industry itself. The computer manufacturers, including those providing materials and supplies, represent over $40 billion a year in sales. The communications industry is a $70-billion market, and office equipment adds another $10 billion. Publishers and other disseminators of information have sales of $30 billion. The total is something over $150 billion a year that is in some way associated with computers and information processing.

Only a small fraction of the individuals employed in these industries actually work on the development of computer products and services. That small fraction is important, and there is a shortage of individuals who are able to fill these positions. What do these specialists do? Professionals employed by computer vendors develop software that is often sold commercially. They might design any or all of the following:

■ Operating systems
■ Utility programs
■ Languages
■ Compilers
■ Query languages
■ Database management systems
■ Dedicated applications (e.g., payroll packages)
■ Communications systems

Any of the software on this list may be developed for micros, minis, or mainframe computers.

Some of the development work—for example, developing languages and compilers—requires a strong computer-science background. A firm designing a new spreadsheet package for a micro may want to have it programmed in assembly language for speed of execution. However, few applications require this kind of talent for programming; computer science graduates are likely to work for firms in the business of building hardware and/or software systems.

Other types of software may demand a business or industry specialization on the part of the computer professional. If one's employer is designing software packages for the banking industry, at least a part of the project team will need to have a knowledge of banking. One of the most frequent complaints from users is that computer personnel do not understand the areas of business, like accounting or finance. It behooves the systems analyst and programmer to learn something about different business functions when designing a system for a firm.

A TYPICAL ORGANIZATION

A large number of individuals are employed who apply computer technology to solving problems in the firm. Computer departments range from one person to thousands. As an example, American Airlines employs over a thousand programmers, programmer/analysts, and systems analysts in support of its finance, marketing, administration, personnel, and subsidiary operations, including its Sabre reservations system. These employees work in three separate organizations, and Data Processing and Communications Services is a separate division of American Airlines.

Within the computer industry itself, there are many jobs that are not related to the development of computer products; computer professionals like systems analysts and programmers work to develop

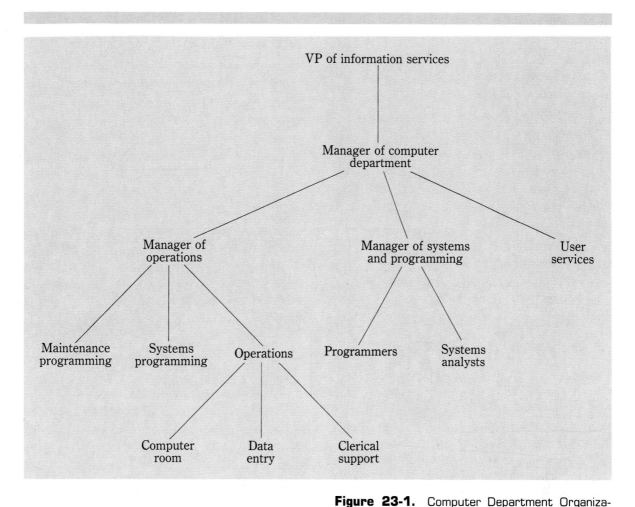

Figure 23-1. Computer Department Organization. Another way to organize an information services function; this one includes a subunit for user services.

applications to support the business, such as systems for sales reporting, accounting, and inventory control. In this section, we shall review some of the roles for computer professionals in the organization. (See Figure 23-1 for a typical computer department's organization.)

Senior Management

As budgets for information processing have increased and the critical importance of systems to the firm has become evident, organizations have moved the reporting relationship of the senior information-systems officer to higher levels. Early in the days of data processing, the head of the department reported several levels below the controller because many early applications were in accounting. Because the computer department cuts across many traditional department boundaries in the firm, it is probably a good idea to have it report somewhere other than to a department like accounting or finance.

One solution is to create a ***vice-president of in-***

Figure 23-2. (a) Computer operations area at McKesson Corporation for their Economost system. (b) Computer operations area at Chemical Bank, New York.

a

b

formation services or of administration with responsibility for information processing. This individual must be aware of corporate plans and the needs of management. He or she serves to link information systems planning to corporate plans. The role also includes working with other senior managers to be sure that adequate resources are devoted to systems in their areas.

Of course, this manager has to provide leadership for information processing itself. Budgets and plans plus requests for new resources come to the vice-president of information services; he or she must gain the approval of the plans from the most senior levels of management. Typical of these requests is the need for new hardware, such as a large mainframe computer, where the investment may run into the millions of dollars.

Computer Department Management

There are a number of management positions in the computer department, depending on its size. Usu-

Figure 23-3. I/O Control at Chemical Bank in New York.

ally, we find a single manager responsible for all of the activities in the department. This manager must be a skilled organizer; he or she is responsible for budgeting, planning, and keeping abreast of the technology.

The job also calls for working with the users (and for project management skills.) It is a very difficult position and many have been unsuccessful in it. The computer department manager almost always has inadequate resources to accomplish all of the requests that come from users. Some of these managers develop steering committees. Users are often in the majority of such a committee, which allocates resources. As a result, the computer department does not look arbitrary in selecting what applications will be developed.

We can divide the computer department into three main areas, each of which will have its own manager:

1. *Operations,* which is responsible for running the firm's computers.

2. *Systems development,* which builds new applications.
3. *User services,* which trains and consults with users. We shall now examine each of these areas in more detail.

Operations. The computer department has a diverse set of responsibilities. *Operations* is the firing line. The *operators* must keep the computers running (see Figure 23-2).

For batch systems, they must see that the work assigned to their shift is placed on the computer and executed correctly. Operators must load magnetic tapes and forms for the printer as well.

More important, for batch or on-line systems, operators must recognize hardware and software errors and take the appropriate action. It may be necessary to restart the system, to call a programmer or to call the computer vendor for service.

Input/output control is responsible for preparing the input for batch systems (see Figure 23-3). Any data not entered from a terminal in user areas must be keyed for the computer. The control group also checks the output reports. Are the totals correct? Do the accounting systems balance from run to run? The movement toward on-line systems has reduced the number of individuals in **input/output control** in many firms.

Maintenance programming is something that we have not discussed yet. Unlike the programmers of a new system, maintenance programmers work primarily with changes in existing programs. Some of these changes are due to errors in the original system. (Remember that it is impossible to test exhaustively every part of a program; as new conditions arise during program execution, they may trigger an error not found before.) Studies suggest that errors or bugs do not take the majority of the maintenance programmer's time. Instead, the maintenance work load is dominated by **enhancements,** changes requested by users in existing systems. An enhancement may be as simple as a new format for a report or as complex as major surgery to restructure files and reports. On the average, about 50 percent of a department's resources for programming are devoted to maintenance. We hope that in the future, end user programming will satisfy some of these requests for ad hoc reports and queries.

There have been reports of dramatic reductions in change requests once users are given tools and training to do some of their own programming. IBM, Ltd., in Canada found that the maintenance requirements took 40 percent of the computer staff, down from about 70 percent, when about five hundred users started working with end user tools. About half the project requests are being completed by the users.

Maintenance programming is difficult because one is generally changing a program written by someone else. It is very hard to look at and understand another programmer's code. Some organizations rotate programmers between new development and maintenance, possibly to encourage programmers to write clear programs and **document** them (describe what the programs do).

Another type of programmer, the systems programmer, usually works in the operations area. This individual is most often found working with mainframes or minis. He or she is a specialist in the operating system and the systems software. Why is such an individual needed? Computer vendors are constantly updating their systems software; they fix bugs and errors and provide new functions. As a result, the customer must install the new software. Frequently, various types of systems programs require some modification so that they will all work together. The systems programmer would interface, for example, a telecommunications monitor, the operating system, and a database management system so that all would cooperate together. Systems programming is highly specialized and requires a strong technical background.

Systems Development. Systems development is very unlike operations. The time horizon is long, and the computer professionals here must be creative. They often work in groups to design a system. Typically, there is a design team that includes users.

Often the work here has a strong research-and-development flavor. Although the designers know how to develop a system, each application presents some new features or a unique set of problems. It has proved very difficult to anticipate all of the problems that will arise in developing a system. As a result, systems usually take longer than anticipated to complete; they often cost more than predicted; and sometimes, the original design specifications are compromised so that the project can be completed.

The roles in systems development are changing, though many long-term staff members are resisting the change. Two major trends are affecting analysts and programmers.

The first trend is due to the problems in the length of time required to develop custom systems. One group of researchers studying large corporations found a large backlog of systems authorized for development, but waiting to be started. This backlog extended three years and longer into the future.

Although this discovery was alarming in itself, the researchers also found an equally large number of applications that users had not suggested yet because they were discouraged by the current backlog. Most professionals realize the something has to

backlog - accumulation of work or business not yet attended.

be done to reduce both the visible and the invisible backlogs.

One approach to this problem is the use of more packaged programs. However, often the computer professional feels that a package is unsatisfying; it is more fun to build a system than to try to get someone else's to work. We have seen that there is still a need for systems analysis and design when a dedicated package is purchased, but some organizations do not realize it. Thus, the analyst may feel that his or her skills are diminished by packages.

The second trend to help solve productivity problems is to move toward higher-level or fourth-generation languages and transactions processors. Some analysts view these tools as a real advantage, and others resist them. Possibly, the resistance is rooted in a fear of deskilling or replacement, and possibly, it is due to a desire to not have to learn new techniques. Clearly, the future will bring a greater use of these tools. No good analysts need worry that their skills will not be needed. There are many new applications just waiting for attention.

User Services. The growing backlog of applications, *fourth-generation languages,* query languages for databases, and microcomputers has brought **end users** rapidly into computing. These end users need consulting help and support to work with computers. End users of fourth-generation languages want to be able to access corporate data; computer professionals are usually necessary to help locate the data and copy them to a file or download them to a personal computer for the user. Usually, we do not want the user to modify the original data, so the computer department makes a copy of them.

A number of firms have established user services groups to assist end users. One popular mechanism for user support is an *information center,* a place that provides users with help on query and fourth-generation languages. The information center staff also locates data for users and frequently merges or combines data from different files to make it easier for users to access them.

An information center can also function as a computer store; that is, it has various brands of microcomputers and software for demonstration pur-

poses. The user can receive advice and actually try a machine in a supportive environment. Consulting help is available for the most popular microcomputer software being used in the firm (see Figure 23-4).

South Pacific Communications Company offers a good example of the use of an information center. The firm sells communications services in the United States; it is the largest private microwave trunk carrier in the United States. The company has eight hundred sales agents around the country who are independent; they are paid on the basis of new accounts generated and the volume of use of the communications services they sell. The firm did not plan to issue IRS 1099 forms, but the agents complained that they needed them for their taxes. A 1099 is a summary of earnings for an independent contractor who is not a regular employee of the firm and for whom the firm withholds no federal income taxes.

There was no way to go through a year's payment record manually to produce the needed 1099's. However, an employee of the finance department used the tools in the information center to sort the names of all the agents in alphabetical order and to subtotal the payments for each. With that information, it was possible to prepare the 1099's in about two days.

The result was a happy user in the finance department and eight hundred sales agents who received the output they wanted. More important, the request was handled in a timely manner without the involvement of programmers. Without an information center and end user tools, the user would have to make a formal request for maintenance; the request would have had to be prioritized and then placed in the queue of pending requests waiting for a maintenance programmer. Finally, with luck, the program would have been written and tested. It is hard to imagine a task like that being completed in less than a week, and some users wait months for requests to be fulfilled. If such a request were given a high priority by management, the computer department would have to interrupt work on some other request to work on this project. As a result, another user would be displaced. The information center will not solve all problems, but it can help

Figure 23-4. An information center at Manufacturers Hanover Trust Company headquarters in Manhattan. Financial planning workers receive instruction from a computer staff member.

remove some of the pressure on the computer department.

User services is a precursor of a new role for many professionals, that of a consultant and teacher. For many years, systems analysts and programmers practiced a mystical art. However, many users are getting involved with computers; they want help in doing the job themselves rather than waiting for a staff member to take over the job completely. More and more, the computer professional in the organization will become a teacher and a consultant to users.

Different Organizational Structures

There are many different structures for information processing; we have discussed centralized, decentralized, and distributed. We can have hardware, operations, and systems analysis in various organizational structures from **centralized** to **decentralized.** Do the roles of computer staff members

change under these different structures? Some of the activities will be different, as will the hardware and the software, but the basic functions remain the same.

The highly centralized operation may have economies of scale (proportionately less expensive equipment and fewer employees are needed for a larger operation than for many smaller ones) and greater specialization than smaller units; for example, for mainframe computers, there is often a systems programmer who tends software like the operating system and the telecommunications monitor. If Multicorp were centralized, it could afford a systems programmer. However, three decentralized centers might not have enough work for one systems programmer at each location.

The major challenge to centralized departments is to be responsive to users. Some users feel that decentralized operations are more responsive because they are responsible to local management. The challenge to management under decentralization or *distributed* processing is to see that there is coordination and some semblance of standards. If we fail to coordinate, each decentralized operation may develop the same application, which would probably be a waste of resources.

Thus, the activities of programmers and analysts are the same under the various forms of organizational structure, but management and the computer professional have to recognize the multiple roles that they play and adjust their style for the structure of the firm. The type of management appropriate and the type of coordination required do differ for alternative organizational structures for computing. Centralization requires effort to be responsive to users; decentralization requires effort to coordinate different computer locations.

USERS

An organization consists of many different individuals. A manager is in charge of some work unit, and he or she may request a new application. When the system is under development, the manager needs to stay aware of the logic of the system and to see that users in the department work on the project. Managers must lead the systems development process in their departments.

Users take part in systems analysis and design. They must spend time explaining requirements and reviewing the system. The user provides test data and accepts the application as complete. Without commitment on the part of users, systems have little chance of success.

The movement toward end user computing helps to bring users closer to the computer professional. Managers and other users now have personal computers and routinely access corporate data. More user orientation on the part of the computer professional and greater knowledge by the end user should help to improve the effectiveness of information processing in the organization. The potential of computer technology is great, and the opportunities for this technology to contribute to the user and to the organization are unlimited.

CAREER PATHS

We have discussed a number of different positions in this chapter, all of them involved in the computer field. How do you begin a career in this area? How do you progress to higher-level positions?

Figure 23-5 is an example of how one might move in an organization by starting in information systems. We are assuming here a typical firm with a mature computer operation. The firm has a mainframe computer and some micros, and there is quite possibly a minicomputer or two also available.

Staff Positions

Beginning with the lower-left-hand side of the figure, we have the systems programmer, who works with the operating system, systems programs like those for handling communications between the computer and the on-line terminals, and the installation of new software. This individual probably has a computer science background and is interested in working with software. He or she has to understand hardware but will probably not be involved in developing or modifying it. There is limited contact with users; most interactions will take place in the computer department itself.

Maintenance programmers also generally report to the operations area. These individuals have the same skills as an applications programmer (programmers who work in new applications); in fact, maintenance programmers may be more skilled because they must understand someone else's program and modify it. Unlike systems programmers, maintenance programmers may have contact with users. Sometimes, they respond to written requests as submitted, but more often, they have to check with the user making the maintenance request to determine exactly what is wanted.

The operations staff in the computer department has the lowest required level of education. The operations staff consists of computer operators, input/output (I/O) control clerks, and data entry operators. Most systems programmers have a computer science or technical background, and maintenance programmers usually have at least a two-year college degree; often, they have a bachelor's degree. The operations staff may have some college training, but it is not a requirement. Operators are trained on the job and at computer vendors' schools to run a specific computer with a specific operating system. Data entry personnel and I/O clerks are also involved in operations, and no special educational background beyond high school is usually required for these positions.

Moving to the right in the figure, we find programmers for applications, who come from a variety of backgrounds. Some may be technical majors who are interested in applying their knowledge; others are from business programs. We predict that, more and more, the programmer for applications will come from a business background. Programming is becoming less technical as we move to higher-level languages and new tools. The programmer needs to be able to communicate with users and to understand the functional requirements for a system. An entry-level programmer today probably will need a college degree for most organizations.

The *systems analyst* needs a good business background; this individual works with users and suggests how technology can help solve their information-processing problems. The job is less technical than programming; it requires good interpersonal communications skills and an ability to reason logically.

In the past, many systems analysts had a background in programming; when a programmer reached the top of a salary scale in programming, he or she became a systems analyst because these jobs were considered more demanding and paid better than programming. Unfortunately, this career path has not always been successful. Today, many firms recognize that they need senior programmers, individuals who want to remain in programming rather than to move to another job. Many programmers are far better at designing algorithms and programs than they are at dealing with users. As a result, we would expect to see fewer programmers moving into analysis in the future.

Looking at the lowest level of the figure, we can see that there are several paths for individuals with programming jobs. The maintenance or systems programmer who is really interested in management can become the manager of operations. However, as has already been mentioned, organizations are recognizing the need for senior programmers, just as many industries have senior engineers. it may become quite acceptable for a programmer to remain in this job category and simply to progress in skill levels and salary.

The applications programmer or systems analyst can move into management or can remain and progress to become senior in her or his present staff job. The analyst might become manager of systems and programming or of user services. Because user departments are doing more computing, an analyst might decide to move from the computer department to become a user department analyst in some department like marketing, accounting, or finance.

Middle Management

The manager of operations is like any line manager; he or she occupies a position similar to that of a factory manager. The computer department has resources and jobs to do; they must be scheduled, and the facilities must be kept available to users. The manager of operations also has to "fight fires." Unanticipated machine downtime, the failure of a program that is in production, and a communications line that becomes unavailable all create problems to which this manager must respond.

The manager of systems and programming faces an entirely different environment. Here, the work is more project-oriented. It also has a lot of uncertainty of the kind that we find in research-and-development efforts. No one knows all of the problems that will be encountered on a development project, and it is even hard to know how complete a system actually is. This manager must obtain reports from the staff on progress and then adjust resources to try to keep projects on schedule.

The manager of user services has a job that is midway between the requirements of the other two managers at this level. User services is an ongoing activity, but in most instances, it does not have the responsibility for running specific jobs on computers. There are systems development projects, but their duration is far shorter than that of the large-scale

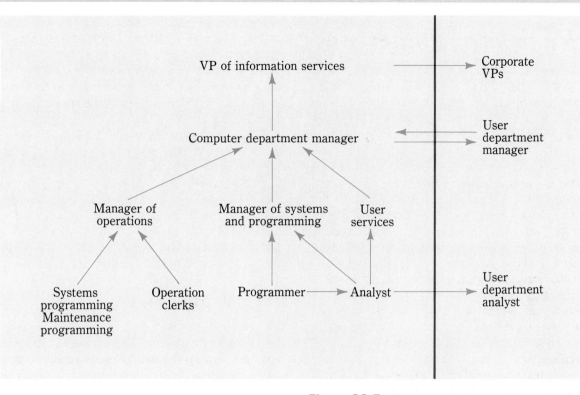

Figure 23-5. Computer Profession Career Paths. There are many different career paths within the information services area. Computer staff members can also move into other parts of the organization.

applications. The pressures come from trying to be responsive to users. User problems should be given a quick solution, which often requires extensive research by a computer-department staff member in user services. This staff member needs to be very user-oriented; he or she functions as a consultant and teacher for users.

Senior Management

We discussed earlier some of the duties of the computer department manager. This individual has often come from the ranks of technical positions in the department. In the future, it is likely that this position will be filled by someone with a management background. The technical issues are not as important today as are management problems. The technical staff can support the manager in the technological aspects of his or her job.

The basic problem has been that many technical staff members who have moved into management lack the ability to communicate. These individuals are conditioned to seeing very detailed, very technical problems. Sometimes, they have had trouble adapting to the scope of the manager's responsibilities. The computer department manager is concerned with the entire organization, not a technical computer problem. Certainly, at the vice-presidential level, we will find managers who are skilled in organization, leadership, and communications.

Review of Chapter 23

REVIEW

The computer profession offers numerous opportunities. In general, salaries for jobs demanding at least an associate's degree are quite good. Working in a well-managed computer department can be very satisfying. There is an opportunity to see systems make a major contribution to the firm and to the individuals working for the firm.

We have reviewed the tasks associated with different positions in the computer department. One objective was to dispel the notion that a computer science background is required for developing computer applications in a firm. As we have seen, a good knowledge of the functions of a business and the ability to think logically are far more important. We need computer department staff members who can communicate and present alternatives to users. The future will demand that a systems analyst act more as a consultant and an educator than as the person in charge of a project.

The computer field offers one the opportunity to stay in a job that is appealing, like that of a programmer or an analyst, and to become a senior professional in that specialty. Options to move into management also exist if such a move should become more appealing. As computer applications continue to expand and as more users work with computers, there will also be opportunities to move into other parts of the firm.

Whether or not you choose the information systems field directly, you will continue to be influenced by this technology. Computer professionals, end users, and managers of all types influence information systems and at the same time are influenced by them. The future of this technology is their responsibility. The purpose of this text is to prepare you to take full advantage of the opportunities offered by information-processing technology.

KEY WORDS

Career paths	Fourth-generation
Centralization	language
Decentralization	Information center
Distributed	I/O control
Documentation	Maintenance
End users	programming
Enhancements	Operating system

Operations   Users
Operator   User services
Programmer   Vice-president of
Systems analyst   information
Systems development   services
Systems programmer

BUSINESS PROBLEMS

23.1. The classical role of the systems analyst has been to meet with users, to ask questions to determine their needs for information processing, and to design a system. The analyst has clearly been in charge of this process, and the user has responded to him or her. There have been a number of problems with this model, communications are sometimes distorted and systems end up looking quite different from what the user expected.

Enter the era of end user computing. We have talked about packages, end user programming, fourth-generation languages, and a multitude of applications for microcomputers. All of these trends suggest that the systems analyst's role, at least in a large number of projects, will change.

We will still have some systems that follow the classical development model, especially large transactions systems or database systems. However, when the user is taking a larger role in information processing, the analyst will have to act differently. No longer will he or she be in charge. Instead, the analyst must become more of a teacher and a consultant to the user.

What strategy can you suggest to the organization for developing individuals with modern analysis talents? Should the firm try to reeducate existing analysts or hire new ones? What background would be best for the new analysts? Do new trends actually open up a new profession?

23.2. A chairman of the board of a corporation once asked, "How much money should we be spending on computing? How can we know what we are getting for it?"

These questions are hard, and possibly they do not have answers, at least answers that will satisfy the board chairman.

Try to outline a response to the chairman. Think about the issues covered in the text, and develop a series of recommendations for evaluating the return from the firm's investment in information processing.

Is the first question relevant? If not, why not? Can you help the chairman?

REVIEW QUESTIONS

1. Describe the major components of the computer industry.
2. What background is required to develop systems software?
3. What are the roles of senior information-systems management?
4. Why should the senior systems officer not report to an area like accounting or production?
5. Is the systems area important enough to be headed by a vice-president?
6. What are the various demands on the computer department manager?
7. What are the three main activities of the computer department?
8. How do operations differ for batch and on-line systems?
9. How would you describe the function of the I/O control group?
10. What is maintenance programming?
11. What kind of changes do maintenance programmers make?
12. How is the role of the computer professional changing?
13. How can an information center potentially reduce maintenance requests?
14. What is the management challenge of the decentralization of the computer department? Of the centralization of the computer department?
15. What should users do in systems development?

THOUGHT QUESTIONS

16. How does the design of an operating system differ from the design of an applications program?
17. Why are new languages being designed?
18. Why would a computer vendor develop a system using assembly language?
19. How can an operator tell if there is a hardware or a software error?
20. Why will the operations group shrink with on-line systems? Do you think that it will ever disappear?

21. What would you describe as the impact of systems analysis and design on maintenance programming?
22. How does systems development differ from operations?
23. Why do developers often work with teams of users?
24. Why might analysts and programmers resist some of the new approaches to systems development?
25. How can we break the applications backlog? Describe two approaches.
26. How are end users and computer professionals being drawn closer together?
27. What kind of consulting help do end users need with fourth-generation languages? With microcomputers?
28. How do computer professionals' roles change under different forms of computer department organization?
29. Where do you see conflict developing between users and computer professionals?
30. How will computer staff members and users have to interact in order to achieve the potential of the computer?

RECOMMENDED READINGS

Datamation. A widely read periodical in the computer profession; contains frequent articles on various positions in the field.

Computer Decisions. Another journal devoted to the profession with articles about the management of the computer department.

Lucas, H. C., Jr., *The Analysis, Design and Implementation of Information Systems.* (3rd ed.). New York: McGraw-Hill, 1985. See particularly the chapter on the computer department.

BASIC Appendix

Prepared by Robert Saldarini, Bergen Community College.

This segment is dedicated to the "art" of programming. Although many individuals believe programming is a science, in many ways it qualifies as an art. Each programmer designs and creates a program that incorporates his or her own expertise and style. Novice programmers often duplicate the programming methodology of more experienced programmers. As they gain programming experience, their own unique style usually emerges. The outcome of one's skill and creativity is the computer program, a carefully thought out list of instructions which, when executed, solves a problem efficiently and accurately.

TOOLS OF THE TRADE

As in any other trade, programmers have certain tools, predefined procedures, and technical jargon. The tools include such items as a flowchart template, layout forms, diskettes, and, of course, a computer system. Special-purpose software routines called *algorithms* and structure design techniques are examples of predefined procedures. Finally, the thousands of acronyms, such as IBM,

VSAM, and UNIX, are one example of the programmer's jargon.

Regardless of the programmer's level of experience, an analysis of the problem must be completed before the **coding** (writing) of the program solution. In a manner of speaking, the computer can be viewed as a student with a great desire to learn; the programmer fulfills the role of the teacher. Before the programmer can teach the machine how to solve a problem, he or she must be able to solve it manually. Problem analysis may take a considerable amount of time if the task is very involved or complex. Take a moment to remember how much time you required to solve for your first unknown element in chemistry, or how much time it took you to analyze and completely understand the registration system at your college. Even though the problems presented in these pages are fundamental, taking time for problem analysis is still essential.

The **program flowchart,** an analytical tool, is a graphic solution to a given problem. The programmer draws it using a stencil-like guide called a **flowchart template.** The flowchart provides a reference for coding the program because it details all processing logic. The American National Standards

567

FLOWCHART SYMBOLS

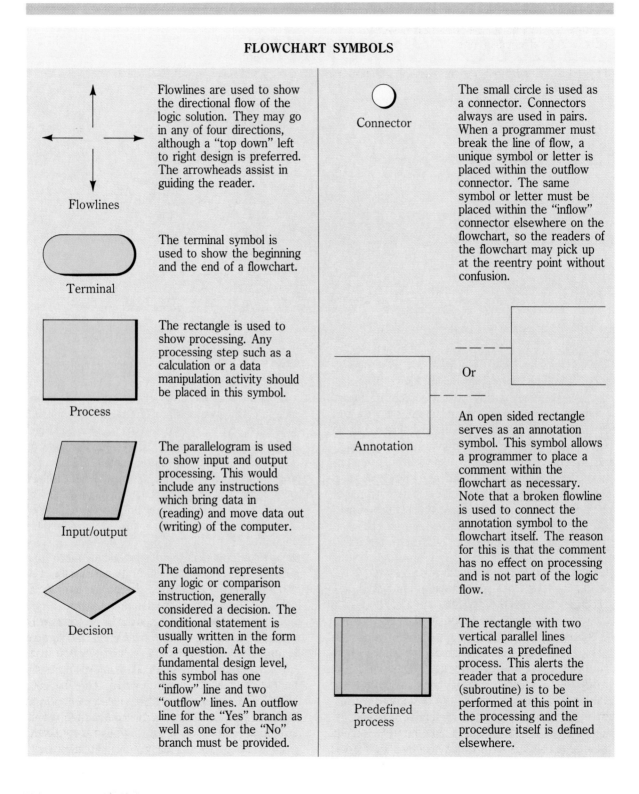

Flowlines

Flowlines are used to show the directional flow of the logic solution. They may go in any of four directions, although a "top down" left to right design is preferred. The arrowheads assist in guiding the reader.

Terminal

The terminal symbol is used to show the beginning and the end of a flowchart.

Process

The rectangle is used to show processing. Any processing step such as a calculation or a data manipulation activity should be placed in this symbol.

Input/output

The parallelogram is used to show input and output processing. This would include any instructions which bring data in (reading) and move data out (writing) of the computer.

Decision

The diamond represents any logic or comparison instruction, generally considered a decision. The conditional statement is usually written in the form of a question. At the fundamental design level, this symbol has one "inflow" line and two "outflow" lines. An outflow line for the "Yes" branch as well as one for the "No" branch must be provided.

Connector

The small circle is used as a connector. Connectors always are used in pairs. When a programmer must break the line of flow, a unique symbol or letter is placed within the outflow connector. The same symbol or letter must be placed within the "inflow" connector elsewhere on the flowchart, so the readers of the flowchart may pick up at the reentry point without confusion.

Annotation Or

An open sided rectangle serves as an annotation symbol. This symbol allows a programmer to place a comment within the flowchart as necessary. Note that a broken flowline is used to connect the annotation symbol to the flowchart itself. The reason for this is that the comment has no effect on processing and is not part of the logic flow.

Predefined process

The rectangle with two vertical parallel lines indicates a predefined process. This alerts the reader that a procedure (subroutine) is to be performed at this point in the processing and the procedure itself is defined elsewhere.

Figure 1. (opposite) Select ANSI flowchart symbols with brief descriptions.

Figure 2. (a) (right) The sequential order of instructions.

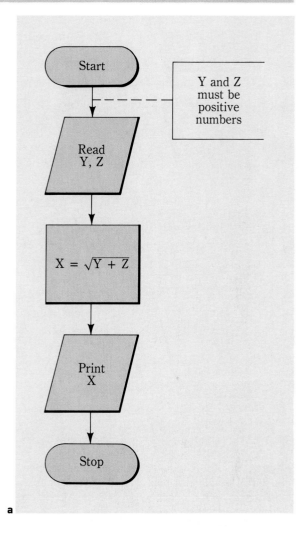

a

Institute (ANSI) has adopted several symbols for use in the flowcharting effort. All programmers are encouraged to use these symbols so that flowcharts may serve as a communications tool. Selected symbols are shown in Figure 1.

Flowchart solutions are tested for accuracy by the performance of a *walk-through.* This method of verification requires the programmer to invent test data and to proceed through the flowchart while actually carrying out each instruction as it is encountered. If the results of conducting the walk-through with pencil and paper are correct, the flowchart is considered logically correct. If the results are erroneous, a logic problem exists that must be corrected before the program is coded.

The computer executes instructions sequentially, line by line, unless the program directs otherwise. Figure 2(a) illustrates this *simple-sequence* structure of processing. Notice that the flow begins and then terminates after only one X has been computed. In order to calculate another X, the potential program must be executed again. Although the results are accurate, the program design is inefficient.

In order to process many X's, one can create a

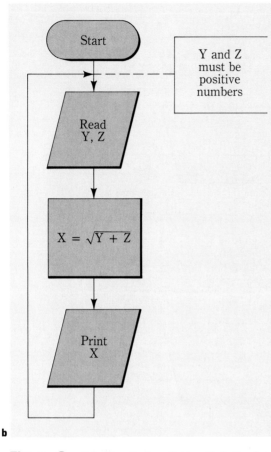

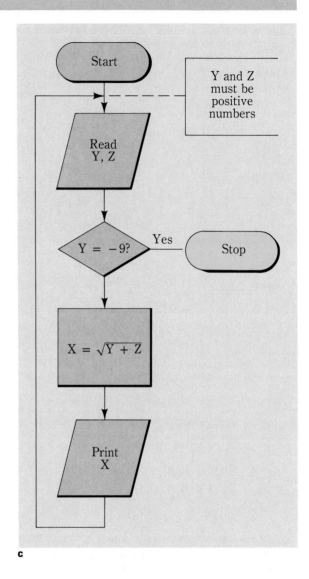

Figure 2. (b) The logic of the "infinite loop," caused by an unconditional branch. (c) A successful loop design with an unconditional branch that provides a means of terminating the loop.

loop. A simple loop contains a few instructions that are performed repetitively. Often an ***unconditional branch*** instruction passes control to a specified location that continues the repetition. The logic shown in Figure 2(b) creates a loop. Unfortunately, the loop is continued ad infinitum, calculating X's forever. This type of loop, ***an infinite loop,*** is often a trap set by the novice programmer.

To avoid an infinite loop, the programmer must insert a decision symbol into the flowchart logic to represent a ***conditional branch*** instruction. A conditional branch is usually expressed in the form of a question that has only a "Yes" or "No" answer. The question is selected based on the overall problem. During every occurrence of the loop, the programmer must ensure that the computer will determine whether the loop should continue. Figure 2(c) uses the question "$Y = -9$?" as the decision on whether to exit or to continue the loop. This choice is based on the fact that no valid Y could be negative

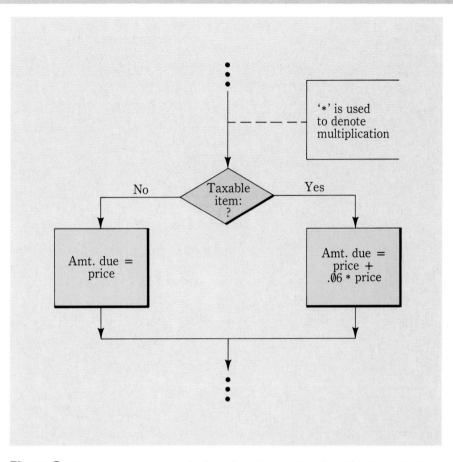

Figure 3. A decision segment of a flowchart illustrating the selection structure of processing.

(see the flowchart annotation). The users can supply all the data they wish and simply terminate the program by supplying a "−9" for the value of Y.

To summarize, a simple loop structure may require the use of two types of branching. The first, the unconditional branch instruction, is used to transfer control to a specific location that causes a segment of code to be executed repetitively. In the flowchart, the unconditional branch is represented by a flowline directing the reader forward or back past one or several symbols. Second, the programmer must provide a conditional branch instruction (represented for flowcharting purposes by a decision symbol) in order to terminate processing and to

avoid an infinite loop.

Conditional branching instructions serve other purposes, such as allowing for the **processing of alternatives.** The ability to handle alternatives easily enables the programmer to be selective in processing. For example, assume that a 6 percent sales tax is applied to all taxable items. At the point where the total amount due from a customer is calculated, a decision must be made. If the item being purchased is taxable, then the amount due is equal to the price plus the applicable tax. If the item is nontaxable, the amount due is equal to the price. This decision or **selection structure** is illustrated in Figure 3.

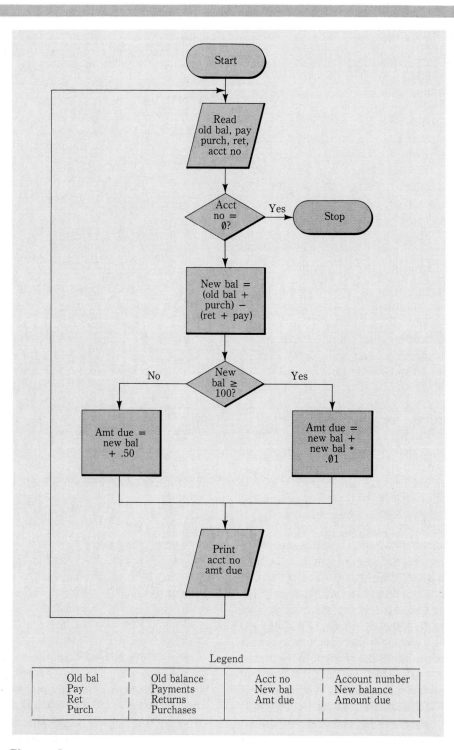

Figure 4. A complete flowchart showing the logic solution for Ms. Syms's credit report request.

Flowchart Analysis

Problem. Connie Syms, owner of CS Auto Parts, requires a program that will calculate the total amount due from each of her credit customers (see Figure 4). A new balance is calculated monthly, which is equal to the old balance plus purchases, less payments and returns. If the newly calculated balance is greater than or equal to $100, a 1 percent finance charge is assessed on the new balance; otherwise a fixed amount of 50 cents is applied. No customer has an account number of zero. (For simplicity, ignore the possibility of a negative account balance.)

Before continuing, note the following:

1. The appropriate usage of ANSI symbols.
2. The sequence of instructions.
3. The well-designed loop using the question "Acct no. = 0" to create a conditional branch.
4. The use of the selection structure to calculate the amount due with the appropriate finance charge.

Accumulation is a common procedure in programming. One needs to "accumulate" whenever a running total is required for a **data item** that increases by unknown amounts. A payroll clerk may need to know the total of the wages paid for a given period, or a sales supervisor may require the total amount of all the sales for the northeast region. These are examples of quantities that would have to be accumulated.

Figure 5 shows the logic involved in the accumulation of total wages. Notice that the amount of total wages is initialized to zero. After each wage calculation, the product is added to the accumulator (total wages). The value of the accumulator is printed just before the termination of processing. One can prove the accuracy of this flowchart by performing a walkthrough with a small set of test data.

Another common procedure in programming is *counting.* Counting involves increments in equal amounts. One may count by increments of 1, 2, 10, and so on, but always in a fixed amount. Figure 6 calculates the average of five test scores, each of

which is entered individually. The counter (count), initialized to 1 in this case, is increased by 1 before the next input ("Read") instruction. This design requires no fictitious data; the solution is based on the internal counting logic. Even though the counting procedure is used often in various forms, counting to a result that ends processing is rare. Such a design would make a program very inflexible. When most programs are written the number of data items is unknown. Some advanced applications may use selected counting procedures to terminate processing.

Flowchart Analysis

Problem. Bill Richards, personnel manager for VT Enterprises, would like a listing of part-time employee wages (see Figure 7). His request includes a list of both Type 1 employees, who are clerks, and Type 2 employees, who are sales representatives. Clerical personnel receive a wage equal to their rate of pay multiplied by the hours they work. In addition to a wage ascertained by multiplying the rate of pay by the hours worked, sales representatives receive a 10 percent commission based on their weekly sales. Mr. Richards would like to know the total number of part-time employees as well as the total gross pay for the period.

Before continuing, note the following:

1. The report has a heading that occurs before the loop. If the unconditional branch directs control to return and reenter before the heading, a heading will print before every line of printed detail information.
2. The total employees number is derived by counting.
3. The total gross pay amount is derived by accumulating.

When a programmer wishes to divide the overall processing job into various independent segments of code, **subroutines** are created. A subroutine is a selected group of instructions that perform a certain procedure or accomplish a specific programming task. A subroutine may be invoked by some type of "calling" statement. After the subroutine processing

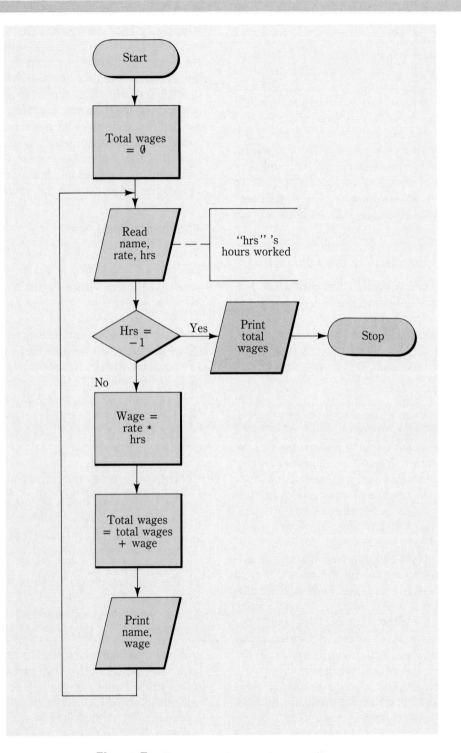

Figure 5. The accumulation of total wages.

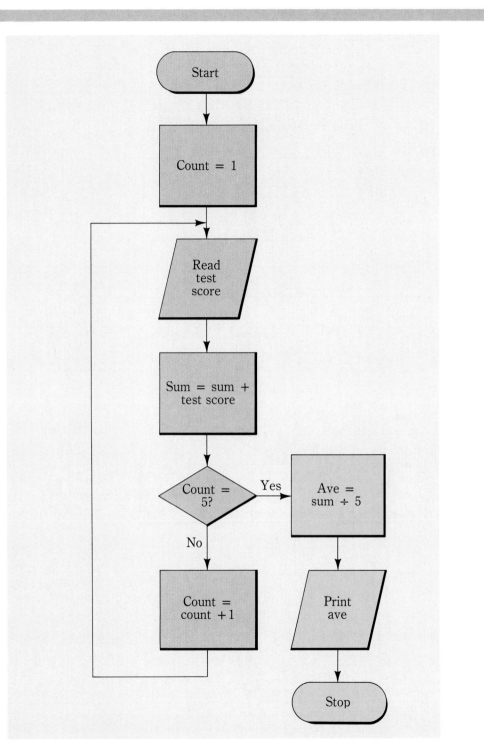

Figure 6. Counting logic by an interval of 1.

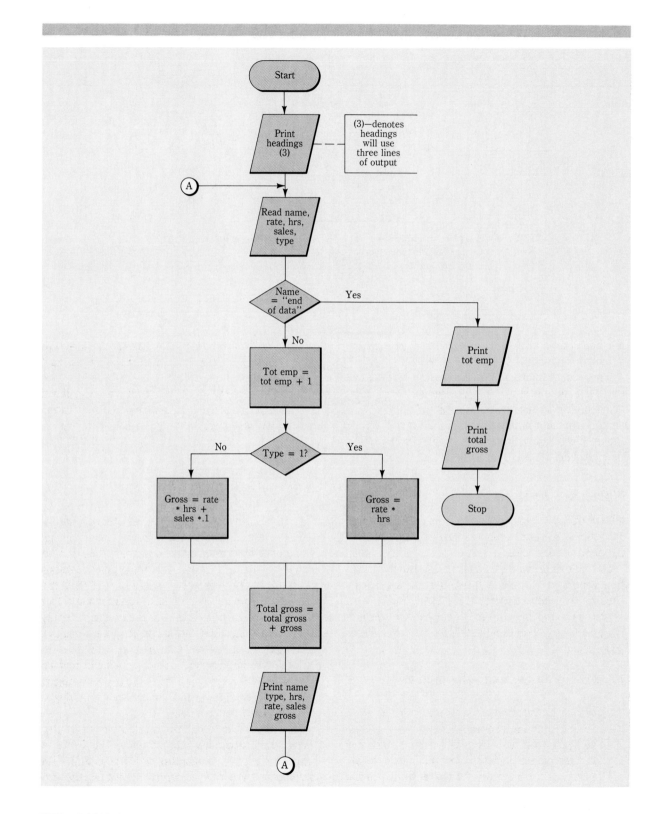

Legend			
Hrs	Hours worked	Tot emp	Total employees
Rate	Rate of pay	Type	Employee type
Sales	Weekly sales	Gross	Gross pay

Figure 7. (opposite page and above) A complete flowchart showing the logic solution for Mr. Richards's payroll report request.

is complete, control is passed back to the next executable instruction following the "call."

The use of subroutines aids the programmer in obtaining an efficient solution. Redundant code is avoided; when the same procedure is to be repeated, the subroutine need only be "called" again. Figure 8 uses a headings subroutine to ensure that a new heading will be printed at the top of each page.

Flowchart Analysis

PROBLEM. Paulene DiQuattro needs a listing of the names and addresses of her one-hundred-fifty-member Garden Club.

In order to provide Paulene with a visually attractive report, a three-line heading must appear on each page of output. Also, three blank lines should be left at the top and bottom of each page to serve as margins. A zip code of −99999 is used to terminate processing.

Before continuing, note the following:

1. The use of the predefined process symbol.
2. The line counting procedure.
3. The eject to a new page is accomplished only when the page is logically over (63 lines). Recall, three lines are required for the bottom margin.

(In BASIC, ejecting to a new page is accomplished by a series of PRINT instructions, as illustrated in Figure 25.)
4. The placement of the "Return" in the subroutine's terminal symbol. Control must be returned to the next executable statement following the "call" instruction.

BASIC CONSIDERATIONS

The BASIC language has been in existence since the 1960s. Beginning as a simple fundamental language to be used in an educational setting, BASIC has become one of the most popular languages for personal computing. There are many versions of BASIC that offer the same statements, with variations in regard to syntax. *Syntax* is defined as the rules and regulations of the language. A violation of syntax results in a *syntax error.* If such an error occurs, the programmer must examine the objectionable instruction, locate the error, and make the appropriate correction. (See Figure 9 for a summary of the syntax notation used in this appendix).

The BASIC instruction is divided into three sections: the line number, the statement, and the optional variable(s), constant(s), or expression(s). The instructions are *free-formatted;* that is, the pro-

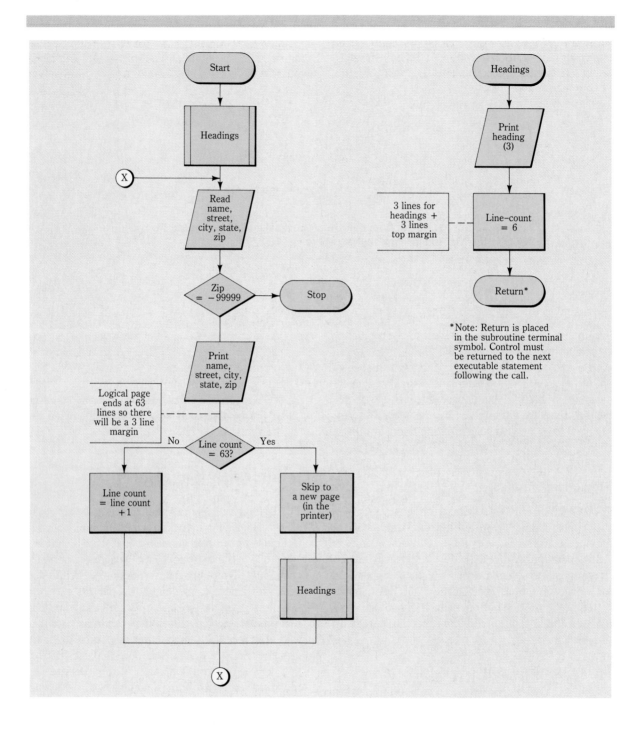

Figure 8. (opposite) A complete flowchart showing the logic solution for Ms. DiQuattro's listing· using a headings subroutine that is "called" to prevent a duplication of code.

Figure 9. (below) Syntax notation may vary from one source to another. It is important to become familiar with the author's method of presentation.

A Word About Syntax Notation

The syntax notation used within this section follows the following conventions:

Notation	Explanation
line #	A BASIC line number is required.
UPPERCASE WORDS	BASIC terms that are required in the instruction to ensure proper processing.
lowercase words	Programmer supplied terms.
Braces $\{\ \}$	Braces represent alternatives. One of the alternates must be selected in order for processing to occur.
Brackets $[\ \ ]$	When syntax is placed in brackets it is considered optional. Programmer discretion must be applied to determine if the option is needed for processing.
Ellipsis . . .	The ellipsis indicate an item may be repeated any number of times.
< >	When a certain key is to be pressed on the keyboard, it's name is placed within this notation.
var. N or con. N	Used to denote the last programmer supplied variable or constant to guarantee successful processing.
. ; : ( )	Punctuation is illustrated as required.

grammer may leave spaces where he or she wishes in order to make the program more readable. IBM-PC BASIC does require that at least one blank space follow a statement. One must remember it is the line number that initiates a new instruction. Periodically, an instruction may "wrap around" to the next line if it is longer than eighty characters and thus occupies more than one line on the screen.

After the code is keyed into the computer, the programmer may request a *LIST*ing. It is considered good practice to "sight-verify" the listing for obvious syntax errors before an execution. When the programmer believes that the program will work, it is time to *RUN* (execute) the program. If the desired results are achieved, the program is considered logically correct. If there is an error, the programmer must rework the logic, make the appropriate modifications, and run the program again.

Line Numbers

BASIC instructions are used to inform the computer of the actions that must be taken to complete processing. These instructions are executed sequentially unless the program statements direct the computer to do otherwise. BASIC statements must be preceded by a *line number* that indicates placement. Line numbers may be assigned by the programmer manually or may be specified by the computer if the AUTO function is enabled (see the section on IBM-PC operations).

One might think that line numbers should appear in increments of one. In actuality, line numbers are spaced by a predetermined interval, usually 10, in order to allow for the easy insertion of additional code between any two previously coded lines, if the need arises.

Because the line numbers are ordinal and may have uneven intervals, they reflect sequence only: it would be incorrect to assume that a BASIC statement with the line number 30 is the thirtieth statement in the program.

At certain times, a programmer may want two or more BASIC statements to have the same line number. This is possible if the two statements are separated by a colon.

Constants

A *constant* is a data item that cannot change in value. There are two types of constants in BASIC programming: numeric constants and string constants.

A number such as 2433 is a numeric constant. *Numeric constants* are composed of the digits 0 through 9 and, if desired, a decimal point and a positive or negative sign. Unsigned numbers are assumed by the computer to be positive. The comma and the dollar sign, which are used often when one is writing out numeric amounts by hand, are not allowed within a constant.

When very large or very small numbers are to be used, the programmer may have to represent these numeric constants in *exponential notation.* Exponential notation, which is a variation of scientific notation, requires the number to be simplified by the use of the powers of 10. Assume that the programmer would like to use the numeric constant 4000000000000000000. This number would exceed the computer's storage capability for a constant, which is a maximum of sixteen digits plus a sign. In exponential notation, this number could be expressed as 4 times 10 to the 18th power. In BASIC notation, the constant is written as $4E+18$. The E is symbolic for "exponent," and the positive sign shows the magnitude of the number. For very small numbers, the negative sign would be used instead.

Among the valid numeric constants are

+23.23	23.23	5E + 13	3.33E − 16
−122.33			

Invalid numeric constants would include

23.44−	2.344	$E + 13$	12,223
$23.00			

String constants, called *literals* by many programmers, are alphanumeric constants. An alphanumeric data item can be a composite of letters, digits, and special characters, such as the asterisk, the colon, and the percentage sign. These characters are not used in arithmetic calculations and are often enclosed within quotation marks, which make them easily recognizable. The maximum length for a given string is 255 characters.

String constants often provide headings ("XYZ Corporation"), and labels ("Total Ending Value ="") for reports; serve as messages to the user ("Please enter your name"); and enable the programmer to perform many conditional tests (IF RESPONSE$ = "YES").

Examples of string constants are

"YES"   "22%"   "XYZ CORPORATION"   "22.120"

Invalid string constants include:

"YES   'YES'   any constant larger than
                  255 characters

Variables

A *variable* is a term that represents a value that can change. Usually, when the program is being written, the programmer does not know the values of many of the variables. Unknown values have no impact on one's ability to program. What must be known is whether the variable is to be of the numeric or the string classification.

When selecting the name of a variable, the programmer should keep in mind the intent of the value that the variable represents. A person reading the program listing should immediately see a relationship between the variable name and its value. For example, it would be poor programming style to use the variable T to represent the value of a zip code.

IBM-PC BASIC allows a variable name to have from one to forty characters. If a variable name has more than forty characters, the system *truncates* (shortens) the name to the first forty characters. The only allowable characters to form the name are letters, numbers and the decimal point. Many variable names have special ending characters (%, $, # or !) to denote their data type.

The programmer should familiarize herself or himself with the BASIC statements. These statements have been predefined for the computer and cannot serve as variable names. For example, the BASIC statement "PRINT" cannot be used as a variable name.

Numeric variables are used in calculations or in the storage of numeric quantities. There are three types of numeric variables: integer, single-precision, and double-precision. These variables are automatically initialized (set) to zero when they are defined.

Integer variables represent whole-number amounts in the range of -32768 to $+32767$. To denote an integer variable in IBM-PC BASIC, one must include a percentage sign (%) as the last character of the variable name.

Examples of acceptable integer variables are

TOTAL.STUDENTS%   LINE.COUNTER%
EMP.TYPE%

Invalid integer variables include

TOTAL STUDENTS%   LINE.COUNTER
%EMP.TYPE

Single-precision variables represent real numeric values that can be stored as six digits ($+9999.99$ to -9999.99). A single-precision variable may have the exclamation point (!) as the last character to denote its type. If the exclamation point is not present, a single-precision numeric variable is assumed.

Examples of acceptable single-precision variables are

RATE.OF.PAY   SALES.TAX!   GROSS.PAY

Invalid single-precision variables include

RATE OF PAY   SALE.TAX%   GROSS.PAY$

Double-precision variables also represent real numeric values. Double-precision provides space for sixteen digits plus a sign. To inform the computer that this extra storage space is desired, the programmer must include the number sign (#) as the last character of the variable name.

Acceptable double-precision variable names include

TONS.OF.CARGO#   AVE.STATE.INCOME#

Among the invalid double-precision variable names are

TONS OF CARGO#   TONS.OF.CARGO!
TONS.OF.CARGO%

String variables represent alphanumeric values. These variables are identified by the use of the dollar sign ($) as the last character of the variable name and can have a maximum length of 255 characters. String variables cannot be used in mathematical calculations even if their values fall under numeric definition.

Acceptable string-variable names include

FIRST.NAME$ ADDRESS$ STATE$ SEX$

The following would be unacceptable string-variable names:

NAME% $NAME   NAME   EMPLOYEE NAME$

Arithmetic Operations

BASIC provides a variety of arithmetical operators. Included are exponentiation, division, multiplication, addition, and subtraction. All mathematics are represented in "algebraic-like" expressions using the following symbols:

exponentiation	$\wedge$	(up arrow)
division	/	(forward slash)
multiplication	*	(asterisk)
addition	+	(plus sign)
subtraction	−	(minus sign)

BASIC follows the rules of algebra in regard to the order of operations: Exponentiations are performed first, followed by multiplication and division as they occur from left to right. Finally, additions and subtractions are performed as they occur from left to right. This natural order can be altered by the use of parentheses; the operations within the innermost parentheses are solved for first. For example, if the calculation of a mean average for a group of four test grades is desired, the expression MEAN.AVE = TEST.ONE + TEST.TWO + TEST.THREE + TEST.FOUR / 4 would be incorrect. This calculation would divide the value of TEST.FOUR by 4 and would add the result to the sum of the values of TEST.ONE, TEST.TWO, and TEST.THREE. The correct expression would be MEAN.AVE = (TEST.ONE + TEST.TWO + TEST.THREE + TEST.FOUR) / 4.

An important difference exists between the BASIC language and algebra in regard to the equals sign. In BASIC, the equals sign serves to assign a value to a variable instead of as an indication of equality. For example, if the programmer uses the expression $X = Y * 2$, the product will be stored in the location represented by the variable name X after the arithmetic process is complete.

This concept of value assignment allows for the possibility of statements like $R = R + 3$. In this calculation, the computer first adds 3 to the original value of R. After this addition, the sum is placed in the storage location named R, thus destroying R's original value.

A BASIC LESSON

As discussed previously, prior to any programming, the analysis of the problem must be complete. At the point where the programmer is ready to code, the appropriate BASIC statements must be selected and written in acceptable syntax. The BASIC statements fall into one of four categories of instructions: processing, input/output, decision and branching, or documentation.

Processing Instructions

One of the most common BASIC processing instructions is the LET statement. The *LET* statement serves as the catalyst for many mathematical processes. The main intent of this instruction is, however, to store the value of a variable, that is, the result.

$$\textit{Syntax:} \quad \text{line \# LET variable} = \begin{Bmatrix} \text{variable} \\ \text{expression} \\ \text{constant} \end{Bmatrix}$$

It is important to note that the syntax requires the variable representing the value to be stored to be placed on the left side of the equals sign. Also, it is the programmer's responsibility to ensure that appropriate variable types are used. Care must be taken to avoid a "type mismatch" error, which is generated when there is an inconsistency of variable types. For example, notice the string variable SALES.TAX$ in the following LET statement. This would cause a "type mismatch" error:

305 *LET TOTAL.PURCHASE*
    = SALES.PRICE + SALES.TAX$

The following are valid LET statements:

120 LET GROSS.PAY
    = RATE.OF.PAY * HOURS.WORKED
107 LET SALES.TAX.RATE = .06
476 LET EMP.NO.HOLD$ = EMP.NO$

The following are invalid LET statements:

137 LET RATE% = "SALES RATE"
407 LET (X + Y)/Z = RESULT

The END statement terminates the processing of a BASIC program. Although in IBM-PC BASIC this statement is optional, its use is highly recommended. The END statement has the highest line number and is therefore placed at the end of the BASIC program.

Syntax: line# END

Input/Output Instructions

When the data are known at the time that the program is being coded, it is possible to use the READ/DATA set of instructions for input processing. READ and DATA are considered dependent BASIC instructions and are therefore termed a **statement** set. Whenever a programmer uses a READ instruction, at least one DATA statement must be used as well.

Syntax: line #
        READ var.1 [,var.2, . . . ,var.N]
        line #
        DATA con.1 [,con.2, . . . ,con.N]

Remember that *var.1* and *con.1* are abbreviations for "variable.1" and "constant.1," respectively.

The **READ** statement accepts the values for each variable from the **DATA** statement. It is most common to have only one READ statement and many DATA statements. If the READ statement is placed in a loop, sufficient data must be made available to ensure complete processing. Failure to supply sufficient data causes an "out-of-data" error during execution of the program. An internal pointer controlled by the computer keeps track of the appropriate location of the next data item to be read so that no duplication ever occurs.

For simplification, a DATA statement is often supplied for each anticipated occurrence of a READ instruction. In actuality, one DATA statement may supply the program with all the data required for processing. The following example contrasts both usages of the DATA statement for the three values required to process *X*:

Multiple DATA Statements	Single DATA Statement
100 READ X	100 READ X
120 DATA 23.25	120 DATA 23.25, 332.44, 12.56
130 DATA 332.44	
140 DATA 12.56	

The constants supplied for each DATA statement must correspond to the definition specified in the READ instruction. For example, assume the following READ instruction:

200 READ STUDENT.NAME$, GPA, STUDENT.NO%

Take notice of the order of the variables. The computer reads first a string variable, then a single precision variable, and lastly, an integer variable. An appropriate DATA statement which corresponds to the above could be:

500 DATA "Joan Shields",4.0,11223

Although the READ and DATA statements are a set of instructions, there is no need for them to be next to or even near one another. As long as the DATA statements are within the boundaries of the program (not after the END statement), contain sufficient data for processing, and comply with the variable types defined in the READ instructions, no errors should arise during program execution.

A valid READ/DATA set would be

105 READ PURCHASES, RETURNS,
     BEG.BAL, PAYMENTS, NAME$
600 DATA 126.79,0,205.49,100.00,"Theresa Cillo"

Invalid READ/DATA sets are

105 READ PURCHASES, RETURNS,
     BEG. BAL, PAYMENTS, NAME$
600 DATA "Theresa Cillo",126.79,0,205.49,100.00
407 READ SALE.TAX%
709 DATA 5.90

The **PRINT** statement provides the ability to generate a **softcopy** (visual) display on the computer's screen. **LPRINT,** a modification of the PRINT statement, generates a **hardcopy,** or a line of print on the computer's printer. There are many variations of the PRINT and LPRINT instructions. This section explores a Format 1 syntax that makes use of the comma, the semicolon, and the tab options.

Format 1

Syntax:
$$\text{Line \#} \left\{ \begin{array}{c} \text{PRINT} \\ \text{LPRINT} \end{array} \right\} \text{[tab]} \left\{ \begin{array}{c} \text{constant.1} \\ \text{variable.1} \\ \text{expression.1} \end{array} \right\}$$

$$\left[\ldots \left\{ \begin{array}{c} \text{tab} \\ ; \\ , \end{array} \right\} \left\{ \begin{array}{c} \text{constant.N} \\ \text{variable.N} \\ \text{expression.N} \end{array} \right\} \right]$$

In the simplest form, just a line number and a PRINT command create a blank line. This blank is important in creating adequate vertical spacing of either reports or screen displays. In the previous section, it was mentioned that, at certain times, a programmer may wish to have many BASIC statements with only one line-number reference. If, for example, the programmer needs three blank lines between the heading and the body of a display, she or he can easily create this space within one line instead of coding three lines:

100 PRINT : PRINT : PRINT

PRINT statements tend to get very elaborate and fully utilize the print positions available for display or paper. Often a special form called a **print/display spacing chart** is used to assist the programmer in creating a report that is appealing to the eye. Under the Format 1 syntax requirement, spacing across the screen or the printed page can be accomplished by the use of the comma, the semicolon, or the TAB function.

IBM-PC BASIC provides the programmer with a standard seventy-column format for output, divided into five print zones of fourteen characters each. Zone 1 begins at Column 1 and ends at 14: Zone 2 begins at 15 and ends at 28. This pattern continues through Zone 5, which begins at Column 57 and ends at 70. The comma in the PRINT statement acts as an automatic tab to the *next* available zone. Examine the following statements:

1. 100 PRINT "A","B","C","D","E"
2. 200 PRINT "Account Number Reference",
     "Number"
3. 300 PRINT "A","B","C","D","E","F"
4. 400 PRINT ,,,"ABC"

Statement 1 will generate one line of display, each string constant being placed in the first column of each zone, that is, "A" in Column 1, "B" in Column 15, . . . "E" in Column 57. Inspecting Statement 2, one may quickly assume that the second constant "Number" is to be printed in Zone 2. The constant "Number" actually prints beginning in Zone 3, which is Column 29. Recall that the comma automatically tabs to the next available zone. The first constant, "Account Number Reference," requires more than one zone to print or display all the characters.

Statement 3 (Line 300) requests that six constants be printed; therefore two lines of print are generated. Constants "A" through "E" print out on Line 1 in their respective zone positions. Constant "F" prints on Line 2 in Zone 1. Finally, Statement 4 (Line 400) instructs the computer to skip the first three zones and to print "ABC" at the beginning of Zone 4.

The **semicolon** allows the programmer to take advantage of all eighty columns of output media. It is used to separate variables, constants, or expressions within the PRINT statement. The computer provides no automatic spacing. The programmer must insert adequate spaces to ensure that the data will be properly spaced. Examine the following print statements that use the semicolon:

```
100 PRINT "A";"B";"C";"D";"E"
200 PRINT "A ";"B ";"C ";"D ";"E "
```

Unlike the comma, the semicolon generates no spacing: the first PRINT statement yields a display of "ABCDE," beginning in Column 1. In the second statement, the programmer provides spacing between the constants: this statement displays as "A B C D E ." In regard to numeric items, when a semicolon is used a number is always followed by one space, and positive numbers are preceded by a space.

In industry, the comma is seldom used because of the strong control over spacing imposed by the computer. The semicolon alone is often viewed as a burden. When using just the semicolon, one must account for almost every column, often inserting string constants containing blank spaces to move the next item to its proper print position. Most programmers take advantage of the TAB function or, as explained in the next section, the PRINT USING statement. These two options, like the semicolon, provide the programmer with a full eighty-character line of display or print.

The **TAB function** enables the programmer to set a tab stop exactly where he or she wishes. The syntax requires the use of the word TAB followed by the desired column position placed in parentheses. For example, to print "XYZ Corporation" beginning in Column 32, the programmer need only code

```
330 PRINT TAB(32);"WYZ Corporation"
```

Note that there is no space between the word TAB and the left parenthesis. If a space exists, the error message "subscript out of range" is displayed during execution. Most programmers, when using the TAB option, also use the semicolon to separate items in the PRINT instruction. To guarantee the desired output when using this function, one should make sure that the space between the tab stops is large enough to fit the material being printed.

The following are valid PRINT statements using the TAB function:

```
105 PRINT TAB(32);"RICH AND SONS, Inc."
205 PRINT TAB(12);STUDENT.NAME$;TAB(30);G.P.A;
         TAB(35);STUDENT.NO%;TAB(50);RANK%
```

The following are invalid PRINT statements using the TAB function:

```
300 PRINT TAB32;"RICH AND SONS, Inc."
405 PRINT TAB (32);"RICH AND SONS, Inc."
```

As stated previously, string constants or literals are used extensively to create headings and labels and as a vehicle to provide directions to a user in an interactive environment. Variables are printed to provide detailed information and to present the results of processing.

Another alternative available is to use the PRINT statement to generate a calculated result from a given expression. For example, the following code may take advantage of the PRINT instruction using an expression:

```
10 READ NAME$, RATE.OF.PAY, HOURS.WORKED
20 Let GROSS.PAY
     = RATE.OF.PAY*HOURS.WORKED
30 PRINT "The Gross Pay is "; GROSS PAY
```

```
LIST
10   PRINT TAB(35);"PAYROLL REPORT" : PRINT
20   PRINT TAB(8);"EMPLOYEE NAME"; TAB(27);"TYPE"; TAB(38);"HOURS";
     TAB(48);"RATE"; TAB(59);"SALES"; TAB(70);"GROSS PAY"
30   READ EMP.NAME$, RATE.OF.PAY, HOURS.WORKED, SALES.AMT, EMP.TYPE%
40   LET GROSS.PAY = RATE.OF.PAY * HOURS.WORKED + SALES.AMT * .1
50   PRINT TAB(7); EMP.NAME$; TAB(28); EMP.TYPE%; TAB(38); HOURS.WORKED;
     TAB(47);RATE.OF.PAY;TAB(59);SALES.AMT;TAB(72);GROSS.PAY
60   DATA "Donna Piccuirro",5.50,10,375.00,2
70   END
Ok
RUN

                              PAYROLL REPORT


        EMPLOYEE NAME      TYPE       HOURS       RATE       SALES       GROSS PAY
        Donna Piccuirro      2         10         5.5        375          92.5
Ok
```

Figure 10. Sequential BASIC program using the
PRINT, LET, READ, DATA, and END instructions.

Lines 20 and 30 can be combined as

> 20 PRINT "The Gross Pay is ";
>   RATE.OF.PAY*HOURS.WORKED

In conclusion, the PRINT statement has many variations and therefore is very powerful. Column spacing can be manipulated by the use of the comma, the semicolon, and the TAB function. Although the previous examples illustrate many methods of spacing, the programmer may use a number of combinations within the same instruction. The following PRINT instruction illustrates a valid combination:

> 205 PRINT "Answer to",PROB.NO;" page ";
>   PAGE;TAB(50);R * X

It takes time, patience, and some trial and error to fully master the PRINT statement.

Program Analysis

The following program illustrates a simple calculation of a salesperson's gross pay (see Figure 10). The individual receives a wage equal to the rate of pay multiplied by the hours worked, plus a 10 percent commission on the weekly sales.

Before continuing, note the following:

1. The multiple statements in Line 10 of the sample program, using the colon as a separator.
2. The appropriateness of the variable names and definitions.
3. The relationship between the READ and DATA statements.
4. The use of the TAB function in Lines 10, 20, and 30 as it relates to the output.

Branching and Decision Instructions

An unconditional branch in BASIC programming is initiated by the *GOTO* command. The GOTO transfers control from one part of the program to another.

> *Syntax:*   line# GOTO   line#

The destination line number must exist. An unconditional branch to a nonexisting line causes an "undefined-line-number" error on execution of the program. A successful GOTO instruction appears in line 107 of the following code:

```
 30 READ X
    (Additional lines of BASIC code)
107 GOTO 30
500 DATA 32.7
    (Additional lines of BASIC code)
```

The **IF** statement provides the mechanism for decision making in the BASIC language. In IBM-PC BASIC, there are two formats for the IF statement. Format 1 uses the IF statement as a conditional branching tool. Format 2 uses the IF statement for decision processing.

Format 1

Syntax: line # IF relational expression GOTO
 line #

The transfer of control to the destination line number following the GOTO occurs only when the relational expression is true. If the expression is false, the next sequential statement is executed. As in the GOTO statement, should the destination line number not exist, an undefined-line-number error is displayed on the screen during the execution of this instruction.

The simple relational expression is the comparison of two values (constants, variables, or expressions). In IBM-PC BASIC, the following **relational operators** may be used:

equal to	=
not equal to	<> or ><
greater than	>
greater than or equal to	>= or =>
less than	<
less than or equal to	<= or =<

Examine the following IF statement:

400 IF POINTER$ = "YES" GOTO 500

In an evaluation of this expression, transfer is made to line 500 when the value of POINTER$ is equal to the constant "YES." If the value of POINTER$ is anything other than "YES," the next statement following 400 is executed. One should make an effort to remember this rule of thumb: ***"Branch only when true."***

Format 2

Syntax:
line # IF relational expression
$$\text{THEN} \begin{Bmatrix} \text{line \#} \\ \text{statement} \end{Bmatrix} [: \text{statement.2} \ldots : \text{statement.N}]$$
$$\left[\text{ELSE} \begin{Bmatrix} \text{line \#} \\ \text{statement} \end{Bmatrix} [: \text{statement.2} \ldots : \text{statement.N}] \right]$$

The Format 2 IF statement allows for decision processing without branching as well as transfer of control. As in the Format 1 IF statement, the relational expression is evaluated first. If the outcome is true, the "THEN" path of the statement is executed. For example:

```
340 IF ITEM.CODE$ = "TAX"
    THEN LET TOTAL.SALES
    = SALES.AMT + SALES.AMT * .06
```

As stated previously, if the result of the expression proves to be false, control is passed to the next statement in sequence. By using the ELSE option, the programmer can perform processing before the next instruction when a false condition is determined. The ELSE option is illustrated in the following instructions:

```
340 IF ITEM.CODE$ = "TAX"
    THEN LET TOTAL.SALES
    = SALES.AMT + SALES.AMT * .06
    ELSE LET TOTAL.SALES = SALES.AMT
350 PRINT TOTAL.SALES
```

Before printing, the above code produces a different assigned value for TOTAL.SALES that depends on the outcome of the relational expression. If the ITEM.CODE$ is equal to "TAX," the THEN path is executed, calculating a TOTAL.SALES value equal to the SALES.AMT plus the appropriate tax. If the expression proves to be false, the TOTAL.SALES amount is assigned the value of the nontaxed item.

```
10    REM *******************************************************************
20    REM *                                                                 *
30    REM *   This program calculates the gross pay for two different types *
40    REM *   of employees.  "Type 1" employees are paid a wage equal to    *
50    REM *   their hours worked times their rate of pay.  "Type 2" employees *
60    REM *   receive a wage equal to their rate times hours, as well as a   *
70    REM *   commission of ten percent of their weekly sales.               *
80    REM *                                                                 *
90    REM *******************************************************************
100   REM
100   PRINT TAB(35);"PAYROLL REPORT" : PRINT
110   PRINT TAB(8);"EMPLOYEE NAME"; TAB(27);"TYPE"; TAB(38);"HOURS";
      TAB(48);"RATE"; TAB(59);"SALES"; TAB(70);"GROSS PAY"
120   READ EMP.NAME$, RATE.OF.PAY, HOURS.WORKED, SALES.AMT, EMP.TYPE%
130   IF EMP.NAME$ = "END OF DATA" GOTO 340
140   LET TOTAL.EMP% = TOTAL.EMP% + 1
150   IF EMP.TYPE% = 1
         THEN LET GROSS.PAY = RATE.OF.PAY * HOURS.WORKED
      ELSE LET GROSS.PAY = RATE.OF.PAY * HOURS.WORKED + SALES.AMT * .1
160   LET TOT.GROSS.PAY = TOT.GROSS.PAY + GROSS.PAY
170   PRINT TAB(7); EMP.NAME$; TAB(28); EMP.TYPE%; TAB(38); HOURS.WORKED;
      TAB(47);RATE.OF.PAY;TAB(59);SALES.AMT;TAB(72);GROSS.PAY
180   GOTO 120
190   DATA "Robert Saldarini",5.00,20,0,1
200   DATA "Patti De Sopo",6.5,35,100,2
210   DATA "Flory Sung",7.50,5,0,1
220   DATA "Jeffery Volkhiemer",5.00,20,250,1
230   DATA "Kenneth Rasmuson",4.50,10,0,1
240   DATA "Frank O'Grady",7.25,20,0,1
250   DATA "Denise Pelosi",4.50,20,275.50,2
260   DATA "Donna Piccuirro",5.50,10,375.00,2
270   DATA "Adele Hartig",6.50,20,0,1
280   DATA "Roanne Angiello",7.50,10,0,1
290   DATA "Pat Mauro",5.75,15,0,1
300   DATA "Steve Gerard",6.75,10,550.50,2
310   DATA "Charles McNerney",7.25,20,0,1
320   DATA "END OF DATA",0,0,0,0
340   PRINT : PRINT                          'Double spacing before totals
350   PRINT TAB(7);"TOTAL EMPLOYEES ";TOTAL.EMP%
360   PRINT
380   PRINT TAB(7);"TOTAL GROSS PAY ";TOT.GROSS.PAY
390   END
```

Figure 11. Coded solution to Mr. Richards's pay-roll report as presented in Figure 7.

Documentation Instructions

Use of the **REM** statement (derived from the word *remark*) is the most common method of **documenting** a BASIC program.

Syntax: line # REM [comment entry]

The comment entry can consist of any message that the programmer wishes to convey to the reader of the listing. This statement does not generate any output; its function is to enhance the readability of the source listing.

IBM-PC BASIC allows for a comment to be made on the same line as an executable statement. One need only use the apostrophe following the statement that is to be documented. Here is an example of the use of the apostrophe:

100 LET RRR = .215   ' RRR is the required rate of return.

```
RUN
                           PAYROLL REPORT

        EMPLOYEE NAME      TYPE    HOURS     RATE      SALES     GROSS PAY
        Robert Saldarini    1       20       5          0          100
        Patti De Sopo       2       35       6.5       100         237.5
        Flory Sung          1        5       7.5         0          37.5
        Jeffery Volkhiemer  1       20       5         250         100
        Kenneth Rasmuson    1       10       4.5         0          45
        Frank O'Grady       1       20       7.25        0         145
        Denise Pelosi       2       20       4.5       275.5       117.55
        Donna Piccuirro     2       10       5.5       375          92.5
        Adele Hartig        1       20       6.5         0         130
        Roanne Angiello     1       10       7.5         0          75
        Pat Mauro           1       15       5.75        0          86.25
        Steve Gerard        2       10       6.75      550.5       122.55
        Charles McNerney    1       20       7.25        0         145


        TOTAL EMPLOYEES   13

        TOTAL GROSS PAY   1433.85
Ok
```

Figure 12. A reproduction of the screen display produced by the execution of the program listed in Figure 11.

The fact that IBM-PC BASIC has lengthy variable names enables the programmer to produce code that is almost self-documenting: thus this documentation technique is rarely needed.

Program Analysis

The program shown in Figure 11 is the coded solution to the payroll report problem flowcharted in Figure 7. A fresh walk-through of this flowchart is suggested before a review of Figure 11. A copy of the screen-image payroll report is shown in Figure 12.

Before continuing, note the following:

1. The comments supplied in the REM statements, Lines 10–100.
2. The counting procedure in Line 140.
3. The accumulation procedure in Line 160.
4. The conditional branch instruction (Format 1 IF statement) in Line 130, which will terminate the loop caused by the unconditional branch instruction (GOTO statement) in Line 180.
5. The Format 2 IF statement used for decision processing in Line 150.
6. The multiple DATA statements for the one READ statement in Line 120.
7. The use of the apostrophe to add a comment to instruction Line 340.

A BASIC FACE-LIFT

There is nothing more exciting to the novice programmer than to have her or his first program run correctly. Assume that the program illustrated in Figure 11 is your first work of art. Even though the output as shown in Figure 12 is correct, some would view it as unattractive. Although the data are in neat columns, the numbers do not line up, the numeric data align on the left instead of the right of the column. The dollar figures are not represented properly. At times, the dollar amounts are missing the two positions to the right of the decimal point for cents, not to mention the appropriate dollar signs.

```
10   REM *** EXAMPLE ONE ***
20   REM    Use of fixed dollar sign, comma, decimal point, number sign and space.
30   REM
40   LET X = 3148.33
50   LET Y% = 4578
60   LET Z = 34.44
70   LET FORMAT.LINE 1$ = "    $###,###.##        #####        ####.##      "
80   PRINT USING FORMAT.LINE.1$; X; Y%; Z
90   END
RUN
     $  3,148.33        4578           34.44
Ok
```

```
10   REM *** EXAMPLE TWO ***
20   REM    Use of floating dollar sign, comma, decimal point, number sign
            and space.
30   REM
40   LET X = 22.35
50   LET Y% = 34
60   LET Z = 12.78
70   LET FORMAT.LINE.2$ = "    $$###,###.##        #####        ####.##      "
80   PRINT USING FORMAT.LINE.2$; X; Y%; Z
90   END

RUN
         $22.35          34         12.78
Ok
```

```
10   REM *** EXAMPLE THREE ***
20   REM    Use of literal, space, and string variable.
30   REM
40   LET X$ = "Mary Jane Smith"
50   LET FORMAT.LINE.3$ = "   CHILD'S NAME:  \                 \ "
60   PRINT USING FORMAT.LINE.3$; X$
70   END

RUN
  CHILD'S NAME:  Mary Jane Smith
Ok
```

```
10   REM *** EXAMPLE FOUR ***
20   REM    Example showing truncation of a string variable due to inadequate
            space.
30   REM
40   LET X$ = "Mary Jane Smith"
50   LET FORMAT.LINE.4$ = "   CHILD'S NAME:  \       \ "
60   PRINT USING FORMAT.LINE.4$; X$
70   END

RUN
  CHILD'S NAME:   Mary Jan
Ok
```

```
10   REM *** EXAMPLE FIVE ***
20   REM    Example of misuse of the comma.
30   REM
40   LET X = 3.43
50   LET FORMAT.LINE.5$ = "  ,###.##"
60   PRINT USING FORMAT.LINE.5$; X
70   END

RUN
  ,  3.43
```

```
10 REM *** EXAMPLE SIX ***
20 REM    Example of a disagreement of print image and variable type.
30 REM
40 LET X$ = "Richardson's Mill"
50 LET FORMAT.LINE.6$ = "   ########    "
60 PRINT USING FORMAT.LINE.6$; X$
70 END

RUN

Type mismatch in 60
Ok
****
```

Figure 13. (opposite page and above) Examples using various PRINT USING images.

"Type 1" clerical employees have a zero sales amount printed; this area would look better if it were left blank.

PRINT USING, the second format of the PRINT statement, enables the programmer to create a very elaborate line of print with many output-editing features. Because of the complexity of the PRINT USING instruction, this section presents only a survey of this powerful statement.

Format 2

Syntax

line # $\left\{ \begin{array}{l} \text{PRINT} \\ \text{LPRINT} \end{array} \right\}$ USING print format [;var.1 . . . ;var.N]

A print format may be created by the use of the LET statement. Recall that the LET statement can store the value of a constant, that is, the print format. The print format is a string constant composed of individual data items' images. The format must be placed in quotes.

The programmer can select from a group of so-called PRINT USING image characters to design the print format. Eight selections are outlined here:

Selection   Printing Results

.   **DECIMAL POINT**—prints a decimal point in a numeric field. Only one decimal point is allowable for a given numeric image.

,   **COMMA**—is inserted in a numeric image for each group of three digits. When a significant digit greater than zero is to the left of the comma, the comma will print. The comma should not be the left-most character of the image.

\#   **NUMBER SIGN**—(pound sign) is used to represent each numeric digit.

$ **DOLLAR SIGN**—is used as the left-most character in a numeric image to print a fixed dollar sign.

$$ **FLOATING DOLLAR SIGN**—is used as the left-most character position in a numeric image to denote a dollar sign that prints next to the left-most significant digit greater than zero.

literal   **LITERAL**—prints exactly, character by character, what is expressed in the image.

(space)   **SPACE**—provides one or more blank spaces between individual images.

\ \   **BACK SLASH**—provides space for printing string variables. The programmer must allow ample space between slashes or the variable will be truncated (shortened) to the space provided.

Figure 13 provides six illustrations of print formats and data item images. Study these examples closely so that you understand them before coding your own program.

```
10    REM ****************************************************************
20    REM *                                                              *
30    REM *  This program calculates the gross pay for two different types *
40    REM *  of employees. "Type 1" employees are paid a wage equal to    *
50    REM *  their hours worked times their rate of pay.  "Type 2" employees *
60    REM *  receive a wage equal to their rate times hours, as well as a   *
70    REM *  commission of ten percent of their weekly sales.             *
80    REM *                                                              *
90    REM ****************************************************************
100   REM
110   LET FORMAT.1$ = "   \              \ #       ##.##     $$#.##
          $$###.##"
120   LET FORMAT.2$ = "   \              \ #       ##.##     $$#.##     $$##
#.##     $$###.##"
130   LET FORMAT.3$ = "   TOTAL EMPLOYEES              ###"
140   LET FORMAT.4$ = "   TOTAL GROSS PAY   $$###,###.##"
150   PRINT TAB(35); "PAYROLL REPORT" : PRINT
160   PRINT TAB(4);"EMPLOYEE NAME"; TAB(24);"TYPE"; TAB(35);"HOURS";
      TAB(45);"RATE"; TAB(56);"SALES"; TAB(67);"GROSS PAY"
170   READ EMP.NAME$, RATE.OF.PAY, HOURS.WORKED, SALES.AMT, EMP.TYPE%
180   IF EMP.NAME$ = "END OF DATA" GOTO 410
190   LET TOTAL.EMP% = TOTAL.EMP% + 1
200   IF EMP.TYPE% = 1
          THEN LET GROSS.PAY = RATE.OF.PAY * HOURS.WORKED : GOTO 240
      ELSE LET GROSS.PAY = RATE.OF.PAY * HOURS.WORKED + SALES.AMT * .1
210   LET TOT.GROSS.PAY = TOT.GROSS.PAY + GROSS.PAY
220   PRINT USING FORMAT.2$; EMP.NAME$; EMP.TYPE%; HOURS.WORKED; RATE.OF.PAY;
          SALES.AMT; GROSS.PAY
230   GOTO 170
240   LET TOT.GROSS.PAY = TOT.GROSS.PAY + GROSS.PAY
250   PRINT USING FORMAT.1$; EMP.NAME$; EMP.TYPE%; HOURS.WORKED; RATE.OF.PAY;
          GROSS.PAY
260   GOTO 170
270   DATA "Robert Saldarini",5.00,20,0,1
280   DATA "Patti De Sopo",6.5,35,100,2
290   DATA "Flory Sung",7.50,5,0,1
300   DATA "Jeffery Volkhiemer",5.00,20,250,1
310   DATA "Kenneth Rasmuson",4.50,10,0,1
320   DATA "Frank O'Grady",7.25,20,0,1
330   DATA "Denise Pelosi",4.50,20,275.50,2
340   DATA "Donna Piccuirro",5.50,10,375.00,2
350   DATA "Adele Hartig",6.50,20,0,1
360   DATA "Roanne Angiello",7.50,10,0,1
370   DATA "Pat Mauro",5.75,15,0,1
380   DATA "Steve Gerard",6.75,10,550.50,2
390   DATA "Charles McNerney",7.25,20,0,1
400   DATA "END OF DATA",0,0,0,0
410   PRINT : PRINT
420   PRINT USING FORMAT.3$; TOTAL.EMP% : PRINT
430   PRINT USING FORMAT.4$; TOT.GROSS.PAY
440   END
```

Figure 14. A modified version of Mr. Richards's payroll report with output editing, generated by the PRINT USING instruction.

Program Analysis

The program in Figure 14 is similar in all respects to the listing in Figure 12, with the exception that it generates a formatted report utilizing the PRINT USING statement. A sales amount is printed only for "Type 2" employees. The reproduction of the screen image of the payroll report in Figure 15 shows all the editing characteristics requested.

```
RUN
                                        PAYROLL REPORT

             EMPLOYEE NAME          TYPE      HOURS      RATE        SALES      GROSS PAY
             Robert Saldarini        1        20.00     $5.00                   $100.00
             Patti De Sopo           2        35.00     $6.50      $100.00      $237.50
             Flory Sung              1         5.00     $7.50                    $37.50
             Jeffery Volkhiemer      1        20.00     $5.00                   $100.00
             Kenneth Rasmuson        1        10.00     $4.50                    $45.00
             Frank O'Grady           1        20.00     $7.25                   $145.00
             Denise Pelosi           2        20.00     $4.50      $275.50      $117.55
             Donna Piccuirro         2        10.00     $5.50      $375.00       $92.50
             Adele Hartig            1        20.00     $6.50                   $130.00
             Roanne Angiello         1        10.00     $7.50                    $75.00
             Pat Mauro               1        15.00     $5.75                    $86.25
             Steve Gerard            2        10.00     $6.75      $550.50      $122.55
             Charles McNerney        1        20.00     $7.25                   $145.00


          TOTAL EMPLOYEES              13

          TOTAL GROSS PAY    $1,433.85
Ok
```

Figure 15. A reproduction of the screen display produced by the execution of the program listed in Figure 14.

Before continuing, note the following:

1. Each print format as a contiguous group of characters in the form of a string constant.
2. The use of the various data images that produce the desired output.
3. The overall report presentation found in Figure 15 as contrasted with the report found in Figure 12.

INTERACTIVE BASIC

When a majority of programs are written, the data to be processed are unknown. In most cases, the data are supplied by the user and change every time the program is run. The previous payroll program works, but every execution provides the same results. This problem is solved quickly when the program is made interactive. The term *interactive* implies a two-way communication between user and machine. The user is asked to supply the data when they are required for processing by the computer. Interactive BASIC is put into action with the use of the *INPUT* statement.

Syntax:
line # INPUT [literal prompt]
    var.1 [,var.2 . . var.N]

When a program is interactive, the INPUT statement replaces the READ/DATA statement set for input processing. When this statement is encountered during execution, the computer halts processing, displays a question mark on the screen, and waits for the user to key in data. After the data are supplied, processing is resumed. Examine the following actions when the instruction "200 INPUT RATE.OF.PAY" is executed:

Step 1. Processing is halted until the user supplies a value for RATE.OF.PAY. To indicate that data are required, a question mark appears on the screen:
    ?

```
Ok
RUN
?
?Redo from start
? 43,John Smith,32
?Redo from start
? 23,34,John Smith
?Redo from start
? John Smith
?Redo from start
? John Smith 33 45
?Redo from start
? John Smith,33,45
Ok


LIST
20 INPUT X$,Y,Z
Ok
```

Figure 16. (left) A user's haphazard attempts to provide the computer with data when only a question mark prompt is supplied.

Figure 17. (opposite) Examples of prompt messages that ensure proper data entry.

Step 2. The user supplies a data item and then presses the enter key:
  ?5.25 ⟨enter⟩
Step 3. The processing continues.

Note that a question mark is generated for each INPUT statement, not for each variable. When data are entered for multiple variables, a comma must separate each data item from the others. If the user supplies only some data when more are expected, or if the data do not conform to the variable definition, the computer responds with the message "Redo from start" and displays another question mark. Examine the trials of the user in Figure 16 in attempting to supply data for the instruction "20 INPUT X$,Y,Z."

Prompting the User

Imagine that you have sat down at a microcomputer and executed a depreciation program, and only a question mark appears on the screen:
  ?
After looking at the question mark, you might consult the documentation that would provide operation guidelines. Or you might just key "WHAT DO YOU WANT ME TO DO"; the computer's reply to this input may be "Redo from start." It is almost impossible to function in a processing environment where the user must try to outguess the computer in regard to data entry.

The programmer supplies **prompts** to the users of the programs, showing them how to enter the data for processing. Prompting is accomplished by one of two methods. One method is to code various PRINT statements that supply the user with one or more lines of guidance that will secure proper data entry. Another way is to use the INPUT statement itself to prompt the user.

If the PRINT statement is followed by an INPUT statement, the question mark is displayed on the line immediately following the message. Use of the literal prompt option of the INPUT statement forces the question mark to be displayed on the same line as the message, as in the following code:

100 PRINT "ENTER IN THE RATE OF PAY"
110 INPUT RATE.OF.PAY

Execution yields:

   ENTER IN THE RATE OF PAY
   ?

Whereas:

100 INPUT "ENTER IN THE RATE OF PAY";
  RATE.OF.PAY

```
10   REM *** EXAMPLE ONE ***
20   REM   Use of the PRINT statement to prompt the user.
30   REM
40   PRINT "DO YOU WISH TO CONTINUE?  ENTER <YES> OR <NO>.
50   INPUT RESPONSE$


RUN
DO YOU WISH TO CONTINUE?  ENTER <YES> OR <NO>.
?
```

```
10   REM *** EXAMPLE TWO ***
20   REM   Use of the INPUT statement to prompt the user.
30   REM
40   INPUT "WHAT IS YOUR NAME"; USER.NAME$


RUN
WHAT IS YOUR NAME?
```

```
10   REM *** EXAMPLE THREE ***
20   REM   Creation of a menu for data entry using both the PRINT and INPUT
           statements.
30   REM
40   PRINT TAB(33);"*** MAIN MENU ***" : PRINT
50   PRINT TAB(30);"ACTION";TAB(55)"COMMAND"  : PRINT
60   PRINT TAB(20);"ADDITION OF A NEW ACCOUNT";TAB(57);"<A>"    : PRINT
70   PRINT TAB(20);"CHANGE OF AN EXISTING ACCOUNT";TAB(57);"<C>"    : PRINT
80   PRINT TAB(20);"DELETION OF AN EXISTING ACCOUNT";TAB(57);"<D>"   :  PRINT
90   PRINT : PRINT
100  INPUT "                  WHAT IS YOUR SELECTION";RESPONSE$


RUN
                              *** MAIN MENU ***


                    ACTION                    COMMAND

          ADDITION OF A NEW ACCOUNT              <A>

          CHANGE OF AN EXISTING ACCOUNT          <C>

          DELETION OF AN EXISTING ACCOUNT        <D>



          WHAT IS YOUR SELECTION?
```

would yield:

ENTER IN THE RATE OF PAY?

In order to comply with good English usage, it is recommended that the programmer prepare "question-type literals" when using the literal prompt option of the INPUT statement. Although the programmer did not intend to ask a question in the INPUT instruction just quoted, the "computer-supplied question mark" has turned the sentence into an awkward question. A better instruction would be:

100 INPUT "WHAT IS THE RATE OF PAY"; RATE.OF.PAY

Figure 17 provides examples of good prompting. Try not to make the literals too long. As users be-

```
10    REM  *****************************************************************************
20    REM *                                                                           *
30    REM *   This interactive program calculates gross pay for two types             *
40    REM *   of employees. "Type 1" employees are paid a wage equal to               *
50    REM *   their hours worked times their rate of pay.   "Type 2" employees        *
60    REM *   receive a wage equal to their rate times hours, as well as a            *
70    REM *   commission of ten percent of their weekly sales.                        *
80    REM *                                                                           *
90    REM  *****************************************************************************
100   REM
110   INPUT "DO YOU WISH DIRECTIONS ON HOW TO RUN THIS PROGRAM";RESPONSE$
120   CLS
130   IF RESPONSE$ <> "Yes" GOTO 200
140   PRINT "THIS PROGRAM ALLOWS YOU TO PROCESS GROSS PAY FOR TWO EMPLOYEE TYPES.
      "
150   PRINT "TYPE 1 EMPLOYEES ARE THE CLERICAL STAFF.   WHEN ASKED, PLEASE"
160   PRINT "ENTER THEIR RATE OF PAY AND THE HOURS THEY WORKED.   TYPE 2 ARE THE"
170   PRINT "SALESPEOPLE.   YOU WILL HAVE TO PROVIDE THEIR WEEKLY SALES SO"
180   PRINT "THE APPROPRIATE COMMISSION WILL BE PAID."
190   INPUT "PRESS ENTER TO CONTINUE. . . ";RESPONSE$
200   LPRINT TAB(35); "PAYROLL REPORT"
210   LPRINT
220   LPRINT TAB(8);"EMPLOYEE NAME"; TAB(27);"TYPE"; TAB(38);"HOURS";
      TAB(48);"RATE"; TAB(59);"SALES"; TAB(70);"GROSS PAY"
230   CLS
240   PRINT TAB(22); "INTERACTIVE PAYROLL PROGRAM DATA ENTRY"
250   PRINT : PRINT : PRINT
260   PRINT "ENTER 'End' FOR EMPLOYEE NAME TO STOP THE PROGRAM" : PRINT : PRINT
270   INPUT "WHAT IS THE EMPLOYEE'S NAME"; EMP.NAME$ : PRINT
280   IF EMP.NAME$ = "End"
          THEN GOTO 410
290   LET TOTAL.EMP% = TOTAL.EMP% + 1
300   INPUT "WHAT IS THE EMPLOYEE'S TYPE"; EMP.TYPE% : PRINT
310   INPUT "WHAT IS THE EMPLOYEE'S RATE OF PAY"; RATE.OF.PAY : PRINT
320   INPUT "HOW MANY HOURS DID HE OR SHE WORK"; HOURS.WORKED : PRINT
330   IF EMP.TYPE% = 2
          THEN INPUT "WHAT IS THE EMPLOYEE'S WEEKLY SALES AMOUNT"; SALES.AMT :
          LET GROSS.PAY = RATE.OF.PAY * HOURS.WORKED + SALES.AMT * .1 : GOTO 380
340   LET GROSS.PAY = RATE.OF.PAY * HOURS.WORKED
350   LET TOT.GROSS.PAY = TOT.GROSS.PAY + GROSS.PAY
360   LPRINT TAB(7); EMP.NAME$; TAB(28); EMP.TYPE%; TAB(38); HOURS.WORKED;
             TAB(47); RATE.OF.PAY; TAB(72); GROSS.PAY
370   GOTO 230
380   LET TOT.GROSS.PAY = TOT.GROSS.PAY + GROSS.PAY
390   LPRINT TAB(7); EMP.NAME$; TAB(28); EMP.TYPE%; TAB(38); HOURS.WORKED;
             TAB(47); RATE.OF.PAY; TAB(59); SALES.AMT; TAB(72); GROSS.PAY
400   GOTO 230
410   LPRINT : LPRINT
420   LPRINT TAB(7);"TOTAL EMPLOYEES ";TOTAL.EMP%
430   LPRINT
440   LPRINT TAB(7);"TOTAL GROSS PAY ";TOT.GROSS.PAY
450   END
```

Figure 18. A recorded solution of Mr. Richards's payroll-report program incorporating an interactive method of processing.

```
RUN
DO YOU WISH DIRECTIONS ON HOW TO RUN THIS PROGRAM? Yes




                 --------   NEW  SCREEN   --------



THIS PROGRAM ALLOWS YOU TO PROCESS GROSS PAY FOR TWO EMPLOYEE TYPES.
TYPE 1 EMPLOYEES ARE THE CLERICAL STAFF.   WHEN ASKED, PLEASE
ENTER THEIR RATE OF PAY AND THE HOURS THEY WORKED.   TYPE 2 ARE THE
SALESPEOPLE.   YOU WILL HAVE TO PROVIDE THEIR WEEKLY SALES SO
THE APPROPRIATE COMMISSION WILL BE PAID.
PRESS ENTER TO CONTINUE. . . ?



               --------  PROCESSING  SCREEN  --------




              INTERACTIVE PAYROLL PROGRAM DATA ENTRY


ENTER 'End' FOR EMPLOYEE NAME TO STOP THE PROGRAM

WHAT IS THE EMPLOYEE'S NAME? Robert Saldarini

WHAT IS THE EMPLOYEE'S TYPE? 1

WHAT IS THE EMPLOYEE'S RATE OF PAY? 5.00

HOW MANY HOURS DID HE OR SHE WORK? 20
```

Figure 19. A screen reproduction of the prompts and data supplied by the user, which were requested by the program shown in Figure 18.

come more and more familiar with the program, the prompts tend to become a nuisance.

Often programs provide an option for user directions, keeping operational messages to a minimum.

The Clear Screen statement (CLS) assists the programmer in preparing uncluttered screen designs. When the computer encounters the CLS instruction, all text is removed and the screen becomes blank. The cursor, a small dash of light used to show where on the screen a character is to be displayed when entered, is returned to the left-most corner, at the top of the screen. This area is known as the *home position:*

Syntax: line # CLS

Program Analysis

Figure 18 is a rewritten version of the program shown in Figure 11. This modified program illustrates the interactive method of processing. A hard copy (Figure 19) is produced similar to that shown in

Figure 12. There is one exception, a sales amount is printed for "Type 2" employees only.

Before continuing, note the following:

1. The option for user directions. Notice the programmer temporarily halts processing until the user is ready (see line 190). After he/she presses the enter key, RESPONSE$ will equal spaces.
2. The screen presentations in Figure 19 caused by the interactive code.
3. The appropriateness of the prompts.
4. A more realistic approach to data entry. At line 330, a sales amount request is made only when it is determined that EMP.TYPE% = 2.
5. Use of the CLS instruction to clear the screen in Lines 120 and 230.

MORE BASIC INSTRUCTIONS

This section covers two of the more advanced BASIC concepts: the FOR/NEXT statement set, which creates an automatic loop, and the GOSUB/RETURN set, which enables the programmer to perform subroutines. These statements facilitate the programming effort and accomplish a task that would otherwise necessitate the use of many individual instructions.

FOR/NEXT Loop

The *FOR/NEXT loop* creates an automatic counter. The instruction set enables the programmer to start a counter at a predefined value and to increase or decrease it by the value of 1 or by any other fixed amount.

Syntax:
line #   FOR counter.var = initial value TO
                                    ending value
                    [STEP interval amount]
                        (Body of Loop)
line #   NEXT counter.var

Like READ and DATA, FOR and NEXT are a statement set. The FOR begins the loop by setting the counter.var to the initial value stated in the instruction. The body of the loop is then processed. When the NEXT statement is encountered, the counter.var is automatically increased. Unless the STEP option is supplied (this option is discussed later), the counter.var is increased by +1. An internal test is performed to determine if counter.var has exceeded the stated ending value. If it has, the loop is finished, and the statement following the next instruction is executed. If the outcome of the test is false, control is automatically transferred back to the FOR statement, causing the loop to be reentered.

The following code illustrates a simple FOR/NEXT loop:

```
100 FOR COUNTER = 1 TO 5
1100        PRINT COUNTER
120 NEXT COUNTER
```

The FOR statement initiates the loop by setting COUNTER to 1. Processing the body of the loop entails printing COUNTER. Line 110 is indented for readability only. When the NEXT statement is executed, COUNTER is checked to see if it is greater than 5. If COUNTER is found to be greater than 5, the statement following Line 120 is executed; otherwise, control is transferred back to Line 100. Figure 20 shows the power of the FOR/NEXT statement set by contrasting the FOR/NEXT instructions with code simulating the same processing.

The *STEP* option allows the programmer to count by a predefined interval other than +1. This amount may be positive or negative, depending on whether the programmer wishes to increase or decrease the count. The STEP interval may be an integer or a real numeric value. When "STEP" is present in the FOR instruction, the computer adjusts the counter by the value of the declared interval. When a decreasing loop is created, the NEXT statement terminates the loop when the counter.var is less than the ending value. For example:

```
100 FOR COUNTER = 100 TO 10 STEP −2
110        LPRINT COUNTER
120 NEXT COUNTER
```

The code just shown creates a descending hard-

```
LIST
10   REM ***  FOR/NEXT LOOP ***
20   FOR N = 1 TO 5
30      PRINT N
35      LET SUM.OF.N = SUM.OF.N  + N
40   NEXT N
50   PRINT : PRINT "The sum of N is equal to "; SUM.OF.N
60   END

RUN
 1
 2
 3
 4
 5

The sum of N is equal to  15
Ok
```

```
LIST
10   REM *** CODE REQUIRED TO SIMULATE THE ABOVE FOR/NEXT LOOP ***
20   LET N = 1
30   PRINT N
40   LET SUM.OF.N = SUM.OF.N + N
50   LET N = N + 1
60   IF N > 5 GOTO 80
70   GOTO 30
80   PRINT : PRINT "The sum of N is equal to "; SUM.OF.N
90   END

RUN
 1
 2
 3
 4
 5

The sum of N is equal to  15
Ok
```

Figure 20. Contrast of the FOR/NEXT statement set to individual instructions performing the same task.

copy listing that counts backward from 100 to 10 by 2's. Note that the high value (100) is the initial value and that the low value (10) is the ending value in a decreasing FOR/NEXT loop.

The initial value, the ending value, and the interval amount in a FOR/NEXT instruction set may be represented by numeric variables. The variable must be assigned a value before the initiation of the loop. If no value is assigned, zero is assumed by the computer. A variable is useful when the beginning value or the ending value of the loop must be supplied by the user. For example, the counting-specific program just illustrated can become a general-purpose program with the use of variables:

```
10 REM *** EXAMPLE ONE ***
20 REM    FOR/NEXT Loop with an ending value variable.
30 INPUT "WHAT IS THE ENDING VALUE OF THE LOOP"; END.VAL
40 FOR COUNTER = 1 TO END.VAL
50     PRINT COUNTER
60 NEXT COUNTER
70 END

RUN
WHAT IS THE ENDING VALUE OF THE LOOP? 4
 1
 2
 3
 4
Ok
```

```
10 REM *** EXAMPLE TWO ***
20 REM    FOR/NEXT Loop using all variables supplied by the user **ASCENDING**
30 INPUT "WHAT IS THE BEGINNING VALUE OF THE LOOP"; INT.VAL
40 INPUT "WHAT IS THE ENDING VALUE OF THE LOOP"; END.VAL
50 INPUT "AT WHAT INTERVAL DO YOU WISH TO COUNT"; INTERVAL
60 FOR COUNTER = INT.VAL TO END.VAL STEP INTERVAL
70     PRINT COUNTER
80 NEXT COUNTER
90 END

RUN
WHAT IS THE BEGINNING VALUE OF THE LOOP? 10
WHAT IS THE ENDING VALUE OF THE LOOP? 20
AT WHAT INTERVAL DO YOU WISH TO COUNT? 2
 10
 12
 14
 16
 18
 20
Ok
```

```
10 REM *** EXAMPLE THREE **
20 REM    FOR/NEXT Loop using all variables supplied by the user **DESCENDING**
30 INPUT "WHAT IS THE BEGINNING VALUE OF THE LOOP"; INT.VAL
40 INPUT "WHAT IS THE ENDING VALUE OF THE LOOP"; END.VAL
50 INPUT "AT WHAT INTERVAL DO YOU WISH TO COUNT"; INTERVAL
60 FOR COUNTER = INT.VAL TO END.VAL STEP INTERVAL
70     PRINT COUNTER
80 NEXT COUNTER
90 END

RUN
WHAT IS THE BEGINNING VALUE OF THE LOOP? 20
WHAT IS THE ENDING VALUE OF THE LOOP? 10
AT WHAT INTERVAL DO YOU WISH TO COUNT? -2
 20
 18
 16
 14
 12
 10
Ok
```

```
10 REM *** EXAMPLE FOUR **
20 REM    FOR/NEXT Loop using all real variables supplied by the user.
30 INPUT "WHAT IS THE BEGINNING VALUE OF THE LOOP"; INT.VAL
40 INPUT "WHAT IS THE ENDING VALUE OF THE LOOP"; END.VAL
50 INPUT "AT WHAT INTERVAL DO YOU WISH TO COUNT"; INTERVAL
60 FOR COUNTER = INT.VAL TO END.VAL STEP INTERVAL
70    PRINT COUNTER
80 NEXT COUNTER
90 END

RUN
WHAT IS THE BEGINNING VALUE OF THE LOOP? 9.5
WHAT IS THE ENDING VALUE OF THE LOOP? 12.5
AT WHAT INTERVAL DO YOU WISH TO COUNT? .5
 9.5
 10
 10.5
 11
 11.5
 12
 12.5
Ok
```

Figure 21. (opposite page and above) Examples of various loops illustrating the FOR/NEXT statement set.

```
100 INPUT "WHAT NUMBER DO YOU WANT
      TO START COUNTING FROM"; INT.AMT
110 INPUT "WHAT NUMBER DO YOU
      WANT TO STOP AT"; END.AMT
120 INPUT "WHAT INTERVAL DO YOU
      WANT TO COUNT BY"; INTERVAL
130 FOR COUNTER = INT.AMT TO
      END.AMT STEP INTERVAL
140    LPRINT COUNTER
170 NEXT COUNTER
180 END
```

Figure 21 demonstrates four different FOR/NEXT statement sets.

The complexity of this statement set provides greater potential for error. Errors can result from one or more of the following:

1. Misplacing the NEXT statement creates logic errors and therefore produces erroneous results.
2. If the NEXT statement is used without a FOR instruction, a "NEXT without FOR" error terminates processing.
3. If the FOR statement is used without a NEXT instruction, a "FOR without NEXT" error terminates processing.
4. A conditional or unconditional branch into or out of a FOR/NEXT loop may yield erroneous results. Try to design the program so that the loop contains statements that can be executed sequentially.
5. When you are increasing the intervals, if the value of the counter.var is greater than the ending value when entering the loop, no processing is performed.
6. When you are decreasing the intervals, if the value of the counter.var is less than the ending value when entering the loop, no processing is performed. When the design requires the counter to decrease, use the higher value as the initial value and the low value as the ending value. The STEP option must be used with a negative interval value.
7. When the initial or the ending values are represented by variables, the variables must be assigned their values before the execution of the loop.

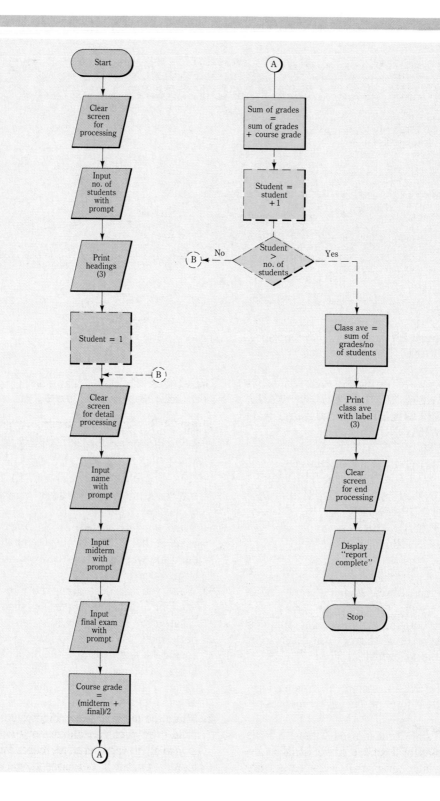

```
10   REM  ********************************************************************
20   REM  * THIS PROGRAM WILL BE USED ONLY BY PROFESSOR LASSITER FOR COMPUTING *
30   REM  * THE FINAL GRADE FOR EACH STUDENT ENROLLED IN HER CLASS.            *
40   REM  ********************************************************************
50   REM
60   CLS
70   INPUT "Good day Professor Lassiter.  How many students are enrolled";
          TOT.STUDENTS
80   LPRINT TAB(20); "PROFESSOR LASSITER'S FINAL GRADE REPORT" : LPRINT
90   CLS
100  LPRINT TAB(14); "STUDENT'S NAME"; TAB(35);"MIDTERM";TAB(45);"FINAL EXAM";
          TAB(60); "COURSE GRADE"
110  FOR STUDENT = 1 TO TOT.STUDENTS
120      CLS
130      INPUT "What is the student's name";STUDENT.NAME$
140      INPUT "What grade did he/she receive on the midterm exam"; MIDTERM
150      INPUT "What grade did he/she receive on the final"; FINAL
160      LET COURSE.GRADE = (MIDTERM + FINAL)/2
170      LET SUM.OF.COURSE.GRADES = SUM.OF.COURSE.GRADES + COURSE.GRADE
180      LPRINT TAB(12); STUDENT.NAME$; TAB(36); MIDTERM ; TAB(48); FINAL;
              TAB(65); COURSE.GRADE
190  NEXT STUDENT
200  LET CLASS.AVE = SUM.OF.COURSE.GRADES / TOT.STUDENTS
210  LPRINT : LPRINT
220  LPRINT TAB(25); "THE CLASS AVERAGE IS. . . "; CLASS.AVE
230  CLS : PRINT "REPORTING COMPLETE"
240  END
```

Figure 22. (opposite) A complete flowchart showing the logic solution for Dr. Lassiter's student grade report. Broken lines represent logic generated by the system.

Figure 23. (above) Coded solution to the flowchart logic detailed in Figure 22.

Figure 24. (below) Hard-copy course grade report produced by the program shown in Figure 23.

```
              PROFESSOR LASSITER'S FINAL GRADE REPORT

        STUDENT'S NAME        MIDTERM    FINAL EXAM      COURSE GRADE
        Richard D. Jenkins       88          90              89
        Janet Cowan              89          92              90.5
        Joseph Conti             88          96              92
        Judith DeFelice          80          84              82
        Victor R. Long           67          75              71
        Richard Considine        88          80              84
        Jasper T. Book           76          92              84
        Mary Ellen Samson        45          63              54
        Mary Grace Abel          88          76              82
        Alice G. Duey            54          65              59.5
        Jennifer Anne Peterson  100          89              94.5
        Nancy R. Barrison        73          62              67.5

            THE CLASS AVERAGE IS. . .   79.16666
```

Program Analysis

Problem. Professor Lassiter of the English Department wants a program that will create a final hard-copy grade report (see Figures 22, 23, and 24). Dr. Lassiter gives only a midterm and a final exam, each having a weight of 50 percent. The number of students enrolled in her class ranges from ten to forty. The program should also include the calculation for the overall class average and should have descriptive headings.

Before continuing, note the following:

1. In regard to the FOR/NEXT instruction set, the flowchart shows the systems logic.
2. The use of a variable as the ending value in the FOR statement is found in line 110.

Subroutines

As stated previously, a subroutine is an independent group of instructions that is called upon to perform an individual task. In BASIC, it is the *GOSUB* (GO to the SUBroutine) statement that serves as the call instruction. After a subroutine is completed, control must be transferred back to the next sequential statement following the GOSUB. It is the ***RETURN*** statement that transfers the control back again:

Syntax: line # GOSUB line #
Syntax: line # RETURN

The line number following the GOSUB must be the first line of the subroutine that is to be performed. The RETURN must be the last instruction of the subroutine:

```
250 GOSUB 600
260 PRINT AMT.DUE
      (Additional lines of BASIC code)
600 INPUT "What is the amount of the sale";SALES.AMT
610 LET AMT.DUE = SALES.AMT * .06 + SALES.AMT
620 RETURN
```

This code illustrates a subroutine. Line 250 "calls" the subroutine starting at Line 600. Line 600 requests input data and is followed by 610, which computes the AMT.DUE. Line 620 returns control back to the next executable statement following the call, which in this case is Line 260, causing the amount due to be displayed on the screen.

Without the GOSUB statement, two GOTO instructions would be required to accomplish the task:

one GOTO to branch to the desired line of code and a second GOTO to return. The programmer should avoid the GOTO statement as much as possible. Too many GOTO instructions make the program logic very difficult to follow.

An often asked question is "Why use subroutines?" The reasons may be vague to the novice programmer, but as programs increase in size, much of the coding becomes redundant. If this redundant code can be collected into groups of individual procedures, these procedures can be called upon when needed. A myth exists that states, "The longer the program, the more important it is." This myth is false. The programmer should strive to make his or her program as efficient as possible. Subroutines are used heavily in a contemporary method of coding called ***structured programming.*** In this design, a main control module calls all subordinate subroutines.

When working with subroutines, the programmer must be careful of certain conditions that cause errors. Some of these conditions are the following:

1. Care must be taken not to permit an unconditional branching out of a called subroutine, for this may yield unpredictable results. When a subroutine is "called," the computer anticipates a return.
2. A RETURN statement encountered when a subroutine has not been called causes a "RETURN without GOSUB" error, which terminates processing.
3. A GOSUB that contains a nonexistent line number as the destination of a subroutine causes an "undefined-line-number" error, which terminates processing.
4. A GOSUB statement must never call a line number that ultimately causes the same GOSUB to be executed again. Such a routine causes an infinite loop and generates an "out-of-memory" error. For example:

```
100 LET R = X * 5
110 GOSUB 100
120 PRINT R
130 RETURN
```

```
10   REM ***********************************************************************
20   REM * THIS PROGRAM WILL BE USED ONLY BY PROFESSOR LASSITER FOR COMPUTING *
30   REM * THE FINAL GRADE FOR EACH STUDENT ENROLLED IN HER CLASS.            *
40   REM ***********************************************************************
50   REM
60   CLS
70   INPUT "Good day Professor Lassiter.  How many students are enrolled";
        TOT.STUDENTS
80   GOSUB 210
90   CLS
100  FOR STUDENT = 1 TO TOT.STUDENTS
110      CLS
120      INPUT "What is the student's name"; STUDENT.NAME$
130      INPUT "What grade did he/she receive on the midterm exam"; MIDTERM
140      INPUT "What grade did he/she receive on the final exam"; FINAL
150      LET COURSE.GRADE = (MIDTERM + FINAL) / 2
160      LET SUM.OF.COURSE.GRADES = SUM.OF.COURSE.GRADES + COURSE.GRADE
170      LPRINT TAB(12); STUDENT.NAME$; TAB(36); MIDTERM; TAB(48); FINAL;
                TAB(65); COURSE.GRADE
180      IF LINE.COUNTER = 63
             THEN LPRINT : LPRINT : LPRINT : GOSUB 210
             ELSE LET LINE.COUNTER = LINE.COUNTER + 1
190  NEXT STUDENT
200  GOTO 300
210  REM ***********************************************************************
220  REM *                       HEADING SUBROUTINE                           *
230  LPRINT : LPRINT : LPRINT ' Three lines top margin of the new page.
240  LPRINT TAB(20);"PROFESSOR LASSITER'S FINAL GRADE REPORT" : LPRINT
250  LPRINT TAB(14); "STUDENT'S NAME"; TAB(35); "MIDTERM"; TAB(45);"FINAL EXAM";
                TAB(60); "COURSE GRADE"
260  LET LINE.COUNTER = 7
270  RETURN
280  REM *                                                                    *
290  REM ***********************************************************************
300  LPRINT : LPRINT
310  LET CLASS.AVE = SUM.OF.COURSE.GRADES / TOT.STUDENTS
320  LPRINT TAB(25); "THE CLASS AVERAGE IS . . . "; CLASS.AVE
330  CLS : PRINT "REPORTING COMPLETE"
340  END
```

Figure 25. Coded modification of Dr. Lassiter's final-grade-report program (see Figures 22 and 23) using a heading subroutine.

Program Analysis

Problem. Dr. Lassiter wishes to have her grade-report program modified (see Figure 25). She will be offering a special lecture section.

The number of students will range from fifty to seventy in one class. The continuous paper has sixty-six lines, and a heading must appear on the top of each page.

Before continuing, note the following:

1. The incorporation of the line counter for adequate spacing.
2. The method of skipping to a new page. The user must physically start the paper at the top of a new page before executing the program.
3. The use of the subroutine to avoid duplicating the code that produces the heading. Notice that there are two GOSUBs, and one RETURN.

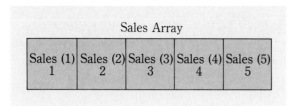

Sales Array

Sales (1)	Sales (2)	Sales (3)	Sales (4)	Sales (5)
1	2	3	4	5

Figure 26. Graphic illustration of the one-dimensional array "SALES," containing five elements.

BASIC ARRAY PROCESSING

Periodically, certain data values may have to be referenced many times during processing. Data can be stored in a table, more commonly called an *array*. An *array* is a set of related data *elements* represented in one contiguous storage location. Each individual element within the array has a *subscript* that denotes its relative position.

Assume that each salesperson has five sales, one for each day of the work week. The data may be stored as one item, called SALES. Because SALES represents only one list of data, it is referred to as a one-dimensional array. Figure 26 shows a graphic portrayal of the SALES array.

As illustrated in Figure 26, each day's sales are qualified by the use of a subscript. The subscript clarifies to the computer which element of the set is to be referenced.

Numeric constants or variables may be used as subscripts. If a variable is used, the programmer must be sure that it has the proper numeric value that points to the desired element, before referencing the array. If the variable has a value other than the value anticipated by the programmer, either an execution or a logic error will result.

Defining Storage

Memory is allocated to an array by the use of the *DIM* instruction. One must dimension (DIM) an array to the correct size before executing any statements that reference this area.

$$\textit{Syntax}$$
$$\text{line \# DIM var.1} \begin{cases} \text{(variable)} \\ \text{(constant)} \\ \text{(expression)} \end{cases}$$

$$\left[\dots \text{ var.N} \begin{cases} \text{(variable)} \\ \text{(constant)} \\ \text{(expression)} \end{cases} \right]$$

To save coding time, many arrays may be created in one DIM statement. The syntax allows the size of the array to be described in the form of a variable, a constant, or an expression. The size specification, regardless of the type of definition, must be placed in parentheses.

A numeric integer constant is used when the size of the array is fixed in length. If the salespeople work only five days a week, the easiest method of defining SALES would be

100 DIM SALES(5)

A variable-size array is very beneficial when the number of data items to be stored is unknown at the time the program is being designed. To avoid an array with zero elements, assign the value of the variable before defining the array.

100 INPUT "HOW MANY SALES AMOUNTS DO YOU
    WISH TO ENTER"; NUM.OF.SALES%
110 DIM SALES(NUM.OF.SALES%)

This code illustrates a variable-length array. The size changes to meet the requirements of each particular processing situation. The use of this type of array helps to save storage. Some programmers who have developed poor habits assign the storage of variable-length arrays based on what they think is the maximum size. This practice is inefficient and could result in a processing error in the future if the estimated maximum becomes insufficient.

The use of an expression to dimension an array is the practice of the more advanced programmer. The

Figure 27. Screen-image reproduction of user-directed processing to build the POSTAGE.RATE array.

```
HOW MANY POSTAGE RATES ARE TO BE ENTERED? 5

ENTER THE POSTAGE RATE FOR   1   OUNCES
? .22

ENTER THE POSTAGE RATE FOR   2   OUNCES
? .38

ENTER THE POSTAGE RATE FOR   3   OUNCES
? .49

ENTER THE POSTAGE RATE FOR   4   OUNCES
? .56

ENTER THE POSTAGE RATE FOR   5   OUNCES
? .73
```

size of the array is predicated on the outcome of some mathematical process. One must guarantee that the result will yield a positive amount: storage of a negative number of values is meaningless.

Building the Array

The DIM statement only sets aside memory for the array: it does not store data. It is the programmer's responsibility to store each data item in its proper location or, in other words, to build the array.

A FOR/NEXT loop structure is perfect for this task. It performs the appropriate processing to fill each element of the array sequentially with data. Assume that the following data represent postage amounts per ounce:

Weight in Ounces	Rate
1	.22
2	.38
3	.49
4	.56
5	.73

The following code builds the postage rate array:

```
100 DIM POSTAGE.RATE(5)
110 FOR OUNCE% = 1 TO 5
120    READ POSTAGE.AMT
130    LET POSTAGE.RATE(OUNCE) = POSTAGE.AMT
140 NEXT OUNCE%
150 DATA .22,.38,.49,.56,.73
```

Space is allocated by the DIM instruction. The

FOR statement initializes OUNCE to 1. Line 120 reads one postage amount. The LET statement assigns POSTAGE.RATE(OUNCE) to the value read. The first time through the loop, POSTAGE-.RATE(OUNCE) (pointing to Element 1 of the array) is assigned to the postage amount of 22 cents. The NEXT statement increases the counter "OUNCE" by 1 and checks the ending limit. This process continues until the POSTAGE.RATE array is loaded with data. Do a walk-through of this code to be sure that you understand the processes required to build an array.

The code can be modified to create a general-purpose procedure as follows:

```
100 INPUT "HOW MANY POSTAGE RATES ARE TO BE
        ENTERED"; NUMBER.OF.RATES
110 DIM POSTAGE.RATE(NUMBER.OF.RATES)
120 FOR OUNCE = 1 TO NUMBER.OF.RATES
130 PRINT "WHAT IS THE POSTAGE RATE FOR ";
        OUNCES; " OUNCES"
140    INPUT POSTAGE.AMT
150    LET POSTAGE.RATE(OUNCE) = POSTAGE.AMT
160 NEXT OUNCE
```

Figure 27 provides a copy of the screen image generated from processing these instructions.

Notice that the size of the array depends on the response of the user. Also, the prompt in the FOR/NEXT loop used to obtain the POSTAGE.AMT incorporates the internal counter to enhance the message. (It takes a little more logic to avoid the plural OUNCES for the first request of one ounce.)

```
10   REM ******************************************************************
20   REM *   THE PURPOSE OF THIS PROGRAM IS:                              *
30   REM *         1.   DEFINE STORAGE FOR A ONE DIMENSIONAL ARRAY        *
40   REM *         2.   BUILD THE ARRAY BY LOADING THE AREA WITH DATA.    *
50   REM *         3.   PROCESS THE ARRAY                                 *
60   REM ******************************************************************
70   REM
80   CLS
90   INPUT "HOW MANY POSTAGE RATES ARE TO BE ENTERED"; NUMBER.OF.RATES
100  DIM POSTAGE.RATE(NUMBER.OF.RATES)
110  FOR OUNCE = 1 TO NUMBER.OF.RATES
120      PRINT : PRINT "ENTER THE POSTAGE RATE FOR "; OUNCE; " OUNCES"
130      INPUT POSTAGE.AMT
140      LET POSTAGE.RATE(OUNCE) = POSTAGE.AMT
150  NEXT OUNCE
160  CLS
170  PRINT TAB(30);"PROCESSING SALES" : PRINT : PRINT
180  INPUT "WHAT IS THE AMOUNT OF THE SALE"; SALES.AMT
190  INPUT "WHAT IS THE SHIPPING WEIGHT IN OUNCES"; SHIPPING.WEIGHT
200  LET AMOUNT.DUE = SALES.AMT + POSTAGE.RATE(SHIPPING.WEIGHT)
210  CLS
220  PRINT "THE SALES AMOUNT FOR THE ORDER IS . . . . "; SALES.AMT
230  PRINT "THE SHIPPING WEIGHT FOR THE ORDER IS. . . "; SHIPPING.WEIGHT;
         "OUNCES"
240  PRINT "THE COST TO SHIP IS . . . . . . . . . . ";
             POSTAGE.RATE(SHIPPING.WEIGHT)
250  PRINT "THE TOTAL AMOUNT DUE FOR THIS SHIPMENT . . "; AMOUNT.DUE
260  PRINT : PRINT : PRINT
270  INPUT "DO YOU HAVE ANY MORE SALES TO PROCESS <YES> OR <NO>"; RESPONSE$
280  IF RESPONSE$ = "YES" THEN GOTO 160
290  END
```

Figure 28. A listing of the program that processes using the one-dimensional POSTAGE.RATE array.

```
                         PROCESSING SALES


     WHAT IS THE AMOUNT OF THE SALE? 100.00
     WHAT IS THE SHIPPING WEIGHT IN OUNCES? 3
a
     THE SALES AMOUNT FOR THE ORDER IS . . . .   100
     THE SHIPPING WEIGHT FOR THE ORDER IS. . .   3 OUNCES
     THE COST TO SHIP IS . . . . . . . . . . .   .49
     THE TOTAL AMOUNT DUE FOR THIS SHIPMENT . .   100.49



     DO YOU HAVE ANY MORE SALES TO PROCESS <YES> OR <NO>? YES
b
                         PROCESSING SALES


     WHAT IS THE AMOUNT OF THE SALE? 236.78
     WHAT IS THE SHIPPING WEIGHT IN OUNCES? 40
     Subscript out of range in 200
     Ok
c
```

Figure 29. The subscript SHIPPING.RATE is provided unknowingly by the user. (b) Results of processing the user's request for the total amount due after accessing the POSTAGE.RATE array. (c) A request for an element not in the POSTAGE.RATE array, resulting in a processing error.

```
10   REM *******************************************************************
20   REM * THIS PROGRAM PRODUCES A REPORT OF CORPORATE STOCK SOLD BY DISTRICT *
30   REM *******************************************************************
40   REM
50   DIM DISTRICT$(5), SHARES.SOLD%(5)
60   FOR COUNT% = 1 TO 5
70       READ DIST.NAME$
80       LET DISTRICT$(COUNT%) = DIST.NAME$
90   NEXT COUNT%
100  CLS
110  PRINT "ENTER <0> FOR THE NUMBER OF SHARES SOLD TO END PROGRAM"
120  PRINT : PRINT
130  INPUT "WHAT ARE THE NUMBER OF SHARES SOLD"; NO.SOLD%
140  IF NO.SOLD% = 0 THEN GOTO 190
150  PRINT
160  INPUT "FROM WHICH DISTRICT (USE APPROPRIATE CODE)"; DIST.CODE%
170  LET SHARES.SOLD%(DIST.CODE%) = SHARES.SOLD%(DIST.CODE%) + NO.SOLD%
180  GOTO 100
190  LPRINT TAB(17); "CORPORATE SHARES SOLD BY DISTRICT" : PRINT
200  LPRINT TAB(20); "DISTRICT"; TAB(40); "SHARES SOLD"
210  FOR PRINT.COUNT% = 1 TO 5
220      LPRINT TAB(15); DISTRICT$(PRINT.COUNT%); TAB(45);
                  SHARES.SOLD%(PRINT.COUNT%)
230  NEXT PRINT.COUNT%
240  DATA "North Eastern States"
250  DATA "Midwest"
260  DATA "Southern States"
270  DATA "West Coast"
280  DATA "Central States"
290  END
```

Figure 30. Coded solution to Mr. Driscoll's request for a program to calculate the sale of corporate stock by district.

Processing the Array

After an array is loaded with data, the programmer may process the array elements as desired. When an element in the array is required for processing, a subscript *must* be used. The computer has multiple elements defined by the DIM instruction. It is the subscript that denotes the relative storage position of the element to be processed.

Figure 28 provides a listing of the program that processes the POSTAGE.RATE array. Line 190 requests the shipping weight in ounces. Once the weight has been entered, the computer uses this value (SHIPPING.WEIGHT) to retrieve the appropriate postage rate from the array. Assume that the user answers the input prompts as illustrated in Figure 29(a). The computer uses the value 3 entered for the variable SHIPPING.WEIGHT to obtain the third element from the POSTAGE.RATE array valued at 49 cents. The results of processing can be seen in Figure 29(b).

One must always remember to stay within the boundaries of the array or the system will generate a "subscript-out-of-range" error. Figure 29(c) illustrates the error with a request of relative position 40 from a table containing only five elements.

Program Analysis

Problem. Michael Driscoll, director of finance, would like to do a summary report showing the sale of corporate stock by district (see Figure 30): each of the five districts is identified by a code number as shown below.

```
     CORPORATE SHARES SOLD BY DISTRICT
        DISTRICT            SHARES SOLD
   North Eastern States        1432
   Midwest                     1239
   Southern States             3273
   West Coast                   652
   Central States              5662
```

Figure 31. A hard-copy stock distribution report produced by an execution of the program shown in Figure 30.

District	Code
North Eastern States	1
Midwest	2
Southern States	3
West Coast	4
Central States	5

For data entry purposes, only the number of the shares sold and the respective code for the district are entered to expedite processing. Mr. Driscoll wants the report to show each district by name (see Figure 31).

Before continuing, note the following:

1. The size of the array is fixed: there are only five districts.
2. The FOR/NEXT loop (Lines 60 through 90) places the district names in the array.
3. Subscripts are used in Lines 80, 170, and 220 to identify the elements of the array.
4. The processing involves the use of the district code for input and the district name for output.

IBM-PC OPERATIONS

The PC configuration includes the central processing unit (CPU), two disk drives, the monitor, the keyboard, and the printer.

Step 1—Turn on the computer.

At first, one may guess that the on-off switch would be located on the keyboard. In actuality, it can be found on the right-hand side of the CPU. IBM, like many other computer manufacturers, places the on-off switch where it cannot be pressed accidentally.

When the machine is turned off, its main memory is cleared of all entries made by the user or programmer. An unintentional power-off can destroy hours of work.

When turning on the computer, also turn on the monitor and the printer. Within a few seconds, the computer will enter the BASIC mode of processing. You can now key the BASIC program.

Step 2—Key in the program.

The IBM-PC keyboard is very similar to a typewriter keyboard. The standard return key on the typewriter is replaced by an ⟨enter⟩ key (denoted on the keyboard by ↵). The ⟨enter⟩ key provides communication with the computer. This key must be pressed after the keying of every BASIC instruction, as well as after each command.

Two additional sets of keys, not common to a typewriter, are also provided. The minikeyboard to the left defines ten computer function keys. Each key is represented with a function number, F1 through F10. These function keys are provided to save time for the user or programmer. One need press only one key to have the computer perform a predefined function instead of keying the entire function manually. For example, pressing ⟨F2⟩ in the BASIC mode of processing executes the program residing in memory.

The group of keys located to the right provides a vehicle for entering numeric data in a method similar to that used on a calculator. To invoke this option, press the ⟨Num Lock⟩ key. The cursor can be manipulated by the use of these same keys when the numeric key pad option is not in effect.

It is recommended that the new programmer become comfortable with the keyboard by keying the BASIC program found in Figure 11. A summary of keyboard actions is provided in Figure 32.

```
                    IBM-PC Keyboard Usage Summary

        Desired Action                    Key Stroke(s)

Move the cursor to the right                < → >

Move the cursor to the left                 < ← >

Move the cursor up                          < ↑ >

Move the cursor down                        < ↓ >

Communicate with the computer               < ↵ >
when entering data, code or
commands

Repeat a character multiple          Hold the desired
times                                key for a second

Clear the screen not alter-
ing memory                          <CTRL> and <HOME>

Key in UPPERCASE                       <CAPS LOCK>

To use of the number pad               <NUM LOCK>

To get a hardcopy list of the
screen image                        <shift> and <PRTSC>

To backspace                         < ← > on top row
```

Figure 32. IBM-PC keyboard Usage Summary.

To facilitate entering the program, the automatic line-numbering function can be engaged by keying AUTO and ⟨enter⟩. The computer supplies a new line number, increasing by 10, every time the programmer presses the enter key. To disengage the AUTO function, hold down the ⟨CTRL⟩ key and press ⟨BREAK⟩.

To renumber the entire BASIC program, key RENUM and ⟨enter⟩.

Step 3—Get it running.

After keying is complete, the programmer should request a listing to sight-verify her or his work. The programmer obtains this listing by keying the word LIST or pressing ⟨F1⟩ followed by ⟨enter⟩. A hard-copy listing can be secured by keying LLIST. Make sure the printer is turned on and that it is on-line before requesting a listing.

If a correction is desired, a line may be rekeyed by its respective line number or it can be edited. To edit, key EDIT and the line number that is to be edited, then ⟨enter⟩. By using the ⟨INS⟩ key for character insertion and the ⟨DEL⟩ key for character deletion, correct the line. Remember to press ⟨enter⟩ after editing is complete, in order to alter the contents of memory.

After all syntax errors seem to be corrected, execute the program by keying RUN followed by ⟨enter⟩ or by pressing ⟨F2⟩. If the results of the execution are correct, congratulations. If there are any execution errors, list the program, make the necessary corrections, and then rerun the program.

DISK BASIC

In order to process using diskettes, you need a copy of the IBM-PC operating system. Insert the operating system diskette in the left drive (Drive A), and

```
Current date is Tue  1-01-1980
Enter new date: 9-13-85
Current time is  0:00:20.98
Enter new time: 9:32:00


The IBM Personal Computer DOS
Version 2.10 (C)Copyright IBM Corp 1981, 1982, 1983

A>FORMAT B:
Insert new diskette for drive B:
and strike any key when ready

Formatting...Format complete

    362496 bytes total disk space
    362496 bytes available on disk


Format another (Y/N)?N
A>
```

Figure 33. Screen reproduction of successful results of formatting a new diskette on Drive B.

Figure 34. IBM-PC DOS command summary.

IBM-PC Operating System Command Summary
(Systems diskette resides in Drive A (A)command)

Desired Action	Required Procedure
Format a diskette in Drive B	Key FORMAT B: and (◄─┘) Example: A>FORMAT B:
Format a diskette in Drive A	Key FORMAT A: remove the operating system, insert the new disk and press (◄─┘) Example: A>FORMAT A:
Enter the BASIC mode of processing	Key BASIC and (◄─┘) Example: A>BASIC
Delete a BASIC program from	Key ERASE filename.BAS and (◄─┘) Example: A>ERASE PRO1.BAS
Backup the diskette	Key DISKCOPY source-drive: distination drive: and (◄─┘) Example: A>DISKCOPY A: B: Backup disk on drive A to B.
To see the directory of a diskette	Key DIR drive: and (◄─┘) Example: A> DIR B:

then turn on the computer. In a few seconds, the machine will request the date in a month-day-year format. If a correct date is provided, the computer will then request the time in the format hours (military 0–24):minutes:seconds. You may avoid entering the date or the time by pressing the ⟨enter⟩ key.

It is common practice for a programmer to store the application programs on a separate diskette. Most of the space on the operating-system diskette, often called the *systems disk,* is taken up with manufacturer-supplied software.

Before the programmer can use a new diskette, it must be formatted. To format, insert the new diskette in the right drive (Drive B), leaving the systems

IBM-PC BASIC Command Summary
(Systems diskette resides in Drive A)

Desired Action	Required Procedure
To automatically increment line numbers by ten	Key AUTO and 〈◄—┘〉 Example: AUTO
To automatically increment line numbers at a specific starting point	Key AUTO beginning line # and 〈◄—┘〉 Example: AUTO 250
To disengage the AUTO function	Press 〈CTRL〉 and 〈BREAK〉
To delete a line of BASIC code	Key DELETE line # and 〈◄—┘〉 Example: DELETE 120
To delete a sequential group of lines	Key DELETE beginning line # -ending line # and 〈◄—┘〉 Example: DELETE 130-160
To edit a line of BASIC code	Key EDIT line # and 〈◄—┘〉 Example: EDIT 410
To request a directory of the a diskette when in the BASIC mode of processing	Key FILES "drive*.*" and 〈◄—┘〉 Example: FILES "B*.*"
To execute the program	Key RUN and 〈◄—┘〉 or press 〈F2〉
To list the entire program	Key LIST or press 〈F1〉 and 〈◄—┘〉
To list certain lines of the the BASIC program	Key LIST beginning line of number-ending line number Example: LIST 100-200
To load a file from diskette	Key LOAD"filename" and 〈◄—┘〉 Example: LOAD "PRO1"
To clear memory	Key NEW and 〈◄—┘〉
To save a file on diskette	Key SAVE"filename" and 〈◄—┘〉 Example: SAVE "PRO1"
To delete a file off a diskette	Key KILL"filename.BAS" and 〈◄—┘〉 EXAMPLE: KILL"PROB1.BAS"
To renumber a BASIC program by intervals of ten	Key RENUM and 〈◄—┘〉

Figure 35. IBM-PC BASIC command summary.

disk in Drive A. Key in the command:

FORMAT B: (and 〈enter〉)

Follow the computer-supplied prompts. A format procedure is illustrated in Figure 33.

Once the application disk is formatted, enter the BASIC mode of processing by keying BASIC (and 〈enter〉). Figures 34 and 35 summarize the major IBM-PC system and BASIC commands, respectively.

PROBLEMS

The following assignments are designed to provide practice in the areas of problem analysis, creating flowchart solutions, and coding BASIC programs. It is highly recommended that all solutions be executed on a microcomputer to ensure understanding.

1. Create a three-line hard-copy listing of an individual's name, street address, and city, state, and zip code.
2. Calculate the simple interest (principal × rate × time) of a $3,000 car loan for two years at 12.5 percent.
3. Create a listing for the dean of students by selecting all seniors with a grade-point average of 3.5 or more. There are approximately 10,000 students. A grade-point average can never be negative. (Test for accuracy using a select sample of data.)
4. Modify Problem 3 to provide the following totals at the end of the report: the total number of students selected; the total number of students rejected.
5. Design and code an interactive statistical program that will calculate a mean average regardless of the number of observations.
6. Create an interactive computing environment for checkbook processing. Add all deposits to the account during the month and subtract all the withdrawals. Make sure that the beginning balance is requested. Assume that the bank imposes a flat service charge of two dollars, plus a five-cent charge for each withdrawal. Provide the user with a hard-copy listing of each transaction and a final balance at the end of processing. Fully disclose all finance charges. (This is a good application for incorporation of the PRINT USING instruction.)
7. Design and code a payroll program that calculates net pay using subroutines. An individual's gross pay is equal to the hours that the employee worked times her or his rate of pay. If the employee works overtime, time-and-a-half is paid for all the hours worked in excess of the weekly requirement of thirty-five hours. For simplicity, assume that the federal tax rate is equal to 20 percent and the FICA rate is equal to .05 percent of the gross pay. Provide appropriate headings and totals.
8. Create an interactive auto-insurance-payment listing based on the following risk classifications and amounts:

Risk Class	Insurance Amount
A1	256.38
A2	329.98
B1	405.33
B2	455.78
C1	506.45
C2	589.99

Use only the risk classifications for input purposes.

IBM-PC Operations

1. Which key on the keyboard provides communication with the computer?
2. How does one use the number pad keys located to the right of the main keyboard?
3. What is the purpose of the AUTO function? How does one engage it? How does one disengage it?
4. Why must a disk be formatted before its use?
5. Explain in your own words the purpose of the following IBM-PC system commands:
   FORMAT
   BASIC
   ERASE
   DISKCOPY
   DIR
6. Explain in your own words the purpose of the following IBM-PC BASIC commands:

DELETE	EDIT
LIST	RETURN
READ	LET
DATA	IF
PRINT	THEN/ELSE
LPRINT	FOR/NEXT
PRINT USING	END
GOTO	
GOSUB	

BASIC Array Processing

1. What is an array?
2. What is the purpose of a subscript?
3. Explain the DIM statement. Contrast the use of the variable and the constant to dimension the array.
4. Using the DIM instruction, create an array of twenty employee names.
5. Using the DIM instruction, create an array of employee names. The size varies, depending on the number of employees.
6. What is meant by the phrase "building the array"?
7. Code the necessary BASIC instructions to create and build an array that will hold the names of the twelve months of the year. Use the READ/DATA instruction set.

For Questions 8 through 10, use the array created in Question 7.

8. Code the necessary BASIC instructions to process the array and print "March" only.
9. Code the necessary BASIC instructions to process the array and print only the summer months.
10. Code the necessary BASIC instructions to print the month requested by the user, via the keyboard.

More BASIC Instructions

1. What is the purpose of the FOR/NEXT instruction set?
2. Discuss the dynamics behind the logic of the FOR/NEXT instruction set.
3. Code a FOR/NEXT loop that will sum twenty test scores.
4. What is the purpose of the STEP option?
5. Code a FOR/NEXT loop that will count backward from 1055 by fives to 100.
6. Examine the following:
   100 FOR X = 5 TO 3
   110 PRINT X
   120 NEXT X
   How many X's will be printed?
7. Examine the following:
   100 FOR Y = Z to 0 Step −1
   110 PRINT Y
   120 NEXT Y
   How many Y's will be printed?
8. What type of error, if any, occurs when a FOR is used without a NEXT instruction?
9. When a FOR is misplaced in the program, what type of error, if any, will result?
10. What is the purpose of the GOSUB instruction?
11. Why do programmers use subroutines?
12. What processing procedures occur when a RETURN instruction is executed?

Interactive BASIC

1. What is meant by the term *interactive* in regard to programming?
2. What is displayed on the screen when the computer executes an INPUT instruction?
3. What is a user prompt? Why should the user be prompted? What may occur if the user is not prompted?
4. Discuss the differences between using the PRINT statement and the INPUT statement in regard to prompting the user.
5. When the "literal prompt" option of the INPUT instruction is used, should the message to the user be in the form of a statement or question? Support your answer with a reason.
6. What is the purpose of the CLS instruction?
7. Should user prompts be lengthy? Why?
8. Assume that the user is to enter in her or his name, last name first. Supply an appropriate prompt.

A BASIC Face-Lift

1. What is meant by *print image?*
2. Contrast a floating dollar sign with a fixed dollar sign.
3. When is the back slash required?
4. When a comma is used in a print image, when will it actually print on the report?
5. Code a print format that will hold a fifteen-character string variable beginning in column 12 and a

numeric integer variable of four characters beginning in Column 30.

6. Code a print format that will hold the following data items:

   The literal "Name . . . " beginning in Column 5.

   A twenty-character string variable beginning in Column 18.

   The literal "Department Code . . ." beginning in Column 45.

   A five-character integer variable beginning in Column 68.

7. Code a print format that will hold the following data items:

   An eight-character dollar amount using a decimal point, a comma, and a floating dollar sign, beginning in Column 10.

   A three-character string variable beginning in Column 30.

   A two-character dollar amount using a fixed dollar sign beginning in Column 38.

A BASIC Lesson

1. Code a LET instruction that will perform the following calculation of X (use Line 400).

$$X = \frac{3r^2}{2 + Y}$$

2. Given the following,
   ```
   100 READ N$, R, C
   110 GOTO 100
   120 DATA "John Smith", 23.14, 32.17, 42.19,
       32.47, 2.12
   ```
   what will occur during the execution of this code?

3. What is the difference between the PRINT and the LPRINT instructions?

4. Given the following PRINT instruction,
   ```
   210 PRINT A, B; C,"XYZ"
   ```
   in which column will "XYZ" display? (Assume that A, B, and C are each less than eight print characters.)

5. Contrast the GOTO instruction with the Format 1 IF instruction.

6. What is a relational operator? Give two examples.

7. What is the purpose of the REM statement?

8. Examine the following BASIC instructions for possible syntax errors. If an instruction is in error, recode it appropriately.
   a. LET A = C
   b. READ R$, C, R, T!
   c. 140
   d. END
   e. 170 REM
   f. 195 IF A EQUALS C THEN GOTO 500
   g. 244 IF C < R2 THAN GOTO 201
   h. 290 IF A = 7
          PRINT "Error for variable A"
          ELSE LET R = A * .4332
   i. 105 GOTO 300
   j. 190 LPRINT G; R#; X + 7
   k. 200 PRINT TAB(40); NAME$; TAB (60);
      ADDRESS$

9. Given the following BASIC program,
   ```
   100 LET X = 0
   110 READ Y
   120 IF Y = −99 THEN GOTO 200
   130 LET X = X + Y
   140 GOTO 110
   150 DATA −12
   160 DATA 42
   170 DATA −2
   180 DATA −99
   190 DATA 23
   200 LET ANSWER = X/2
   220 PRINT "The answer is "; ANSWER
   230 END
   ```
   What will be the value printed for ANSWER after the program has been executed?

BASIC Considerations

1. What is a syntax error?
2. What is meant by *free-formatted instructions?*
3. What are the three components of a BASIC instruction?
4. What is the purpose of line numbers? Will every line on the screen have a number when you are keying BASIC code?
5. Why is the colon used in BASIC? Give an example.

6. What is a numeric constant? Give an example.
7. What is meant by *exponential notation?* Why is it used?
8. What is a string constant? Give an example.
9. List the types of BASIC variables and discuss their differences.
10. Identify the following variables as:
    A. Single-precision
    B. Double-precision
    C. Integer
    D. String
    E. Invalid
    a. REAL ESTATE%
    b. GROSS.PAY!
    c. STOCK$
    d. INTEREST.Y.T.D
    e. $NAME
    f. X$
    g. P#
    h. 372
    i. ZIP.CODE%
    j. "ADDRESS"
    k. Q
    l. %POSTAGE.RATE
11. Write the following formula in BASIC arithmetic notation:

$$\frac{3R + X^3}{2Y}$$

12. Discuss the difference between the use of the equals sign in algebra and in BASIC.

Tools of the Trade

1. Place each of the following instructions in their appropriate flowchart symbols:
   a. 3 * 4R
   b. Is the student number > 400
   c. Print heading
   d. Start
   e. X = 4 * Y
   f. Write check number
   g. Display error message
   h. Read employee name
   i. Stop
   j. Input Y
   k. Note: Processing is done daily.
2. Why does a decision symbol require two outflows?
3. What is an infinite loop? How can it be avoided?
4. Describe counting and accumulation. How are they different?
5. What is a subroutine? How is it shown in a flowchart?

Glossary

Acceptance test. Tests designed by users for a new system to see that it is working properly before the users agree to accept the new system for routine use.

Accounts receivable. In business, the task of keeping a record of what customers owe our firm, sending bills to customers, and keeping track of customer payments to us.

Address. The location of something like a piece of data in primary memory or like a record on secondary storage.

Algorithm. A specified step-by-step approach to solving a problem.

Amplitude. The height of a wave, like a sine wave.

Analog. Analog signals are continuous, like a sine wave. They can be contrasted with digital signals which are discrete ones and zeros.

Analytical Engine. The name given by Babbage to his planned mechanical computer.

Application. The use of a computer for some specific task, like an accounts receivable application.

Applications program. A program that processes data for a user; it contains the logic of the information-processing task for which the computer is being used.

Architecture. The basic structure of a computer or a computer application.

Array. A table in memory. A two-dimensional array has rows and columns, and each element in the array is referenced by a row and a column number.

Artificial intelligence. Programs that perform computations on symbols rather than numbers; the programs exhibit behavior that we would call intelligent if exhibited by a human.

Artificial limb. A mechanical limb, like an arm or a leg which is worn by an amputee.

ASCII. A code used by most non-IBM manufacturers; it features seven bits plus a check digit.

Assembly language. A language close to machine language that features alphabetic mnemonics for instructions and symbols for variables.

Assignment statement. A statement in a programming language that assigns the value of one variable to another. A typical assignment statement would be $X = Y$ which assigns the current value of the variable Y to the variable X.

Asynchronous communications. Data are transmitted as entered; this mode of transmission is the opposite of *synchronous*, in which the sending and receiving ends are coordinated. Characters are marked with start and stop bits.

Automation. A term describing the use of machines and computers to reduce the amount of human labor required to perform some task, like building an automobile.

Backup. The availability of a second position, e.g., a second copy of a computer file in case something happens to damage the original. Also a second computer ready to take over if the primary computer fails.

Base. The foundation of a number system. The decimal system is base 10, the binary system is base 2.

Baseband. A method of sending digital data over communications lines that is suitable for short distances and low transmission speeds.

BASIC. A higher-level language used extensively for time-sharing and on microcomputers.

Batch. Processing that occurs at one point in time after a batch of transactions has been prepared. The batch is used to update a master file once, and no further changes are made until the next update.

Batch processing. The assembly of all transactions to be processed at one time. The transactions are processed against files and the files are updated on a single run.

Baud. In communications, the number of times per second that a signal changes.

BCD (binary coded decimal). A six-bit code used in early computers. BCD is still used as a communications code.

Binary. A number system using base 2. The number system used by most computers.

Bit. Binary digit; either a 0 or a 1.

Block. A group of characters or a group of logical records.

Blocking. The placement of many logical records in one physical record to make input/output more efficient.

Block mode. A block of characters is transmitted together at one time.

Broadband. A method for sending digital signals over communications lines that is suitable for long distances and high transmission speeds.

Bubble memory. The use of tiny magnetic bubbles to store data.

Buffer. A location in memory where data are held temporarily.

Bus. A connection among the components of a computer system.

Bus architecture. A computer system in which components like memory and the CPU are connected using a data bus.

Byte. Usually eight bits; enough to store two digits for computation purposes or a single character.

Career path. The sequence of jobs that an individual holds during his or her career.

Carrier. A firm that provides communications services for sale.

Cell. The intersection of a row and a column in a spreadsheet program.

Centralization. The placement of computers and/or computer staff members in a central location.

Centralized. Located in a central location.

Central processing unit (CPU). The unit that contains all of the logic of the computer and includes the arithmetic unit, the instruction register, and other logic devices.

Chained file. A list of pointers runs through a file linking together records with similar data in a given field.

Channel. A unit of a mainframe computer with its own logic for handling input/output operations; peripherals like tapes, disks, and printers are connected to controllers, which connect to the channel.

Character. Usually the smallest type of data of interest, e.g., the word *character* consists of the characters c, h, a, etc.

Character mode. Data are transmitted one character at a time, usually with a start and a stop bit.

Check digit. A digit that is computed to check for errors in data transmission.

Chip. A small semiconductor, usually of silicon, that contains hundreds of thousands of electronic components. The chip may have memory or logic or both.

COBOL. A high-level computer language used extensively in business processing.

Code. The representation of a message using another medium. For example various bit patterns are used to indicate different letters in a computer.

Commands. Statements that tell a computer what it should do.

Commission. A form of payment often used to compensate sales personnel in which the sales person's income is based on a percentage of the value of the goods he or she sells.

Communications. The transmission of data or voices between two or more points.

Communications satellite. A communications device placed in orbit around the earth. Signals from earth are sent to the satellite which relays them to another location. Signals might be sent via satellite from New York to Paris and vice versa.

Compiler. A program that translates a high-level language like COBOL into machine language.

Complement. The complement of a number is the number subtracted from its number base.

Complexity. The more different states that a system has, the greater its complexity.

Computer conferencing. An electronic mail-like system for conducting a conference with participants in remote locations. Each communicates with a computer system, which maintains a record of the conference.

Conditional. In a computer language, statements that tell the computer to take action depending on some variable. For example, the statement IF X < 0 THEN Y = 2 says that if X is less than 0, set the value of Y to 2.

Conglomerate. A firm that is made up of a number of different subsidiary businesses, often in different lines of business.

Control. The comparison of actual performance with standards, e.g., the thermostat controls the heating system. Also, assuring the accuracy and integrity of the information provided by a computer system.

Controller. A device that interfaces peripherals like a disk or a printer with a computer; the controller takes similar commands for input/output from the computer and changes them to the signals required by the different peripherals.

Conversion. The change from one type of system to another.

Core. A magnetic medium used for the first through third generation of computers for primary memory.

Core storage. Small metal doughnuts that store a 0 or a 1, based on the direction in which they are magnetized. A predominant medium for primary storage during the first twenty-five years of computers.

Cost avoidance. An action that avoids future costs.

Cost-performance ratio. The cost of equipment divided by some measure of its performance. A metric used to compare alternatives.

Cost savings. An action that reduces costs.

CPU. See central processing unit.

Critical Path Method (CPM). An approach to project management that uses a network to represent the completion of tasks in a project and arranges the tasks in the order in which they must be completed. One can use the network to calculate the earliest finish date of a project and the latest start date for each task.

CRT. A terminal with a televisionlike screen.

Cursor. The bright spot of light on a CRT that shows the user's place on the screen.

Custom programming. Writing a program specifically for a given problem as opposed to buying a package program.

Cylinder. A cylinder consists of the set of tracks that are under the read/write heads of a disk when the heads are stationary.

Data. Numbers, characters, or symbols.

Database. A collection of files in an organization.

Database administrator (DBA). An individual charged with the responsibility of defining and maintaining the data structures and the data stored, through the use of a database management system.

Database management system (DBMS). A piece of systems software that provides a dictionary of data items, access routines, and management services for the purpose of creating and maintaining easily accessible data.

Data definition language (DDL). A set of commands used in a database management system to define the characteristics and structure of the data.

Data dictionary. A list of field names and record identifications in a database system.

Data flow diagram (DFD). A type of flowchart that encourages clear representation of an information-processing task; DFDs encourage top-down analysis, moving from a high conceptual level to lower ones in turn.

Data structure. The logical or physical relationship among various entities being stored in memory or on secondary storage.

Decentralization. The presence of computer equipment or staff members at various locations or in different departments. Contrast with centralization.

Decentralized. At a number of different locations.

Decision support. The use of a computer to help aid an individual or a small group of decision makers. Often the decision is ad hoc or may not occur again in the near future.

Decision Support System (DSS). A system designed to help a decisionmaker solve a problem as opposed to a system designed primarily to process transactions.

Dedicated package. A package program that is oriented to one area of business, like accounts receivable.

Delete. To remove information, generally to remove a record no longer needed from a computer file.

Demodulation. The decoding of a modulated digital signal from an analog carrier.

Density. The number of bits stored per unit of area.

Dictionary. A type of file directory that contains a list of the key values and the address at which the first record with that key value is stored on a direct-access file.

Dimension (DIM). A statement that tells BASIC how much room to allow for a matrix.

Direct access. Storage in which any record can be accessed at random.

Directory. The method of transforming the input key of

a query into the record address, where the data about the record with that key are stored on a direct-access device.

Disk. A magnetic disk offers direct-access secondary storage.

Diskette or floppy disk. A disk in which the read/write heads actually come in contact with the diskette medium. Used extensively with personal computers.

Distributed. Partway between centralized and decentralized; communication links decentralized locations.

Documentation. Information that describes something like the logic of a computer system, the instructions for a user to work with a system, etc.

Documented. Refers to a system or subsystem for which documentation is available.

EBCDIC. An eight-bit code used by IBM mainframes and some IBM minicomputers.

Economic order quantity (EOQ). The most economical amount of a product to order. A formula is used to compute the EOQ; it balances the cost of ordering against the cost of having items in inventory.

Electrode. A terminal connected to an electrical supply.

Electronic mail. A communications system using a computer and electronic mailboxes. Individuals at terminals send and receive messages on the system.

Electronic spreadsheet. A computer program like Lotus or Visicalc that facilitates the construction of two dimensional tables which relate different cells through formulas.

Electronic spreadsheet programming. Using a spreadsheet program to solve a problem such as the analysis of a firm's sales.

Emulation. The use of microprogramming and software to make one computer execute the programs of a different computer.

Encryption. The coding of data to make it unreadable by individuals for whom it is not intended.

End of file. A special mark on a computer file that indicates there are no more records on the file.

End user. An individual who is a user of computers, but for whom working with computers is not the major part of his or her duties.

End-user programming. Computer users rather than professionals employ fourth-generation languages, personal computers, and query languages to answer their own questions without requiring programs from professionals.

Enhancements. Changes to a computer program or system to improve the way it functions.

ENIAC. The first electronic computer.

Entry. The process of inputting information into a computer or data entry device.

Environment. The conditions surrounding something, like the environment of a computer room. Also the environment of a firm which refers to the kind of market it faces, the competition, the nature of customers, and so forth.

Error. Data that are incorrect in some way.

Error checking. Human or machine techniques to look for errors in data.

Execute cycle. The central processing unit does what the instruction in the instruction register indicates should be done.

Expert system. A type of decision support system in which the rules followed by a human expert are encoded in a computer program. The system is used for training and for making expert knowledge widely available.

Expression. A mathematical statement relating two variables or constants, e.g., $Y + 2 \times X$ is an expression.

Fail-safe computers. Computers that suffer a fault of some type but continue to process data accurately.

Feasibility. Determining whether a new computer application is advisable and desirable.

Fetch cycle. The central processing unit accesses data or an instruction during a fetch cycle.

Fiber optics. The use of narrow tubes of glass and a laser to communicate voice and data.

Field. A collection of characters in a record; the lowest-level grouping to which one wants to assign a name, like a person's social security number.

Fifth Generation. The next generation of computers.

File. A file contains data for processing on a computer. The data are organized into a series of records, which are stored in the file.

Finished goods. The manufactured items of a firm that are completed and awaiting shipment to customers.

Firmware. Microprogrammed instructions.

Fixed-length record. A record whose number and size of fields are of fixed length.

Fixed-point number. A number in which the decimal point is assumed to be to the right of the rightmost digit; for example, the number 1,223 is a fixed-point number.

Floating-point number. A number in which the decimal point is explicitly included; for example, 123.456 is a floating-point number.

Flowchart. A diagram using symbols and connectors to produce a graphic depiction of a process, like the flow of information in a firm.

Forecast. A prediction of the future.

Format. The way in which something is arranged. In a

computer system, the place in which various fields are located on a record including their contents and size.

Formula. An expression in which one variable is equal to some algebraic combination of other variables.

FORTRAN. A computer language designed for engineering and scientific calculations. The name stands for FORmula TRANslation.

Fourth-generation language. A very-high-level language with a conceptual level above languages like COBOL. Comes close to a nonprocedural language, where one tells the computer what to do rather than how.

Full duplex. Data are transmitted in both directions at once; requires the use of two communications lines.

Functions. A mathematical expression that returns a value to some variable in a programming language.

General-purpose package program. A package program that can be used to solve problems rather than a package dedicated to a particular application; for example, a spreadsheet package for a microcomputer.

Generators. A series of programs that create applications programs when an analyst provides a definition of inputs, the data to be kept on files, and the output for the application.

Gigabyte. One billion bytes.

GOSUB. A statement in BASIC that transfers control to a new part of the program. When that part is finished, it returns control to the statement after the GOSUB.

Graphics. The creation of figures and geometric shapes in contrast with textual information.

Half duplex. Data are transmitted in both directions, but not at the same time.

Hardware. The components of a computer system that can be physically seen and touched.

Harrassment. Repeatedly disturbing an individual or group.

Hexadecimal. A number system with a base of 16 used in many IBM mainframe and minicomputers.

Hierarchical data. A data structure in which records are arranged in a hierarchy like a family tree.

Higher-level language. A language that is at a higher level conceptually than assembly language, such as COBOL, FORTRAN, or BASIC.

IF-THEN-ELSE. A conditional statement in BASIC and other languages.

Impact printing. Printing in which a hammer presses a wire or a character against a ribbon and paper.

Inception. The first stage in the development of a computer application.

Indentation. The practice of offsetting various statements in a computer program from the left hand margin to make the program easier to read and understand.

Index. A table that relates input keys to addresses on a direct-access storage device.

Information center. A center established to help users access computer data themselves. Generally, it provides consulting help and assistance in locating data and putting them into a form for processing by the user.

Information system. A combination of manual and computer procedures which help reduce uncertainty about some state or event and/or helps to control operations in an organization.

Information worker. An individual who primarily works with data and information as opposed to physical products.

Input/output (I/O). Entry or display of data in a computer system.

Input/Output (I/O) control. A group in a computer department that checks to see that input and output is correct.

Insert. To place one thing in another, e.g., to put a new record in its proper place in a computer file.

Instruction. An order to a computer to perform some operation.

Instruction location counter. The register that keeps track of the next instruction in the program to be executed. Unless changed by the central processing unit, it will be the next sequential instruction in the program.

Instruction register. A register in the central processing unit that holds an instruction while it is being decoded and executed.

Instructions. Commands to computer hardware causing it to perform certain actions.

Instruction set. The repertoire of instructions of a given computer.

Integrated circuits. The connection of various circuit components electronically rather than through mechanical means.

Interdependence. A condition in which two individuals or groups depend on each other to accomplish something.

Interorganizational system. A computer application that connects two different organizations together.

Interpreter. A program that examines instructions, determines what they mean, and then takes the action that the instructions indicate. A computer interprets machine language.

Interrecord gap. The physical space between physical records on a secondary storage device.

Inventory. Items stored for future use.

Inverted directory. A directory that contains a list of all records containing a particular key, e.g., all parts to be shipped on August 30.

Involvement. The inclusion of computer users in the development and/or operation of information processing systems.

Iteration. A repetitive procedure for solving a problem; in a programming language, an iteration is implemented with a looping instruction or instructions.

Justification. The alignment of text on one or both margins of a page.

Key. A field in a data record of particular interest; for example, the field used for retrieving records from the file.

Knowledge workers. Individuals who work primarily with information, such as employees in an office.

Large-scale integration (LSI). The fabrication of thousands of transistors on a single chip of silicon.

Laser. A device capable of generating light in a narrow frequency band. Lasers can be turned on and off very rapidly and hence are able to send signals.

Launch-on-warning. A nuclear defense strategy in which a country launches its nuclear missiles when it receives warning that an opponent has launched its missiles. The strategy does not have a country wait to see if the missiles are definitely coming or to see if one actually strikes before launching a counterattack.

Local area network (LAN). A network that connects devices in a small physical area, such as one floor of an office building.

Local intelligence. Some type of computer logic in a local device, like a terminal.

Log. A file in an on-line system containing a history of all input transactions.

Logic. The precise steps required to accomplish some goal, like the logic necessary to compute the payroll for a company.

Logical operator. A mathematical operator that compares two quantities. The operator in A < B is true of A is less than B and false otherwise.

Logical record. The record as defined by the programmer.

Loop. A part of a computer program that is executed n times where n is greater than 1.

LSI (Large Scale Integration). The construction of computer chips with thousands of transistor-like elements on each chip.

Machine language. The language actually understood by the computer's circuits. The computer can execute a program in machine language directly.

Magnetic ink character recognition (MICR). A type of input used by the banking industry to read and sort check destinations. The checks are encoded with magnetic ink.

Mainframe. A large, general-purpose computer capable of running simultaneously a variety of jobs, including batch processing, time-sharing, and on-line processing.

Maintenance. In programming, the task of correcting errors in running programs and making enhancements to existing applications.

Maintenance programming. The repair and enhancement of existing programs and systems.

Mark 1. An early computer developed at Harvard.

Mass storage. Very large capacity storage devices; slower than disk storage.

Master file. A file containing records that are semipermanent. A master file is typically updated and maintained as an active set of data.

Matrix. A table consisting of rows and columns. A table is two dimensional, but in general a matrix can have n dimensions.

Megaflops. Million of floating-point instructions executed in a second; a measure of supercomputer processing speed.

Memory. In a computer, a device that stores data.

Menu. A type of computer input in which the user is given a numbered list of choices and indicates the number of the item desired (like a restaurant menu).

Microcomputer. A small computer often serving one user; may have eight-, sixteen-, or thirty-two-bit data path, CRT, printer, and floppy or hard disks.

Microinstructions. Instructions at a lower level of detail than machine language, which can be used to build a machine language instruction.

Microprocessor. An entire computer on one or a small number of chips. Microprocessors process 4 to 32 bytes of data at a time.

Microprogramming. The construction of programs out of microinstructions.

Microwave. A signal with a very small wave length that is sent at a high frequency. Microwaves are used extensively to transmit voice and data communications.

Minicomputer. A medium-sized computer of sixteen- or thirty-two-bit data path; used for time-sharing and dedicated applications.

Modem. A device for converting digital data to analog by coding the digital data on an analog signal. A modem at the receiving end also demodulates, changing the analog signal back to a digital signal.

Modulation. The coding of a digital signal on an analog waveform.

Module. A piece of a program, usually one that has minimal dependency on other modules and that accomplishes a single function.

Motivation. A force encouraging an individual to take certain actions.

Multiprogramming. In a computer, the presence of more than one semi-active program in the computer at one time.

Natural language. A language like English.

Network (communications). A group of devices connected through communication links forms a network.

Network or plex structure. A data structure in which the data form a network.

Node. A location with a sending or receiving device on a network.

Nonimpact printing. Printing in which the print mechanism does not come in direct contact with the paper, such as a thermal or ink-jet printer.

Nonprocedural language. A language in which the user tells the computer what to do rather than how to do it.

Octal. A number system with base 8.

Office automation. The use of electronic mail, word processing, and calendar and reminder systems to assist managers and other office workers.

On-line. Pertaining to direct interaction with a computer over a communications line; the user works at some kind of terminal device.

Open. In processing computer files, the command that makes the file ready for reading or writing.

Operating system. A program that controls the resources of the computer. It is superior to other programs running on the computer.

Operations. The part of a computer department that is concerned with running computers and doing routine processing.

Operator. In mathematics, the symbol that stands for an operation like + means to add two numbers.

Optical character recognition. See *Scanner*.

Optical storage. Data storage that uses laser-modulated light to store data on optical disks.

Order entry. A function in business that involves recording and processing an order from a customer for some product or service.

Package. A program written by a vendor for sale to vari-

ous users of a computer system. The package might actually include the computer on which it is to run.

Packet switching. Data are assembled into bunches or packets. Each packet has an address and is routed through a network to its destination.

Parallel processors. Two or more processors working on parts of the same processing task.

Parity bits. Extra bits in a character or message for transmission that are used to check for errors.

Pascal. A high level language widely used in computer science.

Personal computer (PC). A microcomputer dedicated in general to a single user. At a minimum, a personal computer usually has a CRT, a CPU, and a primary memory.

Physical record. The number of bytes actually read or written by the operating system at one time.

Planning. The act of preparing for the future.

Plex. A network data structure.

Pointer. A number in a record that points to the next record in a file that contains the same value for a particular field, such as a pointer to the next record with a shipping date of August 30.

Point-of-sale (POS) terminal. A terminal that collects data where a sales transaction is taking place, such as in a grocery store.

Position. The relative location in a record of some field, e.g., name is in the first through the 15th position of the record.

Primary memory. Memory in a computer that is directly accessible by the CPU.

Primary storage. The storage or memory that the central processing unit of a computer can directly access. On early computers, generally consisting of cores; today, most primary memory is made of semiconductors.

Print. To transfer information to paper.

Private Branch Exchange (PBX). A telephone exchange that is owned and operated by a private organization (as opposed to the phone company) for its own use.

Problem-oriented package. A computer programming language or package program that is designed to solve a particular type of problem, for example, the statistical analysis of data.

Procedural language. A computer language in which the programmer must specify each of the major procedures or steps for how some processing is to be accomplished.

Professional programmer. An individual whose primary job is writing computer programs.

Program. A series of instructions telling a computer what to do.

Programmer. An individual who writes code to solve an information-processing problem.

Prompt line. A line on a computer input device that helps tell the user of the device what to enter into the computer next.

Protocol. A convention for how devices are going to communicate with each other during data transmission.

Prototyping. The process of building a small working model of a system or part of a system before undertaking the final design.

Quality. The level of excellence. In manufacturing, seeing that a product meets its standards.

Query. A question that a user asks of a computer system.

Query language. A language designed for asking questions about information stored in a computer database.

Random access memory (RAM). Memory that the central processing unit can access directly; the CPU can read from or write to RAM.

Read-only memory (ROM). Memory that the computer can only read; it cannot modify ROM. ROM's are used to store microinstructions.

Real time. Information is processed quickly enough to control some process such as a rocket launch or a factory's functioning.

Record. A collection of fields about some entity, such as an individual who works for a company.

Register. A device that holds a small number of data; usually, a register has some logic ability, such as being able to perform arithmetic.

Relational database. A structure in which data are maintained as two-dimensional tables; commands facilitate the processing of the tables.

REM or Remark. A statement in BASIC that the computer does not execute. It is included in a program to make the program easier to read and understand.

Replace. To substitute one entity for another.

Report generators. Languages designed for ease of programming; they can be used to quickly generate reports, and advanced versions are employed for developing entire applications.

Requirements analysis. Determining the requirements or needs when designing an information system.

Response time. The time from the completion of data entry to a response from the computer.

Retraining. To train someone for a new task who has already been trained and working on some other task.

Retrieval. The location and display of a particular record.

Return. A program statement that ends a subroutine and directs control back to the statement immediately after the one that invoked the subroutine.

Robot. An electromechanical device usually capable of moving and of grasping objects. Used in manufacturing for painting, welding, and a variety of similar tasks.

Rotational delay time. The time required for a disk drive to rotate to the beginning of a record after the read/write heads have located the track on which the record is located.

Rules. A series of statements that describe a condition and what should be done if that condition occurs.

Save. In a computer system, to put data on a file to be saved for later use.

Scalar. A quantity described by a single number as opposed to a vector or array.

Scanner. A device that reads data directly, such as a device that reads the words on a printed page with an optical character recognizer. Also a grocery store scanner that reads the universal product code.

Scroll. The movement of data vertically on a computer screen as one reads "down" a document.

Search. The process of looking for a specific entity like a particular key in a computer file.

Secondary storage. Devices that store data that cannot be directly accessed by the central processing unit. The CPU must read these data onto files in primary memory before it can process the data.

Seek time. The time it takes for the heads on a movable-head disk to seek the track containing the desired record.

Semiconductor. A substance, like silicon, that conducts electricity only under certain conditions, such as when a voltage is applied to it.

Sensor. A device that sends a signal when some event occurs. For example, a car has a sensor that signals if the oil pressure is too low.

Sequential-access file. A computer file in which records are located one after another in order based on some key.

Sequential storage. Storage in which only the next record in a sequence is accessible.

Simplex. Data are transmitted in one direction.

Single precision. A number with the normal precision of the computer on which a language executes.

Soft keys. Keys on a terminal or a keyboard that are defined by the program. They may mean different things in different parts of the program.

Software. The instructions that tell a computer what actions to perform. Software can be seen in the form of listings, but it cannot be seen when it is executing in the computer.

Sort. Rearranging records to place them in some order, such as numerical or alphabetic.

Sort program. A program which rearranges the order of data based on keys supplied by the user.

Specifications. The detailed requirements needed to prepare a new system.

Spreadsheet program. A program that constructs a financial spreadsheet on a computer. The user enters data, including formulas, at row and column intersections. The program automatically recalculates after changes.

Storage. A place where data and program instructions are kept.

Storage address register. The register in which the central processing unit places the address of data it wants from primary memory.

Strategy. The underlying mission and objectives of an organization and plans for how to accomplish them.

String. A series of characters. A string variable for "NAME" might have the value "Jones."

Structure. The way in which something is constructed.

Structured design. A disciplined approach to systems analysis and design that helps in communications among users and professional designers.

Style sheet. A specification for how a document is to be prepared in word processing.

Subroutine. A portion of a program that is called from a main program to do a specific task.

Supercomputer. The fastest computers today designed for heavy computational chores.

Superminicomputer. The fastest minicomputers generally processing 32 bits of data at a time.

Switch. A device that is capable of being turned on and off. Alternatively, a device that directs data along one of several paths.

Synchronous. In data transmission, the sending and receiving units are coordinated.

Synchronous transmission. The sending and receiving units are synchronized in data communications; usually associated with bloc mode transmission.

System. A set of components organized to achieve some goal. For a computer, generally the use of a compu-

ter to solve a problem requires the development of a system.

Systems analysis. The process of understanding a system and what it does. The process of systems design is often included in systems analysis.

Systems analyst. A computer professional who guides a design team of users and other analysts in developing a new computer application.

Systems development. The process of developing a new system.

Systems programmer. A programmer primarily concerned with systems software, like the operating system.

Systems software. Programs that control the resources of the computer, like operating systems and database management systems.

Tape. Magnetic tape is a sequential secondary-storage medium. The tape is very similar to the tape used in a home tape recorder.

Telecommunications handler. A program that controls and processes messages coming to a computer from various telecommunications lines.

Terminal. A device used by a human to communicate with a computer.

Testing. In programming, the process of seeing that a program works properly.

Text. Symbols and words that make up a written document.

Throughput. The amount of work processed by a computer in a given time period.

Time-sharing. The use of a single computer by a number of individuals simultaneously. The users share the time of the central processing unit and have the ability to write and execute programs.

Top-down analysis. Analysis that begins at a high conceptual level and then fills in the details at lower levels in different stages.

Touch screen. A CRT that is able to determine a user's choice of input by where he or she touches the screen with a finger or a pointing device.

Track. A circle on a disk on which data is stored.

Trade-off. Two factors that must be balanced against each other in the making of a decision or choice.

Training. Teaching an individual or group something new.

Transactions. Incoming data that are used to update existing information. For example, an item you charged on a credit card becomes a transaction that updates your records at the credit card company.

Transactions file. A file of transactions used to update a master file.

Transistor. A semiconductor device capable of amplifying a signal. A transistor can also be constructed to have one of two states representing a $\emptyset$ or a 1.

Undo. A command in some computer applications that reverses the last action taken.

Univac 1. An early commercial computer of the first generation.

Update. The addition, modification, or deletion of records in a computer file.

User. An individual in a firm who is not a computer professional, but who wants assistance from a computer.

User interface. The part of a computer system seen by the user such as the dialog that appears on a terminal.

User services. The part of a computer department that is designed to work with users to help solve their problems.

Variable. A symbol that stands for some value, such as $X = 45$.

Variable-length record. A file consisting of records with differing lengths.

Very-high-level languages. Languages above the level of FORTRAN and COBOL; often called fourth generation languages (4 GL).

Very-large-scale integration (VSLI). The fabrication of hundreds of thousands of components on a chip.

Very Large Scale Integration (VLSI). The fabrication of chips with hundreds of thousands of transistor-like elements on them.

Virtual memory. A combination of hardware and software techniques that provides the programmer with an extremely large logical memory. The operating system maps the logical addresses into physical memory.

Vision. In a computer, the ability to recognize shapes and objects, such as in a robot for factory automation.

Vocoder. A device used with a digital transmission system to encode the human voice digitally for transmission.

Voice grade. A telephone line that is capable of clearly transmitting voice communications.

Voice mail. A communications system like electronic mail in which the participants record voice messages for each other; the messages can be forwarded and distributed widely.

von Neumann. A Princeton mathematician who was instrumental in the design of early computers. Today, a von Neumann computer is one that has a CPU and primary memory. The CPU fetches instructions and data from the primary memory for processing.

"What if" questions. The simulation of various alternatives by a decision maker; the user changes various numbers to determine the result if some assumption or prediction is altered.

Window. The partitioning of the screen of a CRT so that multiple items appear, such as two pieces of a long document.

Word. A unit of computer storage which often consists of 4 bytes or 32 bits.

Word processing. The use of a computer-based device and a program to assist an individual in entering, editing, revising, and producing the final copy of a document.

Word wrap. In word processing, the ability to type without using a return key; the computer automatically goes to the next line.

Workstation. A set of tools for an individual, usually including a personal computer with powerful software for doing spreadsheets, word processing, and other office or engineering tasks.

Index

Absolute reference, in electronic spreadsheet, 355

Access, user understanding, 476–477

Accounts receivable, as application, 32, 33

Accumulation, in programming, 573

Addition
  in binary, 99–100
  floating point number and, 101
  machine language for operations in, 166–169

Addresses, of computer, 84, 86, 167

Aiken, Howard, 51

Airlines, computer systems used by, 37–39, 552

Algebra, BASIC and, 582

Algorithms, 422, 567

Alphanumeric printers, 156

Alternatives
  conditional branching instructions and, 571
  systems design and analysis considering, 267–268

American Airlines, 552

American Express, 512–513

American Hospital Supply Corporation, 455–457

American National Standards Institute (ANSI), flowchart and, 567, 568

American Standards Code for Information Interchange (ASCII), 235, 236

American Stock Exchange (AMEX), touch-screen terminal of, 144

Analyst, users role with, 478

Analytical engine, 47, 48

Anderson, C. D., 545

Annotation, in flowchart, 568

APL, 176, 178, 179

Apple, 81
  Apple II, 61, 62, 120, 151
  McIntosh, 146

Applictions, 18, 19, 20, 21, 35, 260–261
  dedicated, 118
  logic of, 20, 23, 24, 26, 27–28, 30, 33
  in managerial plan, 482, 484
  see also Logical design, for business application; Processing

Applications generator, 300, 301

Applications program, 20, 166

Applications programmer, 559, 560

Arc Welding System, 542

Arithmetic
  BASIC and, 582
  computer performing, 98–103, 108
  machine language for operations in, 166–169

Array processing, in BASIC, 606–610

Arrays, 422, 423
Article format, in word processing, 375, 377
Artificial intelligence (AI), 63, 529–530
Artificial limbs, computer used with, 498
ASCII (American Standards Code for Information
    Interchange), 235, 236
Assembler, 170
Assembly language, 53, 170
    for high-level systems, 528
Assignment statements, on BASIC, 422, 427, 428
Assumptions, in planning document, 482
Asynchronous transmission, 237
Atanasoff, John, 50, 51, 53
AT&T, 242, 526, 527
AT&T Telecommunications, 249
Augusta, Ada. *See* Lovelace, Lady
AUTO, on IBM-PC, 611
AUTO function, 580
Auto racing, computers used with, 35–37
Automated-teller machine (ATM), 512–513
Automation
    in factory, 414–419, 541
    in office, 463–466, 530, 539
Automobile bumper, computer-aided design for, 405

Babbage, Charles, 46–48
BACK SLASH, in BASIC, 591
Backlogs, custom systems and, 556–557
Backups, using floppies, 150, 151
Banking
    automated teller-machine, 512–513
    Electronic Funds Transfer, 513
    Pronto system for, 544–545
Bar chart, business graphics producing, 500
Baseband system, of local area network, 247
Bases, 98
    8, 102
    16, 102, 103
    10, 88, 103
    2, 82–83, 98–103
BASIC, 58, 59, 175, 420–446, 577–613
    arithmetic operations in, 582
    array processing in, 606–610
    comma in, 585
    conditional branch in, 587
    constants and, 580–581

disk, 611–613
documenting, 588–589
files in, 440–445
Format 1 syntax requirement, 584–586
free-formatted instructions in, 577, 580
graphics and, 446
home position, 597
IBM-PC running, 610–613
Input/Output in, 422, 583–586
interactive, 593–598
line numbers and, 580
LISTING request and, 580
loops and, 428–429, 430
matrices in, 434
modules in, 429, 430–432, 433
nonprocedural, 294
operators in, 428
semicolon in, 585
statements in, 426–427
    assignment, 427, 428
    CLS, 597
    conditional, 428, 429
    DATA, 434–440, 583–584
    DIM, 434, 606–607
    ELSE, 587
    END, 583
    FOR/NEXT, 598–604, 607
    GOSUB, 432, 433, 604
    GOTO, 586–587
    IF, 587
    INPUT, 593–594
    iteration, 422, 428–429, 430
    LET, 582–583
    LPRINT, 584
    OPEN, 440
    PRINT, 584–586
    PRINT USING, 591
    READ, 434, 583–584
    REM, 588
    remark, 427
    RETURN, 604
    RUN, 580
    STEP, 598
structuring program in, 422–423, 429–434
subroutine in, 432–434, 604
syntax and, 577, 579

BASIC, *Continued*
   TAB function, 584, 585, 586
   unconditional branch in, 586
   user prompted in, 594–597
   variables in, 423, 426, 581–582
Batch-processing, 114, 115, 118, 138
   direct-access files for, 202
   flowchart for, 197
Batch systems, operators and, 555
Baud, 240
BCD (Binary Coded Decimal), 105–106, 235
Bell Laboratory, 526, 527
Binary, hex conversion and, 102
Binary digits, 82
Binary number system, 82–83, 98–103
Biochips, 528
BISYNC Protocol, 241
Bits, 82, 83
   start and stop, 235
Bivariate normal distribution, business graphics
   producing, 400, 402
Blind, computers used for, 498, 499
Block mode transmission, of data, 237
Blocking the tape, 199
Boldface, in word processing, 368, 372
Book inventory, 329
Booting the system, 313
Branching, in simple loop, 570, 571
(BREAK), on IBM-PC, 611
Broadband system, of local area network, 247–
   248, 249
Brokerage firm, computers used by, 454–455
Bubble memory, 136, 152
Budgets, in managerial plan, 484
Buffer, 199
Bumper, computer-aided design for, 405
Burroughs A9 mainframe computer, 125
Bus, 80, 83, 89, 247
   local area network using, 247, 248
   trends in, 520
Bus architecture, trends in, 520
Business
   graphics for, 400–403
   systems design for. *See* Logical design, for
     business application
Byte, 83

CAD. *See* Computer-aided design
Calculations. *See* Arithmetic
Capacity, computer system considering
   requirements for, 266–267
Career paths, for computer profession, 559–561
Case Western Reserve University, 496–497
Cash management account (CMA), computers
   used with, 454–455
Casino Management System, 90–91
Cathode ray tube (CRT), 89, 134, 141, 156
Cells, in electronic spreadsheets, 347–348
Central processing unit (CPU), 81–82, 85
   machine language program for, 166–169
Centralization, as organizational structure, 462
   for computer department, 558–559
Centralized computer network, 242
Centralized processing, for systems, 265
Chained list, 203–204, 204–205
Changes, in storage, 205–208
Channels, 89
Character mode transmission of data, 236–237
Character readers, for input, 136, 146–147
Character string, in BASIC, 426
Charging, for computer services, 485–486
Chart template, 567
Chemical Bank, 554, 555
   Pronto home banking service, 544–545
Children, hierarchical file and, 219
Chip, 56
   coprocessor, 102
   microprocessor and, 119–121
   see also Silicon chips
Cincinnati Milacron robot, 543
Clauses, in BASIC, 428
Clear Screen statement (CLS), in BASIC, 597
COBOL, 55, 173–175
CODASYL committee, 173
Coding, by computer, 103–107, 108, 235
Comma, in BASIC, 585
COMMA, in BASIC, 591
Commission report, system generating, 336, 337
Communications. *See* Data communications
Communications terminal, workstation providing,
   78
Competitive advantage, use of computer gaining,
   454–462

Compiler, FORTRAN and, 170–171
Complements, subtraction using, 100–101
Complexity, computers and, 512
Components of computer. *See* Hardware
Computer-aided design (CAD), 156, 404–414, 541
   for engineering workstation, 404–410
   Louvre renovated using, 411–413
Computer-aided manufacturing (CAM), 541
Computer-aided tomography machine (CAT
   scanner), 544
Computer conferencing, 466
Computer department, 11–13
   end-user assisted by, 394
   management positions in, 554–558
Computer education, 511–512
Computer file. *See* File
Computer languages. *See* Software
Computer matching, 507–510
Computer profession, 9–13, 551–561
   in computer industry, 552
   future and, 528–529
   manager, 11–12
   operations personnel, 11, 12
   organization for, 552–559
      computer department management, 554–558
      senior management, 553–554
      structure of, 558–559
   programmers, 11, 12
   systems analyst, 11–12
   users and, 559
   see also Management; Organization, computers
   and
Computer system. *See* Information system
Computervision
   for computer-aided design, 411–413
   workstation offered by, 404, 405, 406
Conditional branch instruction, 570, 571
Conditional branching, in BASIC, 587
Conditional statement, in BASIC, 428, 429
Conferencing, computer, 466
Connector, in flowchart, 568
Constants, BASIC and, 580
Control of information processing, framework for,
   482–488
Control statements, on BASIC, 422

Conversion
   second-to-third generation computers and, 57–
     58
   in systems life cycle, 262, 263, 264, 280
   user's role in, 479
Coprocessor, 102
Copying, in electronic spreadsheet, 353–355, 356
Counting, in programming, 573
CPU. *See* Central processing unit
Crime
   computer, 512
   computer matching and, 507–510
Critical path method, for monitoring progress, 264
Croy 1 supercomputer, 126
CRT. *See* Cathod ray tube
Cruise line, records for passengers for, 208–210
(CTRL), on IBM-PC, 611
Cursor, 145
   in electronic spreadsheets, 347–348
Custom programming, 279
   backlogs in, 556–557
Customer services, computer systems for, 463

Daisy wheel, for serial printer, 154
Data banks, 507
Data bus. *See* Bus
Data communications, 234–252
   coding in, 235–236
   electronic mail facilitating, 463, 464–465
   hardware for, 250
   Hewlett-Packard and, 250–251
   input/output, 89
   line speed and, 240
   M&C Electronics and, 252
   networks, 240, 242–249
      centralized, 242
      distributed, 243
      local area, 244, 246–249
      packet switching, 242–243, 244, 250
      structures for, 243–244, 245
      switched, 242–243, 244
   protocol for, 240, 241
   signals in, 237–240
   software for, 250

Data communications, *Continued*
  sources of service for, 249–250
  3M and, 251–252
  transmission in, 236–237
  trends in, 526–529
  see also Networks
Data definition language (DDL), 221–222
Data dictionary, 222
Data entry operators, 559
Data flow diagram (DFD), 269, 272
  for inventory control, 323, 324
  menus with, 313, 314
Data item, 573
DATA statements, in BASIC, 434–440, 583–584
Data structures, 203–204, 217–220
  hierarchical, 218–219
  logical, 219–220
  physical, 219
  plex (network), 219
  relational, 219, 220
Database
  capacity and size of, 266, 267
  contents of, 337
  updating, 326, 328–330
Database administration (DBA), 220–221
Database concept, 220
Database management packages, 291
Database management systems (DBMs), 58, 214–228
  data definition language in, 221–222
  data dictionary of, 222
  database administration for, 220–221
  execution of, 223, 224
  goals of, 220
  query language of, 222–223, 295, 298–299
  types of, 223
  use of, 225–227
  user understanding, 476, 477
Decentralized operation, 559
Decentralized processing, for systems, 265
DECIMAL POINT, in BASIC, 591
Decimal system, 103
  binary conversion and, 99
Decision, in flowchart, 568
Decision-support system (DSS), 23, 34

computer used for, 458
  spreadsheet programs for, 347
Declarations, on BASIC, 422
Dedicated application, 118
Dedicated packages, 180, 184, 185, 292, 293
Defense systems, computers and dangers in, 16
(DEL) key, on IBM-PC, 611
"Delete," in electronic spreadsheet, 359, 360
Deleting, in word processing, 370, 372
Design, 288
  as application, 33–34
  manager's role in, 479
  systems development and, 556–557
  trade-offs in, 78–81
  user's role in, 478
  see also Logical design, for business application;
    Systems analysis and design
Dictionary, 202
Difference engine, 46–47
Digital Equipment Corporation (DEC), 116–118, 539
  PDP-8, 60
  PDP 11/70 minicomputer, 90
DIM statement, in BASIC, 606–607
Dimensions, in BASIC, 434
Direct-access device, hard disk as, 148, 150
Direct-access files, 200–202, 205, 206
  problems connected with use of, 216–217
Direct wiring, 80–81
Directories, 202
  for cruise lines, 209–210
  inverted, 205, 206, 208
Dishwasher, automated manufacturing techniques
    for, 414–419
Disk BASIC, 611–613
Disk drives, trends in, 523–524
  see also Storage
Diskettes. *See* Floppy disks
Disks
  floppy, 6, 86–88, 136, 150–151, 182
  hard, 136, 148–150
Display, symbols for, 24
Distributed computer network, 243
Distributed processing, 257, 265, 559
Division, floating point number and, 101
Division-level format, in word processing, 375

Documentation, 269
  BASIC and, 588–589
  during programming, 264
  see also Flowcharts
DOLLAR SIGN, in BASIC, 591
Dot matrix printer, 154–156
Double-precision variables, in BASIC, 426, 581
Downloading data from network to computer, 477–478
Drug supplies company, computer used by, 457–458
Dumped, data as, 202
Dun & Bradstreet Corporation (D&B), 186
Dun's Financial Profiles, 186

EBCDIC code, 104, 105, 235
Eckert, W., 51, 53
Economost system, 457, 554
EDIT, on IBM-PC, 611
Edit program, for on-line input, 141
Editing, in word processing, 370, 372–374
Editor, of microcomputer operating system, 182
Education, about computers, 511–512
Electronic accounting equipment, 48, 49
Electronic Data Systems, Inc., 251
Electronic Funds Transfer (EFT), 513
Electronic mail, 463, 464–465, 530, 539
Electronic spreadsheets, 6–7, 9, 122, 181, 294, 344–362
  cells in, 347–348
  commands of, 346
  copying by, 353–355, 356
  cursor in, 347–348
  for decision support systems, 347
  formulas in, 346, 349–350
  functions in, 346, 356, 358–359
  graphs in, 361–362, 400
  labels in, 346, 348
  "move" in, 359
  numeric data in, 349
  popularity of, 346–347
  printing by, 359–360
  range in, 359
  storage ability of, 359
  table look-up function in, 359
  user understanding, 476
  variables in, 350–353
  Visicalc, 120, 121
  windows in, 355–356, 357
  worksheets in, 346, 359, 360
  wordstation providing, 78
Electronic walker, computer used for, 496–498
ELSE option, in BASIC, 587
Employees, computers and. *See* Organization, computers and
Emulation, 58
Encoding, amplitude modulation and, 238, 239
End of file, in BASIC, 440
END statement, BASIC and, 583
End user computing, 12, 393, 476–478, 484
  computer professional and, 559
  with FOCUS, 393–395
  future and, 529
  maintenance and, 556
  programming by, 294–295
  user services for, 557–558
  see also under User
Engineering workstation, computer-aided design for, 404–410
Enhancements, in planning document, 483
ENIAC, 51, 53
Entry, in word processing, 369–370, 371
Epson, 155
Equipment, in managerial plan, 484–485
Equity Funding Corporation of America, 16, 17
Errors, 513
  checking, 235–236
    by codes, 106–107
  computers causing, 510–511
Ethenet, 246
Execution of the program, 169
Executive steering committee, to control information processing, 488
Executive summary, in planning document, 482
Expert systems, 63, 530, 531–538
Exponential notation, in BASIC, 580
Expression, in BASIC, 428
Eye tumors, computers used for, 498

Factory automation, 414–419, 541–544
Fail-safe computers, 524, 526
Fairchild Camera and Instrument, 61
Feasibility study
  in systems life cycle, 261, 263, 269
  user's role in, 478
Federal Reserve, computer and fraud in, 17–18
Fetch, 166
Fiber optics, for long distance communication,
  526, 527
Fifth generation computers, 62–63, 64, 529, 530
File operations, of microcomputer operating
  system, 182
File system, workstation providing, 78
Filene's, 298
Files, 7, 194
  in BASIC, 440–445
  direct-access, 200–202, 216–217
  master, 195
  sequential, 195–199, 202, 205, 208
  symbols for, 24
  transactions, 198
  user understanding, 476
Finished-goods inventory, 28, 30
Firmware, 80
First generation computers, 53–54
  assembly language of, 170
Fixed length, record as, 195, 196
Fixed-point number, 101, 102, 103
FLOATING DOLLAR SIGN, in BASIC, 591
Floating-point fixed-point scalar, 423
Floating point number, 101–102, 103
  in BASIC, 426
Floppy disks (diskettes), 6, 86–88, 136, 150–151,
  182
  of IBM-PC, 611–613
Flow of information or documents, symbols for,
  24
Flowchart. See Program flowchart
Flowchart analysis, 573–577
Flowcharts, 269, 270–272, 567–577
  batch processing and, 197
Flowlines, in flowchart, 568
FOCUS, 181, 393–399
FOR/NEXT loop, in BASIC, 598–604, 607

Forecasts, 24
  computer systems for, 463
  graphics used for, 400, 402
FORMAT B, of IBM-PC, 613
Format 1 syntax requirement, in BASIC, 584–586
Formatting, in word processing, 369, 372, 375–
  376, 377
Formulas, in electronic spreadsheets, 346, 349–
  350
Forrester, Jay, 53–54
FORTRAN, 55, 59, 170–172
Fourth generation computers, 62
Fourth Generation Languages, 181, 289–290,
  294, 557
  FOCUS, 393–399
  user learning, 478
Fraction, computer representing, 103
Free-formatted, BASIC instructions as, 577, 580
Frito-Lay, 463–464
Full duplex transmission, 237
Functions, 432
  in electronic spreadsheets, 346, 356, 358–359
Future. See Trends

Gallery, in word processing, 375
Gateways, for local area network, 248
General Electric, 143, 414–419
General Motors, 405, 541, 544
General-purpose packages, 181
Generators, 298–301
  applications, 300, 301
  report, 295, 296–297
Goals, in planning document, 482
GOSUB statement, in BASIC, 433
GOTO statement, in BASIC, 586–587
Government, computer matching and , 507–510
Graphics
  BASIC and, 446
  for business, 400–403
  by electronic spreadsheets, 361–362
Graphics pads, for input, 144–145
Graphics terminals, 156–157, 159
Grocery store scanner, as point-of-sale terminal,
  142

Hal, 498
Harassment, computers causing, 510–511, 513
Hard copy, 157, 584
Hard disks, 136, 148–150
Hardware, 78–93
    addresses, 84, 86
    capacity requirements considered in, 266–267
    central processing unit, 81–82, 85
    input/output, 89
    memory, 82–84, 85
    secondary storage, 86–87, 89
    systems design and analysis considering, 265–266
    trade-off in design of, 79–81
    for transmission of data, 250
    trends in, 521, 523–526
Health care, computers used for. *See* Process control applications, of computer
Hewlett-Packard (HP)
    data communications operations of, 250–251
    150 micro-computer, 144
    plotter, 157
    32 bit processor, 392
Hexadecimal (hex), 102
Hierarchical data structure, 218–219
Hierarchical network configurations, 243, 245
Higher level languages. *See* Software
Highlighting, in word processing, 368, 372
History of computers, 46–68
    Babbage, 46–48
    fifth generation, 62–63, 64, 529, 530
    first computers, 51–53
    first generation, 53–54, 170
    fourth generation, 62
    Hollerith, 48, 49, 137
    second generation, 54–56
    third generation, 56–62
    von Neumann, 51–53
Hollerith, Herman, 48, 49, 137
Hollerith card, 48, 137
Home computers, 123
Home medical-alert system, computer used for, 500–501
Home position, in BASIC, 597
Homes, as offices, 544–545
Hospital supply firm, computer used by, 455–457

IBM, 9, 48, 51, 53, 56
    EBCDIC code of, 104, 105, 235
    1404 computer, 54
    mainframe computers, 104
    microprograms and, 58
    personal computer, 81, 90, 102, 121, 122, 246
        BASIC run on, 610–613
    360 computer, 56–57, 105, 137
IBM, Ltd., 556
IF statement, 587
IF-THEN-ELSE statement, in BASIC, 428, 429
Inception, in systems life cycle, 261, 263, 268–269
Index, 204
    on direct-access file, 200–202
Infinite loop, 570
Information center, for end users, 557–558
Information services department. *See* Computer department
Information system, 18, 23–34, 260
    components, 18–21, *see also* Application; Technology
        organization, 19, 20, 21
        user interaction, 19, 21
    environment of, 24
    input, 23
    query capacity of, 23
    reporting by, 23
    symbols describing, 24
    transactions processed by, 23
Ink-jet printer, 156
Input, 23, 136–147
    character readers, 136, 146–147
    graphics pads, 144–145
    joystick, 145–146
    key to tape on disk, 136, 137–139
    mouse, 145, 146
    OCR, 136
    on-line, 140–142
    punched cards, 48, 49, 136, 137
    punched paper tape, 136–137
    symbols for, 24
    terminal, 136, 141–142
    touch, 144
    voice, 136, 142–143, 160

Input/output (I/O), 89
  on BASIC, 422
  control, 555
  in flowchart, 568
  of microcomputer operating system, 182
  operators and, 555–556
  see also Input; Output
Input/output (I/O) control clerks, 559
Input/output instructions, in BASIC, 583–586
INPUT statement, in interactive BASIC, 593–594
Inquiries
  as capability of information system, 23
  on status of items in inventory, 330–3332
  see also Query language
(INS), on IBM-PC, 611
"Insert," in electronic spreadsheet, 359, 360
Installation, user's role in, 479
Instruction location counter, 166
Instruction set, 57
  in machine language, 166, 168
Instructions. See Software
Integer variables, in BASIC, 426, 581
Intergrated circuits, 56, 57, 61
Intel 8088, 81, 84, 121, 122, 144
Interactive BASIC, 593–598
Interactive output, 156–157
Interdependence in organizational structure,
    information systems and, 462
International Business Machines, Inc. See IBM
International Species Inventory System, 39–40
Internist, 530, 534–538
Interorganizational systems, computer and, 539–
    541
Interpreter, 120–121
Inventory, 27, 28, 30, 208–209, 308–337, 463
  see also Logical design, for business application
Inventory movement report, system generating,
    333–334, 335
Inverted directories, 205, 206, 208
I/O. See Input/output
Iterative statements, on BASIC, 422, 428–429,
    430
ITT system, XTRA as, 96, 143

Japan
  factory automation and, 541

fifth-generation computer and, 62, 64, 530
Job control language (JCL), 184
Joystick, 145
Juki, 155
Justification, in word processing, 369

Kemeny, John, 58, 175, 422
Key-to-disk devices, 136, 137–139
Key-to-tape devices, 136, 137–139
Keypoint, 186
Knowledge workers, 7, 9
Kurtz, Thomas, 58, 175, 422

Labels, electronic spreadsheets and, 346, 348
Languages. See Software
Large-scale integration (LSI), 60, 116
Laser
  for communications, 526, 528
  for printers, 156
Launch-on-warning policy, 502
Leasing lines, in computer networks, 242–243,
    244
Least squares regression analysis, business
    graphics producing, 400, 402
Lexis, 458–459, 460–461
Lifeline Systems Inc., 500–501
Line numbers, BASIC and, 580
Line printers, 154
Line speed, transmission and, 240
Linked list, 203–204
LISTING, BASIC and, 580
LITERAL, in BASIC, 591
Literals, in BASIC, 580
LList, on IBM-PC, 611
Local area network (LAN), 244, 246–249
Local committee, to control information
    processing, 488
Log tape, of direct-access files, 202
Logic, 263
  of application, 20, 23, 24, 26, 27, 28, 30, 33
  in CPU, 81
  in information system, 20, 23
  of processing, 194
  vacuum tubes for, 54

Logic chips, trends in development of, 523, 524
Logical data structures, 219–220
Logical design, for business application, 308–337
  decisions for, 312–313
  inventory control system in, 323–332
    database contents for, 337
    database updates for, 326, 328–330
    inquiries handled by, 330–332
    inventory receipts processed by, 326, 327
    menu for, 323, 324
    reorder point in, 323, 326
    reports from, 332–337
    returns recorded in, 323, 325–326
    sales recorded in, 323, 325–326
  messages as capability of, 313, 315–317
  ratifying reorders in, 319–322
  re-order application for grocery store, 310–311
  sales reported in, 322
  shutdown, 317–318
  strategy for, 308, 312–313
  transmission in, 319–322
Logical operators, in BASIC, 428
Loop network configuration, 243, 245
Loops, 570–571
  in BASIC, 428–429, 430
  NEXT, 598
Lotus 1-2-3, 6, 291, 346
  see also Electronic spreadsheets
Louvre, computer-aided design for, 411–413
Lovelace, Lady, 47–48
LPRINT statement, in BASIC, 584

M&C Electronics, 252
McDonnell Douglas, 458
Machine language, 53, 101, 166–169
McKesson Corporation, 457–458, 554
Macmillan, 476
Magnetic core storage, 54
Magnetic disks. See Hard disks
Magnetic ink character recognition devices
    (MICR), 146
Magnetic tape, 136, 147–148
Mailing lists, privacy and, 507
Mainframe computers, 88, 89, 102, 117, 121,
    122, 124–126

database management system for, 223
  in network, 521
  on-line application and, 119
  operating systems of, 183–184
Maintenance, in planning document, 483
Maintenance committee, to control information
    processing, 488–489
Maintenance programmers, 556, 559, 560
Maintenance transactions, 195
Management, 476–489
  alternatives selected by, 479
  committees formed by, 488–489
  of computer department, 11, 554–558
  design as concern of, 479
  end user computing and, 476–478, 484
  framework for control of information processing
    by, 482–488
    applications, 484
    charging for computer services, 485–486
    equipment, 484–485
    organizational structure, 483–484, 485
    planning, 482–483
    staff needs, 485
  policy objectives stated by, 481
  project management and, 481
  resources controlled by, 481
  rewards used by, 481
  role of in organization, 481
  system impact considered by, 481
  system understood by, 479
  systems analysis and, 478–479
  see also Computer profession; Organization,
    computers and
Management committees, to control information
    processing, 488–489
Managerial workstation, 380
  engineering workstation as, 410
Manufacturers Hanover Trust Company, 558
Manufacturing, computers and robotics in, 414–
    419
Marine Terminals, 458
Mark 1 electronic-sequence calculator, 50, 51, 53
Mark sense reader, 146–147
Market share, computer used to increase profit
    and, 454–458
Mass storage, 136, 152, 521

Master file, 195
Master file key, 198
Materials Requirements Planning II (MRP II), 293–294
Matrices, in BASIC, 434
Matrix printers, 154–156
Mauchly, J. Presper, 51, 53
Mead Data Central, 458–459, 460–461
Megaflops, 520
Memorex 3680 Disk Storage Subsystem, 150, 525
Memory, 82–84
　primary, 82, 86, 88, 147, 192
　random access, 83
　virtual memory system, 184–185
　see also Storage
Menu, 7, 141
　data flow diagrams with, 313, 314
　touch screen for, 144
　in word processing, 374
Merrill Lynch, 192, 454–455
Messages
　design allowing for, 313, 315–317
　system transmitting, 319–322
Microcomputers, 60–61, 61–62, 80, 81, 119–123, 247
　components of. *See* Hardware
　graphics capability of, 400
　operating system of, 182–183
　trends in, 520
Microfilm, as output, 157–158
Microinstructions, 58, 59
Microprogramming, 58, 59, 80, 81
Microsoft Word, 368
　see also Word processing
Microwave stations, for data transmission, 250
Middle management, 560–561
Mill, of analytical engine, 47
Minicomputers, 116–118, 121, 122, 123–124
　database management system for, 223
Mobil Oil Company, 227–228
Modem, 238, 239
Modulation, transmission and, 238, 239
Module, 279, 280
　in BASIC, 429, 430–432, 433
MONY Financial Services in New York, 393, 400

Motivation, employees and computers and, 469–470
Motorola, microcomputer of, 520
Mouse, 145, 146
"Move," in electronic spreadsheets, 359
Movement report, on inventory, 333–334
Multiplication, floating point number and, 101
Multiprogramming, third generation computers and, 58

Nanoseconds, 136, 192
NATURAL, 181, 182
Natural language, 160
Neon laser welding assembly, 542
Network data structure, 219
Networks
　access to data on, 476–477
　downloading data from to microcomputer, 477–478
　trends in, 521, 523
　workstation providing, 78
　see also Data communications
Node's parent, hierarchical file and, 219
Nonimpact printers, 154–156
Nonprocedural languages, 294
Nuclear defense, computer and communications systems and, 502–504
NUMBER SIGN, in BASIC, 591
Number system, 98
　see also Binary number system
Numbers, codes representing, 103–107
　see also Arithmetic
Numeric constant, in BASIC, 580
Numeric data, in electronic spreadsheets, 349
Numeric variables, BASIC and, 581

Objectives, manager's role in, 481
OCR. *See* Optical character recognition
Octal, 102
Office automation, 463–466, 530, 539
On-line system, 56, 60, 115, 117, 119, 138
　operators and, 555
　sequential files in, 202
OPEN, in BASIC, 440
Operating system. *See* Software

Operations, 11
  in computer department, 555–556, 559–560
  in planning document, 482, 484
  in systems life cycle, 262, 263, 264, 280–281
  user's role in, 479
Operators, in BASIC, 428
Optical character recognition (OCR), 136, 147
Optical storage, 136, 152–153
Optomation 11 Bin Vision, 506
Orbiting communications satellites, 528
Order entry, 28, 30
Order processing, as application, 26–28
Orders, inquiries about, 330–332
Organization, computers and, 19, 20, 21, 454–474
  competitive advantage gained by, 454–458
  individuals and, 469–470
    involvement, 470
    motivation, 468–469
  interorganizational systems, 539–541
  quality improved by, 459
  revenue increased by, 454–459
  savings from, 459
  structure of organization and, 462–468, 483–484, 485
    centralized, 462, 558–559
    decentralized, 559
    distributed, 257, 265, 559
    interdependence, 462
    new structure development, 462–463
    office automation, 463–466
    in planning document, 483
    teleconferencing, 466–468
  as system component, 260, 261
  see also Computer profession; Management
OSI Laser Drive, 153
Output, 136, 153–158
  graphics, 156–157, 159
  interactive, 156–157
  microfilm, 157–158
  paper reports, 136, 154–156
  plotters, 136, 157
  terminal, 136
  voice, 136, 157

P code, 176, 178
Packages, 178, 180–181, 289–294, 557
  advantages and disadvantages of, 289
  for data communication, 250
  database management and, 223
  dedicated, 180–181, 184, 185, 292, 293
  fourth-generation, 181, 289–290
  framework for classifying, 288
  general purpose, 181
  problem-oriented, 290, 291
  selecting, 184–185, 186, 292–293
  systems software, 290–291
  see also Electronic spreadsheets
Packet-switching, 242–243, 244
  value-added carriers and, 250
Pages, 184
Paragraph formatting, in word processing, 375
Parallel processors, 520–521
Paralysis, computers used in cases of, 496–498
Parity checking, 106–107
  in data communications, 235–236
Pascal, 175–176, 177, 178
Pascal Compiler, 178
Payroll processing, 138, 139
Pei, I. M., 411
Peripherals, 134, 136
  see also Input; Output; Storage
Personal computer, 6, 61–62, 89
  end-user working on, 393–395
Photoresist, 387
Physical data structure, 219
Physical inventory, 329
  see also Inventory
Physical pointers, 204
Physical records, 148
  updating of sequential files and, 198–199
Pie chart, business graphics producing, 400, 401
Planning, 24
  for managing information processing, 482–483
Plex data structure, 219
Plotters, 136, 157
Point-of-scale (POS) terminals, 141–142
Pointers, 204, 211
Policy decisions, manager's role in, 481
Popple Harry, 530
Predefined process, in flowchart, 568
Presentation graphics, workstation providing, 78
Primary memory, 82, 86, 88, 147, 192

Prime 9955, 124
Print/display, in BASIC, 584
PRINT statement, in BASIC, 584–586
PRINT USING, in BASIC, 591
Printing, 154–156
 by electronic spreadsheets, 359–360
 in word processing, 374
Privacy, computer and, 507
Private branch exchange, 248–249
Problem-oriented packages, 290, 291
Problems, computer use causing
 complexity, 512
 computer matching, 507–510
 crime, 512
 errors and harassment, 510–511, 513
 nuclear defense, 502–504
 privacy, 507
 security, 501
 unemployment, 505–507
Procedural languages, 294
Process
 in flowchart, 568
 symbols for, 24
Process control applications, of computer, 496–501
 with artificial limbs, 498, 499
 for blind, 498, 499
 for eye tumors, 498
 for Lifeline Systems Inc. home medical-alert
  system, 500–501
 for paraplegics, 496–498
 for spinal disorders, 498
Processing, systems design and analysis
  considering, 265–266
 see also Batch-processing; On-line system;
  Time-sharing
Processing of alternatives, conditional branching
  instructions and, 571
Processor, of microcomputer operating system,
  182
Product. See Output
Production control, as application, 27, 28–31
Production scheduling, as application, 24, 26, 27
Professional programmers. See Computer
  profession
Program flowchart. See Flowcharts

Programmer
 applications, 559, 560
 maintenance, 556, 559, 560
 staff, 559
 systems, 556, 560
Programming
 custom, 279, 556–557
 end user, 294–295
 manager of, 560
 in systems life cycle, 262, 263, 264, 279–280
 trends in, 528–529
 user's role in, 478
 see also Software
Programs, 6, 82
 modules, 279, 280
 see also Software
Project MAC, 56
Project management, 481
 control, 486
PROLOG, 529, 530
Prompts, in BASIC, 594–597
Pronto banking service, 544–545
Protocol, for data communications, 240, 241
Prototyping, 300–301
 trends in, 528–529
Punched card, 48, 49, 137
Punched paper tape, 136–137

QTAT (Quick Turn Around Time), 390
Quadriplegics, computer used for, 497–498
Quality, computer systems improving, 459
Quality control
 for dishwasher, 417, 419
 statistical chart for, 400, 402
Queries. See Inquiries
Query language, 290, 295, 298, 299
 of database management system, 222–223
 user knowing, 477

Racing cars, computers used with, 35
Radio Shack, TRS-80, 83
RAM. See Random access memory
Ramada Inns, 108
RAMIS, 181

Random-access device, hard disk as, 148, 150
Random access memory (RAM), 83, 84
Range, in electronic spreadsheets, 359
Re-order application, for grocery store, 310–311
Read-only memory (ROM), 83–84
READ statement, in BASIC, 434, 583
Real time, 56
Recorders
    system ratifying, 319
    system transmitting, 319–322
Records, 194–195
    physical, 198–199
    storage of, 194–195, 196
    updating, 202
Register, in CPU, 82
Regression techniques, graphics illustrating, 400–402
Relational data structure, 219, 220
Relative copying, in electronic spreadsheet, 353, 355
Relative reference, in electronic spreadsheet, 355
"REM" statements, in BASIC, 427, 588
Remark statements, in BASIC, 427
RENUM, on IBM-PC, 611
Reorder point, in inventory record, 323, 326
Repeaters, 247
"Replace," in word processing, 372
Report generators, 295, 296–297, 300, 301
Reporting, by information system, 23
Reports
    on inventory, 332–337
    printed, 154–156
    symbols for, 24
Requirements, in systems life cycle, 262, 263, 272–279
Resorts International, 90–91
Resources, managers controlling, 481
Response time
    capacity considering requirements for, 266, 267
    time-sharing and, 56
Restaurants, computers used by, 35
Retrieval languages, 295
"Retrieve," in electronic spreadsheets, 359
RETURN, in BASIC, 604
Returns, systems recording, 323, 325–326

Revenue, from information-processing technology, 458
Review, for control, 486
Rewards, managers using, 481
Ring
    local area network as, 247
    network structure as, 243, 245
Risks, in planning document, 483
Robotics, 505, 507
    for automated factories, 414–419, 541–543
    intelligent, 414
    simple, 414
    vision capabilities and, 414
Robovision, 542
ROM. See Read-only memory
Root, hierarchical file and, 219
Rotational delay time, 148
Rounding off, by computer, 102–103
RPG Program, 295, 296–297
RUN, BASIC and, 580

Sales
    inquiries about, 330–332
    reports on, 322, 332–333, 336
    FOCUS and, 396–399
    system recording, 323, 325–326
Satellite offices, 544
Satellites
    for communication networks, 528
    for data transmission, 250
"Save"
    in electronic spreadsheets, 359
    in word processing, 372, 374
Savings, due to computer applications, 459
Scalars, 422, 423
Scenario, in planning document, 482
Scrap, deleted text as, 372
Scrolling, in word processing, 374–375
Seagate drive, 149
"Search," in word processing, 375
Seasonal data, graph of, 400, 402
Second generation, of computers, 54–56
Secondary storage, 86–87, 89, 134, 147, 192
    see also Storage

Security, computers and, 501
Selection structure, 571
Selling short, 18
Semicolon, in BASIC, 585
Senior management, 561
　of computer department, 553–554
Sensing robots, 541–543
Sequential access, 202
Sequential files, 195–199, 205
　changes and, 208
Sequential medium, magnetic tape as, 148
Serial printers, 154
Shierson Racing, 35–37
Shipping, as application, 31, 33
Shutdown, logic for in system, 317–318
Signaling, in data communications, 237–240
Silicon chips, 56, 60
　manufacturing of, 386–392
　substances replacing, 528
Simple loop, 570–571
Simple-sequence structure, of processing, 569
Simplex transmission, 237
Single-precision variables, in BASIC, 426, 581
Slot machines, computers monitoring, 90–91
Soft keys, 144
Softcopy (visual) display, 584
Software, 55, 107, 166–187
　Ada, 48
　assembly language, 170
　capacity requirements considered in, 266–267
　definition of, 82
　fourth generation computers and, 62
　higher level languages, 55, 170–178, 557, *see also* BASIC
　　APL, 176, 178, 179
　　COBOL, 55, 173–175
　　FORTRAN, 55, 59, 170–172
　　Pascal, 175–176, 177, 178
　machine language, 166–169
　for new products, 186
　operating system, 20, 56, 166, 183–186
　　of mainframes, 183–184
　　virtual memory, 184–185
　procedural, 294
　strategy for selecting, 184–186

systems design and analysis considering, 265–266
third generation computers and, 58
trade-off of, 79–81
for transmission of data, 250
trends in, 528–529
see also Fourth Generation Languages; Packages
Solid drafting package, of Computervision, 405, 406, 407
Sort algorithm, 422
Sorting, 195
South Pacific Communications Company, 557
SPACE, in BASIC, 591
Spacing chart, in BASIC, 584
Specialized processors, 521
Specifications
　in systems life cycle, 262–264, 272–279
　users understanding, 478
Sperry Corporation, 63, 154
Sperry Rand, 53
Spinal disorders, computers used for, 498
Sports teams, computers used by, 36, 37
Spreadsheets. *See* Electronic spreadsheets
SPSS (Statistical Package for the Social Sciences), 290, 291
Staff positions, for computer profession, 559–560
Staffing, management assessing, 485
Star
　local area network as, 247
　network structure as, 243, 245
Start bits, 235
Statement set, in BASIC, 583
Statgraphics program, 400
Statistical quality control chart, 400, 403
STEP option, in BASIC, 598
Stop bits, 235
Storage, 83, 136, 147–153, 191–210
　in BASIC, 606–607
　bubble, 136, 152
　chained or linked list, 203–205
　changes and, 205–208
　in electronic spreadsheets, 359
　file, 194, *see also* update, *below*
　floppy disks, 6, 86–88, 136, 150–151, 182

Storage, *Continued*
  hard disks, 136, 148–150
  inverted directory and, 205, 206
  logic of processing and, 192, 194
  magnetic tape, 136, 147–148
  mass, 136, 152
  optical, 136, 152–153
  records, 194–195, 196, 202
  secondary, 86–87, 89, 192
  streaming tape drive, 136, 151
  update, 27, 195–202
    direct-access files, 200–202, 206
    in information system, 23
    physical records and, 198–199
    sequential files and, 195–199, 202, 208
  see also Memory
STORE, 7
Store, of analytical engine, 47
Streaming tape drive, 136, 151
String characters, in BASIC, 428
String constants, in BASIC, 580
String variables, in BASIC, 426
Structured design, 269, 272
Structured programming, subroutines in, 604
Style sheet, in word processing, 375–376
Subroutines, 573, 577
  in BASIC, 432–434, 604
Subtraction
  in binary, 100–102
  floating point number and, 101
Super-minicomputer, 124
Supercomputer, 121, 122, 126–128
  in network, 521
  on a wafer, 520
Supervisor, operating system as. *See* Software
Switched computer network, 242–243, 244
Symbols
  computer processing, 103–107
  computer representing, 108
Synchronous transmission, 237
Syntax, BASIC and, 577
Syntax error, BASIC and, 577
System, 23, 90, 260
  for business. *See* Logical design, for business
    application
  managers of, 560

operating. *See* Software
see also Information systems
Systems analysis and design, 11, 260–282
  alternatives provided for, 267–268
  capacity requirements, 266–267
  components of system, 260–261, *see also*
    Application; Organization; Technology; User
  definitions, 260
  implementation failure and, 281
  processing configurations for, 265–266
  responsibilities of user at stages of, 478–479
  systems life cycle, 261–282
    conversion, 262, 263, 264, 280
    feasibility, 261, 263, 269
    inception, 261, 263, 268–269
    operations, 262, 263, 264, 280–281
    programming, 262, 263, 264, 279–280
    specifications, 262–264, 272–279
    system analysis, 262, 263, 269–273
    testing, 262, 263, 264, 279–280
    training, 262, 263, 264, 280
  trade-offs in, 79–81, 264–265
Systems analyst, 11–12, 560
Systems development, 556–557
Systems disk, 612
Systems life cycle. *See* Systems analysis and
  design
Systems programmer, 556, 559, 560
Systems software, 290–291
Sytek, broadband local area network of, 246, 249

TAB function, in BASIC, 584, 585, 586
Table look-up function, in electronic spreadsheet,
  359
Tandem computers, 251
  nonstop, 526
Targeting Systems, 507
Technology, 261
  in information system, 19, 20, 21
  systems design and analysis considering, 265–
    266
  see also Hardware; Robotics; Software
Telecommunications handler, 250
Telecommunications monitor, 291
Teleconferencing, 466–468

Telenet, 545
Telephone network, 240, 242
Terminal
    in flowchart, 568
    for on-line input, 141–142
    time-sharing and, 56
Testing
    in systems life cycle, 262, 263, 264, 279–280
    user's role in, 478–479
Third generation, of computers, 56–62
Three-dimensional analysis, 541, 544
    business graphics producing histogram for, 400
3M, data communications and, 251–252
Through-the-arc vision system, 543
Throughput, third generation computers and, 58
Time-sharing, 56, 58–59, 60, 115, 116
    APL for, 176
    local area networks and, 245, 247
    minicomputers and, 117–118
    original equipment manufacturers and, 118–119
Top-down design, 256, 272
Top-down programming approach, 423, 429
Touch screen input, 144
Track, of magnetic tape, 147
Trackball controller, 544
Tracks, storage by, 148
Trade-offs, in systems design and analysis, 79–81, 264–265
Trade *Plus system, 545
Training
    employees and computers and, 469
    in systems life cycle, 262, 263, 264, 280
    user's role in, 280, 479
Transaction key, 198
Transactions, 194, 195
    capacity considering number and types of, 266
    information systems processing, 23
    maintenance, 195
Transactions file, 198
Transactions processor, 300, 557
Transistors, 54, 61
Translator, 170
    FORTRAN and, 170–171
Transmission, in data communications, 236–237
    of messages and recorders in system, 319–322
Tree structure, for local area network, 247

Trends, 520–545
    in communications, 526–528
    in components, 521, 523–526
    in expert systems, 530, 531–538
    in factory automation, 541–544
    in fifth generation computing, 529–538
    in hardware, 520–521
    in interorganizational systems, 539–541
    in office automation, 530, 539
    in software, 528–529
    in work from the home, 544–545
TRS-80 Color Computer 2, 83
Truncating, variables and, 581

Unconditional branch, in BASIC, 586
Unconditional branch instruction, 570, 571
Underlining, in word processing, 368, 372
Unemployment
    automation and, 505–507
    computerization and, 469
Univac I, 53
Update. See Storage
User acceptance tests, 280
User interaction procedures, in information system, 19, 21
User interface, fifth-generation computer and, 62–63, 64
User satisfaction questionnaires, for control, 486, 487–488
User services
    for end users, 557–558
    manager of, 560–561
Users
    capacity considering number of, 266
    computer profession and, 559
    as system component, 260, 261
    training for, 280, 479
    see also End-user computing
Utilities, 184

Vacuum tubes, 54
Value-added carriers, 250
Variable-length records, 195

Variables
    in BASIC, 423, 426, 580–581
    in electronic spreadsheeets, 350–353
Vertical recording, 523
Very-high-level languages. *See* Fourth Generation
        Languages
Very-large-scale integration (VLSI), 62, 63
    trends in chips using, 521, 523
Vice-president of information services, 553–554
Videodisk technology, 523–524, 525
Virtual memory, 184–185
Visicalc, 120, 121, 291
Vision system, robots and, 541, 542, 543
Vitalink, 250, 251
Voice
    for input, 160
    as output, 157
Voice data, transmission of, 240
Voice mailboxes, 464
Voice-recognition systems, for input, 136, 142–
        143
Von Neumann, John, 51–53

Wafer-scale integration, 520
Walk-through, 569
Walker, computer used for, 496–498
Warren Communications, 293–294
Westar IV satellite, 250
"What if" questions, electronic spreadsheets
        handling, 347
Wideband transmission, 240

Winchester disk, 150
Windows
    in electronic spreadsheet, 355–356, 357
    in word processing, 376
Word, address and, 86
Word processing, 122, 366–380, 463, 539
    editing in, 370, 372–374
    entering text in, 369–370, 371
    formatting in, 369, 375–376, 377
    justification in, 369
    quality improved by, 459
    scrolling in, 374–375
    user understanding, 476
    users of, 368–369, 378–379
    windows in, 376
    work station providing program for, 78
Word wrap, in word processing, 369
Worksheet, 346
    see also Electronic spreadsheets
Worksheet command, in electronic spreadsheets,
        359, 360
Workstation, 78, 380
    engineering, 405–410
    future and, 528, 529
Wright State University, 497

XTRA, 143

Zoo, computers used at, 39–40

Picture Credits

Part openers and Chapter openers are identified in this list by page number. Figure number refers to the text reference.

Page 3 © Joel Gordon
Page 5 Courtesy Intel Corporation. Used by permission.
1-1 PAR/NYC
1-2 PAR/NYC
1-3a PAR/NYC
1-3b PAR/NYC
1-4a © Charles Harbutt/Archive
1-4b © Michael O'Brien/Archive
1-5 © David Burnett/Contact-Woodfin Camp & Associates, Inc.
1-6a © Sepp Seitz/Woodfin Camp & Associates, Inc.
1-6b © Ben Asen
1-7 © David Burnett/Contact-Woodfin Camp & Associates, Inc.
Page 15 Photo courtesy of Hewlett-Packard Company. Used by permission.
2-1 Copyright © 1973 by The New York Times Company. Reprinted by permission.
2-8 Courtesy INTERMEC Corporation. Used by permission.
2-15 Photo courtesy of Hewlett-Packard Company. Used by permission.
2-16 Courtesy Remanco® Systems Inc. Used by permission.
2-17 Photo by Ron McQueeney, courtesy Indy 500 Photos. Used by permission.
2-18 © Sam Stone, San Diego and the San Diego Chargers.
2-19(a) © W. Marc Bernsau
2-19(b) Courtesy American Airlines, Inc. Used by permission.
2-19(c) Courtesy American Airlines, Inc. Used by permission.
2-20 © Tom Kelly
Page 45 © Ivan Massar/Black Star
3-1 National Portrait Gallery, London, England NPG Cat. Number 414
3-2 The Science Museum, London, England
3-3 Crown Copyright. National Physical Laboratory.
3-4(a) U.S. Department of Commerce, Bureau of the Census.
3-4(b,c,d) The Computer Museum, Boston, Massachusetts
3-5(a,b) Courtesy of Cruft Photo Lab, Harvard University

3-6(a,b) Courtesy Iowa State University
3-7 Courtesy Moore School of Electrical Engineering, University of Pennsylvania, Philadelphia.
3-8(a) Harris & Ewing/Photo Trends
3-8(b) Courtesy of Cruft Photo Lab, Harvard University
3-10 Courtesy IBM Archives. Used by permission.
3-11(a,b) The M.I.T. Museum, Cambridge, Massachusetts
3-12 Courtesy IBM Archives. Used by permission.
3-14 Courtesy IBM Archives. Used by permission.
3-16 The Computer Museum, Boston, Massachusetts
3-17(a) Courtesy of AT&T Bell Laboratories. Used by permission.
3-17(b) Fairchild Camera and Instrument Corporation Photo. Used by permission.
3-17(c) The Computer Museum, Boston, Massachusetts
3-18 © Tom Kelly
3-19(a,b) Courtesy Sperry Corporation Computer Systems. Used by permission.
Page 73 © Joel Gordon
Page 77 © Joel Gordon
4-3 © W. Marc Bernsau
4-4 Courtesy of Apple Computer, Inc. Used by permission.
4-5 Courtesy of Radio Shack, A Division of Tandy Corporation. Used by permission.
4-6 Courtesy of Apple Computer, Inc. Used by permission.
4-9(a) © W. Marc Bernsau
4-9(b) Courtesy Sperry Corporation Computer Systems. Used by permission.
4-9(c) Photo (c) Control Data Corporation. Used by permission.
Page 97 Courtesy Mead Data Central. Used by permission.
5-6 Courtesy Hilton Hotels Corporation. Used by permission.
Page 113 © Chuck Fishman/Woodfin Camp & Associates, Inc.
6-4 Courtesy Sperry Corporation Computer Systems. Used by permission.
6-6 PAR/NYC
6-7 Photo (c) Control Data Corporation. Used by permission.
6-9 © Tom Kelly
6-10 Courtesy of Prime Computer, Inc. Used by permission.

6-11 Courtesy Burroughs Corporation. Used by permission.
6-12 © Mark Godfrey/Magnum Photos Inc.
6-13 Courtesy American Petroleum Institute. Used by permission.
6-14(a,b) U.S. Department of Commerce, National Severe Storms Laboratory
Page 135 Courtesy American Petroleum Institute. Used by permission.
7-2 © Erich Hartmann/Magnum Photos Inc.
7-3 © Brody/Art Resource
7-6 © W. Marc Bernsau
7-7 © Rob Kinmouth/Gamma-Liaison
7-8 © Tom Kelly
7-9 © ITT Information Systems. Used by permission.
7-10 Photo courtesy of Hewlett-Packard Company. Used by permission.
7-11 © Ben Asen
7-12 © Roger Tully/Black Star
7-13 Courtesy National Computer Systems, Minneapolis, MN. Used by permission.
7-14 © Paul Fusco/Magnum Photos Inc.
7-15 Photo Courtesy Seagate. Used by permission.
7-16 Photo Courtesy Seagate. Used by permission.
7-17(a,b) Courtesy Memorex Corporation. Used by permission.
7-18(a,b) Courtesy Apple Computer, Inc. Used by permission.
7-19 © Dan McCoy/Black Star
7-20 Courtesy 3M, St. Paul, MN. Used by permission.
7-21 Courtesy Sperry Corporation Computer Systems. Used by permission.
7-22 © Erich Hartmann/Magnum Photos Inc.
7-23(a) © Joel Gordon
7-23(b) Courtesy Epson America, Inc. Used by permission.
7-24 Courtesy Computervision Corporation, Bedford, Massachusetts. Used by permission.
7-25(a,b) Courtesy Hewlett-Packard Company. Used by permission.
Page 165 © Joel Gordon
Page 191 © Paul Fusco/Magnum Photos Inc.
9-2(b) © Erich Hartmann/Magnum Photos Inc.
Page 215 Courtesy Motorola Corporation. Used by permission.
Page 233 Courtesy Motorola Corporation. Used by permission.